The Great Australian
BIRDFINDER

The Great Australian
BIRDFINDER

MICHAEL MORCOMBE

LANSDOWNE PRESS
Sydney • Auckland • London • New York

HOW TO USE THIS BOOK

The numbers that appear on photographs and paintings throughout this book and on the bird entries in the Habitats and Regions sections refer the reader´ to the Bird Reference section where bird species are listed 1–647 and basic data is supplied for each species.

The cross referencing below each bird entry throughout the book refers the reader to photographs, and further information on the bird.

Numbers provide a quick reference to basic data on these birds in the Bird Reference section, where birds are listed 1–647.

Page numbers indicate where photographs and further information can be found.

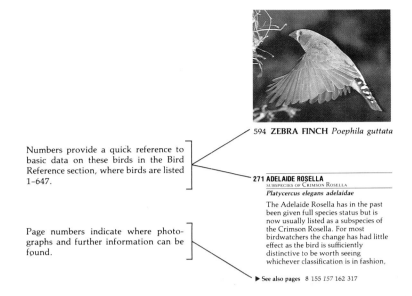

594 **ZEBRA FINCH** *Poephila guttata*

271 **ADELAIDE ROSELLA**
SUBSPECIES OF CRIMSON ROSELLA
Platycercus elegans adelaidae

The Adelaide Rosella has in the past been given full species status but is now usually listed as a subspecies of the Crimson Rosella. For most birdwatchers the change has had little effect as the bird is sufficiently distinctive to be worth seeing whichever classification is in fashion,

▶ See also pages 8 155 *157* 162 317

AUTHOR'S NOTE

The description and maps of birdwatch walks are intended only as a general indication of the location, approximate route and extent of the walk, and should not be used as the sole guide to walking, especially where the proposed walk does not follow a made track or road. It is the responsibility of the user of this book to satisfy himself that he has adequately detailed and accurate maps, equipment and provisions if undertaking any of the suggested birdwatching activities, and to obtain the advice of rangers or landowners regarding safety, current conditions and other relevant information. When in doubt, walkers should keep to made trails or roads, and should not walk alone or without advising someone of routes and times. Unknown swamps and lakes should not be entered alone, and caution should be taken in case of deep mud, deep water or other hidden hazards.

Bushwalkers and travellers should obtain the permission of the owner or occupier of any private land likely to be traversed, observe all required precautions if using camp or cooking fires, and leave all gates as found.

Designer: Susan Kinealy
Design concept: Ted Barlowe
Editors: Louella McFarlane & Doreen Grézoux

Published by Lansdowne Press
a division of RPLA Pty Limited
176 South Creek Road, Dee Why West, N.S.W., Australia, 2099
First published 1986

© Copyright Michael Morcombe 1986
Produced in Australia by the Publisher
Typeset in Australia by Savage Type Pty Ltd, Brisbane
Printed in Australia by Griffin Press Limited
Colour separations by Colour Scanners Pty Ltd, Sydney

National Library of Australia Cataloguing-in-Publication Data

Morcombe, Michael.
The great Australian birdfinder.

Bibliography.
Includes index.
ISBN 0 7018 1962 6.

1. Birds — Australia — Identification. I. Title.
598.2994

CONTENTS

88 BLACK-SHOULDERED KITE *Elanus notatus*

INTRODUCTION

This book is designed for the birdwatcher who is moving beyond familiar birding territory in the expectation of seeing new species of birds in their natural habitats.

Bird observers who would travel the breadth of the continent to find new birds in the wild, often would not bother to see the same birds close to home in an aviary. The sighting of an Eclectus Parrot in the rainforests of Cape York, though the bird may be 100 metres away and not clearly seen, brings excitement and satisfaction far beyond that experienced in a close study of the same species in a cage. Most of us gain immeasurably greater satisfaction from seeing a species for the first time in the wild rather than in captivity, even if we catch but a fleeting glimpse of it. The sighting of a riflebird in a tropical rainforest, or a sea-eagle over a spectacular coastline, is an experience intensified by the beauty of the setting. The satisfaction of finally locating and identifying the bird is probably proportionate to the difficulty in making the sighting. This book is intended to encourage enthusiasts to extend their birdwatching into new territory and to assist them in finding birds in regions beyond the familiar home environs.

But 'new territory' can have widely differing meanings. For the great majority of people with a casual interest in birds, their own back yard and neighbourhood have very many kinds of birds unknown to them; at the other extreme are birdwatchers who have travelled to many distant parts of Australia in search of rare species. The majority of those with an interest in birds fall between these extremes, usually having a good knowledge of the birds of their district, or a substantial part of their State, and perhaps some experience of the birds of several distant localities.

Within the familiar territory of each bird observer will be a number of favoured birding sites, as near to home as the back garden, but usually a local patch of bush, a swamp, a coastal mudflat, perhaps within a national park or other public land, or private land, where both the birds and their environment are familiar. Here the bird observer has learned where many kinds of birds may be found, their preferred terrain and vegetation, and the best time of day and season in which to see them.

Most importantly, birdwatchers within their familiar range of places will know many, perhaps most of the bird calls. The distinctive song or alarm call of each bird is one of the most important aids to the sighting and often the identification of the bird. In home birding territories, observers can become so familiar with the sounds of the birds that they can wander through the bush and be told a great deal about the surrounding birdlife by calls alone.

When travelling into new regions, however, the bird observer is deprived of this accumulated experience. The new territory may be the first visit to a new habitat very close to home; the transition, within the distance of a few metres, perhaps from woodland into rainforest, or swamp, can give a greater number of 'new' species than do some trips of several thousand kilometres. But usually travel over long distances is more likely to find distinctively new bird habitats, and consequently new birds. Not only is the landscape of ranges, rivers, or coast new, but so also are the climate and the vegetation.

To travel from Melbourne, Adelaide or Perth to far northern Australia is to go from a predominantly winter rainfall to a summer rainfall pattern. In those southern regions, most nesting is finished by late December or early January, but in the tropical north, many species are only just beginning to breed with the onset of the wet season. Some species, like the Rainbow Pitta, will call much more often and loudly with the approach of the wet season, making them much easier to find. Other species become more difficult to see, like the waterfowl, which in the dry season congregate in huge flocks on northern lagoons, but disperse to breed in remote swamps as these fill during 'the wet'.

Not only the season, but also habitats will differ from those of home, and there is the difficulty here of locating accessible examples of habitat that are likely to be rich in birds. The use of the habitat by individual species may also be unknown: whether a particular species is likely to be seen in treetop foliage or undergrowth, rainforest edges or deep within the rainforest.

The predominance of unfamiliar bird calls, while exciting, leaves the birdwatcher with little chance of recognizing birds by their calls. Many a time has a rare or exciting bird been overlooked because its call is not recognized, being quite unlike the calls of others of its genus. For example, the call of the Yellow-billed Kingfisher is quite different from that of the other Australian kingfishers, yet the bird is extremely difficult to see without the guidance of those very distinctive calls.

Location of many places and most species should be possible using this book, with the appropriate input of time and effort that is inseparable from any search for species that are scarce or of restricted range. When further assistance must be sought, the queries can be made with some basic knowledge of local birds and sites.

This book is in three major sections. The first section covers the major habitats, for the location of the appropriate habitat is almost invariably the prerequisite for finding the birds Also discussed here are some birds confined to, or mainly found within, each habitat. These are mainly species widespread within their respective habitats.

The second section is the major part of the book, where each of fourteen regions is covered in detail. Attention is concentrated upon the birds unique to each region, whether they be full species, or subspecies. Birds that may best be seen in the region, that are of special interest in some other way, or form part of the bird character of the region are also covered. This section also gives attention to bird experiences unique to particular localities, although the birds themselves may be common or widespread. For example, the spectacle of massed birdlife at Kakadu, the Brolga flocks of Townsville Common, and the immense wader congregations of the continent's north-western beaches are discussed.

Some regions have many more endemic birds than others, Cape York and the Atherton Region being especially rich. Others, such as the Top End and the Kimberley, the south-western corner of Western Australia, the South East and Tasmania all have their lists of unique species, and usually a greater number of locally unique subspecies. Some regions have few unique birds, but within their birdlife have other facets of significance or interest. The birds discussed in detail are mainly of restricted range, for it is upon these less easily found species that the book concentrates. The information given on habitat, behaviour, daily routines and calls are designed to assist in finding and recognizing the bird sought.

For most bird observers the bird calls are extremely important, locating birds hidden in dense cover, where the presence of some species would otherwise go undetected. Many of the rare or localized species seem to fall into this category, although some common species are also very secretive and keep beneath dense cover. Such birds include the two species of scrub-birds, the whip-birds, bristlebirds, and emu-wrens. Other birds such as the pardalotes, the small lorikeets, and some others of the treetop foliage, although not secretive, would often be unnoticed among the leaves of forest or woodland canopy but for their calling. Often the presence of one of the raptors soaring so high overhead that it is but a speck in the sky, will be revealed by calls. At the other extreme, the birds of open habitats, the waders and shorebirds, are usually fairly easily spotted, though calls may assist identification.

Considerable attention has therefore been given in this book to describing, within the limitations of imitating bird sounds through the written word, the calls of the birds, especially those for which the calls are essential or important for detection and location.

The places described are, of course, far from being the only localities where rewarding birdwatching is possible, but they give a selection of starting points for observers coming into new territory. With these as examples, they may find other, and perhaps in some respects better, birdwatching sites for some or many of the species. In a few instances the text deliberately avoids being too specific in giving precise locations, especially where the habitat is fragile, or the birds so rare or so sensitive to disturbance that numbers of visitors could be damaging. For example, nesting Peregrine Falcons might desert their nest after a very few intrusions of humans into their breeding territory, and a colony of breeding seabirds could be endangered by excessive visitor disturbance to their islands. So it is better that some species and sites be found only by birdwatchers who are sufficiently dedicated to follow up the leads given in this book with some further research, and local enquiry, and probably a great deal of work in the field.

The third section of the book, the Bird Reference, presents the basic data of recognition, habitat, call, range and status of all species, the widespread and common as well as rare and confined species. The coverage of the book matches that of the *Atlas of Australian Birds*, compiled by the Royal Australasian Ornithologists Union, which surveyed 647 species. Included in this book are an additional 103 uncommon and vagrant species, some of which are mentioned in lists of sightings at specific sites, and in the main birdlist at the back of the book.

The frequent 'lumping and splitting' of species, with resultant apparent elimination or creation of species, often with new names, must be confusing to readers. The names of birds are substantially different in current books, compared with those published a few years ago. In this book, previous names are included in the index and under the Other Names heading, to bridge the gap between old and current names. Where previous full species have been reduced to subspecies, these birds may be discussed in detail equal to that given to full species, provided these birds are distinctive in appearance, are well known by a common name, and are of interest within the local or regional avifauna. Examples are the Helmeted Honeyeater, Adelaide and Yellow rosellas, Black-and-white and Lavender-flanked fairy-

339 RUFOUS SCRUB-BIRD *Atrichornis rufescens*

447 STRIATED GRASSWREN *Amytornis striatus*

wrens, Golden-backed
Honeyeater, Plumed Frogmouth,
and the three subspecies of fig-
parrot: Marshall's, Macleay's
and Coxen's. These and other
subspecies are often of special
interest to ornithologists, usually
for their rarity, or restricted range.
They will undoubtedly continue to
be known by these common
names, though omitted from many
books because they are no longer
full species. There is every chance
that some will be returned to full
species status at some time.

The bird distribution maps in
this section, and other maps
throughout the book, use the same
projection as those of the *Atlas of
Australian Birds*, to facilitate cross
referencing. The Atlas distribution
maps were an important reference,
but only one among many used to
build up the bird distribution maps
of this book. The boundaries of
range of each species are set, as an
outermost limit, where there is still
a reasonable though perhaps slight
chance of finding that species,
rather than at the most outlying
limits, where the possibility of
finding the species would be very
remote.
All native species are illustrated,
either by photographs taken in the
wild, or in paintings. The use of
paintings, with around ten species
per panel, has allowed the
inclusion of a far greater volume of
reference material within the book
than would have otherwise been
possible. The paintings usually
contain a mixture of very large and
very small birds, making
unsuitable the use of a fixed scale
of size within each panel. Instead,
the larger species have been placed
further back into the background,
the small species closer and on a
larger scale, following the rules of
perspective. The scale, however,
must vary from foreground to
background; species on the same
distance plane will be of
approximately similar scale.

561 **WESTERN SPINEBILL** *Acanthorhynchus superciliosus*

All birds shown here have been
photographed in the wild, and not
confined or constrained in any
way. The selection includes
photographs at, and away from
nests. Varied techniques were
employed to overcome the natural
timidity of birds: hides on steel
towers, and in trees at heights
sometimes over 25 metres, hides in
swamps, and on the ground. Birds
have been photographed at
waterholes and feeding, and at
nests, from the concealment of
these hides but also on occasions
by remote-controlled cameras, and
often by stalking of the subject
with powerful telephoto lenses.

This book does not, however,
aim to be a field guide; the users of
this book will probably have one
of the many field guides widely
available. While the illustrations
will generally provide
identification of the main list of
species, it is beyond the scope of
this book to equal a field guide
devoted solely to bird
identification including all rare
vagrant species, nor can it depict
each and every subspecies, every
male-female difference, or seasonal
plumage change.

This book primarily shows the
birds through habitat and regional
groupings, though cross referenced
to a summary, in the Bird
Reference section, of the basic data
on each species in the usual

zoological sequence. Not only does
this gather together all the species
of special interest for each region,
for convenient reference when
travelling within that region, but
also emphasizes the vital
relationship between birds and
their habitats.

The text of this book,
particularly that part covering bird
places, is partly from personal
experience, especially from western
and northern parts of the
continent, and has also drawn
heavily upon the immense mass of
information within the periodicals
and newsletters of ornithological
associations and bird observers'
clubs of all States. Especially
valuable have been surveys of the
birds of specific localities, and
accounts of club excursions to
various local birding sites known
to be rich enough in birdlife to
warrant a day trip or weekend
campout.

Success in birdwatching will
always be proportional to the time
and effort put into the search; very
early risings and long hours of
searching are the only guarantee of
success in finding a significant
number of the less commonly
sighted species. The information
given here should assist in finding
Australia's birds, but finally the
degree of success will depend upon
enthusiasm and often upon
stubborn determination.

HABITATS

Most species of birds have a preferred habitat, but many may be found through a variety of other habitats, and some occur in almost all. Habitats which have a clearly defined boundary, where the vegetation and other elements change abruptly, tend to contain a higher proportion of endemic birds. Rainforests, mangroves, wetlands, and the coast are precisely identifiable and have many species confined within their boundaries, or very nearly so. Forests, woodlands, mallee, mulga, heathlands and grasslands usually have much less obvious boundaries, and a far greater interchange of birds.

The birds chosen here as examples of the avifauna of each of the major habitats are those that are unique to a particular habitat, or very typical of it, but at the same time are geographically widespread. The text covers predominantly the bird in its habitat, especially any distinctive behaviour, song, or other information which could assist in the sighting of the species.

Coastal heathlands, north coast of New South Wales

HEATHLANDS

Heaths are communities of shrubs of many families; they are usually less than 2 m in height and often under 0.5 m. The foliage tends to be hard and often prickly, while grasses and herbaceous plants are rare. Plant families dominating the heathlands include the Proteaceae, Myrtaceae, Mimosaceae, Casuarinaceae, Epacridaceae and Xanthorrhoeaceae.

The density of shrub cover varies greatly, allowing descriptions of heaths as closed or open. Often trees, banksias, eucalypts or casuarinas are scattered through the heathland, and where these trees become more numerous the heathland can blend to woodland with the heath continuing as the understorey.

Within the broad heathland habitat are several distinct types. These include sandplain-heaths on low fertility sands, both coastal and inland, in localities ranging from high to low rainfall, and also the swamp-heaths, including alpine and button-grass types.

Heathlands are widespread but are mostly near-coastal with a few inland areas. This habitat is absent from the major part of the interior of the continent and from the northern to north-western coasts; there is some heathland along the north-eastern parts of Cape York Peninsula.

Most heathland types, with the exception of alpine and button-grass, are rich in birds. Their wealth of plant species, a great many prolific in nectar-bearing flowers, and their dense cover together provide a very favourable habitat especially for honeyeaters, wrens and other small passerines.

The swamp-heaths, waterlogged for part of the year, tend to have a poorer variety of bird species, while the sandplain-heaths have a larger list, especially where they intermix with open banksia, mallee

Sandplain-heath, Fitzgerald River National Park, Western Australia

banksia or mallee, sharing many of their species. But the heathlands usually tend to have fewer bird species than forest habitats; there appears to be a correlation between the number of layers of vegetation and the total species that can be supported. Forest, with at least two and often three strata, can support many more species than the single stratum of heathland; the more complex the vegetation structure, the richer its avifauna tends to be.

While the number of species utilizing the varied heathland habitats is substantial, there are only three or four virtually confined to it, and of these the Ground Parrot and the bristlebirds are rare and localized.

The following are species widespread and typical of heathlands; heathland species of restricted range are covered in their respective regions.

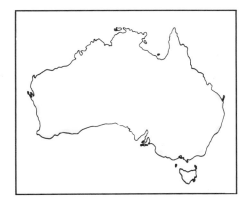

228 BRUSH BRONZEWING

Phaps elegans

Although largely an inhabitant of
heathlands and coastal tea-tree scrubs,
the Brush Bronzewing is found also in
mallee scrubs and undergrowth
thickets of forests and woodlands. It is
rather scarce, probably due to clearing
of its habitat and its tendency to nest
low. The Brush Bronzewing is most
likely to be seen when flushed from
near the ground or as it travels in swift
flight low across heath or forest
undergrowth. At times its muffled,
repetitive 'oom-oom-' if followed may
result in a sighting, especially in the
breeding season when it calls almost
incessantly. The chestnut of nape and
sides of the neck, and chestnut throat-
patch help to identify it; in flight it
looks smaller, more rufous than the
Common Bronzewing.

▶ See also pages 17 307–8

265 GROUND PARROT

Pezoporus wallicus

The Ground Parrot has suffered
considerable reductions in its range
since European settlement, primarily
from the loss of habitat through
clearing, burning, and drainage of
swamps. The species occupies varied
heath and heath-like habitats: sedge
swamps, temperate shrub heathlands,
open heaths, and sedge plains where
there are usually grasstrees.

The main habitat requirement
appears to be the low, very dense
ground-cover. The parrots will use
more open heathlands, and sites
thinned by grazing, but may be
inhibited from nesting except where
there is very dense vegetation in which
to hide the nest.

Ground Parrots return to burnt
areas within two to five years and
build up to a maximum population in
five to 15 years, after which the
populations very gradually fall away
to zero, 20 to 25 years after the
burning. It appears that fire, at lengthy
intervals, is required to maintain
suitable habitat. It is also evident that
as the heaths need many years to
recover before the parrots return and
build up in numbers, burning at close
intervals will eliminate these birds
altogether. Repeated burning at
intervals of less than six to eight years
apart was found to cause loss of plant
species and local extinction of the
species.

Tasmania's Ground Parrot
populations are on the island's western
and southern button-grass plains.
Victoria's habitat includes parts of
Wilsons Promontory and East
Gippsland; New South Wales has

Wallum heath, coastal Queensland

populations at Nadgee and Barren
Grounds; Queensland has this species
in the Fraser Island and Cooloola
heaths, and Western Australia at
isolated points including Fitzgerald
River National Park, along the south
coast. The species is now extinct in
South Australia.

The Ground Parrot is difficult to
sight unless flushed, usually
accidentally, from its dense cover,
particularly as the species is mainly
nocturnal. Activity begins at dusk,
while there is still light enough to see,
with a song of high-pitched 'tee-tee-
teee-eee' or 'tee-tee—stit', loud enough
to carry on a still evening but lost if
there is much wind.

Often at this time they will begin
flying about low over the heath, giving
brief sightings but with colours usually
rather poor in the half-light of dusk.
This period of activity lasts half to
three-quarters of an hour and is
repeated with the first light of dawn.
During the day the parrots are silent.

If flushed during the day the Ground
Parrot will fly low and fast, zigzagging
away to pitch abruptly down into the
heath again rarely more than 100 m
away.

▶ See also pages 15 *17* 123 124 126 142 152
242 316

452 EASTERN BRISTLEBIRD

Dasyornis brachypterus

Although apparently quite common along Australia's eastern coast from south-eastern Queensland to north-eastern New South Wales, the Eastern Bristlebird suffered so heavily from destruction of habitat and feral predators that for a time it was feared extinct. The species has been found to exist in a number of localities, many now protected within reserves, and this has ensured that, though rare, it is relatively safe.

The Eastern Bristlebird occupies rank, wet vegetation bordering heath and, near the coast, dense scrub and thickets. It moves mouse-like beneath this dense, low cover, where it is always difficult to observe, though it has been observed, but rarely, feeding in more open situations than the usual leaf-litter layer, and at times among low foliage.

In the breeding season the Eastern Bristlebird calls loudly, greatly increasing the chances of a sighting. The calls are piercing whistles, yet melodious, variable, and seeming to have ventriloquial qualities. Phrases have been described as 'it-wood-weet-sip', sweet yet penetrating and with something of a whipcrack ending. A bird may call repeatedly for several minutes then remain silent. However it will respond well to imitations or tape recordings of its call.

If the bird can be glimpsed at all it is likely to be seen as brownish, moving furtively beneath the vegetation, the long tail usually raised and often fanned. Probably the best opportunity for a clearer view is when the bird is calling, for it usually sings from bushes. If the Eastern Bristlebird is flushed it flies low, for but a short distance; its preference when disturbed is to keep to the ground where it can move beneath the dense, low cover with amazing speed and stealth.

▶ See also pages 123 124 362

454 RUFOUS BRISTLEBIRD

Dasyornis broadbenti

At the time of European settlement the Rufous Bristlebird occurred in both south-eastern and south-western Australia but the western subspecies, which occupies coastal heathland habitat in the extreme south-western corner of Western Australia, has not been reliably recorded for many years and may be extinct. It was found in dense heath, about 40 cm high, along the coast between Cape Mentele and Cape Naturaliste.

The south-western subspecies *litoralis* was recorded as feeding on

insects and taking seeds of seashore and heath plants; it was seen to cross open dune and beach sand to feed among banks of seaweed near the water's edge. In crossing these open spaces this bird was described as 'running at top speed . . . tail depressed . . . dwarf, rounded wings used as an aid to its running . . . neck outstretched to the utmost . . .'.

228 **Brush Bronzewing** *Phaps elegans*
265 **Ground Parrot** *Pezoporus wallicus*
452 **Eastern Bristlebird** *Dasyornis brachypterus*
454 **Rufous Bristlebird** *Dasyornis broadbenti*
467 **Striated Fieldwren** *Sericornis fuliginosus*

In south-eastern Australia the Rufous Bristlebird still occupies its historical range along a narrow strip of heathland along the Victorian and South Australian coasts from near Anglesea to the Murray mouth. Here the species seems to be maintaining its numbers even near settlement; the recorded habitats include dense coastal heath and thickets, sand dunes and clumps of wire-grass.

Although apparently not as shy as the other species of bristlebird, the Rufous keeps well hidden, scurrying into clumps of vegetation with head lowered and tail slightly raised, and rarely flying. Observers record success in sighting by sitting quietly and imitating the calls, and the birds are easily brought into the open with use of tape recordings of the calls.

The Rufous Bristlebird is best located by its loud calls, the usual and most distinctive being like the creaking of a slow-turning wooden cartwheel, which gave it the name 'Cartwheel Bird'. The song has been described as a squeaky-grating 'cheep-cheep-chew-chew-ee-ee', and by some as being rather rollicking, loud and melodious, ventriloquial. Pairs sing in duet.

▶ **See also pages** *17 121 126 163 363*

467 STRIATED FIELDWREN

Sericornis fuliginosus

Ornithologists seem unable to decide whether there is a single species of two subspecies, or two separate species; current fashion seems inclined towards the latter. These are the Striated Field-wren of the south-east and Tasmania and the Rufous Fieldwren of the southern drier country to the west and north of the range of the Striated, through to the southern half of Western Australia.

The habitat of the Striated is of damp heathlands and button-grass

554 TAWNY-CROWNED HONEYEATER *Phylidonyris melanops*

plains, moorlands and samphire, while the Rufous species (or subspecies) inhabits heath, mallee-heath, saltbush and samphire, usually on sand and gibber plains.

These birds are secretive and rather wary but are fairly easily located by their song, especially at dawn and early morning during the breeding season from midwinter to early summer. The song, a sweet and musical outpouring of rather sad notes, not extremely loud, but far-carrying on calm, crisp morning airs, is given by the male from an exposed twig atop a bush within his territory. With the site known, patient observation should give sightings, especially of the male in song.

▶ **See also pages** *17* 18 124 150 152 162 163 223 366

554 TAWNY-CROWNED HONEYEATER

Phylidonyris melanops

The Tawny-crowned Honeyeater will often seek out the heath habitat in localities dominated by other vegetation. In the heavy forest country it can be found, often nesting, in sites where a more open canopy has allowed small patches of heathy undergrowth, and it has been found nesting in low-cut heathy vegetation along firebreaks surrounded by unsuitable forest. Both nectar and insects are taken from the flowers of the heath shrubbery.

▶ **See also pages** *18* 122 124 150 152 163 232 242 245 386

571 WHITE-FRONTED CHAT

Ephthianura albifrons

This is one of the most common birds of the heathlands across southern Australia, where it shows a preference for the damp coastal heaths. It does occur also well inland, on sandplain-heaths and the samphire margins of saltlakes. These birds are generally conspicuous, often perching on small bushes where the bold black-and-white plumage is obvious. When a nest is nearby they go to great lengths to be seen and followed away from the site.

▶ **See also page** 390

571 **WHITE-FRONTED CHAT** *Ephthianura albifrons* Top: *Male* Bottom: *Female*

Mangroves, northern Queensland

MANGROVES

Mangroves are trees or bushes that usually grow below the high-tide line of coasts and estuaries. The term 'mangrove' as generally used applies to both the individual mangrove tree species and also to this type of vegetation and habitat. However, the mangrove community as a whole is more correctly known as the mangal.

The mangrove tree and shrub species belong to many different families, some but distantly related, but having in common special characteristics for survival in this marine habitat. They are, of course, all well adapted to salty and waterlogged soils and the frequent inundations of the rising and falling of tides. Foremost are their modifications that allow them to 'breathe' in the oxygen-deficient soil, and to support them in the soft mud. Many have slender, air-filled pneumatophore roots which rise vertically in great numbers from the mud to facilitate the transfer of gases to and from the main root system beneath the mud. Others have knee-like kinks where their roots rise above the mud then turn sharply down again. Others again have long, arching, air-filled stilt roots curving down from lower trunk to mud, and aerial roots hanging from lower limbs.

Buttressing stilt roots serve also to brace the trees to the radiating cable roots beneath the mud, which intermesh with other roots, anchoring and supporting against waves and winds which are sometimes of cyclonic strength.

Mangroves grow in many tropical parts of the world. In Australia they occur mainly around the northern coastline, from the north coast of New South Wales around to Shark Bay on the Western Australian coast, with isolated small pockets around the southern coast. They favour sites protected from the open sea,

Coastal mudflats and mangroves, west Kimberley

typically in sheltered bays and estuaries and along tidal reaches of rivers.

Mangroves, like rainforest, form a closed-canopy forest, and share with the rainforests many species of birds, particularly where rainforest adjoins the landward side of the mangrove belt, as is the case on many parts of the Queensland coast. Often such rainforest serves as a corridor between blocks of mangroves, allowing movement of species. The tall mangrove forests of Cape York and other parts of the northern coast are very much like rainforest, with closed canopy and very open beneath, except for the maze of stilt roots low down. But the stunted, shrubby mangroves of north-western Australia also, though low in stature, retain a rainforest-like closed canopy.

Australia has about 25 species or subspecies of birds that are largely dependent upon mangroves. This compares with about 11 for New

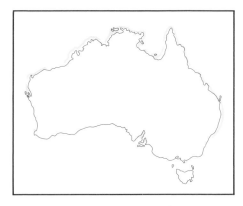

47 GREAT-BILLED HERON *Ardea sumatrana*

Guinea, which has a similar extent of mangrove habitat. Again, looking at specific parts of the Australian coastline, it is apparent that there are more mangrove bird species in north-western Australia than elsewhere. This is believed to be due to the more broken nature of the north-west mangrove belt and the lack of any rainforest connecting corridor, so that birds have been more effectively isolated, resulting in independent evolution towards new races and species.

The following are birds entirely or almost entirely dependent upon, and confined to, the mangrove habitat. In addition, there are many subspecies that are virtually confined to mangroves. Other birds are predominantly mangrove inhabitants but occur also in adjoining rainforest and monsoon scrubs.

47 GREAT-BILLED HERON

Ardea sumatrana

The Great-billed Heron is found right around Australia's northern coastline but it usually inhabits mangrove swamps so remote and inaccessible that it is difficult to observe. Nests are rarely found; there was only one breeding record in the extensive Royal Australasian Ornithologists Union survey. The Top End of the Northern Territory probably offers the best opportunity of a sighting, for here it occurs further inland on river lagoons, some of which carry quite heavy traffic of small boats, mainly barramundi fishermen but also tour boats at some sites. Although this species remains always very wary, sightings at moderate distances are possible, perhaps within 50 m, compared with the usual closest approach of 300 m or more.

The Great-billed Heron is usually solitary and in daylight hours is most likely to be seen standing in mangroves at the edge of a lagoon or mangrove creek. It feeds on mudflats at low tide, but may be at least partly nocturnal. In flight it appears ponderous, travelling with deep wingbeats, neck folded in closely.

The presence of this heron may be revealed by the call, often given at night, and sounding like the bellow of a bull or a crocodile, hence the alternative name 'alligator-bird'.

▶ **See also pages** 96 98 188 196 197 198 199 208 262

56 STRIATED HERON

Butorides striatus

The Striated Heron, perhaps better known as the Mangrove Heron, is confined almost exclusively to mangrove swamps, tidal estuaries and mudflats; it is also occasionally to be seen on exposed reefs. Its daily routine is determined by the tides, roosting in dense mangroves at high tide, hunting on the mudflats when these are exposed. The squat, rather bittern-like shape, short-legged for a heron, makes the species easily identified; there are grey and rufous forms.

▶ **See also pages** 98, 122, 223, 264–5

127 CHESTNUT RAIL
Eulabeornis castaneoventris

An elusive species confined entirely to mangroves of the Kimberley and Northern Territory. Except where it has become accustomed to power boats it is shy and very difficult to sight. Rivers where tour boats operate frequently, as on the Adelaide River and the Kakadu lagoons, and localities frequented by fishing boats, offer the best chance of a sighting. The presence of this large rail is often revealed by its loud call, a raucous and steadily repeated 'wack-wacka'. Sometimes when it emerges from the dense mangroves to feed on mudflats exposed at low tide it may be less wary. The large size, dusky chestnut breast and tail-flicking habit assist identification.

▶ **See also pages** 196 197 210 283

329 COLLARED KINGFISHER
Halcyon chloris

The Collared or Mangrove Kingfisher is very widespread outside Australia. One of its many subspecies occurs in Australia's mangroves and occasionally in adjoining woodland. The call can be helpful in locating the bird; it is quite loud, a slower and more deliberate version of the familiar 'kek-kek-kek-' of the Sacred Kingfisher. Kingfishers sighted in this habitat cannot be assumed to be the Collared, as the Sacred commonly uses mangroves. The Collared has a heavier, longer bill, blacker crown, and is whitish rather than buff-coloured beneath.

▶ **See also pages** 98 110 223 332 333

369 MANGROVE ROBIN
Eopsaltria pulverulenta

In Australia this species appears confined entirely to the mangroves of the northern coastline, where it is usually in pairs, sometimes small parties. Within this habitat it seems patchily distributed, often being absent from mangroves that appear suitable. The call is a soft, clear whistle which, if imitated or replayed, will attract the bird. The difficulties of moving through this habitat, and the

bird's tendency to remain motionless much of the time, makes the Mangrove Robin more difficult to sight, though it is tame rather than timid.

▶ **See also pages** 110 196 199 210 223 343

56 **Striated Heron** *Butorides striatus*
127 **Chestnut Rail** *Eulabeornis castaneoventris*
329 **Collared Kingfisher** *Halcyon chloris*
369 **Mangrove Robin** *Eopsaltria pulverulenta*
386 **Mangrove Golden Whistler** *Pachycephala melanura*
389 **White-breasted Whistler** *Pachycephala lanioides*
402 **Broad-billed Flycatcher** *Myiagra ruficollis*
473 **Mangrove Warbler** *Gerygone laevigaster*
527 **Mangrove Honeyeater** *Lichenostomus fasciogularis*
566 **Red-headed Honeyeater** *Myzomela erythrocephala*
581 **Yellow White-eye** *Zosterops lutea*

Coastal mudflats and mangroves, west Kimberley

386 MANGROVE GOLDEN WHISTLER

Pachycephala melanura

The Mangrove Golden Whistler keeps closely to its mangrove habitat, rarely venturing into rainforest even when it is adjoining, while the Golden Whistler is a bird of eucalypt forests and woodlands and is seen only rarely in the adjacent rainforest. Consequently the habitat is useful in identification. The plumages are very much alike but the yellow of the Mangrove is deeper and makes a wider collar across the nape, the tail is black and the bill distinctly longer. There is little, if any, difference in the loud, ringing calls.

▶ See also pages *23 98 192 196 208 347*

402 BROAD-BILLED FLYCATCHER

Myiagra ruficollis

Although predominantly a mangrove species, the Broad-billed Flycatcher occurs also in monsoon scrubs and paperbark swamp-woodlands along the far northern coastline. Some observers report it to be a somewhat silent bird, with an occasional harsh 'shwek', and possibly also a whistled 'too-whee-'. In the field it is difficult to separate from the female Leaden Flycatcher, but seems to be noticeably bluer on the upperparts and is less inclined to quiver the tail.

▶ See also pages *23 110 196 210 350–1*

473 MANGROVE WARBLER

Gerygone laevigaster

Usually a bird of the mangroves, but occasionally in monsoon forest, rainforest, or paperbarks bordering the mangroves. This species advertises its presence with song, which in the north can be heard most of the year, and throughout its range almost constantly in the breeding season. The Mangrove Warbler is generally common and is usually seen foraging, often hovering, around foliage.

▶ See also pages *23 196 199 210 218 367*

An Eastern Reef Egret hunts among the low mangroves of the Pilbara coast, Western Australia

527 MANGROVE HONEYEATER

Lichenostomus fasciogularis

The Mangrove Honeyeater is a noisy and conspicuous species. When many birds congregate at flowering trees they chatter and fight among themselves, while in the breeding season they sing almost continuously, their calls and song loud and quite musical. This species is almost confined to mangroves but will visit flowering trees of adjoining vegetation, including gardens.

▶ **See also pages** *23 98 379–80*

566 RED-HEADED HONEYEATER

Myzomela erythrocephala

The Red-headed Honeyeater occupies mangroves and nearby eucalypt woodlands mainly along streams and in swampy localities. The abundance of this species varies greatly as the birds flock together and move with the flowering of trees; often they are in mixed associations with other small mangrove birds. These are very active birds and the males are conspicuous as they flit about the treetops; they are inquisitive and will respond to imitations of their calls.

▶ **See also pages** *23 77 110 196 199 208 389*

581 YELLOW WHITE-EYE

Zosterops lutea

Although usually in mangroves, the Yellow White-eye is not confined to that habitat but may be found up to several kilometres away in monsoon and river-edge vegetation, paperbark woodlands and, occasionally, eucalypt woodlands. Usually the species is in conspicuous flocks, noisily foraging among the foliage for insects. Nesting is invariably within the mangrove belt.

▶ **See also pages** *23 208 210 231 392–3*

Spinifex-hummock grasslands, Pilbara, Western Australia

GRASSLANDS

Grasslands form Australia's most extensive habitat, covering much of the northern arid and semi-arid country. The grasslands are in some places treeless, but usually with very sparsely scattered trees and shrubs. There are three major types: arid hummock grassland or spinifex, the tussock grasslands of Mitchell grass and, along the tropical northern coast, the grasslands of the coastal black-soil floodplains.

Spinifex-hummock grasslands cover Australia's most arid regions but it blends with other vegetation types so that precise boundaries are often hard to define. In the north spinifex merges into tropical woodlands, its sparse trees and shrubs gradually becoming more numerous until it becomes better described as woodland or shrubland. Similarly, in many places in the interior and around its boundaries the sparse mulga shrubs that occur through most spinifex country increase in density until the habitat becomes better described as mulga scrubland. But the spinifex continues through much of the northern scrubland as ground-cover, so that the boundaries between the habitats are blurred rather than sharply defined.

In other regions the spinifex is without even the most sparsely scattered trees or large shrubs, usually in sand-dune deserts such as the Great Sandy and Simpson deserts.

Spinifex is described as hummock grassland for the domed or hummocked shape of its clumps. Sand swept from the bare surfaces builds up into hard mounds within the shelter of each spinifex clump. This is most evident on sandy deserts. Spinifex on clay or rocky country usually holds small or negligible mounds, though the clumps still have the rounded,

Spinifex on sandy desert, central Australia

hummocked shape typical of this needle-leaved vegetation.

Although the ground between the spinifex hummocks is usually bare, after rain it carries many ephemeral plants, some, like the Sturt desert pea and the many papery everlastings, temporarily transforming the deserts.

The tussocky Mitchell grass covers plains mainly across the eastern parts of the Northern Territory and western Queensland. The grass tufts are spaced about a metre apart, and the ground between is often bare.

The grasslands of the tropical floodplains are also distinctive. They occur mainly close to the coast in the Northern Territory and around the southern parts of the Gulf of Carpentaria. These are

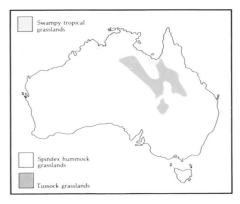

Swampy tropical grasslands

Spinifex hummock grasslands

Tussock grasslands

closed grasslands, where the massed plants are so closely packed that their leaves intermix in a continuous low 'canopy', under which many small herbaceous plants occur. This grassland occurs on heavy black soils flooded in the wet season.

Australia's grasslands as a whole are used to some extent by at least 87 species of birds, with about 15 species largely confined to this habitat. Among the latter are the Spinifex Pigeon, Rufous-crowned Emu-wren, Spinifexbird and several species of grasswren. The following are widespread species typical of the grasslands habitat. Other grassland species that are endemic to various parts of Australia, or representative of regional avifauna, are covered within those regions.

229 FLOCK BRONZEWING

Phaps histrionica

Records before the turn of the century are of Flock Bronzewings in 'countless multitudes' and in the 1930s there were reports of 20 000 to 100 000. Since then records have been usually well under 5000, with a sighting estimated at 3000 in 1980. The Flock Bronzewing is usually seen in numbers near water; away from the waterholes, tanks and bores the flocks break up into small parties or pairs.

The Flock Bronzewing is an inhabitant of tussock grassland country, where if disturbed while feeding it will at first squat, sitting tight, colours inconspicuous, taking flight at quite close quarters. When coming to water the flocks wheel in tight formation before dropping briefly to drink. Sightings have been scattered across the northern arid and semi-arid country, the stronghold of the species appearing to be from the Barkly Tablelands of the Northern Territory into western Queensland.

This species seems to undergo cycles of abundance, perhaps not due as much to the arrival of great numbers from distant parts but rather from the build-up of numbers over a series of good seasons.

A sighting of a flock of around 400 birds at a windmill on Brunette Downs, on the Barkly Tableland, was of flocks of 50–100 birds wheeling and dipping over the water, coming lower each time, and silent but for the sound of wings. Dropping suddenly to the ground, the birds walked to the water's edge, drank briefly, then were up and away. This was an early morning sighting; Flock Bronzewings

Tussock grassland

are reputed to come to water more often towards dusk but have been recorded at most times of the day. A sighting seems to depend very much upon being at the right place at the right time.

▶ **See also pages** *29* 175 223 308

266 NIGHT PARROT

Geopsittacus occidentalis

Always rare, and for some time thought possibly to be extinct, the Night Parrot has been reported on but very few occasions in recent years. During the preceding long interval when there were no sightings, some ornithologists suggested this lack of contact with the species to be a consequence of its nocturnal and secretive habits and remote range, and that far from being extinct it may in fact be moderately common.

Until recently the only knowledge of the species came from early records. It was rarely seen by day, apparently then only when flushed from its hiding place in a clump of spinifex or dense, low saltbush. Two superficially different habitats were recorded, one of spinifex on stony ridges and breakaways, the other the saltbush-bluebush margins of saltlakes. The habitats have in common that they are virtually treeless, and that the vegetation is of low, very dense clumps of bushes with bare ground between.

Early observers noted that this parrot preferred to run from bush to bush rather than fly unless extremely hard-pressed. It would then rise abruptly, darting off low and erratically, to pitch to the ground some distance away, then running to cover. Feeding flights to water occur after dark. The birds usually arrive in small parties, landing right at the water's edge, drinking and perhaps bathing for a few seconds, before flying away again.

Calls may be helpful in identifying birds seen in half-light conditions. Only two calls were recorded in the past. One was a short, sharp, croaky and sometimes repeated alarm when flushed. The other seemed to be a contact call, a drawn-out whistle, soft, rather mournful, repeated at intervals of about three seconds, and said to be far-carrying. A possible sighting of a Night Parrot during a field survey of the birds of the Keep River National Park in April 1982 was in sandstone and spinifex breakaway country.

Other sightings of recent years have been in the Pilbara and goldfields of the interior of Western Australia and the Lake Eyre region of the eastern interior. There were also reports from north-western Victoria in the period 1974–79 in the Big Desert area; the birds on those occasions were always located by flushing from spinifex by day.

▶ See also pages 198 316

310 EASTERN GRASS OWL

Tyto longimembris

Field observations are usually but a brief glimpse as the owl is flushed from its daylight roost or nesting place in tall dense grass clumps. The call is recorded as a soft-pitched trill, unlike the usual Barn Owl screech, probably unlikely to be very useful in revealing the presence of this species. Occasionally, perhaps at times of stress, it will hunt during the day; there is a record of 30 in the air at the one time. However the species is generally regarded as scarce and localized.

Most observations appear to have resulted from chance encounters — the accidental flushing of an owl while searching for other species through habitat suiting these owls. A systematic patrolling of such sites may give this result. Probably the most successful way of sighting is to watch out over suitable or known habitat at dusk when the owls first take to the air to begin hunting. The best times are in the first half or three-quarters of an hour after sunset and just before visibility is lost in darkness. In flight the Grass Owl's legs hang down much further than those of the Barn Owl and the head and neck look shorter. A typical suitable site is along the road to Trebonne, 7 km west of Ingham, where there are areas of high grass between sugarcane clumps.

▶ See also pages 175 196 210 326-7

341 SINGING BUSHLARK

Mirafra javanica

A widespread species of open grasslands, conspicuous in the breeding season, when it performs typically lark-like song-flights, rising steeply to hover on rapidly quivering wings while pouring out a rich and

229 **Flock Bronzewing** *Phaps histrionica*
266 **Night Parrot** *Geopsittacus occidentalis*
310 **Eastern Grass Owl** *Tyto longimembris*
341 **Singing Bushlark** *Mirafra javanica*
428 **Spinifexbird** *Eremiornis carteri*
432 **Brown Songlark** *Cinclorhamphus cruralis*

430 **GOLDEN-HEADED CISTICOLA** *Cisticola exilis*

varied succession of notes, before dropping back to ground or perch. In these display flights the Singing Bushlark could be confused with the introduced Common Skylark, but has a song that is more varied and tinkling.

▶ **See also pages** *29 223 336*

428 SPINIFEXBIRD

Eremiornis carteri

In the Hamersley, Chichester and other ranges of the Pilbara region the Spinifexbird is common in suitable habitat; it favours the slopes and valley sides of arid ranges, where the additional runoff of the meagre rain causes the spinifex clumps to be large

and close-packed. Convenient habitat is within 100 m of Wittenoom, along the lower slopes of the Hamersleys, as well as in countless gullies higher on the range. The distribution of the species extends from the west coast through central Australia to western Queensland.

From its dense needle-leaved cover the Spinifexbird is usually heard before being sighted. When its sharp alarm call (like the striking together of stones) is known, the species can readily be found simply by walking through likely habitat. The Spinifexbird will respond with the alarm call and will usually climb onto the seeding stalks above the spinifex for a brief look at the intruder before scuttling down into its dense cover. Identifiers are the rich rufous plumage, and the long, dark brown tail often carried cocked upwards.

▶ See also pages 28 *29* 175 219 230 357

430 GOLDEN-HEADED CISTICOLA

Cisticola exilis

The habitat of the Golden-headed Cisticola is the tall dense grass of the wet margins of swamps and lagoons, where in the breeding season the almost incessant buzzing calls of the males make this bird very obvious. Although the habitat is dense, the cisticolas readily show themselves, often perching in clear view on grass stems and shrubs.

▶ See also pages *30* 138 192 357

432 BROWN SONGLARK

Cinclorhamphus cruralis

In the breeding season the Brown Songlark is so obvious that its presence can hardly be overlooked. In his conspicuous song-flight the male takes off singing, rising steadily upwards in a fluttering flight that includes glides with wings steeply upswept, legs dangling, all the while pouring out a reeling succession of notes, many of metallic 'scratchy' quality, yet pleasant and far-carrying.

▶ See also pages *29* 358

590 PAINTED FIRETAIL

Emblema picta

The rich red-and-black plumage of the Painted Firetail makes it unmistakable; it is quite abundant where there is spinifex on rocky ranges so long as there is water in the gorges. These finches are inconspicuous while feeding in pairs and small parties, taking seeds from the ground among the spinifex clumps, and are not usually noticed until flushed at quite close range. The best opportunities of sighting are at pools, where they will be arriving in steady succession throughout the day in warm dry weather.

▶ See also pages 184 221 233 395

590 **PAINTED FIRETAIL** *Emblema picta* Top: *Male* Bottom: *Female*

The waterlily surface of Fogg Dam, Northern Territory

WETLANDS

Wetlands are a valuable bird habitat but all too scarce on this largely arid continent. This habitat covers all inland waters, fresh and saline, permanent and temporary. The wetlands are mostly coastal and can conveniently be grouped into four major segments of the continent: the northern and north-eastern coasts, the Murray-Darling drainage, the south-west and south-east coastal, and the interior region of occasional and temporary wetlands.

The scarcity of swamps, lakes and other wetlands across this dry continent, and the fact that most of these birds are entirely restricted to the wetlands, with no alternative habitat, make the retention of wetlands vital if the waterbird populations are to be maintained. Large areas of coastal wetlands have already been drained or filled.

Some of Australia's outstanding wetlands are those of the river systems of the Northern Territory and north-eastern Queensland, where annual summer wet season flooding of the billabongs, swamps and plains along their lower reaches provides breeding and refuge for huge numbers of waterfowl. Many of these wetlands are now within national parks.

In the south-east, the occasional flooding of the Murray-Darling system creates vast areas of temporary swamps, while many of its billabongs are more permanent. The inland south-west also has chains of lakes, mainly temporary, along some of its rivers. Although clearing of surrounding farmlands has caused most to become saline, they remain important to the south-western birdlife.

The greater part of the continent, the dry interior, has no permanent wetlands but when heavy rains occur temporary wetlands of great extent can be created. Some species of

Paperbark swamp

waterbirds are able to take advantage of the additional habitat, moving to those localities and beginning to breed almost immediately.

These inland waters include not only the extensive shallow salt lakes, but also the temporary claypans, and pools retained for months in river channels that are for most of the year dry. Some of the salt lakes when flooded become breeding sites for huge colonies of birds, including Banded Stilts.

Although the Australian land mass extends from tropic to southern mid-temperate regions it is the poorest of the continents in number of waterfowl, probably a direct consequence of the very restricted wetlands. The extent of wetlands available varies greatly, and even on such major rivers as the Murray fluctuates enormously; consequently the nomadic habit is strongly developed among Australia's waterbirds.

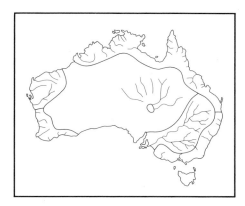

63 **SACRED IBIS** *Threskiornis aethiopica*

About 120 species make some use of wetland habitats, with the quite large proportion of over half, about 70 species, virtually confined to this habitat. The following are some widespread wetland species.

58 LITTLE BITTERN

Ixobrychus minutus

The Little Bittern is extremely secretive, solitary, keeping to the most dense of swamp vegetation where the cryptic plumage and pose make it very difficult to sight. When disturbed it either adopts a frozen posture, bill pointing skywards, effectively blending into the vegetation, or quietly steals away through the reeds. Rarely can it be put to flight but if one is flushed it takes off suddenly, seemingly awkward, legs trailing, then flies heron-like with neck folded back. The species is apparently at least partly nocturnal. The presence of the species is usually revealed by the regularly repeated deep croaking of the male in spring, or the finding of a nest in the reed-beds.

▶ **See also pages** *35 99 137 163 242 244 265*

A salt lake of the interior

59 BLACK BITTERN

Dupetor flavicollis

The Black Bittern is a solitary bird of swamps, lagoon margins, mudflats, flooded paperbark woodlands and mangroves. Some of these habitats are quite open, and this bittern seems more inclined to venture out, where it may be seen by a quiet and patient observer, especially near shaded pools or shallows where it may hunt. It is a rather quiet species, sometimes giving a low, regular 'whoo-oo-'.

▶ See also pages   208 210 265

60 AUSTRALASIAN BITTERN

Botaurus poiciloptilus

In some localities the Australasian Bittern is present throughout the year, in others it appears only during favourable local conditions. It occurs alone or in groups, favouring areas of extensive and dense reed-beds, where its presence may be revealed by feeding platforms, the trampled reeds littered with remnants of yabbies and other prey. When this large bittern emerges to feed on mudflats it seems not particularly shy, stalking and stabbing at prey with the heavy, dagger-like, straight bill. If flushed it seems to lift clumsily into the air with heavy wingbeats. The repeated booming 'woomph' is heard mainly at night.

▶ See also pages   163 242 265

63 SACRED IBIS

Threskiornis aethiopica

In Australia the Sacred Ibis has greatly increased its range and has become common where previously unknown. In the South-West Region it was unknown until 1952, was first reported breeding in the wild in 1979, and now seems to be regularly sighted on wetlands throughout that region. It is a conspicuous species which is unique in its combination of all-white plumage and typically ibis sickle-shaped bill.

▶ See also pages   34 79 136 137 161 174 198 264 266

86 MUSK DUCK

Biziura lobata

Through its long breeding season the male Musk Duck draws attention to itself in displays that are both visible and audible at a considerable distance. The breeding cycle of the male begins early in the year and the displays may begin in autumn, though nesting seems

non-breeding plumage

breeding plumage

to be mainly from spring to early summer. In display the male kicks jets of water out and back, this accompanied by 'plonking' and 'whistling', the 'plonk' evidently caused in striking the water, the 'whistle' purely vocal. These remarkably far-carrying sounds often attract attention to the Musk Duck

58   **Little Bittern** *Ixobrychus minutus*
59   **Black Bittern** *Dupetor flavicollis*
60   **Australasian Bittern** *Botaurus poiciloptilus*
69   **Plumed Whistling Duck** *Dendrocygna eytoni*
71   **Freckled Duck** *Stictonetta naevosa*
86   **Musk Duck** *Biziura lobata*
115   **Brown Quail** *Coturnix australis*
125   **Buff-banded Rail** *Rallus philippensis*
130   **Australian Crake** *Porzana fluminea*
136   **Dusky Moorhen** *Gallinula tenebrosa*
145   **Painted Snipe** *Rostratula benghalensis*

163 **RED-NECKED AVOCETS** *Recurvirostra novaehollandiae*

Temporary claypan; bird tracks in the mud show its value as a feeding site

when it otherwise would not have been noticed, perhaps screened by reeds; on open waters the splashes are conspicuous.

▶ **See also pages** *35 125 272*

115 BROWN QUAIL

Coturnix australis

The Swamp Quail is often treated as a subspecies of the Brown and is confined to Tasmania; whether species or subspecies, they appear identical in the field. Both occupy lush vegetation of damp ground, backwaters of reservoirs, margins of swamps, and islets in irrigated pastures. These quails are most likely to be noticed when flushed, or perhaps when calls are heard, usually very early in the morning, towards evening and at night.

▶ **See also pages** *35 279*

125 BUFF-BANDED RAIL

Rallus philippensis

This bird often occupies lush vegetation around the margins of swamps, lagoons and watercourses but although quite common it is seldom sighted, being very shy and retiring. Rarely are more than one or two birds sighted. When alarmed this rail will run into concealing vegetation rather than fly, but if it is put to flight it rises with extended neck and trailing legs. It is difficult to flush or to see by day but is more active towards dusk when the calls are usually heard. As well as the colourful plumage, the frequent flicking of the tail aids identification.

▶ **See also pages** *35 82 124 137 242 282*

130 AUSTRALIAN CRAKE

Porzana fluminea

Although never far from dense sheltering vegetation of the wetlands, this crake will fly out over open waters between reed-beds and forage along exposed shorelines. Although in this respect it is probably the boldest of the crakes, it is quick to run or fly low into cover if alarmed. If the observer waits quietly the bird is likely to return after a short time to carry on feeding. The Australian Crake is a permanent inhabitant of many swamps, both fresh and saline, but will also colonize or abandon wetlands as conditions require.

▶ **See also pages** *35 82 183 242 283*

136 DUSKY MOORHEN

Gallinula tenebrosa

The easiest sightings of this species are
in the parks and gardens of cities and
suburbs where there are lakes or large
ponds bordering open lawns. In the
wild the species, though common, is
shy, keeping to dense vegetation of the
freshwater swamps or river banks.
The Dusky Moorhen is active by day
and usually feeds on shallow waters,
dabbling at surface plants and insects,
or upending, duck-like. The strident
harsh 'kerk' may help to locate it in
dense vegetation.

▶ **See also pages** *35 82 99 285*

145 PAINTED SNIPE

Rostratula benghalensis

The Painted Snipe is most active at
dusk and dawn, and probably much of
the night, probing for aquatic and
other insects and some plant seeds.
During the day it shelters quietly
within dense wetlands vegetation
where the disruptive patterning of the
plumage makes it difficult to see. The
Painted Snipe tends to occur in small
groups, with up to 25 birds nesting
within an area of about 1 ha. The calls
seem to be limited to alarm and
courtship sounds, probably not helpful
in locating these birds.

▶ **See also pages** *35 163 183 288*

425 CLAMOROUS REED-WARBLER

Acrocephalus stentoreus

The spirited, loud song of the
Clamorous Reed-Warbler is likely to
be heard from any reed-bed no matter
how isolated it may seem. This bird
travels or disperses widely and
colonizes the reed-beds of any pools of
gorges or river pools which are
sufficiently permanent to support such
vegetation. Although its presence is so
loudly proclaimed, it is secretive and
not easily sighted unless it chooses to
come to the edge of its reed-bed. It is
much more often reported through the
spring and summer when breeding and
calling, but is evidently also
migratory, moving into, or becoming
more common in, southern wetlands
in spring and summer.

▶ **See also pages** *356 384*

425 **CLAMOROUS REED-WARBLER** *Acrocephalus stentoreus*

Arid woodland, interior of Western Australia

Woodlands cover a large part of the Australian continent and contain a diversity of habitats, in both coastal areas and much of the interior. There are very many species of woodland eucalypts, while the understorey vegetation is varied but usually of low scrub or grass.

The trees of the woodlands are much more widely spaced than those of the forests, though the transition from open forest to tall woodland may be almost imperceptible. As with rainforest and forest, woodland is defined in terms of canopy cover and tree proportions. The wider spacing of woodland trees gives a canopy cover from 50 per cent down to less than 10 per cent. The trees have space and light to expand laterally, more of the lower limbs are retained than in forests, so that the length of their boles, up to the first large limbs, is less than the remaining distance to the treetops.

Within this broad description, woodlands have great variety, ranging from grasslands with sparsely scattered trees to woodlands of tall trees quite closely spaced and almost of forest character.

Like the forests, woodlands are usually dominated by eucalypts, but sometimes by paperbark, or acacias such as pindan or brigalow. The understorey is most commonly of grasses but in south-western Australia usually of a low undergrowth scrub, made up of a bewildering variety of plants, many bearing large and often bird-pollinated flowers.

The grass understorey in much of the semi-arid regions takes the form of spinifex, and the terrain can range from flat or gently undulating plains to rough, broken sandstone country, yet with its scattered trees it still qualifies as woodland.

Tall woodland of salmon gums

Within the broad classification of 'woodland' are included many vegetation names applied at various times to distinctive types of woodland. These include riverine forest, river red-gum and timbered country, paperbark woodland or swamp, brigalow, pindan, tropical deciduous woodland, tropical mixed woodland, temperate mixed woodland, and other specific types.

The varied character and wide distribution of woodland makes it Australia's richest bird habitat, used by about 320 species. The main regions of woodlands are sufficiently separated, usually by semi-desert country, that no one region has so large a woodlands birdlist. The isolated south-western woodlands in particular lack a great many of the species found in northern and eastern woodlands, but have some unique species.

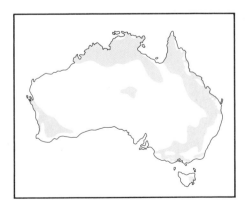

223 **PEACEFUL DOVE** *Geopelia placida*

223 PEACEFUL DOVE

Geopelia placida

A widespread and common species of open grassy woodlands and open forests where it is most often to be seen at the forest edges, close to the more open grassland. It is always quite close to a supply of water, so that in drier parts of its range it is confined to the vicinity of the more permanent rivers or river pools. The soft calls are among the best known of woodland bird calls.

▶ See also pages   211 223 306–7

254 VARIED LORIKEET

Psitteuteles versicolor

This is a species of the tropical lowlands where it inhabits most types of country where there are flowering trees, but is most common in woodlands, especially the eucalypts and melaleucas along streams. In northern Queensland it frequents the drier woodlands and open forests. The Varied Lorikeet is common, but locally scarce or absent for long periods. These nomadic movements follow the flowering of trees, sometimes seasonal but mostly irregular; at times the birds are scarce

even in areas of heavy flowering. Attention is likely to be drawn by the loud screeching in flight, or the high-pitched chattering while feeding. These lorikeets drink where branches or logs give access to the water.

▶ See also pages   175 193 208 313

260 RED-WINGED PARROT

Aprosmictus erythropterus

Usually seen in pairs or family parties, but sometimes, after the breeding season, in flocks of up to 20. Red-winged Parrots spend most of their time feeding among the foliage of trees and shrubs, coming only occasionally to the ground to feed on fallen seeds, or to drink. They tend to be wary and difficult to approach. Often attention is drawn by their contact call, given in flight, a sharp metallic 'crillik-crillik'. When sighted in flight the Red-winged is unmistakable, even when the bright colours are not visible, for its unusual flight, weaving erratically through the air with slow, deep wingbeats. It is quite common but patchy and nomadic along the southern edge of its range.

▶ See also pages   41 136 137 207 208 314–15

Alpine woodland, Victoria

272 EASTERN ROSELLA

Platycercus eximius

Although woodlands and open forests are the Eastern Rosella's natural habitat it is now also very much a bird of lightly timbered farmlands where there are trees remaining along roadsides, creeks and stony rises. In coastal eastern Victoria it is often in banksia woodlands. This species is common almost throughout its range and has benefited from clearing of heavier forests; it occurs in suburbs of Canberra and Sydney. The flight is swift and undulating and the plumage bright and distinctive.

▶ See also pages 136 317 318

278 RED-RUMPED PARROT

Psephotus haematonotus

This parrot inhabits most types of lightly timbered country including open woodlands, open mallee, grasslands and farmlands with scattered trees. In the more arid parts of its range it keeps to the tree-lined watercourses. It is quite common around Canberra and it occurs in eastern suburbs of Sydney. Usually seen in pairs or small parties, or larger flocks in winter. Although conspicuous and often calling noisily in flight, this species is much more difficult to sight while feeding on the ground.

▶ See also pages 129 136 319

355 WHITE-WINGED TRILLER

Lalage sueurii

This triller occurs in open woodlands, scrublands and lightly treed grasslands almost throughout Australia. In southern parts it is a summer migrant. When breeding the male attracts attention by loud and spirited song from treetops and while in flight.

▶ See also pages 173 340

376 JACKY WINTER

Microeca leucophaea

The small, active flycatcher affectionately known as Jacky Winter is very widespread through inland and drier coastal parts of Australia. It is probably most typically a bird of open woodlands but is also in mallee and at the edge of eucalypt forest adjoining open country. It takes frequent, quick flights to catch flying insects and returns to a conspicuous position on a dead limb or other open perch where it restlessly wags its tail.

▶ See also pages 42 80 213 344–5 373

406 RESTLESS FLYCATCHER

Myiagra inquieta

The Restless Flycatcher is probably part-migratory, many of the southern birds moving north in winter; in other areas it is resident. It is certainly more obvious in spring and summer when its loud grinding calls reverberate through the woodlands. These calls are given while the bird hovers a metre or two above the ground, searching for insects.

▶ See also pages   41 213 351

422 WHITE-BROWED BABBLER

Pomatostomus superciliosus

Although predominantly a bird of the woodlands, the White-browed Babbler occurs also in open forest and arid scrublands. Like other babblers it lives in groups of up to about 12 individuals. This group as a whole noisily defends the territory against intrusion by other babblers, and combines to direct loud, scolding alarm calls and harassment at possible predators. It is a common and obvious bird which should be easily found within the appropriate habitat.

▶ See also pages   41 135 220 355 356

477 WHITE-THROATED WARBLER

Gerygone olivacea

The White-throated Warbler's delightful song is almost always the first indicator of the presence of the species, the delicate cascade of silvery notes carrying far through the woodlands. When the source of the song is tracked down it is a bird equally attractive, and easily identified with white throat and pale lemon-yellow underparts. The song may be heard in woodlands, open forests and lightly timbered grasslands.

▶ See also pages   41 162 208 324 367 368

498 BROWN TREECREEPER

Climacteris picumnus

This rather plain treecreeper is common and widely distributed through woodland and adjacent open forest, grasslands, and farmlands with scattered living and dead trees. The Brown Treecreeper spirals up trunks and limbs of trees both living and dead in search of insects, but spends up to half its time foraging on fallen logs and on the ground. The species is quite conspicuous and attracts attention to itself with typical sharp treecreeper calls.

▶ See also pages   41 92 373

376 **JACKY WINTER** *Microeca leucophaea*

Tropical woodland of eucalypts and pandanus, west Kimberley

579 STRIATED PARDALOTE *Pardalotus striatus*

579 STRIATED PARDALOTE

Pardalotus striatus

Found almost throughout Australia in open eucalypt country, typically woodland and the woodland-like tree-lined margins of inland rivers, and also in mallee and open-forest country. The four subspecies are sufficiently distinctive to have been previously regarded as separate species. The Striated Pardalote is common but so small and inconspicuous when feeding among tree foliage that it would often be overlooked but for its loud and continuous calling.

▶ See also pages 153 392

627 APOSTLEBIRD

Struthidea cinerea

The Apostlebird is never far from water, needed for the mud nest. Woodlands are the usual habitat, but also mallee, and timber along watercourses. These birds are usually in groups of around eight to 20, noisy and obvious, and often fairly tame around outback habitations.

▶ See also pages 41 136 403–4

631 WHITE-BROWED WOODSWALLOW

Artamus superciliosus

The very widespread White-browed Woodswallow is usually found in woodlands and, to a lesser extent, in open forests, grasslands, pastoral land and farmlands with scattered timber and in mulga scrublands. It is usually in pairs or parties, but most often in larger flocks, often in company with Masked Woodswallows. These gatherings are made all the more conspicuous by the musical 'chap-chap' flight calls.

▶ See also pages 41 405

Rocky coast

COASTS AND ISLANDS

The coast is a composite of many distinct habitats. These include islands and reefs, shores both sandy and rocky, bays, estuaries and mudflats. Included also is the land immediately behind the shore, often of dunes or cliffs. The coastal seas extend out to the edge of the continental shelf, beyond which are the open oceans. While many birds of the coastal habitat will occupy several or even most of these, some show preference for, or are confined to, one or other part.

Of all bird habitats, islands are the site of some of the most intensive use by birds, with colonies of thousands, sometimes tens of thousands of birds packed into the confines of a breeding colony, often on a flat, sandy cay of only a few hectares in area. But of course such an islet is but a central focus for these birds, their habitat including the surrounding seas and reefs.

Rivalling the seabird colonies for massed birdlife are the coastal mudflats where migrant waders gather in passage to and from their breeding grounds in the Northern Hemisphere. The huge expanses of beach and mudflats exposed by the tides along the coasts of north-western Australia and the southern parts of the Gulf of Carpentaria attract waders in concentrations totalling hundreds of thousands, as they rest and feed before continuing their journey.

Through the summer months the coasts almost right around Australia are the habitat of many species of waders, though never in such immense numbers as the northern sites of arrival and departure. These birds favour the sheltered waters, sandbanks or mudflats of bays and river estuaries, and many also utilize the shores of lakes.

Those parts of the coastline that are rocky attract other birds, some,

Sandy coast

like the Sooty Oystercatcher, specialized for feeding on the marine life of reefs and rocks. Other birds, including the White-bellied Sea-Eagle, Osprey, Little Penguin, Fairy Prion, Common Diving Petrel, Gannet, Great Cormorant, Black-faced Shag and Red-tailed Tropicbird, utilize the coastal waters.

Coastal seas extend out to the edge of the continental shelf and include the entirety of the Great Barrier Reef, Bass Strait, the Gulf of Carpentaria, Torres Strait and the Timor and Arafura seas. Where the oceans meet the coastal seas at the edge of the continental shelf the upwelling of deep currents brings food to the surface and attracts oceanic birds, making the edge of the shelf a rich birdwatching location.

The following are some widespread coastal species.

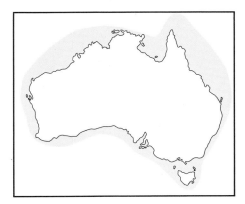

15 GREAT-WINGED PETREL

Pterodroma macroptera

In Australian waters, the Great-winged Petrel breeds only on islands of the south coast of Western Australia. Outside Australia, the species also breeds in New Zealand and birds seen off the coast of south-eastern Australia are predominantly of the New Zealand subspecies.

In the south-west, the Great-winged Petrel is present most of the year near its breeding sites on the high granite islands from the Recherche Archipelago west to Cape Leeuwin. In this region sightings were recorded throughout the year but were more widespread in spring; in the south-east, sightings were throughout the year.

▶ **See also pages** 47 253

31 WHITE-FACED STORM-PETREL

Pelagodroma marina

The White-faced Storm-Petrel breeds on a great many islands around the southern coasts of Australia. These birds come to their nest burrows only at night; even moonlight results in a decrease in activity. Some of the colonies on record in recent years have contained up to 35 000 birds. These birds are rarely seen close inshore by day. They are usually sighted from boats at sea, characteristically fluttering across the wave-tops, long legs dangling and often pattering on the surface.

▶ **See also pages** 47 151 164 244 256-7

35 RED-FOOTED BOOBY

Sula sula

In Australia this booby breeds only on Raine Island and Pandora Cay, off the north-east coast of Cape York Peninsula. Usually there are few sightings away from the seas and coasts in the region of the breeding colonies. The colonies on these islands are quite small, just several hundred birds. This booby requires vegetated islands for nesting. It seeks squid and flying fish, sometimes at dusk and dawn.

▶ **See also pages** 47 97 258-9

146 **PIED OYSTERCATCHER** *Haematopus longirostris*

Coastal lagoon

45 LEAST FRIGATEBIRD

Fregata ariel

Widespread on northern Australian coasts and seas, and occasionally reaching southern coasts, the Least Frigatebird breeds on islands of the north-western and north-eastern coasts. These Australian colonies are much smaller than those of the central Pacific. In the north-west, in 1982 Adele Island had about 11 400 birds, the Lacepedes 2700, and Bedout Island 4580. In 1980, Australia's north-eastern colonies were Raine Island with about 2670, and Quoin Island with about 1000.

▶ See also pages 81 97 110 218 219 262

55 EASTERN REEF EGRET

Egretta sacra

Usually seen hunting on exposed mudflats and reefs, and on rocky shores and beaches, often crouching with wings partly open, ready to jab at the prey. The two colour phases, dark grey and white, can be confused with immature White-faced Herons, or various egrets. White phase Reef Egrets generally predominate, except on southern coasts where the grey form is more common.

▶ See also pages 25 82 264

94 BRAHMINY KITE

Haliastur indus

The Brahminy is most likely to be seen along the more sheltered parts of northern coasts, in bays, estuaries and lower tidal reaches of rivers, especially where there are mangroves and mudflats. It takes mainly fish, often those stranded in mudflat pools, but also small crabs and carrion. This species is often to be seen scavenging around northern coastal towns.

The call can be useful in drawing attention to its presence when it is perched out of sight in mangroves. Once sighted, identification presents no problem except perhaps confusion of brownish immatures with Whistling Kites; the Brahminy has a much shorter tail.

▶ See also pages 80 82 83 98 122 223 274

144 BEACH THICK-KNEE

Burhinus neglectus

The Beach Thick-knee inhabits beaches, reefs and mudflats, particularly of islands, around Australia's northern and eastern coasts. Records south of Queensland are very sparse. Like the Bush Thick-

knee, the species is most active at night when its wailing calls are usually heard. But most sightings are by day, when Beach Thick-knees may be seen standing around, seemingly idle, occasionally moving to take small crabs or other marine creatures. Though generally reputed to be very wary, it may sometimes on remote

15 **Great-winged Petrel** *Pterodroma macroptera*
31 **White-faced Storm-Petrel** *Pelagodroma marina*
35 **Red-footed Booby** *Sula sula*
45 **Least Frigatebird** *Fregata ariel*
55 **Eastern Reef Egret** *Egretta sacra*
94 **Brahminy Kite** *Haliastur indus*
144 **Beach Thick-knee** *Burhinus neglectus*
147 **Sooty Oystercatcher** *Haematopus fuliginosus*
164 **Ruddy Turnstone** *Arenaria interpres*
185 **Sanderling** *Calidris alba*
203 **Black-naped Tern** *Sterna sumatrana*

coasts be less shy, even somewhat inquisitive. Most far northern beaches seem to have at least one pair. At a distance the bustard-like stance and heavy bill are useful identifiers.

▶ See also pages 47 80 81 197 223 287–8

147 SOOTY OYSTERCATCHER

Haematopus fuliginosus

An inhabitant of Australian coasts generally but more commonly recorded on southern coasts, its

occurrence across much of the far northern coasts being restricted by the presence of mangroves and mudflats rather than the preferred habitat of reefs and rocky shores. Breeding is usually on rocky islands or promontories, after which small flocks form to move to mainland coasts for the autumn and winter. Locally, these movements may determine the most likely sites for the species.

▶ See also pages 45 47 82 122 124 288

177 **BAR-TAILED GODWIT** *Limosa lapponica*

204 **SOOTY TERN** *Sterna fuscata*

164 RUDDY TURNSTONE

Arenaria interpres

A summer migrant to Australia, but with some birds, probably immatures, remaining through the winter. The Ruddy Turnstone occurs on beaches with a rocky intertidal zone. This small bird draws attention to itself with its constant activity, turning over stones, shells and seaweed in search of small marine creatures. Although usually solitary or in very small parties, or in company with other waders, it is sometimes seen in large numbers. As many as 2060 were recorded at Roebuck Bay in the Kimberley region when on migration in February, and lesser but still considerable numbers on beaches at Darwin, Eyre Peninsula and some Barrier Reef islands.

▶ See also pages 47 149 150 293

177 BAR-TAILED GODWIT

Limosa lapponica

This distinctive wader occupies coastal sandy and muddy shores and the adjacent estuaries, lagoons and marshes, feeding in the shallows. This is an abundant wader in widely separated parts of Australia. Along the north-western beaches between Broome and Port Hedland counts of this species have reached 58 000 as the birds stop over on their migration in November. Along the Queensland coast it is the most abundant wader, with counts of over 7000, and at Victoria's Corner Inlet around 7000 are recorded each summer.

▶ See also pages 80 122 123 124 149 150 218 *219* 296

185 SANDERLING

Calidris alba

A bird of the ocean beaches, and occasionally lagoons or estuaries, it feeds on small aquatic insects where the sand is washed by the ebb and surge of waves along the beach. It feeds by jabbing the bill into the wet sand, running or flying up to avoid each wave, then settling again.

▶ See also pages 47 297

203 BLACK-NAPED TERN

Sterna sumatrana

The Black-naped Tern is to be seen on coastal and occasionally inshore waters of far northern and north-eastern Australia. It feeds mainly from the surface, taking fish and some other forms of marine life. When fishing it

210 **COMMON NODDY** *Anous stolidus*

makes diving swoops to take food
from the surface, flying with short,
choppy wingbeats. The Black-naped
Tern often mingles with Roseate or
other terns, or noddies. Its colonies on
island beaches have been found to
suffer considerable losses to gulls,
high-tide flooding and human
disturbance. This species, and indeed
most other colonial-nesting seabirds,
should not be unnecessarily subjected
to close human approach.

▶ **See also pages** 47 81 82 96 203

204 SOOTY TERN

Sterna fuscata

There are large breeding colonies of
the Sooty Tern on islands around
northern Australia, in the Coral Sea
south to Cairns, and on Ashmore
Reef, Bedout Island, and the Houtman
Abrolhos islands on the north-west
coast. Some of these colonies have
contained up to 40 000 birds but
usually are much smaller.

▶ **See also pages** 48 82 96 97 237 244 302–3

210 COMMON NODDY

Anous stolidus

In Australian waters the Common
Noddy occurs off the north-eastern
and north-western coasts, with large
colonies in both regions. There are
also colonies much farther south, on
the west coast of Pelsart Island and in
the Houtman Abrolhos group, nest
site of the pair shown here.

▶ **See also pages** 81 96 97 219 237 244 304

Rainforest, north-eastern New South Wales

RAINFORESTS

Rainforest is closed forest, where the crowns of the closely spaced trees intermingle to form a dense and mostly continuous canopy of foliage, excluding almost all direct sunlight from the lower parts of the forest. By comparison with the luxuriant upper levels it is but sparsely vegetated, relatively open, often very gloomy, and almost always very humid. Rainforest is distinguished from other closed-canopy forests, such as mangroves and brigalow, by its abundance of lianes, epiphytes and, towards ground level, a covering of ferns, mosses and fungi upon moist earth and damp, decaying logs.

At the edge of the rainforest the foliage canopy slopes down to the ground forming a dense and seemingly impenetrable wall of lush, tangled vegetation. But once through into the great space beneath the canopy the forest floor is more open and movement is generally not too difficult. Here, as well as the light being far more subdued, temperatures are much more stable, usually much cooler than where the full heat of direct sunlight beats down to the coarse grass undergrowth of the open forest, but occasionally it is warmer, blanketed against the chill of cold wind or frosty morning. The trees of the rainforests are often more than 30 m tall and in the more luxuriant tropical rainforests support several canopy layers.

Rainforest occurs along almost the full length of Australia's eastern coast and in western Tasmania. As monsoon forest it continues in small patches across northern Australia, mostly near the coast. The character of the rainforest varies greatly and has been classified into a number of types based on broad latitudinal regions, together with such features as leaf size of the trees and the predominance of certain classes of plants such as lianes, epiphytes, ferns and palms.

Tropical rainforest occurs south to about Mackay, reaching its peak where temperature, rainfall and soil fertility are all high. The trees are of a bewildering diversity of species, many are large-leaved, with an abundance of woody lianes and plank buttresses; in places where there are poorly drained soils there are palm forests.

In tropical rainforest is the greatest diversity of plant and animal species, most of its plants, birds and other life forms not occurring outside this habitat.

Further south, on ranges and lowlands from Mackay to south-eastern New South Wales, the diversity of tree species is progressively reduced. The tropical characteristics of plank buttresses, large leaves and wealth of epiphytes continue to reduce with distance southwards, where the subtropical rainforest in many places meets with temperate rainforest, the subtropical on the lowlands and eastern slopes of the Great Dividing Range, the temperate confined to the highlands.

The subtropical rainforests have few lianes and an increasing abundance of mosses, lichens and filmy ferns. There are far fewer tree species. Higher altitudes have much the same effect as higher latitude, extending the occurrence of temperate rainforest much

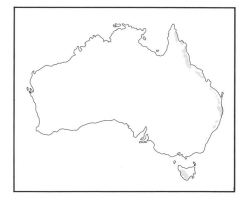

Palm forest, Fraser Island, Queensland

farther north along the mountain tops, and extending the range of the mossy Antarctic beech forest type into south-eastern Queensland.

Temperate rainforests tend to be dominated by a single species of tree and to be rich in mosses and terrestrial ferns. They extend patchily through eastern New South Wales and Victoria to western Tasmania, but with decreasing species of rainforest birds.

The birdlife of the closed forests is distinctive, particularly that of Cape York north of Cooktown, being an attenuation of the Papuan bird fauna, and is both biogeographically and ecologically separated from the closed-forest bird fauna farther south. During the most recent increases in aridity the McIlwraith Range–Iron Range area and other rainforests of Cape York have acted as refuges for these species. There is no species endemic to the region but many are shared with New Guinea.

But in the extensive rainforests (or rather the remnants of these) farther south, in the Cooktown–Atherton–Townsville area, there are 10 endemic species, seven of them restricted to the uplands.

In another distinctive region of extensive rainforests, including highlands, in south-eastern Queensland and north-eastern New South Wales, there are five endemic rainforest birds — the Paradise Riflebird, Regent Bowerbird, Logrunner, Rufous Scrub-bird and Albert Lyrebird. Altogether, five distinct groups of rainforest birds have been identified along Queensland's eastern coast south of Cape York.

Three groups contain rainforest birds of the higher altitudes, one of birds found only in the north-east, one of birds unique to the south-east, and one of birds found the entire length of the highland rainforests.

Of lowland rainforest birds, there seem to be two groups, one confined to north-eastern Queensland and one group of birds occurring throughout lowland rainforests.

The following are some of the birds of the rainforests.

111 ORANGE-FOOTED SCRUBFOWL
Megapodius reinwardt

In north-eastern Australia this is a bird of the rainforests but it also inhabits the monsoon scrubs, sometimes the mangrove edges and the narrow river-edge strips of broad-leaved scrub. Across northern Australia it is in small patches of monsoon forest and scrub on swampy ground, river banks and at springs below cliffs. Its extension into mangroves occurs mainly in the extreme north, on islands, and in New Guinea. The incubation mound requires a sufficient rainfall and steady high humidity for fermentation of the vegetation; it is usually placed in a shaded position. The Orange-footed Scrubfowl can be seen in most areas of rainforest along the northern coasts and on many of the continental islands. It is common near the coast and adjacent islets, but not usually more than 20 km inland except along major rivers. In the far north it also occurs in mangroves, dense acacia thickets and thickets under eucalypt forest. In the Kimberley the Scrubfowl is confined to the north-west coast and islands.

▶ **See also pages** *53 91 98 209 278*

214 SUPERB FRUIT-DOVE
Ptilinopus superbus

In the Atherton and Cape York regions this species is moderately common in the thickest parts of the closed forests. Although feeding mainly in lowland and highland rainforests, it is recorded as quite often nesting in open forest, with breeding as far south as the Eungella Range. Around Innisfail the species is widespread at all altitudes. Mission Beach is a convenient and reliable site for sightings. Here it feeds upon fruits of the upper forest canopy, occasionally descending to lower vegetation. The Superb Fruit-Dove may also be seen in mangroves or adjoining eucalypt forests. All four Australian members of this genus are connected at species or subspecies level to populations in New Guinea, Indonesia or other northern islands and seem to be comparatively recent

Riverine forest, Top End of Northern Territory

colonists which have established themselves in habitats similar to those of their main range. At least part of the Australian population of the Superb Fruit-Dove apparently maintains its link with New Guinea by migration across Torres Strait, probably wintering in New Guinea.

▶ See also pages 81 111 305

222 BROWN CUCKOO-DOVE

Macropygia amboinensis

In south-eastern Australia this species is found only in pockets of lowland rainforest, but in the north of its range it is very common in humid highland forests and moderately common in the lowland rainforests. It is a South-East Asian species, with the Australian population listed as an endemic subspecies. The Brown Cuckoo-Dove favours the lower levels of the rainforests, especially the edges and clearings where it feeds on weeds and on berries of the undergrowth. It feeds mainly on the ground, making observation easier.

The Brown Cuckoo-Dove will sometimes fly several hundred metres from rainforest to feed in regrowth and wild tobacco, but always returns to the forest to roost. It tends to be relatively tame and if disturbed does not usually fly far.

▶ See also pages 81 122 306

236 WONGA PIGEON

Leucosarcia melanoleuca

Found right through the full extent of the rainforest habitat, common at the margins, most often where on deep red soils the forest is tall and lower levels relatively open. Timber tracks that rise from rainforest to ridges clad with eucalypts seem ideal for sightings, for the birds seem to feed in the rainforest but spend some time, and often nest, on the intervening hardwood ridges.

The Wonga belongs to a genus endemic to Australia. It may have affinities with the bronzewings, but the data available seem insufficient to establish close relationship with any other pigeon, and it would appear to be a rainforest bird of Australian origins. Unlike many other rainforest pigeons, it spends much of its time on the ground.

▶ See also pages 123 309

311 LESSER SOOTY OWL

Tyto multipunctata

Confined to the rainforests of north-eastern Queensland, unlike the Sooty

Owl (*T. tenebricosa*) of the south-east which is similar but larger and inhabits both the rainforests and the wet eucalypt forests. The Sooty and Lesser Sooty owls were previously listed as subspecies of a single species but at present are separated into two species.

The Lesser Sooty is found mainly in highlands and foothills from Cedar Bay south to Paluma and inland to

111 **Orange-footed Scrubfowl** *Megapodius reinwardt*
214 **Superb Fruit-Dove** *Ptilinopus superbus*
222 **Brown Cuckoo-Dove** *Macropygia amboinensis*
236 **Wonga Pigeon** *Leucosarcia melanoleuca*
311 **Lesser Sooty Owl** *Tyto multipunctata*
314 **Marbled Frogmouth** *Podargus ocellatus*
335 **Noisy Pitta** *Pitta versicolor*
377 **Pale-yellow Robin** *Tregellasia capito*
397 **Black-winged Monarch** *Monarcha frater*
412 **Chowchilla** *Orthonyx spaldingii*
459 **Large-billed Scrubwren** *Sericornis magnirostris*

377 **PALE-YELLOW ROBIN** *Tregellasia capito*

Julatten, Atherton and Ravenshoe. In rainforests within this region the species is quite common, with pairs occupying comparatively small territories of 50–60 ha. The birds can sometimes be seen hunting along the sides of roads passing through rainforests, and out over adjoining cleared land.

▶ **See also pages** *53* 327

314 MARBLED FROGMOUTH

Podargus ocellatus

This small and richly patterned frogmouth is primarily an inhabitant of rainforests of tropical, lowland and monsoon types. The northern population, on Cape York, is

moderately common on ridges in dense tangles of lawyer vine and bamboo, while the southern population is now very rare in remnants of lowland rainforest. The species is widespread from New Guinea to the Solomon Islands. The Australian birds are probably isolated remnants of one or several invasions of the species from New Guinea, now isolated long enough to be distinct subspecies.

▶ **See also pages** *53* 74–5 328

335 NOISY PITTA

Pitta versicolor

Usually an inhabitant of rainforests but venturing into adjacent mangroves and eucalypt forest or woodland in damp situations where it feeds on ground invertebrates, often snails. The species also occurs in New Guinea, and part of the Cape York population migrates across Torres Strait to New Guinea. The family is centred towards South-East Asia, with three or four species, all dominantly rainforest inhabitants, touching upon northern and eastern coastal Australia.

The species can be heard and, with patience, seen in many easily accessible rainforests including national parks and reserves along the east coast and ranges, including Lamington, New England, Dorrigo, Tooloom, Gibraltar Range, Eungella, and Bunya Mountains and Atherton Tableland reserves. This pitta also occurs on many heavily vegetated continental islands.

▶ **See also pages** *53* 81 105 111 121 127 334

377 PALE-YELLOW ROBIN

Tregellasia capito

Apparently entirely confined to rainforests, often in areas of very dense vegetation, especially of lawyer vines, both coastal and high altitude. Although the genus occurs also in New Guinea, this species is an Australian endemic. It appears to have a strong affinity for areas of lawyer vine within the rainforest, so that the presence or absence of the species may depend very much upon whether this vine is abundant. Its unobtrusive behaviour and preference for the gloomiest parts of the rainforest makes this species easily overlooked. It is however quite active, often taking insects on the wing.

▶ **See also pages** *53* 55 97 121 127 345

*Monsoon forest, Top End of
Northern Territory*

397 BLACK-WINGED MONARCH

Monarcha frater

Usually found in rainforests, but
occasionally also in adjacent eucalypt
woodland and open forest. This is a
New Guinea species which migrates to
Cape York for the wet season; there
appear to be no winter records. It is
moderately common at the Claudie
River, where there is one breeding
report, and occurs at Iron Range,
where it has arrived by the beginning
of November. The calls are very much
like those of the more common and
widespread Black-faced Flycatcher and
it is usually to be seen about the
foliage of the rainforest edges and
where there are breaks in the canopy.

▶ See also pages *53* 111 349–50

459 LARGE-BILLED SCRUBWREN

Sericornis magnirostris

Predominantly a bird of rainforests
but also occurring in dense
undergrowth of damp gullies in
eucalypt forests. Although fairly
common it is quiet and unobtrusive
but if suddenly disturbed usually
betrays its presence with a sharp alarm
note. Although this species is endemic
to Australia, others of the genus occur
also in New Guinea.

    Unlike most scrubwrens, which are
ground feeders, the Large-billed works
over the foliage of the mid-levels of the
forest, seeking insects from leaves and
bark. It is widespread in suitable
habitat.

▶ See also pages *53* 92 121 126 363–4

518 LEWIN'S HONEYEATER *Meliphaga lewinii*

518 LEWIN'S HONEYEATER

Meliphaga lewinii

Lewin's Honeyeater is widespread in
rainforest from the Atherton Region to
south-eastern Victoria. It is not as
closely tied to the rainforest habitat as
the Pale-yellow Robin and may also be
found in eucalypt forest and
woodland. In the Atherton Region it is
a bird of the highlands, being replaced
by the Graceful and Yellow-spotted
honeyeaters at lower altitudes; in
southern parts, where the Graceful
and Yellow-spotted do not occur,
Lewin's Honeyeater is more common
in the lowland forests.

▶ See also pages 92 97 126 378

Mulga scrub after rain

MULGA, MALLEE AND OTHER DRY SCRUBLANDS

These scrublands cover a vast area of Australia, mainly in the interior, but also reaching drier parts of the coast. Two vegetations are dominant: in northern and central arid regions, acacia scrub such as mulga, gidgee, myall and boree are the dominant vegetation over huge areas, while across southern Australia is a scrub dominated by small, multi-stemmed eucalypts, both these and the vegetation type being known as mallee.

The acacia scrubs form a cover usually around 2–5 m in height, sometimes quite dense, but more often quite open, and with ground-cover of diverse small drought-resistant shrubs such as eremophila, saltbush and bluebush. The brigalow scrubs of Queensland, however, are different from the mulga type of acacia scrubland, tending to form quite dense forests in places, elsewhere a woodland structure, and again further inland is a lower, more open scrub.

Mallee eucalypts can form thickets where the massed slender stems are so close together that there can be a foliage canopy of up to 70 per cent, and the ground so littered with shed strips of bark, twigs and leaves that very little undergrowth exists. Usually the mallee eucalypts are much more widely spaced, with varied ground-cover, in some regions of spinifex, elsewhere of low scrub or of low sandplain-heath where the mallee may be in very sparsely scattered clumps.

Australia's arid scrublands form a habitat that either can be very sparsely populated with birds, or extremely rich. Seasonal factors have immense effect. In drought, which tends to be the usual condition, its birdlife seems comparatively poor, made up of those hardy species that can

Mulga along a temporary watercourse

tolerate the hot dry conditions. But after good rains the landscape is transformed, the bare earth covered with ephemeral plants, insect life abundant, and the birds present in great numbers and variety of species.

Many of the birds of the arid scrublands are nomadic, moving to regions of favourable conditions, often to adjoining habitats such as woodlands, spinifex and other grasslands, and to some of the drier heathlands. This use of varied habitats results in the acacia and mallee scrublands, while having a list of around 135 species, having relatively few (about 12) that are predominantly confined to this habitat.

The following are some of the most typical and widespread of the scrubland birds. Others of this habitat are described in regions where they are endemic or most readily seen.

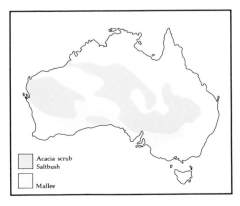

Acacia scrub
Saltbush

Mallee

366 **RED-CAPPED ROBIN** *Petroica goodenovii*

276 MALLEE RINGNECK

Barnardius barnardi

Early in the day these parrots are often to be seen in pairs or small flocks feeding on the ground or among the outer branches, but by mid to late morning they have usually retreated to shady foliage to shelter from the heat of the day. Towards evening they become active again, feeding and going to drink. Early mornings provide the best chance of sightings, when the Mallee Ringnecks leave roost trees to drink at waterholes, dams or troughs, and then to feed. Their flight is undulating and the birds often call in flight. When feeding in trees they may chatter softly but are silent and timid when on the ground.

▶ See also pages   *59* 129 136 137 139 158 175 318

361 SOUTHERN SCRUB-ROBIN

Drymodes brunneopygia

This inhabitant of the southern mallee and acacia scrubs is unobtrusive and shy, usually keeping just out of clear view and giving but fleeting glimpses as it crosses the ground with a bouncing run, long tail held partially raised. Often its presence is revealed only by its song, a persistent, clear, loud, rollicking 'chip-per-perp-ree', 'chip-pip-ee', given from a low perch in a shrub, and a clear piping 'pee-pee-peee' from under cover. When disturbed, it will also give a harsh scolding. However, it is quite inquisitive and may come closer to a quiet and patient observer.

▶ See also pages   *59* 130 137 139 162 242 341

366 RED-CAPPED ROBIN

Petroica goodenovii

The Red-capped Robin is common and widespread throughout the drier parts of Australia, generally absent from most of the tropical north and northern interior and from the wetter and more heavily forested regions. While the acacia scrublands comprise the major part of the range of the species it also occurs in the drier woodlands. It is one of the species that will almost inevitably be seen by any bird observer in these habitats and its cheery ticking trill is one of the most common sounds of the interior.

▶ See also pages   231 *246–7* 342

366 **RED-CAPPED ROBIN** *Petroica goodenovii*

384 GILBERT'S WHISTLER

Pachycephala inornata

This whistler's plumage is very plain and it is known more for its powerful, rich and far-carrying calls. For most of the year it is fairly quiet and easily overlooked but in the spring the loud calls often indicate the presence of the species long before it can be sighted. The calls are typical of the whistlers, yet distinctive. Included is a clear whistle 'like man whistling dog', a 'perwheee, perwheee, perwheee', 'jok-jok-jok' given repeatedly, also 'pew-pew-pew' rising in volume, and 'eee-chp, eeechop—'. When disturbed, it tends to move on ahead of the observer in strong, undulating flight.

▶ See also pages 137 138 139 164 213 220 232 346

389 WHITE-BREASTED WHISTLER

Pachycephala lanioides

This whistler is confined almost entirely to the narrow mangrove belt around Australia's northern coast, occasionally moving into adjoining rainforest patches in the Darwin area and perhaps also in the northern Kimberley. Breaks in the continuity of the mangroves have allowed the evolution of three subspecies. The White-breasted Whistler is difficult to sight as it tends to sit quiet and still, watching for prey. The bird is easily found when it is calling — four to six deep whistled notes and an outpouring of rich, mellow song, most likely to be heard at dawn. The plumage is quite distinctive.

▶ See also pages 23 192 196 208 347–8

416 CHIMING WEDGEBILL

Psophodes occidentalis

The Chiming Wedgebill is abundant through the mulga scrublands where it is heard far more often than seen. The clear, chiming calls are one of the most characteristic sounds of the mulga habitat.

The Chiming Wedgebill is very shy, so that it is difficult to get more than a fleeting glimpse. Once the ringing 'pipity-boo' call is known, one realises that these are among the most common of mulga-scrub birds for they keep up the call almost incessantly and, on moonlight nights, through the night also. But if the bush where it sings is approached it will slip silently away, flying low to the next dense cover and giving very little chance of a clear view. Its behaviour at the nest is similar. Rarely can a Chiming

Wedgebill be sighted on its nest even with a quiet approach. By the time the nest, which is placed in a dense shrub, can be seen, the wedgebill is usually singing from another bush, pretending there is no nest.

▶ See also pages 61 179 184 231 353 354

276 **Mallee Ringneck** *Barnardius barnardi*
361 **Southern Scrub-robin** *Drymodes brunneopygia*
384 **Gilbert's Whistler** *Pachycephala inornata*
465 **Shy Heathwren** *Sericornis cautus*
466 **Redthroat** *Sericornis brunneus*
483 **Slaty-backed Thornbill** *Acanthiza robustirostris*
492 **Banded Whiteface** *Aphelocephala nigricincta*
497 **White-browed Treecreeper** *Climacteris affinis*
563 **Black Honeyeater** *Certhionyx niger*
576 **Yellow-rumped Pardalote** *Pardalotus xanthopygus*

490 **SOUTHERN WHITEFACE** *Aphelocephala leucopsis*

465 SHY HEATHWREN

Sericornis cautus

Timid, but often curious, the Shy Heathwren bounces across the ground among the mallee stems and litter of bark, twigs and heathy ground-cover. The tail is carried erect, so that the fiery chestnut rump is often glimpsed. This species normally forages alone, feeding mainly upon insects. The song is most valuable in locating and assisting identification. The pleasant 'chee-chee-chickadee' is given most often in spring, early in the morning.

▶ See also pages   *59* 130 137 139 162 232 365–6

466 REDTHROAT

Sericornis brunneus

An inhabitant of arid mulga and other acacia scrublands, especially along watercourses. The Redthroat forages low, in and around saltbush and other small shrubs. As the species is sedentary it should be present in suitable habitat even under drought conditions. The Redthroat tends to attract attention by singing from the top of a shrub or scrubby tree.

▶ See also pages   *59* 130 232 323 366

483 SLATY-BACKED THORNBILL

Acanthiza robustirostris

Dense mulga and spinifex, especially along foothills of ranges, is the preferred habitat of this species. It feeds both among the foliage and on the ground. The call is loud and vigorous, attracting attention and helping to separate it from the similar Chestnut-rumped Thornbill; most characteristic is a high 'wi-pu-chew'. The iris of this species is dark, that of the Chestnut-rumped is whitish.

▶ See also pages   *59* 173 230 370

490 SOUTHERN WHITEFACE

Aphelocephala leucopsis

The Southern Whiteface is common through the mulga and mulga-spinifex country of the southern interior and to

A dense stand of mallee eucalypts

some drier coastal parts. It is usually to be seen busily foraging in pairs or small flocks on the ground and seems especially common about the yards of farm and station homesteads.

▶ See also pages *60* 171 232 371 372

492 BANDED WHITEFACE

Aphelocephala nigricincta

This species is moderately common to abundant almost throughout the open country of the southern interior where it is often in mixed flocks with Yellow-rumped Thornbills. Usually this whiteface is seen hopping busily across the ground in search of seeds and insects. It is quite tame and easily approached, and favours the surrounds of outback station homesteads.

▶ See also pages *59* 171 183 371 372

497 WHITE-BROWED TREECREEPER

Climacteris affinis

The White-browed Treecreeper can be found in the same localities throughout the year, irrespective of seasonal conditions. It is usually solitary or in pairs but has occasionally been reported in small parties. It favours arid country dominated by mulga or sheoak, where it takes insects from treetrunks and fallen timber. In this open country it is not easily overlooked, though it tends to be quiet; when it calls, the notes are unmistakably those of a treecreeper — thin and sharp.

▶ See also pages *59* 130 373

563 BLACK HONEYEATER

Certhionyx niger

The Black Honeyeater has a wide range covering most of the drier parts of the continent. It is highly nomadic in most parts, with evidence of regular seasonal movement in some regions; the south-eastern limits of its range also appear to fluctuate year to year. At any time this species may be abundant or completely absent, depending upon local seasonal conditions and the resultant flowering of shrubs, especially various red-flowered species of eremophila. Breeding will occur at any time after rain; at such times the species is usually locally abundant and the high, thin 'see-' of its calls prominent among the sounds of the mulga country.

▶ See also pages *59* 137 173 175 219 220 231 388

416 **CHIMING WEDGEBILL** *Psophodes occidentalis*

576 YELLOW-RUMPED PARDALOTE

Pardalotus xanthopygus

This pardalote occupies mallee and occasionally adjoining open woodland. This tiny, gum-leaf sized bird can easily be missed as it feeds among the foliage. The soft calls may attract attention, for although similar to those of the well-known Spotted Pardalote, they are sufficiently distinctive to warn that a different species is close by.

▶ See also pages *59* 213 242 391–2

Mountain ash forest, Gippsland, Victoria

FORESTS

Other than rainforests, the most dense vegetation cover is provided by the forests. These are predominantly of eucalypts and more precisely referred to as sclerophyll forests for their vegetation has foliage that is, by comparison with the soft and delicate foliage of rainforests, hard and leathery. The trees and shrubbery of the forests are able to withstand much more arid conditions than those of rainforests. The timber of the trees is much more dense than that of most rainforest trees, hence the description of these as hardwood forests and that of rainforests as softwood forests.

Eucalypt forests have few tree species, usually with but one or two species dominating, although there are often other much smaller trees beneath their canopy. But with eucalypt forests widespread through the heavier rainfall areas of Australia, and with their dominant tree species differing from place to place, the total number of forest tree species is quite large, and with most of these the principal component is a distinct kind of eucalypt forest.

So strongly is the character of the eucalypt forests set by their dominant trees that the forests of many localities are known by the names of those trees, so that 'mountain ash forests', 'blue-gum forests', 'karri forests', 'jarrah forests', are names not only describing the dominant tree of each, but giving, for anyone who is at all familiar with them, an image of the total landscape of a place or region. Rainforests, with their multitude of intermingled tree species, are usually named by place of occurrence, although there are some exceptions including the Antarctic beech forests of the south-eastern highlands.

Forests, as a defined vegetation, are differentiated from the more open woodlands on the basis of tree cover. The transition from forest to woodland is gradual, so that it is usually difficult to say just where one ends and the other begins. The relative density of cover is reflected in the shape of individual trees making up the forests and woodlands.

In forests the trees are more closely spaced, forced upwards in competition for space and light, becoming not only tall, but also with the length of bole from ground to lower branches comparatively greater and making up at least half the total height of the tree.

The canopy also is a reflection of forest density, with an overhead canopy coverage of 50 to 70 per cent of the sky, much greater than that of woodlands but less than the almost totally closed canopy of rainforest.

Forests may be further differentiated. Where rainfall is heavy and soils rich, 'wet' eucalypt forests occur, with trees often exceeding 30 m in height, a near-closed crown canopy, and a lush shrub understorey. Dry sclerophyll occurs in regions of lower but moderate rainfall, with trees usually under 30 m in height and a more open foliage canopy. The understorey is drier, with a more open covering of smaller and drought-resistant shrubs.

The forests habitat has a rich bird population, with some species

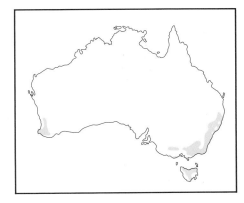

found only in this habitat. But without the sharp boundary of habitat that encloses rainforests, mangroves, wetlands and some other habitats, many of the birds that use forests also use other more open habitats. On the other hand, some find sufficient similarity between the dense vegetation of the wet eucalypt forests and that of rainforests to be able to occupy both.

In the forests, flowering trees and understorey shrubs are important in supporting large numbers of nectar-eating birds. With but few trees dominating each tract of forest, flowering of the trees of adjoining forests may occur at different times of the year. Great numbers of lorikeets and other nectar-seeking birds move nomadically through forests and woodlands, briefly bringing much activity and noise to the treetops as they seek nectar and insects among the gum blossoms.

With forests confined to the higher rainfall coastal parts of Australia, their distribution is considerably broken by intervening drier habitat, causing isolation of some forest species and subsequent evolution of new subspecies or species. This is particularly evident away from the major and comparatively continuous forest belt down Australia's east coast. In particular

Alpine forest, Kosciusko

365 **SCARLET ROBIN** *Petroica multicolor*

the dry Nullarbor separates the heavily forested south-west from the east-coastal forests, and there now exist in that isolated block of forest species derived from eastern birds, but now unique.

The following birds are characteristic of eucalypt forests, and most are quite widespread in this habitat; other forest species of restricted range are covered within the regions to which they are most closely confined or common.

98 GREY GOSHAWK

Accipiter novaehollandiae

One of Australia's more exciting raptors, more solid and powerful than the Brown Goshawk, it is widely distributed through forested country but nowhere is it common. Of the two colour phases, white predominates in the north-west and south-east, the grey elsewhere. This raptor is usually within the heavier forests but will hunt out over open country. In that setting the white form has been likened to a white cockatoo when perched or gliding. But given reasonable visibility any confusion should be brief. From below, the wings appear very broad

and rounded and at closer range the deep yellow of legs and talons, and possibly the cere, stand out against the smooth white or pale grey of the tight plumage.

In most parts of its range the Grey Goshawk is scarce. While it is usually confined to forests, non-breeding birds may be found in more open country.

Though the white form of this species is distinctive among Australian raptors, the grey form can be confused with the much more common Brown Goshawk. When the light is poor, as when seen against white cloud, the usual rounded-winged silhouette and quick shallow wingbeats suggest a goshawk, while the distinctly shorter tail helps separate it from the Brown Goshawk. The call is similar to that of the Brown, but is a slower, deeper, more mellow 'yuik, yuik, yuik'.

▶ **See also pages** *65* 80 82 97 121 123 126 136 152 208 210 275

298 SHINING BRONZE-CUCKOO

Chrysococcyx lucidus

This bronze-cuckoo is an inhabitant of the wetter eucalypt forests, mainly areas of more than 380 mm annual rainfall, and to a lesser extent of the rainforests and woodlands. The loud, clear and continuously repeated whistled call is almost certain to attract attention before the bird is sighted, for the green-plumaged birds are inconspicuous among foliage. In the breeding season the male will often call from exposed high perches and indulge in display and chase; flight is swift, slightly undulating, the wings noticeably long and pointed.

▶ See also page 324

305 POWERFUL OWL

Ninox strenua

The massive Powerful Owl inhabits heavy, wet eucalypt forest, where it roosts by day where the vegetation is most dense along streams. The usual roosting site is bare horizontal branches 5–20 m above ground under dense canopy, in a position giving a commanding view. The presence of a roost is indicated by the spattering of undergrowth foliage and shrubbery with creamy-white excreta, and on the ground by pellets and fur. Sometimes the harassing chatter of small birds will pinpoint the roost. The drawn-out hooting territorial and contact calls are given from a high perch and can carry several kilometres.

▶ See also pages 80 82 121 123 136 325

316 WHITE-THROATED NIGHTJAR

Caprimulgus mystacalis

These nightjars inhabit eucalypt forests and woodlands, showing preference for the drier ridges where the undergrowth is sparse but where abundant leaf-litter and dappled shadows suit their patterned plumage. Often they will not flush until almost trodden upon, and then quickly drop back to cover again, or perch, frogmouth-like, lengthways along a limb. Hunting begins at sunset, their hawking for insects most active at dawn, dusk and on moonlight nights. The White-throated Nightjar calls persistently only in breeding season.

▶ See also pages 328–9

358 AUSTRALIAN GROUND-THRUSH

Zoothera lunulata

A secretive inhabitant of the heavier wet forests, both rainforest and eucalypt, usually in sites of dense canopy and ground-cover, where it keeps mostly to the leaf-litter of the forest floor. When disturbed it will often run for an instant then stop abruptly and remain motionless, relying upon the blending of its mottled brown plumage into the litter surrounds, effective in the dim light of

the forest. The calls are rarely heard, more often in winter and spring and then usually but briefly at dawn.

In gloomy forest environs it will probably usually be difficult to separate this species from the Russet-tailed Ground-Thrush where the ranges of the two species overlap.

▶ See also pages 116 121 139 141 340 341

98 **Grey Goshawk** *Accipiter novaehollandiae*
239 **Glossy Black-Cockatoo** *Calyptorhynchus lathami*
298 **Shining Bronze-Cuckoo** *Chrysococcyx lucidus*
305 **Powerful Owl** *Ninox strenua*
316 **White-throated Nightjar** *Caprimulgus mystacalis*
358 **Australian Ground-Thrush** *Zoothera lunulata*
399 **White-eared Monarch** *Monarcha leucotis*
404 **Satin Flycatcher** *Myiagra cyanoleuca*
417 **Spotted Quail-thrush** *Cinclosoma punctatum*
485 **Buff-rumped Thornbill** *Acanthiza reguloides*

365 SCARLET ROBIN

Petroica multicolor

In eucalypt forests of southern Australia and Tasmania the Scarlet Robin is a common bird. Breeding pairs occupy forest habitat, but at other times may wander locally into adjoining open country of woodland, heathland, or partly cleared farmland. The juveniles wander further afield in autumn, which gives the impression that the species is more extensively nomadic. As a nesting site the Scarlet Robin prefers forest with an open understorey, usually in localities drier than used by the Flame Robin in the south-east or the White-breasted Robin in the south-west. The cheery trilling call often attracts attention when otherwise it might not be noticed in the dense forest setting, for it perches motionless much of the time, scanning the ground.

▶ **See also pages** *64* 342

399 WHITE-EARED MONARCH

Monarcha leucotis

The White-eared Monarch is a bird of the upper foliage canopy, flitting about the crowns of forest eucalypts, along the edges of rainforests and the denser vegetation of creeks, and sometimes mangroves, taking insects in flight and from the leaves. It favours situations where breaks in the canopy allow penetration of sunlight. This activity tends to make it fairly conspicuous, especially in the breeding season when it is noisiest. The call, useful in locating the species, is double-noted, a sharp short whistle immediately followed by a longer, drawn-out descending whistle. The species is readily seen on and around the Atherton Tableland, but less common farther south; the plumage is quite distinctive.

▶ **See also pages** *65* 121 350

404 SATIN FLYCATCHER

Myiagra cyanoleuca

When breeding, the Satin Flycatcher retreats to the heavily vegetated gullies of the wet eucalypt forests, but usually avoids rainforests. When the young are fledged the family parties move to more open country. These birds are almost incessantly active, darting out from high perches in pursuit of flying insects. While perched they often sway the body from side to side, quiver the tail, and call loudly.

▶ **See also pages** *65* 123 139 142 151 350 351

Forest habitat, Fraser Island, Queensland

417 SPOTTED QUAIL-THRUSH

Cinclosoma punctatum

Although mainly an inhabitant of eucalypt forests, the Spotted Quail-thrush extends also into some woodlands. It prefers the drier forests where it is most likely to be met with on the sunny northern slopes of ridges, especially where the ground is rocky and with litter of bark, twigs and fallen leaves. The species is very wary and elusive, with the cryptic colours making sighting more difficult. If flushed or pressed too closely it will burst into flight with a quail-like whirring of wings. The high-pitched warning whistle is inaudible to some people but otherwise may help to indicate the presence of the species.

▶ **See also pages** *65* 121 122 136 162 354

501 RED WATTLEBIRD *Anthochaera carunculata*

575 **SPOTTED PARDALOTE** *Pardalotus punctatus*

485 BUFF-RUMPED THORNBILL

Acanthiza reguloides

A bird of the drier open forests, especially where there is a grassy or shrubby understorey, but occurring also in the taller woodlands. In the north it is also to be found along the margins of, and occasionally within, the rainforests. Foraging for insects is done mainly on the ground but in the far north more often about the lower foliage. This species is usually in flocks and when disturbed departs with 'bouncing' flight, showing the buff of the rump.

▶ **See also pages** *65* 370

501 RED WATTLEBIRD

Anthochaera carunculata

A very common and generally familiar large honeyeater of south-eastern and south-western Australia, often a visitor or resident in suburban gardens. The Red Wattlebird is usually a bird of eucalypt forests, woodlands and mallee, feeding upon nectar and insects. It often draws attention with harsh calls and aggressive behaviour towards other smaller honeyeaters.

▶ **See also pages** *66* 148 245 374 375

575 SPOTTED PARDALOTE

Pardalotus punctatus

Common in forests and also occurring in woodlands of eastern and south-western Australia, this tiny bird is difficult to sight among the foliage. It is most likely to be noticed when its calls are heard, or the sharp clicking of the bill as it takes insects from the leaves.

▶ **See also pages** *2–3* 61 136 148 153 391

REGIONS

This section concentrates upon birds of each of fourteen regions, and describes a selection of birdwatching sites. The text covers birds that are unique to a single region, have a restricted distribution, are rare, or are difficult to find. It also includes some species that are a typical or particularly interesting segment of the local birdlife. Emphasis is placed upon information likely to be helpful in finding these birds of special interest, especially the calls, behaviour, routine, use of habitat, and, for migratory species, months of the year when they can be seen. In addition to illustrations of the species discussed, some photographs of more common or widespread species are included.

The bird places covered within each region are usually localities that have acquired some recognition as rewarding birdwatching sites, especially for the species endemic to the region or which are of local interest. Selected listings are given of bird 'highlights' for individual sites; there is a complete list of birds and their regions at the back of the book.

436 VARIEGATED FAIRY-WREN *Malurus lamberti*

EASTERN QUEENSLAND

The Eastern Queensland Region extends 1200 km down Australia's north-eastern coast and inland to include the Great Dividing Range and its western slopes. Its northernmost part includes the base of Cape York Peninsula but excludes the coastal Atherton Region from Cooktown south almost to Townsville. From Townsville south to Brisbane this region takes in the coast and up to 400 km inland, and extends a similar distance seawards to include the islands of the southern Great Barrier Reef.

Between these limits the Eastern Queensland Region links mountainous and heavily rainforested areas of the Atherton Region and south-eastern Queensland, but has the effect of keeping apart and distinctive the bird faunas of those parts. This Eastern Queensland Region has only isolated patches of rainforest, widely separated by much drier eucalypt savannah-woodland.

From the Atherton highlands almost to the New South Wales border the main chain of ranges of the Great Dividing Range curves well inland, in some places 300–400 km inland from the coast, mostly low and not receiving the rainfall needed for rainforest. On the coast there are some high ranges which carry luxuriant rainforest, but these are isolated and surrounded by far more extensive areas of eucalypt forest and woodland.

Eastern Queensland has heavy summer rainfall and usually an almost completely dry winter. The alternating extremes of flood and drought put great stress upon both plant and animal life. The long dry season, when for most of the time high temperatures exacerbate the drought, severely restricts the occurrence of rainforest to a few most favourable localities so that

by the end of the dry months the extent of waterbird habitat has been reduced to a fraction of that available at the end of the wet.

Rainforest birds are thus confined to small and isolated localities, while the possible population of waterbirds is largely determined by their ability either to find sustenance on the remnant wetlands through the late dry season, or to migrate to other regions at this time.

Eucalypt savannah-woodland dominates this region and provides a continuous habitat for its birds, linking the woodlands avifauna of the far north with that of south-eastern Australia. A quick look through the distribution maps of Australian birds will show that a great many of Australia's birds occupy this Torresian bioclimatic region, across the north, from western Kimberley to Cape York Peninsula, then south through the eastern Queensland woodlands to coastal New South Wales.

Mangroves too comprise an almost continuous habitat along the Queensland coast, without the very wide gaps that occur in the mangrove belt of north-western Australia. This has ensured a spread of most mangrove species along this coast, but there are fewer isolated populations and not as many local endemic subspecies of mangrove birds as in the north-west.

The distribution of rainforest birds, many confined to isolated blocks of rainforest, is more complex, with the composition and number of endemics for each region differing substantially.

Eastern Queensland is a transitional region for rainforests, with tropical rainforest in the north and as far south as Mackay, then subtropical southwards from Mackay to the south-east coast of New South Wales before giving way to temperate rainforest.

Compared with the numbers of

endemic birds in the great blocks of rainforest of the Atherton Region and of the Border Range to the south, the rainforests of the Eastern Queensland Region are undistinguished. Most of the birds of the Eastern Queensland Region's rainforests occur also in either the rainforests farther north or in those farther south, or both. There is one exception, this only since the recognition of a new species of honeyeater, the Eungella Honeyeater, in the highland rainforests of Eungella in 1977. There is also at Eungella an isolated and endemic subspecies of the White-throated Treecreeper.

Included within this Eastern Queensland Region is the southern section of the Great Barrier Reef; here it lies well offshore, some parts 150 km out from the coast. The reef supports a huge population of seabirds. Within this southern part the Capricorn and Bunker groups are important, containing all the major breeding colonies of Black Noddies, a large proportion of the large colonies of Crested and Roseate terns, several large colonies of Brown Boobies, and one of the largest colonies of Wedge-tailed Shearwaters.

The seabird islands present considerable conservation problems, the islands being easily accessible and the colonies obvious, thus attracting attention. But the birds are easily disturbed, to the extent that some eggs can be deserted and young killed.

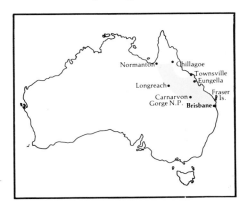

90 **PACIFIC BAZA** *Aviceda subcristata*

BIRDS OF EASTERN QUEENSLAND

83 COTTON PYGMY-GOOSE

Nettapus coromandelianus

The Cotton Pygmy-Goose is almost confined to this Eastern Queensland Region and the adjoining Atherton Region, with possible vagrant records farther afield. It shows a preference for the deeper lagoons with abundant submerged and floating vegetation, where it feeds upon the seeds and other parts of these plants. This species will usually be seen in pairs or small flocks, almost always on the water and very rarely on banks. It is difficult to observe, being shy and retiring, by day keeping far out among the waterlilies and feeding most actively in the evening and night.

During the summer wet, when inland waterways fill, the Cotton Pygmy-Goose moves as far as 100 km inland. Although it is now only a rare vagrant in the southern parts of its range — south-eastern Queensland and north-eastern New South Wales — it is moderately common on the coastal swamps near Townsville and Ingham where flocks of up to several hundred birds may be seen in the dry season. In the early 1960s, when estimates of the total population were as low as 1500 birds, it seemed threatened with extinction in Australia but it appears to have maintained its numbers in north-eastern Queensland.

▶ **See also pages** 75 110 271

90 PACIFIC BAZA

Aviceda subcristata

The Pacific Baza occurs throughout this region and in adjoining regions, in tropical forests, woodlands and the edges of rainforests. It is usually in pairs or family parties. At moderately close range this hawk is unmistakable with its mainly grey plumage, barred breast and small crest. But, as with most raptor sightings, it is most likely to be seen in flight and at a distance. The Pacific Baza's flight is a lazy soaring and floating above and about the canopy of forests and trees. The deep, slow wingbeats are reminiscent of a harrier. The wings are long and broad and held almost flat while soaring. Large insects, such as mantids, are snatched from the foliage.

▶ **See also pages** 82 121 196 197 208 210 273

121 BLACK-BREASTED BUTTON-QUAIL

Turnix melanogaster

The recorded range of this button-quail extends from the Atherton Region south to north-eastern New South Wales but, like many of the button-quails, it is difficult to detect in the dense cover that it occupies. During the RAOU Field Atlas bird survey in 1977–81 it was recorded only from south-eastern Queensland and appears to have suffered considerable reduction in range.

The Black-breasted Button-quail is usually seen in low closed forests including the drier rainforests, vine forests and brigalow, where a deeper and drier leaf-litter layer accumulates than in the wetter rainforests. Recent reports of the species have been from the Upper Brisbane and South Burnett valleys, where it is sometimes also recorded from lantana thickets and hoop pine plantations.

To some extent the scarcity of records must reflect the secretive nature of the species rather than its true status. In this dense vegetation it relies upon stealth instead of bursting into flight when disturbed. The presence of this button-quail can most easily be assessed by searching for the characteristic scrapes, 150–200 mm across, which go through the litter but not far into the soil and tend to be in clusters.

If scrapes are located, a very quiet investigation or a wait in the area may give a sighting. The rustling of the dry leaves while the birds are scratching about among them might attract attention and allow an observer to sneak closer.

The decline of this species may be attributed to the widespread and in many areas complete clearing of low closed forests.

▶ **See also pages** 75 82 121 280–1

140 SARUS CRANE

Grus antigone

The Sarus Crane is a native of India and South-East Asia and was first reported in Australia near Normanton in 1966. It has since become common and widespread in north-eastern and eastern Queensland, with scattered reports from the Top End and Kimberley regions.

The Sarus Crane can be separated from the Brolga by the extension of the scarlet of the face onto the upper neck, and pink rather than grey legs. Large numbers can be seen where they roost at Bromfield Crater and Willetts Swamp on the Atherton Tableland.

▶ **See also pages** 75 99 286

143 BUSH THICK-KNEE

Burhinus magnirostris

The Bush Thick-knee is found almost throughout mainland Australia, with north-eastern Queensland appearing to be a stronghold, perhaps because the grassy woodland which is the preferred habitat is, in most parts, the most widespread vegetation.

When crouched on the ground this bird is extremely difficult to locate, its presence in a locality often revealed by the wailing 'ker-looo' call given at

143 **BUSH THICK-KNEE** *Burhinus magnirostris* Protecting young

night. The calls are given often and loudly when breeding, the bird standing, wings outspread, as it calls.

The Bush Thick-knee puts on a great show of aggression and bluff in defence of its territory or young. The wings are out, arched so that the tips touch the ground, and showing the white bars on the primaries. The tail is raised and fanned, again showing white bars. The head and sharp bill are thrust out, and the bird may make short, quick rushes at the intruder.

▶ **See also pages**   47 138 184 287 288

154 MONGOLIAN PLOVER

Charadrius mongolus

The Mongolian Plover is a summer migrant to Australia, regularly recorded along the east Queensland coast and on other coasts around the continent. It is far more abundant in Queensland than elsewhere, some February counts being of 1770 in Moreton Bay, 1430 in the Great Sandy Strait and Hervey Bay area, and 650 in the Mackay area.

This small wader utilizes both sandy and muddy shores, usually in small flocks of up to 100 birds.

▶ **See also pages**   75 80 98 290

166 WHIMBREL

Numenius phaeopus

This wader has a distinctive, long bill, downcurved towards the tip, and long legs. It is a summer migrant to beaches right around Australia but is most common on the north-eastern coasts. On the southern coasts most sightings are of single birds or very small parties, but along the Queensland coast there can be flocks of up to about 50. The foraging is done along tidal mudflats, with roosting on coral cays, rocky islets or in mangroves.

▶ **See also pages**   75 123 149 150 293

212 BLACK NODDY

Anous minutus

The only Australian breeding colonies of the Black Noddy are on islands of the Queensland coast. On Heron Island, southern Barrier Reef, there is a steadily expanding colony which has grown from 17 000 birds in 1983 to 60 000 in 1983. On nearby Masthead Island a large colony was estimated at 170 000 birds in 1972. These noddies remain at the colonies throughout the year, leaving for the open sea early in the morning and returning at dusk.

▶ **See also pages**   71 75 82 97 304

208 **CRESTED TERN** *Sterna bergii*

231 SQUATTER PIGEON

Petrophassa scripta

The distribution of the Squatter Pigeon covers most of the Eastern Queensland Region, except the south-east, and extends into some adjoining regions. A northern subspecies that has the bare skin around the eye coloured reddish extends south to the Valley of Lagoons; the nominate subspecies in the southern part of the range has bluish skin around the eye. Intermediate forms have been collected from the Burdekin Valley.

This terrestrial pigeon prefers open woodlands with sandy soils, near permanent water, usually in pairs but sometimes in flocks of up to 30. Recognition is aided by the white edgings down the sides of the breast, forming a 'V' from the front, and there is a distinctive black-and-white facial pattern.

▶ **See also pages** 75 110 121 308 309

273 PALE-HEADED ROSELLA

Platycercus adscitus

The major part of the range of the Pale-headed Rosella falls within the Eastern Queensland Region. It is principally a bird of woodlands and heathlands and occasionally the edges of rainforest. It may be seen in pairs or flocks, feeding among foliage or on the ground. At closer range the plumage is distinctive, the head very pale yellow.

At a distance the strongly undulating flight is helpful, with the pale head visible at a considerable distance. In the mornings and evenings it tends to be conspicuous, with almost incessant chatterings and short flights. But when feeding on the ground, especially among dry grass, it is quiet and easily missed. Over most of its range and habitats this is the only rosella, and where it meets other rosellas the plumages are distinctively different.

▶ **See also pages** 75 80 121 317–18 387

248 **SULPHUR-CRESTED COCKATOO**
Cacatua galerita

282 PARADISE PARROT

Psephotus pulcherrimus

The former range of the Paradise Parrot included the south-east of the Eastern Queensland Region. Until the 1880s it was commonly reported from the lower part of the region, then it declined rapidly. The last confirmed sightings came from Casino in 1926, the Burnett River in 1927, and near Dhoneyeter also in 1927. The preferred habitat was grassland with scattered trees and termite mounds, in which it nested. It fed on the seeds of grasses and herbaceous plants.

Possibly it was always scarce, perhaps locally common, so that some alteration in habitat, such as the replacement of native grasses with introduced species, was enough to hasten its extinction.

▶ **See also pages** 75 319–20

314 PLUMED FROGMOUTH

SUBSPECIES OF MARBLED FROGMOUTH

Podargus ocellatus plumiferus

The Marbled Frogmouth has two widely separated populations. One, known by the common name of Marbled Frogmouth, is confined to northern Cape York Peninsula. The second, the subspecies *plumiferus*, restricted to a small part of south-eastern Queensland and New South Wales, is known as the Plumed Frogmouth and has at times been listed as a full species. Whether a species or subspecies, it is a rare and unique bird of great interest. Confirmed sightings during the RAOU Field Atlas survey of 1977–81 were from the Conondale Range of south-eastern Queensland and the Tweed and Nightcap ranges of north-eastern New South Wales. Other sites on record are Mt Tamborine, before 1973, Booloumba Creek 1977, Manning River 1941, Big Rocky Creek north of Lismore 1972, and near Bellingen in 1975 and 1976.

It is possible that the records of sightings of nocturnal birds do not reflect their true status; there is little observation of birds at night, and daylight sightings tend to be a matter of chance. It seems probable that the Plumed Frogmouth is not as rare as the recorded sightings would suggest and that it occurs throughout the subtropical rainforests. Since about 1980, the use of the calls to locate and identify has resulted in the Plumed Frogmouth being found in a number of additional localities.

This bird indulges in a bout of calling that begins about 30 minutes before dawn and continues until at least 20 minutes after the diurnal birds have begun calling. The purpose seems to be to advertise to others of its kind the position of its roost for the day. From these calls it should be possible to locate and positively identify the bird as the light strengthens.

The calls are diverse and varied; some carry for at least 200–300 m through the forest. Often it begins with a rapid 'wooloo-woolook-woolook-' or more deliberate 'kook-kook-kook-', then a succession of rapidly accelerating gobbling notes, beginning abruptly, loudly, then rapidly decreasing in volume. These calls may be made by both members of a pair. Another common call is 'whoor-loop, whoor-loop-' repeated four to six times, each 'whoor-loop' lasting about one second.

Sites where the Plumed Frogmouth has been located with the use of calls include the Whian Whian State Forest on the Nightcap Range, and Wiangaree State Forest in the Tweed Range.

The Plumed Frogmouth may be confused with the reddish phase of the Tawny Frogmouth. The former has a proportionately longer tail, making up more than half the total length of the bird; the plumage is brownish and much less streaked, the underparts having small black streaks with white spots, and the facial plumes are larger.

▶ **See also pages** 11 82 121 328

356 VARIED TRILLER

Lalage leucomela

Along the eastern Queensland coast and into north-eastern New South Wales the Varied Triller is a common species of a wide range of habitats. It is usually high in the foliage where it might not be noticed until it calls, with a distinctive loud, rolling, harsh trill, repeated four to eight times. Another population, a subspecies, occurs in the Top End and Kimberley regions.

▶ **See also pages** 79 208 209 340

405 SHINING FLYCATCHER

Myiagra alecto

This magnificent flycatcher inhabits northern and north-eastern Australia, where it is present throughout the year. The Shining Flycatcher prefers rainforest, especially along streams; it also occurs in mangroves but only rarely in eucalypt forests. This is a very lively flycatcher, flitting about branches, foliage or roots, flying out to take insects or hopping about near the ground to take small creatures from leaf-litter or mangrove mud. It has a frog-like call, often given while hunting near the ground.

This species is usually seen in pairs, and always near water, whether in mangroves, tidal rivers or rainforest pools. The plumage is distinctive, with such great difference between the sexes that they look like different species.

▶ **See also pages** 79 80 98 111 208 210 351

83 **Cotton Pygmy-Goose** *Nettapus coromandelianus*
121 **Black-breasted Button-quail** *Turnix melanogaster*
140 **Sarus Crane** *Grus antigone*
154 **Mongolian Plover** *Charadrius mongolus*
166 **Whimbrel** *Numenius phaeopus*
212 **Black Noddy** *Anous minutus*
231 **Squatter Pigeon** *Petrophassa scripta*
273 **Pale-headed Rosella** *Platycercus adscitus*
282 **Paradise Parrot** *Psephotus pulcherrimus*
301 **Common Koel** *Eudynamis scolopacea*
314 **Plumed Frogmouth** (subspecies of Marbled Frogmouth) *Podargus ocellatus plumiferus*

426 TAWNY GRASSBIRD

Megalurus timoriensis

The Tawny Grassbird is widespread in the islands to the north, and in Australia is most often recorded from the east coast; it occurs also in the Top End and Kimberley regions. This is a bird of the margins of wetlands, within reed-beds, dense damp heath, tall grass, sometimes tall rank grass around crops or forest edges. Its presence in the breeding season may be revealed by the male's display flights above the vegetation, singing, or the sharp 'jk, jk' alarm calls may be heard. It is larger and tawnier than the Little Grassbird.

▶ **See also pages** 79 210 356

476 FAIRY WARBLER

Gerygone palpebrosa

The Fairy Warbler is confined to eastern Queensland including the Cape York and Atherton regions. It is a bird of the rainforest canopy, best or most likely seen in places where the foliage is low, as along streams, and at the forest edges. It is also to be seen in mangroves, where it favours the shore side. The lively high warbling can often attract attention to this very small bird.

▶ **See also pages** 79 368

524 EUNGELLA HONEYEATER

Lichenostomus hindwoodi

This honeyeater is confined to the highlands of the Clarke Range, west of Mackay, and takes its name from the Eungella National Park within which it was discovered. Birds of this species had been seen on previous occasions by ornithologists, and in 1962 an article in *The Emu*, the journal of the Royal Australasian Ornithologists Union, gave description, measurement and photograph, but under the name of Bridled Honeyeater. The bird was seen, recorded, and mentioned in writings by other ornithologists, and a single specimen, collected in 1975, was lodged at the Australian Museum with specimens of the Bridled Honeyeater.

In 1976 the discrepancies of that single specimen from Eungella were noticed and suspicions were aroused that it was not a Bridled Honeyeater but apparently an undescribed species. Finally, in November 1978, the mist-net capture of one of these birds at Eungella confirmed the existence of a new species, later given the name Eungella Honeyeater. Endemic to this range, it has the smallest distribution

441 **RED-BACKED FAIRY-WREN** *Malurus melanocephalus*

of any Australian honeyeater. The Bridled Honeyeater, for which this species was mistaken, does not occur here and must be removed from any birdlists of this region.

The Eungella Honeyeater occurs in rainforest at altitudes above 1000 m. It has been observed in pairs and small parties feeding among the outer foliage, about bunches of palm seeds, and seems to be very much attracted to mistletoe. The Eungella Honeyeater seems to be common within its very restricted range.

▶ **See also pages** 71 79 80 81 379

529 YELLOW HONEYEATER

Lichenostomus flavus

This small honeyeater of eucalypt woodlands and forests is found in north-eastern Queensland and the Atherton and Cape York regions. It is also to be found in mangroves and melaleuca swamplands. In Townsville it is one of the most abundant birds, and occurs in larger numbers in the city streets and gardens than in surrounding woodlands. The bright yellow plumage makes it conspicuous. It has an undulating flight with a noisy 'flop-flop' sound from the wings and loud, clear whistled calls.

▶ **See also pages** 79 380

565 DUSKY HONEYEATER

Myzomela obscura

The Dusky Honeyeater occurs in New Guinea and in Australia, where it has two isolated subspecies: in the Top End (NT) and in eastern Queensland. It is confined to the more humid regions where it occupies strips of rainforest and monsoon forest along

253 **SCALY-BREASTED LORIKEET**
Trichoglossus chlorolepidotus

streams, swampy paperbark
woodlands, mangroves, and adjoining
drier eucalypt woodland.

The Dusky Honeyeater is active,
noisy and often pugnacious when
feeding about flowering trees; it is
often in company with Red-headed,
Scarlet or other honeyeaters.

▶ **See also pages** *79* 198 210 389

573 YELLOW-BELLIED SUNBIRD

Nectarinia jugularis

Australia's sole species of sunbird is
restricted to north-eastern Queensland,
including the Eastern Queensland,
Atherton and Cape York regions. It is
a bright, active and generally
conspicuous small bird of the
rainforest and mangrove edges, often
hovering in front of flowers and while
taking insects from the vegetation.
Within this and the Atherton Region it
is common, and certain to be seen
somewhere along the north-eastern
coast.

▶ **See also pages** 81 *82* 96 388 390–1 *391*

598 BLACK-THROATED FINCH

Poephila cincta

The Black-throated Finch is restricted
to north-eastern Queensland,
principally in the Eastern Queensland,
Atherton and Cape York regions. The
range of this finch has contracted and
it is now rare in south-eastern
Queensland and north-eastern New
South Wales.

The habitat is the grassy understorey
of eucalypt woodlands, especially
along watercourses. It is usually in
small flocks.

▶ **See also pages** *79* 175 396

599 PLUM-HEADED FINCH

Aidemosyne modesta

The Plum-headed Finch occupies drier
country to the mid-west and south-
west of this region. It takes seeds from
the ground and from standing grass. It
is nomadic, being present irregularly
in various localities, probably as a
result of rainfall and subsequent grass
growth. There are from time to time
irruptions of large numbers into areas
where they are uncommon or do not
usually occur.

This species is usually in pairs, small
parties or flocks of up to several
hundred. The flight is undulating, and
large flocks are noisy.

▶ **See also pages** *79* 396–7

611 FIGBIRD

Sphecotheres viridis

Two previously recognized species of
figbird are now combined as a single
species of two subspecies. The
northern is brightly coloured and has
yellow underparts, the southern is
duller and is green beneath. Figbirds
live about the edges of rainforest, in
eucalypt forest and in parks and
gardens. In winter flocks of up to 100
birds may be seen. In general, it is a
conspicuous species which will be
recorded by most birdwatchers
working within its range.

▶ **See also pages** *79* 175 209 399

543 **WHITE-THROATED HONEYEATER** *Melithreptus albogularis*

148 **MASKED LAPWING** *Vanellus miles*

BIRD PLACES OF EASTERN QUEENSLAND

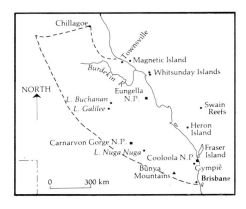

BURDEKIN-TOWNSVILLE WETLANDS

Some of the most extensive wetlands habitat in Australia occurs around the mouth of the Burdekin River, along about 150 km of coastline from the Townsville Town Common south-east to Cape Upstart. Much of this habitat is preserved within reserves, the Townsville Common being an environmental park, and wetlands are in national parks at Cape Cleveland and Bowling Green Bay. Other parts have been reserved as fauna sanctuaries, one of the most important being the Jerona Fauna Sanctuary on Baratta Creek.

While these swamps have a large and diverse waterbird population during the wet season, their greatest value is in providing a refuge during the late dry season when the wetlands of the interior have dried out, and in drought years when the inland swamps remain dry. In this region, as with most of northern Australia, 90 per cent of the rain falls from November to April. The long winter dry season, when there is almost no rain, ensures that many swamps dry completely and most of those that remain are greatly reduced.

The inland swamps are on the lower reaches of the western Queensland rivers in the channel country. These are vast wetlands in years of heavy rainfall but are irregular and temporary; when they dry out the birds that breed there must come with their young to the coastal wetlands.

The Burdekin-Townsville wetlands are set among a diversity of other habitats, with ranges along their inland boundary rising to 1234 m at Mt Elliot. Habitats include patches of rainforest and deciduous vine thicket, extensive areas of savannah-woodlands, and mangroves along the coast. These areas of mangrove are most extensive along the sheltered coast of Bowling Green Bay and Cleveland Bay and line the banks of

estuaries of rivers and creeks. On the inland side of the mangrove belt are expanses of bare saltpan country and grassy marine plains, lying between the coast and the swamplands.

Waterbirds are more attracted to some coastal wetlands than to others. These Burdekin-Townsville swamps support a prolific waterbird population, probably because of the diversity even within the wetland areas. Some parts on the seaward side have brackish water and beds of club rushes, while the shallow freshwater swamplands to the northern and western areas of these wetlands are covered almost entirely by bright green reed-like bulkuru sedge.

Near Cromarty, at the foot of Mt Elliot, deeper lagoon channels hold permanent water and are partly covered by pink and blue lilies. Where freshwater creeks from the ranges meet the swamps there are floating mats of nardoo and white-flowered water snowflake. Among the major permanent waterholes are the large oxbow Pinklily and Horseshoe lagoons.

68 WANDERING WHISTLING-DUCK
Dendrocygna arcuata

The great expanse of swamps that attract these birds are a product not only of the landforms here, but also of the climate of this part of the northern Queensland coast. At this point the coast has an east-west orientation, so that its ranges do not extract such heavy rainfall from the summer monsoons. The result is a wet season that is heavy enough to fill the swamps but insufficient to encourage expansion of mangroves or other heavy vegetation right across the open flats.

The waterbird populations and activities vary with the cycle of the seasons. With the onset of the wet season in about December, the coastal and inland swamps begin to fill. Some species, such as the Grey Teal, leave the coastal swamps for the newly filled wetlands of the interior. Others, including the Magpie Geese, move from the deep lagoons that have been their summer refuge to the wide

shallow parts of coastal swamps as these become covered with sheets of water and begin to change from brown to green.

By the end of February the Brolga flocks have broken up, a few remaining on the large coastal swamps, most spreading out to the many smaller swamps farther inland. With just one or a few pairs at each site a greater territory and food supply is available for the time when there are young in the nest.

The Magpie Geese begin nesting with the regrowth of the bulkuru sedge, usually where this reedy vegetation is thickest, building platforms of broken-down sedge. Black Swans nest in small colonies on islands of the brackish areas of the coastal wetlands, but sometimes build isolated floating nests.

Other species move out to deeper swamps and lagoons of the higher country. Wandering Whistling-Ducks, Plumed Whistling-Ducks and Black Ducks hide their nests in dense grass of swamp islets or margins.

By about the end of May, after several rainless months, some of the small wetlands used by many of the breeding birds throughout the hinterland dry out. From this time onwards there is a steady stream of arrivals at the large coastal swamps, the number growing steadily so that the waterbird population reaches a peak in number of species and total population through June to July or August. From August onwards the shrinking of the large coastal swamps again forces the birds to move, some to deeper lagoons and rivers, others leaving the region altogether.

But in those few midwinter months when the wetlands are at their optimum in extent and depth of water and abundance of food, the bird population is impressive. At this time of year 15 families of waterbirds have been recorded on the Burdekin-Townsville wetlands.

Brolgas are present in huge numbers, with up to 12 000 on the Cromarty Swamps south of Townsville and 1000–3000 on Townsville Common. Flocks of Magpie Geese here total thousands of birds. Most others, such as the various spoonbills, ibises, egrets and herons, are in smaller flocks or parties. The ability of these swamps to support such diversity and numbers is due to the variety of food niches, so that no two species are too closely in competition for the same plant or animal food.

By late October most of the remaining waterbirds are concentrated upon the semi-permanent deepwater lagoons of the coast from Bowling Green Bay to Ingham. But large flocks of Brolgas continue to forage across the swamps where a dry crust covers deep moist mud from which they continue to dig the bulkuru tubers.

The habitats of the Burdekin–Townsville wetlands support more than 230 species of birds, including 17 species of raptors. The RAOU Field Atlas survey recorded 338 species in an area north and east to include the upland rainforests of Paluma, Magnetic Island, the coast and wetlands, and inland for about 150 km. No species is unique to the district; those of the rainforests are shared with the greater blocks of rainforest farther north while the waterbirds and raptors are all widespread species. The distinctiveness of this place lies in the spectacle of huge numbers, rather than endemics.

Baratta Creek, just north of Ayr, has a rookery, first discovered in 1952, of egrets and other species. It is located wholly within mangrove swamps at the mouth of the creek, on a mangrove island, where access is difficult. The species nesting here in February include the Great Egret, Intermediate Egret, Little Egret, Rufous Night Heron, Sacred Ibis, Little Pied Cormorant and Little Black Cormorant. Numbers vary in these swamps, but inaccessibility makes counting very difficult.

The Burdekin River, on its way to these coastal wetlands, flows through a large valley with many lagoons and lakes, known as the Valley of Lagoons, with many waterbirds.

LAKE GALILEE AND LAKE BUCHANAN

In north-eastern central Queensland, some 400 km inland from the Mackay–St Lawrence coast, on the western side of the Great Dividing Range, a sandy tract of country long known as The Desert, for its poor grazing qualities, holds a chain of wetlands. The largest of these are Lake Galilee and Lake Buchanan, while around and between them are a great many small lakes and swamps.

Lake Galilee has an area of 15 000 ha and occupies a shallow basin in alluvial silt and sand deposits. When filled by heavy rain it contains a number of islands, the largest being Dolphin, St Helena and Swan islands. The floods bring great numbers of waterfowl, which use these islands as roosting and breeding sites. Lake Buchanan, with an area of 6100 ha, has a higher salt concentration and very little fringing vegetation.

female   male

More interesting for birdlife are some of the smaller lakes and swamps nearby. Lake Constant, a small salt lake set between the ridges of old beach lines on the western side of Lake Buchanan, is used by Black Swans, whose large floating nests dot the open waters.

One of the most valuable of these wetlands is Caukingburra Swamp, just 2 km east of Lake Buchanan yet

356 **Varied Triller** *Lalage leucomela*
405 **Shining Flycatcher** *Myiagra alecto*
426 **Tawny Grassbird** *Megalurus timoriensis*
471 **Large-billed Warbler** *Gerygone magnirostris*
476 **Fairy Warbler** *Gerygone palpebrosa*
506 **Helmeted Friarbird** *Philemon buceroides*
524 **Eungella Honeyeater** *Lichenostomus hindwoodi*
529 **Yellow Honeyeater** *Lichenostomus flavus*
565 **Dusky Honeyeater** *Myzomela obscura*
598 **Black-throated Finch** *Poephila cincta*
599 **Plum-headed Finch** *Aidemosyne modesta*
611 **Figbird** *Sphecotheres viridis*

142 **COMB-CRESTED JACANA** *Irediparra gallinacea* Top: *Adult* Bottom: *Young*

containing freshwater. The 10 sq. km of its surface have extensive reed-beds providing nesting sites for its abundant waterbirds. Large river red-gums fringe the swamp and grow on several small islands which are heavily used by waterbirds.

CARNARVON GORGE-CENTRAL HIGHLANDS

Also in the drier inland country, but farther south in the Central Highlands, is a region of deeply dissected sandstone tablelands, of which the Carnarvon National Park is the best-known part. The erosion of the white sandstone has formed vertical cliffs on the gorges and tablelands, and in some areas all that remains of the old tableland level are huge sandstone pillars rising from the plains.

About 40 km east of Carnarvon Gorge, where Carnarvon Creek joins the Brown River, a tributary of the Comet River, are the Arcadia Wetlands. This is the largest system of lakes and swamps in east-central Queensland. The main feature is Lake Nuga Nuga, with an area of 2000 ha, the surface often covered with pink *Nymphaea* waterlilies. A short distance downstream, the Four Mile Swamp is a large wetland close to the

junction of Carnarvon Creek and Brown River. These wetlands provide waterfowl habitat and add diversity to the bird fauna in the Carnarvon Gorge area.

Among the birds of these central highlands are the Pale-headed Rosella, Eastern Yellow Robin, Jacky Winter, Variegated Fairy-wren, White-throated Treecreeper, Spangled Drongo, Scarlet Honeyeater and White-eared Honeyeater. The RAOU Atlas survey listed 224 species, 77 breeding, in this locality.

THE GREAT SANDY COAST

Included within this area are Fraser Island, the Cooloola coast south to Noosa, and the mangroves and tidal wetlands of the Great Sandy Strait and Tin Can Bay.

Fraser Island is a diverse environment. It has broad sandy beaches backed by high dunes, some rising to 240 m above sea level. In hollows and valleys between these dunes are numerous freshwater lakes, some to 130 m above sea level. The interior of the island is heavily vegetated, with rainforest-like vine forests, blackbutt, scribbly gum and melaleuca forests, and banksia-dominated wallum.

Mangroves are restricted to the sheltered western side of the island, mostly along the sides of the Great Sandy Strait, and in the inlet of Tin Can Bay. The Fraser Island birdlist stands at more than 200 species, with a wide range of habitats utilized. It includes albatrosses and petrels of the open waters, the many seabirds and waders that use the long sand beaches, and the birds of the dense palm and vine forests. Among the birds recorded have been the Grey Goshawk, Beach Thick-knee, Powerful Owl, Barn Owl, Rose Robin, Shining Flycatcher and Regent Bowerbird.

The extensive areas of sandbanks and mudflats of Tin Can Bay have large numbers of waders and other birdlife; this small township is north-east of Gympie. The birding opportunities depend upon the tides. At high tide the birds are pushed up close to the shore near the town. Observers here in mid-February found some 400 Bar-tailed Godwits, along with a few Black-tailed Godwits, Mongolian Plovers, Large Sand Plovers, Red-capped Plovers, Lesser Golden Plovers, Silver Gulls and a congregation of about 50 Pied Oystercatchers.

As the tide falls the flocks spread out onto the exposed mudflats. A small boat will give the best viewing, following the tidal channels. Other birds to be seen here include the

Jabiru, Beach Thick-knee, Brahminy Kite, White-bellied Sea-Eagle and Osprey. Across the many kilometres of exposed mudflats are scattered great numbers of waders, busily feeding.

In the RAOU national wader count, this Hervey Bay–Great Sandy Strait area ranked seventeenth among Australia's wader sites, with a count of 13 800 birds.

326 **FOREST KINGFISHER** *Halcyon macleayii*

EUNGELLA

The high and rugged Clarke Range, lying close to the east of Mackay, is best-known for the magnificent scenery and rainforest of Eungella National Park, which covers more than half the range. This 1277 m range and its rainforests are isolated from the ranges and rainforest north of Townsville, and those of south-eastern Queensland, by wide expanses of much drier open eucalypt woodland country, so that its avifauna contains elements from both those regions and has some of its own unique species and subspecies.

The rainforest birds of Eungella show closest affinities to the avifauna of south-eastern Queensland, being the northern limit for such birds as the Regent Bowerbird and Brown Thornbill. Eungella was the site of an exciting discovery in 1977 of a new species of bird, subsequently named the Eungella Honeyeater. It had been seen previously but was recorded as the Bridled Honeyeater. It now replaces the Bridled Honeyeater on the Eungella birdlist, the latter being confined to the Atherton Region. Eungella has also an isolated endemic subspecies, *intermedia*, of the White-throated Treecreeper.

The most accessible part of the Clarke Range is within the national park, where roads pass through rainforest and give access to some

87 **OSPREY** *Pandion haliaetus* Adults and large young

lookout points with spectacular views over the Pioneer Valley. From a camping area set in rainforest at Broken River, trails allow closer contact with superb highland rainforest, some routes following the Broken River where the Eungella Honeyeater occurs. Trails include a 2.4 km Broken River Circuit, a 6 km Broken River Track, and a 7.6 km Palm Walk Track.

These Eungella tracks pass through some superb rainforest, winding between large buttressed trees, and often among palms. In the dimly lit slopes of the hillside above and below the track Rainbow Pittas can often be heard calling, Black-faced and Spectacled Monarchs dart about the lower strata of the rainforest, the calls of Eastern Whipbirds ring out from undergrowth thickets, a Rufous Fantail flits about beside the track, its rufous and often-fanned tail bright even in this subdued light.

Of considerable interest among the birds of the area are the White-rumped Swiftlets, which nest in caves in the cliffs of some of the gorges.

Rainforest pigeons are well represented, with Rose-crowned Fruit-Doves, Superb Fruit-Doves, Wompoo Fruit-Doves, Topknot Pigeons, Brown Cuckoo-Doves and Emerald Doves.

On the coast close to Eungella, the small Cape Hillsborough National Park has forest of hoop pine, rainforest and open eucalypt forest; the shoreline has sandy and rocky beaches, with areas of fringing mangroves. The bird list here is over 130 species, with 12 species of raptors, the Beach Thick-knee, Noisy Pitta and Yellow-bellied Sunbird.

THE SOUTHERN BARRIER REEF

Offshore from this part of the coast, the Whitsunday Islands form a maze

of islands, most small but a few very large and mountainous. Their birdlife is typical of the coastal ranges of the nearby mainland. Farther out to sea lies the Great Barrier Reef where the islets are low coral cays ringed by extensive reefs. Among these are some outstanding seabird islands.

On the Swain Reefs of the south-eastern Great Barrier Reef, 10 species of seabirds were recorded breeding on eight of the coral cays. These islands are situated 84–203 km from the mainland coast and are low, flat, and vegetated with dense or sparse low grass and herb cover.

The breeding seabirds here are the Crested Tern, Lesser Crested Tern, Black-naped Tern, Bridled Tern, Roseate Tern, Silver Gull, Common Noddy, Brown Booby, Masked Booby, and Least Frigatebird.

The Bunker–Capricorn Group, closer inshore and about 50–100 km east of Gladstone, has about a dozen

573 **YELLOW-BELLIED SUNBIRD**
Nectarinia jugularis

islets, some with dense vegetation of low pisonia trees. One of these vegetated islands is Heron Island, where Black Noddies nest in thousands, their nests being flattened platforms of leaves cemented to the branches with droppings, many nests in each tree.

In January many nests have a single egg, others have chicks of various sizes. Throughout the day such a colony is a bedlam of yelping birds, the noise rising to a crescendo every time another group arrives from the sea and each bird is greeted by its mate at the nest. Away from the pisonia trees and noddies, much of the island's sandy soil is honeycombed with the nest burrows of Wedge-tailed Shearwaters; during the day the colony appears deserted, most birds being at sea, others in their burrows.

Because it is so well wooded, Heron Island does not have any tern or gull colonies; for these one must visit islands such as One Tree or Masthead, also on the Capricorn–Bunker group. Both are low coral cays with large areas of grass or low exposed shrubbery. They have colonies of thousands of birds, mainly Crested Terns, but also Black-naped Terns, Sooty Terns, Bridled Terns, Lesser Crested Terns, Black Noddies, Silver Gulls, Eastern Reef Egrets and Sooty Oystercatchers. Fifteen other species of seabirds have been recorded but do not breed here.

The largest of the coral cays, with an area of 82 ha, is nearby North West Island with dense vegetation and tens of thousands of nesting seabirds.

325 **BLUE-WINGED KOOKABURRA**
Dacelo leachii

THE BLACKALL-CONONDALE RANGES

The Blackall and Conondale ranges are situated only about 140 km north of Brisbane and about 30–50 km inland from the Sunshine Coast. The range carries a diversity of habitat, including rainforests, vine forest, and wet and dry sclerophyll forests.

The rainforests here are superb, much of the setting rugged with ferny creeks and gorges. These rainforests have an abundance of epiphytic ferns and orchids, woody lianes, climbing palms and walking-stick palms growing on and beneath strangler figs. In some parts of the forest tall bunya pines and rose-gums rise high above the canopy. On drier slopes are forests of brush-box, tallowwood and rose-gum.

The Conondale forests are in many ways similar to the lowland rainforests of north-eastern New South Wales, with similarities in avifauna. The bird-list for the range is near 180 species. Among the more exciting species recorded here have been the Red Goshawk, Black-breasted Button-quail, Powerful Owl, Sooty Owl and Plumed Frogmouth.

The raptors of the Blackall–Conondale ranges and adjoining lowlands total 22 diurnal species and six owl species. Among these is the rare Red Goshawk, usually seen soaring late morning to midday, often to the south-west of Kenilworth, and also on nearby parts of the Blackall Range. Many of the sightings have been in the vicinity of major watercourses; there seem to be only one or two pairs within this district.

The Grey Goshawk is an uncommon breeding resident, both grey and white phase sighted, grey predominant; the dense moist forests are favoured. Other species of *Accipiter* here are the Brown Goshawk, a common breeding resident, and the Collared Sparrowhawk, an uncommon resident.

Other diurnal raptors of the district are the Black-shouldered Kite, Pacific Baza, Black Kite, Square-tailed Kite, Brahminy Kite, Whistling Kite, Wedge-tailed Eagle, Little Eagle, Spotted Harrier, Marsh Harrier, Peregrine Falcon, Australian Hobby, Brown Falcon, Australian Kestrel, and as an irregular visitor from the coast, the Osprey.

Among the owls, the presence of the rare Sooty Owl is of interest. It is known only from dense forests at Kilcoy, Booloumba Creek and Maleny. The presence of this owl is usually revealed by its 'falling bomb' call. Also rare here are the Powerful Owl, Masked Owl, and Barking Owl; common are the Southern Boobook and Barn Owl.

Although rainforest and open eucalypt forest are the dominant habitats of the range, there are small areas of freshwater streams, ponds, marshes and swamps which are known to support a total of 56 species including a number of rails. Most are considered migratory, and are probably present from August to April.

The rare Lewin's Rail has been seen at Booloumba Creek, Maleny and Conondale; it is very shy and keeps to dense vegetation. The Buff-banded Rail is the most common here, seen in dense vegetation around ponds and swamps. Baillon's Crake has been seen regularly on freshwater swamps in the Woodford area. There has been a single sighting of the Australian Crake in dense vegetation at Little Yabba Creek. Also rare, the Bush-hen is known to frequent dense vegetation along the edges of Little Yabba Creek, and at Maleny. Common here are the Dusky Moorhen, Eurasian Coot and Purple Swamp-hen. A visitor to marshes, wet pasture and shallow freshwaters is Latham's Snipe, a migratory wader.

TOWNSVILLE COMMON BIRDWATCH

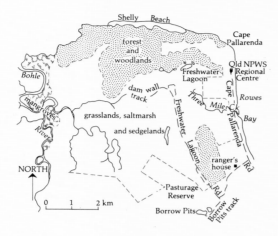

In 1981 an extensive area of swamplands and surrounding habitats close beside the city of Townsville became one of Queensland's largest environmental parks in recognition of its immense value as a bird habitat. The Townsville Town Common, with the spectacle of its massed waterbirds, has long attracted ornithologists and tourists from far and wide, yet it is just a ten-minute drive to the city's international airport.

The reputation of the Townsville Common is built upon its spectacularly large numbers of waterbirds.

Following the flooding rains of the midsummer wet, the plains of the Common become a vast shallow swamp attracting huge numbers of Brolgas, Magpie Geese, spoonbills, herons, egrets, ibises and other waterbirds. The waterlevel falls steadily through the long dry season, until the swamps become damp grassland with isolated pools, and finally dry grasslands and bare salt flats, forcing many of the waterbirds to leave. Large flocks of Brolgas remain, and some species of waterbirds concentrate on the permanent waterholes.

From the gate the Freshwater Lagoon Road extends about 3 km into the Common, passing through a variety of habitats and terminating at the earthen dam wall of Freshwater Lagoon. A track along the top of the dam wall provides elevated viewpoints overlooking the grassland and saltmarshes of the Common to south and west, and across the sedgeland of Freshwater Lagoon.

The birdwatching experiences here will depend upon the time of year and day. The Common is renowned for its flocks of Brolgas but there are also large and noisy flocks of Magpie Geese and smaller numbers of ibises, spoonbills, egrets, herons, a few stately Black-necked Storks and a great many smaller waterfowl, raptors and birds of shrubland, woodland, forest and rainforest.

The Brolgas provide the most spectacular sights at the Common. These birds congregate on the coastal wetlands as inland swamps dry out, the numbers increasing steadily through the early months of the dry season, with up to 3000 birds massed together through the latter part of the dry season.

From the vantage points on the dam or elsewhere the Brolgas can be watched probing in the shallow water to feed on the rhizomes of the bulkuru sedge. Although there are huge numbers, they are clustered in small family parties or pairs. Often a pair, or the birds of a group, will cease feeding to dance, gracefully leaping with flapping wings, bowing, then with wings arched throwing their heads back to give their far-carrying whooping, trumpeting calls.

While the flocks are feeding, parties may be flying in from other feeding grounds to join the main flock, their arrival announced by the trumpeting calls floating down from above. The great grey birds glide down, broad wings spanning well over 2 m, and touch down lightly with a few beats of the great wings, run a few bouncing strides, fold their wings, shuffle their feathers, and nonchalantly begin to feed. One of the most beautiful sights here is in the evening, when from the usual vantage points the flocks of Brolgas, Magpie Geese and other birds land silhouetted against the sunset.

Farther out on the swamp, where there are reeds and bulkuru sedges rising above the water, many hundreds, sometimes thousands of Magpie Geese feed, those in deeper water upending, tails skywards, reaching with long necks to dredge bulbs from the muddy bottom.

Through the pools, groups of Royal and Yellow-billed spoonbills march steadily forward in tight formation, swinging their long, flat-tipped bills from side to side to filter tiny water creatures.

Wherever there is floating vegetation Comb-crested Jacanas will be seen, mainly on Manypeaks Dam and other weedy waterholes. Later in the dry season these birds are confined to the old borrow pits as shallower pools dry out.

The Common has a varied raptor population, the diverse habitats suiting the hunting of the raptors of coast, swamp and forest. Often when mobs of birds fly up in alarm, attention will be drawn to the brown, white-rumped Marsh Harrier floating lazily over the open swampland. It is usually seen flying low over the reed-beds, occasionally dropping out of sight in taller vegetation, and sometimes circling higher, when the waterfowl on the open waters will take off in panic from its path.

White-bellied Sea-Eagles frequently soar over, inspecting the flats for carrion or prey; they are distinctive, with their broad wings held in an upswept position, and an extremely short tail. Ospreys are present but keep more to the coast and can at times be seen fishing off Shelly Beach.

The third coastal raptor here is the Brahminy Kite, unmistakable with its white head and rusty-brown wings and body. It tends to favour the mangrove areas but will occasionally quarter the open wetlands. Also likely to be seen hunting over the open grasslands is the small Australian Kestrel, often hovering skilfully.

The Townsville Common, with its diversity of habitats, has also some of the raptors of forests and woodlands, including the Peregrine Falcon, Australian Hobby, Brown Falcon, Brown Goshawk, Black Kite and Whistling Kite.

In addition to the dam wall track, there is a waterbird circuit, a track to the deeper pools of the borrow pits, and a forest track.

The Common is situated 5 km out via the Cape Pallarenda Road. Turn left near the Rowes Bay Country Club. The gates are open from 6.30 am to 6.30 pm. The Queensland National Parks and Wildlife Service regional office is about 5 km farther along the Cape Pallarenda Road, should ranger advice be needed.

322 **AZURE KINGFISHER** *Ceyx azurea*

ATHERTON REGION

The birds of north-eastern Australia owe much of their diversity and distinctiveness to the east coast landforms, in particular the Great Dividing Range which extends the full length of this coast, some parts very high and rugged, some sections rising steeply from the sea, others curving well inland.

Where the ranges are high and interrupt moisture-laden winds the heavier rainfall has allowed the development of rainforests of both lowland and upland types. Along the coast and ranges from Cooktown south to Ingham the rainfall is Australia's heaviest. It is over this section that some of the continent's most luxuriant tropical rainforests have developed.

Between these rainforests and those of Cape York Peninsula a wide belt of drier open eucalypt and paperbark woodlands forms a barrier, about 200 km wide, to a large number of rainforest birds.

While the Cape York Peninsula rainforests have many birds found in no other part of Australia, those species are shared with New Guinea. On the other hand, the rainforests of the Atherton Region, separated by that dry, open woodland, have 11 species, and many subspecies, that are unique to Australia. In addition, some of the New Guinean birds are able to cross the woodlands barrier and add to the already rich avifauna of the Atherton Region.

The height of the ranges of the Atherton Region, and their close proximity to the sea, has allowed the development of rainforests unique to the misty heights, different in composition and character from the lowland rainforests along the narrow coastal strip between mountains and sea. Many of the endemics of the Atherton Region — the Tooth-billed Catbird, Golden Bowerbird,

Mountain Thornbill, Atherton Scrubwren, Australian Fernwren, Grey-headed Robin, Bower's Shrike-thrush and Bridled Honeyeater — are confined to the upland rainforests. Others whose range is mostly within the Atherton Region, both highland and lowland, are the Pied Monarch, Macleay's Honeyeater and Victoria's Riflebird.

Although mountain ranges dominate the Atherton Region, there is great variety of landform and habitats, resulting in an impressive total of bird species, often in settings of superb scenery.

The coastline is varied. In the north between Cooktown and Daintree the steep slopes of the rainforest-clad ranges run right down to the sea. Southwards, there is low coastal plain broken by numerous river and creek channels with extensive mangrove swamps in their estuaries. Behind these mangroves and sand beaches the flat coastal plain is swampy, with woodlands of eucalypts and paperbarks. In some localities are swamps, some with fan palms and patches of lowland rainforest.

Further inland again the eastern slopes of the great mountain block rise abruptly. The steep, rainforest-clad, often cloud-capped massif of the Mt Bartle Frere and Bellenden-Ker Range rises to a height of 1600 m and dominates both the coastal plains to its eastern side and the Atherton Tableland to the west.

The broad, gently undulating tableland is mostly at an altitude of around 900–1000 m but is almost encircled by higher ranges with many parts over 1200 m. Although much of the tableland rainforest has been cleared, most of the surrounding ranges are still forested.

The highlands of the northern parts of the Atherton Region are even more rugged and certainly more difficult to reach. These are

606 METALLIC STARLING *Aplonis metallica* Immature

the ranges around the Daintree and Bloomfield rivers, overlooking Mossman, where they reach altitudes above 1200 m and include Mt Lewis and Mt Spurgeon.

Although the major mountain wilderness areas have among their birds the upland endemic species, these can be seen much more conveniently at several of the smaller but easily accessible national parks of the Atherton Tableland.

Tableland birding spots well worth a visit include Lake Barrine, Lake Eacham, The Crater, and then perhaps some lesser-known sites for hard-to-find species.

On the coast, Cairns Esplanade for waders, the lowland rainforests and fan palm forests at Mission Beach and Clump Point, Eubenangee Swamp near Innisfail, and the seabird islands of the northern Great Barrier Reef.

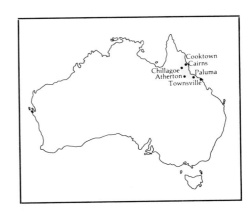

BIRDS OF THE ATHERTON REGION

117 RED-BACKED BUTTON-QUAIL

Turnix maculosa

In the Atherton Region the Red-backed
Button-quail is widespread in cleared
grassy areas up to 900 m altitude,
favouring the heavier grassy and
herbaceous growth beside
watercourses. It also occurs at edges of
rainforests, in woodlands, crops, and
gardens. It tends to 'freeze' under
cover rather than fly.

This button-quail is usually found in
pairs or coveys and is reputed to be
not easily flushed. When it is, it flies
fast and far before dropping back to
cover. The female, with a distinctive
rufous patch on the upper back, is
much more easily identified. The call is
a subdued booming which may be the
first indicator of its presence. It is tame
around habitation on some Great
Barrier Reef islands.

▶ See also pages 87 280

128 RED-NECKED CRAKE

Rallina tricolor

The Red-necked Crake is most often
reported from the Atherton Region but
occurs also down the east coast of
Cape York Peninsula. It appears that
at least part of the Cape York
population migrates to New Guinea
when the rainforest floor dries out in
the winter months. Some birds seem to
remain throughout the year in the
more permanently wet rainforests of
the Atherton Region.

In this region it lives where the
rainforest undergrowth is most dense,
favouring areas of vine thickets where
ground and leaf-litter are permanently
wet. Although occasionally seen
during the day it forages mostly at
dusk and dawn and often calls during
the night. The evening's activity often
begins with a late afternoon visit to a
pool to drink and bathe, the birds
usually calling at intervals as they
move, well concealed, towards the
water. Such sites, if found, provide
some of the best chances of a view of
this secretive and wary species,
otherwise there is usually little chance
of any more than a fleeting glimpse as
it scuttles for cover.

The call, when known, gives the
best and usually the only practical way
of discovering the presence of this
crake. In the dense vegetation there is
little chance of approaching such a
wary bird, but the calls carry several
hundred metres. Its territorial call is a
loud, harsh, penetrating series of
notes, becoming more rapid as they
fade away: 'ARK, ark, ark-ark-ark-

128 **RED-NECKED CRAKE** *Rallina tricolor*

ar-', and sometimes also a single loud
high 'aak'. It is reported to give a
monotonous 'tok, tok, tok', which it
may continue for hours.

Except when coming to water in the
middle to late afternoon, these birds
are seldom seen during the day. They
probably have roosting platforms in
dense foliage and have occasionally
been flushed from crowns of palms.
When disturbed they are quick to take
cover, hiding, running, swimming, but
rarely flying.

Feeding is usually recorded around
dusk when these crakes forage along
creek-banks and in the wet litter of
waterlogged depressions in the
rainforest, where they seek mainly
aquatic invertebrates.

The loud, harsh territorial calls
usually begin towards evening and are
taken up by pairs in neighbouring
territories. The monotonous 'tok, tok'
call is most evident through the
breeding season, going on for hours,
well into the night. Territories focus
on a central point, such as a creek,
with the calling indicating that these
territories are maintained throughout
the year.

The Red-necked Crake inhabits the
swampy rainforest around the
boardwalk in the Centennial Lakes in
Cairns. It has also been recorded at
Cooktown, Mossman, Atherton,
Innisfail, Hinchinbrook Island and
other rainforest habitats.

▶ See also pages 98 283

133 BUSH-HEN

Gallinula olivacea

The Bush-hen appears to be locally
nomadic, restricted to areas of
permanent water in the dry season,
then spreading out when heavy rains
of the wet season arrive. It keeps
mostly to dense vegetation, swampy
thickets, especially lantana intermixed
with tall grass, usually near fresh
water but sometimes up to 0.5 km
away.

This is a secretive species, best
located by its call, which is more
frequent and prolonged during the
summer wet than in the dry season.
The loud, shrieked 'knee-you'
territorial calls of breeding pairs are
often heard at night.

The Bush-hen has been recorded
also in the Brisbane area, including
outer suburbs, and around Eungella.

▶ See also pages 82 87 284

216 WOMPOO FRUIT-DOVE

Ptilinopus magnificus

This dove prefers large undisturbed
areas of rainforest. It is abundant most
of the year where fruit-bearing trees,
palms and vines are best developed,
where the understorey is dense,
especially along rainforest watercourses.
Even where common the Wompoo
Fruit-Dove is usually solitary or in
pairs, but sometimes in numbers on
trees with ripe fruit.

Although large and quite colourful, the bird tends to be unobtrusive, flying through or just below the canopy, often entering feeding trees unnoticed. The calls, a deep 'bollock-a-boo' or 'whom-poo', are usually the only indication of its presence. Even then it can be hard to detect; a useful ploy is to stand beneath the tree and look vertically upwards for the yellow of the undertail-coverts.

▶ **See also pages** 81 98 111 121 305

217 TORRESIAN IMPERIAL-PIGEON

Ducula spilorrhoa

The Torresian Imperial-Pigeon is distributed across northern Australia but is probably most easily seen in north-eastern Queensland. It is a migratory species, birds banded in Queensland being recovered in western New Guinea. This large, distinctive pigeon arrives in northern Australia around mid-August and departs by March or April.

This pigeon is unique in its wide segregation of breeding and feeding sites. The mainland rainforests provide the fruits upon which it feeds, while the mangroves of the Barrier Reef islands provide the nest colony sites, with the pigeons traversing the intervening sea each day.

On the mainland these pigeons are conspicuous; white with dark grey flight feathers. They can be seen flying about the rainforest canopy of the ranges overlooking the western parts of Cairns and feeding in the lowland rainforests at Mission Beach. The islands with large colonies tend to be situated close to the forests where the best feeding is available. There are major colonies on Low Island, with numbers as high as 25 000 birds, and many other islands around the northern coast. In the Kimberley Region it occurs in small numbers and does not seem to nest communally.

The use of islands as breeding sites is thought to give this pigeon greater security against predators.

The groups and flocks are conspicuous as they fly to and from the mainland feeding grounds and as they wander over the rainforest canopy. When feeding high in the rainforest canopy their presence is revealed by a low, double-noted advertising call, 'coo-WOO', and by short, sharp, screech-like sounds while skirmishing among themselves in the tops of the food trees.

The Torresian Imperial-Pigeon is not confined to rainforest but will feed at fruiting trees in eucalypt, melaleuca or mangrove forests.

▶ **See also pages** 97 98 196 209 305

219 WHITE-HEADED PIGEON

Columba leucomela

Although primarily a rainforest species, the White-headed Pigeon may also be found in patches of regrowth, isolated remnant patches and individual trees of former rainforest, and sometimes in introduced trees. It is more common at the rainforest edges.

117 **Red-backed Button-quail** *Turnix maculosa*
133 **Bush-hen** *Gallinula olivacea*
216 **Wompoo Fruit-Dove** *Ptilinopus magnificus*
217 **Torresian Imperial-Pigeon** *Ducula spilorrhoa*
219 **White-headed Pigeon** *Columba leucomela*
304 **Rufous Owl** *Ninox rufa*
319 **White-rumped Swiftlet** *Collocalia spodiopygia*
323 **Little Kingfisher** *Ceyx pusilla*
331 **Buff-breasted Paradise-Kingfisher** *Tanysiptera sylvia*

Although usually seen feeding on the fruits of trees, it is sometimes seen foraging on the ground.

Identification presents no problem, this being the only Australian pigeon with a dark body and white head, these visible at a considerable distance in open country. In dark rainforest, the wing-claps it makes in flight and its low, mournful 'oom-coo' or single, low, soft 'oom' are helpful.

▶ See also pages 87 121 306

258 DOUBLE-EYED FIG-PARROT

Psittaculirostris diophthalma

Three subspecies of the Double-eyed Fig-Parrot occur in Australia: *marshalli* in the Cape York Region, *coxeni* in south-eastern Queensland and north-eastern New South Wales, and, shown here, *macleayana* in the Atherton Region. The Double-eyed Fig-Parrot is principally a rainforest bird. It feeds upon the seeds of native figs of the rainforests, roosts and nests in rainforest, and pays but fleeting visits to, or through, areas of eucalypt forest. The nest hollow is drilled into the soft decayed wood of a dead limb of a rainforest tree.

The three Australian populations of fig-parrot were formerly separate species but later regarded as subspecies of the Double-eyed Fig-Parrot of New Guinea. Each subspecies has carried a common name which is often still used.

The subspecies confined to the Atherton Region, *macleayana*, sometimes called Northern or Red-browed Fig-Parrot, occurs in both the highland rainforest of the Atherton Tableland and surrounding ranges, and the lowland coastal rainforests. The Cape York subspecies, *marshalli*, the Cape York or Marshall's Fig-Parrot, is found in lowland rainforests, monsoon forests and coastal scrubs. The third subspecies, *coxeni*, the Southern or Blue-browed Fig-Parrot of south-eastern Queensland and north-eastern New South Wales, also occurs in both high and low rainforests.

The Double-eyed Fig-Parrot spends most of the day in rainforest, sometimes in isolated feeding trees in other surrounds, and moves through the drier habitats in the early morning and towards dusk. In the Atherton Region it is reported occasionally in wet eucalypt forest. The Cape York and Atherton subspecies are common within their limited range but the southern subspecies is rare.

The flight is swift and direct, without undulations, generally above the forest canopy rather than twisting

258 **MACLEAY'S FIG-PARROT** *Psittaculirostris diophthalma macleayana* Male feeding female

258 **MACLEAY'S FIG-PARROT** *Psittaculirostris diophthalma Macleayana* Male at the nest

and turning through the trees. The contact call is a sharp, penetrating 'tseet-tseet-tseet-', given in flight, on landing, and immediately prior to take-off. The alarm is a shrill, rolling screech, sometimes also a softer screech in flight. It responds to imitations of its calls.

At Iron Range it seems to feed almost exclusively on fruits of the fig *Ficus hispida*, a tree of rainforest edges. In the Atherton area it feeds on several species of figs. Once the favoured individual local feeding trees are known they can be watched from time to time, when the fruit are at a suitable stage, for signs of these birds. When feeding in fig trees the birds will descend to where the fruits of some figs grow low down on the trunk, giving excellent sightings.

▶ See also pages 97 98 114 314

304 RUFOUS OWL

Ninox rufa

The Rufous Owl roosts during the day in dense vegetation of monsoon forest, thick river-edge forest, or mangroves. A daylight sighting is probably a matter of chance or the result of very thorough searching in likely situations. By night, the Rufous Owl hunts mainly over adjacent open eucalypt woodland country. Typically it appears to have a number of roost sites and, being very shy, often slips silently away to another site as an intruder approaches, before being seen; however it is said to defend the nest site strongly.

The call is a deep 'woo-hoo' or 'woo-woo', which if heard at night in an appropriate site could lead to a sighting.

By day the Rufous Owl roosts under thick foliage on a bare horizontal limb in a position giving a commanding outlook in several directions. There are usually several such roosts within the territory, which is occupied permanently. A pair will occupy one or other roost site in a seemingly haphazard sequence day by day, the position often disclosed by the chattering and harrying of smaller birds.

Although it appears that Rufous Owls hunt separately, male and female roost together, or at least in trees within calling distance. Females are typically more timid and are the first to flush from the roost tree if disturbed. The smaller male is more inclined to stand his ground, calling her back after the danger has passed.

Hunting begins at dusk and the owls settle to roost about sunrise. In the half-light of dusk and dawn the Rufous Owl hunts in the heavier, darker forests then moves out into more open areas in the darkest part of the night. Most calling is done at dusk and dawn, with soft hooting for contact and to advertise territory. The contact call is a drawn-out 'whooooo-hoo', this given repeatedly in territorial calling. Sites on record include Atherton, Mareeba, Herbert River Gorge, Dunk Island, Mt Mulligan, Byfield, upper Burdekin River, the mouth of the Watson River, and the Claudie River. The Northern Territory subspecies is occasionally recorded from monsoon forest just north of Cooinda, and the Mary River Crossing.

▶ See also pages 87 97 196 209 325

313 PAPUAN FROGMOUTH

Podargus papuensis

The Australian range of the Papuan Frogmouth is almost entirely within the Cape York and Atherton regions where it lives at the edge of the closed forest, rainforest, monsoon forest, vine thicket or mangrove swamp.

The dense cover of the closed forest serves as their daytime roost, the roosting branches being well overhung with dense vegetation. At night they hunt in the open eucalypt woodland.

The Papuan Frogmouth has been able to tolerate some clearing, provided that patches of dense roost forest remain. It seems to be plentiful in those suburbs of Cairns that are close to the forested ranges.

▶ See also pages 97 110 327–8

313 PAPUAN FROGMOUTH
Podargus papuensis

319 WHITE-RUMPED SWIFTLET

Collocalia spodiopygia

This swiftlet nests and roosts in caves, the colonies varying from a few pairs to more than a thousand. There are only about six known breeding areas: on the Upper Mitchell River, Chillagoe Caves, Tully Gorge, Mt Peter Mines, the Family Islands, and in Finch Hatton near Eungella. The frequency of sightings farther north, at Iron Range and between Cooktown and Cairns, suggests that there may be other colonies in those areas. As human interference is one factor in reduced breeding success, the precise localities are better not publicized.

This species is of particular interest for its echo-locating ability, needed when flying within dark caves which are occupied only during the breeding months. The birds then probably disperse over north-eastern Queensland.

This swiftlet is most common in areas under 500 m altitude. It is often seen in parties or small flocks hawking for insects over the rainforest canopy, over river gorges, and on reef islands. The flight appears erratic and bat-like.

▶ See also pages 81 87 329

323 LITTLE KINGFISHER

Ceyx pusilla

In this region the Little Kingfisher occurs both on the coast and in highlands up to 700 m altitude, along small creeks heavily screened by mangroves, monsoon forest, paperbarks and similar dense vegetation, usually tidal, but also inland freshwater streams.

The Little Kingfisher, like the Azure, spends most of its time sitting motionless on a low perch over water, often in a position screened by foliage. From time to time it will dive into the water or dart along the river to another perch or to the nest tunnel, giving several shrill squeaks as it flies. These calls are much like those of the Azure. The best chance of seeing either of these kingfishers seems to be to sit quietly at the edge of a watercourse in a likely site and watch for movement along the river and listen for the high squeak it may give as it dashes past. Even if there are no kingfishers, the other birdlife that comes by chance along almost any rainforest stream will make such a watch well worthwhile.

Size is often difficult to judge at a distance and the Azure can look very small. The Little Kingfisher has white underparts where the Azure is deep buff.

▶ See also pages 87 98 110 196 197 198 330–1

331 BUFF-BREASTED PARADISE-KINGFISHER

Tanysiptera sylvia

The Buff-breasted Paradise-Kingfisher is present in north-eastern Australia only in the summer wet season, arriving during November. Although some references suggest that this bird arrives in the Cape York Region later than in the Atherton Region, it was quite common at Iron Range by mid-November in 1985, when members of the Queensland Ornithological Society spent a week observing the birds of that locality.

In the Atherton Region the Buff-breasted Paradise Kingfishers arrive in the last week of October or the first week of November and most appear within a few days so that the rainforests, almost overnight, are noisy with their calls.

This kingfisher occurs in high density in suitable patches of rainforest. Near Innisfail, at least eight pairs occupied one site of 10 ha, and on the Whitfield Range, Cairns, there can be three or four pairs in some of the rainforest gullies. Often from one nest site the kingfishers of the surrounding territories can be heard calling.

Finding this bird should present no great difficulty provided that the time, locality and habitat are right, for its calls are loud, distinctive, and frequent during the breeding season. The call most likely to be heard is a steady, ascending 'chok-chok-chok-'. The birds are most easily seen immediately after their arrival when, with calls and feverish activity, they establish their territories.

These are birds of the upper levels of the rainforest but they often fly through the more open mid-level spaces. They appear to float through the forest, the long tail streaming behind, and will perch on bare horizontal limbs or vines, usually high, but often low by the nest mound. A tape recorded replay of the calls is usually effective in bringing the birds closer.

Localities include: Cairns, the Whitfield Range trail; Julatten; Innisfail district; Finch Hatton Gorge near Eungella; Cape York, Iron Range.

▶ See also pages *87 97 98* 333

352 YELLOW-EYED CUCKOO-SHRIKE

Coracina lineata

The Yellow-eyed Cuckoo-shrike is a sociable species, being seen in flocks of up to 50 birds roosting together in the non-breeding season. Communal nesting does not seem to occur. The chattering calls, given in flight, often attract attention, as does their activity as they forage among the foliage. The barred underparts and pale yellow eye are distinctive.

▶ See also pages *93* 339

380 GREY-HEADED ROBIN

Poecilodryas albispecularis

The Grey-headed Robin is confined to rainforests above 200 m altitude in the ranges of the Atherton Region and closely adjoining parts of the Eastern Queensland Region. It shelters and nests a little way into the rainforest but is most often seen foraging along the margins or just outside. It spends much of its time on low perches from which it darts out to take insects from the ground.

The Crater is a convenient observation site, for here the Grey-headed Robins are frequent visitors to the rainforest-surrounded picnic grounds.

▶ See also pages *85 97* 345

380 GREY-HEADED ROBIN
Poecilodryas albispecularis

391 BOWER'S SHRIKE-THRUSH

Colluricincla boweri

This species is almost entirely confined to the Atherton Region. It was thought to be restricted to rainforests of ranges and tableland above 250 m altitude but several coastal winter sightings suggest it either occurs at lower levels where the habitat is suitable, or moves lower in the winter months. Bower's Shrike-thrush is a quiet and unobtrusive bird, foraging about the foliage of the middle and lower strata. Only during the breeding season does it draw attention to itself with its rich and varied repertoire of calls. The species with which it is most likely to be confused is the Little Shrike-thrush, which is smaller, less streaked, and has a more slender bill.

▶ See also pages *85 93 97* 348

395 YELLOW-BREASTED BOATBILL

Machaerirhynchus flaviventer

Australia has two subspecies of the Yellow-breasted Boatbill, one in the Cape York Region, the other isolated within and endemic to the Atherton Region. In appearance it is unmistakable, especially if close enough to show clearly the unique broad, flattened bill. It is active about the foliage of the lower and mid-levels of the rainforest, taking insects from leaves and in flight. The call, a soft, musical trill, is different from that of other flycatchers. When known, it will reveal the presence of the species much more often than if sight alone is relied upon, confirming that it is quite common, though usually out of sight in the forest canopy.

▶ See also pages *93 97 98 111* 349

401 PIED MONARCH

Arses kaupi

This conspicuous and boldly plumaged flycatcher is almost entirely confined within the Atherton Region and restricted to the forests on the eastern side of the Great Dividing Range. Although similar to the Frilled Monarch of the Cape York Region, it is clearly distinguished by the black breastband; it is also separated in distribution, this species being found only as far north as Cooktown. It shares the treecreeper-like bark-foraging habits of the Frilled Monarch and captures insects on the wing, tail fanned, often calling. This activity makes the species quite conspicuous, and as it is present throughout the year should readily be found in suitable rainforest stream-edge habitats.

▶ See also pages *85 93 97 106* 350

412 CHOWCHILLA

Orthonyx spaldingii

The Chowchilla is endemic to the Atherton Region where it is a sedentary inhabitant of rainforest, feeding among the leaf-litter of the forest floor. Territories of about 3 ha are occupied by breeding pairs and often by parties of three to five birds.

The members of such parties keep within sight or sound of each other while foraging, occasionally communicating with low sounds.

When feeding among litter the usual sequence is to sweep aside the litter with one or other foot, scratch at the exposed soil, peck at any prey, then move on to repeat the process. The tail, which has strong shafts and bare spine-like tips, is used as a prop while one foot is sweeping aside the leaf- and twig-litter.

Chowchillas have a loud, unusual and beautiful song — a 'chow-chilla-chow-chow-chow-choo-choo-' which appears to be directed at groups in other territories. It can be heard from several hundred metres away and at close range can be deafening. It appears that individuals take turns in singing, so that the outpouring of sound can be maintained. The call is heard at dawn and dusk and there may be brief, quieter snatches of song during the day. Once known, the song is the most convenient way of finding this species, provided that the observer is on site at dawn or dusk.

Some sites include Josephine Falls, Palmerston National Park and Lake Barrine.

▶ See also pages *53 97 353*

412 **CHOWCHILLA** *Orthonyx spaldingii*

437 LOVELY FAIRY-WREN

Malurus amabilis

The male of the Lovely Fairy-wren looks very much like that of the Variegated Fairy-wren, but the female is distinctive with much light blue about the head and back. This species is also exceptional among fairy-wrens in its preference for rainforest and other dense habitats, including mangroves. It is most likely to be found along the scrubby margins where these densely canopied habitats meet the open grassy woodlands, and in adjoining lantana thickets. Here the Lovely Fairy-wrens, usually in small family parties, forage partly in the low grass, but also often quite high in the foliage of the rainforest-edge canopy.

Over most, if not all, of its range it is the only chestnut-shouldered fairy-wren. Previously a subspecies of the Variegated Fairy-wren, it is now separated again as a full species.

The Lovely Fairy-wren is common around Cairns and the Atherton Region generally, in appropriate habitat.

▶ See also pages *93 96 98 111 359*

457 AUSTRALIAN FERNWREN

Crateroscelis gutturalis

The Australian Fernwren is almost entirely confined to the Atherton Region. It is found only in damp gullies of rainforested ranges, usually above 600 m altitude. In those situations it can forage in damp litter throughout the year, lifting and turning leaves in search of small invertebrates.

Little is known of the habits of this species, though it is common in the misty wet highland rainforests from Cooktown south towards Townsville. It is most likely to be seen along one of the tracks in the rainforest, where it may be flushed from the ground if near the track, or heard rustling about in the leaf-litter. Otherwise its sombre olive-brown plumage makes it difficult to distinguish in the gloom of the rainforest. The white eyebrow and throat and the black breast bib are usually visible even in dim lighting. If the bird calls, its high whistle or harsh staccato warning chatter will certainly attract attention.

Fernwrens are usually in pairs. They are not shy, and very actively hop and fossick, with much bowing, uplifting of tail and flicking of leaves. They have been seen foraging in company with the Orange-footed Scrubfowl, apparently benefiting from the larger bird's raking of the leaf-litter.

This species is quite common on the Atherton Tableland, at The Crater and Lake Barrine.

▶ See also pages *85 93 97 363*

458 ATHERTON SCRUBWREN

Sericornis keri

The Atherton Scrubwren is confined to the tablelands and ranges within this region, above an altitude of about 600 m. Its plumage is very much like that of the Large-billed Scrubwren, which also occurs in this region. The

Atherton Scrubwren tends to be more terrestrial in its foraging and has darker brown plumage, slightly shorter wings, heavier legs and feet and a slightly smaller bill. While any dull brown scrubwren feeding on the ground in highland rainforest could well be an Atherton Scrubwren, positive identification should not be assumed on this basis alone. Nests of the Atherton Scrubwren have been found very close to the ground.

The Crater, southern Atherton Tableland, is a good site for this species.

▶ See also pages 85 93 97 363

471 LARGE-BILLED WARBLER

Gerygone magnirostris

The Large-billed Warbler is present throughout the year in coastal mangroves, paperbark woodlands and lowland rainforests, where it forages for insects, taken mainly from the foliage of the forest canopy. The plumage is very plain and it has a bill that is slightly larger than that of other warblers. But its song is outstanding, with a series of descending, clear, liquid notes. The nest of the Large-billed Warbler is more distinctive than the bird itself, suspended from a slender branch over water of swamp or forest stream. It is large for the size of the bird, domed, with a long tail, and looks like suspended floodwater debris.

When a plain brownish warbler is seen flitting about the foliage and visiting one of these distinctive nests, it is a factor that helps in identification.

▶ See also pages   79 98 228 324 364 367

478 MOUNTAIN THORNBILL

Acanthiza katherina

This little-known thornbill of the mountain rainforests between Cooktown and Townsville was given species status in 1968; the first nest was not found until 1971. It is a bird of the high outer canopy of rainforests above 450 m altitude, where it takes insects from the leaves, though it rarely flutters about the foliage. Its preference for the upper levels makes it difficult to observe but at mid-range, with the aid of binoculars, the pale yellowish iris of the eye may be visible. This feature separates the Mountain Thornbill from the Brown Thornbill, which has a dark red eye. The very large, moss-covered domed nest is usually suspended fairly high.

Sites include Mt Bellenden-Ker, Mt Lewis and Mt Baldy.

▶ See also pages 85 93 97 368

495 LITTLE TREECREEPER

Cormobates leucophaea minor

The range of the Little Treecreeper falls almost entirely within the Atherton Region. Previously a full species, it is now considered to be a subspecies of the White-throated Treecreeper. This subspecies is unique among treecreepers because of the extent to which it is confined to rainforests. It is usually working about the high limbs of the rainforest canopy where light penetration encourages growth of epiphytic mosses and lichens. These tend to be most abundant near the forest margins and where there are breaks in the canopy, as over clearings and roads, and are largely confined to highland rainforests. The moss and lichen clumps apparently conceal more insects than the often smooth limbs and trunks of lower and darker parts of the rainforest.

The Little Treecreeper has plumage and calls similar to the White-throated Treecreeper but as the localities of the two are widely separated, no identification problem arises. The other local treecreeper, the Brown, is obviously different in plumage and occupies woodland habitat.

Sightings of the Little Treecreeper should be sought along roads, streams and margins where a clear view can be obtained of limbs and trunks protruding from the general mass of foliage. Any treecreeper-like calls heard in these environs would be worth investigating.

▶ See also pages 97 372–3

516 MACLEAY'S HONEYEATER

Xanthotis macleayana

This honeyeater, while almost confined within the Atherton Region, is common within that restricted range. Recognition of the calls, which may be louder or more frequent during the breeding season late in the year, seems to be important for easy or frequent sightings. This is the reason why some visiting observers recorded the species infrequently and reported it uncommon, quiet and shy, while local resident birdwatchers considered it common and conspicuous, largely because of its loud calls.

Macleay's Honeyeater is found singly or in pairs about the upper and middle strata of both eucalypt forest and rainforest, and at times in nearby gardens and orchards. It forages about the foliage and flowers in a deliberate, thorough manner, probing among suspended debris of treetops and vine tangles for insects and fruits, and occasionally briefly hovering.

▶ See also pages 85 97 99 377

519 YELLOW-SPOTTED HONEYEATER

Meliphaga notata

The Yellow-spotted Honeyeater is confusing in its likeness to the Graceful Honeyeater and covers almost the same range and habitats. It is, however, a more conspicuous bird, very active in the foliage about the middle and lower levels, especially of the rainforest edges and margins. This species is noisy and aggressive, the harsh, petulant calls being quite different from those of the Graceful and Lewin's honeyeaters. It can be called up by making squeaky noises.

The range of the Graceful Honeyeater within Australia covers both the Atherton and Cape York regions, where it is predominantly a bird of the lowland rainforests, but it also occurs, in smaller numbers, on highlands. Within its range this species is widespread and moderately common. A lively bird, it favours rainforest fringes and also visits flowering trees outside the rainforest.

The Graceful Honeyeater closely resembles the Yellow-spotted and Lewin's honeyeaters but it tends to forage and nest higher in the forest. It has a tenuous whistle and short, sharp sounds that help to separate it from the Yellow-spotted Honeyeater. The Lewin's Honeyeater, in this region, is mainly on highlands. It has a loud, staccato, rattling chatter, is larger, and is not as close in plumage pattern as the Graceful and Yellow-spotted honeyeaters.

▶ See also pages 55 99 378

523 BRIDLED HONEYEATER

Lichenostomus frenatus

The range of the Bridled Honeyeater extends very little beyond the Atherton Region, where it is present throughout the year at altitudes above 450 m. There seems to be some uncertainty about its occurrence at lower altitudes; however it does appear that it is present on low foothills near the coast at least during the drier months. The species is quite conspicuous, being active, aggressive when feeding with other birds around flowering trees, and fairly noisy.

The Bridled Honeyeater forages in the upper canopy of both rainforest and eucalypt forest, often in groups; insects, nectar and fruits are taken. It is common on the Atherton Tableland, Cape Tribulation, Cairns foothills and Cardwell.

▶ See also pages 76 80 85 97 99 379

526 VARIED HONEYEATER

Lichenostomus versicolor

In Australia, the Varied Honeyeater is confined to coastal parts of the Cape York and Atherton regions. It is principally a bird of the mangroves and adjoining vegetation. It is present throughout the year but at Cape York a fluctuation of abundance has been reported. This may occur elsewhere as well and may be due to some local movement, or the birds' behaviour may be more conspicuous at certain times of the year. Both insects and nectar are taken, often obtained at flowers of mangroves. These honeyeaters are usually quite inquisitive and bold. They are constantly active, often noisy, especially in groups, with loud whistling and aggressive behaviour among themselves and towards other birds.

▶ See also pages *99 379*

555 BROWN-BACKED HONEYEATER

Ramsayornis modestus

The Brown-backed Honeyeater occurs in New Guinea and north-eastern Australia where its range is largely within the Cape York and Atherton regions. It appears migratory, arriving in August and departing in May, with possibly part or most of the Australian population wintering in New Guinea.

This species will be found in mangroves and coastal swamp-woodlands and watercourse thickets; it visits flowering trees of nearby woodlands and rainforest. Although usually in pairs, flocks will be seen around the time of their migration. These are lively and noisy birds, with much chattering as they feed, often with other honeyeaters, on flowering trees.

▶ See also pages *98 99 387*

604 BLUE-FACED FINCH

Erythrura trichroa

The Blue-faced Finch is widespread on islands to the north but within Australia is confined to the Cape York and Atherton regions, with almost all records from the latter. In Australia this finch seems mainly an inhabitant of rainforests, where it favours the lower vegetation of edges and regrowth, and the adjacent eucalypt undergrowth.

The Blue-faced Finch feeds in rainforest trees; it eats also the seeds of casuarinas and grasses near rainforest margins and along tracks through

rainforest. At Mt Lewis it is seen regularly when the introduced guinea-grass along the forestry track is seeding.

Recognition of the call is helpful. It is a rapid series of high thin notes of descending pitch, described also as a metallic whistle. The Blue-faced Finch is not often sighted even by local observers familiar with its habits, but

352 **Yellow-eyed Cuckoo-shrike** *Coracina lineata*
391 **Bower's Shrike-thrush** *Colluricincla boweri*
395 **Yellow-breasted Boatbill** *Machaerirhynchus flaviventer*
401 **Pied Monarch** *Arses kaupi*
437 **Lovely Fairy-wren** *Malurus amabilis*
457 **Australian Fernwren** *Crateroscelis gutturalis*
458 **Atherton Scrubwren** *Sericornis keri*
478 **Mountain Thornbill** *Acanthiza katherina*

613 **GOLDEN BOWERBIRD** *Prionodura newtoniana* Male decorating his bower

619 **TOOTH-BILLED CATBIRD**
Ailuroedus dentirostris Male calling over the display ground

its generally quiet and inconspicuous behaviour, and dense habitat terrain, could cause it to remain unnoticed in mountainous or remote parts of north-eastern Australia.

Sites on record include Mt Lewis, Julatten, Mt Fisher, and the highlands between Helenvale and Ravenshoe.

▶ See also pages 97 99 397–8

606 METALLIC STARLING

Aplonis metallica

Most of the population of the Metallic Starling migrates during the months of March to August, presumably to the northern islands. Breeding occurs while in Australia; the nests are massive communal apartments, many nests clustered together, usually in rainforest but at times in parks and gardens, including those of the suburbs of Cairns. One such colony was made up of 188 individual nests. When the young have left the nest, flocks of 3000 to 5000 birds may be seen. The species is abundant and easily seen at Cairns and in the vicinity of other north-eastern towns.

▶ See also pages 85 398

606 **METALLIC STARLING**
Aplonis metallica

613 GOLDEN BOWERBIRD

Prionodura newtoniana

The Golden Bowerbird occurs throughout the Atherton Region and beyond, south to the Paluma Range. Within this range the species is fairly common in highland rainforest at altitudes between 1500 m and 900 m, and occasionally down to 600 m in winter. The species is present throughout the year on the Atherton Tableland, with occasional visits to the bowers during the year. Activity is intense during the breeding season.

Although brightly coloured, the male Golden Bowerbird is unobtrusive and not often seen except in the vicinity of the bower. The bower itself is usually large, eventually becoming massive, with one of the towers of sticks sometimes reaching 3 m in height. The bowers are built in the open lower level of the rainforest and are often seen before their owners. Bowers in sites easy to visit become well-known among ornithologists, and the bird appears to become accustomed to the audience in the background as he carries on with decoration or display. The Crater, a small national park near Yungaburra, has for many years had a bower at one or other point along its walk track, and is probably the best-known site. Other sites are Mt Lewis and Paluma.

▶ See also pages 85 *94 97* 400

619 TOOTH-BILLED CATBIRD

Ailuroedus dentirostris

The range of the Tooth-billed Catbird does not extend far beyond the Atherton Region, where it is usually confined to rainforests at altitudes of 600–1400 m. The male makes a playground of leaves placed face down; fresh leaves are brought early each morning and withered ones removed. From a perch over this carpet of leaves he displays and sings, his powerful notes carrying a considerable distance through the rainforest, and very helpful in obtaining a sighting.

The Tooth-billed Catbird has a great variety of calls both soft and loud. The songs are improvised day by day and sounds are imitated, including elements of the song of the males of adjoining territories and, in one instance, the chatterings from a nearby camp of fruit-bats. The sounds have qualities similar to those of bowerbirds and will probably be recognized as belonging to the bowerbird family by those familiar with other species of this family. Among the calls are loud shrieks, melodious whistles, and cloth-

620 **SPOTTED CATBIRD** *Ailuroedus melanotis*

tearing or grating sounds. This activity, which begins around August and ends late January, assists greatly in locating this species.

Localities include rainforests of the Atherton Tableland.

▶ See also pages 85 *94 97* 401

620 SPOTTED CATBIRD

Ailuroedus melanotis

The Spotted Catbird is widespread and quite common. It attracts attention to itself with loud nasal wailings and cries and, in the breeding season, clicking sounds. Sometimes the female joins in as a duet. This rainforest species has a preference for the dense thickets, as where a break in the rainforest, or a road, provides light to allow prolific low growth.

▶ See also pages 97 *111* 401

623 VICTORIA'S RIFLEBIRD

Ptiloris victoriae

Almost endemic to the Atherton Region, where it is a common resident of coastal and mountain rainforests. Males maintain territories within rainforest but females may wander out into nearby eucalypt woodland. There is a preference for the edges, clearings or breaks of rainforest. These birds, the dark-plumaged male in particular, would often not be noticed among the epiphytic mosses and ferns of the rainforest canopy but for the strident and prolonged 'yaa-aaas' as it forages among bark and debris. The males display from stages, which may be high limbs or tall stumps of broken-off trees.

Victoria's Riflebird should be relatively easy to find in rainforest national parks of the Atherton Tableland. These include The Crater, Lake Barrine and Lake Eacham; it is also at Mt Spec, near Townsville, and at Paluma. These riflebirds are to be seen displaying on top of power or telephone poles. The breeding season, and the best time to watch a display, is September to January.

▶ See also pages 85 *97 99* 402

635 BLACK BUTCHERBIRD

Cracticus quoyi

The Black Butcherbird occurs in mangroves and rainforest in New Guinea and northern and north-eastern Australia. It is a skulking predator that takes nestling birds, small reptiles and large insects. The rich yodelling calls and loud 'ah-ooo-ah, ah-ooo-ah' help to locate the bird which, in dark plumage, can be difficult to sight. It is quite common throughout its range.

▶ See also pages *99* 406

BIRD PLACES OF THE ATHERTON REGION

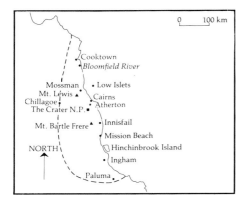

CAIRNS COASTAL LOWLANDS

The coastal lowlands of the Cairns district have a number of bird sites that are conveniently close to the city and accessible for visitors not able to reach more distant areas within this Atherton Region.

Closeness to the city in this instance does not mean second-rate birding. The harbour foreshore along the Cairns Esplanade has a reputation as one of the best wader sites on the east coast of Australia and is regarded as a 'must' for all ornithologists visiting northern Queensland. It is a wide expanse of mudflats and some areas of sandy beach extending between mangrove forests at Ellis Point in the north and Trinity Inlet to the south of Cairns harbour.

Australia is the main wintering area for the majority of the Arctic-breeding waders that migrate south through the Asian–Pacific region.

The Cairns Esplanade mudflats were chosen as the most suitable site in Australia to conduct regular countings of waders, for although it is somewhat artificial in that seedling mangroves are removed to retain the open habitat, it has proved to be one of the richest sites for birdlife in northern Australia. The site is of international renown, and overseas ornithological groups give it high priority when on bird study visits to Australia.

Despite the abundance of birdlife and the numbers of tourists, these mudflats are threatened from time to time by reclamation proposals which could result in a rich bird habitat being replaced by apartments, motels and carparks.

Mangrove forests to the north and south give roosting and shelter and the tidal flats provide feeding grounds. The site is easily accessible for birdwatchers, both resident and tourist. The location is also important, north-eastern Queensland being an entry and departure point for many of the Northern Hemisphere waders, but at the same time accessible, most other northern wader staging points being much more distant and more difficult of access.

Of the few lowlands swamps in this region, one of the best is Eubenangee Swamp about 20 km north of Innisfail. Among the species recorded here are the Great-billed Heron, Little Egret, King Quail, and Little Bronze-Cuckoo.

MISSION BEACH

Conveniently situated and easily accessible on the coast almost midway between Tully and Innisfail, the lowland rainforests of the Mission Beach area, at Kurrimine, Bingil Bay and Clump Mountain, are popular sites for the sighting of birds of this habitat. Lowland rainforest once covered much of the strip between sea and mountains, but most has been cleared for sugarcane, so that these remnant areas are most important as bird habitats.

The Clump Point–Kurrimine parks contain islands, coastal lowlands, plains, mountain ridges and watercourses. Clump Mountain and Maria Creek are important bird habitats, with a number of vegetation communities of scientific and scenic importance. They contain representative samples of coastal lowland rainforest along the seafront and on deep flood-soils.

Along this part of the coast the rainforest meets the sea, at the shoreline mangroves. In places there are depressions which become waterlogged in the wet season and support stands of fan palms.

Mission Beach is best known for its Southern Cassowaries. These may occasionally be seen crossing roads through the rainforest and some become semi-tame and wander about homes set in rainforest. Local enquiry may determine whether there are any to be seen in the locality.

Although so large, and with brilliant blues and reds on the bare head, neck and wattles, cassowaries are surprisingly difficult to see in the rainforest. Sometimes one will be heard treading on the dead leaves, the sound not unlike that of a man walking. Often these great birds make rumbling and booming sounds. They can be dangerous, especially when defending eggs or young.

The cassowary can run with surprising speed through thickly entangled rainforest undergrowth, the great hard feet brought up under the chin with each stride to beat downwards the undergrowth, the helmet on the head deflecting low vines upwards. In July, the cassowary lays its green eggs on a bed of leaves on the rainforest floor; the chicks at first are delightful in downy brown and cream stripes.

The Mission Beach rainforest and coast has many other birds. Yellow-bellied Sunbirds are common here, as they are through much of the Atherton Region; their long nests will be seen suspended from the verandahs of many houses. These lively birds bring bright colour and cheerful sounds to the open woodlands, scrubby rainforest edges, plantations and gardens, often hovering in front of flowers as they take nectar, or chasing each other about the shrubbery. In the grassy undergrowth of the woodlands, Lovely Fairy-wrens trill merrily; they often enter the rainforest edges and at times ascend well up into the foliage. The female is especially distinctive and it seems this species must have been named for her.

The lowland rainforests have many interesting birds. In particular, a large variety of rainforest fruit-doves and pigeons, some of which have been the subject of detailed studies in these rainforests.

MICHAELMAS CAY

Among the many north-eastern Queensland reef islets, Michaelmas Cay is an exceptional bird site. This tiny coral cay set among reefs 40 km north-east of Cairns is used by many thousands of nesting seabirds and is one of the largest colonies on the Great Barrier Reef.

The greatest nesting activity is through the summer months when there can be more than 30 000 birds on the island. It is then a spectacular sight with many thousands in the air overhead at any time, the whole island incredibly noisy with their calls. The most abundant breeding species are the Crested and Lesser Crested terns, the Sooty Tern and the Common Noddy.

The islet has an area of only 1.8 ha and a height of just 3.5 m. The vegetation is of low mat-grass and herbs. Access to the island is restricted to the northern side; under Queensland National Parks and Wildlife Service regulations, only the northern beach can be approached by boat or landed upon. Access to the vegetated area and other beaches is prohibited to avoid excessive disturbance to nesting birds as this can cause desertion or loss of eggs or young.

Breeding species here are: Black-naped Tern in small numbers; Sooty Tern, up to 10 000 pairs in January;

Crested Tern, up to about 4000 pairs; Lesser Crested Tern, over 10 000 pairs in October; Common Noddy, all year round, with a peak of about 6000 in January.

Among the many seabird islands of the northern Great Barrier Reef are: Bird Islands, near Cape Grenville, a pair of low wooded islands with a colony of some 4000 pairs of Black Noddies, Great Frigatebirds and Least Frigatebirds. Raine Island, on the outer northern Great Barrier Reef, 88 km north-east of Cape Grenville, with an area of about 30 ha, is a major breeding site for the Brown Booby, with at least 2000 species, and also the Red-footed Booby, Masked Booby, Least Frigatebird, Red-tailed Tropicbird and Sooty Tern. Maclennan Cay nearby has about 1000 breeding Brown Boobies.

Nesting seabirds are extremely sensitive to human intrusion and should not be excessively disturbed.

Low Island, near Mossman, is well-known as the nesting site of large numbers of Torresian Imperial-Pigeons, beginning about September and reaching a peak in November.

ATHERTON TABLELAND: LAKE EACHAM AND LAKE BARRINE

The twin lakes of the Atherton Tableland — Lake Barrine and Lake Eacham — are among the richest and at the same time most accessible of the highland rainforest sites. These wide and deep lakes fill ancient craters of volcanoes.

Each lake retains a wide belt of encircling rainforest typical of that which once covered much of the Atherton Tableland. The rainforest here has developed under conditions of high altitude, rich soil, high rainfall and almost constantly high humidity, a complex mesophyll forest that contains a wide variety of large-leaved trees. There are about 80 different tree species, including the red tulip oak which is endemic to the Tablelands.

The tracks that encircle the lakes provide the opportunity to walk slowly and quietly through the rainforest without the bird-frightening noise and movements that often result from pushing through the thicker parts of trackless forest.

The birdlist for the lakes and environs stands at about 105 species, which is not a large total compared with a listing for the Atherton Shire of around 315 species. But the latter, though not covering a huge area, has a much greater variety of habitats, including eucalypt forests, woodlands, swamplands and lake shores suitable for waders, as well as rainforests. There is further diversity between the east with its heavy rainfall and the western parts where the rainfall is much lighter.

Only one habitat, closed forest, is well represented at Lake Eacham and Lake Barrine. The lakes are mostly too steep-sided and deep to be good waterbird habitat, and the one other habitat, grassland, touches only upon the edges of these reserves.

The species unique to the Atherton Tableland, and found here, are the Fernwren, Mountain Thornbill, Atherton Scrubwren, Grey-headed Robin, Bridled Honeyeater, Spotted Catbird and Tooth-billed Catbird. The Little Treecreeper, at present a subspecies of the White-throated Treecreeper, previously a full species, is also endemic to the highlands.

Those found not only in upland rainforests, but also on the lowlands, and occurring at Lake Eacham or Lake Barrine, and above all endemic to the broader Atherton Region, are: the subspecies *macleayana* of the Double-eyed Fig-Parrot; subspecies *queenslandica* of the Rufous Owl; the Chowchilla; Bower's Shrike-thrush; Macleay's Honeyeater; Graceful Honeyeater, and Victoria's Riflebird.

Another group of interest are those occurring here but of slightly wider range, confined to north-eastern Queensland generally. These are the Southern Cassowary, Yellow-breasted Boatbill and Graceful Honeyeater.

MT LEWIS

Mt Lewis, situated at the northern part of the Atherton Region, near Julatten, rises to a height of 1227 m and overlooks the coast near Port Douglas.

The rainforest here contains a rich variety of birds, of which the most sought after is the elusive Blue-faced Finch, which is regularly seen at Mt Lewis. When the guinea-grass is seeding along the edge of the road, from February to May, this finch emerges from surrounding rainforest, where it is very difficult to see, and feeds on this grass and a blue-flowered herbaceous plant.

The uplands rainforests of Mt Lewis contain most if not all the endemic birds of the region. Recorded here have been the Topknot Pigeon, Sooty Owl, Chowchilla, Atherton Scrubwren, Bridled Honeyeater, Golden Bowerbird, Grey-headed Robin, Mountain Thornbill, Tooth-billed Catbird, Papuan Frogmouth, Victoria's Riflebird and Bower's Shrike-thrush, and, among endemic subspecies, the Little Treecreeper and Macleay's Fig-Parrot.

DAVIES CREEK NATIONAL PARK

Davies Creek National Park is situated approximately midway between Kuranda and Mareeba. The road in to the camping area continues on into forestry country, at first through open eucalypt woodland and casuarinas, then passing into rainforest at a higher altitude. Sightings here have included the Golden Bowerbird and Buff-breasted Paradise-Kingfisher in or near rainforest. In the casuarina groves are the White-cheeked Honeyeater, King Quail, Yellow Robin, Red-browed Finch and, rarely, the Blue-faced Finch.

THE CRATER (Mt Hypipamee)

Probably the most renowned birding site on the Atherton Tableland, The Crater is a small national park with a huge crater shaft dropping vertically 60 m to deep water. It is situated on the high south-eastern edge of the Tableland, at an altitude of about 1000 m, at the headwaters of the Barron River.

The Crater is a superb site for seeing the endemic species of the upland rainforests of the Atherton Region and of north-eastern Queensland. Birds of extremely confined distribution occurring here are the Mountain Thornbill and Australian Fernwren, both quite common at The Crater. The Grey-headed Robin and Spotted Catbird are frequent visitors to the picnic area, where Victoria's Riflebird will occasionally forage on the high limbs overhead and draw attention with loud rasping calls.

But it has been for the Golden Bowerbird that The Crater has become best-known among birdwatchers. Over many years there have been various bowers in the rainforest here, some close by the tracks. Also here, perhaps not as easily found, though drawing attention to itself with its calls, is the Tooth-billed Catbird. Otherwise, the birds found here are typical of the Atherton upland rainforests, so that it is possible to see the Lewin's Honeyeater, Bridled Honeyeater, Macleay's Honeyeater, Bower's Shrike-thrush, Chowchilla, and many more widespread species including the Yellow-breasted Boatbill, Pale-yellow Robin, Rufous Fantail, Pied Monarch, Spectacled Monarch, Black-faced Monarch, Grey Goshawk, and a number of species of rainforest pigeons, fruit-doves and lorikeets.

CAIRNS BIRDWATCH

Cairns has, within its boundaries, birdwatching potential equalled by few, if any, other cities. In addition to the renowned waterfront wader habitat within sight of the waterfront motels, the city has on its western side the rainforest-clad foothills of some of Queensland's highest ranges.

Unlike similar natural mudflats of northern Queensland mangrove coasts, Cairns Esplanade gives easy access and elevated viewpoints from along the sea wall. Early morning and late afternoon are usually best, especially when a rising tide gradually forces the waders in and they huddle together in large roosting flocks closer to the wall.

Many unusual migrant wader species have been recorded on the Cairns mudflats, and the Esplanade wader list is at least half of Australia's total wader species list. For most of their stay they are in dull winter plumage, but towards the end of their stay many waders begin to show traces of the usually more colourful breeding plumage.

Some other bird visitors to the mudflats are nomads, wandering the coast and resting on mudflats or in mangroves. Among these are pelicans, various egrets, herons, oystercatchers and several raptor species.

The Cairns harbour birdlist is expanded by the variety of habitats available. The mangroves, saltmarshes and inlet channels, together with the tidal flats, combine to give abundant wildlife resources of shelter and food, and contribute to the richness of the area. The mangroves at Ellis Point and Trinity Inlet have a different birdlist, including the Striated Heron, Collared and Little kingfishers, Large-billed Warbler, Mangrove Honeyeater, Shining Flycatcher, and Mangrove Golden Whistler. A convenient access to the Trinity Inlet mangroves is via the CSR jetty site, where the Great-billed Heron has been recorded.

From the Esplanade can be seen, across the mudflats, many large and obvious birds, but there are also abundant small species, needing high-powered binoculars or better still a telescope mounted on a tripod to see the detail often needed for identification. Among them could be some

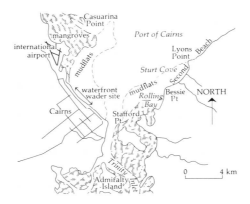

of the rarities, such as the tiny Red-necked Stint, the Pectoral Sandpiper with charcoal-grey breastplate, the Mongolian Plover, Great Knot, and the smaller Red Knot.

Among the more common waders are the Sharp-tailed Sandpiper, Curlew Sandpiper, Common Sandpiper, Greenshank, Eastern Golden Plover and Grey Plover. Out over the water, sometimes patrolling the outer mudflats and mangroves may be sighted Brahminy Kites, Whistling and Black kites, perhaps an Osprey snatching fish from the harbour, and Gull-billed Terns patrolling.

Some of the waders remain through the winter months but the great influx occurs through September to November, as the flocks arrive from the Northern Hemisphere, stay a while, rest and feed on these tidal flats, then continue their journey to southern Australia. The pattern is reversed through March and April.

Set beneath rainforested ranges, the Centennial Lakes and Botanical Gardens have a low-lying area of rainforest with a ground stratum that in the summer wet is boggy and at times partly flooded. To allow visitor access to this 'jungle' a boardwalk has been constructed.

The prized sighting here is the Red-necked Crake, which might be seen stalking the boggy parts at dawn and towards dusk. The dark brown plumage will not be easily seen if the light is poor, but the bird will be on the move, foraging. Its loud call may help to locate it. Also to be seen here, in addition to the more common lowland rainforest species, are the White-

browed Crake, Little Kingfisher and Brown-backed Honeyeater. Double-eyed Fig-Parrots have been recorded nesting in this rainforest.

Alongside the Centennial Lakes the rainforested Whitfield Range rises steeply, a spur of the mountain ranges that dominate Cairns on the eastern side, overlooking the northern and north-eastern parts of the city and the airport.

The Queensland National Parks and Wildlife Service has provided a walk trail, beginning near the Centennial Lakes. The first part of the trail is through a rainforested gully, then climbs steeply for a short distance. Soon it reaches open grassy clearings along the summit ridge, with views over the coastal plains to the mangrove swamps around Trinity Point.

The rainforested slopes often have a pair or so of the Buff-breasted Paradise Kingfisher. This beautiful bird will not be seen here until early to mid-November, but will then be easily found once the call is known, for the pairs call back and forth almost continuously as they endeavour to establish their territories.

Through the rainforest gully and climb, and in later rainforest parts of the track, birds that might be seen are the Orange-footed Scrubfowl, Red-crowned Pigeon, Wompoo Fruit-Dove, Torresian Imperial-Pigeon, Double-eyed Fig-Parrot, Chestnut-breasted Cuckoo, Yellow-breasted Boatbill, Black-faced Monarch, Spectacled Monarch and Rufous Fantail.

Where the trail emerges into open woodland and along rainforest edges the list of species changes. Helmeted Friarbirds call as they raid the flowering eucalypts, a Mistletoebird's piercing call rings out as he darts from tree to tree, a family party of Red-backed Fairy-wrens work their way through the tall grass to the accompaniment of high trills, a pair of Lovely Fairy-wrens search the foliage of rainforest-edge shrubbery, and a flock of Chestnut-breasted Mannikins climb among the grass-stems in search of seeds. Overhead, Rainbow Bee-eaters twist and turn as they hawk for insects, and the calls of a Pheasant Coucal can be heard coming from tall grass down the slope.

ATHERTON WETLAND HABITATS

The high, gently undulating Atherton Tableland has a number of wetland areas where waterfowl, waders and others favouring marshy habitats may be seen. There are three areas — the Bromfield Crater, Tinaroo Dam, and the swamps to the south of Atherton, near Walkamin.

Bromfield Crater is a wide, deep crater of an extinct volcano situated between Malanda and the Kennedy Highway. The floor of the crater is taken up by a huge swamp with many pools surrounded by grasses, sedges, rushes and stunted paperbarks.

The rim of the crater in places rises several hundred metres above this swamp, giving a commanding view. The swamp is used as a roosting place by many hundreds of Brolgas and Sarus Cranes. An observer, recording the calls of incoming flocks of these birds in September 1983, arrived at the rim at 5.45 pm when there were only several of each crane species in the crater. Over the next hour some 750 Brolgas and 300 Sarus Cranes arrived in flocks which were always of one species or the other, never intermixed. The following morning the thousand or more birds departed for distant feeding grounds by 8.30 am. In flight the Sarus Cranes and Brolgas could be separated by the greater extent of red down the necks of the Sarus, the orange to pinkish legs of the Sarus compared with the grey of the Brolgas, and the more raucous calls and deeper honkings of the latter.

The wetland habitat provided by Tinaroo Dam is different in that it attracts many waders to its 200 km of shoreline, while its great body of water is almost an inland sea.

To the south and south-west of Atherton and west of Wongabel an area of swamp-woodland includes two important swamp-wetlands, Hasties Swamp and Willetts Swamp. The birds recorded here, unlike the rainforest avifauna, are of cosmopolitan species, including such birds as the Australasian Grebe, Little Pied Cormorant, various species of herons and egrets, the Cattle Egret, Rufous Night Heron, Little Bittern, spoonbills and ibises, the Magpie Goose, Wandering Whistling-Duck, various ducks, the Brolga, Dusky Moorhen, Purple Swamp-hen, Lotusbird, some of the waders including the Curlew Sandpiper, Sharp-tailed Sandpiper, Australian Snipe, and many others.

Unlike the rainforests with their high level of endemism, the Atherton swampland species are very widespread.

516 **Macleay's Honeyeater** *Xanthotis macleayana*
519 **Yellow-spotted Honeyeater** *Meliphaga notata*
520 **Graceful Honeyeater** *Meliphaga gracilis*
523 **Bridled Honeyeater** *Lichenostomus frenatus*
526 **Varied Honeyeater** *Lichenostomus versicolor*
555 **Brown-backed Honeyeater** *Ramsayornis modestus*
604 **Blue-faced Finch** *Erythrura trichroa*
623 **Victoria's Riflebird** *Ptiloris victoriae*
635 **Black Butcherbird** *Cracticus quoyi*

407 RUFOUS FANTAIL *Rhipidura rufifrons*

CAPE YORK PENINSULA

Cape York Peninsula is one of Australia's last great wildernesses and is unique within this continent for its close links with the flora and fauna of South-East Asia. The Great Dividing Range forms the Peninsula's major physical feature, reaching a height of about 800 m near Coen. To the east of the Divide are some of Australia's most extensive areas of lowland rainforest, and there are wetlands with a vast array of lakes, lagoons and swamps. Westwards the country is drier and flatter, carrying predominantly open eucalypt woodlands, with gallery rainforests along some of the rivers. The climate here is one of almost constant heat, except in the pleasantly warm winter months. Through the summer wet season, December to April, heavy cloud and rain moderate the heat but bring very high humidity.

While most of Cape York Peninsula is wilderness, some areas are of outstanding environmental significance. These include the Iron Range–McIlwraith Range lowland rainforests, the Jardine River catchment and swamps, and the Laura Basin where the Normanby and North Kennedy rivers form extensive wetlands where they wind across their coastal floodplains.

Much of the ornithological interest of Cape York Peninsula arises from its close proximity to New Guinea. Its list of New Guinean birds is far in excess of that for any other region of Australia, so that most birdwatchers arriving here encounter new species in a variety otherwise to be seen only by travelling outside Australia.

Remarkably, the region has no endemic bird species. The many birds that are found here and nowhere else in Australia are not endemic to Cape York Peninsula for they are shared with New Guinea and often with other northern islands. For most birdwatchers this window into New Guinea's renowned birdlife is more than sufficient reason to visit some of the Peninsula's bird localities. The best way to do this, at least on the first trip into this remote region, is within a tour organized by one of the national or state ornithological associations.

The rainforests of Australia's east coast are like a tenuous chain of islands, each surrounded and isolated by the comparatively dry and far more open eucalypt woodland country. The rainforests of Cape York Peninsula are separated from those farther south by a wide expanse of woodland, and many New Guinea birds have been unable to cross this barrier to reach the more extensive rainforests between Cooktown and Townsville.

The bird fauna of these northern Peninsula rainforests is essentially an extension of the Papuan avifauna, and because of the increasing aridity of the continent these rainforests are serving as the only refuge on this continent for many of those bird species.

The rainforests of Cape York Peninsula are less luxuriant than those of the Atherton Region. They are best developed on moist ground beside the rivers, where the trees are massive and support a high canopy where there are epiphytic orchids and ferns. At their lower levels the character is more of monsoon forest, with undergrowth scarce except at edges of clearings and beneath breaks in the canopy. In some low-lying parts of the forest there are thickets of bamboo, pandanus and lawyer vine, but most of the forest floor is quite open, thickly carpeted with fallen leaves and similar to monsoon forest in character. Away from the main river channels the smaller watercourses have narrow edgings of similar but much lower, less luxuriant, gallery forest.

Beyond these closed forests of the rivers the dominant vegetation is of open woodland with scattered eucalypt and melaleuca trees and a ground-cover of tall blady grass. On some areas of higher ground are heaths, while low-lying swampy areas may have stands of pandanus or nipa palms. Along the coast are extensive areas of tall mangrove forest.

Among the birds are many that can be seen in rainforests and tropical woodlands farther south, but the centre of attention here is always upon those that, in Australia, are found only on the Peninsula. Most exciting are the Red-cheeked and Eclectus parrots, Great Palm Cockatoo, Yellow-billed Kingfisher, Red-bellied Pitta, White-faced Robin, Pearly Flycatcher, Manucode, the Magnificent Riflebird and, away from the rainforest, the Golden-shouldered Parrot.

Other significant habitats are Queensland's largest perennial stream, the Jardine River catchment, with its vast network of perennial swamps and waterways, and the Olive River–Cape Grenville area where there is a concentration of lakes, lagoons and swamps. There is an isolated and distinctive small patch of rainforest at the very tip of Cape York Peninsula.

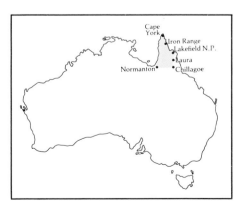

65 ROYAL SPOONBILL *Platalea regia*

54 INTERMEDIATE EGRET *Egretta intermedia*

BIRDS OF CAPE YORK PENINSULA

120 BUFF-BREASTED BUTTON-QUAIL

Turnix olivei

There have been very few observations of this species. Discovered in 1894, it was not collected again until 1921–22 near Coen and there have been later sightings near Iron Range since 1970. The status of the species is uncertain with few recent sightings. One of these, at Davies Creek on the Atherton Tableland, is the only record for a region other than Cape York Peninsula.

This button-quail was apparently common near Coen when it was collected there, being found in short grass of open stringybark forests in March, late in the wet season. At this time it was breeding and calling; at other times it was more obvious. It has also been recorded in patches of rainforest and swampy country.

The apparent rarity of this button-quail may be due to the scarcity of observation during the wet season, or local populations may fluctuate, and only rarely is it as common as recorded near Coen. The Atherton sighting suggests that this species may be more widespread but is not reported because of its secretive habits and, usually, small numbers.

▶ See also pages 105 280

237 PALM COCKATOO

Probosciger aterrimus

A clear view of a Palm Cockatoo must be one of the most impressive of all possible Cape York bird sightings. Though fairly common along the Claudie River, these huge cockatoos are most often only briefly glimpsed flying above the forest. But a powerful, harsh screech from a treetop may draw attention to a massive black shape among the foliage. Usually these birds are too wary to allow much movement by birdwatchers trying to get a clearer view and are likely to depart for another part of the forest.

When a Palm Cockatoo alights in an exposed position nearby, or is sighted through a break in the canopy, binoculars are slowly lifted and the massive-crested, red-cheeked black head is brought into focus, the observers tense lest sudden movement or noise puts the wary bird to flight.

Brought close by the glasses the Palm Cockatoo in the wild is awe-inspiring, seeming immense, made to look larger by the radiating black crest, and with the red of the bare cheek patches in bold contrast against the sooty tones of the plumage; compared with the head, the body seems small.

Unlike some of the other New Guinean birds here, the Palm Cockatoo is present on Cape York Peninsula throughout the year. Its preferred habitat is an intermix of rainforest and woodland, where it may feed on the fruits of pandanus and other trees.

The usual daily routine begins about an hour after sunrise with the cockatoos calling to each other, usually resulting in a small group gathering in a tall tree in open woodland, often the same tree being used for the purpose. At this time they frequently engage in various playful antics, such as tipping forward, hanging head down, wings outstretched, and giving a whistled contact call. This is thought to be a congregating display.

The birds feed in open woodland until mid-morning then move to rainforest where they spend the hottest part of the day. While in open country they are very wary but in rainforest seem more at ease and can be approached more closely.

The calls are helpful, particularly in rainforest where the dense vegetation makes the initial sighting more difficult. The contact call, given in flight and upon alighting, is a disyllabic whistle made up of a deep, mellow note followed by a shrill, high note that is drawn-out and has an upwards inflexion. The alarm call is a short, harsh screech.

Most sightings result from the deep, harsh screeches of flying birds, seen then as heavy-headed, broad-winged dark silhouettes, travelling with deep wingbeats or gliding on downcurved wings.

▶ See also pages *105* 310

249 ECLECTUS PARROT

Eclectus roratus

The Eclectus lives within the rainforest but often forages out into adjoining woodland. It is exceptional among parrots for its communal behaviour, usually feeding, roosting and nesting in small groups of six to eight birds. It is a conspicuous bird at Iron Range and is often seen flying overhead, although from below it tends to look black, especially the dark red of the females. Loud rasping 'kraaach-kraaak-' screeches are given frequently while in flight, so that one rarely passes over unnoticed. While feeding the birds often give a disyllabic wailing and a mellow flute-like whistle.

The Eclectus Parrots have a definite daily routine, flying in the morning from their rainforest roosts to the trees currently favoured for feeding. The flight is distinctive, usually well above the forest canopy, rather slow and direct, interspersed with brief glides on downcurved wings and with deliberate wingbeats in which the wings do not lift above the level of the body. The characteristic flight and the loud, harsh screeches soon allow recognition even when the birds are but indistinctly seen through treetop foliage as they pass overhead.

Eclectus Parrots are extremely wary, especially about the nest. If disturbed they will fly off or circle overhead, screeching. This species appears to be fairly common in the rainforests along the Claudie River.

▶ See also pages 7 101 *105* 111 312

250 RED-CHEEKED PARROT

Geoffroyus geoffroyi

Most records of this colourful small parrot come from the Iron Range area but it is believed equally common in other less accessible areas of lowland tropical rainforests between the Pascoe and Rocky rivers. It is present throughout the year, though locally nomadic.

The Red-cheeked Parrot inhabits rainforests, especially along watercourses, and is most often seen at the rainforest edges where foliage grows low beside rivers and roads, or where rainforest meets woodland. It is usually seen in pairs or small parties and will sometimes congregate in large groups on fruiting trees. The Red-cheeked Parrot is conspicuous, calling loudly in flight and tending to alight in the open on dead branches where it usually calls again. It will sometimes fly around noisily just outside the rainforest early in the morning and again towards nightfall. The flight is swift, direct, with fast, shallow wingbeats, without undulations or any glide when it comes in to land, more like the flight of a lorikeet than a parrot.

But although noisy, the species is not easy to see within the rainforest. While closely associated with rainforest, it passes through the woodlands and often pauses in woodland trees, perhaps only while travelling between patches of rainforest. This movement out to food trees is mostly in the mornings; by 10 am it has usually settled into the shady canopy of the rainforest where it can be hard to see. It sometimes roosts and possibly nests just out of the rainforest.

The calls are important as visibility is often difficult in rainforest. The contact call is a harsh, metallic and quite rapid 'aaank-aaank-aaank', given in flight, on stopover perches and in alarm. The bird responds to recordings or imitations of the calls. It also gives various chatterings and high screechings, some similar to those of Rainbow Lorikeets.

▶ See also pages 101 *109* 111 312

280 GOLDEN-SHOULDERED PARROT

Psephotus chrysopterygius

The range of this beautiful parrot has declined since settlement, with confirmed reports now only from eastern parts of its former range. It is usually seen in eucalypt and sometimes in paperbark woodlands where there is a grassy understorey. It feeds on grass seeds, which it takes from standing grass and from the ground.

As an indication of the present scarcity of this species, a researcher during 71 days over a five-year study period found only three groups with six to 10 birds, pairs on eight occasions and single birds on seven occasions. This decline may be due in part to nest robbing but is thought to be more due to an alteration of habitat, perhaps caused by grazing and frequent burning.

During the breeding season, from April to June, the Golden-shouldered Parrots occupy woodlands on alluvial flats near watercourses. After breeding they disperse across a wider variety of habitats, sometimes even to coastal mangroves.

The call can be helpful in drawing attention to the birds: a whistled 'fweep-fweep', several times, sometimes drawn-out as 'feew-weeep, feew-weeep', given in flight and just after landing. While perched in trees a sharper 'weet, weet, weet-', or a mellow 'fee-ooo-' may be given.

▶ See also pages 101 *105* 110 319

294 CHESTNUT-BREASTED CUCKOO

Cuculus castaneiventris

A New Guinean species with a small outlier population on Cape York Peninsula and possible occurrences in the Atherton Region. At least part of the population appears to migrate to New Guinea.

This species is principally a rainforest bird but it moves well out into the open forest and may be sighted near the rainforest edges. Although regarded as uncommon in Australia it

318 **LARGE-TAILED NIGHTJAR** *Caprimulgus macrurus*

is usually recorded by birdwatchers visiting Iron Range. Its rich colours make it unmistakable.

This cuckoo is said to be restless and shy, keeping to the tops of the tallest of rainforest trees. However, it will respond well to taped recordings of its calls and may then perch close enough to be observed.

▶ **See also pages** 98 *107* 111 322

318 LARGE-TAILED NIGHTJAR

Caprimulgus macrurus

This nightjar species is sedentary; it calls throughout the year, maintaining a permanent territory. Its preferred habitat is at the rainforest margin and the woodland bordering the rainforest. The bird announces its presence loudly and clearly with calls that are among the most familiar and easily recognizable sounds of tropical northern woodlands at night. Its calling is most evident at dusk and again as the sky begins to lighten towards dawn. Hunting activity likewise is then most intense, though in bright moonlight it may hunt throughout the night.

This species feeds exclusively upon insects taken in flight, fluttering about like a great silent moth it circles tightly among the trees.

The loud calls serve not only to announce the presence of the Large-tailed Nightjar but also reveal the location of individual territories where the birds may then be seen hunting at dusk, or perhaps flushed from the ground by day. The call is a repetitive

chopping, in the distance it sounds like an axe repeatedly and evenly striking timber, at the rate of about one blow per second. Close at hand, the calls are a rich, deep, double-noted 'tch-aunk, tch-aunk'.

The calls are given sporadically throughout the year but are far more frequent in the breeding season. The birds also seem much more vocal in localities of optimum habitat where there is more population pressure on territories.

During the day male and female roost separately but not far apart; the pair bond is maintained throughout the year. The usual daytime roost is just within the rainforest, close to the margin or close to a clearing, in shadows beside a treetrunk or between buttresses, where there is abundant leaf-litter. They rarely flush unless almost walked upon, fluttering suddenly upwards then gliding away with rather erratic flight to pitch to the ground again, or onto a low horizontal limb or log. If pressed, the nightjars then circle back to remain within their territory.

▶ **See also page** 329

330 YELLOW-BILLED KINGFISHER

Syma torotoro

This unusual and colourful kingfisher is confined to undisturbed pockets of rainforest in northern Cape York Peninsula where it appears to be resident. But as it is silent most of the year it is very difficult to detect, probably because it sits very still,

usually on a rather low perch, scanning the ground for its prey.

The Yellow-billed Kingfisher is usually heard in rainforest, most often just inside the rainforest edge; it will often hunt and nest in the adjacent eucalypt woodland. Even in the breeding season when calling often and loudly it is surprisingly hard to sight. Although brightly coloured it sits so still that it seems to blend with the foliage, where the gold and orange of new shoots and the yellowed tones of dying leaves are common.

The call is both loud and distinctive and quite unlike that of any other Australian kingfisher. It consists of a rapid trill, not very high pitched, rising, then falling as it gradually fades away after three or four seconds to be repeated after an interval of perhaps 10 seconds. There will usually be three to five, sometimes up to 10, such trills in a sequence, each slightly stronger and more insistent than the one before.

Irrespective of the length of the sequence of calls, one trill is always recognizable as the last of the series immediately it begins, for it starts more abruptly, more sharply, rises more slowly in pitch and lasts much longer, then falls away in an attenuated, fading ending after perhaps 10 or 15 seconds. The kingfisher will then usually be silent for some time, perhaps for only five or 10 minutes, sometimes an hour or more. Even when giving its sequence of trills close by, the calling bird is remarkably difficult to find, suggesting that the calls may have some ventriloquial quality.

The Yellow-billed Kingfisher is likely to be heard calling strongly in November and probably December when it is in the early stages of breeding and beginning to drill out a nest tunnel. A pair watched at Iron Range were flying in to strike an arboreal termite nest with a thud that could be heard 30 m away.

▶ **See also pages** 7 101 *107* 111 333

334 RED-BELLIED PITTA

Pitta erythrogaster

This is a New Guinean species and part of that population migrates to northern Cape York Peninsula to breed. Some birds arrive as early as October but usually later, sometimes apparently not until December. In some years birdwatching groups visiting Iron Range in mid-November have been unable to find this species in its usual haunts.

The Red-bellied Pitta is confined to the rainforest and feeds upon ground-dwelling invertebrates but spends some time well up in the trees. There are but two species of pitta on the Peninsula and, provided the site is not too gloomy, identification should not be difficult.

The call is distinctive, totally unlike that of the Noisy Pitta, or indeed any other bird of the region, a deep, throaty or rasping, resonant 'quorrrrr', rising and drawn-out, repeated several times. The rich resonance of the call is like that of the Noisy Pitta but each note is much more drawn-out, quite distinctive and very useful in location and identification. It is said to respond to imitation or tape recording of the call.

While foraging, this pitta moves erratically across the litter with an occasional jerking of head and tail. In flight it usually keeps close to the ground, unless moving up into the trees.

▶ See also pages 101 *107* 334

360 NORTHERN SCRUB-ROBIN

Drymodes superciliaris

A New Guinean species with two Australian subspecies, one of which is known only from two specimens collected from the Northern Territory in 1909, the second confined to Cape York Peninsula.

The Northern Scrub-robin is found in rainforests and vine scrubs where it seems to favour thickets close to the margins and probably where there are breaks in the canopy. It appears common in localities of optimum habitat and is present throughout the year.

The call of the Northern Scrub-robin is a drawn-out whistle, often closely preceded or followed by harsh scoldings which may only be given in alarm in the presence of intruders. If an observer waits quietly within the rainforest glimpses may be obtained as the shy but evidently rather curious birds bounce across the leaf-litter, contriving most of the time to keep behind a screen of foliage or forest debris.

The Scrub-robin appears to respond to imitations and recordings of its calls. If a sighting can be obtained where the light is not too dim, with luck in a patch of sunlight, this robin is unmistakable, larger and much longer-legged than other robins, with an upright, alert stance, rich rust tones on the back and the conspicuous black vertical eyeline. Even where the light is very poor, the bounding gait and the call give almost certain identification.

▶ See also pages *107* 341 363

373 YELLOW-LEGGED FLYCATCHER

Microeca griseoceps

The Yellow-legged Flycatcher is confined to northern Cape York Peninsula although there is a possibility of it occurring in the Atherton Region. It is a rainforest species, moderately common but sometimes keeping high in the canopy

99   Red Goshawk *Erythrotriorchis radiatus*
120 Buff-breasted Button-quail *Turnix olivei*
237 Palm Cockatoo *Probosciger aterrimus*
249 Eclectus Parrot *Eclectus roratus*
280 Golden-shouldered Parrot *Psephotus chrysopterygius*

618 FAWN-BREASTED BOWERBIRD
Chlamydera cerviniventris
Male arranging ornaments at the bower

where it can be difficult to identify or observe, flitting about the uppermost foliage. Generally, however, it seems to prefer the margins rather than the depths of the rainforest, so that these places, where the bird will be lower, are the best sites to watch.

The Yellow-legged Flycatcher will at times move out of the rainforest, sometimes up to 50 m into adjoining eucalypt or melaleuca woodland.

▶ See also pages *107* 192 344

378 WHITE-FACED ROBIN

Tregellasia leucops

The White-faced Robin is a New Guinean species which is represented in Australia by a subspecies confined to the northern part of Cape York Peninsula. Within the rainforests of this very restricted range it is moderately common.

A delightful and unmistakable little bird, it has large black eyes set in a white face, giving it a clown-like appearance. Usually it gives only a rather harsh, scolding 'chee-', but in the breeding season it has a musical song of about five notes. The White-faced Robin is always found well inside the rainforest where the vegetation is dense and the light gloomy. It favours situations where there is a denser lower strata vegetation of saplings and lawyer vines.

This is a very quiet and inconspicuous bird, more likely to be noticed by the observer who sits quietly to watch the comings and goings of the rainforest birds. It may then become very confiding and inquisitive, coming to sit on a low perch close by, dropping every now and then to the ground to take some small insect. In the dim light

of the rainforest the bird's colours are not conspicuously bright but once sighted the bold facial pattern is distinctive. This robin is usually not noticed until it moves, when the brief flitting between perches, or down to the ground, catches the eye.

▶ See also pages 101 *107* 111 345

400 FRILLED MONARCH

Arses telescophthalmus

Within Australia this boldly plumaged monarch flycatcher is confined to northern Cape York Peninsula and is an extension of the main New Guinean population. It occurs in rainforest and appears to be sedentary. Among the monarchs this and the similar Pied Monarch are unusual in their habit of finding insects on the bark of trees rather than only about the foliage. Early observers recorded this species as being not plentiful but more recent birdwatchers in these rainforests have found it common. It is most often or most easily sighted along the outside edge of the rainforest and in the closely adjoining woodland, working sittella-like over the bark of trees, tail often fanned and propped against the bark as it spirals up trunks and limbs.

The plumage of this bird is distinctive and it could only be confused with the Pied Monarch, which does not occur in this region. The call is a low 'quark', typical of monarch flycatchers. It is a fairly conspicuous bird and will almost certainly be seen by birdwatchers visiting the Iron Range area.

▶ See also pages 90 *107* 111 350

461 TROPICAL SCRUBWREN

Sericornis beccarii

This is essentially a New Guinean bird, its range extended to Australia by the presence of two subspecies on Cape York Peninsula. It is confined to rainforests and is common along the Claudie River at Iron Range, in rainforest and vine thickets.

The Tropical Scrubwren feeds in the middle stratum of the rainforest, finding insects on the foliage of saplings and other shrubbery. In this it differs from most scrubwrens, which tend to forage on or near the ground. It is therefore more likely to be seen where breaks in the canopy admit light and allow the emergence of undergrowth.

In appearance, the bill is noticeably large for a scrubwren and the face and wing patterns are not too difficult to discern because of its preference for

the relatively open mid-levels. The calls include harsh, scrub-wren raspings and some soft musical notes.

At the Claudie River this species was foraging very actively at heights of around 1–4 m, moving among foliage, sometimes fluttering flycatcher-like to inspect the leaves.

▶ See also pages *109* 111 364

517 TAWNY-BREASTED HONEYEATER

Xanthotis flaviventer

The Tawny-breasted Honeyeater occurs in New Guinea and, within Australia, northern Cape York Peninsula. It appears to be sedentary, inhabiting rainforests, mangroves and woodlands. It keeps mainly to the foliage of the rainforest canopy and is not easily spotted except where the canopy is low at the rainforest edges. Here the bird comes down to the lower foliage and extends its feeding into the adjoining woodland especially if there are trees in flower. It takes insects from upper branches and foliage, also some nectar and fruits.

This is a large honeyeater whose tawny colour and long, downcurved bill give a superficial resemblance to the female Magnificent Riflebird.

▶ See also pages *109* 378

546 GREEN-BACKED HONEYEATER

Glycichaera fallax

The Green-backed Honeyeater in Australia is confined to an extremely small area of Cape York Peninsula around the Claudie River and possibly north towards the Pascoe River. Within this restricted range it is quite common. It also occurs in New Guinea.

This small honeyeater is usually high in the rainforest canopy but comes down lower where the canopy slopes to the ground at the edge of the rainforest and in the foliage of trees and shrubs immediately adjoining the rainforest. Though not brightly coloured it attracts attention with its activity, fluttering and hovering about the foliage and blossoms, taking insects and perhaps also nectar; it tends to be in pairs or small parties.

Its soft twitterings are not loud enough to attract attention but if it is imitated or its calls are replayed on a tape recorder the Green-backed might be enticed down to lower foliage for a closer view. It has been sighted where the road along the Claudie River runs beside rainforest.

The Green-backed Honeyeater is unusual because its behaviour is more like a flycatcher, fluttering about the foliage. It is often in mixed feeding parties with other species, especially fantails, warblers and monarch flycatchers.

▶ See also pages *109* 111 384

548 WHITE-STREAKED HONEYEATER

Trichodere cockerelli

Although on one occasion collected in the Atherton Region, the White-streaked Honeyeater is a species that requires a visit to northern Cape York Peninsula for any realistic chance of a sighting. Unlike so many of the other birds restricted to the Peninsula, this honeyeater does not occur in New Guinea. It appears at least locally nomadic and localities where the species was abundant on a previous occasion later appear to be devoid of the bird.

Habitats are varied and the use of these depend upon the flowering of trees, whether paperbarks of swamp woodlands, or grevilleas, eucalypts, rainforest trees, or mangroves. It is often in eucalypt and heath areas.

This honeyeater is said to be seldom silent, its loud scoldings and melodious whistlings similar to those of the Brown Honeyeater. Together with its active, restless nature, its habit of taking insects in flight and its preference for more open habitats, the species is easily sighted when present.

▶ See also pages *109* 384–5

580 PALE WHITE-EYE

Zosterops citrinella

This white-eye is found only on islands down the eastern coast of Cape York, south as far as Eagle Islet. Towards the southern end of its range it could be confused with the Silvereye, of which the subspecies inhabiting the northern Barrier Reef islands also has whitish underparts; however the Pale White-eye has a distinctive yellowish forehead.

The Pale White-eye inhabits scrubby thickets on those of the offshore islands that carry vegetation.

▶ See also pages *109* 392 393

618 FAWN-BREASTED BOWERBIRD

Chlamydera cerviniventris

The Fawn-breasted Bowerbird is predominantly a New Guinean species with a very restricted population on northern Cape York Peninsula. Here it occurs in eucalypt woodlands, especially scrubby coastal woodlands

close to mangroves, and is to be found in the Portland Roads area of the coast near the Claudie River.

The bower is of the avenue type, similar to that of the Great Bowerbird but with a more bulky, higher base platform and heavily decorated with green berries.

This bowerbird, like the Great Bowerbird, is likely to be revealed by

258 **Marshall's Fig-Parrot** (subspecies of Double-eyed Fig-Parrot) *Psittaculirostris diophthalma marshalli*
294 **Chestnut-breasted Cuckoo** *Cuculus castaneiventris*
300 **Gould's Bronze-Cuckoo** *Chrysococcyx russatus*
330 **Yellow-billed Kingfisher** *Syma torotoro*
334 **Red-bellied Pitta** *Pitta erythrogaster*
360 **Northern Scrub-robin** *Drymodes superciliaris*
373 **Yellow-legged Flycatcher** *Microeca griseoceps*
378 **White-faced Robin** *Tregellasia leucops*
400 **Frilled Monarch** *Arses telescophthalmus*

624 MAGNIFICENT RIFLEBIRD *Ptiloris magnificus* Male calling from a display perch, the iridescent blues and greens of the throat and upper breast changing with every movement

the extremely noisy behaviour of the male in the vicinity of the bower, the loud rasping sounds, metallic churrings, chatterings and hisses being easily recognized as bowerbird calls.

At Iron Range the Fawn-breasted Bowerbird is solitary and timid, seldom seen except at the bower, which is the focal point of the territory, so that a wait near a known bower is a certain way of seeing this species. In the non-breeding season it is sometimes seen in small parties, usually heard before being seen.

▶ See also pages *106* 110 401

624 MAGNIFICENT RIFLEBIRD

Ptiloris magnificus

The Magnificent Riflebird is a New Guinean species which, in Australia, reaches only northern Cape York Peninsula where it inhabits rainforests and monsoon scrub along creeks. In these forests the Magnificent Riflebird frequents mainly the mid to upper levels, keeping to the trunks and heavier limbs which are often festooned with ferns and mosses, and where it is often hidden from below.

Even when calling loudly the bird often cannot be detected, or only momentarily as it flies to another tree. Sometimes its location will be betrayed by the sounds of its attack upon the bark for insects. Females seem to be sighted more often; perhaps they are less wary and more inclined to descend into the rainforest vegetation. Their rich cinnamon plumage also tends to make them more conspicuous.

The calls of the males reverberate through the rainforest, their deep, ringing whistles betraying the abundance of the species along the Claudie River; otherwise, from sightings alone, the bird could be thought to be rare. The call is likened to a deep, wolf-whistled 'aaa-ooo-whip', the pitch falling for the second part and rising sharply in the final 'whip'.

Selected perches, often horizontal limbs, sometimes quite low, serve as display or calling perches. One such display perch photographed over two days at Iron Range in November was visited only in the afternoon, with the male Magnificent Riflebird staying only briefly to call and preen. No females were sighted in the vicinity. Within a distance of perhaps 15–20 m the flight of the riflebird is noisy, the silken rustling sounds heard also with any sudden movement or shuffling of feathers. Every shift of position changes the plumage colours, especially across the fan-shaped area of throat and upper breast, which one instant would be velvety-black, the next moment iridescent turquoise or purplish-blue, especially as the bird throws back its head and points its long bill skywards to call. The last 'whip' note is given with a convulsive jerk of the head, as if expelling the final crescendo of sound with all the power it can muster.

▶ See also pages   101 106 *108* 111 402

624 MAGNIFICENT RIFLEBIRD
Ptiloris magnificus

625 TRUMPET MANUCODE

Manucodia keraudrenii

A bird of the New Guinea region, with northern Cape York Peninsula its only Australian representation. It is probably present throughout the year and keeps to the larger and heavier rainforests. It has not been recorded in woodlands even if close to rainforest, nor is it seen in the narrow strips of monsoon forest along watercourses. It is a bird of the upper stratum of the rainforest where it can be difficult to sight as it moves through the canopy in search of fruits and insects.

The Trumpet Manucode is generally reported to be shy and wary. It has been labelled as inquisitive, an observation supported on one occasion when a manucode descended to investigate photographic equipment set up at a Magnificent Riflebird's display perch.

The call, likened to a low-pitched blast from a trumpet or the deep creaking of a heavy door, is usually the key to a sighting. The sound is unique, loud, and if recognised can lead to the bird, even if only seen as a distant silhouette high in the rainforest canopy.

▶ See also pages   111 402

250 **Red-cheeked Parrot** *Geoffroyus geoffroyi*
379 **White-browed Robin** *Poecilodryas superciliosa*
461 **Tropical Scrubwren** *Sericornis beccarii*
517 **Tawny-breasted Honeyeater** *Xanthotis flaviventer*
546 **Green-backed Honeyeater** *Glycichaera fallax*
548 **White-streaked Honeyeater** *Trichodere cockerelli*
580 **Pale White-eye** *Zosterops citrinella*
625 **Trumpet Manucode** *Manucodia keraudrenii*
637 **Black-backed Butcherbird** *Cracticus mentalis*

BIRD PLACES OF CAPE YORK PENINSULA

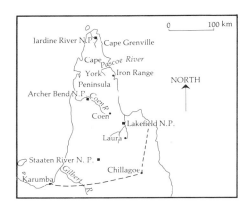

609 YELLOW ORIOLE *Oriolus flavocinctus*

IRON RANGE

Iron Range has a well-earned reputation as one of Australia's outstanding bird sites. Most of the species which, within Australia, are confined to Cape York Peninsula can be seen here. Rainforest here, including that along the Claudie River and partly contained within the Iron Range National Park, forms Australia's largest remaining area of tropical lowland rainforest. Within short distances are intermingled rainforest and open woodlands, with areas of heath on higher ground. Mangroves are easily accessible at nearby Portland Roads.

Birdwatching groups, which usually stay about a week in the area, often record birdlists of around 100 species. But more exciting is the probability of recording most of the Peninsula's list of about 22 species that in Australia are unique to this region.

The coast at Portland Roads area has stands of very tall mangroves, forest-like, with an almost-closed canopy high above and open beneath, except for the entangled stilt roots; access is easy except perhaps at high tide. Here Mangrove Robins, Broad-billed Flycatchers, Red-headed Honeyeaters, Little and Collared kingfishers can be found, with probable sightings of Least Frigatebirds and Brown Boobies over the open waters. Scrub behind the mangrove belt nearby is one of the localities where the Fawn-breasted Bowerbird may be found.

Other areas of mangroves are accessible at Quintell Beach and along the lower section of the Claudie River, where also are stands of nipa palms.

LAKEFIELD

On the Pacific side of the Great Dividing Range, where it curves inland to the north of Cooktown, is a great lowland basin. Here, the Normanby, Bizant and North Kennedy rivers wind across the flats from their headwaters in the ranges to reach the sea at Princess Charlotte Bay.

During the wet season these rivers overflow into swamps, lagoons, lakes and waterholes, joining in a vast network of flooded waterways and boggy plains. Through the following dry, the water recedes to the deeper channels where permanent water attracts birds in great variety of species and numbers.

Interspersed with these wetlands are grassland plains and woodlands with scattered paperbarks and eucalypts. The river channels are edged with eucalypt open forest and gallery forest, while patches of monsoon forest occur in areas of sandstone escarpment. Where the rivers approach Princess Charlotte Bay their estuary channels are lined with mangroves and there are large expanses of mudflats.

During the wet season the waterfowl and other wetland birds are scattered across the swampy plains, hidden among reeds and lush tall grass. As the dry season advances the water is confined to the permanent lagoons, which have areas of open water and floating waterlilies. At this time it is easier to see the birds where they concentrate in tens of thousands on the remaining water.

Almost every kind of tropical Australian waterbird might be seen here, with huge flocks of Magpie Geese, Plumed Whistling-Ducks, Brolgas and Cotton Pygmy-Geese. Egrets, spoonbills, ducks, ibises, plovers and various raptors add to the interest. Lakefield has a birdlist of about 175 species. Large crocodiles also occur in these waterways.

Lakefield is a national park and, in common with other parts of the Peninsula, becomes inaccessible after heavy rain. Camping permits are required and these, together with access advice, are available from the Queensland National Parks and Wildlife Service, Cairns.

CENTRAL CAPE YORK PENINSULA

Inland from the wetlands of Lakefield, where the headwaters of its rivers rise among the low hills of this part of the Great Dividing Range, the Peninsula Development Road traverses open woodland country. From its crossing of the Hann and Moorhead rivers, north-west to the Coen River, is country that has captured the attention of ornithologists.

Undoubtedly the primary attraction here is the beautiful but rare Golden-shouldered Parrot, but in the course of searching out that species several observers have listed other birds of the district. The National Photographic Index of Australian Birds Expedition to central Cape York Peninsula spent some time here in October 1974 and compiled a list of 138 species. In addition to a very small number of Golden-shouldered Parrots, among several species of interest which are uncommon or unique to north-eastern Queensland were the Squatter Pigeon and the Papuan Frogmouth.

The Golden-shouldered Parrot has suffered a considerable decline, probably partly due to taking of young and possibly also due to changes in the environment, including widespread burning. It is probably best that precise sites for this species, especially of nest localities, are not widely publicised, although the raiding of nests is said to have been curtailed in recent years.

Although the drier open woodlands of this part of Cape York Peninsula do not have the wealth of New Guinean birds that occur in the rainforests of Iron Range, there is much activity of friarbirds and other honeyeaters, lorikeets, the more common species of parrot, and finches.

There are no visitor facilities in the area and roads may be closed by rain.

IRON RANGE BIRDWATCH

A delightful narrow dirt road inland from the coast at Portland Roads follows the Claudie River for part of the way to the Iron Range airfield and inland along the West Claudie. There are numerous crossings of the river and its tributaries where the road plunges into tropical lowland rainforest, dips into a river or creek crossing and emerges again to open woodland within 50–100 m. It then runs flat through woodland again for a few hundred metres before the next branch or tributary is encountered.

Along this road the rainforest is largely confined to areas close beside the river and its major branches, so that the road alternates between open woodland and tongues of rainforest, often skirting the rainforest edge.

The vegetation here constantly changes, rainforest and woodland alternating and intermingling, so that even at walking pace there seems unending variety. It is this edge zone, the ecotone between rainforest and open woodland, that is so incredibly rich in birdlife. The road, merely a dirt track which usually carries very little traffic, provides an outstanding route for birdwatching without the need to venture far into rainforest or woodland where becoming lost is always a possibility.

Most of the rainforest birds are best seen near the edges, comparatively few are deep in the rainforest. So rich in birdlife is this vicinity that newcomers to the Iron Range–Claudie River area will find that they have sighted a number of new species within hours and have a lengthy list of new sightings within a week.

In the open woodlands and along rainforest edges a typical series of bird encounters might include fig-parrots feeding on fruits clustered down the trunk of roadside fig trees. These birds are quiet and seem unafraid of observers even when close; their brightly coloured faces are clearly visible whenever they lift their heads.

Close by, its scanty twig platform precariously supporting a single white egg, a Superb Fruit-Dove watches timidly from behind screening foliage, inconspicuous though brightly plumaged. In the tall blady grass of the open a little farther down the track,

trilling calls attract attention to a family party of Lovely Fairy-wrens. The male is similar to others of the red-shouldered group but the female, with an exceptional amount of blue in her plumage, is distinctive.

The edge of the rainforest along this track gives many sightings of tropical flycatchers. At the very edge of the track a male Yellow-breasted Boatbill seems unafraid and easy to approach as he forages about the foliage just a couple of metres above the ground. Higher, clinging to trunk and limbs more in the manner of a treecreeper than a flycatcher, a Frilled Monarch can easily be identified by its pied plumage but all-white underparts.

Also along the rainforest margins, a 'whee-whee-whee' call, sometimes trilled as 'whrree-', may draw attention to the Chestnut-breasted Cuckoo. It will come in close to a taped replay, showing not only the rich chestnut of its entire underparts but also its prominent white eye-rings.

In the open woodland, particularly early morning and evening, there are often the sharp, harsh, abrupt screeches of Red-cheeked Parrots dashing through the treetops; unless they stop to feed or rest there is little chance to study their plumage. The magnificent Eclectus Parrots too are most often seen in flight, the rich red and blue of the females tending to look black against a sky that here is mostly cloudy white. Their screech is harsh and powerful, soon recognized and a useful warning that an Eclectus is ap-

proaching. To see one perched and obtain a careful look through binoculars is a result of both good fortune and alertness, for they are wary and easily put to flight.

Where the track cuts through or follows close beside the rainforest it is most likely that a Yellow-billed Kingfisher may be heard, and probably often, but the bird is remarkably difficult to sight although brightly coloured. At the beginning of the breeding season in November it is likely to be drilling a tunnel into an arboreal termite mound; the thud of the kingfishers striking the hard surface can be heard 30 m away.

Where the track slopes down to each river and creek crossing it forms a deep cutting or tunnel into the riverside belt of rainforest. Here the bird calls are more often of those that keep within the dense canopy of foliage. The river itself seems a particularly rich bird habitat. From each crossing it is usually not difficult to walk along the river bank a little way, perhaps only 50 m, find a comfortable log and watch the comings and goings of the birds. Here are likely to be seen Tropical Scrubwrens, Magnificent Riflebirds, Spotted Catbirds, Noisy Pittas, Green-backed Honeyeaters, Northern and Rufous fantails. There may be Shining Flycatchers active in the lower vegetation, a Black-winged Monarch fluttering about the mid-level foliage, or a pair of Wompoo Fruit-Doves preening quietly on a high limb.

Across the river one might gain rare glimpses of the male Magnificent Riflebird, which is quite abundant here and often heard but difficult to sight. In rainforest farther along this road a fallen limb caught up in a horizontal position 4–5 m above the ground was being used as a display perch. In two days of observation the male riflebird was seen to come to the perch at intervals of perhaps 30 to 90 minutes, staying only very briefly to call and sometimes to preen. In the long waits between visits other birds around that site included a pair of White-faced Robins, quiet and easily overlooked in the gloom of the rainforest, and a Trumpet Manucode, which announced its presence with most uncouth braying sounds.

522 **YELLOW-FACED HONEYEATER** *Lichenostomus chrysops*

SOUTH-EAST

The South-East Region, compared with the greater part of the Australian continent, enjoys a substantial and reliable rainfall and holds a large part of Australia's forests. The region is essentially a coastal strip, from the ocean to the inland slopes of the Great Dividing Range. Its northern boundary lies through Brisbane and Toowoomba, and in the south follows the Victorian coast to the South Australian border.

Although by far the most heavily populated region, the South-East retains a substantial forest cover, but only because the Great Dividing Range and other adjoining ranges are, through much of the region, so rugged that destructive exploitation has been delayed. The comparatively recent widespread interest in the Australian natural environment has now ensured the preservation of an increasingly significant area of remaining wilderness in national parks and similar reserves. For the coastal rainforests and other easily accessible country this interest has developed too late and the reserves hold only small remnants of these habitats.

The region is surprisingly diverse: its landforms include Australia's highest mountains — the only mainland alpine country; the great gorges and cliff-rimmed ridges of the Blue Mountains and surrounding sandstone heights; areas of sandy coastline with lakes and river estuaries and, in western Victoria, levels out to extensive plains now largely cleared for agriculture.

The vegetation is equally varied. It includes some superb subtropical rainforests along the ranges of the northern parts; relic patches of temperate rainforest on some northern highlands; heathlands along parts of the coast and ranges; alpine vegetation on the highest parts of the Great Dividing Range; extensive eucalypt forests and woodlands; and wetland vegetation around coastal swamps, rivers and lakes.

The South-East Region has a large and varied bird population. The continuity of its major habitats, especially of woodland and forest, both within the region and as a continuation of these habitats in adjoining regions, allows many of the birds of northern Australia to occur much farther south than on the western side of the continent where deserts break the continuity of habitat.

The number of species endemic to the region fluctuates from time to time in line with changes in the classification of bird species, but currently there are about a dozen species that are found entirely or almost entirely within this region. In addition, among the numerous subspecies that are unique to the South-East, some are sufficiently distinctive to warrant mention — usually those that, like the Helmeted Honeyeater and Coxen's Fig-Parrot, have at one time been listed as full species.

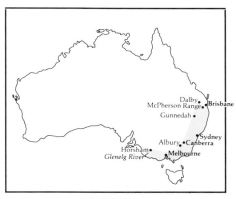

South-East

BIRDS OF THE SOUTH-EAST

18 GOULD'S PETREL

Pterodroma leucoptera

The Australian subspecies of this petrel breeds only on Cabbage Tree Island, near Port Stephens, where the total number of birds is around 500–1000. These birds are not noticeable at the colony because they arrive after dark and leave before first light each morning. Gould's Petrel is usually recorded only in the general vicinity of the colony, except for the period between May to October when they are absent from the colony.

On Cabbage Tree Island most of the petrels nest under cover of a forest of palms, among rocks or in short burrows. Eggs are laid from about November to December, chicks hatching in January and fledging by April.

▶ See also pages 117 254

242 GANG-GANG COCKATOO

Callocephalon fimbriatum

The richly coloured Gang-gang Cockatoo is almost confined to this region, where it is usually found in mountain forests. Some seasonal movement occurs and occasional wanderings by individuals over longer distances. The Gang-gang Cockatoos of the higher south-eastern mountain ranges move to lower ranges and coastal forests during winter, becoming much more common around Canberra from April to September. In the northern part of its range it is present on the higher parts throughout the year and is always more often seen at higher altitudes.

This cockatoo is mainly a bird of the forests but some birds move into more open country in winter and may then be seen in parks and gardens. During their winter visits to the lowlands the birds may gather into small flocks but after returning to the mountain forests for the spring and summer breeding, pairs or small family parties are usual.

The stronghold of this magnificent cockatoo is the south-east corner, in the mountainous forests of south-eastern New South Wales and eastern Victoria, where it is quite common and secure. In common with other cockatoos it could be threatened by forestry clear-felling which eliminates older trees with large hollows suitable for nesting.

Gang-gang Cockatoos feed in the treetops or lower shrubbery, returning methodically to the same site until the supply of seeds or berries is exhausted. While feeding they can be remarkably tolerant of close approach before climbing higher or flying a short distance to continue feeding. During hot weather they may spend the middle of the day quietly perched in dense foliage.

In heavy forest these dark-plumaged birds might not be noticed among dense foliage but for their distinctive drawn-out screech, which is unique: rasping, with scratchy and squeaky sounds intermixed. While feeding they give low growling sounds from time to time.

The Gang-gang Cockatoo may occasionally be spotted in the air. It is a powerful flier, with deep, heavy wingbeats, and often travels high and far across the mountain valleys.

▶ **See also pages** *117* 122 123 311

258 COXEN'S FIG-PARROT
SUBSPECIES OF DOUBLE-EYED FIG PARROT

Psittaculirostris diophthalma coxeni

The Double-eyed Fig-Parrot has three Australian subspecies, two of which are discussed in their respective regions, the Cape York and Atherton regions. This southern subspecies is very much isolated from those of north-eastern Queensland and occurs northwards perhaps as far as the Maryborough district.

Coxen's Fig-Parrot has become very rare, possibly the result of the extensive clearing of lowland rainforest. It inhabits both highland and lowland rainforests, though the latter, within its range, has been almost entirely cleared. There were no confirmed reports of this subspecies during the RAOU Field Atlas survey, 1977–81. It was recorded at Lamington National Park in December 1976; two were reported at Koreelah Creek, Tooloom Scrub area, in February 1976. Previous sites include Kenilworth State Forest south of Gympie and Bunya Mountains National Park in the 1960s. In New South Wales it is confined to a few rainforest areas north of the Richmond River.

The breeding of Coxen's Fig-Parrot has never been positively recorded. A set of eggs collected near Maryborough in 1934, and thought to

271 **CRIMSON ROSELLA** *Platycercus elegans*

be of this subspecies, appear to have been mis-identified. The birds of this subspecies are larger than those of the northern subspecies, there is only a little orange to the lower face and no red on the forehead. The sexes are almost identical; behaviour and calls are presumably the same as for the northern birds.

▶ **See also pages** 11 88 113 *117* 121 314

337 ALBERT'S LYREBIRD

Menura alberti

The Albert's Lyrebird is confined to a small area in the north of the South-East Region. It includes south-eastern Queensland from the vicinity of the Mistake Mountains and Cunninghams Gap, around the Scenic Rim to Springbrook, Tamborine Mountain,

the McPherson Range including Lamington, and adjacent ranges of north-eastern New South Wales including the Tweed and Richmond ranges. This species is confined to wet sclerophyll forest, intermixed sclerophyll and rainforest, and subtropical rainforest, where there is dense ground-cover of vine and scrub understorey or clumps of tree-ferns.

Several song or display platforms of Albert's Lyrebirds found at Dalrymple Creek, Queensland, were described as small, roughly circular clearings among the ferns. All debris had been raked from the ground but no attempt had been made to construct any built-up mound nor were the display platforms hidden in dense undergrowth. Display platforms at Tamborine Mountain, Springbrook and vicinity were in dense undercover and had an intermeshed layer of vines, sometimes of lawyer canes, usually just above the raked ground. The agitated movements of the bird displaying on the vines would be transmitted to surrounding vegetation, setting the foliage shaking.

In a locality frequented by the Albert's Lyrebird one might think that to locate a calling bird may not be too difficult, but even a distant and brief sighting is rare, for the bird is usually in a tangled vine thicket where visibility is poor in the dim light and the birds extremely wary.

The display of the male seems similar to that of the Superb Lyrebird, although the shorter tail does not seem to hang over as low in front. Observers have commented on the strength of the song and the excellent mimicry.

In full song the use of mimicry by the Albert's Lyrebird is significantly different from the Superb Lyrebird. In each case the song consists of segments that are purely their own, interspersed with mimicry. Both species have song that is very loud and continuous, but whereas the Superb Lyrebird mimics a wide range of clearly identifiable bird calls, Albert's Lyrebird restricts itself to mimicry of just four or five species, and some other calls which do not seem to be identifiable. Being winter breeders, these birds are usually in full song in June and July.

▶ See also pages *117* 120 121 335

338 SUPERB LYREBIRD

Menura novaehollandiae

The Superb Lyrebird is famed for the spectacular display of the male. With shimmering tail fanned wide and arched over his back so that he is enveloped in its lace-like filaments, he sings with incredibly loud but beautiful notes, interwoven with the mimicked calls of other birds.

The principal habitat of the Superb Lyrebird is wet sclerophyll forest but it also occurs in, and breeds within, subtropical and temperate rainforest and in some localities may be found in quite dry eucalypt forest. It occurs from Stanthorpe in southern Queensland to the Dandenong Ranges near Melbourne, at altitudes from sea level up to 1500 m.

Superb Lyrebirds studied at the Tidbinbilla Fauna Reserve, 40 km south-west of Canberra, were at an altitude of about 1000 m, close to a walking track known as the Lyrebird Trail. The habitat here is of wet sclerophyll forest with tree-fern and broad-leaf shrubbery along the creeks and acacia scrub on the slopes.

The territory of a male Superb Lyrebird appears to encompass the territories of several females and there appears to be a degree of pair-bonding with each. The distance between the territories of males is usually sufficient to allow for several of the smaller female territories between.

At Tidbinbilla the male Superb Lyrebirds have territories averaging 2.4 ha in area, and within those territories they have on average 42 display mounds. The pattern of use of these mounds is influenced by the male's need to defend his territory and to attract a mate. Breeding commences in winter when the temperature is lowest and humidity high. The peak of singing coincides with egg-laying and is strong from about May to the end of July, but this can vary with abnormal seasons.

Both sexes seem to prefer the cooler, damper parts of the territory, though during the breeding season the male is forced to higher, drier parts to defend his territory. Rival males may be as much as 450 m apart, the intervening country heavily forested and usually rough. To defend his territory by song the male must be heard across such distances and often over valleys or ridges. He must use the more elevated sites so that he can direct the calls at his neighbours more effectively than would be possible from within the muffling confines of densely vegetated gullies. The male thus tends to have his attention divided between his desire to be in the lower part of the territory and the need to maintain a persistent territorial defence.

The female Superb Lyrebirds, on the other hand, are usually fully occupied within the lower areas where the denser vegetation and wetter soil are best for nesting and finding food for the young: tasks which they must undertake without help from the male.

When they do visit upper parts of the territory the females appear to be attracted to the freshly raked earth of the display mounds. It is thought that the male, in maintaining large mounds of freshly scratched earth, is simulating in these higher, drier parts of his territory the feeding conditions found in the valleys, thus tempting the females to occasionally visit the sites where he must remain most of the time to effectively defend his territory by song. The male not only selects sites for display mounds on the basis of acoustics, he also chooses the coolest situations, in keeping with the simulation of preferred creekside habitat.

The male Superb Lyrebird usually roosts in a tall tree near the highest part of his territory. His first song at

614 SATIN BOWERBIRDS *Ptilonorhynchus violaceus* Top:*Male* Bottom:*Female*

dawn is from this perch and he then descends from limb to limb, calling, then proceeds to the nearest song-point, usually a mound. During the morning he works his way downhill, singing at mounds and other points. The middle of the day is usually spent in the lower parts of the territory.

The Superb Lyrebird is not always an inhabitant of lush wet forests. At Mt Marula, 12 km east of Goulburn, it inhabits dry sclerophyll forest, in this instance without wet sclerophyll or rainforest nearby and without surface water within 6 km.

The best-known site for the Superb Lyrebird is Sherbrooke Forest, in Victoria's Dandenong Ranges near Melbourne. Although normally extremely shy, the Sherbrooke lyrebirds have become accustomed to visitors and can be seen feeding and sometimes displaying.

▶ See also pages *117* 118 121 122 123 124 126 335

339 RUFOUS SCRUB-BIRD *Atrichornis rufescens*

339 RUFOUS SCRUB-BIRD

Atrichornis rufescens

The Rufous Scrub-bird inhabits temperate and subtropical rainforest and wet sclerophyll forest. It keeps to the very dense undergrowth that develops where the canopy has been opened up, usually by the felling of a tree.

Like the similar Noisy Scrub-bird of Western Australia, the Rufous is famed for its powerful and varied song, which peaks in the breeding season. In the mimicry which is part of its outpourings of loud song, the Rufous Scrub-bird often includes the calls of the Logrunner and other birds, but the Noisy Scrub-bird does not normally use mimicry in full song. However, both species include mimicry in their much quieter sub-songs outside the breeding season.

The Rufous Scrub-bird is quite rare and restricted to comparatively few localities. Its range extends from the tops of Queensland's Mistake Mountains, Little Liverpool Range and McPherson Range, southwards along the highest rainforested summits, including Mt Warning, Gibraltar Range, New England Tableland and Barrington Tops; most of its better-known populations are within national parks. Before 1900 the Rufous Scrub-bird was known also from lowland rainforests but that habitat is almost entirely cleared.

The habitat requirements of the Rufous Scrub-bird seem to include a dense layer of ground-cover around a metre high, abundant leaf-litter, and a site within rainforest or in wet sclerophyll forest at the edge of rainforest. A sighting of the Rufous Scrub-bird at Mt Banda Banda, about 45 km north-west of Wauchope, was at an altitude of about 1000 m, under tall eucalypts with a rainforest understorey varying in height between 6 and 10 m and dense ground cover of shrubs, fallen limbs and litter.

In spring the ringing calls can be heard from hundreds of metres away. Beneath the low dense cover the male scrub-bird will sometimes come to within a metre or so, when the calls become quite deafening, though the bird can only rarely be glimpsed. The female is usually silent and rarely seen.

The Rufous and Noisy scrub-birds, and probably the two species of lyrebird, may have had their origins in the cool, damp Antarctic beech forests which were once much more widespread. Although now in other habitats, they all keep to the coolest parts, where it is moist and shady, and most nest at the coldest time of the year. Their nests are well suited to the cold wet situations, both the lyrebirds and scrub-birds building substantial and well-lined domed nests.

▶ See also pages *9* 52 120 121 127 235 335 336

359 RUSSET-TAILED GROUND-THRUSH

Zoothera heinei

Among the birds that have suffered frequent confusing name changes is the species which was once known as the Ground Thrush, Scaly Thrush, and then White's Thrush. Recent studies have resulted in that species being split into two full species. One, the Australian Ground-Thrush, has been given the species name of *Zoothera lunulata* and has a subspecies *cuneata*. The second is the Russet-tailed Ground-Thrush, *Zoothera heinei*. The Australian Ground-Thrush is discussed within the Habitats section as a bird of the forests.

These species inhabit coastal forests of eastern and south-eastern Australia. The Australian Ground-Thrush has one subspecies in north-eastern Queensland, the other in coastal south-eastern Australia, from south-eastern Queensland to Kangaroo Island and Tasmania. The Russet-tailed Ground-Thrush inhabits north-eastern, central to south-eastern coastal Queensland and extends into north-eastern New South Wales.

In south-eastern Queensland and north-eastern New South Wales the breeding ranges of the two species overlap but there is no evidence of interbreeding. In the area around the Richmond and Tweed rivers they are partially separated by altitude, the Australian Ground-Thrush usually being found above 550 m altitude and the Russet-tailed below 750 m.

The Russet-tailed Ground-Thrush is identified by its shorter russet tail and rufous-tinged rump. It has a loud double-noted whistle, sounding like 'wheer-doo' or 'pee-pooo', of very even tone. The Australian Ground-Thrush has a longer tail, olive rump, and a melodious, subdued song of whistles and trills, given at dawn and probably at dusk in the breeding season, and also a piping hiss of one to three notes.

In localities where both species occur their calls would appear to give the best chance of identification, given the similarity of appearance and the poor light often prevailing in the dense forests.

▶ See also pages 65 *117* 121 341

411 LOGRUNNER

Orthonyx temminckii

The Logrunner is a bird of the rainforests where it feeds among the damp leaf-litter of the forest floor. It forages very actively and in the quiet of the forest attention may be drawn to this bird by the rustlings of its

searching. Sideways kicks send leaves
and twigs aside, exposing underlying
layers of litter and earth, where it
pecks at any small creatures that it
finds. It then runs forward a little way,
to repeat the process. Small circular
patches of bare soil remain as evidence
of its activities.

Logrunners have loud calls, most
often given at dawn. Although they
may not be immediately obvious in the
gloom beneath the rainforest canopy
and undergrowth, these are colourful
birds, their upperparts richly mottled
in rust and black. They are unusual in
that the female is the more colourful,
with a bright orange-rufous throat-
patch, where the male is entirely white.
The Logrunner is quite common in
south-eastern Queensland and likely to
be seen by most birdwatchers giving
more than superficial coverage to the
rainforests. It is uncommon in the
southern parts of its range, in New
South Wales.

▶ **See also pages** 52 121 122 127 353

411 **LOGRUNNER** *Orthonyx temminckii*
Top: *Male* Bottom: *Female*

413 EASTERN WHIPBIRD

Psophodes olivaceus

The name 'whipbird' comes from the
whipcrack calls of this long-tailed,
predominantly olive-green bird. But
despite the far-carrying calls it can be
very difficult to see, keeping to the
thickets and densely tangled
undergrowth.

18 **Gould's Petrel** *Pterodroma leucoptera*
28 **Fluttering Shearwater** *Puffinus gavia*
155 **Double-banded Plover** *Charadrius bicinctus*
165 **Eastern Curlew** *Numenius madagascariensis*
206 **Little Tern** *Sterna albifrons*
218 **Topknot Pigeon** *Lopholaimus antarcticus*
242 **Gang-gang Cockatoo** *Callocephalon frimbriatum*
258 **Coxen's Fig-Parrot** (subspecies of Double-eyed Fig-Parrot) *Psittaculirostris diophthalma coxeni*
259 **Australian King-Parrot** *Alisterus scapularis*
285 **Blue-winged Parrot** *Neophema chrysostoma*
337 **Albert's Lyrebird** *Menura alberti*
338 **Superb Lyrebird** *Menura novaehollandiae*
359 **Russet-tailed Ground-Thrush** *Zoothera heinei*

413 **EASTERN WHIPBIRD** *Psophodes olivaceus*

gorges near water. Water seems important to the Rock Warbler as it appears to abandon sites where the creeks dry up, otherwise it is mainly a sedentary species.

The Rock Warbler is similar to a robin: dark brown above and rich rufous beneath, restlessly active, with almost constant sideways flicks of the tail. Foraging is done mainly among boulders in flowing streams, but often also along the stream banks and occasionally onto the lower branches of nearby trees or shrubs.

The Rock Warbler is most remarkable in choosing a cave for its nest site. A favoured position is a cave or deep hollow in the sandstone behind a waterfall where the bird may have to fly through the spray of the water to enter. The domed nest is suspended from the cave ceiling or the underside of a ledge, often in a situation that is quite dark.

▶ **See also pages** *119* 122 363

The call is often given as a duet between male and female, with the male's drawn-out explosive whipcrack so quickly answered with the female's quieter 'shoo-choo' that there seems to be just the one bird calling. The Eastern Whipbird has a wide range, taking in most of Australia's east coast. Over this great distance the calls vary somewhat and are more evident in the response of the female than the whipcrack of the male.

The calls of the Eastern Whipbird are among the more common of the sounds along rainforest walk trails. A sighting of this species usually depends upon persistence in trying to spot the long-tailed dark olive shape in the thickets.

▶ **See also pages** 81 159 353

455 PILOTBIRD

Pycnoptilus floccosus

The small brown Pilotbird was so named in the belief that it has some special relationship with the Superb Lyrebird in that it acted as a pilot for the larger bird. There are numerous records of sightings of this bird in company with the lyrebird, taking small creatures exposed by the raking aside of large amounts of the leaf-litter by the lyrebird or visiting the freshly scratched moist earth of the display mound.

But the Pilotbird in this respect is little different to some other small insectivorous birds. The White-browed Scrubwren and Eastern Yellow

Robin often accompany the lyrebird, hopping about near the freshly turned litter and earth and darting in to take some insect that would probably be too small to be of much interest to the lyrebird.

Although the range of the Pilotbird is largely within that of the Superb Lyrebird, it extends northwards only to the central New South Wales coast and ranges, while the Superb Lyrebird reaches south-eastern Queensland. In a few localities the Pilotbird extends beyond the range of the Superb Lyrebird, being recorded south to Wilsons Promontory. Locally, either bird may be present where the other has not been recorded, again indicating that the association is one of convenience rather than necessity for the Pilotbird.

The Pilotbird is quite common and is of course most likely to be seen when one is watching for the lyrebird; it has a loud and piercing call which once known will betray its presence in dense vegetation where it would otherwise not have been noticed.

▶ **See also pages** *119* 122 123 124 126 363

456 ROCK WARBLER

Origma solitaria

The Rock Warbler is confined not only to this South-East Region but is also the only bird species unique to New South Wales. It is found only in the Hawkesbury sandstone and limestone country around Sydney and the Blue Mountains, where it inhabits rocky

464 CHESTNUT-RUMPED HEATHWREN

Sericornis pyrrhopygius

This is a remarkably secretive bird whose brownish plumage and skulking habits make it difficult to observe. Fortunately it has a distinctive and very beautiful song which will betray or confirm its presence and give a starting point in tracking the bird.

The Chestnut-rumped Heathwren is principally a bird of heathlands and low dense scrub but it also occurs in woodlands where there is a dense low understorey. It is often in small parties, foraging on the ground and through the low vegetation and usually keeping beneath the shrubbery, the tail carried upright.

The clear, sweet and melodious song is to be heard most often in the spring breeding season between August and December. From a perch on top of a small shrub the male sings with notes that are at first soft, then swell in volume, the variety of sound enriched with mimicry of the songs of other birds. It has a resemblance to the full-voiced song of a Canary, or of the Skylark, but given with far greater variety and accomplishment.

A heathwren is likely to burst into song at any time of day but most reliably and most frequently towards sundown. Others within hearing quickly follow until the area for a while resounds with song. Cool, fine, clear weather is best for hearing heathwrens; they are mostly silent in very windy conditions.

▶ **See also pages** *119* 121 122 126 139 365

532 HELMETED HONEYEATER
SUBSPECIES OF YELLOW-TUFTED HONEYEATER

Lichenostomus melanops cassidix

The very attractive and rare Helmeted Honeyeater was Victoria's sole claim to a bird species unique to that State. It is now included within the more widespread Yellow-tufted Honeyeater as a subspecies but should continue to be known by the common name of Helmeted Honeyeater. This is a distinctive bird, more beautiful than the other subspecies of the species into which it is now placed. It is no less worthy of our interest and conservation efforts because of a taxonomic change which, like so many others, may in time prove temporary.

There are now four subspecies making up the species known as the Yellow-tufted Honeyeater. Of these the Helmeted Honeyeater is the most restricted in occurrence.

The species as a whole extends slightly beyond the boundaries of this region, from south-eastern Queensland to the south-east of South Australia. The Helmeted Honeyeater was probably at one time quite widespread through Gippsland but has declined in numbers and range until only a few colonies remain along the Woori-Yallock and Cardinia creeks just east of Melbourne. The latter is now the stronghold of the Helmeted Honeyeater, though with only a few hundred individuals remaining. Part of its habitat has been protected within the Yellingbo Fauna Reserve.

The Helmeted Honeyeater is a very active and vocal species, usually in pairs or parties foraging about tree and shrub foliage. The golden crown, separated from an equally bright golden throat by a bold black line through the eye, and the short golden crest or 'helmet' on the forehead, make the Helmeted Honeyeater conspicuous. The adjoining subspecies *gippslandica* is similar but lacks the forehead tuft, and the transition from gold of crown to olive of back is gradual rather than sharply defined.

▶ See also pages 8 113 381

Michel K. Macabe
1986

615 REGENT BOWERBIRD

Sericulus chrysocephalus

A Regent Bowerbird in flight against the dark greenery of the rainforest must rank among the most startling and enthralling of Australian bird sights. The black of the body is all but lost against the dark backdrop, but the flickering gold of its wings immediately commands attention. For a moment it could be taken for a great gold-and-black tropical butterfly; given another second or two there would be few birdwatchers who would not be able to name the bird. So magnificent is its plumage that most observers will know it from guidebook paintings or photographs where even its likeness on paper is spectacular enough to leave a permanent image in the memory.

The Regent Bowerbird is associated

362 Rose Robin *Petroica rosea*
455 Pilotbird *Pycnoptilus floccosus*
456 Rock Warbler *Origma solitaria*
464 Chestnut-rumped Heathwren *Sericornis pyrrhopygius*
489 Striated Thornbill *Acanthiza lineata*
494 White-throated Treecreeper *Cormobates leucophaea*
496 Red-browed Treecreeper *Climacteris erythrops*
510 Regent Honeyeater *Xanthomyza phrygia*
512 Bell Miner *Manorina melanophrys*
532 Helmeted Honeyeater (subspecies of Yellow-tufted Honeyeater) *Lichenostomus melops cassidix*
560 Eastern Spinebill *Acanthorhynchus tenuirostris*
622 Paradise Riflebird *Ptiloris paradiseus*
640 Pied Currawong *Strepera graculina*

615 **REGENT BOWERBIRD** *Sericulus chrysocephalus*

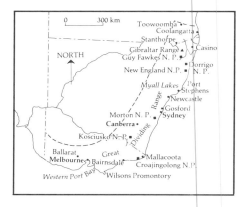

BORDER RANGE TO GLOUCESTER TOPS

From the Mistake Mountains south-east of Toowoomba to the McPherson Range overlooking Coolangatta, the great arc of ranges of the Scenic Rim sweeps down to the New South Wales border, with 25 peaks exceeding 1000 m in height. Along the crest of the rim a chain of national parks preserve segments of the ranges and provide access; best-known of these are Cunninghams Gap, on the Cunningham Highway, and Lamington National Park.

From the McPherson Range, the Tweed Range, Mt Warning and farther inland the Richmond Range extend southwards into north-eastern New South Wales. Here also the national parks provide road and foot access to the prime sites on the range-tops and in the forests. Two convenient parks are the Nightcap National Park, north of Lismore, and Mt Warning National Park west of Murwillumbah. It is not only the national parks that provide good birding sites; some forestry areas have acquired a reputation as being excellent for birding, including Tooloom and Whian Whian.

Farther inland again the Great Dividing Range carries the mountain chain southwards, broadening to form the New England Tableland, with a series of reserves along its eastern escarpment. The major national parks here are Gibraltar Range, Guy Fawkes, Dorrigo, New England and Barrington Tops.

The birdlist in these rainforested ranges is similar throughout but with local variations. The Albert's Lyrebird is confined to the northern parts, in and near the ranges of the Scenic Rim, and south to the Tweed Range and Mt Warning; the Rufous Scrub-bird is found on the summits of the McPherson Range, Mt Warning, Gibraltar Range, New England and Barrington Tops, and some other less well-known sites. Among the rare subspecies, Coxen's Fig-Parrot seems

with forests which contain elements of subtropical rainforest. There it can be locally abundant in optimum habitat, particularly in the river valleys along the lower coastal slopes of the Great Dividing Range, but being shy and retiring it can easily be overlooked. After breeding, some Regent Bowerbirds move to more open country and in winter months may visit orchards and gardens seeking cultivated fruits.

The Regent Bowerbird is not as noisy around the bower as some of the other bowerbirds. At the bower the male keeps up a low chattering, its usual call being a grating, scolding sound. Its relative quietness and preference for a site among very dense undergrowth makes finding this bird more difficult. The best opportunities of a sighting are at some national parks, such as Lamington, where Regent Bowerbirds are more accustomed to people. Other localities include Iluka Scrub, Tooloom Scrub and the Gosford–Wyong district.

▶ **See also pages** 52 80 121 122 127 400

622 PARADISE RIFLEBIRD

Ptiloris paradiseus

The Paradise Riflebird is found in rainforests of southern Queensland,

where it occurs in the Bunya and McPherson ranges, and in northern New South Wales where it extends southwards to such localities as the Richmond Valley, Tooloom Scrub and Barrington Tops.

This riflebird is not confined to rainforest but also uses adjoining dry eucalypt woodland. Nor is it much restricted in altitude, being found in the Antarctic beech forests of the tops of the ranges and down onto the foothills.

Like the riflebirds of northern Queensland, this species keeps mostly to the high limbs of the trees, moving in rather treecreeper-like manner over the bark and dead limbs, using the long, curved bill to prise into the crevices for insects. When the birds fly the rustling sounds that the wings make may often be heard.

The male Paradise Riflebird has display perches or 'stages': conspicuous limbs high in tall trees that are lit by early morning and late afternoon sun. In display it spreads the wings, bows low, then with body feathers fluffed out, points the bill skywards giving strident calls; these and other sequences of movements and calling may attract the female to the perch.

▶ **See also pages** 52 *119* 120 121 127 402

now confined to the McPherson and nearby ranges, and the Plumed Frogmouth to the vicinity of the Tweed and Nightcap ranges. Otherwise, the birdlists from the Border Range to Barrington Tops are broadly similar, with a strong rainforest element and with a greater or lesser number of species where a wider variety of habitat is included.

Some localities have an extremely varied vegetation, perhaps including subtropical and temperate rainforest, eucalyptus forests and woodlands, alpine woodland and areas of heath, but most places have fewer habitats. The birdlists — 113 species at Gibraltar Range, 220 species at Barrington Tops, 170 for the Scenic Rim and Border Range, 89 species for Lamington and 130 species for Whian Whian State Forest — show up a varied total. The RAOU Field Atlas survey lists for three 1° blocks southwards from Cunninghams Gap to Barrington Tops were each near 270 species, including a wider variety of tablelands and coastal lowlands as well as the ranges.

Birds of interest include the Pacific Baza, Noisy Pitta, Albert's Lyrebird, Superb Lyrebird, Paradise Riflebird, Rufous Scrub-bird, Logrunner, Regent Bowerbird, Grey Goshawk, Spotted Quail-thrush, Rose-crowned Fruit-Dove, White-headed Pigeon, Wompoo Fruit-Dove, Topknot Pigeon, Emerald Dove, Black-breasted Button-quail, Chestnut-rumped Heathwren, Powerful Owl, Sooty Owl, Masked Owl, Australian Ground-Thrush, Russet-tailed Ground-Thrush, Spectacled Monarch, White-eared Monarch, Pale-yellow Robin, Olive Whistler, Large-billed Scrubwren, Rufous Bristlebird, Red-browed Treecreeper and Yellow-throated Scrubwren.

Further variety of habitat is given by the granite belt country of the higher parts of the Great Dividing Range between Stanthorpe and Tenterfield, conveniently accessible at Girraween National Park, where the granite domed ranges reach an altitude of 1267 m. Farther south, the more open country of the New England Tableland in the Inverell district, largely open woodland and farmlands, offers an excellent variety of birds, many that are not found in the heavily forested areas to the east. The district birdlist is over 200, with Turquoise Parrot, Square-tailed Kite, Squatter Pigeon, Yellow-tailed and Glossy black-cockatoos, Pale-headed Rosella and Yellow-tufted Honeyeater.

396 **BLACK-FACED MONARCH** *Monarcha melanopsis*

434 **SUPERB FAIRY-WREN** *Malurus cyaneus*

NORTHERN COAST

Northern coastal New South Wales, from the Queensland border southwards to Newcastle, has a significant amount of remaining natural environment but has lost most of its lowland rainforest. There are small remnant patches of rainforest along the coast, some with a reputation as good bird sites. Otherwise this coastal strip has mainly heaths, swamps, eucalypt forests and woodlands, and the habitats of ocean beaches and river estuaries.

The Myall Lakes and Wallis Lakes area, of which part is within the Myall Lakes National Park, has numerous interconnected lakes, some so large that the far banks are almost out of sight and in other parts are narrow waterways lined with swamp oaks, paperbarks and casuarinas. The varied soils of its small rocky hills, swamps, sand ridges and wet hollows have given great diversity of habitat, including some isolated pockets of rainforest.

The rainforests at Myall Lakes have a rich breeding avifauna of at least 34

460 YELLOW-THROATED SCRUBWREN
Sericornis citreogularis

species, including the Australian King-Parrot, Superb Lyrebird, Rufous Fantail, Black-faced Monarch, Crested Shrike-tit, Regent Bowerbird and Satin Bowerbird. In littoral rainforest near Seal Rocks more than 76 species have been recorded. The wet sclerophyll avifauna is similar to that of the rainforest but that of the dry forest is more distinctive, with Olive-backed Oriole, Yellow-faced Honeyeater, Rufous Whistler and Brown Thornbill as typical species. Myall Lakes also has extensive heath; typical birds here are White-cheeked, New Holland, Yellow-faced and Tawny-crowned honeyeaters, the Noisy Friarbird and the Little Wattlebird.

Much of the northern coast is now protected within a chain of national parks — Broadwater, Bundjalung and Yuraygir — that take up a large section of coast from Broadwater, just south of Ballina, southwards through Iluka and Yamba to Angourie. Within these is a range of habitats that ensures an excellent variety of birds.

Behind the long sweeping beaches and rocky headlands are areas of dune vegetation, heathlands both wet and dry, paperbark and reedy wetlands and, farther inland, eucalypt woodlands. Birdlife is excellent, ranging from Black-necked Stork and Brolga to tiny Southern Emu-wren and Red-backed Fairy-wren. Near the

mouths of the Richmond and Evans rivers and at the southern end near the Clarence River are patches of rainforest on coastal sand. Around the mouth of the Clarence are numerous good birding sites: Woody Head and Iluka Scrub on the north side, Yamba and Angourie to the south.

Iluka Scrub, a relatively small patch of coastal rainforest, is known among birdwatchers as a good site for the Regent Bowerbird and at times the Spangled Drongo. There are also extensive areas of river estuary, mudflats and fringing mangroves. Birds to be seen around the mouth of the Clarence River could include the Osprey, Brahminy Kite, White-bellied Sea-Eagle, Brolga, Black-necked Stork, Striated Heron, Royal Spoonbill, Sooty Oystercatcher, Blue-faced Honeyeater and Scarlet Honeyeater. The Myall Lakes birdlist is in excess of 280 species.

Farther south, around the lower parts of the Hunter River, on the northern and western fringes of Newcastle, are sites covering a variety of habitat including river mudflats, mangroves, paperbark swamps, rainforests, open forest and heathlands. So rich is this district that within a 30 km radius of Newcastle there are to be found a total of at least 324 species; the RAOU Field Atlas survey recorded almost 330 species for the 1° block extending from Newcastle north to Barrington Tops and including the lower Hunter River.

One of the most rewarding wader sites here is Kooragang Island in the Hunter estuary. Here it is possible to see some 70 species in a day, with as many as 200 birds visible at some sites. The list includes the Eastern Curlew, Broad-billed Sandpiper, Terek Sandpiper, Marsh Sandpiper, Black-tailed Godwit, Bar-tailed Godwit, Mongolian Dotterel and Greenshank. Birds other than waders include egrets, ducks, the Black-necked Stork, White-bellied Sea-Eagle and Scarlet Honeyeater. Studies here have shown that the waders begin to arrive about mid-August, peak at around 10 000 birds in October or November, and leave for the Northern Hemisphere between March and May.

Other sites around Newcastle are Wallsend, Minmi, Black Hill, Stockton Beach, Swansea and Buttai.

BLUE MOUNTAINS AND SYDNEY ENVIRONS

To the west of Sydney a great sandstone plateau has been sculptured into cliff-rimmed gorges and ridges in what is known as the Blue Mountains. In equally spectacular fashion this

259 AUSTRALIAN KING-PARROT
Alisterus scapularis

landform extends northwards to the rugged wilderness areas in and around Wollemi National Park, and to the south-west is partly within Kanangra-Boyd National Park.

The mainly flat plateau tops, above cliffs of both the coastal sandstone national parks and those of the Blue Mountains, are mainly of banksia-heath and scribbly gums, with areas of woodland and forest. On the Blue Mountains plateau the heath and woodland hold around 140 species, including many typical of heathlands, such as the Tawny-crowned Honeyeater, Southern Emu-wren, Chestnut-rumped Heathwren, Variegated Fairy-wren, Spotted Quail-thrush, Rufous Whistler, Eastern Spinebill and Beautiful Firetail; in gullies with creeks the locally endemic Australian Rock Warbler might be seen.

In the gorges and valleys the vegetation is much heavier, with forests of massive eucalypts in the Blue Mountains, and scattered patches of rainforest.

The avifauna of the heavier forests of the valleys is quite different from that of the heights and includes Brown Cuckoo-Dove, Topknot Pigeon, Yellow-tailed and Glossy black-cockatoos, Gang-gang Cockatoo, Brush Cuckoo, Superb Lyrebird, Flame Robin, Golden Whistler, Rufous Fantail, Yellow-throated Scrubwren, Pilotbird, Logrunner, Black-faced Monarch, Yellow-tufted Honeyeater and Satin Bowerbird.

The Botany Bay area has become known for rewarding birdwatching conveniently close to Sydney. Favourable sites around the bay are the Kurnell Peninsula, Towra Point, Boat Harbour and Eastlakes. The vegetation is of banksia-heath, with areas of eucalypts and angophoras. The mudflats at Botany Bay are famous as the feeding grounds of quite large flocks of migratory waders.

At Towra Point the waterbirds on

one occasion included skuas, terns, gulls, ibises, spoonbills, herons, egrets, pelicans, cormorants, moorhens, ducks and swans; among waders on the nearby beach were large numbers of Bar-tailed Godwits, small numbers of Grey-tailed Tattlers and Whimbrels, and a Pied Oystercatcher. There are numerous Common Terns, an Arctic Tern, a White-bellied Sea-Eagle and a Brown Goshawk.

ILLAWARRA COAST AND HINTERLAND

Although Lake Illawarra is within an industrial area, the coast and hinterland offer a diverse bird environment and protect some rare species. Lake Illawarra itself has a birdwatching site of interest at Windang, at the lake entrance, with Black Swans, terns and waders. Shoalhaven Heads and Comerong Island at the entrance to the Shoalhaven River form another good locality for waders and terns, while Jervis Bay Nature Reserve is also worth visiting for sightings of birds of beach and ocean. Nearby Coomonderry Swamp is an area of excellent waterbird habitat.

Farther down the coast near Batemans Bay, Burrewarra Point projects well out beyond the general trend of the coast. It has proven to be a favourable site for observing seabirds, from a vantage point near the tip of the Point at about 15–20 m above sea level. Some species that might be seen are the Black-browed Albatross, mainly in June and July, the Wandering Albatross in August and September, the Shy Albatross in October, while the Yellow-nosed Albatross is generally a rare visitor; giant-petrels may be sighted from June to October. Among other seabirds passing along the coast are various shearwaters, petrels, prions, diving-petrels, cormorants, skuas, gulls, terns and the Australian Gannet.

Inland are some major habitat reserves, including Morton National Park. The RAOU Field Atlas birdlist for the 1° block covering the coast from Jervis Bay to Moruya and inland to Morton totalled 268 species.

Morton, situated 17 km south of Moss Vale, has some spectacular scenery at Fitzroy Falls; the surrounding eucalypt forests and patches of subtropical rainforest have a rich and varied birdlife. The national park has a visitor centre able to provide advice on wildlife, tracks and places of interest.

A bird place well-known among ornithologists is the reserve established for the protection and study of several rare heathland species including the Ground Parrot and Eastern Bristlebird. The Barren Grounds Bird Observatory serves as a centre for bird research, with scientists from various academic institutions spending time here to gather data in the field. The Observatory is managed by two full-time wardens and hosts various study courses, workshops and seminars on subjects related to the natural environment, including general bird courses. Subjects have included bird banding, nature photography, studies of insects, mammals, wildflowers, and bird groups such as honeyeaters. Of particular interest are the local species: the Ground Parrot and Eastern Bristlebird. Accommodation is limited to a dozen people so that bookings are necessary; contact can be made through the RAOU.

The Barren Grounds Nature Reserve is situated on a sandstone plateau inland from Kiama, at an altitude of about 600 m. It is an area of impoverished and poorly drained soil, with a climate that can be very cold. While heathland is an important vegetation as habitat for the Ground Parrot and Eastern Bristlebird, there are substantial areas of woodland and forest, especially on the escarpment slopes. Research here has included studies of the effect of fire upon the habitat. The Barren Grounds birdlist stands at about 135 species.

AUSTRALIAN CAPITAL TERRITORY AND SNOWY MOUNTAINS

Canberra has an abundance of birdwatching areas close at hand, with a variety of habitat provided by forested ranges and open farmlands. In the winter months the local bird population is boosted by birds such as the Flame Robin, Gang-gang Cockatoo and Australian King-Parrot which then move down from the alpine areas. Locally, Lake Burley Griffin and the Jerrabomberra Wetlands at its eastern end are worth a visit. The latter are sewerage farm ponds, where migratory waders may be seen. For local bush birds, Mount Ainslie, the Black Mountain Reserve and the Cotter Reserve on the Murrumbidgee River are convenient localities. The Black Mountain list of about 120 species includes the Yellow-tufted Honeyeater, Olive-backed Oriole, Western Warbler, Hooded Robin and Crescent Honeyeater.

Tidbinbilla Fauna Reserve, about 35 km from Canberra via the Monaro Highway, across ridges and spurs of the eastern side of the Brindabella Range, has forested areas with fern gullies that are the habitat of Superb Lyrebirds. Tracks within the reserve give easy access to these areas. Parts of the valley previously cleared have waterfowl enclosures where these birds can be viewed from hides.

A larger site, the Gudgenby Nature Reserve, 34 km south-west of Canberra via Tharwa, covers rough forested ranges adjoining the Kosciusko National Park. Habitats include grassy valleys, heathy swamps, alpine woodlands and alpine sphagnum bogs. Many of its higher peaks are snow-capped in winter. This reserve provides, within a short distance of Canberra, the habitats and birdlife of the greater alpine areas of the Snowy Mountains, with peaks to 1829 m on its eastern side. Birds that could be found here or at Tidbinbilla are the Wonga Pigeon, Yellow-tailed Black-Cockatoo, Gang-gang Cockatoo, Australian King-Parrot, Powerful Owl, Superb Lyrebird, Olive Whistler, Superb Fairy-wren, Pilotbird, Satin Flycatcher and Rose Robin.

In complete contrast to the mountainous sites to the south-west of Canberra, Lake George beside the Federal Highway 30 km north-east of Canberra is a great expanse of shallow water, or sometimes of dry lakebed. The value of the lake as a birding area will depend upon seasonal conditions, but with around 190 species recorded here, including Great Crested Grebe and Freckled Duck, it can be a bird site of considerable interest.

Kosciusko National Park provides an example of alpine habitat and its birdlife. Its high, glaciated plateau has extensive winter snowfields which causes some birds, including the Flame Robin, to move to lower country for the winter months.

The vegetation is of alpine woodland and meadow on the highest parts, wet and dry sclerophyll forests and woodland on the lower slopes. Bird sites of interest are the Lower Snowy River, Geehi, Yarrongobilly Caves, and the Tom Groggin area.

The Kosciusko birdlist of just over 200 species includes the Grey Goshawk, Gang-gang Cockatoo, Superb Lyrebird and Olive Whistler.

THE SOUTH-EAST CORNER

Croajingolong National Park extends along more than 100 km of Victoria's easternmost coast and at the border joins the Nadgee Nature Reserve in the extreme south-east corner of New

South Wales. It is accessible by a number of roads off the Princes Highway, to the coast at Mallacoota Inlet, Wingan Inlet and the mouth of the Thurra River.

The river estuaries are focal points of the park, the largest estuary being that of Mallacoota Inlet; farther west along the coast are the inlets or estuaries of the Wingan, Mueller, Thurra, Cann and Bemm rivers. Except for the roads into the inlets, most of the coast is accessible only to bushwalkers. But for bird observations, the estuaries and their vicinity provide a large number of species, with habitats of ocean and beaches, sheltered estuary and inlet waters, coastal heath and dune vegetation. Inland, along the various roads leading to the sea, is good bird habitat with both wet and dry sclerophyll forest and some patches of temperate rainforest.

This great diversity of habitat results in a birdlist for the park of almost 250 species. Among these are the Little Tern, White-bellied Sea-Eagle, Sooty and Pied oystercatchers, Ground Parrot, Southern Emu-wren, Striated Fieldwren, Eastern Bristlebird, Black-faced Monarch and Tawny-crowned Honeyeater. The RAOU Field Atlas list for the 1° block taking in the coast from Eden to Bemm River was of 278 species, 143 with breeding records.

Mallacoota Inlet provides a variety of good birding sites. Local bird sites include the west side of The Narrows between Top Lake and Bottom Lake, the coastal heathlands, and the rainforest of the Howe Range, reached via Harrison Creek at the north-west corner of the inlet. Camping facilities at Mallacoota are good.

On the New South Wales side of the border, Nadgee Nature Reserve and Ben Boyd National Park extend the protected coastline around the 'corner' to the east coast. Nadgee in particular has valuable bird habitat. Its broad expanses of heathlands, like the heaths right around this south-eastern coast, are often colourful with wildflowers. These heaths are a major refuge for the rare Ground Parrot and are used by many other heathland birds. Farther inland, along the Table and Coast ranges, are areas of rainforest and wet eucalypt forest with tree-fern undergrowth, where Superb Lyrebirds may be heard.

GIPPSLAND LAKES

The Gippsland Lakes area consists of a complex of inlets, coastal lakes and swamps, although in parts closely bordered by farmlands. The lakes have formed behind the great sweep of sand coast and dune of the Ninety Mile Beach, behind which is sheltered the long narrow Lake Reeve, and many other waterways including lakes Victoria, Wellington and Tyers.

Part of the complex of waterways near Lakes Entrance forms The Lakes National Park, while the coast near Orbost is within the Ewings Morass Game Reserve. There are also game reserves along Lake Tyers and at Dowds Morass beside Lake Wellington. These, and McLeods Morass Game Reserve south of Bairnsdale, are all usually good birding sites. Altogether there are some 43 000 ha under reservation and the lakes and swamps of the area regularly support an estimated 40 000–50 000 ducks, swans, coots and other waterfowl. About 17 500 waders use the lakes during summer. Lake Reeve alone has had wader counts of 9000 Red-necked Stints, 1000 Sharp-tailed Sandpipers, 1800 Curlew Sandpipers and 5000 Red Knots.

A swamp in this area supports nesting White-bellied Sea-Eagles and one of Victoria's two breeding colonies of Pied Cormorant. Where natural vegetation remains, it includes saltmarsh, swamp paperbark, tea-tree and coast banksia, with areas of forest country inland. Other interesting birds in the area are the Little Penguin, Brown Bittern, Buff-banded Rail and Azure Kingfisher.

Rotamah Island Bird Observatory, situated in the heart of the Gippsland Lakes, serves as a field study and visitor centre. Courses and workshops are held here from time to time on subjects mainly ornithological. The island has an area of 260 ha with samphire, coastal scrub and open forest. Enquiries should be directed to the Royal Australasian Ornithologists Union.

WILSONS PROMONTORY

This is a rugged promontory where a granite-domed range extends southwards into Bass Strait. Once an island, it is now connected to the mainland by a narrow neck of sand. The promontory is a national park, with superb scenery and walk trails through deep forested gullies to parts of the coast and hilltop lookouts.

The more exposed areas are mainly low dense coastal scrub and heath, with scattered taller shrubbery or stunted trees of banksia, hakea and casuarina; there is an abundance of wildflowers, making this habitat attractive to the birds that find nectar or insects around flowers. In the more sheltered valleys are forests, with some large trees of blue-gum, stringybark and peppermint. In a few places, where there is permanent seepage, the most sheltered valleys hold small patches of temperate rainforest. Some of the best bird sites are Oberon Bay, Whiskey Bay, Lilly Pilly Gully, the tracks to the lighthouse and Sealers Cove, and Millers Landing in Corner Inlet. Around the promontory, birds of shore and ocean are conspicuous; Silver Gull, Pacific Gull, Sooty Oystercatcher and Hooded Plover. The Crimson Rosella is abundant, and New Holland and Tawny-crowned honeyeaters common. Inconspicuous or scarce species recorded here are the Southern Emu-wren and Ground Parrot.

Between the hilly part of the promontory and the mainland, the almost landlocked Corner Inlet is an important wader site. Here, on more than 50 000 ha of habitat, are supported an estimated 29 000 waders including many of the uncommon species such as the Grey Plover, Bar-tailed Godwit, Red Knot and Great Knot. It has been estimated that around half the total population of the migratory waders wintering in Victoria use the Corner Inlet. In addition, the southern portion of the inlet supports about 2000 Chestnut Teal.

En route to Wilsons Promontory, a detour to Tarra Valley and Bulga national parks allows a study of birds of the mountain ash forests, where the Superb Lyrebird, Rose Robin, Pink Robin, Eastern Yellow Robin, Pilotbird, Golden Whistler, Olive Whistler, White-browed Scrubwren and Crescent Honeyeater occur. Also while travelling to or from Melbourne, a visit to the Coolart Reserve can provide a few hours or a full day of interest. At Coolart the main attraction is an area of reedy wetlands where a permanent hide has been constructed overlooking an area of open water where a large number of waterfowl and various other birds can be watched. The reserve, near Somers on the southern side of the Mornington Peninsula, is open Tuesday, Wednesday, Thursday and Sunday.

DANDENONG RANGES

Best-known of bird places near Melbourne is Sherbrooke Forest, about 48 km east of the city in the Dandenong Ranges. Sherbrooke is renowned for its population of Superb Lyrebirds, some of which are almost tame. They may be observed at almost any time of the year, but their powerful song and elaborate displays are most likely to be seen on winter mornings. Walking tracks wind through the tree-fern undergrowth beneath the tall gums of the forest.

PHILLIP ISLAND

Situated at the entrance to Western Port Bay, Phillip Island is well-known for its 'penguin parade', when large numbers of penguins come ashore watched by visitors. Waterbirds such as the Black-faced Cormorant, Short-tailed Shearwater, Royal Spoonbill and many others can be watched from points around the coast, including Observation Point, The Nobbies, and Rhyll Sanctuary.

At Rhyll Swamp the Fisheries and Wildlife Division has constructed a hide which allows birdwatchers to view swamp birdlife at close range. Species likely to be seen here are ibises, Royal Spoonbill, Blue-billed and Musk ducks, Grey and Chestnut teal.

Also in Western Port Bay, French Island has some of the last undamaged bushland in south-central Victoria. The large areas of tea-tree swamp, heathland and areas of mangroves support about 200 species of birds including many wetlands species. Wader surveys have shown Western Port to support about 10 000 waders during summer and around 10 000 swans and ducks. Other birds recorded have included the Orange-bellied Parrot, Lewin's Rail and White-bellied Sea-Eagle.

PORT PHILLIP BAY

This great body of water, so landlocked that it is like an inland sea, is almost encircled by sites of birdwatching potential. Port Phillip Bay and nearby areas have long been known to have a large variety of those birds dependent upon coastal wetlands and protected waters, to the extent that the area is of international significance for its great numbers of migratory waders, waterfowl and seabirds. In terms of the total number of waders using the area it ranks seventh on the list of Australian wader sites, with a peak usage of around 65 000 waders. Not only waders occur here in large numbers. The Werribee Sewage Farm eriodically supports tens of thousands of swans, Eurasian Coots and ducks on its ponds, irrigated grasslands and adjoining mudflats; once there were an estimated 15 000 Pink-eared Ducks there.

621 **GREEN CATBIRD** *Ailuroedus crassirostris*

Port Phillip Bay is also of national significance for the variety of species found there and the large concentrations of cormorants, Pied Oystercatchers, Banded Stilts, Red-necked Avocets, Great Crested Grebes, Straw-necked Ibises and Royal Spoonbills. The bay has also large numbers of seabirds, including shearwaters, and is visited by small numbers of albatrosses. Seven species of terns and three species of gulls feed over the shallow waters and roost in flocks around the shores.

The waders concentrate in a number of main areas of the bay: the Altona area at the north-west of the bay, the Werribee–Avalon area, the Geelong Saltworks area and the Swan Bay area. For waterfowl the most important areas are at Werribee, Point Wilson, Avalon, the Altona Saltworks and Swan Bay, while most other waterbirds are more widely scattered across the bay.

The rare Orange-bellied Parrot winters around the bay's coastal vegetation, mainly at Werribee, Point Wilson, Swan Bay and Swan Island. Other bird sites around the bay are the Mud Islands, Point Nepean and Lake Coonewarre Wildlife Reserve. The RAOU Field Atlas survey birdlist for the 1° block covering the Geelong environs and most of Port Phillip Bay totalled 316 species, 143 breeding.

610 **OLIVE-BACKED ORIOLE** *Oriolus sagittatus*

OTWAY RANGES

This lush outlier of the forested ranges of Gippsland, 150 km to the south-west, is an isolated wilderness island, separated from other wet forests by cleared and drier country. Its position, projecting into Bass Strait, together with its high ranges ensures a substantial and reliable rainfall allowing not only wet sclerophyll forests of tall blue-gums but also temperate rainforests of ancient and mossy Antarctic beech.

The isolation of the Otways has caused the absence of some birds that would usually be expected from such habitat: the Superb Lyrebird, Pilotbird, Large-billed Scrubwren and Lewin's Honeyeater. In addition to the forests, the Otway Ranges have areas of wet coastal heath where Southern Emu-wrens are common and both the scarce Rufous Bristlebird and Ground Parrot were recorded during the RAOU Field Atlas survey.

Birds of the Otway forests include the Grey Goshawk, Barking Owl and Rose Robin. Among the prime birdwatching sites around the ranges are the heathlands at Carlisle, Blanket Bay and Marengo, the Paradise Fern Gully and the Parker, Calder and Aire rivers.

LOWER GLENELG AND PORTLAND DISTRICT

The Discovery Bay coast and lower reaches of the Glenelg River are included in the national parks and conservation parks. There is some delightful scenery along the lower reaches of the Glenelg, and the long sweep of sandy beach at Discovery Bay is backed by the largest area of coastal sand-dune country in Victoria. The comparative isolation has allowed some rare species to find refuge, and the coast's exposure to westerly gales has occasionally led to the discovery of remains of rare oceanic birds on the beach.

This area is an important part of the habitat of the rare Rufous Bristlebird which inhabits heathlands close to the coast. The very rare Orange-bellied Parrot has also been recorded in the area. Other birds of special interest in the district are the Chestnut-rumped Heathwren, Southern Emu-wren and Beautiful Firetail.

The hinterland, although mostly cleared for farming, has some excellent bird sites including wetlands on the headwaters of the Glenelg River, which in its upper parts becomes the Wannon River. These include Bryan Swamp Game Reserve, Lake Linlithgow, east of Hamilton, Wannon Falls Reserve, Lake Bulrush and Lake Kennedy.

The RAOU Field Atlas survey, in the 1° block covering the coast for about 90 km east of the border, and the near hinterland and ocean, recorded 274 species of birds, 72 breeding.

BALLARAT DISTRICT

Although agricultural rather than wilderness district, Ballarat and its environs have retained considerable diversity of habitat and a large variety of birds. In many respects the opening up of the land may have increased the bird variety by allowing entry of birds of open habitats into the district, while most of the bushland species have been retained in surviving natural habitat.

Among the localities that usually have good birdlife are Lake Wendouree in Ballarat, with about 160 species including many waterbirds; the Clunes Swamp Game Reserve with lake and woodland, and over 140 species listed; Lake Goldsmith Game Reserve; the Flax Mill Swamp; and the various areas of forest such as that at Mount Beckworth, Fells Gully and Mount Cole State Forest. The Bird Observers Club has a reserve, Clarkesdale, in the district.

LAMINGTON BIRDWATCH

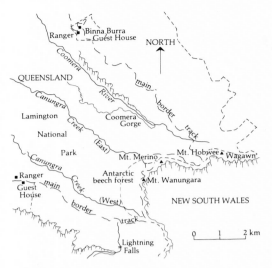

An encounter with the birds of Lamington's mountain-top rainforest should begin with the first glimmer of pre-dawn light, when the high ridges of the McPherson Range are often still enshrouded in the fine mists that have settled about the summit overnight. Already birds are welcoming the first signs of dawn with their calls as they stir on their roosts, restlessly waiting for the strengthening light to penetrate the rainforest canopy and enable them to begin their day.

A Logrunner is among the first of the birds to call. His loud and vigorous 'be-kweek-kweek-kwek-kwek-', as if chiding the rest of the forest birds into activity, is quickly answered by another Logrunner, probably from an adjoining territory. For the next half hour the rainforest quiet is well and truly broken as the Logrunners do battle with song, along an invisible line that marks the meeting of their territories. All around, the other birds greet the new day with their calls.

In Lamington National Park, atop the McPherson Range, a 21 km walking track connects the ranger stations, guest house and camping centres of Binna Burra to similar facilities at O'Reilly's lodge, and from each end of the track other tracks radiate out to places of interest. Where one of these tracks plunges into rainforest close by the national park camping grounds at O'Reilly's, a pre-dawn battle of Logrunner song had reportedly awoken campers every morning. A stealthy approach found two pairs of Logrunners, one on each side of the track, conducting a vigorous battle of song. The birds moved from one low vantage point — a log or rock — to the next and at each spot they paused and, with bill uplifted and throat pulsating, directed another torrent of sound at the rival pair across the track.

Many birds can be seen without venturing far from the clearings of picnic and camping grounds; the clearings create a change of habitat, bringing in birds, such as the Crimson Rosella, that are unlikely to be seen along tracks under rainforest canopy. At O'Reilly's, some of the birds of the surrounding rainforest have become sufficiently tame to venture out into the open or to the edges of the rainforest. Among them are the Australian Brush-turkey, Satin Bowerbird, Regent Bowerbird, and possibly a Paradise Riflebird in one of the larger trees at the edge of the rainforest.

There are many tracks into the rainforest, leading to scenic features such as waterfalls or to clifftops with spectacular views over the valleys to the coast of northern New South Wales. The Border Track, which links the two settlements, climbs steadily from either end until the rim of the highest parts of the Lamington Plateau is reached, in the vicinity of Mt Merino, Mt Wanungra, Mt Tooloona and Mt Bithongabel, all at an altitude of between 1160 and 1165 m.

An early start along the Border Track will find birdlife most active. Often the first hour or so will be misty as the wind pushes up the banks of mist that have collected overnight in ravines around the plateau, or sweeps clouds across the high plateau. In the first light the dark columns of the great rainforest trees fade upwards into the grey fog that drifts through their crowns, but in the dim forest on all sides the many birds are becoming active, their calls following those of the early-rising Logrunners. By the time birdwatchers are out along the trail the cloud or mist could be lifting, allowing several hours' birding along the track before the activity towards the middle of the day.

The Border Track climbs steadily through subtropical rainforest until along the highest parts of the route it enters temperate rainforest of mossy Antarctic beech. Here some of the trees may be more than a thousand years old, their trunks broken and decayed, many with limbs broken, dead or stripped of foliage by the strong winds of this exposed situation, but heavily festooned with mosses and very often enveloped in the mist and fine rain of the clouds.

But the beeches are not the only relics of the past. One of the most primitive of Australian birds, the Rufous Scrub-bird, occurs here. If calling, its loud, ringing notes could not be overlooked but a sighting can be very difficult for it manages always to keep beneath dense low undergrowth.

The Rufous Scrub-bird populations are remnants of much more widespread distribution when the climate was colder and wetter. The globular nest is well suited to such conditions.

Also occurring in the Antarctic beech forests is the Olive Whistler, which here is of a subspecies found almost exclusively in the isolated mountain-top patches of beech of the northern parts of this region.

A Rufous Scrub-bird would be the pinnacle of possible sightings but there are many other interesting and much more likely sightings along the Border Track. In contrast to the dawn calling of Logrunners, the deep throaty 'walk-to-work' whistles of the Noisy Pitta can be heard through much of the day.

The Green Catbird, even more than the Noisy Pitta, advertises its presence with loud calls — unmistakably cat-like wailings — but like many of the birds of the rainforest foliage it can be quite difficult to sight. Easier to see are the small birds of the middle and lower levels. Among those that might be encountered along any of the Lamington trails are the Black-faced Monarch, Rufous Fantail, Rose Robin, Pale-yellow Robin and Yellow-throated Scrubwren.

92 **SQUARE-TAILED KITE** *Lophoictinia isura*

MURRAY-DARLING REGION

The great rivers of the western plains of New South Wales are among the most significant features of the Australian interior. The Murray River and its major branches, the Darling, Lachlan and Murrumbidgee rivers, make up Australia's only really extensive interior river system and drain a basin that covers a substantial part of the Australian continent.

The Murray–Darling basin reaches well into the southern half of Queensland where tributaries of the Darling, Balonne, Condamine and Macintyre rivers spread across much of inland south-eastern Queensland. Farther inland another tributary, the Warrego River, extends far into central Queensland, with its headwaters in the Great Dividing Range close to Carnarvon Gorge National Park.

In north-eastern New South Wales the easternmost tributaries of the Darling have their origins on the gentle slopes of the New England Tableland, where the Great Dividing Range exceeds 1500 m altitude at several points between Armidale and Tenterfield, and often receives snowfalls. Snow, in far greater area and depth, also feeds the headwaters of the Murray and Murrumbidgee rivers, at the south-eastern corner of this region.

The Murray itself is the greatest of these rivers, rising in the Australian Alps and fed by melting snows. From these south-eastern mountains it flows in a north-westerly course, across country that becomes steadily drier as this river, like the Darling far to the north, winds its way across plains that slope very gradually from the coastal ranges into drier, and then into semi-desert country.

Once out into the semi-arid interior these rivers create their own distinctive local habitat, carrying an almost certain supply of water that maintains the fringing belt of river red-gum woodland. So isolated by dry surrounds is this riverine forest that some of its bird species are almost confined to it, or have the river as a place of retreat when conditions become too adverse beyond the tree-lined watercourses. The bird most tightly tied to this river system is the Yellow Rosella; it occurs nowhere else but the Murray and close tributaries, and adjacent timbered plains. To a lesser degree, the Superb Parrot is closely associated with the river and its adjoining woodlands.

But the tree-lined river channels are heavily used by a great many birds for food, water, shelter and nest sites. Most conspicuous are the Galahs, Little Corellas, Sulphur-crested Cockatoos, Cockatiels, Budgerigars, Mallee Ringnecks and Red-rumped Parrots. The big trees of the river channels provide high nesting sites for the birds of prey. Far up the wide Murray and Darling rivers can be seen the White-bellied Sea-Eagle, while the woodlands of the floodplains and of the north-eastern headwaters are the habitat of the uncommon Square-tailed Kite. The limbs of the highest trees provide nest sites for the Whistling Kite, Australian Hobby, Brown Falcon and Wedge-tailed Eagle, while a Peregrine Falcon may find a high hollow in one of the big old gums. The foliage of the rivergums provides for many small birds: honeyeaters, whistlers, weebills and pardalotes.

When heavy rain in the distant coastal catchments sends floodwaters down the Darling, or along the Murray from rain and melting snow on the Alps, the immense volume of water rises above the high banks in many places, spreading far out over the floodplains and filling lakes and swamps. Some of these, like the Macquarie Marshes in north-central New South Wales, are renowned for their waterbirds. Farther downstream, where the Darling flows through semi-desert country near Broken Hill, the Menindee Lakes are filled as part of the Darling's overflow. Similar wetlands occur on the Murrumbidgee and Murray, among them the swamps and lakes of the Mildura district, Hattah Lakes on the Murray near Swan Hill, and the Kerang wetlands.

Downstream from Mildura the Murray, now joined by the Darling, flows through mallee country as it enters South Australia and turns south towards Lake Alexandrina, and to the ocean at The Coorong. In Victoria the main block of mallee is south of the Murray, in the Sunset Country, towards the South Australian border at the Big Desert, Little Desert and Wyperfeld.

In South Australia the river continues through the Murray mallee district where some large blocks of mallee habitat remain within reserves. In these remnant islands of mallee habitat, often isolated by cleared land, are birds unique to the region, some found only in this mallee district and others that are found farther afield but are rare wherever they occur.

Bird species unique to this mallee district, or very nearly so, are the Red-lored Whistler and the Black-eared Miner; among distinctive

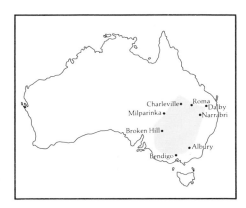

subspecies are the Mallee Emu-wren and Western Bristlebird. Almost endemic to the woodlands along the Murray, but sometimes feeding in adjoining mallee, is the Yellow Rosella (subspecies of Crimson Rosella).

The western and north-western parts of this region, whether of mallee or other vegetation, are the edge of the range of many birds of the interior. Consequently, for birdwatchers of the south-eastern corner of Australia, they are the closest places for seeing such birds. Among them are the Southern Scrub-robin, Chirruping Wedgebill, Chestnut and Cinnamon quail-thrushes, White-winged Fairy-wren, Striated Grasswren, Shy Heathwren, Redthroat, Slender-billed Thornbill, White-browed Treecreeper and Purple-gaped Honeyeater.

104 **MARSH HARRIER** *Circus aeruginosus*

104 **MARSH HARRIER** *Circus aeruginosus* Chicks

BIRDS OF THE MURRAY-DARLING REGION

92 SQUARE-TAILED KITE

Lophoictinia isura

A bird of open forests and woodlands, the Square-tailed Kite is most often recorded in the north-eastern parts of this region. It follows the woodland belt of the western slopes of the Great Dividing Range from eastern Queensland into northern New South Wales, along the extremities of the Darling, Warrego, Condamine, Moonie and Macintyre rivers.

The Square-tailed Kite is also sparsely scattered through the southern and western parts of the region, where the Darling and Murray rivers are bordered by belts of rivergum woodlands. Beyond this region, the Square-tailed Kite is most often seen in the south-west of Western Australia and sparingly through the tropical woodland areas of the far north and inland Queensland.

Except in the vicinity of the nest this is a solitary bird, usually seen circling low over the treetops, gliding slowly and easily, with an occasional leisurely flap of the broad wings. Because it keeps low the white of the forehead, face and crown are easily visible. The shape of the tail is not a reliable characteristic in separating it from other soaring raptors. Apart from the white on the head, the large broad wings, with fingered primaries widespread, are a helpful identifier. In flight the wings show dark-tipped primaries, with large white patches near the base of the primaries.

A typical sighting of a Square-tailed Kite was in a broad, shallow valley of low ranges where the hillsides carried forest, opening out in places to woodland with areas of treeless heath. The kite was sighted low in the valley, gliding below treetop level along the gently sloping sides, only occasionally giving a leisurely flap of the wings and perhaps gaining lift from a slight breeze up the valley. For the most part it concentrated on the open and sparsely treed heaths where it floated just 2–3 m above the dense low vegetation, its forward movement seeming almost down to walking pace against the breeze, and often circling back. At times the kite's path would take it into the woodland areas where it would thread its way among the trees or lift to glide just above.

During the breeding season the Square-tailed Kite preys almost entirely upon the nestlings and fledglings of small birds, and

presumably also at other times. During photography and observation of the nest on page 128, the female remained constantly on the nest with the single downy-white young, while the male hunted. On every observed visit of the male to the nest, the prey was a nestling or fledgling and sometimes the nest itself was brought in with the young, apparently of the Yellow-plumed Honeyeater, abundant in that locality, or possibly the nest of a Silvereye. The sharp-eyed female on the nest would always be aware of the male in the vicinity well before he could be located by observers. She greeted him with yelping calls and was answered by the male as he circled in low over the treetops. On these visits to the nest the male stayed but a few seconds, leaving the female to dismember the prey. She offered it to the young by holding small pieces at the tip of her bill; large young are reported to swallow small prey whole.

The Square-tailed Kite appears to make regular migratory movements, at least in some parts of Australia: south in spring, northwards in autumn.

▶ See also pages 82 121 *128* 129 136 138 *179* 183 245 273

104 MARSH HARRIER

Circus aeruginosus

The Marsh Harrier within Australia is remarkably widespread. Far from being restricted to coastal wetlands it occurs across the far north and in scattered localities through much of the interior, though it is absent from the sandy deserts and waterless limestone of the Nullarbor Plain. At the other extreme it can be seen patrolling rocky islets of Bass Strait.

Breeding records of the Marsh Harrier, however, come from southern Australia, the northern limit of breeding apparently being at about 30–31° south. As the Marsh Harrier is found north to the Kimberley, Top End, and Cape York regions, these birds must all be winter migrants from the south. In their northwards migration the Marsh Harriers reach southern New Guinea, where there is also a resident population. In Australia this raptor was listed as a species distinct from the almost world-wide Marsh Harrier, and known as the Swamp Harrier, *Circus approximans*, then comparatively recently changed to Marsh Harrier, *Circus aeruginosus*. It now appears that the earlier names, both common and scientific, will be used again for this harrier.

Whether known as Marsh Harrier or Swamp Harrier, the habitat of this bird is indicated by the name: it inhabits open wetlands, hunting over open water, reed-beds and surrounding grasslands. It will at times use tall crops which provide a habitat similar to that of reed-beds. When hunting, the harrier often flies low, quartering the reed-beds and occasionally dropping from sight among the reeds where it might be after frogs or rats. When keeping low the distinguishing white rump is visible, with binoculars, at a great distance. Over open water it often keeps higher, then swoops down with some speed at the slowest of the waterbirds, often the young of coots or ducks.

Among birds of prey, the Marsh Harrier has acquired a reputation for being very timid and likely to desert a nest that has been disturbed. On the other hand, it is a species not often observed closely, especially at the nest. For photographs of this species a hide was placed in water just over 1 m deep, at a distance of about 8 m, initially with intervening reeds left in place. Three precautions were taken: firstly, the young were several weeks of age before photographs were taken; secondly, the hide was put in place during the morning rather than the afternoon; and thirdly, the effect of this activity upon the birds was observed. A convenient hillside vantage point allowed an overview of the swamp from a distance of about 0.5 km.

When neither bird had returned to the young after a reasonable time, the hide was taken down and then re-erected two days later, 5 m farther back. On this second occasion the harrier, again watched from a distance, returned within the hour and stayed on the nest. If on the first occasion the hide had been put in place late in the day, and if the effect upon the Marsh Harrier had not been monitored, the nest might have been left unattended through the night, or perhaps even deserted.

After the first attempt at photography the harriers did not return, although a usually effective technique was used: two persons approaching the hide, one departing. The second and third attempts with the hide placed farther away, resulted in three photographs, after a total of 12 hours in the hide. For the fourth occasion there was an experimental change of tactics, after noting that the harrier did not appear to spend the night on the nest, with the young becoming larger. The swamp was entered at 4.30 am, in almost total darkness and without helpers to act as decoys. The difference in the behaviour of the Marsh Harriers was

remarkable. They arrived at the nest soon after sunrise and then made three more visits with food, all before 9.30 am. The harriers seemed much more at ease, their attention appearing to be directed towards the young rather than the hide, even though photographs were being taken using fill-in flash.

The dramatic change of behaviour by the birds, their earlier arrival, and the rapid succession of feedings compared with the lengthy waits when the hide was entered shortly after sunrise, suggested that this extremely wary bird is made very nervous by the sight of humans among the reeds, and this may be the cause of the slow return. By entering the hide in the pre-dawn darkness, when the young were several weeks of age, the problem was avoided.

Other bird photographers have noted that for this species the hide must be placed down-wind from the nest, suggesting that this bird has a strong sense of smell. At the nest mentioned above, no attention was paid to wind direction, but rather to finding a position causing least disturbance while obtaining a clear view; however, the prevailing easterly winds of November would probably have blown from hide to nest.

The prey brought in to the nest was mainly the introduced *Rattus rattus*, but also occasionally the young of the Eurasian Coots and various ducks.

▶ **See also pages** 82 83 *130* 137 139 142 151 153 161 163 172 183 224 242 244 276

124 PLAINS-WANDERER

Pedionomus torquatus

The Plains-wanderer is the sole species of a family unique to Australia. Its classification has been debated ever since its naming by Gould in 1840, for it is like the button-quails in appearance, and in that the female is the dominant and more colourful of the pair. But unlike the button-quails, which lack the hind toe, the Plains-wanderer has a hind toe like a true quail. As with the button-quails, the male incubates the eggs and tends the young. Its eggs and some aspects of its behaviour are wader-like, while its plumage is similar to that of the bustards. Consequently it is not linked to any of these families, but recognized as unique.

The Plains-wanderer is appropriately named, occupying grassy plains where it was once far more widespread and common. It is nomadic, breeding in times and places of heavier than usual rainfall. The food seems to consist of small grass

525 **SINGING HONEYEATER** *Lichenostomus virescens*

100 **WHITE-BELLIED SEA-EAGLE** *Haliaeetus leucogaster*

seeds, beetles and other insects.

The range of the Plains-wanderer has contracted. It used to be found over most of south-eastern Australia, from Victoria, southern and north-eastern South Australia, to central-eastern Queensland. Today it is more frequently seen in the Riverina district of New South Wales and north-central Victoria, with occasional sightings farther inland. There are also rare reports from eastern New South Wales. They are often seen around Deniliquin.

Plains-wanderers are usually seen in

52 **GREAT EGRET** *Egretta alba*

pairs or small family parties. They pause at frequent intervals to stand very upright, necks stretched vertically for the best view. When alarmed they may run, or even very rarely take flight, but a common reaction is to flatten themselves against the ground where the cryptic coloration and patterning of the plumage will make them hard to detect. Such is their faith in this concealment that they can occasionally be picked up while in this 'frozen' position. Any calls are soft, and useless for location.

For study purposes Plains-wanderers are usually located by spotlight at night, by driving across the paddocks sweeping the spotlight from side to side. Breeding groups of Plains-wanderers seem to be concentrated in relatively small, compact areas across the great expanse of the Riverina plains. These small areas are difficult to locate, and the birds, at night, are most active in grass taller than themselves.

▶ See also pages 131 138 282

189 AUSTRALIAN PRATINCOLE

Stiltia isabella

The Australian Pratincole is migratory; it travels to northern regions in winter, some birds going as far as Indonesia and New Guinea and returns in spring and summer to inland south-eastern Australia to breed. This bird is well adapted for life in arid environs. It occupies the arid and almost bare, flat, stony plains and claypans of the interior, using the shoreline of saltpans, lakes and dams as feeding areas. Nesting will also occur at such sites if the ground is gravelly or has a gibberstone surface. This is a gregarious species, seen in small loose flocks of 15–20 birds, occasionally to 50 near water. Breeding is usually loosely colonial, the distance between nests being from 50 to several hundred metres.

Usually the nesting sites have to be away from the water to obtain the preferred stony surface and scattering of very small shrubs, and may be as far as 2 km from water. Insects are the principal food, taken in a quick dash along the ground, or by leaping into the air, or in full flight. Even with the insect diet, the Australian Pratincole drinks often, and because it has salt-excreting glands can drink salt water.

Several aspects of behaviour have been observed which assist the pratincole to survive in the often very hot interior. It will sometimes stand near a very small bush or rock which will cast a shadow over its feet. It will also pant when very hot.

The chicks, when hatched, very soon find shelter in one of the small shrubs, where the adults then bring the food. These chicks are very difficult to find, thanks to the guile used by the adults and the disruptive patterning of the down; the true feathers begin to appear when the chicks are about three weeks old.

▶ See also pages *136* 137 138 173 220 290 298

124 **Plains-wanderer** *Pedionomus torquatus*
189 **Australian Pratincole** *Stiltia isabella*
244 **Long-billed Corella** *Cacatua tenuirostris*
261 **Superb Parrot** *Polytelis swainsonii*
271 **Yellow Rosella** (subspecies of Crimson Rosella) *Platycercus elegans flaveolus*
283 **Blue Bonnet** *Northiella haematogaster*
383 **Red-lored Whistler** *Pachycephala rufogularis*
423 **Hall's Babbler** *Pomatostomus hallii*
424 **Chestnut-crowned Babbler** *Pomatostomus ruficeps*
488 **Yellow Thornbill** *Acanthiza nana*
505 **Striped Honeyeater** *Plectorhyncha lanceolata*
515 **Black-eared Miner** *Manorina melanotis*
549 **Painted Honeyeater** *Grantiella picta*

247 **PINK COCKATOO** *Cacatua leadbeateri*

247 PINK COCKATOO

Cacatua leadbeateri

Throughout the dry inland regions that are usually its home, this beautiful cockatoo will for a long time be better known by the more distinctive name of Major Mitchell Cockatoo. A variety of country is utilized, the principal requirements being fresh surface water and trees with large hollows. The rivers and watercourses of inland Australia provide these needs, with the deeper river-bed pools often lingering months after the flowing of the watercourse, and old river red-gums having the large, deep hollows preferred by this and other cockatoos.

Out of the breeding season Pink Cockatoos may be seen in pairs or small parties, in the earlier part of the day, feeding on the ground or in seeding shrubs, often well away from the river. They go to water very early in the morning, late afternoon and occasionally at other times of the day. In the heat of the day the Pink Cockatoos are more likely to be amid the shady foliage of riverside gums.

When breeding, each pair of Pink Cockatoos requires a large territory of around 500 ha, which they rarely

leave. The size of the territory forces these cockatoos, unlike the communal Galahs, to spread out at wide intervals along the watercourses, severely limiting the number of nesting pairs, even where there are abundant hollows and plentiful food and water.

The Pink Cockatoo is a very conspicuous bird, with distinctive flight, when the deep pink of its underwings shows in contrast to the pale body plumage. Together with the peculiar quavering screech, this makes it obvious even when there are just one or two intermingled in a large flock of Galahs. In the vicinity of the nest it becomes much more wary and usually silent.

▶ See also pages *1* 137 138 139 164 184 185 219 220 231 312

261 SUPERB PARROT

Polytelis swainsonii

The Superb Parrot is very nearly confined to the Murray–Darling Region and probably does not breed outside that region. Its habitat is the river red-gum and other woodland which in the drier parts of its range fringe the river channels; but in the

eastern parts, where woodland is more widespread, it can be found much farther from the rivers. Within this restricted range the Superb Parrot is quite common. Flocks are often to be seen along the middle section of the Murrumbidgee River, between Darlington Point and Narrandera.

The Superb Parrot appears to remain in flocks throughout the year but in early spring the females disappear, presumably to incubate the eggs, leaving the flocks predominantly of males. After the breeding season the flocks break up into smaller parties, made up of several pairs and their fledged young.

These parrots are most likely to be seen feeding on the ground in the early morning and late afternoon, when they are quite approachable. The middle of the day is usually spent in shady foliage, the flocks occasionally breaking out from one tree to fly 100 m or so to another tree. The flight seems swift and easy, that impression heightened by the sleek silhouette of pointed backswept wings and long slender tail.

▶ See also pages 129 *133* 137 315

271 YELLOW ROSELLA
SUBSPECIES OF CRIMSON ROSELLA

Platycercus elegans flaveolus

The distribution of the Yellow Rosella follows the Murray and Murrumbidgee rivers and their tributaries; it is endemic, or very nearly so, to this region. The Yellow Rosella is principally a bird of the river red-gum margins of the river but follows these woodlands where in some places they spread out from the close vicinity of the river. It remains quite common within the restricted range and habitat. Feeding is on the ground, in shrubs, and amid the foliage of trees.

▶ See also pages 8 129 130 *133* 137 138 317

289 TURQUOISE PARROT

Neophema pulchella

Although the Turquoise Parrot is not unique to the Murray–Darling Region, this is where the greater part of its range falls. It favours the margins of woodlands alongside grassy clearings, farmlands with stands of trees, or timbered ridges surrounded by farmlands. It is quite common along the tablelands and western slopes of the Great Dividing Range in northern New South Wales, and in south-eastern Queensland.

The Turquoise Parrot is usually to

289 TURQUOISE PARROT *Neophema pulchella*

be found in pairs or small parties, occasionally in flocks of up to 25 or 30 birds, which for most of the morning and late afternoon feed in the grass; they will then allow a close approach. When in dry grass their green upper plumage is fairly conspicuous, but they are much less noticeable in green vegetation. When disturbed, or moving about, their flight is swift but light and fluttering; on landing the tail is spread showing conspicuous yellow feathers. The calls, high and metallic in flight with softer twitterings while feeding, are only likely to be heard at moderately close range. Convenient sites include, among national parks, the Warrumbungles and Cocoparra.

▶ See also pages 121 136 137 321

383 RED-LORED WHISTLER

Pachycephala rufogularis

The Red-lored Whistler is a bird of very narrow habitat preference. It not only requires mallee environs but also that which has one of several types of ground-cover, including low ground-cover with *Cassytha* creepers in north-western Victoria's Big Desert or, at Pulletop, in New South Wales, mallee with broombush and native pine. This latter population, well to the east of the present main population, has not been recorded for some years and may no longer exist. The range of this species has steadily contracted since it was discovered near Adelaide in 1839. This is largely due to the clearing of the mallee sandplains for agriculture.

Within its remnant mallee country the Red-lored Whistler is evidently quite rare. It is a solitary species, often quiet and easily missed. It does

however have a distinctive loud call of two drawn-out notes, the first a loud, clear, drawn-out whistle of increasing volume, the second abrupt. Out of the breeding season its calls may be restricted to some short, harsh 'chut-chut' sounds. The Red-lored Whistler is a shy and elusive bird, often feeding on or near the ground, usually under or near low cover. If disturbed, it tends to move away, flying some distance with strong, undulating flight.

Localities on record include the Big Desert and Sunset Country, Wyperfeld, Round Hill, the Waikerie area, and Cocoparra.

▶ See also pages 129 *133* 137 138 346

423 HALL'S BABBLER

Pomatostomus hallii

This babbler was not collected until 1963 when it was found at Tyrone, in the north-west of the Murray–Darling Region; its range extends into the adjoining Eastern Deserts Region. Hall's Babbler is found over a quite extensive tract of country west of Longreach, Blackall, Charleville and Cunnamulla, south to the Barrier Range and Mootwingie. Here it is widespread in mulga and other acacia scrublands with grassy understorey, open grassy eucalypt woodlands, and adjoining treeless spinifex country.

The behaviour of this species appears similar to that of other babblers. It is highly gregarious, the members of the group foraging in small, close-knit, noisy flocks of around five to 15 birds, roosting and breeding communally. Many examples of co-operative foraging have been observed, such as the mutual flushing of small insects from the understorey, the sharing of larger items of food, and feeding of incubating females by many members of a group.

This babbler could be mistaken for the White-browed Babbler except that the browns are darker and cover more of the underparts, where the white is constricted to a small bib. It is sedentary and common in localities of suitable habitat. A study site was beside the Eulo road, 35 km west of Cunnamulla.

▶ See also pages *133* 356

515 BLACK-EARED MINER

Manorina melanotis

The Black-eared Miner lacks clear-cut identifying characteristics so that separation of this species from the Yellow-throated Miner in the field is difficult. It does not have black on the

38 DARTER *Anhinga melanogaster*

129 BAILLON'S CRAKE *Porzana pusilla*

crown as does the Noisy Miner, and compared with the Yellow-throated Miner it is more uniformly grey along the upperparts, with a more extensive black facial patch which is broader over the ear-coverts. It is usually seen in mallee country around the junction of the borders of Victoria and its two neighbouring States.

The Black-eared Miner is largely confined to this region, thus overlapping the range of the Yellow-throated and occupying similar habitat so that the two species come into contact. It occurs in small and very localized colonies at sites including Wyperfeld and Hattah Lakes national parks.

▶ See also pages 129 *133* 138 377

BIRD PLACES OF THE MURRAY-DARLING REGION

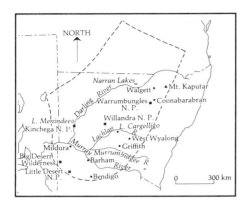

WARRUMBUNGLE RANGE AND PILLIGA SCRUB

Where the western slopes of the Great Dividing Range level out to the inland plains of northern New South Wales, the eroded volcanic peaks of the Warrumbungle Range are a dominating feature of the landscape. The effect of their high peaks and ridges upon the vegetation and animal life is significant. The shaded, moist valleys of the ranges have many of the plants normally associated with the higher rainfall areas much closer to the coast, making the Warrumbungles like an island of eastern habitat on the western plains. Other drier parts, often the north-western flanks of ranges, are more like the surrounding countryside.

The Warrumbungle Range's avifauna likewise has many species both of the dry inland and of the wetter eastern habitats. Birds of the interior and northern woodlands recorded here are the Crested Pigeon, Cockatiel, Mallee Ringneck, Black-eared Cuckoo, Spotted Nightjar, Red-backed Kingfisher, White-backed Swallow, Chestnut-rumped Thornbill, Crimson Chat, Hooded Robin, Singing Honeyeater, Spiny-cheeked Honeyeater, Yellow-throated Miner, Zebra Finch, White-winged Chough, Apostlebird and Little Woodswallow. On record also are some rare visitors from the interior: the Letter-winged Kite, Black Kite, Square-tailed Kite, Black Falcon and Grey Falcon.

Representatives of wetter regions, some found in cooler, wetter valleys of the park, are the Little Lorikeet, Australian King-Parrot, Crimson Rosella, Eastern Rosella, Turquoise Parrot, White-throated Treecreeper, Spotted Pardalote, Yellow-faced Honeyeater, White-naped Honeyeater and Red-browed Finch.

The attractiveness of the Warrumbungle National Park stems from its diverse birdlist and abundance of many of the species, and the scenic beauty of the setting in which these birds are seen. The network of walk tracks gives easy access to diverse habitats and reaches out to the best of the scenery. Tracks through good bird territory are the Spirey Creek trail to Hurleys campsite, the West Spirey Creek trail, and The Boulevard. The national park has camping grounds with necessary facilities.

To the north of the Warrumbungles, Mt Kaputar on the Nandewar Range offers similar environs, with volcanic peaks high enough to be snow-capped in winter. Situated 56 km north-east of Narrabri, it is centred upon an old volcanic peak where there are savannah woodlands of snow-gums and candlebark on the highest parts, and woodland or open forest on the slopes, with scrubby undergrowth. Some colourful local birds are the Australian King-Parrot, Crimson Rosella and Eastern Spinebill. Of special interest are sightings here of Grey Goshawk, Red-winged Parrot, Turquoise Parrot, Flame Robin and White-eared Honeyeater.

Pilliga Scrub Nature Reserve is situated across the Newell Highway about 40 km north of Coonabarabran. It is a large block of dry eucalypt forest with ironbark, yellow-box and various other eucalypts, wattle, casuarina and sandalwood. There are at least 123 bird species, among which are the Spotted Quail-thrush, Painted Button-quail, Square-tailed Kite, Powerful Owl, Speckled Warbler and Turquoise Parrot.

73 AUSTRALIAN SHELDUCK
Tadorna tadornoides

189 AUSTRALIAN PRATINCOLE *Stiltia isabella*

MACQUARIE MARSHES AND NARRAN LAKES

64 STRAW-NECKED IBIS
Threskiornis spinicollis

The Macquarie River, flowing north-east across the northern plains of New South Wales, spreads out into braided channels that form two extensive areas of swampland: the Southern and Northern Macquarie marshes. These make up a nature reserve of 18 000 ha.

The marshes have a diversity of habitat, with large lagoons of open water, clumps of cumbungi, areas of river red-gums that stand surrounded by water when the marshes are full, extensive reed-beds and, surrounding the lush wetlands, vast red-earth plains. In times of flood the water spreads out to link up with the many other creeks, forming a far more extensive wetlands area. The size and diversity of these wetlands makes them one of the most important within Australia.

A bird count covering 25 lagoons and other bird habitats within the southern half of the marshes found an estimated 10 000 birds of 36 species, covering most major bird families: grebes, cormorants, herons and egrets, spoonbills, the Brolga, Black Swan, Australian Pelican, and a great many species of ducks, plovers, terns and gulls. The northern marsh is equally large and rich in birdlife, and there are wetland areas also on private land.

The marshes support large breeding colonies, parts having hundreds of treetop nests of various egrets and spoonbills, Little Pied Cormorants and Little Black Cormorants, and huge numbers of nesting Straw-necked Ibises and Sacred Ibises. The marshes are not exclusively waterbird habitat, the treetops are often enlivened by the chatterings of Budgerigars and Red-rumped Parrots. Other birds of interest here are the Plumed Whistling-

Duck, Australian Pratincole, Glossy Ibis, Red-winged Parrot, Black-eared Cuckoo, Ground Cuckoo-shrike, Crimson Chat, White-winged Fairy-wren and Spotted Bowerbird. This site is about 80–100 km north of Warren, on the road following the west side of the river north to Carinda.

Also in northern New South Wales is another great swamp, but farther west, not as well known, and difficult of access, situated on the Narran River about 80 km west of Walgett. In the vicinity of its crossing from Queensland into New South Wales the Balonne River breaks into numerous channels, one of which, the Narran River, flows into the Terawah or Narran Lake. This is a vast wetland which spreads far wider when filled by floodwaters of Queensland rains. The lake covers some 35 km north to south, 15 km east to west, an area of more than 400 sq. km of lake channels, dense lignum clumps, areas of open water, and river red-gums standing in water.

When the lake is filled it has huge breeding colonies of Straw-necked Ibises and cormorants and large numbers of nesting Royal Spoonbills, Great Egrets, Little Egrets, Intermediate Egrets, Darters, Australian Pelicans and Rufous Night Herons. From the edge of the great swampland the intensity of birdlife is shown by the vast numbers of birds overhead, with formations of ibises, spoonbills, pelicans, cormorants and egrets. The RAOU Field Atlas survey recorded 222 species of birds, 125 breeding, for the 1° block centred upon the Macquarie Marshes.

Access requires the permission of the landowner, and the best time to visit is after there has been sufficient rain to bring this lake to life.

COCOPARRA NATIONAL PARK

The Cocoparra National Park and nearby Pulletop Nature Reserve conserve samples of the habitats of the Riverina district of New South Wales. Situated between the Lachlan and Murrumbidgee rivers about 20 km north-east of Griffith, Cocoparra covers hills with dry sclerophyll forest on the ridges and slopes, and areas of cypress pine on the wide valleys.

The birdlist of 125 or more species here and in the nearby small Pulletop Reserve includes the Malleefowl, Pink Cockatoo, Mallee Ringneck, Turquoise Parrot, Variegated Fairy-wren, Southern Scrub-robin, Black-backed Fairy-wren (subspecies of Splendid Fairy-wren), Yellow-plumed Honeyeater, Gilbert's Whistler,

137 **PURPLE SWAMP-HEN** *Porphyrio porphyrio*

Chestnut Quail-thrush, Shy Heathwren, Chestnut-rumped Thornbill, Spiny-cheeked Honeyeater and Black Honeyeater. The rare Red-lored Whistler also occurs here, but seems not to have been sighted in recent years.

LACHLAN RIVER WETLANDS

About 80 km north, on overflow channels of the Lachlan River, Lake Cargelligo, beside the small town of the same name, is set in an area of considerable birding potential. It is situated just south of the Lachlan River, about 100 km west of Condobolin. There are numerous lakes nearby, and the channels of the Lachlan River. Waterbirds are usually common, including Great Crested Grebe and Blue-billed Duck. There are also in this district the Australian Pratincole, Spotted Bowerbird, Australian Hobby, Glossy Black-Cockatoo, Superb Parrot, Ground Cuckoo-shrike and Orange Chat. Away from the river the vegetation is largely of mallee and native pine.

Lake Brewster, to the south-west, and Lake Cowal, to the east and south of Condobolin, could also be worth visiting. At Lake Cowal both the Royal and Yellow-billed spoonbills breed. While there are usually only a few hundred pairs of spoonbills, the colony of Straw-necked Ibis at Lake Cowal has many thousands of birds. Lake Tarrawong, about 40 km north of Oxley, has river red-gums interspersed with lignum and acacia. There have been occasional records of the Freckled Duck breeding here and at Merrimajeel Creek, about 50 km west of Booligal.

GEMMILS SWAMP

Gemmils Swamp is part of the overflow system of the Goulburn River, near Mooroopna in central Victoria; in addition to a swamp of 30 ha there is a timbered area of about 200 ha. The swamp is of interest for the large rookery of White Ibis and Straw-necked Ibis. The birdlist records sightings of about 143 species, including the Great Crested Grebe, Little Bittern, Royal and Yellow-billed spoonbills, Pink-eared Duck, Marsh Harrier, Australian Hobby, Buff-banded Rail, Masked Lapwing, Southern Boobook, Barn Owl, and a wide variety of passerine species.

BARMAH AND GULPA FORESTS

Along the Murray River near Deniliquin, between Cobram and Swan Hill, are vast areas of river red-gum forest. Along most parts of the rivers these trees are in a narrow belt but where the rivers regularly overflow their banks and flood large areas, they give rise to some extensive forests. Among these are Barmah, Gulpa, Werrai, Koondrook and Little Murray forests. Apart from the river red-gum forests, there are both transient and permanent swamps in the area, the latter with cumbungi, a dense vegetation favoured by breeding waterbirds; there is a large cumbungi swamp in Gulpa State Forest. Away from the river, the plains have grasses, boree trees and saltbush. The birdlist of this district includes the Great Crested Grebe, Spotted Harrier, Marsh Harrier, Black Falcon, Southern Boobook, Barn Owl, Pink Cockatoo, Long-billed Corella, Superb Parrot, Regent Parrot and Yellow Rosella.

Gulpa Island State Forest is one of the best bird sites in the district. It is reached by travelling about 32 km south of Deniliquin, then turning east at Gulpa Siding and taking the Hazelwood Track to the Edward River. The island is a large segment of forest between two branches of the Edward River, just north of their junction with the Murray. The area is primarily a red-gum forest of about 5000 ha but with some sand-hill areas vegetated with Murray pine and wattle. The birdlist for the forest is in excess of 134 species. The RAOU Field Atlas birdlist for the 1° block on the Murray River near Swan Hill recorded 262 species. Farther upstream on the Murray River, opposite the Victorian town of Cobram, near Barooga, between the Murray and the Mulwala Canal, are good birding areas at Cottadidda Forest, Lake Bonney, and Mulwala Canal.

102 **LITTLE EAGLE** *Hieraaetus morphnoides*

SUNRAYSIA AND RIVERLAND DISTRICTS

In the Sunraysia District of Victoria and the Riverland of South Australia the Murray River passes through extensive irrigated fruit-growing areas. The Murray, Darling, and their extensive anabranch systems commonly have wide river flats with many billabongs and vegetation of river red-gums, black-box, lignum and cumbungi.

Swamps near Dareton and Buronga result from drainage and irrigation water spilling over riverine flats. The vegetation is of cumbungi and reeds with low rank vegetation around the margins; the Dareton swamp covers about 11 ha. Other bird sites in the Sunraysia area are Kings Billabong, about 10 km south-east of Mildura on the Victorian side of the Murray, Ryans Swamp about 17 km south-west, Lake Cardross about 12 km south-south-west of Mildura, and the Murray River.

Hattah Lakes National Park, beside the Murray south of Mildura, provides camping facilities and walk tracks around the overflow lakes of the Murray. Many birds can be found by following prepared tracks among the rivergums, or out into the dry scrub; the birdlist for Hattah Lakes exceeds 200 species.

The Sunraysia birdlist, for the area within a 100 km radius of Mildura, stands at more than 260 species. Within that 100 km are habitats ranging from river and swamp to open, semi-arid plains. Among the birds are the Black Falcon, Letter-winged Kite, Black-breasted Buzzard, Square-tailed Kite, Plains-wanderer, Golden-headed Cisticola, Black-eared Miner, Red-lored Whistler, Gilbert's Whistler, Chestnut Quail-thrush, Mallee Emu-wren (a subspecies of the Rufous-crowned Emu-wren), Striated Grasswren, Australian Bustard, Bush Thick-knee, Inland Dotterel, Banded Stilt, Australian Pratincole, Ruff, Purple-crowned Lorikeet, Yellow Rosella (subspecies of Crimson Rosella), Red-backed Kingfisher, White-backed Swallow and the Australian Owlet-nightjar.

KINCHEGA AND WILLANDRA NATIONAL PARKS

Lakes on the overflow of the Darling River are the major feature of Kinchega. Around the two largest, Lake Menindee and Lake Cawndilla, are black-soil floodplains and areas of old red dunes with low scrubby vegetation. Along the Darling are the usual river red-gums and coolibahs.

Kinchega is dominated by the Darling River and its interconnecting overflow channels and lakes. These are filled when the river floods, and until the comparatively recent construction of levees and canals to retain the water, used to drain back into the river as the flood subsided.

The lakes are used as feeding and breeding areas for large numbers of waterbirds, especially of Australian Pelicans, Black Swans, and many species of ducks, cormorants and egrets. The total list is over 160 species, with, among the more interesting birds, the White-bellied Sea-Eagle, Brolga, Gull-billed Tern, Bush Thick-knee, Masked Lapwing, Spotted Harrier and Yellow Rosella (subspecies of Crimson Rosella).

The Willandra Lakes National Park, on the floodplains of the Lachlan River, has various riverine and semi-arid habitats which are used by at least 163 species, the total so far recorded. Water is available to the birds along approximately 60 km of creek frontage. During heavy rain the many billabongs and claypans fill, providing temporary wetlands used by the birds.

THE MALLEE

With the extensive clearing of the mallee sandplains of western and north-western Victoria, and adjoining mallee country in South Australia, a number of mallee reserves were established to retain samples of the mallee habitat. These include, in Victoria, the Pink Lakes State Park north of Linga and Underbool, Wyperfeld National Park north of Rainbow and Yaapeet and, on the border west of Wyperfeld, the Big Desert Wilderness. Farther south, between Dimboola and Nhill, reached via Kiata, the Little Desert National Park retains another sample of mallee country. In the adjoining mallee of South Australia, the large Ngarkat Conservation Park joins Victoria's Big Desert.

Best-known as sites for mallee birds, and most convenient for Victorian birdwatchers, are Wyperfeld and Little Desert national parks. Among the birds that are of special interest in the mallee are the Red-lored Whistler, the subspecies *leucogaster* of the Western Whipbird, the Mallee Emu-wren (subspecies of Rufous-crowned Emu-wren), and the Slender-billed Thornbill.

Differences between published

112 **MALLEEFOWL** *Leipoa ocellata*

birdlists — totals of around 120 species for Ngarkat, 213 each for Wyperfeld and Little Desert — probably reflect the amount of observation time expended at these places. Among the highlights of birdwatching in any of these places might be sightings of Malleefowl, Pink Cockatoo, Regent Parrot, Mulga Parrot, Gilbert's Whistler, Southern Scrub-robin, and Purple-gaped Honeyeater.

BENDIGO DISTRICT

The Bendigo district has a diversity of habitat that provides for a large and varied bird population. Among its vegetation types is that known as the Bendigo whipstick, one of the most southerly large occurrences of mallee in Victoria; some of this country is included in the Whipstick Forest Park, north of Bendigo. Elsewhere in the district are areas of eucalypt forest with understorey of heaths. Wetlands include Lake Cooper, a lake at Eppalock, and swamps to the north near Tandarra and Dingee.

This district appears to be the southern limit for many of the birds of the drier inland areas, such as the Spotted Nightjar, Gilbert's Whistler, Mallee Ringneck and Purple-gaped Honeyeater. It also has in its heavier forests birds typical of the south: the Rufous Fantail, Australian Ground-Thrush, and Pink and Rose robins. Honeyeaters are particularly abundant, and most are resident, including the Yellow-tufted and Black-chinned honeyeaters.

In this area occur both species of heathwren, the Shy Heathwren confined to mallee parts of the Whipstick Forest, and the Chestnut-rumped Heathwren restricted to heathy scrub in forests just south of Bendigo.

WARBY RANGES AND LAKE MOKOAN

The Warby Ranges are situated in north-eastern Victoria between Wangaratta and Benalla, north of the Hume Highway. Parts of the district are State forests. Lake Mokoan is a reservoir used for irrigation and recreation. The ranges, lake and surrounding plains have a birdlist of about 190 species. Among the most exciting of its birds are the Black Falcon, Peregrine Falcon, Australian Hobby, Satin Flycatcher and Crested Shrike-tit. The RAOU Field Atlas birdlist for the 1° block from the Murray River south to Mt Buffalo, and including the Warby Ranges, totalled 265 species, with 188 breeding.

WYPERFELD BIRDWATCH

The Wyperfeld mallee and its birds can be seen along walk trails, both short and lengthy. As an example, the Tyakil Walk extends a distance of 6 km return distance, covered in about three hours, depending on time taken to watch birds along the track. A nature trail leaflet is available at the start of the track, with commentary on track-side features corresponding to numbered markers. The Wyperfeld walks traverse areas of mallee and native cypress pine, passing some of the dry lakes and Outlet Creek which feeds the chain of dry lakes when the Wimmera River flows after unusually heavy rain.

Small mallee eucalypts, mainly the yellow mallee, dominate the vegetation. In some areas there are scrub cypress pine, tea-tree and banksia; spinifex and scattered small flowering shrubs make up the ground-cover. Parts of Wyperfeld have large old sand dunes, some rising as much as 45 m above the intervening flats and stabilized by spinifex and scattered shrubs. The creek and lake environs are dominated by the river red-gums, and some areas of black-box trees.

Probably the most important bird species in Wyperfeld is the Malleefowl, whose mallee habitat in much of the surrounding country has been destroyed, or has deteriorated to the extent that it cannot support the Malleefowl. Up to 14 years is required after fire before the habitat returns to a condition suitable for the successful rebuilding and use of the incubator mounds, as these require abundant old leaf- and twig-litter.

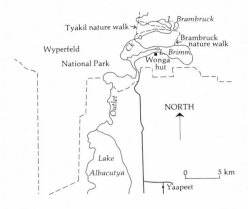

Most likely to be seen by the average birdwatcher wandering along Wyperfeld's tracks is a bird that is characteristic of the mallee country: the Regent Parrot. Its peculiar call, given while in flight, attracts attention and the swift-flying parrots may then be seen, their plumage gold and green, their silhouette graceful, long-tailed and with back-swept wings. Attractive though they may be, the Regent Parrots are possibly surpassed in beauty by another of the Wyperfeld birds, the Pink Cockatoo, probably still better known as the Major Mitchell. This bird's habit of holding out the wings momentarily upon alighting, and of spreading the richly coloured crest, displays the deeper pinks and reds that are usually hidden.

Wyperfeld's birdlist is considerably increased by waterbirds when these lakes hold water. Among the waterbirds to be seen at, or near, the lakes are the Rufous Night Heron, Pacific Heron, a variety of ducks, and the Marsh Harrier.

262 **REGENT PARROT** *Polytelis anthopeplus*

70 **BLACK SWAN** *Cygnus atratus*

TASMANIAN REGION

Tasmania is mountainous almost throughout, particularly in the west, with many ranges reaching 900–1200 m, and some to nearly 1600 m. The island has had a number of periods of separation and alternating connection with the mainland. Sea levels dropped by 100 m during the last glaciation, around 70 000 to 18 000 years ago, then rose until about 8000 years ago the sea was almost at its present level.

Today Bass Strait separates Tasmania from the mainland by a distance of 140 nautical miles, but the effective distance is reduced by King, Flinders and many smaller islands which can act as resting points for migrating birds.

Rainfall is much higher on the west coast, total precipitation reaching 3000 mm annually; the lowest rainfall is in the central and eastern parts at 450 mm. Because of the great range of topography and rainfall there is a diversity of vegetation. Temperate rainforest occurs extensively across the western half of Tasmania, and also in an isolated area in the north-east, at altitudes from sea level to 900 m, wherever rainfall exceeds around 1200 mm. On the mainland of Australia the occurrence of temperate rainforest is confined to small remnant mountain-top patches, so the presence of this habitat in large areas is unique to Tasmania.

Wet sclerophyll forests occur between the rainforests and the more extensive dry forests, with some very large trees, often between 60 and 90 m tall, but spaced sufficiently to allow light to reach a substorey of smaller trees and shrubbery. The dry sclerophyll forests are the dominant vegetation of the eastern half of Tasmania and have a low scrubby undergrowth layer. On the central plains of the midlands, savannah woodlands have plains of native grasses with scattered trees. Heathlands, with a low dense layer of a great variety of shrubs, occur mainly on poorer coastal soils of the north, east and west, extending well inland in places.

The vegetation is in many places zoned by altitude and aspect. With a climate of warm summer sun, and gales, snow and heavy rain for a large part of the year, the effect of aspect can be considerable. The northern slopes of the ranges and steep valleys are exposed to greater intensity of sunlight so that floristically they are quite different from the shadowy, colder and wetter southern slopes, giving a mosaic of habitats through the more mountainous areas. Within the rainforests and the wet eucalypt forests the gullies and steep southern slopes provide a distinctive habitat, usually centred upon a permanent creek, heavily screened and further shaded with tall tree-ferns, sassafras trees or, at higher altitudes, Antarctic beech. Some birds, such as the endemic Scrubtit, have become specialized in the use of such situations.

These Tasmanian forests are lacking in any significant amount of soft fruits that would be used by birds, though the massed blossoming of the eucalypts provides an abundant source of nectar and of insects attracted to the flowers: a food source utilized by parrots, lorikeets and the passerine honeyeaters. The time of heavy flowering of forests varies, depending upon the flowering seasons of their dominant eucalypt species, and other seasonal factors, so that the movements of most of these birds, their occurrence and breeding, likewise can be very erratic.

The abundant seed crop of the island's eucalypt forests seems to be exploited by only one species, the Green Rosella, in contrast to a much wider variety of arboreal seed-eaters on the mainland. The Green Rosella is, however, found throughout Tasmania and is one of its most abundant species.

The great eucalypt forests, especially the ribbon-barked and fibrous-barked species, have in their crevices and beneath strips and flakes of bark, a food supply for birds in the form of small invertebrates which shelter in these crevices. Here an especially interesting adaptation of the birds is evident. With the bark-foraging Varied Sittella and the treecreepers absent from the island, their role has been taken over by several of the honeyeaters. The Strong-billed Honeyeater in particular forages on the bark like a treecreeper, prising into the crevices with its distinctly heavier bill.

Relatively few bird species are common in the cold, wet, high mountain habitats, although these cover a considerable part of the island. This is apparently due to a generally much lower food supply being available. The temperate rainforests, particularly the Antarctic beech forests, are poor in birdlife with relatively few species common, among them the Pink Robin, Australian Ground-Thrush, Scrubtit, Tasmanian Thornbill and White-browed Scrubwren. On the summits of moorlands and alpine woodland there are even fewer species that appear commonly or regularly, among them the Pipit,

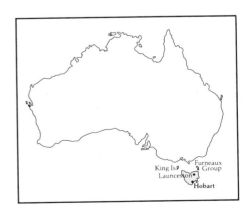

the Peregrine Falcon and the Flame Robin. The wet button-grass sedgelands, mainly around the coastal south-west, do not have a great variety of birds. But for several it is a vital habitat, being the only breeding grounds for the extremely rare Orange-bellied Parrot and the uncommon Ground Parrot. In Tasmania, as a general rule, the number of bird species decreases at higher altitudes and in very cold and wet environs.

At least 21 species of Tasmania's birds migrate to the mainland for the winter, and for about half of these, almost the entire population departs. Among them are the Marsh Harrier, Swift Parrot, Orange-bellied Parrot, Welcome Swallow, Tree Martin, seven species of cuckoos, the Satin Flycatcher, Black-faced Cuckoo-shrike and four species of woodswallows.

As well as this northwards migration to escape the quite severe Tasmanian winters, there is also an altitudinal migration by a number of species that in summer breed in the extensive mountain forests and descend to the lowlands for the winter: the Black Currawong, Flame Robin and Crescent Honeyeater.

Tasmania, compared with the nearest part of the mainland, Victoria, has only about two-thirds the number of species. Several families are missing: the lyrebirds, bee-eaters, sittellas, treecreepers, choughs, magpie-larks and bowerbirds. In total there are about 70 species of the south-eastern mainland that do not reach Tasmania, otherwise the structure of the island's avifauna is basically similar.

On present classifications Tasmania has about 12 endemic species, including those that breed only on the island but migrate to the mainland. These are the Tasmanian Native-hen, Swift Parrot, Green Rosella, Orange-bellied Parrot, Dusky Robin, Scrubtit, Tasmanian Thornbill, Yellow Wattlebird, Yellow-throated Honeyeater, Black-headed Honeyeater, Strong-billed Honeyeater and Forty-spotted Pardalote. This number of endemic species is high compared with other large continental islands.

72 CAPE BARREN GOOSE *Cereopsis novaehollandiae*

BIRDS OF THE TASMANIAN REGION

134 TASMANIAN NATIVE-HEN

Gallinula mortierii

The Tasmanian Native-hen is probably the most easily seen of the endemic birds of the island. It ranges from coasts to highlands but is absent from the heaths and very wet forested mountains of most of western Tasmania. Its preference is for reedy margins of swamps and creeks where there are grassy clearings nearby, providing open feeding on pasture but with dense vegetation for protective cover. It may be seen also on damp river flats, the margins of lagoons and the damp pasture of cleared land where there are creek thickets for shelter.

Although by nature very shy, the Tasmanian Native-hen is common in some situations and will almost certainly be seen by visitors to Cradle Mountain and other national parks. It frequents the camping area at Lake St Clair, where it has both lawns and dense reedy cover close at hand; it may also be seen at Waldheim. In Hobart it has been seen along the waterfront and occasionally visits some suburban gardens. Although it can be seen during the day in places where it is semi-tame and feels secure, this native-hen is most active at night; the loud rasping cry when taken up by many birds of a flock can make the nights near their swamps quite noisy.

Although lacking webbed feet, it not only swims but often submerges and will sometimes swim underwater from bank to bank when crossing narrow waterways. The Tasmanian Native-hen is almost flightless, though it is able to run very fast, with additional bursts of speed given by the short wings lifting it into the air sufficiently to clear obstacles in its path.

▶ See also pages 151 152 284

268 SWIFT PARROT

Lathamus discolor

Although not confined to Tasmania, the Swift Parrot breeds only on that island. Its migration has been mapped out in some detail. Nesting activities begin around the end of September, with egg-laying in October and November. The Swift Parrot is a gregarious species and this trait carries into the breeding so that there are often many pairs nesting in places where there is a strong nectar flow in surrounding forests or woodlands. The breeding range is eastern and central Tasmania, where it uses hollows not only of forest trees but also trees of woodland, partly cleared farmland and the suburbs of towns and cities.

By January the harsh begging cries of young Swift Parrots is a common sound of the Tasmanian bush, and the birds begin occupying the forests of western Tasmania. About this time some birds cross Bass Strait and the mainland sightings begin, in southern Victoria and South Australia, in February. The bulk of the population has migrated to the mainland by May,

134 TASMANIAN NATIVE-HEN
Gallinula mortierii

while in Tasmania the numbers are noticeably fewer after March and usually there are none to be found by May. The return south to the Tasmanian breeding grounds occurs around September. On Flinders and King islands in Bass Strait, Swift Parrots appear to be recorded only as migrants.

On the mainland the concentration of Swift Parrots seems to be in southern and central Victoria, but in some years they travel much farther, to south-eastern Queensland and the Mount Lofty Ranges of South Australia. The movements of the parrot are governed by the flowering of the eucalypt forests and woodlands, the birds appearing in greatest numbers where the eucalypts are flowering most profusely. As heavy flowerings of eucalypts is irregular, the Swift Parrots do not usually invade the same district in large numbers two years in succession.

Swift Parrots are almost always in small flocks, dashing overhead or feeding at flowers in the crowns of trees, where they take not only nectar but also pollen and lerp. They are very noisy and not likely to be missed if in a district in numbers. Their high-pitched, clinking calls, quite distinctive from the screechings of lorikeets, are given most strongly when the birds take off and while in flight overhead; feeding is usually accompanied by more subdued chattering. When they are feeding, Swift Parrots are restlessly active.

▶ **See also pages** *145* 150 151 152 156 316–17

270 GREEN ROSELLA

Platycercus caledonicus

The Green Rosella occurs throughout the Tasmanian Region, including King and Flinders islands, but does not occur on the Australian mainland. It is abundant, being one of the most commonly recorded birds in the region, and appears to be sedentary or only locally nomadic out of the breeding season.

Eucalypt forests form the principal and breeding habitat for the Green Rosella, but it also visits heathlands where there are stands of trees, and rainforests, timbered farmlands, orchards and gardens. Rainforest is also used when breeding, if only rarely. Green Rosellas have been reported feeding young at a nest in a hollow of an Antarctic beech in pure rainforest in north-western Tasmania.

The Green Rosella tolerates extremely cold, wet conditions, being present on Mount Wellington and in

western coastal rainforest through the winter. A wide range of food is taken including seeds of trees, shrubs and grasses; native and introduced fruit; and blossoms and insects.

Although their greenish plumage makes them inconspicuous among high foliage, the yellow underparts are most noticeable when the birds are on an exposed perch or in flight. The Green Rosella is noisy and attention is usually drawn to the calls before the birds are sighted.

▶ **See also pages** 141 142 *145* 151 152 317

288 ORANGE-BELLIED PARROT

Neophema chrysogaster

The Orange-bellied Parrot is one of Australia's rarest birds. With fewer

than 200 individual birds remaining, it is very much an endangered species. It seems that the population was considerably larger before the turn of the century and it is thought that the decline in numbers may be due to habitat loss because of the destruction of coastal vegetation, disturbance of coastal areas, and trapping for aviculture.

The breeding range of the Orange-bellied Parrot is confined to a small part of coastal south-western Tasmania: the sedgelands from just south of Macquarie Harbour to Louisa Bay, with most of the birds using the extreme south-west corner around Port Davey and Bathurst Harbour. The habitat here consists of extensive and in parts swampy sedgeland plains. Scattered throughout this area are

324 **LAUGHING KOOKABURRA** *Dacelo novaeguineae*

3 GREAT CRESTED GREBE *Podiceps cristatus*

small stands of forest, and most of the rivers and creeks are lined with trees. When feeding in this habitat the parrots prefer sedge areas that have been burned seven to 12 years ago.

Breeding activity begins in October with selection of nest sites, usually in the hollow branches of *Eucalyptus nitida* trees. Pairs that have nested successfully use the same hollow again in following years. After the young have fledged and are flying strongly in March and April, the Orange-bellied Parrots make their way gradually up the western coast of Tasmania to islands of the Hunter Group, then to King Island and the coasts of Victoria and South Australia.

The mainland wintering range extends from Jack Smith Lake on the Gippsland coast east of Wilsons Promontory, westwards around the coast to The Coorong, with rare sightings on the coast of Gulf St Vincent.

Port Phillip Bay is now the most important area for the Orange-bellied Parrot during its winter stay on the mainland, and in particular Point Wilson, on the western side of the bay. In some years over 70 of these rare birds, probably representing more than one-third of the population of the species, are on these patches of saltmarsh. Other sites in the bay are Swan Island, Swan Bay and Freshwater Lake. Elsewhere along the Victorian coast the Orange-bellied Parrots utilize saltmarsh and heath at Breamlea on the Bellarine Peninsula, French Island and Jack Smith Lake east of Wilsons Promontory.

About one-third of the population, 40 to 60 birds, use the South Australian coast. The birds are scattered in small groups between Nelson and The Coorong and feed on the dune plants not far from the high-tide line. The Orange-bellied Parrots return to their breeding grounds in Tasmania about October, certainly in smaller numbers than when they left the island in the autumn.

There have never been more than 130 Orange-bellied Parrots accounted for at any one time. When the birds leave Tasmania for their mainland wintering grounds there may be as many as 200, including perhaps 70 juveniles from the nesting just completed. During the journey across Bass Strait, and back again, the mortality rate is high, especially among the young birds, due to predators such as the Peregrine Falcon, leaving perhaps just 100 birds surviving. If their breeding is successful and 60 to 70 young are fledged, the year's losses will be recovered. In balance is the survival of

the species, which at present appears to be just holding its own though it remains in a precarious position. For mainland birdwatchers the species would best be seen at its summer feeding grounds, rather than disturbing the birds in their Tasmanian breeding grounds.

▶ **See also pages** 125 126 142 143 152 163 321

22	**Fairy Prion** *Pachyptila turtur*	
26	**Sooty Shearwater** *Puffinus griseus*	
27	**Short-tailed Shearwater** *Puffinus tenuirostris*	
32	**Common Diving-Petrel** *Pelecanoides urinatrix*	
126	**Lewin's Rail** *Rallus pectoralis*	
195	**Kelp Gull** *Larus dominicanus*	
202	**White-fronted Tern** *Sterna striata*	
268	**Swift Parrot** *Lathamus discolor*	
270	**Green Rosella** *Platycercus caledonicus*	
288	**Orange-bellied Parrot** *Neophema chrysogaster*	
644	**Forest Raven** *Corvus tasmanicus*	

3 SOUTHERN EMU-WREN *Stipiturus malachurus*
Top: *Male* Bottom: *Female*

363 PINK ROBIN

Petroica rodinogaster

Tasmania is a stronghold of the Pink Robin, with breeding throughout the island. On mainland Australia breeding is confined to some extreme south-eastern alpine areas and the high rainfall coastal ranges.

Male Pink Robins appear to remain throughout the year in their territories, which are usually in the damp fern gullies of rainforests and eucalypt forests. There is a dispersal in autumn and winter to open habitats and lower altitudes, but mostly of 'brown birds', the immatures and perhaps females. The fully coloured males are best sought in the fern gullies of the forests.

▶ **See also pages** 124 139 141 *147* 151 152 153 341

368 DUSKY ROBIN

Melanodryas vittata

The dull grey-brown Dusky Robin is endemic to the Tasmanian Region where it is common in most districts and on the Bass Strait islands. It is closely related to the Hooded Robin, these two making up the genus *Melanodryas*. While the adult plumage of the Dusky Robin differs greatly from the crisp black-and-white of the Hooded Robin, they have similarities of behaviour, calls, eggs, nests and ecology.

The distribution of the Dusky Robin throughout Tasmania and the offshore islands reflects the ability of this species to occupy a wide range of habitats and colonize new areas, including cleared farmlands and country regenerating after fire. Otherwise it seems sedentary, pairs remaining within the same territories and sometimes nesting in the same shrub several years in succession.

The Dusky Robin perches motionless on stumps, posts or low branches in forest clearings or open scrub, sometimes in open country, and is inconspicuous until it drops to the ground or flies to another perch. During the nesting season its presence is often revealed by the melancholy 'choowee, cheweeer'.

▶ **See also pages** 142 *147* 151 152 342–3

382 OLIVE WHISTLER

Pachycephala olivacea

A study of Olive Whistlers at Kosciusko National Park showed it to have 10 different song-types in three localities within the park, where populations are isolated from each other by higher alpine ridges. It has

131 **SPOTLESS CRAKE** *Porzana tabuensis*

also been found that the Snowy Mountains Olive Whistlers, the isolated population of Olive Whistlers in the Otway Ranges of southern Victoria, and the northern subspecies around the McPherson Range have quite different territorial songs. In Tasmania the Olive Whistler has a song similar to the southern mainland birds, but some variations would be expected. The sweet and plaintive notes of the Olive Whistler are among the most beautiful whistler songs and are heard to best advantage during the spring breeding season. The song is a repeated, prolonged and melodious 'cheer-weet', 'whip-oo-will', and a sharp whipcrack.

Olive Whistlers remain in permanently mated pairs, using the same dense forest breeding territories year after year, but appear to move into more open vegetation in winter. They are much more common in Tasmania than on the mainland and are found over almost the entire island, as well as Flinders and King islands.

▶ **See also pages** 121 123 124 127 *147* 151 152 163 346

463 SCRUBTIT

Sericornis magnus

The Scrubtit is almost exclusively an inhabitant of the damp and gloomy fern gully undergrowth beneath the eucalypt forests and rainforests in Tasmania, though on King Island it inhabits tea-tree scrub. This small, mostly brownish bird is found only in the Tasmanian Region, mainly down the heavily forested and wetter western half and in the hilly forested north-east.

Finding the quiet and unobtrusive Scrubtit can be complicated by the presence of three other small birds inhabiting these dense forest undergrowths: the endemic Tasmanian Thornbill, the Brown Thornbill, and an endemic subspecies of the White-browed Scrubwren. If a clear view can be obtained the Scrubtit is distinctive enough in appearance, with diagnostic white throat and white spot at the edge of each wing. The confusion arises from the similarity of its calls to those of the scrubwrens and thornbills, accentuated by the reluctance of the Scrubtit to be called up by squeaky imitations of its calls. In the very dense and gloomy fern-gully undergrowth much time can be expended in trying to sight the owner of calls, only to find that it is not the Scrubtit after all.

The Scrubtit can be found in the fern glade on the foot track to Russell Falls, in Mt Field National Park, and in areas of similar habitat in Cradle Mountain National Park; in north-eastern Tasmania it is among tree-ferns at Liffey Falls.

▶ See also pages 141 142 151 152 153 364

481 TASMANIAN THORNBILL

Acanthiza ewingii

Two confusingly similar thornbills occur in Tasmania: one is the endemic Tasmanian Thornbill, the other an endemic subspecies of the Brown Thornbill. The two birds can be difficult to separate in the field but fortunately have differing habitat preferences. The Tasmanian Thornbill keeps to the wet western forests, of both temperate rainforest and wet sclerophyll, and the Brown Thornbill to drier central and eastern forests, so that there is but slight overlap.

Even in localities where both occur they tend to separate themselves by habitat. Along the coast, where the Brown Thornbill occupies the heaths, the Tasmanian Thornbill uses the tea-tree swamps. Where the Tasmanian Thornbill does occur in dry eucalypt forests it is in creekside thickets; it is rarely seen in flocks. The slight differences between Brown and Tasmanian thornbills include, for the latter, a browner forehead without such obvious dark scallopings, flanks and undertail-coverts whiter and breast less obviously streaked.

▶ See also pages 141 142 150 151 152 369

502 YELLOW WATTLEBIRD

Anthochaera paradoxa

Tasmania's endemic Yellow Wattlebird is the largest of Australian honeyeaters, reaching 50 cm in length. It cannot be confused with any other bird in Tasmania, where the only other member of the genus is the Little Wattlebird. The Yellow Wattlebird is

363 Pink Robin *Petroica rodinogaster*
368 Dusky Robin *Melanodryas vittata*
382 Olive Whistler *Pachycephala olivacea*
463 Scrubtit *Sericornis magnus*
481 Tasmanian Thornbill *Acanthiza ewingii*
502 Yellow Wattlebird *Anthochaera paradoxa*
531 Yellow-throated Honeyeater *Lichenostomus flavicollis*
541 Strong-billed Honeyeater *Melithreptus validirostris*
545 Black-headed Honeyeater *Melithreptus affinis*
550 Crescent Honeyeater *Phylidonyris pyrrhoptera*
577 Forty-spotted Pardalote *Pardalotus quadragintus*
588 Beautiful Firetail *Emblema bella*

364 **FLAME ROBIN** *Petroica phoenicea*

found over most of Tasmania, in eucalypt forests, coastal heaths, orchards and suburban gardens, but is absent from the wet eucalypt forests, rainforests, button-grass plains and alpine habitats of the western parts of the island. Like the Red Wattlebird of the mainland, it can be recognized immediately by its calls: various harsh guttural gurgling sounds.

▶ See also pages 142 *147* 150 151 152 374

531 YELLOW-THROATED HONEYEATER

Lichenostomus flavicollis

This common endemic honeyeater is widespread in most habitats and parts of Tasmania and the Bass Strait islands. It occurs in wet and dry eucalypt forests, woodlands, heathlands, orchards and gardens, and from sea level to quite high altitudes though avoiding the bare mountain summits. It was the most commonly recorded of the Tasmanian honeyeaters in the RAOU Field Atlas survey.

The behaviour of this honeyeater attracts attention; it is quite noisy, aggressive towards other birds, and makes many brief, erratic flights.

▶ See also pages 142 *147* 150 151 152 153 380

541 STRONG-BILLED HONEYEATER

Melithreptus validirostris

The endemic Tasmanian Strong-billed Honeyeater is closely related to the mainland Black-chinned Honeyeater, but where the latter feeds among foliage, the Strong-billed Honeyeater finds food on the bark. The flowers of the trees are also visited but make up only a small part of the total foraging activity of this species. The extensive feeding upon bark puts the Strong-billed Honeyeater into the niche

occupied on the mainland by treecreepers, the Varied Sittella and the Crested Shrike-tit, which are all absent from Tasmania.

True to its name, this honeyeater does use its robust bill to forcefully probe and prise into bark crevices. It may be seen in pairs or noisy flocks working over the trunks and limbs; the noise and activity when a flock is working overhead often attract attention to this common species.

▶ See also pages 141 142 *147* 150 151 152 153

545 BLACK-HEADED HONEYEATER

Melithreptus affinis

This honeyeater, endemic to Tasmania and the Bass Strait islands, is common in eucalypt forests, where it is conspicuous, often in small flocks that travel briskly from tree to tree in search of insects. The flocks are noisy, with much calling as they work over the foliage. The all-black head without any white crescent around the nape, and the double-note whistling make identification easier.

Compared with the related Strong-billed Honeyeater, this species is smaller and has a preference for the dry sclerophyll country rather than the wetter forests favoured by the Strong-billed.

▶ See also pages 142 *147* 150 152 153 384

577 FORTY-SPOTTED PARDALOTE

Pardalotus quadragintus

The Forty-spotted Pardalote is not only a Tasmanian endemic but within Tasmania it is also extremely rare and is found only in a few small colonies along the south-eastern coast and several adjacent islands. The great interest in this species in recent years

has led to the discovery of several additional colonies and more will probably be found. Like other pardalotes it is very small, leaf-sized, making it inconspicuous in forest trees.

It appears that the Forty-spotted Pardalote was much more common and widespread over most of the eastern parts of Tasmania before about 1925. Certainly its present range is far more constricted than shown by early collections of the species and records of sightings, but the cause of the decline is still a matter for speculation. Recent research has revealed much more of the biology of this pardalote and lifted the estimates of total population; as a result some additional habitat reserves have been created.

All known colonies of the Forty-spotted Pardalote are in dry sclerophyll forests where the manna gum is the dominant tree and where most feeding occurs. Nests are almost always in mature trees or old stumps where hollows have had time to develop. It is possible that the removal of mature trees by forestry has reduced the available nest hollows to less than the number needed. The similar Spotted Pardalote nests in the ground and remains common.

The total number of Forty-spotted Pardalotes is estimated at about 1200 birds; estimates made several years ago were 850 and then 1000. The latest total results from a revised estimate from the North Bruny Island population from a maximum of 300 birds to about 500. The colony on North Bruny Island is now thought to equal or perhaps be larger than that of Maria Island, previously the largest population.

Although the total population has been revised upwards, this has been due to the discovery of new colonies and more accurate counting and it appears that the species may still be declining. The greatest effect is on the smallest colonies, which may result in localized extinctions.

The first requirement for seeing the Forty-spotted Pardalote is to go to a convenient site where it is known to occur. The call is a useful indicator of the bird's presence. It is a double-note in monotone, like the call of the common Spotted Pardalote but harsher and evidently not as loud. An observation published in 1958 commented on the 'lack of a distinctive call'. It seems, however, that while the call is similar to that of the Spotted Pardalote, those who have heard both can distinguish between them without difficulty. Although the Forty-spotted Pardalote seems inclined to remain silent for lengthy periods it is likely that it would call most persistently in the breeding season, from spring to early summer, and then be more easily found. But if infrequent calling is the norm for the species, it will be harder to pick up the sound and most of the very small birds seen amid the high foliage would have to be keenly watched. There is some evidence that after breeding the species is nomadic, perhaps only locally within the dry sclerophyll forests, which would account for the once-only sightings in some localities.

Most colonies are situated in or near the Derwent Estuary, Tasman Peninsula and nearby coasts and islands. Localities where it appears resident, and the estimated populations, are Maria Island National Park 500, North Bruny Island 500, Tinderbox Peninsula 75, Partridge Island 30, Channel district 30, Tasman Peninsula 20 to 40, Cape Queen Elizabeth 6 to 10, Mt Faulkner 2 to 20, and Flinders Island, uncertain.

▶ See also pages 142 *147* 150 152 392

641 BLACK CURRAWONG *Strepera fuliginosa*

641 BLACK CURRAWONG

Strepera fuliginosa

During the summer months Tasmania's Black Currawong keeps to the highlands, where its loud ringing musical calls are a part of the atmosphere of the mountain peaks and forested valleys. As winter sets in, flocks of a dozen or so make their way to the lowlands and more open coastal country. The Grey Currawong also occurs in Tasmania but it keeps mainly to the drier forests and woodlands of the centre and east.

The Black Currawong is closely related to the Pied Currawong of the Australian mainland but lacks the white rump of the mainland species; there has been some debate on the status of the Black Currawong, some considering it to be only a subspecies of the Pied Currawong.

▶ See also pages 142 151 152 408

BIRD PLACES OF THE TASMANIAN REGION

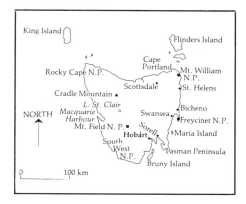

DERWENT ESTUARY

The southern coast of Tasmania lies at the southernmost limit of migration for the Northern Hemisphere waders that winter in Australia. Some important wader sites where these birds are to be found both regularly and in numbers are situated along the south-eastern coast, in the Derwent Estuary near Hobart, and at Pittwater.

Compared with some mainland wader sites the numbers recorded here are very small and it is unusual to find a flock of more than 500 individuals of a species. But there are certain aspects of migration that can best be studied here. Because Hobart is at the southern limit of migration there are no birds passing through to cause fluctuations of numbers, so that assessment of numbers, arrival and departure dates and other data gathering are simplified.

The wader sites fall into two main areas: the Derwent Estuary, south-east of Hobart, and Pittwater, near Sorell on the Tasman Highway about 20 km east of Hobart. Each of these areas has a number of recognized wader sites.

In the Derwent Estuary are Lauderdale, Clear Lagoon, Pipeclay Lagoon, Collins Springs and West Bay within Ralphs Bay. These are clustered on the peninsula separating the Derwent Estuary from Frederick Henry Bay. The habitats here are of mudflats, samphire flats, salt-water lagoons and tidal lagoons. At Clear Lagoon a 400 m diameter pool has sandy edges and is surrounded by samphire, but may dry out at times.

PITTWATER

At Pittwater, the Tasman Highway crosses an earthen causeway which has dammed the Oriolton Rivulet to form Oriolton Lagoon. The waters of the lagoon are brackish, at times with

exposed mudflats, and samphire surrounds. On the opposite, coastal side of the highway, close to Sorell, the shore of Pittwater has an extensive area of sand and mud, some sea-grass and samphire. On the western side of the Coal River Estuary, north of the causeway, Barilla Bay has tidal sand and mud, sea-grass and samphire.

In one period of study a total of 26 species of waders were recorded, of which seven were resident species, 18 species were Siberian migrants and one species was a trans-Tasman migrant.

Barilla Bay is probably the least disturbed of the wader locations in both Pittwater and the Derwent Estuary. It is situated on the north side of the Tasman Highway opposite Hobart Airport. The bay is regularly used by four species throughout the year: Pied Oystercatchers, Masked Lapwings, Red-capped Plovers and Red-necked Stints. Other species recorded include the Lesser Golden Plover, Double-banded Plover, Black-fronted Plover, Eastern Curlew, Greenshank, Curlew Sandpiper, and, rarely, Ruddy Turnstone, Whimbrel, Common Sandpiper, Bar-tailed Godwit, Red Knot, Sharp-tailed Sandpiper, Pectoral Sandpiper and Latham's Snipe.

HOBART AND ENVIRONS

Mount Wellington, dominating Hobart and with its foothills in the western suburbs, has been ravaged by fire on several occasions but still retains most of its bird species. Pottery Road gives access to the lower slopes at Lenah Valley, where there is dry sclerophyll open forest and woodland, with wet sclerophyll forest on the southern slopes and in the gullies — a good locality for bushland birds. This is a site where a number of the endemic honeyeaters can be seen close to the city, and where they are usually quite common. Alternatives with similar habitat are the Waterworks Reserve, several kilometres south-west of Hobart, reached via Huon Highway and Waterworks Road, and Risdon Brook.

TASMAN PENINSULA

Tasman Peninsula, an island but for the low, narrow neck of land joining it to the Tasmanian mainland, is best-known for the historic Port Arthur ruins but has birdwatching interest also. The peninsula is hilly, with spectacular cliffs, headlands and sheltered inlets. Settlement has occurred on a relatively small portion,

The Black Swans when nesting use numerous islands, points and marshes close to the lagoon, the important sites being Cockatoo, Cusicks, Sabinas, Tea-Tree and Bacon Point islands.

The inaccessibility of much of the area delayed appreciation of its importance for waders. There are 10 sites which have been identified as suitable for waders in Moulting Lagoon, including King Bay, Little Bay, Pelican Bay and Apsley Marshes. Apart from Moulting Lagoon, there are three nearby wader sites of interest: the mouth of the Meredith River at Swansea, Belmont Lagoon between the Tasman Highway and the Swan River, and the Friendly Beaches between the northern lagoon and the sea. In a marshy area surrounded by heathland near Coles Bay, Tawny-crowned Honeyeaters and Striated Fieldwrens can sometimes be found.

MARIA ISLAND

Hilly Maria Island has high cliffs on its northern and eastern coasts, giving some impressive scenery. Habitats include dense wet forest and fern gullies, drier open forest, coastal heaths and the shoreline; there are also some lagoons and swamps.

Maria Island is best-known for its colony of the rare and endangered Forty-spotted Pardalote but also has Cape Barren Geese and some of the Tasmanian endemics including Swift Parrot, Yellow Wattlebird, Yellow-throated, Strong-billed and Black-headed honeyeaters, and the Tasmanian Thornbill which appears to completely replace the Brown Thornbill on the island. This national park is accessible by ferry from Triabunna and in 1981 was used as an RAOU campout site, which suggests interesting birdwatching is available. Among other activities, such as a shorebird survey, mist-netting and banding, that group counted 150 Forty-spotted Pardalotes over the three days and saw four nests.

NORTH COAST

The estuary of the Tamar River at George Town attracts migrant waders, with numbers exceeding 400 around mid-September with the influx of birds spending the southern summer in Tasmania. The species recorded here include Lesser Golden Plover, Ruddy Turnstone, Eastern Curlew, Whimbrel, Grey-tailed Tattler, Greenshank, Bar-tailed Godwit, Red-necked Stint and Curlew Sandpiper.

70 **BLACK SWAN** *Cygnus atratus*
Top: *On nest* Bottom: *Cygnets*

the greater part being covered by forest, mostly dry sclerophyll but with some wet forest in the valleys and gullies.

The high cliffs at many points around the coast provide vantage points for observing seabirds. Most convenient are cliffs at Eaglehawk Neck, but those at Point Huay, which juts far out from the main line of the peninsula's western coast, could be very useful sites for recording the passing birds of the ocean. The walk of several kilometres from Fortescue Bay passes through attractive mixed forest and heath and is a good area for small bushland birds.

On the eastern side of Tasman Peninsula, woodland at Saltwater River is the site of a small colony of Forty-spotted Pardalotes.

MOULTING LAGOON

At the confluence of the Apsley and Swan rivers, midway down Tasmania's east coast and sheltered behind the high wall of ranges on Freycinet Peninsula, is the wide expanse of brackish water known as Moulting Lagoon. This 2800 ha area of waterways has extensive surrounding areas of saltmarsh, and on occasion carries more than 10 000 Black Swans.

Although the lagoons here have long been known for their huge concentrations of Black Swans, which use it for both moulting and nesting, they have importance also for other waterbirds. The site is so highly regarded that in 1982 the lagoon was nominated for inclusion on the list of Wetlands of International Importance.

Small numbers of some species remain here during the winter.

Towards the western end of Tasmania's north coast, Rocky Cape National Park has some rugged red-rock coastal scenery backed by an extensive area of coastal heathland and forest, with walking tracks along the coast and through the bushland. Camping and accommodation facilities are available at Boat Harbour and Sisters Beach, the latter also having, in the private Birdland Nature Park, aviaries of Australian birds, a photographic display of the local birds, and a nature trail.

MOUNT FIELD TO CRADLE MOUNTAIN

For birdlife of the mountains, the vicinity of Lake St Clair and Cradle Mountain are attractive birding areas, with about 76 species, including nine of the Tasmanian endemics. Many of the birds can be found within moderate walking distance of the camping areas during the summer months. Some, like the Tasmanian Native-hens and Black Currawongs at Lake St Clair camping grounds, are accustomed to people, allowing a close look at these two endemics.

Walking tracks pass through wet sclerophyll and Antarctic beech forests within a short distance of both places, giving a chance of sighting the Scrubtit and Tasmanian Thornbill, both common here. Other species that might be found are the Swift Parrot, Green Rosella, Flame, Pink and Dusky robins, Satin Flycatcher, Olive and Golden whistlers, Crescent, Yellow-throated and Strong-billed honeyeaters and the Yellow Wattlebird. Along the higher trails, on the alpine heathlands and herbfields above the treeline, the possible sightings are the Wedge-tailed Eagle, Peregrine Falcon, Green Rosella, Black Currawong, Forest Raven and Richard's Pipit.

Mount Field National Park is similar, on a smaller scale, and much closer to Hobart. It has dense wet forests on the lower parts, penetrated by the tracks to Russell Falls, where the Scrubtit and Tasmanian Thornbill might be found, and its higher levels and summit, accessible by road, are likely to have a birdlist similar to Cradle Mountain's alpine country, although the Peregrine Falcon has not been listed among this reserve's 53 species.

SCOTTSDALE DISTRICT

The north-eastern town of Scottsdale is a convenient centre from which to explore the birding sites of north-eastern Tasmania in all directions, from Launceston and the Tamar Estuary, to Cape Portland and Mount William National Park, and south to Moulting Lagoon.

A study conducted by the Tasmanian National Parks and Wildlife Service into the effects of the woodchip industry upon Tasmanian birds was carried out in dry sclerophyll forest near Woodsdale and Tooms Lake. For a very few species the open habitat was beneficial, but for a large list the clearfelling will seriously degrade the habitat for at least 10 years, and for 30 years for some birds.

The study concluded that woodchipping is causing a rapid decline in the amount of good quality east coast dry sclerophyll forest, and as these are areas which hold some of the largest communities of forest birds in Tasmania, many birds and attractive birding localities are being decimated by the woodchipping industry. There is little if any representative reservation of dry sclerophyll forest in eastern Tasmania. Most of Tasmania's large national parks are scenic areas, often not rich in birdlife.

Studies showed that regenerated forests will for a very long time contain greatly reduced numbers of cockatoos, parrots, robins, honeyeaters, button-quails and quail-thrushes. For species like the cockatoos which will not breed in regenerated forest for 80 to 100 years, a re-cutting time of less than that, as is most likely, would mean that those species will never breed in the woodchipped forests. Fortunately, Tasmania's endemic species are not threatened, except that the felling of forest used by the Swift Parrot must reduce their numbers.

THE NORTH-EAST CORNER

Mount William National Park, near the north-east corner of Tasmania, takes in the coast and hinterland between Cape Naturaliste and Eddystone Point. It covers a considerable expanse of granite headlands, beaches, coastal heathlands and ranges. Offshore, several groups of small islands are used by seabirds.

One of these clusters of islets is known as Georges Rocks. The group supports a fairly large number of interesting seabirds, none very rare, but the 12 species breeding here may be a higher number than for any other Tasmanian bird island. Of special interest is the Common Diving-Petrel,

194 **PACIFIC GULL** Larus pacificus

as there are no other known colonies nearby.

In a survey, 24 species of birds were found on the islands and another 11 over surrounding seas. Among the 12 breeding species are the Little Penguin, Short-tailed Shearwater, White-faced Storm-Petrel, Common Diving-Petrel, Black-faced Shag, and the Crested Tern with up to 200 pairs on nests.

Cape Portland is situated at the extreme north-east corner of Tasmania; on its eastern side is Little Mussel Roe Bay, a tidal basin into which flows the Little Mussel Roe River. The basin is covered to a shallow depth with each incoming tide. The basin is an important wintering area for moderate numbers of migratory waders, with about a dozen commonly sighted species.

Raptors which may be seen along this coast are the White-bellied Sea-Eagle, Brown Falcon, Marsh Harrier, Wedge-tailed Eagle, Peregrine Falcon, Australian Hobby, Australian Kestrel and Collared Sparrowhawk.

The birds of the locality include Cape Barren Geese, which can be seen along roads in the area. Oceanic birds can be seen from several headlands in the locality.

BICHENO DISTRICT

The area covered extends from Oxford to St Helens. The locality was the site of an RAOU field outing, based at Bicheno. Some of the areas visited for bird observations were Bicheno Lagoon, beaches and headlands; Diamond Island at Bicheno; Seymour Lagoon and environs; the Apsley River near its entry to the swamps of Moulting Lagoon; Swan River; St Helens; and Coles Bay in Freycinet National Park.

The birdlist compiled during the campout reached 106 species, including most of the Tasmanian a breeding species, is confined to the south-west button-grass but winters in mainland Australia. Also of interest in this habitat is the Ground Parrot, here quite common, the Southern Emu-wren and the Striated Fieldwren. The list of common breeding land birds for the south-west covers 41 species, with a further nine uncommon breeding species; in addition there are nearly 40 species of waterbirds and seabirds of the estuaries, inlets and open ocean. The RAOU Field Atlas survey recorded 138 species, 43 breeding, for the 1° block centred upon the lower Gordon River.

About 13 km south of the mainland, the Maatsuyker Island Group, which includes also De Witt and other islands, has long been isolated. It remains relatively undisturbed by man, and without introduced predators. A list of 24 species, including 14 land birds, has been compiled for Maatsuyker Island, including Grey Goshawk, Ground Parrot, Scrubtit, Tasmanian Thornbill, and Yellow-throated, Black-headed and Strong-billed honeyeaters.

FLINDERS ISLAND (BASS STRAIT)

Flinders Island is the largest of the Furneaux Group, in the eastern part of Bass Strait. The islands are interesting as resting points for birds migrating between Tasmania and the Australian mainland, and because some of their birds have been isolated here since the islands were separated from Tasmania by rising sea levels.

Parts of the island have been cleared but some areas of natural vegetation remain; most significant are Strzelecki National Park and nature reserves covering Logans Lagoon and the Chappell Islands. Strzelecki has rugged high peaks of granite, with scrub, dry eucalypt forest and patches of rainforest. Among the Tasmanian endemics found here are the Tasmanian Thornbill, Yellow-throated Honeyeater and Forty-spotted Pardalote, while there is a doubtful record of the Scrubtit.

Logans Lagoon at times carries a very large population of seabirds, waders both local and migratory, and waterbirds. Large numbers of Cape Barren Geese occur on the island and show a preference for the farm pastures. To minimize conflict, an area of 30 ha of pasture has been fenced off to provide for the geese. The Cape Barren Geese prefer to nest on smaller offshore islands. The birdlist for the group is of at least 161 species, covering island and oceanic species, 88 species breeding.

75 **PACIFIC BLACK DUCK** *Anas superciliosa*

endemics: the Tasmanian Native-hen, Green Rosella, Swift Parrot, Pink Robin, Dusky Robin, Olive Whistler, Tasmanian Thornbill, Scrubtit, Strong-billed, Yellow-throated, Black-headed and Tawny-crowned honeyeaters, Yellow Wattlebird, Beautiful Firetail and Black Currawong.

SOUTH-WEST WILDERNESS

The south-west of Tasmania is famed as a magnificent wilderness area, of spectacular mountain ridges, beautiful lakes, a wild and lonely coast and pristine forests. Its birdlife, in terms of number of species and abundance of birds, is disappointingly low, but it does have one bird (the Orange-bellied Parrot) which, as a breeding species, is confined to the area, and several of the birds endemic to Tasmania are quite common here.

The south-west, roughly the area from Macquarie Harbour to South East Cape, and inland to include

Frenchmans Cap, Mount Anne and Hartz Mountain, is dominated by cold wet habitats. Along the coast its extensive button-grass sedgelands are often wet or flooded, and the ranges carry temperate rainforest, wet eucalypt forest or, on their highest parts, subalpine woodland and alpine moorland. Today these habitats still cover most of the western third of the island.

Antarctic beech is a major component of these temperate rainforests and supports only about a dozen species that could be considered common.

The dense, gloomy, wet gullies and thick forest of the southern slopes is the preferred habitat of two of Tasmania's endemic birds: the Scrubtit and Tasmanian Thornbill. The Scrubtit is of special interest in having taken over the treecreeper role in this habitat, foraging on the bark of trunks and branches, probing bark crevices, moss and debris with its elongated bill.

The bird endemic to the south-west is the Orange-bellied Parrot which, as

SOUTHERN TASMANIAN BIRDWATCHES

0   1   2 km

Mt Field East
high altitude walk
▲1248 m
Lake Nicholls
Lake Fenton
Seager's Lookout
(mid altitude walk)
lyrebird nature walk
Lake Dobson
(steep climb)
Picnic Area
Lady Barron Falls
Nina Creek
NORTH
Russell Falls
Road
high altitude walk
park headquarters
camping area
low altitude walk
Tyenna
River
To Hobart

Mount Field National Park

The forested and often snow-capped bulk of Mount Wellington dominates Hobart, bringing the birds of forest and woodland to the city's doorstep. The mountain has been ravaged by bushfires on a number of occasions but still attracts local and visiting birdwatchers. Not surprisingly, it is also a convenient site for bird studies of a more scientific nature, especially when such studies require frequent visits to the site. The results of these studies can be of interest and help to amateur birdwatchers, and perhaps suggest useful sightings they themselves could be recording.

One study of the birds of Mount Wellington concentrated upon the influence of altitude upon the bird populations of the mountain, from foothills to summit, over altitudes from 240 m above sea level to 1270 m. The slopes of Mount Wellington were divided into a dozen zones, based on altitude and vegetation. A total of 90 visits, over a four-month study period,

mainly between 7.00 am and 11.30 am when bird activity and song were greatest, resulted in a record of 62 species, with every sighting positioned in its appropriate zone.

In a resulting birdlist it could be seen that three species, the Fan-tailed Cuckoo, Flame Robin and Forest Raven, could be considered ubiquitous. A second group of seven species: the Grey Shrike-thrush, Superb Fairy-wren, Brown Thornbill, Yellow-throated Honeyeater, Crescent Honey-eater, Spotted and Striated pardalotes, which generally occur in forest and woodland, are absent or extremely rare on the treeless mountain-top. Among the long list of altitude and habitat preferences, the Pink Robin and Scrubtit are seen as clearly preferring habitats below 800 m and the dense forest undergrowth of the wet gullies; raptors such as the Peregrine and Brown falcons, Brown Goshawk and Marsh Harrier, on the other hand, tend to be ubiquitous but not common.

In the knowledge of the pattern of combined habitat and altitude preferences of species or groups of species, it is possible to walk or drive up such a range and to know where one may expect to see the various birds. Such a study puts into more precise form the impressions of bird habits that most observers, after frequent visits, would have acquired. As well, it helps to make evident unusual patterns of habitat use by the birds and to set these out in an appropriate framework.

Another study was conducted on the lower slopes of Mount Wellington where Pottery Road climbs into bush-land of dry eucalypt forest, with forest and tree-ferns in the gullies. Here the

foraging behaviour of four local breeding species of honeyeater was observed: the Yellow-throated, Strong-billed, Black-headed and Crescent honeyeaters. The Eastern Spinebill was included as a common winter visitor.

The results of this study are of interest as they give some clues to behaviour, the knowledge of which could be of practical benefit in looking for and understanding these birds. Two species, the endemic Strong-billed and Yellow-throated honeyeaters, should be looked for on the trunks and limbs of trees where they forage over the bark, yet both occasionally visit the flowers of the trees as well.

The Black-headed Honeyeater forages almost exclusively amid the foliage, while the Crescent Honeyeater feeds at varied sources: flowers when they are available, at other times among foliage and sometimes on the bark. All four species hawk insects in the air, the Strong-billed least of any. The Eastern Spinebill, an autumn to winter visitor, feeds mainly at flowers, occasionally hawking or foraging in foliage.

Like Mount Wellington, Mount Field National Park encompasses altitudes and vegetations from lowland to alpine. It is relatively undamaged by fire and has walking tracks on the lower as well as the highest parts, and the potential for lengthy and rugged backpacking treks. Birdlife records and observations linked to influencing forces such as altitude, vegetation and other factors may throw new light upon some ornithological mystery, or simply give direction and add interest to the birdwatching.

106 PEREGRINE FALCON *Falco peregrinus*

172 GREENSHANK *Tringa nebularia*

499 **RUFOUS TREECREEPER** *Climacteris rufa*

CENTRAL SOUTH

The central and dominant feature of this region is the high spine of the Flinders and Mount Lofty ranges, a great north–south barrier from desert to ocean. These ranges dominate the surrounding flat lowlands, influencing climate and local bird distribution.

The region's far north is otherwise flat, with but a few low ranges, extensive areas of sand dunes in its north-west, and very arid. Through the central-north to north-east it becomes even more low-lying, with a great number of salt lakes, some very large. The bird habitats and bird species of these northern parts are much like those of the Western Deserts and Eastern Deserts regions.

To the east of the Flinders and Mount Lofty ranges the landscape is again flat, with watercourses that are usually dry, draining to salt lakes that rarely hold water: Lakes Frome, Callabonna, Blanche and many others much smaller. To the north and east of these lakes is semi-desert sand-dune country, continuing across the borders into New South Wales and Queensland.

East of the Mount Lofty Ranges the Murray River winds across flat plains that are largely cleared for farming. Its winding, tree-lined channels, islands and billabongs create an environment distinctly different from the surrounding plains and allow the occurrence of birds that otherwise would not occur in those parts. At its mouth a cluster of large lakes and surrounding wetlands is an outstanding site for waders and waterfowl.

In its south-east corner the region receives much heavier and more reliable rainfall which, with the low-lying landscape of ridges and hollows of ancient coastal dunes, has allowed development of a great many small lakes and swamps. This area has open forest, woodland, and damp heathy vegetation in its low-lying parts. Some of the lagoons and swampy heathlands have been retained in conservation reserves such as Big Heath and Bool Lagoon.

West of the Flinders Ranges, Spencer Gulf extends inland about 300 km and is a major break and barrier between these eastern parts and Eyre Peninsula to the west. The much smaller Gulf St Vincent isolates the narrow Yorke Peninsula, which is very low and flat, mostly cleared as farmland but with natural vegetation remaining at its south-western tip. The coasts of the gulfs have been recognized as being among the best wader sites in Australia.

Kangaroo Island, at the entrance to the gulfs, comes within 14 km of Fleurieu Peninsula but has been separated by that quite narrow stretch of water for about 10 000 years.

At first it appears that this region, and South Australia in general, with such limited variety of habitat, could have but little to offer in the way of unique birdlife, especially by comparison with the more isolated corners of the continent such as Cape York, or even the south-west of Western Australia.

This is only partly correct. On present classification there is no bird species unique to the region, nor to the State. But there are many endemic subspecies, adding greatly to the ornithological interest of the region.

In its position almost midway across southern Australia, and with a transition from quite wet south-eastern parts to a desert in the north, the Central South Region is the outer limit of range for a surprisingly large number of species. Some of these are birds of south-eastern Australia which follow forested and wooded parts of the Great Dividing Range west as far as the forested Mount Lofty and southern Flinders ranges. A few of these birds have a broken range, their westernmost population in the Mount Lofty Ranges being separated by drier habitat from the main population of south-eastern forests, and having subsequently evolved recognizable local subspecies.

This Central South Region is also the limit of range for a third group: birds which occur also in the south-west of Western Australia but extend as far eastwards as either Eyre Peninsula or the Flinders Ranges.

Many birds have subspecies endemic to this region. On Flinders Island these are the Crimson Rosella, Western Whipbird (the same subspecies also on Yorke Peninsula), Southern Emu-wren, Striated Thornbill, New Holland Honeyeater, Purple-gaped Honeyeater, Crescent Honeyeater and Little Wattlebird. Eyre Peninsula has local subspecies of Western Yellow Robin, Thick-billed Grasswren and Southern Emu-wren. In the northern Flinders Ranges there is a unique subspecies of Striated Grasswren, while the southern Flinders and Mount Lofty ranges have endemic local subspecies of the Crimson Rosella (the Adelaide Rosella), Southern Emu-wren, Eastern Spinebill and Red-browed Firetail.

In the RAOU Field Atlas survey, the greatest number of birds for this region and for South Australia was 283 species, 144 breeding, in the 1° block extending from The Coorong north to Adelaide.

BIRDS OF THE CENTRAL SOUTH

39 BLACK-FACED SHAG

Leucocarbo fuscescens

The Black-faced Shag is endemic to southern Australia where it is confined to the rocky parts of the coast and islands. It takes fish from shallow waters and around reefs.

During the RAOU Field Atlas survey of Australian birdlife, this region was reported as having the largest breeding colonies. These are situated in the entrance to Spencer Gulf close to Port Lincoln, the small rocky islets of Dangerous Reef having 5000 birds, English Island 2000 birds and Winceby Island 2000.

Previous large breeding colonies around Tasmania have been destroyed or greatly reduced by fishermen. Any remaining colonies there or elsewhere along Australia's southern coast are very small, usually several hundred birds, rarely much larger. After breeding, there is some dispersal along the coast for distances as great as 1900 km.

▶ See also pages 45 151 *157* 259–60

180 SHARP-TAILED SANDPIPER

Calidris acuminata

The Sharp-tailed Sandpiper has been recorded almost throughout this region in both inland and coastal situations; it has an extremely wide distribution across the continent during its summer migration to Australia, and a preference for inland waters rather than ocean coasts. Its migration route appears to be largely through north-western Australia where large flocks have been recorded. Some very large concentrations occur in south-eastern Australia from about October to March, with few if any surpassing a February count of 54 700 at The Coorong.

While the Sharp-tailed Sandpiper is one of the commonest of waders, there may at times be intermingled in its flocks, or alone, a similar species — the Pectoral Sandpiper — a scarce but apparently regular visitor. The plumage of Sharp-tailed Sandpipers varies considerably from summer to winter, and for immatures, but in all plumages this species appears bulkier, with proportionately smaller head and longer legs than the Pectoral Sandpiper.

Close to Adelaide, the Sharp-tailed Sandpiper can be seen along the coast from Port Adelaide northwards to Port Lincoln, and, south of Adelaide,

on the shores at Goolwa, Lake Alexandrina and The Coorong. The Pectoral Sandpiper has been recorded at the ICI saltworks at St Kilda, Buckland Park, Mullins Swamp, Bool Lagoon and Little Bool Lagoon.

▶ See also pages 98 99 124 149 *157* 218 296 297

207 **FAIRY TERN** *Sterna nereis*

207 FAIRY TERN

Sterna nereis

The major breeding colonies of the Fairy Tern are the southern and western coasts of Australia. This tern is a coastal species, rarely venturing far out to sea or far inland. It takes small fish by plunge-diving into the shallows close to the beaches of the sea, estuaries or coastal lagoons.

Although many nesting colonies are on islands, the Fairy Tern also nests on mainland beaches, sometimes on a sandbar across the entrance of a river, bay, or lagoon, or on a river sandspit.

In the Central South Region the Fairy Tern may be seen along almost all parts of the coast, including that of the gulfs and Kangaroo Island. It nests on Kangaroo Island, on small islands in The Coorong, at Beachport, the Price salt fields on Yorke Peninsula, and the coast and islets of Eyre Peninsula. Close to Adelaide it is most often sighted in and about Lake Alexandrina, Goolwa, the Encounter Bay coastline and Lake Albert; it is also seen around St Kilda and Victor Harbour.

Beyond this region, the Fairy Tern breeds along the Victorian coast as far as Corner Inlet, around the Tasmanian coast and the coasts of Western Australia, where the largest population and colonies occur.

On mainland coasts, especially in south-eastern Australia, human use of beaches, particularly with vehicles and dogs, causes heavy losses in nesting colonies. Birdwatchers should not add to the stress by causing agitation among nesting terns by excessively close approach.

The much larger Caspian Tern also occurs in this region, both on the coast

and inland where suitable permanent or temporary lakes occur. Most records appear to be on the coast or relatively close to ocean or gulf waters. It has been found breeding along the coast between about Ceduna and The Coorong. Colonies are often small, sometimes but a single pair among other nesting seabirds.

▶ See also pages 244 303

255 MUSK LORIKEET

Glossopsitta concinna

The Central South Region is the western limit of range for the tiny Musk Lorikeet, which has populations at the tip of Eyre Peninsula, Kangaroo Island and the Mt Lofty Ranges. Although apparently isolated from the main population of south-eastern Australia, there are no subspecies recognized in this region or elsewhere. The Musk Lorikeet is the common lorikeet of south-eastern Australia in open forest, lightly wooded country and mallee, but uncommon in very dense wet forests.

Although nomadic, the Musk Lorikeet is perhaps less so than some other lorikeets, its movements seasonal rather than erratic. The birds are usually seen in flight, dashing overhead in noisy flocks, with shrill, metallic screechings; the yellow-green of the underwings may then be glimpsed. The Musk Lorikeet is often in company with other lorikeets or Swift Parrots.

When feeding in the treetops, on nectar, fruits or insects, they are inconspicuous, their green plumage

256 **PURPLE-CROWNED LORIKEET**
Glossopsitta porphyrocephala

blending with the foliage. But the almost continuous chattering and the shaking of leaves reveals their presence.

Near Adelaide the Musk Lorikeet is commonly seen throughout the Mt Lofty Ranges.

▶ See also pages 163 313–14

256 PURPLE-CROWNED LORIKEET

Glossopsitta porphyrocephala

Purple-crowned Lorikeets are more often heard than seen, their almost continuous, sharp, high screeches attract attention as flocks or pairs dash through the treetops, the sunlight sometimes catching the crimson of underwings. In the tops of flowering eucalypts, whether forest giants or mallees of the drier country, their green plumage blends into the foliage as they feed upon the nectar, making them remarkably hard to see.

The Purple-crowned Lorikeet is found right across southern Australia, western and eastern populations probably linked through mallee bordering the Nullarbor Plain. The species is highly nomadic, gathering in large numbers where a eucalypt forest or area of mallee is in flower, to feed on the nectar and pollen.

This is the most common and widespread of the lorikeets in South Australia and is probably seen more often here than elsewhere in its range. It is commonly seen in the forests and woodlands of the Mount Lofty Range, Adelaide suburbs and Fleurieu Peninsula.

Nesting occurs wherever the lorikeets happen to find the best conditions in spring months, so that they may nest in a locality and not again for many years. Nesting can be so dense that it could almost be described as colonial. On some occasions almost every suitable small hollow is occupied, some trees with up to four nests, with perhaps five to 20 pairs per hectare over an area of more than hundreds and sometimes perhaps many thousands of hectares.

The nest is a small deep hollow in a limb or knot-hole, usually towards the top of the tree. There can be fierce competition between pairs for use of favoured hollows. At Dryandra State Forest (WA) two pairs fought desperately for a hollow. The birds, locked together in battle, fell 20 m to hit the ground with a thump that was audible 15 or 20 m away, only to fly back up to the hollow and repeat the engagement.

Once ownership of a suitable hollow is established, the Purple-crowned

Lorikeets at first seem to spend much time sitting at and near the entrance. When the female is inside the hollow, the male often remains perched nearby. With any approach his agitated screeches bring her to the entrance.

Occasionally, usually in the warm sunlight of mid-morning, a pair will sit on a twig or at the hollow entrance preening themselves and each other.

39 **Black-faced Shag** *Leucocarbo fuscescens*
180 **Sharp-tailed Sandpiper** *Calidris acuminata*
181 **Pectoral Sandpiper** *Calidris melanotos*
255 **Musk Lorikeet** *Glossopsitta concinna*
271 **Adelaide Rosella** (subspecies of Crimson Rosella) *Platycercus elegans adelaidae*
414 **Western Whipbird** *Psophodes nigrogularis*
533 **Purple-gaped Honeyeater** *Lichenostomus cratitius*
591 **Diamond Firetail** *Emblema guttata*
633 **Dusky Woodswallow** *Artamus cyanopterus*
645 **Little Raven** *Corvus mellori*

The Port Lincoln Ringneck is probably widespread and abundant because it is adaptable and able to utilize a wide variety of habitats, from heavy forests to the arid mulga scrubs of the interior. On Eyre Peninsula it is common wherever there is mallee. It is nomadic in desert regions, where drought often forces travel, but is usually sedentary in the areas of reliable rainfall.

The Port Lincoln Ringneck travels with a swift and seemingly effortless flight, in graceful long undulations, the glides alternating with brief bursts of wingbeats. The call over most of its range is a 'kling-kling-', or for the subspecies in the south-west of Western Australia, 'twen-ty-eight'.

▶ See also pages 213 223 231 233 238 242 318

277 PORT LINCOLN RINGNECK *Barnardius zonarius*

They may stay there for some time, occasionally lifting a wing and showing the crimson underside. Once the young have hatched, the lorikeets seem too busy to sit and preen; they dash endlessly between the nest and the food supply of flowering trees, often a few kilometres away.

▶ See also pages 138 *156* 163 213 220 232 245 314

271 ADELAIDE ROSELLA
SUBSPECIES OF CRIMSON ROSELLA

Platycercus elegans adelaidae

The Adelaide Rosella has in the past been given full species status but is now usually listed as a subspecies of the Crimson Rosella. For most birdwatchers the change has had little effect as the bird is sufficiently distinctive to be worth seeing whichever classification is in fashion, and it is well-known by the common name of Adelaide Rosella. Until the change from full to subspecies status this was an endemic species for the Central South Region, and for South Australia.

The Adelaide Rosella has evolved from the Crimson Rosella. The westernmost part of the Crimson Rosella population was, at some time in the past, effectively isolated in the forested Mount Lofty and southern Flinders ranges. The isolation has been sufficient for the development of the differences that are now apparent in the Adelaide Rosella. Another population of Crimson Rosellas is isolated on Kangaroo Island but has become only very slightly

differentiated from the Crimson Rosellas of the south-eastern mainland; it is sometimes given subspecies status.

In the Mount Lofty and southern Flinders ranges the Adelaide Rosella can be found in forested valleys, along tree-lined watercourses and roadways through cleared land, and occasionally in tall mallee close to these ranges. It is usually seen in pairs or small flocks of four or five and may be feeding in treetops or on the ground. The calls and flight are like those of the Crimson Rosella. The Adelaide Rosella can be seen throughout the hills and coastal plains suburbs of Adelaide, where usually the only other somewhat similar parrot is the Eastern Rosella.

▶ See also pages 8 155 *157* 162 317

277 PORT LINCOLN RINGNECK

Barnardius zonarius

Two species of ringneck parrots meet in this region. The Mallee Ringneck of inland eastern Australia comes as far west as the Flinders Ranges, and the Port Lincoln Ringneck of the west and centre is found as far east as these same ranges. Spencer Gulf also serves as a divider, with the Mallee Ringneck in the forested Mount Lofty Ranges to the east and the Port Lincoln Ringneck on Eyre Peninsula.

The range of the Port Lincoln Ringneck extends across the Nullarbor Plain and Victoria Desert into Western Australia, where the greener birds of the south-west corner are known locally as Twenty-eight Parrots.

287 ROCK PARROT *Neophema petrophila*

286 ELEGANT PARROT

Neophema elegans

The range of the Elegant Parrot at present has a wide break — at the Nullarbor and surrounding arid country — between its south-eastern population and that in the south-west of Western Australia. In south-eastern Australia it is almost confined to this Central South Region but is also recorded in the Murray–Darling Region and south-western Victoria. The break between the populations is probably comparatively recent since there is no differentiation that could justify western and eastern subspecies.

The Elegant Parrot inhabits grasslands, and woodlands with grassy ground-cover, including farmlands. It usually flies quite high when travelling, and would often pass over unseen but for its sharp, tinkling calls.

The alternative name of Grass Parrot is appropriate in that this species is most often seen when flushed from grass or pasture such as clover. It flies up with a succession of sharp calls, usually to perch a while on a nearby tree, often a dead twig, where it and the birdwatcher obtain a good view of each other before it departs for a more peaceful spot. When feeding on the ground, even in short grass, its colours are inconspicuous.

Near Adelaide the Elegant Parrot can best be seen in the more open woodlands to north and south of the heavily forested parts of the ranges. This dainty little parrot usually nests high, perhaps only because most small hollows tend to be in the thinner and higher branches.

▶ **See also pages** 245 320

286 ELEGANT PARROT *Neophema elegans*

287 ROCK PARROT

Neophema petrophila

The Rock Parrot, like the Elegant Parrot, has two populations, one restricted to this region and the other to the South-West Region. Although apart, they are not separable as subspecies.

The plump little Rock Parrot is confined to the coasts, seldom more than a few hundred metres from the sea. It utilizes rocky coastlines, bare rock islets, sandy shores and dunes, and the margins of mudflats and mangroves. Close to Adelaide it can be seen from Torrens Island northwards, among the samphire bushes on the tidal flats.

Many sightings and most breeding records are from Eyre Peninsula,

including Coffin Bay, Point Neill, Louth Bay, Fishermans Bay, and offshore islands including Pearson Island. It also occurs on the shores of Kangaroo Island, and the rocky south-east coast near Robe.

Rock Parrots are inconspicuous when feeding in the low herbage and will usually be first seen when accidentally flushed, or as they fly to and from feeding spots. While feeding they will allow a reasonably close approach and if disturbed will usually fly only a short distance before dropping down to cover again. They usually feed in the morning and late afternoon, especially in hot weather.

▶ **See also pages** 158 162 320–1

414 WESTERN WHIPBIRD

Psophodes nigrogularis

Whipbirds are shy, medium-sized, long-tailed, olive-green, insectivorous birds of the undergrowth. They take their name from the loud, explosive, whipcrack calls of the Eastern Whipbird. There are two species. The Eastern Whipbird inhabits the undergrowth of dense wet forests of coastal eastern Australia where it is abundant. The second, the Western Whipbird, in complete contrast, inhabits the much drier mallee thickets and is so rare that it was at one time thought to be extinct.

The species occurring in the Central South Region is the Western Whipbird. It was discovered in the south-west of Western Australia in 1842 but the known populations were destroyed by widespread clearing and burning.

In 1932 this species was rediscovered more than 1600 km to the east, in Victoria's western mallee country. In 1965 another population of the Western Whipbird was found on southern Yorke Peninsula, in 1966 a third near the tip of Eyre Peninsula, and a fourth on Kangaroo Island in 1967. Also in 1967 the population of western Victoria was found to occur farther west, across the border in the South Australian mallee. Meanwhile in Western Australia the Western Whipbird had been found to survive in mallee country near Gnowangerup and at Two People Bay.

The five scattered populations of the Western Whipbird have been grouped into three subspecies. Those in Western Australia, the first discovered, are the nominate subspecies, as are those of Eyre Peninsula. Those of the Victorian–South Australian border mallee district were given the subspecies name of *leucogaster*, and the whipbirds of

southern Yorke Peninsula and Kangaroo Island became the third subspecies, *pondalowiensis*.

The whipbird has not been seen in Victoria since 1969 despite intensive searches; however the subspecies continues to survive in the adjoining South Australian mallee.

The subspecies of Western Whipbird found on Yorke Peninsula and Kangaroo Island takes its scientific name from the site of its discovery, Pondalowie Bay, at the tip of the peninsula, where its habitat is now protected within the Innes National Park. It is distinguished from other subspecies by the pale edges to the wing feathers and an overall more tawny plumage.

The Western Whipbird is quite common in dense mallee and acacia thickets on coastal dunes, where smaller shrubs and creepers combine to form very dense scrub. It is extremely shy and secretive and was discovered only when the loud calls were noticed. The calls never have the whipcrack quality of the Eastern Whipbird; they are a squeaky sequence of notes, loud and far-

636 GREY BUTCHERBIRD *Cracticus torquatus*

carrying, likened to the turning of a squeaky wooden cartwheel, and articulated as 'itch-a-tee-cha'.

Both sexes contribute to the song, fitting their notes together so well that it seems but a single bird is singing. Another loud call consists of two harsh notes and an upwards trill. The birds are noisiest in the mornings, up to about 10 am, and again in the late afternoon. They seem to be more active and noisy on overcast days and after rain.

Here and at other localities the Western Whipbird is notoriously difficult to observe, keeping for much

438 BLUE-BREASTED FAIRY-WREN
Malurus pulcherrimus

of the time on or close to the ground under or among dense undergrowth. On rare occasions it may give a fleeting glimpse in flight between thickets or perched momentarily in a higher and more open part of a shrub. The white tips of the long tail are then visible.

The Western Whipbird will respond to taped recordings of some of its calls, still keeping under dense cover most of the time. The response may vary from breeding to non-breeding months. Replaying of territorial calls causes some degree of agitation in many birds, which could be harmful in the spring breeding season, so replay should never be continued at a site for lengthy periods.

On rare occasions the whipbirds of Innes National Park have been seen in the open, feeding on the partly vegetated slopes of the dunes, when they tend to keep the tail erect, but dropping it to the ground when alarmed.

The Western Whipbird also appears reasonably common on Kangaroo Island, in sand-dune mallee country of Flinders Chase National Park, Dudley Peninsula and Cape St Albans.

▶ **See also pages** 138 155 *157* 162 164 242 245 353

438 BLUE-BREASTED FAIRY-WREN

Malurus pulcherrimus

The Blue-breasted Fairy-wren is another of the birds whose range is interrupted by the Nullarbor Plain, yet the birds to each side of that break are so near identical that there are no subspecies. In the Central South Region, where it is confined to Eyre Peninsula, and in the south-west of Western Australia, much of the woodlands, mallee and sandplain heath that it inhabits has been cleared for agriculture, leaving natural habitat only in the driest localities or as isolated remnants among farmlands.

The only other species of chestnut-shouldered fairy-wren occurring on Eyre Peninsula is the Variegated Fairy-wren (more precisely its Purple-backed subspecies). The two Variegated and the Blue-breasted fairy-wrens are very much alike: the breast of the former is black, while the breast of the Blue-breasted is deep navy-blue. In poor light it can look black but in strong light it can be seen as a dark navy-blue, distinctly distinguishable as blue against the broad black band across the side of the head and the blackish edging at the lower edge of the breast. Where the ear-covert patch is pale silvery-blue on the Variegated, that of the Blue-breasted is violet-blue, almost as dark as that of the crown.

In Western Australia this species has a small overlap with the range of the Red-winged Fairy-wren, which however has a distinctive call and occupies much wetter and more coastal habitat.

The Blue-breasted Fairy-wren is reported mainly from the western to central parts of Eyre Peninsula, where it is likely to be found in any remnant area of natural vegetation or the national parks of the district. The typical fairy-wren trilling is most likely to draw attention, and observation is then reasonably easy while the birds move about the ground and heathy undergrowth.

▶ **See also pages** 164 240 245 359

499 RUFOUS TREECREEPER

Climacteris rufa

The Rufous Treecreeper occupies a variety of habitats, from the South-West Region's heavy forests of karri and jarrah, to the inland wandoo and salmon-gum woodlands, and the stunted mallee of the Great Victoria Desert. This treecreeper's ability to occupy arid country has given it an unbroken range as far east as Spencer Gulf.

In the Central South Region its stronghold is a belt of mallee extending from the Nullarbor Plain across northern Eyre Peninsula to Spencer Gulf. The continuity between western and eastern populations has preserved uniformity within the species, so that there are no subspecies.

The Rufous Treecreeper on Eyre Peninsula seems less common than in the woodlands of the South-West Region, where this species is abundant. Extensive land clearing has reduced the available habitat in both regions, but the species' more restricted habitat on Eyre Peninsula may have been more severely affected; the mallee habitat has fewer hollows available as potential nesting sites.

Where it does occur, the Rufous Treecreeper is a conspicuous species, the sharp, ringing calls being given almost continuously, while its foraging on treetrunks and limbs keeps it in the open compared with species that feed in undergrowth or treetop foliage. It typically works its way up the trunks and limbs with erratic, jerky hops, then moves on to the next tree with a long, downwards glide, to land near the base and repeat the upward search. Rufous Treecreepers often forage on fallen timber and on the ground. Where hollows are common it seems to be forever ducking in and out, at first giving the impression that every hollow contains a nest. The broad buff bar across the flight feathers is conspicuous in flight.

▶ **See also pages** *154* 164 213 220 232 235 245 373

533 PURPLE-GAPED HONEYEATER

Lichenostomus cratitius

The Purple-gaped Honeyeater has a distribution that follows the mallee belt across southern Australia, from the southern interior of Western Australia to the mallee of north-western Victoria.

The Kangaroo Island population is isolated and was described as a subspecies, said to be larger, brighter, with yellow instead of purplish gape (the strip of bare skin from bill back below the eye). However, a later study concluded that the plumage was no brighter, possibly duller, and that the yellow gape is an immature characteristic present for an equal length of time on both mainland and island birds. There are, however, some other differences. The Kangaroo Island birds have shorter bills, longer wings, and inhabit forest and woodland as well as the mallee-heath of the mainland populations.

▶ **See also pages** 130 139 155 *157*

BIRD PLACES OF THE CENTRAL SOUTH

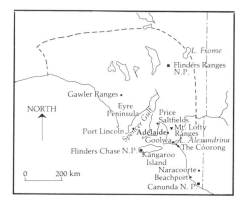

THE COORONG

One of Australia's foremost waterbird and wader areas surrounds a long, narrow coastal waterway known as The Coorong. Before finally reaching the open ocean the Murray River empties into a cluster of lakes separated from the sea by a long strip of sand and silt. Largest is the broad expanse of water of Lake Alexandrina, with Lake Albert adjoining on the southern side. Closest to the ocean, sheltered behind huge beach dunes, is The Coorong.

The Coorong extends southwards for a distance of 130 km from Murray Mouth but its width averages only 2–3 km, while the equally long strip of dunes of the Younghusband Peninsula that separates it from the sea is but 1–2 km wide. The seaward side of the peninsula is an unbroken sweep of beach upon which the surf of the ocean breaks and misty spray drifts inland over the waters of The Coorong.

The sand barrier that separates lagoon from ocean has been built by ocean currents and waves, a process that has been repeated many times along this south-eastern coast. Inland of The Coorong are parallel rows of dunes and swampy or heathy flats, evidence of older coastlines which had similar dune and lagoon formations.

The Coorong's lagoons are shallow, averaging less than 3 m, and the water is often several times more salty than the sea. The shallow lagoons and surrounding habitats provide refuge for a great variety of birds, some in huge numbers. As well as the areas of open lagoon waters, The Coorong and adjoining lakes have areas of reed-beds, mudflats, sedges and salt meadows. Between lagoons and marshes are areas of heathy vegetation. The heaths are on the silted remains of previous lagoons, low-lying and often wet, supporting paperbarks, sheoaks, rushes and sedges.

On the lagoons, pelicans occur in great numbers, particularly in spring. By day they are seen floating in tightly packed 'rafts', probing and reaching down into the shallows or passing overhead in great flocks, to glide down one at a time and congregate again at some favoured feeding or roosting site. They are prolific on the Pelican Islands in The Coorong, and also occasionally in Lake Alexandrina, one site being at Reedy Point where 300–400 have nested.

In Salt Lagoon, a bay at the southern end of Lake Alexandrina, small densely vegetated islands are used by a large number of breeding waterbirds. The breeding species here include the Darter, Great Cormorant, Pied Cormorant, Little Black Cormorant, Little Pied Cormorant, Cattle Egret, Great Egret, Little Egret, Rufous Night Heron, Glossy Ibis, Sacred Ibis, Straw-necked Ibis, Royal Spoonbill, Yellow-billed Spoonbill, Black Swan, Marsh Harrier, and various ducks and smaller birds. Occasionally large numbers are involved, some cormorants having up to 1000 nests, the Great Egret about 100 to 140 pairs, and each of the ibis species with up to 500 nests.

Lakes Alexandrina and Albert cover so great an area and are surrounded by such an extent of dense swampy thickets and reed-beds that some large colonies of breeding birds were still being discovered in the 1960s.

The construction of barrages at the Murray River's outlet to the sea stabilized the waterlevel of Lake Alexandrina and Lake Albert and kept out salt water. Around the very long shoreline are large areas of shallow water, mudbanks and flooded samphire which together provide ideal habitat not only for waders but also for terns and other waterbirds.

The value of The Coorong as a wader site was shown by the RAOU national wader count which recorded numbers of waders at sites around Australia. The Coorong and adjoining lakes ranked third nationally, at peak use having up to 242 000 birds.

Parts of these lakes are national parks or game reserves and a permit is required for entry to some sensitive areas. For relatively brief visits there are some walk trails, such as the Lakes Nature Trail. A park birdlist is available, listing 165 species; the National Parks and Wildlife Service Management Plan list has 238 species, possibly covering a wider area. For information on this and possible entry to other areas the advice of the ranger at Salt Creek is recommended.

150 GREY PLOVER *Pluvialis squatarola*

GULF ST VINCENT AND SPENCER GULF

As well as The Coorong, South Australia has rich wader habitat along the shores of Gulf St Vincent and Spencer Gulf, the former with 67 500 birds and the latter with 38 500 in the RAOU national wader count, placing them fifth and tenth respectively within Australia.

The coast of Gulf St Vincent has been made much more attractive to waders by the development of two saltworks: the ICI saltworks at St Kilda, a short distance north of Adelaide, and the salt fields of Ocean Salt Pty Ltd at Price, near the head of this gulf. Between the two salt fields is about 100 km of mangrove coast, providing mudflat feeding grounds at low tide. When the mudflats are covered at high tide many of the waders move to the salt fields or areas of marshy ground around the head of the gulf.

Towards the southern end of this coast, by the mouth of the Gawler River, the Port Gawler Conservation Park covers areas of mangrove forest and samphire swamp. Nearby are additional habitats of tidal flats, shell-grit dunes, the river red-gum margins of the Gawler River, a freshwater lake, and the extensive shallow water of the ICI evaporation ponds, which are managed as a private sanctuary for the birds that use them.

There is a rookery of Pied Cormorants within the reserve and it is regularly patrolled by birds of prey including the Marsh Harrier, White-bellied Sea-Eagle, Black Falcon, Australian Hobby and Black-shouldered Kite. The birdlist here totals 68 species.

The extensive shallow ponds of the salt fields have proven to be very attractive to waders and some other waterbirds and very convenient for observing these birds. Some are seen in large numbers, with sightings of over 1000 each of Red-necked Stints and

535 YELLOW-PLUMED HONEYEATER
Lichenostomus ornatus

Curlew Sandpipers at Price and over 500 of each at St Kilda.

In the RAOU Field Atlas survey, the 1° block centred upon this coast, including parts of Adelaide and the Mount Lofty Ranges, had 281 species of birds, 138 of them breeding.

Spencer Gulf has wader habitat along its north-western, northern and eastern coasts and bird sites of interest at Redcliffe and Port Broughton. Redcliffe Point is situated on the eastern shore of the gulf, some 25 km south of Port Augusta, and is the site of a petro-chemical project. An environmental impact survey of the birds of the site, over two weekends, recorded 100 species in an area of mangroves, mallee, saltbush-bluebush, tidal flats and other habitats.

Shag Island, near Port Broughton, is a breeding site for Great Egrets, Little Pied Cormorants, White-faced Herons, and possibly Rufous Night Herons.

INNES NATIONAL PARK

Yorke Peninsula has been largely cleared of its natural vegetation though some areas unsuited to farming retain mallee and acacia scrub. At the very tip of the peninsula, the area around Pondalowie Bay has been reserved in the Innes National Park following the discovery there of the rare Western Whipbird in 1965. A sighting of the Western Whipbird requires time and patience, and perhaps good luck. Most sightings have been at the western end of the park, between Pondalowie Bay Road and the coast, but there are some records inland between Spider Lake and Marion Lake.

The birdlist for Innes National Park totals 121 species and includes the Malleefowl, White-bellied Sea-Eagle, Osprey, Mulga Parrot, Rock Parrot, Rufous (subspecies of Striated) Fieldwren, Chestnut Quail-thrush and Southern Scrub-robin.

MOUNT LOFTY RANGES

The Mount Lofty Ranges form the eastern backdrop to the city of Adelaide. Being fairly high and close to the coast these ranges receive an average annual rainfall of nearly 900 mm, much more than the lowlands on the inland side of the ranges. The ranges carry a mixture of dry sclerophyll forest and savannah woodland; the vegetation of the dry plains to the east is of mallee for a great distance, while the country to the north becomes even more arid.

These ranges have, for some thousands of years, been in effect a habitat 'island', upon which many forest species are isolated, unable to cross the intervening arid country to maintain contact with others of their species. Some of these have evolved sufficient distinctive features to be classified as subspecies. Of these, probably only the Adelaide Rosella has become distinct enough from its parental stock to be obviously different in the field and to have acquired a common name.

As with oceanic islands, the number of species that can be maintained must decrease with any reduction in total area of the forests of the ranges. Any clearing of the forests will, sooner or later, result in the loss of some species from these ranges. It has been predicted that if the forest area were to be reduced from its original 300 000 ha to 50 000 ha, the number of species would drop to about 80.

The rarest species would be most likely to go first, possibly including the Swamp Quail, Spotted Quail-thrush, White-throated Warbler, Southern Emu-wren and Black-chinned Honeyeater. It has been suggested that the numbers of these species should be monitored.

While the birdlife can be observed almost anywhere in these ranges, the national parks are convenient sites providing road and walking access, usually freedom from disturbance, and having lists to indicate which species might be found.

The major and well-known national park is Belair, on the range-top south-east of the city. The park has a maximum altitude of 490 m and is vegetated mainly by dry sclerophyll forest and savannah woodland. A list of birds, compiled over several years and through all seasons, totalled 106 species. Another reserve in the Mount Lofty Ranges that is convenient for birding is the Para Wira Conservation Park, north-east of Adelaide. This reserve includes steep gorges of the South Para River and Wild Dog Creek. Vegetation is of dry eucalypt forest, in places of mallee treeforms, and woodlands. A birdlist compiled over a period of 18 months totalled 98 species.

Scott Conservation Park, on the south-eastern scarp of the Mount Lofty Ranges and 10 km north-west of Goolwa, has a different type of vegetation. The rainfall is not much more than half that of Belair. The vegetation includes mallee heath, pink-gum and stringybark scrub, and grassy woodland. A survey of 70 days over 14 months gave a list of 120 species. Honeyeaters and lorikeets were the predominant birds, and flowering trees and other plants were available throughout the year.

Sandy Creek Conservation Park, on the south side of the Gawler–Lyndoch road, is also on the eastern slopes of the Mount Lofty Ranges. The vegetation is complex, giving a variety of habitat which is reflected in the large number of birds, a total of at least 108 species, and a large number of birds that are regularly sighted. Observers have remarked on the abundance of birds usually to be seen.

THE FLINDERS RANGES

The Flinders Ranges, their northern parts extending well into semi-desert country, have a much drier environment than the Mount Lofty Ranges. Here the rugged ranges are not screened by forest, so that the reds and browns of rock and earth rise in contrast against the blue of the sky. Only in gorges and valleys is there much greenery, where river red-gums line the watercourses. But although dry, the northern Flinders Ranges are less harsh than the surrounding arid plains and salt lakes and have a significant influence upon the birds of the north-eastern part of this region.

The Flinders Ranges National Park is probably typical of the central Flinders Ranges, although possibly becoming a richer bird habitat compared with other parts still grazed by stock. The national parks tend to be better known ornithologically than similar surrounding country through the high level of observation by visitors and park rangers.

This national park is centred upon Wilpena Pound and contains high and

530 **WHITE-EARED HONEYEATER** *Lichenostomus leucotis*

rugged ranges, cliffs and gorges as well as wide valleys and tree-lined watercourses, and some areas of mallee-heath. The park birdlist stands at 100 species, plus a dozen that are unusual in the area, or with doubtful records.

A population of the Shy Heathwren occurs on high parts of the ranges, there being sightings on the summit of St Marys Peak and elsewhere in the Flinders Ranges; little is known of the species in this area.

A bird of special interest here is the Striated Grasswren, which occurs on Mt Sunderland and nearby Appealinna Hill, and north to Arkaroola. This is the subspecies *merrotsyi*, endemic to this part of the Flinders Ranges and one of very few really distinctive birds confined to South Australia. It has also been found in the southern Flinders Ranges at Yarah, and between Buckaringa Gorge and Middle Gorge, all within 26 km north of Quorn.

This subspecies is distinguished from Striated Grasswrens elsewhere by its much shorter tail, and in having the black moustache marking almost obscured by heavier white streakings. It occurs in habitats of spinifex with scattered acacia and other shrubs and in places where there are stunted mallee-eucalypts. Another species of grasswren, the Thick-billed, may occur in any of the extensive areas of bluebush, saltbush or cottonbush.

THE SOUTH-EAST COAST

Beachport Conservation Park, 2 km from Beachport, preserves coastal dunes; it includes Lake George, an important site for migratory waders. The birds of its coastal heath include the Olive Whistler and Rufous Bristlebird. On nearby Penguin Island there is a colony of Short-tailed Shearwaters estimated at 3000 pairs.

Canunda National Park, west of Millicent, has a coast of low limestone cliffs and sand dunes, with vegetation of heath and low scrub. The birdlife includes the Rufous Bristlebird and the Orange-bellied Parrot, a very rare species which breeds in Tasmania and winters along this coast.

THE SOUTH-EAST WETLANDS

From the southern parts of The Coorong south to Beachport and inland to Naracoorte is a landscape built of ancient coastal dunes and the remains of lagoons which once lay behind coastal sand spits, in the same way that The Coorong today shelters behind the line of dunes of the Younghusband Peninsula. With the building of the coast farther and farther westwards, the long parallel lines of dunes and intervening lagoons now extend well inland, almost to Naracoorte, a distance of about 100 km.

The old dunes have now largely solidified to limestone, meeting the ocean in low cliffs along many parts of the south-east coast. The lines of lagoons have mostly silted and now are flats between the parallel ridges of low hills, but their remnants are visible in the chains of small lakes, lagoons, swamps and wet heaths.

Many of these wetlands have been drained but enough remain to make this an outstanding district for waterbirds. Most of the sites are within conservation parks or game reserves, some requiring entry permits.

The largest of the south-eastern swamps is in the Bool Lagoon Game Reserve, 17 km south of Naracoorte, where the waterlevel is controlled to provide optimum waterbird habitat, covering 800–2000 ha of water, with large areas of tall reeds and rushes, and of paperbark tea-tree swamp.

Among the 182 species of birds found here, some in large numbers, are the Great Crested Grebe, Hoary-headed Grebe, Little Bittern, Australasian Bittern, Brolga, Freckled Duck, Cape Barren Goose, Magpie Goose, Marsh Harrier, Lewin's Rail, Painted Snipe, Purple-crowned Lorikeet, Musk Lorikeet, Barn Owl, Striated Fieldwren, Southern Emu-wren, White-eared Honeyeater, Tawny-crowned Honeyeater and Spiny-cheeked Honeyeater. Very close by is Hacks Lagoon, a shallow lake with marshy fringes, significant as a summer refuge for waterbirds.

Little Bool Lagoon, in the northern part of the Bool Lagoon Game Reserve complex, is a freshwater wetland, its margins bare or lightly vegetated with sedge, making this site attractive to waders; a rare sighting here has been the Little Ringed Plover, which in this region has also been recorded on Yorke Peninsula.

Big Heath Conservation Park, 32 km south-east of Lucindale, is a complex of low ridges of old sand dunes, plains, shallow depressions and swamps. There are woodlands on the rises, heaths and tussock sedgelands in the depressions. This is a remnant of the once-extensive wet-heathland country of the south-east. The birdlist covers more than 115 species.

Fairview Conservation Park, 9 km west of Lochbar, has semi-permanent lagoons, open heath on seasonally inundated flats, and woodlands on limestone ridges. Over 90 species of birds have been recorded including the Japanese Snipe and Black-chinned Honeyeater. Bucks Lagoon Game Reserve, 30 km west of Mt Gambier, covers a swampy lakebed, with areas of sedges and rushes, making this a significant waterbird habitat.

372 **WESTERN YELLOW ROBIN** *Eopsaltria griseogularis*

EYRE PENINSULA

For many of its birds, Eyre Peninsula is an isolated outpost of their range. A number of species, including the Western Whipbird, Blue-breasted Fairy-wren, Western Yellow Robin and Rufous Treecreeper, are found westwards from Eyre Peninsula into the south-west of Western Australia, providing an opportunity to see these species without having to cross the Nullarbor Plain to do so.

Eyre Peninsula has several endemic subspecies of birds found elsewhere, including the subspecies *parimeda* of the Southern Emu-wren, and the subspecies *myall* of the Thick-billed Grasswren.

The local subspecies of Southern Emu-wren has been recorded from the southern parts of Eyre Peninsula, in heath scrubs, from Sleaford Bay north to Wanilla. In the RAOU Field Atlas survey the Eyre Peninsula subspecies of the Thick-billed Grasswren was recorded only from the north-east of

the peninsula, in the Gawler Ranges, where grasswrens have been recorded previously.

The arid Gawler Ranges, across the northern part of the Eyre Peninsula, have a birdlist of at least 125 species, including the Spotted Harrier, Malleefowl, Pink Cockatoo, Scarlet-chested Parrot, Red-backed Kingfisher, Chestnut and Cinnamon quail-thrushes, Western Yellow Robin, Rufous Treecreeper, Slender-billed Thornbill and Gilbert's Whistler.

Eyre Peninsula has a number of large conservation parks and national parks. Major reserves are Port Lincoln National Park in the extreme south-east tip, and, clustered in the centre of the peninsula, Hambridge, Bascombe Well and Hincks conservation parks. The latter have habitats of mallee, broombush, heath, dunes, and some rocky ranges. Birds are those of dry mallee and heath, such as the Malleefowl and Blue-breasted Fairy-wren.

Around the coasts of Eyre Peninsula many islands have birds of interest. The Sir Joseph Banks Group, in Spencer Gulf near Port Lincoln, is a breeding site for the White-faced Storm-Petrel, with around 500-1000 nest burrows, the Little Penguin, small numbers of the Cape Barren Goose and several other breeding species.

KANGAROO ISLAND

Kangaroo Island was separated from the mainland around 10 000 years ago. The intervening Backstairs Passage, though narrow, is an effective barrier to the movement of many land birds. Some species have probably had isolated populations on the island throughout that time, others may have crossed to the island at some later time and established themselves.

In keeping with a widely recognized tendency for islands to support fewer species than similar mainland environments, Kangaroo Island has only about half the bird species that occur on the Fleurieu Peninsula. A large number of land birds known on the mainland have never been recorded on the island, probably the consequence of a smaller number of habitats available on the island. The RAOU Field Atlas survey recorded almost 130 species on the island and its closely surrounding seas.

Kangaroo Island is of special interest for the slight variations shown by many of its species. Birds whose populations show differences, such as bill length, wing length, or other measurable or visible variation, include the Crimson Rosella, Southern Emu-wren, Brown Thornbill, Striated Thornbill, New Holland Honeyeater, Little Wattlebird and Crescent Honeyeater. Some of these are distinctive to subspecies level, others only doubtfully so. Of the island's birds, of special interest is the Western Whipbird, which appears to be of the same subspecies as that found on Yorke Peninsula.

An annual occurrence of note is the arrival during winter months of many albatrosses and giant-petrels, to feed on cuttlefish in Eastern Cove at the eastern end of the island. Species sighted have been the Black-browed, Yellow-nosed and Shy albatrosses, sometimes the Grey-headed Albatross, and the Southern Giant-Petrel.

The island has many national park and conservation park areas suitable for birding, mainly along its west and south coasts.

SOUTH-EAST WETLANDS BIRDWATCH

The 'birdwatch' concept allows for bird encounters that are more wide-ranging than would be obtained by always keeping to walks in the strict sense; the birdlife of some sites may be best experienced by boat or other means.

At a typical swamp site, a track on dry land around the periphery of the wetlands can give only distant and incomplete observations of the birdlife of this extremely rich habitat. Some birds are likely to be so far out on the open water that the sighting is remote, and the shy species that inhabit reed-beds are usually not seen at all, or give but fleeting glimpses.

If the observer wades into the reed-beds, or forces through with boat or canoe, the resultant unavoidable thrashing about of reeds or rushes alarms birds well in advance, so that few if any will be seen, although some nests may be found. At some wetland sites where large numbers of visitors expect to see waterbirds, observatories have been constructed. These buildings, usually at the swamp edge, or upon piles out on the water, can have screened approach paths and observation windows overlooking the water. But elsewhere, if one wants to watch and perhaps photograph the comings and goings of the secretive birds of the heart of the swamp, one must build a hide.

At times the hide can be erected in a dry position overlooking water and reed-bed. It may be positioned on shoreline, mudbank, logs or stumps in the water, or in a low fork of a tree standing in water. But within reed-beds such convenient sites are rare. Provided the water is not too deep and the mud of the bottom reasonably firm, a simple hide may be built consisting of four posts about 2.3–3 m long, rammed into the mud and covered with screening canvas or hessian; a seat at waterlevel or slightly below is fine if waist-high waders are worn. Some observers use a small flat-bottomed boat with hide attached.

Usually the hide is positioned to watch or photograph the nest of a waterbird. But even without a nest, a hide placed at the edge of a small area of open water that is surrounded by dense reeds, in a swamp well populated by waterbirds, should give bird sightings not otherwise likely to be obtained.

The placing of a hide near any nest must be done with great caution. Reed-bed birds usually build within dense clumps of reeds, closely screened by the massed stems. Initially the hide should be positioned well back, the intervening screen of reeds left in place, to be tied back to reveal the nest only for the duration of the observation; if the bird does not return to the nest within reasonable time the vegetation should be restored to its original position and the hide removed.

Once the timid waterbirds are accustomed to the hide, which may require a few days or perhaps a week, a session in the hide could give sightings, perhaps within reasonable range of a telephoto lens, of some of the birds that normally will not show themselves, especially the crakes, bitterns and rails. It will also afford the chance of seeing and perhaps recording action from birds that are behaving naturally rather than warily watching the birdwatcher.

49 WHITE-FACED HERON
Ardea novaehollandiae

Often when waiting in a swamp hide, one can see birds other than the 'target species', and these can sometimes be the more interesting, like the Baillon's Crakes that kept foraging all over the nest of the much larger Eurasian Coot while that bird was away, or a Purple Swamp-hen feeding in shallow water, or reed-warblers and grassbirds clinging to reed stems, often right alongside the hide.

If the hide has a view over a patch of open water among the reeds, there is a constant coming and going of waterbirds: ducks with attendant downy young, grebes disappearing with scarcely a ripple, to bob to the surface on some other part of the pool. There may be sighted a bittern moving stealthily through the reed-bed, a tall and stately Great Egret stalking forwards a few steps at a time, or a White-faced Heron in relaxed mood, bathing by plunging head-first, to rise with much shaking and shuffling of plumage.

When concealed in a hide in a swamp one is always made aware of the intensity of birdlife of the surrounding reed-beds. Swamps usually have a high density of birds, and many will come within a metre or two of a hide that has been in place a few weeks. The calls of the birds are often loud and very close, the caller frequently remaining hidden, and perhaps unidentified, which maintains a level of anticipation and sometimes breathless suspense. One never quite knows what will emerge from the reeds as rustling sounds draw closer.

By comparison, the quite massive disturbance caused by a human or two thrashing through dense reeds silences every bird and sends most of them to distant parts of the reed-beds, leaving little chance of a sighting. Unless searching for nests in order to compile records, take photographs, or for some other specific task, one may as well remain on the shore and be content with the distant sightings of those birds that will come out into the open.

308 **BARN OWL** *Tyto alba*

EASTERN DESERTS

The Eastern Deserts Region covers an immense area of arid and semi-arid Australia, from the northern interior of the Northern Territory through north-western, central and south-western Queensland to north-eastern South Australia and the north-western corner of New South Wales.

In the north-west its dominant landform is the grassland plateau of the Barkly Tableland. This extends eastwards across the border into Queensland, and then, along a rugged eastern edge through Mount Isa and Cloncurry, breaks up to fall away to the Carpentarian and Central lowlands. The latter form a vast shallow basin drained by the web of watercourses of the Channel Country.

These watercourses are usually dry but carry the occasional runoff towards Lake Eyre. They are chains of dry waterholes and interconnecting braided channels which can be transformed into rivers that are in places 30 km wide. Typically, they are fed great volumes of water along their higher rainfall northern headwaters, so that the floods often will surge steadily south through a parched land, bringing life to plants and animals along the thousands of kilometres of river floodplains, swamps and shallow lakes that they fill.

The main channels are usually lined with coolibahs and other eucalypts, while away from the rivers there are smaller trees, mostly acacias such as boree and gidgee, with Mitchell grass tussock ground-cover, or spinifex on sand dunes and ranges. The rivers converge to the south-west where they wind among dunes and finally disperse their waters among the lakes and lagoons at the eastern edge of the Simpson Desert.

This south-western part of the Eastern Deserts Region can be among the most inhospitable in Australia. However it harbours a number of rare species, some confined to this region, others more likely to be found here than elsewhere. It is a land of contrast, needing only rain, or the flowing of its watercourses from rain farther north, to bring the land and the birdlife to a level of beauty and interest that has attracted many expeditions and excursions over the years.

Across such a great distance there are contrasts of climate. Rainfall across the north of the region comes almost entirely in the summer wet season, with averages as high as 400 mm, fading away to less than 50 mm of highly erratic rainfall in the south-western part, where there is also a small and irregular winter rainfall. But in this southern half, around the great desert lakes and their watercourses, rain that falls far to the north can, for some of the birds, be as effective as local rain.

Local rain can refresh the desert, bringing green growth to dunes and clay-flats, perhaps putting a thin sheet of water over the claypans and lakes; rain in central Queensland can send floodwaters down the Diamantina River, Cooper Creek and Bulloo River, filling Goyders Lagoon, Lake Frome and Caryapundy Swamp, and sometimes reaching Lake Eyre. When these and a great many others are flooded, they attract huge numbers of waterbirds, some of which breed in colonies on islands, or among trees or other vegetation surrounded by the floodwaters. Some of the birds are entirely or substantially confined to this region. For others it is their principal or only breeding site, although they range much farther afield at other times. Two groups of birds are of special interest here: the raptors and the grasswrens.

Nineteen species of raptors are known to occur in this region, the majority breeding; at least 14 species have been recorded nesting along Strzelecki Creek alone. For some of these, such as the Letter-winged Kite, Black-breasted Buzzard, Black Falcon and Grey Falcon, the area around the Diamantina River, Cooper Creek and Strzelecki Creek region is probably their major breeding place. A very few raptors are but rarely recorded in this region, or appear as non-breeding vagrants, these being hawks of the coast or coastal forests, woodlands or grasslands. However the White-bellied Sea-eagle is an occasional visitor to the lakes and billabongs, for this species follows rivers far inland and nests in high gums beside some of the inland rivers.

This is also the region of rare grasswrens, with two species, the Eyrean Grasswren and the Grey Grasswren, apparently endemic, or very nearly, to the southern part of this region. The subspecies *modestus* of the Thick-billed Grasswren, now greatly reduced in range, seems also largely confined to this region. The Dusky Grasswren also occurs here, with both the nominate subspecies touching upon the far north-west, and the subspecies *ballerae* confined to the Mount Isa district and apparently endemic to this region. The widespread Striated Grasswren has also been recorded here, giving a total of five species.

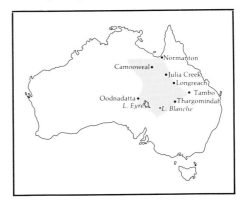

BIRDS OF THE EASTERN DESERTS

89 LETTER-WINGED KITE

Elanus scriptus

Although the Letter-winged Kite has been recorded in most parts of Australia, breeding takes place mainly in the Eastern Deserts Region. Among Australian raptors it is unusual in its colonial breeding, irruptive dispersion and mainly nocturnal hunting.

The Letter-winged Kite might at first be mistaken for the similarly plumaged Black-shouldered Kite, but in flight the underwing markings are distinctive. The wing action is very different, helping identification at distances where the underwing markings are not clear. The wingbeat of the Letter-winged Kite appears slow and floppy, the wings seeming to be held loosely, whereas the Black-shouldered Kite uses quick beats, with stiffly held wings. When perched, the two species are more difficult to separate. Usually the black shoulder-patch of the Letter-winged Kite appears longer and it has the dark patch ahead of, not behind, the eye, which seems to make the eyes appear larger and more owl-like.

On windy days the Letter-winged Kite prefers to roost in densely foliaged trees and may not take flight even when a person walks beneath the tree. At other times it roosts on exposed limbs. Communal roosting seems usual. It is possible that the species is often overlooked and may be more common than supposed.

Hunting begins at dusk, the kites circling low, dropping occasionally to the ground. It is probable that little hunting is done in the late hours of the night. On the other hand, it sometimes hunts on cloudy afternoons.

The Letter-winged Kite responds to widespread heavy rainfall through the desert by nesting, for the good season that follows brings an explosion in the population of the native Long-haired Rat, the principal prey of this kite. Nesting is colonial, sometimes several hundred birds in a locality, though usually only one pair to each tree.

In exceptional years the kite population builds up to numbers far above the normal population. With the inevitable return of drought, and the fall in food supply, there is a mass dispersion from the breeding regions, usually southwards, often into southern Victoria. This seems to be followed by heavy mortality of these displaced birds and probably few, if any, return to the interior.

▶ See also pages   136 138 167 *169 179* 183 184 272–3

93 BLACK-BREASTED BUZZARD

Hamirostra melanosternon

The Black-breasted Buzzard has a very wide range but seems most often recorded and found breeding along the Strzelecki Creek. This is perhaps partly because the area is visited over a number of years by observers working with raptors, probably because it is the closest regular known breeding area to south-eastern Australia.

The buzzard seems sedentary, some pairs nesting year after year in the same locality, probably moving only when forced by prolonged drought. Minor irruptions from time to time give sightings beyond the range over which the species is usually seen. It inhabits open country, woodlands, open dry scrublands, sparsely treed grasslands, preying upon reptiles and birds, including young of other raptors taken from their nests.

The Black-breasted Buzzard is unique to Australia and its relationship to other birds of prey is uncertain. In flight it is distinctive, larger than the common Black Kite, its wings very long and broad. The white 'windows' at the base of the primaries are conspicuous at a distance, being most obvious on the blackish-brown plumage of the dark-phase birds but still apparent on the sandy-brown of the light phase. The Buzzards soar on upcurved wings, with the primaries widely fingered, giving a square-cut wingtip; the tail looks very short. The black breast of dark-phase birds is noticeable at closer range.

Nests of the Black-breasted Buzzard are very large, their bulk surpassed only by those of the Osprey and Wedge-tailed Eagle, and often sited by waterholes in creek-beds. Big old coolibah trees are usually chosen, but even where the species is most plentiful, nests are usually not closer than about 8 km apart.

▶ See also pages   138 167 *169* 173 *179* 183 184 219 220 230 273 274

105 BLACK FALCON

Falco subniger

Although recorded over much of the continent, the Black Falcon is a migrant visitor to some parts, an irregular nomadic or vagrant to others; it is but a rare and irregular vagrant to Western Australia. The breeding range of this species seems confined almost entirely to the south-east interior, especially east of Lake Eyre about the Strzelecki Creek, the Murray–Darling, and the South Australian ranges regions. This falcon nests along watercourses, to which the

larger trees are confined in these dry regions, and hunts through eucalypt woodlands.

In the field this species can be confused with the Brown Falcon. In flight, as these birds are most often seen, the wingtips of the Black Falcon are pointed, those of the Brown are more rounded. The tail of the Black Falcon narrows towards the tip, with a slight step-in as the outermost feathers are shorter than the inner, while the tail of the Brown Falcon widens towards its tip.

When soaring or gliding the wing attitude of the Black Falcon is slightly downcurved, that of the Brown Falcon upswept and with a slight midwing kink. In fast flight the Black Falcon is very much like the Peregrine Falcon, having a rapid flicking action of the wings; the Brown Falcon flies with an erratic 'overarm rowing' action. But in leisurely flight the Black Falcon uses a slow-flapping, crow-like action. In display flight, however, the difference in the wing action of the Black and Brown species may not be as obvious.

The Black Falcon is considerably larger and more heavily built than the Brown, even slightly heavier than the Peregrine. It takes birds up to the size of swamp-hens and Pacific Black Ducks, as well as insects, reptiles and small mammals including rabbits in the southern parts of its range.

The Black Falcon is an Australian endemic with some resemblance to the Indian Lagger Falcon, *Falco jugger*, and the Lanner Falcon, *Falco biarmicus*. In some ways the Black Falcon appears well adapted to its arid environment. The very leisurely flight when not hunting, and the extensive use of soaring flight in thermals, may be an energy-conserving behaviour appropriate to the often limited resources of arid regions.

When good seasons occur in the arid and semi-arid interior the Black Falcon responds by nesting at quite high density; in 1981 four pairs nested along less than 20 km of the narrow Strzelecki Creek floodplain. The fairly high numbers of fledglings, during such favourable seasons, then disperse towards coastal regions.

Sightings in coastal areas are often of the Black Falcon hunting over waters of rivers or swamps, a pair sometimes combining to attack the larger prey, such as Swamphens.

▶ See also pages   136 137 138 139 161 167 169 *169* 173 184 208 219 220 221 277

108 GREY FALCON

Falco hypoleucos

As a breeding species, the Grey Falcon is probably confined to Australia; it was recorded for the first time from New Guinea in 1980. The species seems sparsely distributed through most of inland Australia but the breeding records are concentrated in the Lake Eyre and Murray–Darling districts. It appears resident throughout the year at some sites in the main breeding range but may be nomadic in other areas, especially at the periphery of its range.

Grey Falcons often hunt over river pools and also over open country. Prey recorded includes a variety of birds up to pigeon size, mammals to rabbit size, and quite large lizards. Birds may be taken in fast, low flight or in a steep, Peregrine-like dive. Some observers consider this species possibly the fastest of the Australian falcons. Its apparently lethargic flight when not hunting may, like the similar flight of the Black Falcon, be an energy-conserving technique appropriate to the arid environment.

This is basically a desert falcon, with preference for vast treeless spaces intersected by tree-lined watercourses. Its numbers seem always to have been low; many of those seen in coastal areas are probably wandering juveniles.

The Grey Falcon can be recognized in flight by the black wingtips, which are in strong contrast to the light blue-grey upperparts and even paler underparts. The flight silhouette is similar to that of the Peregrine Falcon but with the wingtips more rounded and a slightly more elliptical outline to each wing. Although almost the size of the Peregrine, the Grey Falcon is considerably lighter.

This falcon often soars to a height of 100–300 m, sometimes to 600 m, usually in the middle to late morning. It is in this high soaring that it is likely to be spotted, and the distinctive flight silhouette evident and useful.

The Grey Falcon uses the deserted nest of a crow or other raptor, and the availability of these may tend to restrict this falcon's numbers.

▶ See also pages 136 167 173 184 185 220 221 230 275 277–8

440 WHITE-WINGED FAIRY-WREN

Malurus leucopterus

The White-winged Fairy-wren is common and widespread through the drier parts of Australia, usually inland, but also along the more arid parts of the coastline. In the Eastern Deserts Region it is perhaps more than usually common as there are extensive areas of suitable habitat. Its range extends into the Central South Region, reaching the sea around Spencer Gulf

and the coast of the Nullarbor Plain. While this fairy-wren occupies a range of arid habitats, it is perhaps most commonly associated with the samphire and saltbush plains and margins of inland salt lakes and claypans, of which habitat there is an abundance to the east, north and west of the Flinders Ranges.

The White-winged Fairy-wren of mainland Australia is a subspecies, the

279 **MULGA PARROT** *Psephotus varius*

nominate subspecies being the Black-and-white Fairy-wren of the Pilbara–Goldfields Region, and discussed under that heading.

▶ See also pages   130 137 *172* 185 216 227 360

---

448 EYREAN GRASSWREN

Amytornis goyderi

This grasswren was discovered in 1874 but was not seen again until 1961 when it was found near the site of the original discovery, on the Macumba River at the northern end of Lake Eyre, a nest with young also being found. Not until 1972 was it sighted again, in the eastern part of the Simpson Desert, on the Queensland–South Australian border between Poeppel's Corner and Eyre Creek, then again farther east.

In 1976 Eyrean Grasswrens were 'abundant' in sandhills of the southern half of the Simpson Desert, inhabiting mainly sandhill cane-grass, and frequently in association with Rufous-crowned Emu-wrens and White-winged Fairy-wrens. That was during a good season; the following year was drier, the cane-grass had no seed, and none of these grasswrens could be found within easy reach of Birdsville.

The Eyrean Grasswren appears to have a wide distribution through the southern Simpson Desert, perhaps even the whole of the desert, but is probably highly nomadic, moving to those parts where conditions are best. The population as a whole seems patchy, sometimes locally abundant in a good season.

This species should therefore ideally be sought several months after good rains, in or near its known range. It has been found mainly on crests and slopes of sandhills, frequenting tussocks of cane-grass, where it is extremely secretive, remaining most of the time within the dense cover of the clumps, and rarely perching in open view on top of tussock or shrub. It usually keeps well ahead of an observer, bounding across intervening bare sand, often using the wings for extra speed so that pairs of footprints left on the sand can become very widely spaced where the bird is nearly airborne. It is usually furtive and difficult to observe, the birds, in pairs or small parties, moving away from intruders.

The calls can be helpful, especially alarm calls when the birds are first encountered but still out of sight in the cane-grass clumps: a high 'seep-seep' or other short sharp note. The song is rich and loud, with excited fast bursts and silvery trills.

▶ See also pages   167 *169* 361

---

449 GREY GRASSWREN

Amytornis barbatus

The Grey Grasswren was not discovered until 1967 although there were possible sightings much earlier. It appears confined to a small area of the overflow country of the Bulloo River, near the western end of the New South Wales–Queensland border, and on the Diamantina River at Goyders Lagoon; more recently it has been recorded on Eyre Creek, 117 km north of Birdsville.

In all these localities the Grey Grasswrens inhabit very dense lignum, intermixed with swamp cane-grass on the Bulloo River and sedge on the Diamantina River. In and about the lignum thickets the Grey Grasswrens feed on seeds and insects, occasionally water snails.

The Grey Grasswren is very secretive, usually sighted only when it chooses to emerge from the dense lignum to perch on the higher canes. Any attempt to move closer will send it down and out of sight in the thickets again, from which it is then difficult to flush. If forced to move on to another clump it will either run with fast, bouncing gait or will fly low above the ground. The Grey Grasswrens occur only where there are dense brakes of lignum or cane-grass covering much of the ground. Sites such as the Bullarine overflow and Goyders Lagoon are flooded once every couple of years to a depth of around a metre, so the grasswrens must have dense vegetation cover rising above that level.

The Grey Grasswrens feed through most of the morning, both on open ground and within the thickets, maintaining contact with much twittering. They are possibly more vocal than other grasswrens, with calls similar to those of Superb Fairy-wrens. When alarmed they emit a single high and piercing 'eeep'.

During the course of foraging, the party of Grey Grasswrens will pause often to perch among the topmost canes of a lignum clump to sunbathe and preen, particularly on a sunny morning after a chilly night. During the heat of midday and afternoon they shelter in shade within the clumps, emerging again to feed in the late afternoon.

The Eyre Creek population, in the overflow area around Lake Machattie, Lake Koolivoo and Lake Mipia, was described as being confiding and easily attracted to the outer edges of the dense and impenetrable lignum clumps by squeaking noises.

▶ See also pages   167 *169* 175 361-2

---

450 THICK-BILLED GRASSWREN

Amytornis textilis

This grasswren occurs in three isolated populations, recognized as three subspecies, of which two have greatly declined, probably through destruction of habitat. It appears to require large dense shrubs with foliage right to the ground, giving low shelter for these largely terrestrial birds. In most parts of its range the cover was bluebush and saltbush but in many places these have been eaten by stock, the bushes becoming too small and bare to shelter grasswrens.

The Western Australian subspecies was widespread but has vanished from most of its range. One of its remaining sites is on Peron Peninsula, Shark Bay, where it inhabits acacia scrubland with smaller bushes of dense mulla-mulla, emu bush and lignum. Also in mid west-coastal Western Australia, this grasswren has been recorded from near the Wooramel River, on the east side of the North-West Coastal Highway. Here the sandplain vegetation is of wanu, a mulga-like scrub. Some areas were burned heavily in the past; the species was reported quite common in this type of fire-regeneration habitat. It has also been seen in saltbush around some remote inland salt lakes.

The two eastern subspecies were recorded during the RAOU Field Atlas survey as remnants of former far more widespread populations. One was confined to country between the northern Flinders Ranges and northern Lake Eyre, the other on Eyre Peninsula, where it was thought to be well distributed though hard to find.

The Thick-billed Grasswren is smaller than the other widespread inland species, the Striated Grasswren. It is often in small parties of five or six which maintain close contact, running and scurrying with 'astonishing rapidity', bouncing along like rubber balls, bush to bush, heads held low, tails erect, seldom flying. They are very elusive. Although their habitat may look open, they can disappear with ease. Through the heat of the day they sit tight, out of sight, rarely flushing unless the bush is shaken, then dashing across to the next cover.

These grasswrens feed early to mid mornings and late afternoons, foraging mainly under and close to protective shrubbery. They often climb to the tops of shrubs to sun themselves and look about. They are the quietest of the grasswrens but have sharp, high alarm notes and the male has a high-pitched 'silvery' musical song.

▶ **See also pages** 155 163 164 167 *169* 178 184 230 232 362

569 **ORANGE CHAT** *Ephthianura aurifrons*

491 CHESTNUT-BREASTED WHITEFACE

Aphelocephala pectoralis

The Chestnut-breasted Whiteface has a very restricted distribution in the north-eastern parts of South Australia, where it is evidently of localized and patchy occurrence as it often cannot be found in localities where it has nested in a previous season. Although first described in 1871, it was not seen again until 1914 when it was rediscovered on gibber plains west of Oodnadatta; the nest and eggs were not found until 1968.

The Chestnut-breasted Whiteface is usually in company with the Southern Whiteface or the Banded Whiteface,

feeding together on the ground; it is said to be more timid, quickly flying to cover if disturbed. The Chestnut-breasted Whiteface resembles the Banded Whiteface but with the narrow black breastband replaced by a broader chestnut zone.

Sighting of this species would seem to require searching in areas of previous records but in a good season examining all individuals of flocks of other white face species. Once known, the weak, tinkling trill may assist.

Sites include Oodnadatta, Coober Pedy, Lake Frome, Myrtle Springs Station, west Leigh Creek and east of the Birdsville Track.

▶ **See also pages** *169* 371–2

536 GREY-FRONTED HONEYEATER

Lichenostomus plumulus

A widespread species through inland Australia, reaching some drier parts of the coast. Eucalypt or acacia woodlands are preferred. Around Mount Isa it is found in localities where there are clumps of low mallee and small watercourses, usually in scattered pairs. At times it congregates in parties of 20–30, sometimes up to 80 birds on flowering trees. In the Great Victoria Desert the usual habitat is mallee with spinifex understorey.

The Grey-fronted Honeyeater is similar to the Yellow-plumed Honeyeater in that it has a sharply defined black line from the bill back over the yellow plume, but the streaks on the underparts are much less distinctive. It is also similar to the Grey-headed Honeyeater, almost certainly resulting in misidentification. Most references show this species to occur in the Hamersley–Chichester ranges area of the Pilbara, where the Western Australian Museum has specimens and records of only the Grey-headed.

▶ **See also pages** *169* 175 197 198 208 220

569 ORANGE CHAT

Ephthianura aurifrons

Although extremely widespread through the interior and drier coastal regions, the Orange Chat is of generally scarce, very patchy occurrence, but at times common locally when conditions are favourable. It occurs on saltbush-samphire margins of salt lakes, areas of low succulent plants, and tussock grasslands.

The Orange Chat is usually quiet and inconspicuous, much less obvious than the Crimson Chat, feeding on the ground among the low dense bushes.

Fortunately it has the habit of perching frequently though briefly on top of these shrubs, where its bright colours and the open environs make it obvious.

A useful search technique is to wander through likely habitat, scanning 20–100 m ahead over a wide arc watching for the momentary flutter of wings as any small bird flies, even momentarily, above the low vegetation. Any that perch, as is the habit of this chat, can then be examined with the binoculars, and for this purpose it is best to search with the sun behind.

The flight call is a weak 'chee-chee-chee'.

▶ **See also pages** 137 173 175 184 220 228 231 389–90

570 YELLOW CHAT

Ephthianura crocea

The Yellow Chat has been recorded widely across the northern parts of this Eastern Deserts Region, where it has colonized the lignum, cumbungi, sedges or other dense vegetation of the swamps that have developed over many decades around bore overflows. Here it seems to be easily sighted and approachable, keeping largely to the muddy edges of the swamps and perching on acacia branches. It may also be found on dry grassy lakebeds and coastal flats.

These chats seem to be recorded regularly at bores on Coorabulka Station and also on Davenport Downs, Lorna Downs, and at Whitula Creek west of Windorah. Other Queensland sites include the Norman River, Mount Isa area and Sudan Dip north of Cloncurry. At times of heavy rain and flooding, areas of suitable

246 LITTLE CORELLA *Cacatua sanguinea*

440 WHITE-WINGED FAIRY-WREN *Malurus leucopterus*

habitat could link many of these locations.

Localities outside this region include Normanton, the Alligator rivers area of the Top End Region, and the Roebuck Plains, Fitzroy River and Kununurra areas of the Kimberley Region.

The best-known of these is on the lower South Alligator and East Alligator rivers where there are open swampy flats. The chats will often perch on the upper parts of tall, coarse grass stems that in places rise above the uniform level of the plains, or on the tops of reeds, when in sunlight their bright, pale yellow is obvious. The calls are distinctive, a thin, high 'pli-pli-' and harsh 'cherr'.

It is sometimes possible to spot Yellow Chats from distances of up to several hundred metres by scanning with binoculars, in wide, slow sweeps across the plains, watching for the yellow when they perch on higher stems.

Although locally common, the Yellow Chat is nomadic and will move away from some sites as they dry out.

▶ See also pages *169* 196 210 218 390

572 GIBBERBIRD

Ashbyia lovensis

The Gibberbird is not only endemic to Australia, but also does not extend far beyond this Eastern Deserts Region. The range of the bird is determined by the occurrence of the sparsely vegetated gibber plains which it inhabits. These plains need not be of great extent; it often occurs where there are small areas of gibber ground between dunes. In most localities the Gibberbird has been found to be resident throughout the year, but there are some records of apparently nomadic movements, perhaps forced by unsuitable conditions.

The Gibberbird bears considerable resemblance to the chats but is larger, runs and tail-wags in pipit-like fashion, and has an undulating display flight similar to that of a songlark. It does not occur in large flocks like the chats, but occasionally in parties of up to six or eight birds, rarely to 20.

The Gibberbird can be difficult to spot unless accidentally flushed.

▶ See also pages *169* 173 175 390

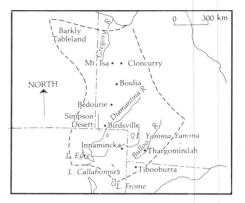

THE DIAMANTINA RIVER, MULLIGAN RIVER AND EYRE CREEK

With its catchment far into north-western and central Queensland, the Diamantina River, after heavy rains in those regions, can carry immense floods south towards Lake Eyre, when its channels and floodplains may become sheets of water many kilometres across. After the floods subside, its almost countless lakes, billabongs, claypans and swamps hold water for months, sometimes years, providing habitat for a great variety of species. The surrounding environs of gibber plains, mulga scrub and spinifex grasslands add to the range of species that might be seen. The Diamantina area is traversed by the Birdsville Track, from Marree in South Australia to Birdsville in south-western Queensland.

The Mulligan, the most westerly river in south-western Queensland, has a catchment along the Queensland–Northern Territory Border. It flows south through dunes to join Eyre Creek at the Muncoonie Lake, forming a wetland oasis at the very edge of the sand-dune expanses of the Simpson Desert.

Many waterholes, some permanent, are scattered along this watercourse and Eyre Creek, which continues south to Goyders Lagoon. These waterholes are frequented by various waterbirds and small waders, while the river-edge trees are used by raptors. Along the edges of the Mulligan River large clumps of lignum occur.

Most of the surrounding country here is of areas of gibber plains or sand ridges. Spinifex and cane-grass are the main ground-cover. An observer at Sandringham Station, near the Mulligan River north-west of Bedourie, over a period of two weeks during a very dry September was able to record 93 species, including the Freckled Duck, Marsh Harrier, Brown

Falcon, Brolga, Inland Dotterel, Australian Pratincole, Whiskered Tern, Gull-billed Tern, Red-backed Kingfisher, White-backed Swallow, Cinnamon Quail-thrush, Slaty-backed Thornbill, Black Honeyeater, Crimson Chat, Orange Chat and Gibberbird.

The Simpson Desert itself requires a thoroughly prepared expedition. As an example of its birdlife, two crossings of the desert in April and July of 1969, the first heading west from Birdsville, the second north-west, yielded a birdlist of 83 species. The desert at that time was in reasonable condition, good rain having fallen the previous February.

In 1973, after heavy rains in Queensland, the Mulligan River and Eyre Creek carried floodwaters sufficient to permit a boat exploration of the watercourse, only the fourth time since 1900 that this has been possible. In the six days that it took to cover the 130 km between Muncoonie Lake and Goyders Lagoon a total of 67 species were recorded. Among these were many raptors, including the Black-breasted Buzzard and Black Falcon, while the most abundant species were the Galah, Budgerigar, Fairy Martin, White-winged Triller and Rufous Songlark.

LAKE EYRE

When containing water, Lake Eyre and surrounding lakes carry large numbers of waterbirds. In 1973–74, when Lake Eyre filled, huge numbers of Australian Pelicans and Silver Gulls nested on the islands of this inland sea. A survey of the birds of the southern

163 **RED-NECKED AVOCET** *Recurvirostra novaehollandiae* With young hatching

and western drainage areas was made in 1977 and 1978, after the flooding of 1973–74 had partly subsided, and 74 species were recorded. The RAOU Field Atlas survey listed 141 species for the Oodnadatta–Macumba River area, and in the wader survey of Lake Eyre in September 1984, an aerial count recorded 95 000 Red-necked Avocets, 23 000 Banded Stilts and more than 6000 migratory waders.

The Pelicans were by then breeding for the second time, with a total of 7000 sitting on eggs on three different islands, and one island had a colony of about 50 Pied Cormorants. On a freshwater lake, probably typical of many in the area, were Pink-eared Ducks, Hardheads, Maned Ducks, Grey Teal and Black-tailed Native-hens. Orange and Crimson Chats were abundant. As a birding site, Lake Eyre has one great drawback: the great intervals between fillings. However, many of the lesser lakes and pools on

inflowing watercourses can be filled by lesser rains and repeat the scene on a smaller scale.

COOPER CREEK

To the east of the Diamantina–Warburton watercourses, Cooper Creek has its beginnings as the Thomson and Barcoo in central Queensland and flows south-westerly to reach the south-east corner of Lake Eyre.

Heavy rain in the central Queensland catchment can cause inundation of the broad Cooper Creek floodplain and the filling of large semi-permanent wetlands of Lake Yamma Yamma and countless river-channel waterholes.

An overflow channel, the Strzelecki Creek, diverges from Cooper Creek near Innamincka, running southwards to Lake Blanche, near the northern end of the Flinders Ranges, a distance of some 200 km. Strzelecki Creek flows only after exceptional rains when its waterholes fill and the numbers of small birds, rodents and rabbits increase rapidly. This tree-lined floodplain, mostly less than 3 km wide, has even in normal seasons an exceptional number of raptors.

A total of 14 species of raptors have been recorded breeding along Strzelecki Creek, including the rare Grey Falcon. A survey by members of the Australian Raptors Association in 1981, along an 18 km section of this watercourse, found 47 active nests of Black Kites, two of Black-breasted Buzzards, two of Whistling Kites, three of Little Eagles, seven of Australian Kestrels, six of Brown Falcons, four of Black Falcons and one of the Australian Hobby. Presumably the numbers would be even greater in a season following heavy rain.

48 **YOUNG PACIFIC HERONS** *Ardea pacifica*

of the Grey Range. The river is eventually dissipated south of the New South Wales border, to the east of Tibooburra and Sturt National Park, in Caryapundy Swamp, the Bulloo Overflow, and numerous cane-grass swamps.

LAWN HILL

The Lawn Hill National Park, on a tributary of the Gregory River between Camooweal and Burketown, takes in 12 200 ha of the eastern edge of the Barkly Tableland. Gorges, permanent water and relict rainforest plant species make the site an oasis in usually dry surroundings. The pool is set among craggy sandstone ridges with spinifex cover, where the Sandstone Shrike-thrush attracts attention with its ringing calls. Other birds seen here have been the White-browed Robin and Banded Honeyeater.

The Gregory River Crossing, between Lawn Hill and Burketown, is a site for the Purple-crowned Fairy-wren, the Northern Rosella, Azure Kingfisher, Fan-tailed Cuckoo, Bar-breasted Honeyeater, Crimson Finch and Masked Finch.

110 **AUSTRALIAN KESTREL** Falco cenchroides

578 **RED-BROWED PARDALOTE**
Pardalotus rubricatus

343 **WHITE-BACKED SWALLOW**
Cheramoeca leucosternum

BULLOO RIVER

Eastwards again from Cooper Creek a third complex of river channels, that of the Bulloo, becomes lost in a confusion of lakes and waterholes at the foot of the Grey Range. Thirty kilometres west of Thargomindah, Lake Bullawarra, which is filled by the overflow of the Bulloo, when it contains water supports many thousands of waterbirds. The lake is edged with a belt of eucalypts and patches of lignum which together provide nesting sites for numerous birds.

Lake Bullawarra also has reed-beds, used by some thousands of ducks and other waterbirds. When the lake fills from time to time to sufficient depth, the many hectares of lignum bushes become the sites of colonies totalling countless thousands of Straw-necked and Sacred ibises. Also nesting here are large numbers of Royal and Yellow-billed spoonbills, three species of egrets, Darters, and seven species of ducks including the Freckled Duck. Breeding records of special interest here have been the nesting of about 50 pairs of Great Crested Grebes.

Other sites of interest along the lower Bulloo are the Dynevor Lakes, and Bulloo Lake along the eastern side

MOUNT ISA

The Mount Isa area offers a variety of birding and has been well-studied by resident and visiting ornithologists.

348 **RICHARD'S PIPIT** Anthus novaeseelandiae

DIAMANTINA BIRDWATCH

The construction of a number of dams in the district has provided water and habitat for local birdlife.

Lake Moonara has developed fringing vegetation, attracting not only waterbirds but many bushland species, some resident around the lake, others migrant visitors. It is situated 20 km north of Mount Isa.

In the district can be found the Spinifexbird, Cloncurry Parrot, Spinifex Pigeon, Painted Finch, Pictorella Mannikin, Black-throated Finch, Blue-winged Kookaburra, White-breasted Woodswallow and Figbird. The Cloncurry Parrot is a subspecies of the Mallee Ringneck, formerly regarded as a full species; it is paler blue-green above, yellower beneath, and lacks the red forehead patch.

When the lake's waterlevel has fallen, late in the dry season, some small islands are exposed; these have been used by Caspian Terns and Silver Gulls as nest sites. Other dams hold large lakes that are improving waterbird habitats; these are Rifle Creek, about 35 km south, and Lake Julius, about 80 km north.

At Mica Creek, near Mount Isa, a permanent soak is a good spot to watch for honeyeaters and finches coming in to drink. Midway between Cloncurry and Mount Isa, Clem Walton Park has a good variety of birdlife, with sightings here of the Cloncurry Parrot, Black-tailed Treecreeper, Spotted Bowerbird, and a colony of Rufous Night Herons.

The northern interior of Queensland has a large and conspicuous honeyeater population, mainly species widespread across northern and central Australia. Among these are the Banded, Black, Brown, Rufous-throated, Yellow-tinted, White-plumed, White-throated, Golden-backed (subspecies of the Black-chinned), Grey-headed, Grey-fronted, White-gaped, Singing, and Spiny-cheeked honeyeaters, Little Friarbird, Silver-crowned Friarbird, and the Yellow-throated Miner. Varied Lorikeets also visit these trees.

The most important sources of nectar are the trees *Tristania grandiflora*, flowering from November to February, and the batswing coral, *Erythrina vespertilio*, flowering from September to December. A number of eucalypt species also contribute. The *Tristania* is an important tree for honeyeaters, attracting them in great numbers; it is widespread along watercourses. For any birdwatcher in the north during those hot months, a wait in shade near one of these trees in flower could be a sensible way of recording the local honeyeaters.

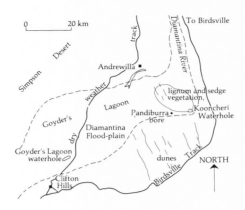

The bird-sighting opportunities along the Diamantina River and Cooper Creek vary enormously depending upon seasonal conditions. A site with potential is Goyders Lagoon, about 100 km south of Birdsville. The lagoon is an extensive floodplain occasionally filled by the Diamantina River across which there are numerous waterholes, especially towards its northern end where the channels of the Diamantina enter. The Birdsville Track here offers alternative routes, a dry-weather track across the lagoon floodplain, and a wet-weather route around the eastern margin. Between these tracks an area of the north-eastern part is of interest as a site for the Grey Grasswren and the Eastern Grass Owl.

Both species have been reported from an area of floodplain extending eastwards from Kooncheri Waterhole to Pandiburra artesian bore, and beyond, a distance of some 15 km. Here the lagoon floodplain is mostly covered with lignum and sedge, merging with lush swampy vegetation around the bore.

Grey Grasswrens have been found in numerous sites to the north-east and north-west of Kooncheri Waterhole and to the north and north-west of Pandiburra Bore. They were most often found in dense areas of lignum with at least some sedge ground-cover, their habitat here more dense overall than in some other localities used by this species. Sightings were difficult; a high 'chip-p-ip' contact call helps in locating and following the bird.

The Eastern Grass Owls, on the other hand, were found where the sedge was thicker, about knee-high, with few lignum clumps; however most of the birds flushed arose from the base of a lignum clump. The numbers of this species will depend upon the abundance of its principal prey here, the native Long-haired Rat. However, there have been sightings of owls on Goyders Lagoon over a number of years, and the very extensive habitat available should ensure that there are at least a few here at most times.

From Goyders Lagoon an interesting route to follow is via Birdsville, Durrie, Innamincka on Cooper Creek, and into New South Wales via Warrie Gate, to Tibooburra and the Bulloo River floodplains.

These tracks traverse a variety of country. Between Birdsville and Durrie, branches of the Diamantina have some areas of lignum swamp, in and around which have been sighted Yellow-billed Spoonbills and Flock Bronzewings. On areas of stony country, Gibberbirds might be seen. Southwards from Durrie the country is flat with some low sandhills, where Cinnamon Quail-thrushes have been recorded, along with Crested Bellbirds and Orange and Crimson chats.

347 **FAIRY MARTIN** *Cecropis ariel*

616 **SPOTTED BOWERBIRD** *Chlamydera maculata*

CENTRAL DESERTS

The Central Deserts Region is a broad belt of semi-arid country that is bordered on the west by the formidable Western Deserts Region and on the east by some equally arid country along parts of its border with the Eastern Deserts Region. The central ranges, made up of the MacDonnell Ranges around Alice Springs, and adjoining ranges, is almost encircled by extremely arid country, largely uninhabited and roadless.

To the north-west are the Tanami Desert and the sand-dune expanses of the Great Sandy Desert, to the west the Little Sandy and Gibson deserts, to the south-west the Great Victoria Desert, and southwards the Nullarbor Plain. Along the region's eastern and south-eastern boundary is probably the most desert-like country anywhere in Australia: the Simpson Desert.

To the north and north-east the Central Deserts Region is linked to the coast by country slightly less desert-like, the grasslands of the Barkly Tableland, and it is from the north that the greater part of the region's rainfall comes.

In the sandy deserts little surface water remains after rain, but the same rain across the rocky terrain of the central ranges gives runoff from the slopes and cliffs of the ranges and a concentration of water in valleys, below the slopes and in the gorges, where the surface water remains widespread much longer in rocky river beds. Deep pools in the shadowy gorges are protected from wind and sun, providing permanent water through long periods of drought. In many places pools are fed by seepages of underground water from crevices low on cliffs and in gorges; even a slow drip or seemingly insignificant trickle can maintain a small pool, some

holding perhaps no more than a cupful of water. On a warm day birds will come to such a seepage to drink and, if the pool is large enough, to bathe.

Almost all the scenic gorges in the MacDonnell Ranges around Alice Springs have pools as the central focus of their scenic beauty, with red cliffs and deep blue desert skies reflected across the mirror surface of the pools.

But in times of extended drought all but the deepest pools will dry out. Across valley flats and plains the ground-cover of temporary everlastings and other small plants, which appear after the rains, become but dry debris in the dust. A great many of the desert birds are nomadic and with the return of drought will have departed for places more hospitable. In so vast a region of desert country there are always some parts that have received rain, either from a summer cyclone sweeping in across the Pilbara coast, or a tropical depression bringing a band of heavy rain southwards from the Gulf of Carpentaria, or an exceptionally strong winter cold front pushing north from the Southern Ocean. Locally, a thunderstorm can bring heavy rain and a rejuvenated landscape to a small patch of desert.

Most birds of arid Australia are quick to take advantage of heavy rain that is sufficient to bring green growth and perhaps some local flooding. One observer was able to list only 30 species of birds around Ayers Rock in May, after many months of drought. In July and August 40 mm of rain fell and by the end of August the species count had jumped to 60, and most were beginning to breed. It is not only the number of species that increases but the numbers of birds. Some, like the Crimson Chat, Pied Honeyeater and Budgerigar, must arrive in thousands, probably tens of thousands, for there can be

nesting pairs every hundred metres or so in all directions over thousands of square kilometres of mulga scrublands.

In coastal regions where rainfall is regular, whether winter or summer, most birds have a clearly defined breeding season, but in the arid regions most species exploit an occasional good season by breeding in either autumn or spring. The extremes of midsummer heat and, except in the northern interior, the midwinter cold, are usually avoided. Some species, such as the Grey Teal, Budgerigar and Zebra Finch, are exceptionally quick to respond to rain, and these are among Australia's most widespread and abundant bird species. The Grey Teal is so quick to respond that it may begin laying eggs within 10 days of heavy rain. The Zebra Finch will continue to produce successive clutches as long as conditions remain favourable, over a year on occasions, and the young mature so rapidly that they are capable of reproducing at less than three months of age. Many other birds will nest in autumn as well as spring and most of the small passerines will probably raise several broods in an extended period of favourable conditions.

On the other hand, some birds adhere rigidly to a regular breeding season irrespective of the weather. These include most of the raptors and parrots.

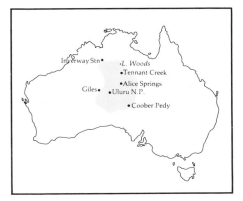

BIRDS OF THE CENTRAL DESERTS

451 DUSKY GRASSWREN

Amytornis purnelli

Except for an outlying population around Mt Isa, the Dusky Grasswren is probably confined to the Central Deserts Region. From the time the Dusky Grasswren was first discovered in 1894 until the taxonomy of the species was resolved in 1972, there has been confusion between this and the Thick-billed Grasswren, of which it was at one time considered a subspecies. To add to the confusion, the Thick-billed Grasswren's population in Western Australia, which appears to be isolated, was listed as a separate species known as the Western Grasswren, while the Thick-billed and Dusky grasswrens, both occupying central regions, were combined as the Thick-billed Grasswren, with the Dusky Grasswren as a subspecies.

In 1972, studies of distributions, habitats and features resulted in recognition of the Dusky Grasswren as a separate species. The Western and Thick-billed grasswrens were combined as a single species.

The Dusky Grasswren in the Central Deserts Region has a distribution which overlaps that of the Thick-billed Grasswren, but the two species occupy different habitats. The Dusky Grasswren is a bird of the rocky slopes of spinifex-clad ranges while the Thick-billed Grasswren keeps to the plains and along watercourses, under dense cover of saltbush, bluebush, and similar small compact shrubs.

The Dusky Grasswren is rarely seen out of spinifex. It seldom flies but if hard-pressed will use the wings to give greater velocity to an already rapid departure. The alarm call is short and sharp, as it hops rapidly, tail up, across the boulders. The Dusky Grasswren shows a preference for the steeper slopes of ranges and the sides and tops of rocky hills, particularly the scree slopes of intermixed broken rock and spinifex below cliffs of ranges and gorges.

In places of optimum habitat the Dusky Grasswren is common, and in general seems more abundant than most other grasswrens. The species is inquisitive and confiding, more easily seen than other grasswrens. Otherwise its routine and behaviour are typical of the grasswrens. It feeds early to mid-morning and again in the late afternoon, then usually retires to shade during the heat of the day.

The crevices and cavities among tumbled boulders provide shady and

504 SPINY-CHEEKED HONEYEATER *Acanthagenys rufogularis*

comparatively cool escape from the central Australian midday heat. These rock refuges also give security. When disturbed, the birds of a group instantly scatter in all directions, bouncing away across bare ground and rocks to vanish within seconds under dense needle-leaved clumps of spinifex or into the hidden recesses between boulders.

The Dusky Grasswren is gregarious and is seen in groups of a dozen or more out of the breeding season, and to some extent during the breeding months. In keeping with this behaviour, the nest territories are quite small and breeding pairs not far apart. Dusky Grasswrens maintain contact with high rippling and twittering calls, while the alarm call consists of two or three short staccato notes. The song is rich, but brief and unobtrusive. Known sites in central Australia include the MacDonnell Ranges, Haasts Bluff, Ellery Creek, Mt Gillen, Mt Benstead, and the Everard, Petermann and Rawlinson ranges. Close to Alice Springs this grasswren may be seen at Simpsons Gap and Ormiston Gorge.

The Dusky Grasswren was thought to be confined to the ranges of central Australia until, in 1966, birds of this species were found isolated much farther east, in ranges near Mt Isa, north-western Queensland, and described as a new subspecies which could be found at the old Ballara Mine near Mary Kathleen.

▶ See also pages   167 *179* 183 184 185 362

482 CHESTNUT-RUMPED THORNBILL

Acanthiza uropygialis

The bright chestnut rump of this thornbill is conspicuous as it flies up from the ground, or lands at its nest. The Chestnut-rumped Thornbill is found almost throughout the drier parts of mainland Australia. It seems often to be seen where dead timber is common, but perhaps this is only because hollows are needed for nesting. Like other thornbills, it builds a domed nest which it places inside a hollow limb, stump or treetrunk; in a fence-post; or in fallen timber. It seems to choose a hollow that is roomy inside, for the nest is thickly lined and bulky; the hollow usually has also a very small crevice or knot-hole as entrance.

This thornbill feeds almost entirely on the ground, in pairs or small parties in the breeding season, at other times in quite large flocks. If disturbed the birds will fly up to a shrub, showing the bright rump. If binoculars are at hand, the eye colour should be observed, for this species has a conspicuous, pale, creamy-white iris which distinguishes it from other reddish-rumped thornbills.

▶ See also pages   60 136 137 184 *218* 369

504 SPINY-CHEEKED HONEYEATER

Acanthagenys rufogularis

Often the distinctive musical chiming, liquid-toned and pleasant calls of the Spiny-cheeked Honeyeater tell of its presence long before it is seen, for the call carries far across the open mulga, spinifex or open, dry woodland country that it inhabits. Like the calls of the Crested Bellbird and the Chiming Wedgebill, these calls seem to have a slightly sad and lonely quality which is in keeping with the harsh and remote outback country in which it is most often seen.

The Spiny-cheeked Honeyeater tends to be shy, so that even where its call is often heard it may not be seen except perhaps at a distance, when calling from the top of a shrub or as it departs with swift, undulating flight. Sometimes a pair will linger close to a profusely flowering eremophila or other shrub where they have been feeding, or in the vicinity of a dense thicket where the nest is concealed, permitting a closer view of a bird which is distinctive with bright pink bill and spiny-looking white streak across the face.

▶ See also pages 136 137 163 175 *178* 183 220 232 375

594 ZEBRA FINCH *Poephila guttata*

34 GREY-HEADED HONEYEATER

Lichenostomus keartlandi

The Grey-headed Honeyeater is common across the central to north-western interior wherever there are eucalypts — the rivergums of the gorges and other watercourses, the stunted range-top trees, or the scattered small eucalypts of the sandy desert country. It occurs right through the Great Sandy and Gibson deserts to the ranges of the Pilbara, north through the Tanami Desert and into central-northern Queensland, wherever there are areas of favourable habitat.

The Grey-headed Honeyeater appears to be locally nomadic rather than migratory. When local shrubs or trees are in full flower, this can be one of the most abundant of birds. A favoured shrub is *Grevillea wickhami*; it has reddish flowers and silvery foliage and is common throughout the

northern deserts, from the northern interior of Queensland, through the northern interior of the Northern Territory, the Great Sandy Desert and Gibson Desert to the Pilbara. Like the honeyeater, this grevillea is found on rocky ranges, sandplains and sand-dune country.

Where gorges of desert ranges hold pools, the Grey-headed Honeyeater is

89 **Letter-winged Kite** *Elanus scriptus* (underwing pattern)

91 **Black Kite** *Milvus migrans* (underwing pattern)

92 **Square-tailed Kite** *Lophoictinia isura* (underwing pattern)

93 **Black-breasted Buzzard** *Hamirostra melanosternon* (underwing pattern)

95 **Whistling Kite** *Haliastur sphenurus* (underwing pattern)

101 **Wedge-tailed Eagle** *Aquila audax* (underwing pattern)

102 **Little Eagle** *Hieraaetus morphnoides* (underwing pattern)

235 **Spinifex Pigeon** (central Australian form) *Petrophassa plumifera*

348 **Richard's Pipit** *Anthus novaeseelandiae*

451 **Dusky Grasswren** *Amytornis purnelli*

647 **Torresian Crow** *Corvus orru*

often among the most common or frequent of all birds in coming to the water. It is usually in pairs to small parties but sometimes in flocks of several hundred birds.

▶ **See also pages** 175 183 185 206 221 230 *232 233 381*

568 CRIMSON CHAT

Ephthianura tricolor

This chat is, like others of the genus, nomadic, arriving often in great numbers following heavy rain and the appearance of lush fresh growth of small ephemeral plants across desert sands or clays. At times there are irruptions towards the coasts, with large numbers of these conspicuous birds in districts where they are not usually seen.

The Crimson Chat occupies open country and feeds on the ground, walking briskly among the low ground-cover plants, taking insects from the foliage. It is not noticed until flushed from the ground, when it flies away with brisk 'chek-chek' calls and usually perches on a twig of a shrub or tree not far away. If there is a nest nearby this will be indicated by the anxious behaviour of the adults. These chats are skilful in approaching and leaving their nest, which typically is placed in a very small shrub, usually within 10–30 cm of the ground. A small, low, dense bush is favoured, often a mulla-mulla or cottonbush, even though there may be taller shrubs nearby.

Invariably the Crimson Chats, when approaching the nest, will land on the ground anywhere from 5 to 20 m away and run erratically back and forth, just as they do when searching for insects, until, as if by chance, the nest bush is reached. A similar deceptive procedure is followed when leaving the nest. From 20 to 30 m viewing distance the chats are out of sight behind bushes more often than in view. Occasionally an incubating bird, male or female, is accidentally flushed from the nest.

▶ **See also pages** 136 137 171 173 175 177 183 *212* 220 231 389

306 **SOUTHERN BOOBOOK**
Ninox novaeseelandiae

109 **BROWN FALCON** *Falco berigora*

354 **GROUND CUCKOO-SHRIKE**
Coracina maxima

97 COLLARED SPARROWHAWK *Accipiter cirrhocephalus*

394 **CRESTED BELLBIRD** *Oreoica gutturalis*

barrier against attack from above by any of the numerous raptors of the northern interior. A male bowerbird, his attention concentrated upon bower construction, maintenance and display, showing bright colour patches and returning again and again to the same site, may be more than usually vulnerable to the sudden dash of a Brown Goshawk or the dive of a falcon, buzzard or eagle, but for the thicket of branches, twigs and foliage usually above and around the bower.

Bowerbirds mimic the calls of other birds and often include the calls of predatory species, perhaps as a defensive measure. The Spotted Bowerbird shown here often gave very realistic imitations of the calls of the Brown Falcon, common in the area, and the 'meow' of the feral cat which, though not seen in the locality, is established in almost every part of the Australian bush.

▶ **See also pages** 137 175 *176* 183 184 197 221 230 232 233 400

574 **MISTLETOEBIRD** *Dicaeum hirundinaceum*
Top: *Male* Bottom: *Female*

616 SPOTTED BOWERBIRD

Chlamydera maculata

This bowerbird is moderately common in the arid ranges, where it inhabits gorges where native figs grow on the steep slopes and from crevices of the cliffs. The calls of the Spotted Bowerbird are loud and harsh and may lead to a sighting as the birds fly to and from trees high on the sides of the gorges, or among the trees or thickets along the floor of the gorge. The males are very noisy around the bower, making harsh, scolding, churring sounds and imitations of other birds. These sounds, accentuated in the confines of a gorge, are the

easiest means to a sighting, possibly of a display at the bower. Some bowerbirds will return to the bower while observers, keeping still and quiet, are watching from a distance of 20 m or more, and will make adjustments to the bower or its decorations.

The bower seems usually to be placed under a large shrubby bush or thicket where low limbs help prevent damage by large mammals such as kangaroos or cattle passing by. The bowerbirds usually approach the bower from above, using the perches provided by the tangle of branches just over the bower. This vegetation above the bower must also be an effective

BIRD PLACES OF THE CENTRAL DESERTS

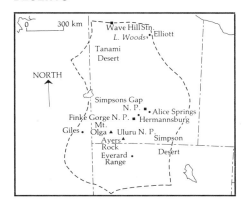

ALICE SPRINGS AREA

Several birdwatching sites near Alice Springs are conveniently close and one at least — the Alice Springs Sewage Ponds — is certain to attract the attention of dedicated birdwatchers, both local and visiting, for it has a reputation as a site for rare species. The ponds are unique as a wetlands area situated in desert country, with no other similar permanent wetlands within many thousands of kilometres. They are situated at the southern edge of the town, just south of Heavitree Gap and to the west of the Todd River. The ponds are a wildlife protection area controlled by the Northern Territory Conservation Commission.

Every year huge numbers of migrant waders arrive on the north-western and northern coasts of Australia, rest a short while, then most continue south across the deserts to spend the summer at the wader sites of the south-eastern, south-western and Tasmanian coasts. For some of these the Alice Springs Sewage Ponds provide a resting and feeding site, breaking the long journey across the deserts. The main influx of waders is in spring and autumn but the ponds are always a worthwhile bird site.

These wetlands are made up of a series of freshwater ponds, separated from each other by earthen levee banks and surrounded by low scrub. Frequent and regular overflow has created a large semi-permanent swamp beyond the southern end of the ponds which is quite heavily vegetated with cumbungi, lignum and other aquatic plants. The waterlevel of the ponds fluctuates, exposing mudbanks where birds can gather.

The birdlist for the wetlands area has about 70 species, not including any bushland species in the vicinity. Some birds occur in fairly large numbers. There are few breeding records, perhaps because of a lack of breeding sites such as hollow trees for ducks, or trees and other dense vegetation standing in water. A large proportion of the birds recorded here had not previously been recorded for central Australia. Among these are the Little Black Cormorant, Darter, Black-necked Stork, Great Egret, Intermediate Egret, Little Egret, Freckled Duck, Australian Crake, Purple Swamp-hen, Painted Snipe, Greenshank, Common Sandpiper, Red-necked Stint, Banded Stilt, Gull-billed Tern, White-winged Tern and Whiskered Tern.

For scenery and habitat that is different from the hilly, rocky MacDonnell Ranges, the road south from Alice Springs towards the Ewaninga rock carvings site and, farther down the track, Deep Well, passes into flat country with spinifex ground-cover and scattered shrubs and small trees. After good rains these plains can be a carpet of colourful everlastings around August to September. In drought this would be very barren but in early spring months, provided there has been some rain in the not-too-distant past, it has a good variety of birds of spinifex and of acacia scrublands.

THE OLD TELEGRAPH STATION

Although primarily of historic interest, the site is close to a large sheet of water, the original Alice Springs. The surrounding environment of scrubby flats and rocky hills has a variety of the birds of semi-arid bushland, while the wetlands area has a diversity of waterbirds totalling around 114 species.

Sightings here include 15 species of birds of prey, among them the Letter-winged Kite, Square-tailed Kite, Black-breasted Buzzard, Spotted Harrier,

638 **PIED BUTCHERBIRD** *Cracticus nigrogularis*

Marsh Harrier and Peregrine Falcon. However, the visiting birdwatcher is unlikely to see more than one or two of these within half a day. More likely to be seen are grebes and ducks, some of the four species of cormorants, or several of the four species of egrets and herons. Among bushland birds here are the Spinifex Pigeon, Mulga Parrot, Red-backed Kingfisher, White-backed Swallow, Ground Cuckoo-shrike, Grey-crowned Babbler, Banded Whiteface, Crimson Chat, Crested Bellbird, Grey-headed Honeyeater, Spiny-cheeked Honeyeater and Spotted Bowerbird.

97 COLLARED SPARROWHAWK
Accipiter cirrhocephalus

MACDONNELL RANGES

The MacDonnell Ranges, the best-known and most accessible of the central ranges, extend in a long curve of parallel ridges to the east and west of Alice Springs. Although these ranges are of only moderate height, the ragged lines of hills hold many fascinating features which compensate for lack of size. Without concealment of heavy vegetation, the rich red of rock and gold of spinifex make spectacular colour contrasts against the usually deep blue of desert skies.

Among these ranges are many wide gaps and deep, narrow canyons where rivers have cut through the rock ridges. Any of these are suitable for bird sighting, and exploration of the varied habitats. A sunrise climb up the flanks of rocky ridges might find Dusky Grasswrens; later in the morning a walk along a watercourse beneath rivergums could give sightings of pigeons and other birds coming in to drink at the pools. Among the gorges along the MacDonnell Ranges are Ormiston Gorge, Ellery Creek, Serpentine Gorge and Simpsons Gap, all to the west of Alice Springs, and Trephina Gorge in the eastern part of the ranges.

One of the most impressive is Ormiston Gorge, which cuts through the ranges near the foot of one of the highest peaks, Mt Sonder. Here a tributary of the Finke River has carved through the dark red rock to make one of the region's most spectacular gorges. To appreciate this scenery fully it is necessary to walk through the gorge, over and around the boulders and ledges of the creek-bed, to reach the entrance to the Pound.

Ormiston Pound has been described as one of the most spectacular parts of the central ranges, a great basin 10 km across, encircled by ranges, with Mt Giles dominating the eastern wall. Ormiston Gorge provides the outlet for this basin, and Ormiston Creek, in its course across the floor of the Pound, has many waterholes, always with the scenery of the encircling ranges in the background. A bushwalk along this creek, where very little tourist traffic penetrates, could be rewarding, with bird observations a part of the excursion. A dawn start for the walk through the gorge would be ideal, particularly in warm weather, and would be timed for optimum bird activity along the creek and in the surrounding scrub of the Pound.

At Simpsons Gap National Park walk tracks have been provided, one a creekside walk, another to Wallaby Gap on higher parts of the range. The rocky spinifex country here is one of the better-known sites for the Dusky Grasswren.

The James and Krichauff ranges, along the south-eastern edge of the MacDonnells, are best-known for the long gorge of the Finke River where unique endemic palms grow along the permanently wet pools of the gorge.

LAKE WOODS

Far to the north of the MacDonnell Ranges, near Elliott on the Stuart Highway, Lake Woods covers an area of some 500 sq. km and extends for a distance of more than 40 km on its longer north-south axis. After exceptionally heavy rain it extends farther over flats to the west, then having an area of up to 900 sq. km and a depth of about 4 m. Such a lake in the arid interior of Australia should attract attention for size alone, except that it is not permanent and in dry periods only a few waterholes remain.

Birdwatchers appear to have had mixed fortunes, some finding little of interest, others finding an abundance of birdlife. The difference is probably seasonal, with, as throughout arid Australia, birds being abundant and active after rain and scarce in drought. Additionally, the lake environs are extensive and there seem to be parts more favoured than others by the local birdlife, and these spots may take more than just a day or two to find.

The eastern shore of the lake is only about 7 km west of the Stuart Highway, 25 km south of Elliott, but a small detour is needed on the part of those passing by. Access is via Elliott, travelling west towards a pool known as Longreach, on Newcastle Waters, but turning off in a southerly direction towards the lake. Local enquiries for directions, track and lake conditions are advisable.

When the lake is flooded the scattered coolibah trees stand deep in water; as the waterlevels fall the lake surrounds become lush with ephemeral vegetation. Waterbirds can be prolific. The water is more permanent at the northern end of the lake where the deeper watercourse channels of Newcastle Waters enter. Here some large breeding colonies of Australian Pelicans and cormorants can at times be found.

An early account of the birds of Elliott and Lake Woods, published in 1945, described the lake as a shallow sheet of water, many miles in extent, the result of a cloud-burst two years previously. After another two years it was entirely dry. A list of 90 species was compiled.

Another published account of Lake Woods in July–August 1969 describes its northern approach as a 'veritable wonderland of birdlife', with 'the air filled with the chatter of vast flocks of Budgerigar'. Large trees along the

367 **HOODED ROBIN** *Melanodryas cucullata*

watercourse channels seemed to attract a great many raptors, to be seen in every direction both in flight and perching.

Recorded on that one-day visit were the Black Kite, Black and Brown falcons, Australian Kestrel, Little Eagle, Whistling Kite, Brown Goshawk and Wedge-tailed Eagle, with the Letter-winged Kite breeding. There was an area of rich tall grass, perhaps occupying part of the vast lakebed, stretching away to the distant horizon, with flocks of up to 50 Brolgas, considerable numbers of bustards, and flocks of many thousands of Little Corellas. The lake at that time evidently held some water, seen glittering in the far distance.

Lake Woods appears to be a bird site that would enjoy or suffer great extremes. Any planned trip should take account of this and recent rainfall records should be obtained.

The watercourse of Newcastle Waters, entering the lake from the north, holds some large pools and could be worth investigating during a visit to this area.

AYERS ROCK-MT OLGA

The birdlife around Ayers Rock and the Olgas is probably little different from that of other ranges of the desert that are less crowded by tourists; this area does have the advantage of being accessible, with camping and other facilities or accommodation available and ranger advice if needed.

As with almost all desert country, rain will transform the land and greatly increase the number of birds to be seen. Assuming a reasonable year, quite a few birds can be seen here. The Uluru National Park checklist, compiled over many years, has at least 144 species.

As would be expected, the birds of prey are well represented with 17 species, including some of the most exciting and in some instances rare birds: the Letter-winged Kite, Black-breasted Buzzard, Collared Sparrowhawk, Little and Wedge-tailed eagles, Spotted Harrier, Black Falcon, Peregrine Falcon, Australian Hobby and Grey Falcon. Among the bushland birds, the reserve has the Australian Bustard, Bush Thick-knee, Spinifex Pigeon, Pink Cockatoo, Bourke's Parrot, Scarlet-chested Parrot, Red-backed Kingfisher, Rufous-crowned Emu-wren, Chestnut-rumped Thornbill, Striated Grasswren, Thick-billed Grasswren, Orange Chat, Chiming Wedgebill, Grey Honeyeater, Pied Honeyeater, Painted Firetail and Spotted Bowerbird.

CENTRAL DESERTS BIRDWATCH

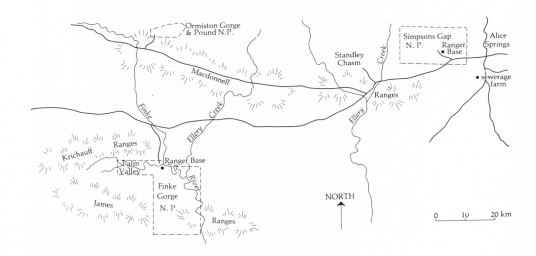

The gorges of the MacDonnell and surrounding ranges of the Central Deserts Region vary considerably in their character, their bird habitats and the makeup of their birdlists. The variety of birdlife is surprising, for the ranges hold not only the birds that are typical of the usual spinifex or mulga habitats but also species that are usually considered to be birds of coastal wetlands.

Two localities, offering such quality of natural environment that they are the two major national parks of the central ranges, are Simpsons Gap and Finke Gorge. Simpsons Gap National Park is only about 8 km west of Alice Springs and covers not only the immediate surrounds of Simpsons Gap but extends over a large part of the rough, dry habitat of the Chewing Range. The rocky spinifex ranges are inhabited by the Dusky Grasswren, a central Australian endemic; flats between the ranges carry scattered ghost gums and acacia scrub.

As an indication of the likely bird sightings for a half-day to a day in this area, the published results of a birdwatching excursion to the Gap by members of the Alice Springs Field Naturalists' Club are worth noting. Although much of the time was concentrated upon the dry gullies and hill slopes, most bird sightings were made in areas of mulga woodland and along the river bed.

On this single trip were found 27 species of birds including some that would be very satisfying sightings for any visiting ornithologist from south-eastern Australia: the Grey Falcon, Red-tailed Black-Cockatoo, Mulga Parrot, Golden-backed Honeyeater (subspecies of Black-chinned Honeyeater), Turquoise Fairy-wren (subspecies of Splendid Fairy-wren) and Grey-headed Honeyeater. Although the rocky slopes were searched, the Dusky Grasswren apparently proved too elusive, for it does not appear on the list of sightings.

Another excursion by the same group covered a contrasting part of the central ranges, within the Finke Gorge National Park. This reserve is situated in the James Range, about 140 km south-west of Alice Springs via Hermannsburg, with the last 19 km along the sandy bed of the Finke River requiring four-wheel drive. At Boggy Hole, a section of the very long, winding gorge where a series of large pools alternate with dry sandy sections of river bed, the bird count yielded about 50 species. Included were some that most visitors to the Centre would not expect to find in desert ranges: the Australasian Grebe, Darter, Little Black and Little Pied cormorants, Pacific Heron, Rufous Night Heron, Yellow-billed Spoonbill, Pink-eared Duck, Hardhead and Pacific Black Duck.

Other birds noteworthy for beauty of plumage or as species of special interest for visiting birdwatchers were the Pink Cockatoo, Purple-backed Fairy-wren (subspecies of Variegated Fairy-wren) and White-winged Fairy-wren.

Finke Gorge National Park is best-known for the cliff-encircled scenery of Palm Creek, a westerly tributary of the Finke River, commonly known as Palm Valley, where livistona palms line the watercourse, especially in Cycad Gorge.

This is a site for the beautiful little Spinifex Pigeon, which seems common in Cycad Gorge, coming in from dry spinifex country of the surrounding range to drink at the permanent pools in this narrow gorge. In these central ranges the Spinifex Pigeons have white on the belly, while those to the western side of the Great Sandy Desert, in the Pilbara region, are cinnamon beneath.

The two forms have in the past been listed as separate species, the white-bellied birds then known as the Plumed Pigeon and the others as the Red-plumed Pigeon. Later the two were combined as a single species, appropriately known as the Spinifex Pigeon. The most recent studies of this species have shown that there are intermediate populations with varying amounts of undersurface white, so that it is not possible to draw a distinct dividing line; the variation is gradual, or clinal, and there should be no subspecies recognized.

In this Central Deserts Region a similar problem occurs with the names of locally distinctive fairy-wrens. Birds that were previously separate species have been reduced to subspecies and have consequently vanished from many birdlists. For example, the Turquoise Fairy-wren is now generally accepted as a subspecies of the Splendid Fairy-wren, and the Purple-backed Fairy-wren as a subspecies of the Variegated Fairy-wren.

50 **PIED HERON** *Ardea picata*

TOP END

The Top End of the Northern Territory is dominated by two major landforms: the great sandstone block of the Arnhem Land Plateau and the coastal lowlands. Together with a tropical monsoonal climate these landforms create an environment that attracts birds in immense numbers and also provides a setting in which there are some bird species that are found in no other place.

The rugged sandstone plateau has a spectacular meeting with the flat coastal river floodplains in western Arnhem Land, where a long escarpment of high cliffs dominate the landscape. The cliffs are broken by several gorges that cut back deeply into the sandstone block of the plateau, or end in towering waterfalls. This escarpment at its northern limit reaches almost to the Arafura Sea coastline, where it is deeply dissected by the upper parts of the East Alligator River.

The line of the escarpment runs to the south-west, broken by gorges of the headwaters of the South Alligator River, then, with slopes rather than cliffs, curves south where it is cut by the magnificent Katherine Gorge. It finally swings back eastwards into Arnhem Land. This western Arnhem escarpment is at its most spectacular where it passes through the eastern and southern parts of Kakadu National Park, where there are immense cliffs, gorges, waterfalls and outlying blocks of eroded sandstone.

The climate here is one of extremes. Summer monsoons with torrential rains are followed by winter droughts and towards the end of this dry season the soaring temperatures burn the parched and dusty land, before the annual deluge begins again in December or January. A description of this region as a 'lake during the wet and a desert during the dry' often seems close to reality.

As the monsoon storms during the summer wet deluge this region, the waterfalls and gorges thunder with the floodwaters escaping the sandstone maze of the plateau and ranges. The lowland river lagoons are filled to overflowing, the water escaping across vast areas of swamps and black-soil plains until parts of the coastal lowlands resemble an inland sea, broken by islands of higher ground and massed treetops of paperbark swamps. Winding belts of darker green mangroves and riverine monsoon forest follow river lagoons that now are but deeper channels beneath the seemingly endless sheet of water.

From March or April the rains cease and the floods begin very slowly to subside. By then the brown landscape of the dry has become green beneath grass, much of it swampy. The waterbirds, most of which have bred in swamps that are very difficult to reach until well after the wet, now congregate in huge numbers, feeding in the shallow waters of the flooded black-soil grasslands, or in the deeper waters of the river lagoons. Here the birds are in immense numbers and become progressively more concentrated as the shallow sheets of water across the plains dry out, leaving only the deeper swamps and lagoons.

Farther inland, south of the Arnhem Land Plateau, the tropical character of the Top End shades into an arid transitional zone, towards semi-desert to the south and the Mitchell grass plains of the Barkly Tableland to the east.

The western part of the Top End is of considerable interest, for here the country again becomes rugged. The Daly, Fitzmaurice and Victoria rivers, which flow into the Joseph Bonaparte Gulf, have carved the land into valleys and residual ranges, in many places of rugged

84 GREEN PYGMY-GOOSE *Nettapus pulchellus*

sandstone with escarpments and gorges. Here the birdlife has Kimberley affinities, the White-quilled Rock-Pigeon and western race of the Purple-crowned Fairy-wren being conspicuous examples.

Within the Top End there are five areas or groupings of 'bird places' with abundant or in some way interesting birdlife. This choice reflects to a considerable extent the comparative ease of access of possible birdwatching places. Much of the Top End is without roads or even rough tracks, while other very large segments are within reserves where access is restricted.

These localities are the greater Darwin area, the Alligator rivers drainage to the east of Darwin, the Katherine area, the Victoria River–Keep River area and the country to the south of the Gulf of Carpentaria.

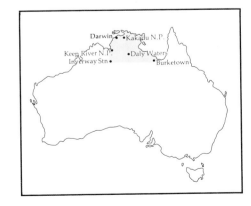

61 BLACK-NECKED STORK
Xenorhynchus asiaticus

BIRDS OF THE TOP END

47 GREAT-BILLED HERON

Ardea sumatrana

The Great-billed Heron is found right around Australia's northern coastline but it usually inhabits mangrove swamps so inaccessible that it is difficult to observe. Nests are rarely found; there was only one breeding record in the extensive RAOU Field Atlas survey. The Top End of the Northern Territory probably offers the best opportunity of a sighting. Here it occurs farther inland on river lagoons, some of which carry quite heavy traffic of small boats, mainly barramundi fishermen but also tour boats at some sites. Although this species remains always very wary, sightings at moderate distances are possible, perhaps within 50 m, compared with the usual closest approach of 100 m or more.

The Great-billed Heron is usually solitary and in daylight hours is most likely to be seen standing in mangroves at the edge of a lagoon or mangrove creek. It feeds on mudflats at low tide but may be at least partly nocturnal. In flight it appears ponderous, with deep wingbeats, neck folded in closely.

The presence of this heron may be revealed by the call, often given at night, and sounding like the bellow of a bull or a crocodile, hence the alternative name of Alligator-bird.

▶ See also pages 22 22 96 98 196 197 198 199 208 262

61 BLACK-NECKED STORK

Xenorhynchus asiaticus

The location of suitable habitat in a region frequented by this very conspicuous tall bird should almost guarantee a sighting. It is almost exclusively a bird of coastal regions, frequenting a variety of swamps and wetlands, wet or flooded grasslands, lake and estuary foreshores, and mangrove mudflats. While the sighting of a Black-necked Stork will be relatively difficult in New South Wales where estimates of the total population have been as low as 30 birds, it will almost certainly be seen by most travellers in coastal Northern Territory, the Kimberley and northern Queensland.

▶ See also pages 80 83 122 183 196 197 198 199 210 223 266 *266*

119 CHESTNUT-BACKED BUTTON-QUAIL

Turnix castanota

In the Top End of the Northern Territory and the Kimberley the Chestnut-backed Button-quail is moderately common, showing a preference for rocky sandstone ridges, with open dry savannah-woodland of stringybark with sparse blady grass (kunai grass) or spinifex. On Cape York Peninsula this species shows a preference for swampy areas. Probably the only way to locate the species is to try to flush the bird by traversing such terrain in a locality where it is known to occur; however it will tend to run rather than fly, so that it may be difficult to obtain more than fleeting glimpses through the grass.

Usually this quail is seen in small coveys of five to 20 birds. If scattered, as when flushed, the quails will give low moaning calls to re-establish contact and re-form the covey, and these sounds may help to locate and give a brief sighting.

The species is moderately common in Kakadu and a group of birdwatchers recently sighted the bird by the roadside 25 km north of Cooinda.

▶ See also pages *189* 280

132 WHITE-BROWED CRAKE

Poliolimnas cinereus

Not particularly shy, this crake feeds in the shallows at the edges of coastal lakes, mangroves and other waterside vegetation, climbing over mangrove roots and walking on floating vegetation. It may ignore a quiet, motionless observer. The call attracts attention, being loud and distinctive, sometimes with several birds in chorus; a chattered 'cutchee-cutchee-'. The White-browed Crake has a distinctive blackish cap and two white facial lines. The toes, especially the middle, are very long and slender, enabling the species to walk on floating vegetation. It is most active and likely to be seen early in the morning and in the evening, but only occasionally through the day. It sometimes flies low, looking somewhat clumsy, its legs dangling, and will take flying insects in this way.

The species appears to be most abundant during the summer wet season in both Darwin and the Atherton Region. It takes aquatic insects from floating vegetation and runs deftly up roots and limbs. The White-browed Crake often gives its presence away by calling in response to sudden loud noises. This crake is common from October to May and can be seen in swamps and lagoons with typha or other dense aquatic vegetation; it is frequently seen in rice crops.

▶ See also pages 98 *193* 197 210 284

167 LITTLE CURLEW

Numenius minutus

The Little Curlew is a summer migrant to northern Australia, arriving in great numbers in October through to December and departing early to mid-April. Sightings within Australia are widespread. The Little Curlew is present in October–November and again in March–April; it is then abundant on damp grasslands, with an estimated quarter million at Fogg Dam in October. Some appear on suburban lawns in Darwin but the species is absent from the Darwin area during the wet season.

These birds evidently reach far north-western Australia in about October, on a broad front, with major concentrations from Broome south to Roebuck Plains and Anna Plains Station. This is about the same time that the species becomes abundant around Darwin. But while the Little Curlews of the Roebuck and Anna plains probably remain, those of the Darwin area move on to the grasslands of the south-western corner of the Gulf of Carpentaria, arriving early December. Some move farther south, so that there are sightings of smaller numbers over a wide area. On their return journey in March the Little Curlews again break their journey to rest and feed on the grassland plains of the Top End, which again become suitable as the flooding of the wet season subsides. The birds evidently do not lay down great reserves of fat and need these last feeding areas at around Darwin and in the north-west before departing for Siberia via Indonesia.

Sites where major concentrations have been recorded include Anna Plains, Roebuck Plains and Broome, Western Australia, Fogg Dam, Northern Territory, and Karumba Plains, Richmond, Queensland.

▶ See also pages 193 196 293

213 BANDED FRUIT-DOVE

Ptilinopus cinctus

The Banded Fruit-Dove is moderately common within its restricted range and habitat, so that a sighting depends in the first instance upon locating likely situations. The species is mainly in monsoon forests of gorges and slopes below escarpment cliffs but the birds fly out to native fig and other fruiting trees on the plateau, and on the lowland plains up to 10 km west of the main line of the escarpment. The Banded Fruit-Doves are most active in the early morning and late afternoon, resting quietly among foliage during the heat of the day.

During the breeding season pairs are spaced widely along the escarpment. The best opportunities to observe this species are when the birds feed in fruiting trees, where up to 10 birds may gather, though usually only one or two. Here the call, a low but quite loud, single-note coo or hoot of about one second's duration, repeated at regular intervals, can assist in locating the birds in the treetop foliage. Alternatively, in the dry season when the birds come to drink at seepages from cliff crevices, they afford a sighting for a patient and reasonably concealed observer. If suddenly alarmed the Banded Fruit-Dove takes flight with a very loud clapping of wings, but if feeding birds are approached cautiously they will usually allow approach to within easy viewing distance using binoculars.

When travelling the flight of the Banded Fruit-Dove is powerful, undulating. It will sometimes alight briefly on an exposed perch, landing with a characteristic forward flip of the tail, and may give a brief clear view for an observer who happens to be in the right position at the time.

Some sites are Cannon Hill, Mt Borrad, Nangalour, El Sharana at Obstacle Creek, and Plum Tree Creek.

▶ See also pages 196 304–5

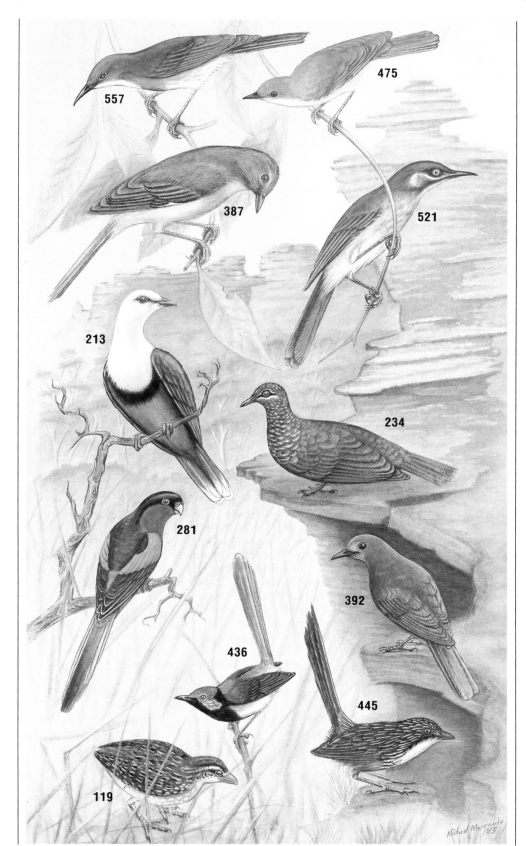

232 PARTRIDGE PIGEON

Petrophassa smithii

There are two subspecies of the Partridge Pigeon. In the subspecies in the Top End the bare skin around the eyes is red while in the Kimberley subspecies this skin is yellow. The preferred habitat is open forest with grassy understorey and moist areas,

119   **Chestnut-backed Button-quail** *Turnix castanota*
213   **Banded Fruit-Dove** *Ptilinopus cinctus*
234   **Chestnut-quilled Rock-Pigeon** *Petrophassa rufipennis*
281   **Hooded Parrot** *Psephotus dissimilis*
387   **Grey Whistler** *Pachycephala simplex*
392   **Sandstone Shrike-thrush** *Colluricincla woodwardi*
436   **Lavender-flanked Fairy-wren** (subspecies of Variegated Fairy-wren) *Malurus lamberti dulcis*
445   **White-throated Grasswren** *Amytornis woodwardi*
475   **Green-backed Warbler** *Gerygone chloronota*
521   **White-lined Honeyeater** *Meliphaga albilineata*
557   **Rufous-banded Honeyeater** *Conopophila albogularis*

and it shows a preference for recently burnt ground, perhaps because fallen seeds are conspicuous. In the Northern Territory the Alligator rivers region is its centre of abundance, while in the Kimberley region it inhabits low open forest in rough sandstone country.

In the late wet and early dry seasons it is usually in pairs or small family parties, occasionally in larger coveys of 15 to 20, rarely to 100 birds.

This species is mainly terrestrial, feeding, roosting and nesting on the ground. When travelling moderate distances, as to water, the coveys usually walk, keeping contact with soft, 'sad' cooing. The birds come to water throughout the day but with a strong preference for the early morning and late afternoon.

When encountered, these birds freeze, some squatting low, some upright. They are difficult to discern, their plumage effectively merging into background colours. If put to flight all 'explode' skyward, some landing in trees. In flight the body looks plump, the tail short; brief bursts of wingbeats are interspersed with glides on downcurved wings.

▶ **See also pages** *193 208 308–9*

234 CHESTNUT-QUILLED ROCK-PIGEON

Petrophassa rufipennis

Fairly common within its narrow range and restricted habitat. This Rock-Pigeon is found along the sandstone escarpments and gorges, where there are pockets of soil along the lower slopes, and among tumbled sandstone boulders with clumps of spinifex, shrubs and trees. The species is confined to this narrow habitat zone, seldom venturing more than 20–30 m out into the woodland of the plains, never perching in trees but at home on boulders and cliff-face ledges.

Early morning and towards evening are the most likely times for a sighting, when the rock-pigeons are most active. They fly out to the flats close to the foot of the cliffs, seeking various seeds, and at the slightest disturbance fly back to the security of the high ledges and boulders where they run among and over the rocks with great agility. On take-off they 'explode' upwards with a loud clapping of wings, then glide on downcurved wings, always keeping close to the cliffs or ground. Small pools where water seeps from cliff crevices, or nearby creek-beds, are visited at intervals during the day and at dusk, giving, for a quiet and patient observer, an opportunity for a close view. The call, though not extremely

374 LEMON-BELLIED FLYCATCHER
Microeca flavigaster

loud, may assist discovery and identification.

In the field the chestnut wing patch is not always obvious in flight and is usually not shown on the folded wing. On the ground this pigeon keeps its long, uniformly dark brown body in a low, horizontal posture, seeming to have an almost reptilian character as it scuttles over the rocks. Localities on record include Kakadu, Oenpelli and Katherine Gorge.

▶ **See also pages** *189 196 198 309*

274 NORTHERN ROSELLA

Platycercus venustus

The Northern Rosella, like other rosellas, is mainly a sedentary species. It is found in eucalypt and paperbark woodlands, often in the vicinity of watercourses, usually in hilly country where pools remain through the dry season. It is more arboreal than most other rosellas, feeding upon seeds and nectar of trees and shrubs but occasionally finding seeds on the ground.

The Northern Rosella is sparse and patchy in occurrence; it is uncertain whether the species has declined or was always uncommon because of limitations of suitable habitat. It is usually seen in small numbers, in pairs or small parties of up to six or eight birds; sometimes it is locally common and this seems to be more often in the taller woodlands.

The Northern Rosella is a quiet species, silent when feeding on the ground and while sheltering among treetop foliage during the heat of the day. When on the ground its plumage blends well with the surroundings, so that it is usually not noticed until flushed; it often feeds at roadsides. These are more wary than most other rosellas and when flushed fly to high

limbs of distant trees. The flight is swift, less undulating, the birds dropping low then swooping up and landing with outspread tails. On longer flights they travel high, over the treetops. They go to water early and late in the day.

Only in the early part of the breeding season, around May to July, does the Northern Rosella become vocal and more conspicuous, with squabbling around nest sites, chattering and tail-wagging.

Sites include: (Northern Territory) Berrimah, Humpty Doo, Katherine, Nicholson River, Queensland border, Mt Bundey Range, Pine Creek. (Kimberley) King Leopold Ranges, Windjana Gorge, Koolan Island.

▶ **See also pages** *174 193 197 208 211 318*

281 HOODED PARROT

Psephotus dissimilis

This beautiful species remains moderately common within its restricted range, on lightly wooded grasslands, spinifex and stringybark vegetated ridges. For a sighting the late dry season is best, if the increasing heat can be tolerated. As the countryside dries out and shallower wetlands and pools vanish, these parrots, together with a great many other birds, are forced to concentrate upon fewer waterholes. At these places a patient observer should have a good chance of seeing these and other local species including the Gouldian Finch.

The Hooded Parrot, in common with most birds of the tropics, is most active in the early morning and towards evening and spends the hottest part of the day near water, sheltering in shady foliage and occasionally coming down to drink. Shallow pools and soaks with sand spits extending out into the water are favoured, so that the parrots can walk out to the water in the open. At one pool these parrots were recorded making their morning visit at 8 am and 8.30 am, in July. The Hooded Parrots feed on seeds which in some localities are more abundant where moisture from roadside drains encourages luxuriant growth, so that there have been reports of flocks feeding along roadsides.

The flight is swift and strong with slight undulations. The contact call is a 'chu-weet, chu-weet'; it is given in flight and after alighting. This species is usually found in open woodland and lightly timbered grassland where there are abundant termite mounds, favouring those on the ridge country. The range has shrunk, probably more due to grazing and burning than trapping.

41 **PIED CORMORANT** *Phalacrocorax varius*

Some sites recorded include the Pine Creek district, Edith River, Daly River, Copperfield Creek, Mainora and Mataranka.

▶ See also pages *189* 196 198 319

336 RAINBOW PITTA

Pitta iris

This richly coloured bird is moderately common in suitable habitat. Even the small patches of monsoon forest near Darwin, known locally as 'jungle', have a few resident pittas. The types of closed forest used by pittas include not only the 'jungles' but also bamboo thickets, dense melaleuca and other scrub in sandstone gorges and mangroves along coastal creeks and lagoons. Within these situations the pitta can best be located by its loud 'wok-a-work' call, especially late in the year as pairs answer between territories. Sighting the bird can be more difficult in the shadowy surroundings; imitating the calls may

bring it into view.

This species can be found throughout the year but the call is heard most often from October to December, the birds calling from trees up to 7 m above ground. At other times of the year it calls only briefly, usually about an hour before dawn.

In the wet season the floor of the 'jungle' is soggy, wet or flooded, but in the dry season a silent and patient observer may detect the presence of pittas by the sound of their hopping over the layer of dead leaves that carpets the ground. The pattern of sound is about four to six hops, a pause, then another burst of hopping.

Sites include: (Northern Territory) Black Jungle, Howard Springs, South Alligator River, Workshop Jungle, Kakadu. (Western Australia) Prince Regent River, Mitchell Plateau, Osborne and St Andrew islands.

▶ See also pages 7 81 *193* 196 197 209 334 – 5

374 LEMON-BELLIED FLYCATCHER

Microeca flavigaster

In the Top End, near the coast, this very small flycatcher favours the denser vegetation in and around monsoon forest, mangroves and paperbark swamps. Farther inland, as at Katherine Gorge, it is confined to the narrow strip of dense water's-edge vegetation. In eastern Queensland it extends to eucalypt and paperbark woodlands and forests, and the margins and clearings of rainforests. The Lemon-bellied Flycatcher is almost ceaselessly active, flitting about the mid-levels of the foliage, catching small flying insects and taking others from leaves and bark. It often uses a dead branch or other open perch from which to sally out in pursuit of passing insects. The call, once known, can be used to locate this bird; it is quite loud, clear and varied, with a jaunty, lively, pleasantly light-hearted quality.

The Lemon-bellied Flycatcher is most likely to be confused with the

Kimberley Flycatcher, but that bird inhabits the Kimberley, merging with the Lemon-bellied near Wyndham. The Kimberley Flycatcher is now regarded as a subspecies of the Lemon-bellied. Another similar bird is the Yellow-legged Flycatcher, seen only on upper Cape York Peninsula.

▶ See also pages *190* 197 198 199 201 202 210 344

387 GREY WHISTLER

Pachycephala simplex

The Brown Whistler was previously a separate species and is confined to the coastal and subcoastal Top End. It is now combined with the Grey Whistler of north-eastern Queensland as a single species under the common name of Grey Whistler. However, the nominate subspecies, the Brown Whistler, is of no less interest. It occupies areas of monsoon forest and is common in paperbark swamps. The calls have the usual exuberant whistler quality, while the plain brown plumage separates it from the other mangrove species, the White-breasted and Mangrove Golden whistlers.

Sites near Darwin are Ludmilla Creek, Shoal Bay, East Point and Lee Point.

▶ See also pages *189* 196 347

392 SANDSTONE SHRIKE-THRUSH

Colluricincla woodwardi

Within its main range, and in optimum habitat areas, the Sandstone Shrike-thrush is moderately common. It is to be found in gorges and areas of rugged escarpments on the sandstone Arnhem Land escarpment. Those familiar with the song of the Grey Shrike-thrush will have no difficulty in recognizing the song of the Sandstone as belonging to the same genus. Its commonly used contact call consists of two strong, clear whistles that echo through the gorges, while there is also a full song of rich, varied notes, more animated than that of the Grey.

If in these regions such song is heard, it should be kept in mind that both the Grey and the Little shrike-thrushes also occur in these regions and that the Grey is listed for the sandstone plateau country of Kakadu, so that although locality, habitat and call are useful locators, only a clear visual identification will confirm a sighting of the Sandstone Shrike-thrush. This species is rich buff on the underparts, with upperparts brownish-grey. In the north the Grey Shrike-thrush is a creamy-brown rather than the cool grey of southern birds.

238 RED-TAILED BLACK-COCKATOO
Calyptorhynchus magnificus

The Sandstone Shrike-thrush will often be sighted perched on a high rock on the rim of a gorge. Its song, considered by some to be more beautiful than that of the Grey Shrike-thrush, echoes between the rock walls.

▶ See also pages   174 *189* 196 197 198 210 211 348

429 ZITTING CISTICOLA

Cisticola juncidis

The Zitting or Streaked Cisticola is much less often reported than the Golden-headed, the coastal Top End being one of the regions where it is often recorded. The two species are difficult to separate, except by song in the breeding season. One observer who is familiar with both describes the song-flight call of the Golden-headed as a rather musical double-note, repeated at intervals of about one second, and those of the Zitting Cisticola as sounding like two sticks being struck together sharply at intervals of about half a second. Both birds have also a 'dzeeep' call. The Zitting appears to be more common on the saline coastal flats, as at Leanyer, while the Golden-headed is dominant in tall grass, as found at East Point.

The habitat here is like that at Ayr, north-eastern Queensland, where the species occupies flat country of low grasses at the edge of saltmarsh. Near Kununurra it has been recorded on the floodplains of the Ord, in saltmarsh grass, which is an important element

of the habitat in the Northern Territory. The Golden-headed was not on this habitat but was common around Kununurra and Lake Argyle.

▶ See also pages   193 210 357

436 LAVENDER-FLANKED FAIRY-WREN
SUBSPECIES OF VARIEGATED FAIRY-WREN

Malurus lamberti dulcis

This subspecies of the Variegated Fairy-wren is confined to the north-west parts of the Arnhem Land Plateau, south to El Sharana. In this region it is moderately common in spinifex and low, sparse shrubbery on the rough sandstone escarpment and plateau country.

The Lavender-flanked Fairy-wren is reported to be usually in small parties where the sandstone ridges are broken by gorges and escarpments and where there are boulders and spinifex. Foraging parties maintain contact with high-pitched squeaks, short, sharp, excited notes and occasional thin snatches of chattering. The song of the male is a reeling trill similar to that of other fairy-wrens; the birds will approach in response to squeaky sounds.

The lavender of the flanks is often not apparent in the field so that identification will usually rely on the fact that no other species or subspecies of chestnut-shouldered fairy-wren comes close to overlapping the range of the Lavender-flanked Fairy-wren.

▶ See also pages 8 *189* 196 198 208 210 211 359

445 WHITE-THROATED GRASSWREN

Amytornis woodwardi

This grasswren is confined within the limits of western Arnhem Land, south onto the divide between the South Alligator and Katherine rivers. It is found on the larger tracts of open, almost treeless habitat where there are large, exposed, flat surfaces of sandstone almost denuded of soil and with scattered clumps of spinifex, and on low, open patches of scrub.

But even in this habitat the species is restricted, avoiding large areas of the unbroken flat sandstone habitat of the plateau tops. It is sometimes numerous in small areas where there are breakaways, gullies and other disruptions of the surface and where there are slopes with sandstone boulders intermixed with large, dense clumps of spinifex, often with low calytrix shrubs. Here it may be seen in small parties of up to six or seven birds, or pairs in the breeding season.

In the breeding season males sing

from prominent points in their territories, the rich and prolonged series of notes rising and falling and audible at a distance of several hundred metres. The alarm and contact calls also are loud, sharp 'trrt' sounds, unlike the weak trills of the fairy-wrens.

The White-throated Grasswren in its behaviour seems not as secretive as some other grasswrens, being recorded as running rapidly across the bare patches of sandstone. But, like the Black Grasswren, it darts into deep crevices between boulders when alarmed. The sighting of the White-throated Grasswren would require recognition of areas of the preferred habitat, at sites where, or near where the species has been recorded, with attention to song, alarm calls and known behaviour.

Sites include: 4 km NNE of El Sharana–Pine Creek Bridge over the South Alligator River; escarpment east of Mt Cullen in an area of boulders and spinifex not burnt for some years; Koolpin Creek; Barramundie Creek; Deaf Adder Creek, El Sharana, Katherine Gorge.

▶ See also pages *189* 196 197 198 361

446 CARPENTARIAN GRASSWREN

Amytornis dorotheae

This species, also known as Dorothy's Grasswren, is known only from a small area south of the Gulf of Carpentaria and recorded from but one or two sites. The habitat here is sandstone broken by gorges and gullies, very rough, and with large clumps of spinifex. The species is usually reported from the McArthur River near Borroloola but has also been recorded in the China Wall area of the Nicholson River drainage. It is one of the most difficult to find and least known of the grasswrens.

A site by the McArthur River near the Old Chance Gold Mine was described as being of sandstone with high ridges and escarpments carrying much spinifex of both the 'normal and old man or bull type'; there were also scattered shrubs and small eucalypts. Here the grasswrens moved across the sandstone 'like animated tennis balls' to disappear into deep spinifex-filled crevices.

The Carpentarian Grasswrens are usually in pairs or parties of up to five birds, often in company with Variegated Fairy-wrens. They have been described as flitting over the rocks so fast that one has to be quick to get any more than a fleeting glimpse. They are wary, rarely staying in sight more than a few seconds at a time, vanishing a few seconds after being flushed, darting into crevices or among boulders. These grasswrens will sometimes take flight when encountered, fluttering like an emu-wren, tail trailing, then dropping suddenly to cover after 20–30 m, to peer at intruders from behind rocks or spinifex.

132 **White-browed Crake** *Poliolimnas cinereus*
167 **Little Curlew** *Numenius minutus*
232 **Partridge Pigeon** *Petrophassa smithii*
254 **Varied Lorikeet** *Psitteuteles versicolor*
274 **Northern Rosella** *Platycercus venustus*
336 **Rainbow Pitta** *Pitta iris*
429 **Zitting Cisticola** *Cisticola juncidis*
446 **Carpentarian Grasswren** *Amytornis dorotheae*
601 **Chestnut-breasted Mannikin**
602 **Yellow-rumped Mannikin** *Lonchura flaviprymna*

441 RED-BACKED FAIRY-WREN
Malurus melanocephalus The north-
western subspecies has a deeper crimson

579 BLACK-HEADED PARDALOTE
Pardalotus striatus melanocephalus
Subspecies of Striated Pardalote

596 MASKED FINCH *Poephila personata*

The Carpentarian Grasswrens are most active from about an hour after sunrise to about 11 am. They forage energetically, tail always cocked, giving occasional high contact calls — a reedy, cricket-like 'sssstz' which carries 30 m or more. Males sing from the tops of higher rocks and shrubs, not only in breeding but occasionally at other times of the year. The song is similar to that of the fairy-wren, a mix of trills and contact churrings, ending with high, metallic and whistled notes. The song might assist in locating the bird at times when the species is especially vocal, early in the breeding season, when breeding territories are being established.

Other sites include the Glyde River area and the Buckalara Range near the Nicholson River.

▶ See also pages *193* 197 361

475 GREEN-BACKED WARBLER

Gerygone chloronota

A New Guinean species which in Australia is confined to mangroves and coastal swamps along the Northern Territory and Kimberley coasts. Its remote and often

inaccessible habitats have ensured that the details of its distribution, habitat and breeding are not well known. The occurrence is not strictly coastal for it has been collected in riverine thickets more than 100 km inland.

The Green-backed Warbler occurs singly or in pairs and is said to be shy. Otherwise it is, like other gerygones, active among foliage and often hovering. The song, though not loud, is helpful in locating this small greenish bird in such closed habitats and dense foliage: a rapid, high twittering of whistled notes, recognizably warbler-like, given repeatedly and with little variation, by both male and female. Although more vocal when breeding, the Green-backed Warbler sings throughout the year and at any time of day.

Although the species tends to be solitary, fluttering about the upper- and mid-levels, taking insects in flight and from foliage, it is often in the company of other species in loose feeding flocks. It is usually in dense, leafy, closed-canopy environs, patches of monsoon forest, waterside thickets, lagoons, rivers, around pools in gorges, mangroves, paperbark swamps, and inland along the moist fringing forests of major rivers.

Sites include: (Northern Territory) Shoal Bay, East Point, Edith Falls, Upper Alligator River, Lower Roper River. (Kimberley) Manning Creek, Windjana Gorge; paperbark swamps on Roebuck Plains near Broome, Drysdale River.

▶ See also pages *189* 198 210 368

521 WHITE-LINED HONEYEATER

Meliphaga albilineata

This rare species occurs in gorges, breakaways, and along broken escarpments of sandstone ranges and plateaus where there are thickets of the broad-leafed shrubs *Xanthostemon*, *Terminalia* and *Gardenia*. It occasionally visits pockets of monsoon forest or paperbark that often occur in the moist lower parts of gorges, or flies up to nearby range or plateau-top shrubbery to feed.

In the broad-leaf shrubbery habitat of such sites this species can occasionally be the dominant honeyeater, locally fairly common, in loose flocks, feeding in the treetops and aggressive towards other honeyeaters. But on other occasions it is much less evident, shy and solitary, foraging in the dense upper foliage of the shrubbery.

The call if recognized is useful, being given at all times of the year and at most times of the day though occasionally rather than consistently. It is a series of whistles, the first always with rising inflexion, the second (sometimes omitted) undulating, the third rising strongly and 'rather wildly' before falling away.

Sites include (Northern Territory) Kakadu escarpments, Arnhem Land, Mary River; probably Katherine Gorge. (Kimberley) Drysdale River, Admiralty Gulf, Prince Regent River.

▶ See also pages *189 196 210 378*

557 RUFOUS-BANDED HONEYEATER

Conopophila albogularis

The Rufous-banded Honeyeater occurs throughout New Guinea and has two separate populations in Australia — on Cape York Peninsula and the Top End of the Northern Territory, from where it seems to have been recorded more often. It appears to be nomadic, its numbers fluctuating greatly. This species may be seen singly, in pairs, in mixed foraging flocks with other species, or in gatherings of up to 30, probably around trees with abundant nectar or insects, the latter often taken on the wing.

This honeyeater draws attention by its activity, especially when in numbers, and its brisk, squeaky song and almost continuous twittering. It is most likely to be seen along rivers in mixed forests and mangroves, in swamps where paperbarks are flowering, occasionally in monsoon forests, and uncommonly in eucalypt forests and woodlands.

▶ See also pages *189 387*

602 YELLOW-RUMPED MANNIKIN

Lonchura flaviprymna

The Yellow-rumped Mannikin, also known as the Yellow-tailed Finch, is endemic to the Top End Region except for a slight penetration into the Kimberley Region where it has been recorded breeding near Kununurra. It prefers swamp margins, wet grasslands and irrigated areas where it feeds on the seeds of various grasses.

This bird is generally scarce and usually seen in company with the Chestnut-breasted Mannikin, not only in mixed flocks but also when breeding. Adult Chestnut-breasted Mannikins are distinguished by the black face. The calls are similar but those of the Yellow-rumped Mannikin are more piercing. It can be locally abundant, as in the Ord River irrigation areas.

▶ See also pages *193 210 397*

67 **MAGPIE GOOSE** *Anseranas semipalmata*

BIRD PLACES OF THE TOP END

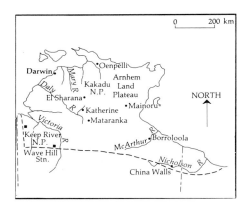

ALLIGATOR RIVERS

The Alligator rivers area, between the Mary River and the East Alligator, but especially the country drained by the South Alligator and East Alligator and largely covered by Kakadu National Park, is exceptionally rich in birds. This wealth is in total number of species, the great abundance of some of these, and in the considerable number of bird species or subspecies which are unique to the area or which occur in very few other places.

The avifauna of the Alligator rivers region includes approximately one-third of Australia's total species, with three largely confined to the area, these being the Banded Fruit-Dove, Chestnut-quilled Rock-Pigeon and White-throated Grasswren. A fourth, the White-lined Honeyeater, once thought to be confined to this region, was later found to occur in similar rough sandstone country of the north-west Kimberley.

Among the subspecies confined to the area are the Lavender-flanked Fairy-wren, Grey Whistler, and a subspecies of Helmeted Friarbird known as the Sandstone Friarbird. The endemics are largely confined to the sandstone escarpment, which encompasses several distinct habitats, principally the open woodland with spinifex ground-cover and the sandstone rainforest of broad-leafed shrubbery. The former is favoured by the White-throated Grasswren, Chestnut-quilled Rock-Pigeon, Sandstone Shrike-thrush and Hooded Parrot, while the latter is used by the Banded Fruit-Dove, Sandstone (Helmeted) Friarbird, White-lined Honeyeater and Rufous Owl, not all confined to this region but species or subspecies restricted at least to far northern Australia.

Coastal mangroves and those fringing the estuarine reaches of the rivers provide nesting, roosting and feeding for many species, some abundant, some uncommon or secretive. None is confined to the Top End but some are found only across far northern Australia and in New Guinea; these tend to be the species sought by visiting birdwatchers. Among the species or subspecies of the area are the Chestnut Rail, Mangrove Kingfisher, Mangrove Robin, Mangrove Golden Whistler, White-breasted Whistler, Broad-billed Flycatcher, Mangrove Fantail, Mangrove Warbler, Red-headed Honeyeater and Yellow Silvereye.

Other habitats, including the coastal woodlands, coastal monsoon forests and wetlands, support some additional species unique to the Top End, for instance the Hooded Parrot, or like the Rainbow Pitta and Red-collared Lorikeet, confined to far northern Australia.

But for most visitors to the Alligator rivers and Kakadu the fascination lies in the spectacle of immense numbers of birds and the ease with which some species can be approached. For example the Black-necked Stork, which in other places would take flight at far greater distance and which at such unaccustomed close range is so much more impressive. The floodplains and swamps of these rivers are major feeding and breeding grounds for a great variety of waterbirds, and as the entire north of the continent becomes parched through the later months of the dry season the remaining deeper lagoons become the major refuge areas. Here the waterbirds of much of the Top End become concentrated and provide a spectacular sight of massed birdlife.

66 **YELLOW-BILLED SPOONBILL**
Platalea flavipes

The species best known for its huge numbers is the Magpie Goose whose population across the coastal Top End, from the Daly River to the East Alligator, was estimated by aerial count at totals varying from 50 000 to 382 000.

The largest congregations were on the South Alligator with 313 930 and on the East Alligator with 31 870, both in 1980, a year when the wet season had been prolonged. In some years when the swamps were not well filled and had dried early very few if any of the young survived to fly. This is probably the reason for lows of 9150 and 3940 birds for these rivers in 1972.

Migrants wintering in Australia swell the bird counts, with waders from the north on mudflats and shores, and several forest species including the Dollarbird, Common Koel and Torresian Imperial-Pigeon. Some of these remain while others, like the Little Curlew, stay just long enough to rebuild their strength to continue to either their wintering or their breeding grounds.

At Kakadu any of the easily located major lagoons, used through the dry season by a steady stream of barramundi fishermen and tourists, will give superb birdwatching opportunities, preferably from a boat, for which there are boat tours from Cooinda. There are several lagoons, the best-known being Yellow-water Lagoon or Yellow Waterhole, and Nourlangie Lagoon, both on the South Alligator River. The birds of the sandstone escarpment country are not as easily seen. Much of the escarpment is difficult to reach or zoned as restricted access. The advice of the national park rangers should be obtained on localities for these species.

Farther downstream, where the Arnhem Highway crosses the lower tidal part of the South Alligator, there are accommodation, caravan and camping facilities, and the opportunity to join the boat tour down the river where sightings of estuarine birds such as the Little Kingfisher and the Great-billed Heron are possible.

A belt of rainforest close by has a walk track where Rainbow Pittas have been seen. Part of this track is through eucalypt woodland and beside a small lagoon where waterbirds, and with luck the White-bellied Sea-Eagle and Pacific Baza, may be seen.

But the most prized bird sightings on this part of the South Alligator are out on the open grassy and somewhat swampy floodplains. To the west side of the main river channel frequent sightings are made of the Yellow Chat and nests quite often located. The Eastern Grass Owl also has been found nesting in this vicinity.

DARWIN AREA

For birdwatching the greater Darwin area can be subdivided into three localities: the coast close to Darwin, the Humpty Doo–Fogg Dam area and the ranges around Mt Bundey and Manton Dam. Even the most distant of these is close enough to allow for half-day trips, and most are much closer.

The birdlist for this area is nearly 260 species, though some are rare vagrants. Habitats include woodland and open forest, small patches of monsoon forest known locally as 'jungle', swamps and lagoons, and the coastline which varies from sandy beaches to mudflats and mangroves.

Of these sites, Fogg Dam is one of the best-known and most accessible. A road across the low earthen dam wall offers convenient viewing across the dam's expanse of water and floating lilies and other aquatic vegetation.

At Fogg Dam can be seen, on a smaller scale, much of the birdlife of the far more extensive lagoons of the Alligator rivers area. Usually there are substantial numbers of Magpie Geese on wet areas below the dam wall, while the waters of the dam have Pied Herons, Little, Plumed and Great egrets, Black-necked Storks, both species of whistling-ducks, Radjah Shelducks, Hardheads, Green Pygmy-Geese, White-browed Crakes and Comb-crested Jacanas. A duck rare in Australia, the Garganey, has been recorded here.

The adjoining Workshop Jungle is a convenient site to see Rainbow Pittas and other monsoon forest species. Rainbow Pittas can also be found at nearby Black Jungle, while Harrison Dam gives further waterbird opportunities. Birds of prey that have been sighted here are typical of the Top End and include Pacific Bazas and Black Kites. At Howard Springs, Rainbow Pittas and Little Kingfishers are seen from time to time.

Darwin, or rather the coast close by, has acquired a considerable reputation as a wader site, especially for first sightings of species not previously recorded in Australia. There are several excellent wader sites, probably the best of these being Lee Point at high tide, but also worth visiting are Buffalo Creek, Mickel Creek, Ludmilla Creek, East Point, Dinah Beach and the east arm of Darwin harbour.

A dinghy and outboard are needed at Buffalo Creek where it is sometimes possible to get a sighting of the Chestnut Rail and Great-billed Heron. There is also some monsoon forest here and at Lee Point.

Sightings along the Darwin coast have included the Hudsonian Whimbrel, Redshank, Eastern Golden Plover, Pectoral Sandpiper, the Beach Thick-knee at Lee Point and the Ruff at Buffalo Point. The Leanyer Swamp, close to the north-east of Darwin between Buffalo and Mickel creeks, has yielded interesting records including the Caspian Plover and Long-toed Stint.

The ponds of the Sanderson

57 **RUFOUS NIGHT HERON** *Nycticorax caledonicus*

Sewerage Works, near Casuarina, have given numerous new or unusual sightings, among them the Little Ringed Plover, Spotted Greenshank, Reeve, Japanese Gull, Grey Wagtail and, unusual for the Top End, the Blue-billed Duck.

More distant Manton Dam and Tumbling Waters, close by the Stuart Highway south of Darwin, and the Mt Bundey area to the south-east, have many of the birds of the drier woodlands including Masked Finches, and Northern Rosellas are common.

THE GULF COUNTRY

Towards its western limits the Top End Region has birds of interest, one very rare, others in huge numbers. The Carpentarian or Dorothy's Grasswren is one of Australia's least-known and most restricted birds, seen by comparatively few ornithologists, while the Gulf mudflats have immense numbers of migrant waders.

A block of relatively low but very rough, broken sandstone extends from the McArthur River west to the Nicholson River. The Carpentarian Grasswren has been found at each end of this sandstone belt and probably occurs in scattered and localized groups through the area between. It may occur farther west, narrowing the gap to the similar White-throated Grasswren of Arnhem Land.

More common and widespread through this southern Gulf country is the Purple-crowned Fairy-wren. This eastern population appears not to have suffered the decline experienced by the species in the Kimberley and western parts of the Top End. It can be seen along the Gregory River and in the Lawn Hill Gorge National Park. Other species in the sandstone country here and at Borroloola along the McArthur River are the Sandstone Shrike-thrush, Northern Rosella, Spotted Bowerbird, and numerous honeyeaters including the Banded, Bar-breasted, Yellow-tinted and Grey-fronted.

The mudflats of the south-eastern corner of the Gulf of Carpentaria around the mouth of the Gilbert River north of Karumba have been surveyed from the air, giving wader counts of up to 250 000 birds in December, including some 50 000 Black-tailed Godwits.

KATHERINE AREA

At Katherine Gorge a great number of birds can be seen around the entrance to the gorge, around the camping and picnic areas, along the side of the escarpment close by, and in the thickets at the river's edge. Some of the species here, most of them quite conspicuous, are Great Bowerbirds, and their bowers, Blue-faced Honeyeaters, Red-winged Parrots, Red-collared Lorikeets, Blue-winged Kookaburras, Crimson Finches abundant in pandanus along the water's edge, White-gaped Honeyeaters, Lemon-bellied Flycatchers in denser

63 **SACRED IBIS** *Threskiornis aethiopica*

river's-edge vegetation, Sulphur-crested Cockatoos, Tawny Frogmouths, boobooks and Black-tailed Treecreepers. From boats along the gorge one can see Darters sunning on logs, and Azure and possibly Little kingfishers along the banks.

The Top End endemics of the sandstone country are not as easily seen. Chestnut-quilled Rock-Pigeons may be seen along walk trails above the gorge, and perhaps the northern subspecies of the Variegated Fairy-wren, the Lavender-flanked Fairy-wren. The White-throated Grasswren inhabits rough and more distant parts of the park. One site is on open spinifex and boulder slopes of the valley of a tributary of the Katherine, the Seventeen Mile Creek, which branches north from near the entrance of Katherine Gorge. Ranger advice should be obtained.

In the dry season, especially late in the year when most small pools have dried out, any remaining pools in areas around Katherine, the Edith River and north to Pine Creek could be worth watching for Gouldian Finches, Hooded Parrots and any other more common birds that might come in to drink. Specific sites are not listed here as the access tracks and local conditions will vary from year to year, and it is possible that such information might be used by bird trappers. The Ranger at the Katherine office of the Northern Territory Conservation Commission may be able to advise on current local conditions and possible sites for seeing these species.

About 100 km south-east of Katherine, Mataranka is a small reserve with a patch of swampy monsoon forest that could be worth a stop for travellers on the Stuart Highway. The birdlist includes a number of closed-forest species.

100 **WHITE-BELLIED SEA-EAGLE**
Haliaeetus leucogaster

VICTORIA RIVER DISTRICT

The western part of the Top End has country that is not only rewarding for its birdlife but also scenically attractive, particularly where the highway winds through the valley of the Victoria River. Scenic areas off the main route include Jasper Gorge to the south near Victoria Downs Station, and Keep River National Park to the north of the highway adjoining the Western Australian border. The landforms include, at the extremes, flat black-soil plains and jagged, broken sandstone ranges.

The birdlife is typical of the Top End and Kimberley, rather closer to that of the latter, as the flat country of the Daly and Katherine rivers' drainage isolates some species of the Kimberley–Victoria River sandstone escarpments from similar species or

81 **HARDHEAD** *Aythya australis*

subspecies of the Arnhem Land–Katherine Gorge sandstone country.

Among birds shared with the Kimberley but not with the more easterly parts of the Top End are the White-quilled Rock-Pigeon, the Lavender-flanked Fairy-wren (Variegated Fairy-wren of the Kimberley, subspecies *rogersi*) and the Kimberley subspecies of the Purple-crowned Fairy-wren. The avifauna generally is a mixture of those of tropical and arid zones, with species such as the Spinifex Pigeon, Budgerigar and Grey-fronted Honeyeater occurring here but not significantly farther to the north-east.

At Keep River National Park, 167 species of birds have been recorded since 1975. Of these, the most exciting is a possible record of the Night Parrot, and perhaps other sightings from Bulloo River and Kildurk stations, nearer the Victoria River. Recent records of the Dusky Honeyeater here, almost on the Western Australian border, suggest that this species will eventually be found in the north-east corner of the Kimberley.

The National Park contains lagoons with such species as the Black-necked Stork, both spoonbills, Green Pygmy-Goose and various ducks. There has been a single sighting of a Great-billed Heron, at a river pool. In the northern part of Keep River is an area of sandstone plateau dissected by a maze of gorges and breakaways, the habitat not only of Night Parrots but also White-quilled Rock-Pigeons, Sandstone Shrike-thrushes and Lavender-flanked Fairy-wrens. Birdlife at the lagoons has increased with the regrowth of vegetation following the fencing-out of cattle.

The Purple-crowned Fairy-wren does not appear to occur at Keep River. The nearby Victoria River is a well-known site for this endangered western subspecies. Farther upstream, on Victoria River Downs Station, it was reported to be restricted in habitat and range and thought to be threatened with local extinction. A survey of the birds at the Station, which is farther inland than the Keep River, produced a list of 181 species including the Green-backed Warbler, White-quilled Rock-Pigeon, Leaden Flycatcher, White-browed Robin, Lemon-bellied Flycatcher, Blue-faced Honeyeater and Northern Fantail. Here, as in many parts of the Kimberley and Northern Territory, many of these birds depend upon the river-edge environment, especially late in the dry season when cattle congregate about the remaining pools, muddying the water and destroying all low vegetation.

KAKADU BIRDWATCH

The lagoons of the Alligator rivers in Kakadu National Park seem to be used more by anglers seeking the barramundi than by birdwatchers. These prized fish are taken either by casting with rod and lure into the murky brown lagoon waters close by banks and snags caused by fallen trees, or by trailing the line behind a dinghy moving with outboard motor only slightly above idle. The keenest of anglers begin before dawn. Almost every morning through seven or eight months of the dry season the pre-dawn darkness is shattered by the sound of outboards starting and anglers speeding away to favoured fishing spots along the many kilometres of river channels.

The immense numbers of birds that use the lily-covered backwaters, flooded grasslands and mangrove fringes around and beside these lagoons have grown accustomed to the almost constant sound and sight of small boats along the waterways. They continue about their business as boats speed or drift by within a few metres, giving sightings from a boat that would never be tolerated at other wetlands. For sightings of an abundance of tropical waterbirds, some remarkably close at hand, others in immense flocks, on Yellow-water or Nourlangie lagoons, all that is needed is a small boat and, preferably, a dawn start, on almost any day in the middle of the dry season.

With the sun still below the eastern horizon the water is usually glassy smooth, reflecting the black silhouettes of the river-bank mangrove trees against the glow of the pre-dawn sky. With a purr of the outboard motor the dinghy glides out onto the broad river, almost immediately passing close by the dark shapes of pelicans huddled on the bank. Overhead, long lines of ibises, geese and ducks begin to make their way from roost to feeding grounds. On the bank a Black-necked Stork stands motionless, silhouetted against the brightening sky it seems huge and majestic. In the semi-darkness below the bank a Rufous Night Heron stalks along the water's edge with slow and deliberate steps, dagger-pointed bill ready to spear forward. Very soon the sun is breaking

above the horizon, flickering between the trunks of the mangroves as the boat glides over the still water. It reveals birds everywhere beginning their hunting. On a perch low over the water an Azure Kingfisher waits motionless, blue of plumage brilliant in the clear early sunlight. It darts ahead

74 RADJAH SHELDUCK *Tadorna radjah*

91 **BLACK KITE** *Milvus migrans*

with sharp calls and vanishes into the darkness of the mangroves.

On the lagoon the Comb-crested Jacanas have appeared and seem to be everywhere, running across the floating lily leaves, incredibly long toes spreading their weight across the floating vegetation. Some pairs are accompanied by their young, seeming all legs and feet.

In places the slightly raised levee-like banks of the channel dip to waterlevel where the grasslands are still flooded with only a few centimetres of water. On the shallow pools huge flocks of Magpie Geese and whistling-ducks have gathered, some probably numbering in the thousands. Among them move the tall white shapes of Royal and Yellow-billed spoonbills and Great Egrets, while Plumed and Little egrets and Pied Herons hunt around the edge.

Along the lagoon edge pelicans glide above their mirrored reflections. The edges of the waterways are thick with floating weeds and lily leaves where, not obvious at first, float Green Pygmy-Geese and various species of ducks.

Ahead of the boat a Pied Cormorant surfaces, a large fish in its bill. It takes off in fright across the water, wings and webbed feet raising a chain of splashes as it struggles to get airborne with heavy fish and wet plumage.

Extremely common along the waterways are Black Kites and White-bellied Sea-Eagles. There is no difficulty getting a good look at these as they snatch food from the water surface or wait patiently for a handout from a successful fisherman.

It is an interesting experience to tie up the boat and explore the fringing mangroves and river-edge forest, always watching for crocodiles. There is usually a good variety of birds, the Yellow Oriole, Lemon-bellied Flycatcher, Mangrove Robin, White-browed Robin, Rufous and Northern fantails, Mangrove Kingfisher, Leaden Flycatcher, Mangrove Warbler and Red-headed Honeyeater. In a quiet backwater, well away from the boats, it might be possible to get a distant glimpse of the wary Great-billed Heron.

252 **RED-COLLARED LORIKEET** *Trichoglossus rubritorquis*

THE KIMBERLEY

In the northernmost part of Western Australia the coast becomes deeply indented, the offshore seas are studded with islands and the ranges of jagged sandstone have been carved into huge gorges. The ocean, rising, has encircled ranges and filled river valleys to create a fiordland-like coast. These are the coastal manifestations of the rugged interior where range and plateau have been carved into a landscape of escarpments, gorges and waterfalls. Not all is sandstone, a notable exception being the Mitchell Plateau where an extensive flat cap of laterite overlies the sandstone.

Eastwards the ragged ranges, often interrupted by broad river valleys, continue almost to the Ord River, making this region as scenically magnificent in the east as it is in the west. Its spectacular landforms include the Elgee Cliffs and Durack Range and the maze of sculptured domes and gorges known as the Bungle Bungle Range.

Southwards, the King Leopold and Mueller ranges were for a long time effective barriers to access, like great walls across the plains, dividing the rugged northern Kimberley from the plains of the southern parts.

Within the mountainous northern Kimberley the summer monsoon rainfall is heavy, with an average of almost 1580 mm at Mitchell Plateau and 1300 mm at the Prince Regent River; in some years the estimated rainfall here has been as high as 4000 mm. Major river systems have developed, carrying huge volumes of water in the wet season. Many deep and shady gorges hold pools right through the dry season. The major rivers of the western and northern Kimberley are the Mitchell, Drysdale, King Edward and Prince Regent. Curving through the south-western and southern sides, with their headwaters in the King Leopold and Durack ranges, are two of Australia's mightiest rivers, the Fitzroy and the Ord.

The southern parts of the Kimberley are mainly of lowland plains, becoming progressively drier southwards and merging into the dune country of the Great Sandy Desert. Climatically the north-western Kimberley is much like the Top End of the Northern Territory with similar rainfall at its wettest parts, around the Mitchell Plateau. There are distinct wet and dry seasons, the intensity and length of 'the wet' varying greatly and depending mainly upon the frequency and route of cyclones. There are usually about four months, December to March, when heavy rain is likely, giving about six 'growing months'; temperatures are consistently high.

Open forests and woodlands dominate. There are a considerable variety of trees: the orange-flowered *Eucalyptus miniata* and *E. phoenicea* and the red-flowered swamp bloodwood are spectacular in flower during the dry season, attracting many birds. These and many other trees and shrubs extend through the Top End, so that there is substantial continuity of habitat, though interrupted for some birds by the drier east Kimberley.

The wettest coastal north-east of the Kimberley, again like the Top End, has rainforest-like vegetation with small patches of low vine-thicket closed forest, usually of 1–25 ha in area, the canopy at about 5–10 m high but with much taller emergent trees, mostly deciduous, which are bare through the winter dry season. The understorey is of shrubs and vines; it has a thin layer of leaf-litter but almost no ground flora. Most of these vine thickets are found on escarpment slopes and in gorges where seepage provides additional moisture through the dry season. There are some very extensive areas of mangroves in river estuaries and other sheltered parts of the coast.

In its wettest and most diverse coastal parts, around the Mitchell Plateau and Prince Regent River, this part of the Kimberley supports about 220 species of birds, a list which could be enlarged with more coastal observations of waders.

In general, the northern Kimberley is in much better condition than most of northern tropical Australia, much of the country being too rugged for cattle.

The Kimberley has one endemic bird species, the Black Grasswren, and several endemic subspecies including the Kimberley Flycatcher and the Dusky Warbler, while the White-quilled Rock-Pigeon and Purple-crowned Fairy-wren are near-endemic, extending over the border into the Victoria River District of the Northern Territory. The Kimberley Flycatcher, a mangrove bird, was formerly a Kimberley endemic species but is now regarded as a subspecies of the Lemon-bellied Flycatcher, confined to the Kimberley. Much of the Kimberley Region north of the King Leopold Range has very limited access for there are few roads and these are usually closed through the wet season. The east Kimberley, around Kununurra, is much more accessible, especially during and following 'the wet'.

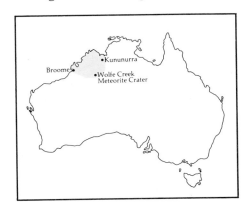

BIRDS OF THE KIMBERLEY

233 WHITE-QUILLED ROCK-PIGEON

Petrophassa albipennis

Throughout much of the Kimberley and into the western parts of the Top End the White-quilled Rock-Pigeon is locally moderately common wherever there is suitable habitat. It is a sedentary species, keeping to rough sandstone country, especially of river gorges and sandstone escarpments near permanent water.

As the habitat includes many scenic areas attractive to the travelling public, including birdwatchers, the species is often seen. Its habits of frequenting cliff ledges around waterfalls and gorges, and of coming to water throughout the day, makes sightings of this species almost inevitable in localities where there are sandstone gorges or cliffs near water.

When on the ground, or, as more often seen, on cliff-ledges, this short-legged brown pigeon seems to scuttle over the rocks in an almost reptilian manner, unlike any other bird within its range. When it takes flight, whether rising from water or flushed, there is a loud clapping of wings which may draw attention when the species would otherwise be overlooked. Between bursts of wing-clapping flight it often glides on stiffly outstretched wings. Coming to water it prefers to walk, moving steadily down over ledges and boulders to the pool.

Nests are flat platforms of sticks built on rock ledges or sheltered rock slabs. It is likely to be seen at such scenic sites as Manning Gorge, the Hidden Valley at Kununurra, Lake Argyle, and occurs also in the Bungle Bungle Range.

▶ See also pages 187 198 201 208 *209* 210 211 309

252 RED-COLLARED LORIKEET

Trichoglossus rubritorquis

The Red-collared Lorikeet is often listed as a subspecies of the Rainbow Lorikeet but whether a species or subspecies it is of interest as a distinctive bird of far northern Australia. This is one of the most common parrots in both the Kimberley and Top End regions and can often be seen, without the need to search. The usual habitat is eucalypt open forest, especially in the vicinity of watercourses, and extends to drier woodlands of eucalypts and melaleucas when trees are in flower.

▶ See also pages 196 197 *200* 208 211 313

344 BARN SWALLOW

Hirundo rustica

Most sightings of the Barn Swallow have been from the Kimberley Region, with occasional records also from the Top End Region of the Northern Territory and along the Innisfail–Mossman coast of north-eastern Queensland; it is a rare vagrant to south-eastern Australia. In the Derby area this species has been a regular visitor since 1960, occasionally in flocks of up to 300 birds. Here it arrives in early November and departs about the end of March.

The Barn Swallow is conspicuous because it perches in open situations, usually on telegraph wires, on top of buildings, and on bare twigs and reed stems but not among foliage. However, the Welcome Swallow, Fairy and Tree martins do likewise so that, without a closer look, perched swallows are generally assumed to be one of the latter. The Barn Swallow is often seen perched or hawking together with these birds and a closer look at all individuals among flocks of martins or swallows, especially across northern Australia, could result in a Barn Swallow sighting. While size and outline are similar to the Welcome, it has glossy blue-black upperparts and its forehead and throat are rich rufous, separated from the creamy white of the rest of the underparts by a narrow black breastband. There are often also juveniles, duller than the adults, with breastband brownish.

The Barn Swallow will usually be seen in open country, near water, often in or near towns, and is highly gregarious. It is possible that the species occurs along other parts of the northern coast, mainly the Gulf of Carpentaria and Cape York Peninsula. Sightings have been in the general area of Derby, Broome, Kununurra, the Darwin area, Innisfail, Mossman, Fraser Island and Canungra.

▶ See also pages *209* 210 337

349 YELLOW WAGTAIL

Motacilla flava

The far north-western coastline of Australia is a regular wintering area for the Yellow Wagtail, with records from the Kimberley, eastern Pilbara and western Top End regions. It is also an uncommon to rare vagrant to eastern and southern Australia. Most sightings have been from November to February but several have been in the southern winter, when the Yellow Wagtail would be expected to be at its breeding grounds in Asia and Alaska.

The Yellow Wagtail frequents lush wet sites, around the shallows of swamps, flooded grasslands and pastures.

▶ See also pages 209 210 338

375 KIMBERLEY FLYCATCHER

Microeca flavigaster tormenti

This small bird of the mangroves, which is probably a subspecies of the Lemon-bellied Flycatcher, is unique to the Kimberley. Although early observers recorded it as living upon small crabs and the like, insects caught on and above the mangrove mudflats are the main diet.

It is usually solitary or in pairs or small parties, keeping low and near the edge of the mangroves. Much of its habitat around the rugged Kimberley coast is inaccessible but it can be seen in the west at Barred Creek near Broome, near Derby, and wherever else mangroves can be reached around the coast east to Wyndham. Early records were from western parts of this range but later specimens from the Cambridge Gulf mangroves have shown it to intergrade with the Lemon-bellied Flycatcher.

Surveys have shown the Kimberley Flycatcher to be moderately common in the mangroves of the Mitchell Plateau and Prince Regent River coasts.

▶ See also pages 192 201 208 *209* 210 344

409 NORTHERN FANTAIL

Rhipidura rufiventris

The Northern Fantail looks more like a flycatcher than does the Grey Fantail. It has a larger bill and white eyebrow but lacks the second small white ear streak of the Grey Fantail. The band across the upper breast is dark grey streaked white, rather than black, and the bird is less inclined to fan the tail or flutter about.

It occurs in all wooded habitats, including mangroves, rainforests, swamps and woodlands. In range and habitats it overlaps substantially the Grey Fantail, so that recognition will depend upon differences of song and appearance. Those familiar with the song of the Grey Fantail in southern Australia will have no difficulty in discerning that the call and song of the Northern Fantail, though similar to the Grey, are recognizably different, the usual call a 'chunk' rather than the 'check' of the Grey. The Northern Fantail also gives various 'chip' notes and a higher and more tinkling song.

▶ See also pages 111 198 199 208 *209* 210 352 409

433 PURPLE-CROWNED FAIRY-WREN *Malurus coronatus*

patrol to one end of their narrow river-edge habitat and then back again, usually keeping within the belt of this vegetation where their position was usually revealed by snatches of song. Although the male was in full colour there was no evidence of any breeding activity.

Much of the northern part of the Kimberley is inaccessible and unsuitable for cattle, so it is possible that this unique fairy-wren will continue to survive in those parts even though it has gone from much of the southern Kimberley. It is regularly reported from the Drysdale River crossing, Manning Creek, the 'beef road' north to Kalumburu, and occasionally from Fitzroy Crossing, Geikie Gorge and the Pentecost and Ord rivers. The Victoria River crossing of the Kununurra–Katherine highway probably offers the best chance of sightings.

▶ **See also pages** 174 187 197 198 201 *203* 208 211 *211* 358

617 **GREAT BOWERBIRD** *Chlamydera nuchalis*

444 BLACK GRASSWREN

Amytornis housei

The Black Grasswren was first collected in 1901 and was not seen again until its rediscovery in 1968. It has since been found in a number of sites in the north-west Kimberley, all in rugged broken country of sandstone escarpments, gorges and boulders, where large clumps of spinifex form the dominant ground-cover. It runs and hops over the boulders rather than flies, and hides in crevices and under spinifex.

The Black Grasswren is probably fairly common through the very rugged and inaccessible sandstone country along the north-west coast of the Kimberley, possibly as far south as the western end of the King Leopold Range and east to the headwaters of the Drysdale and Manning rivers.

Members of the 1985 Bird Observers Club Kimberley Tour found the species plentiful in sandstone country at Mitchell Falls, the Caroline Ranges and about the headwaters of the Charnley and Manning rivers. It has also recently been reported plentiful around the upper Glenelg River.

Along the walk trail to Mitchell Falls the Black Grasswrens were seen near a small stream in typical habitat of rugged sandstone with huge boulders and large clumps of spinifex. Most observers seem surprised at the size of the Black Grasswren, which is considerably larger than the familiar fairy-wrens, perhaps slightly larger than a Willie Wagtail.

Usually these birds keep to the rocks

433 PURPLE-CROWNED FAIRY-WREN

Malurus coronatus

There are two subspecies of the distinctive Purple-crowned Fairy-wren. The western subspecies has suffered severe loss of range and numbers and no longer exists in many places where it once was abundant. The decline is thought to result from destruction of habitat. This fairy-wren is confined to river-edge cane-grass and pandanus thickets, which in many places have been totally destroyed by mobs of cattle congregating about the river pools through the dry season.

The Purple-crowned Fairy-wren is always found close to water, usually in the fringing vegetation along salt or freshwater parts of rivers. It is noticeably larger than other fairy-wrens and has a stronger and distinctive call which makes its passage through cane-grass and other thick vegetation easy to follow. On the lower Victoria River a pair under

observation could easily be located at almost any time of day by their calls, although often intermingling with that of the Red-backed Fairy-wrens.

The calls are not only loud, but perhaps have also a slightly harsher quality. Once the calls of both the Purple-crowned and the Red-backed fairy-wrens have been heard, they can be used to locate, identify and follow the individual species even though the birds may be out of sight in the dense water's-edge vegetation.

Purple-crowned Fairy-wrens, in pairs or small family groups, seem to follow a regular route in their foraging. A pair photographed at the edge of a tidal creek spent most of their time in reedy vegetation along the water's edge, the vegetation being partly under water at high tide. Their territory seemed to extend about 100 m along one side of a tributary creek and perhaps 20 m up onto the higher bank to the edge of open woodland. The birds would regularly and spinifex, darting in and out of crevices and under spinifex and bouncing across boulders. Only occasionally do they fly, rather poorly and keeping low, sometimes for as far as 50 m to cross a gully.

If approached too closely the grasswrens take off with 'chee-chee-chee' alarm calls, members of the group repeating the alarm and scattering. Males are more vocal and often jump to the tops of boulders to chirp or to 'tick' sharply in alarm. The calls are rapid and more metallic than those of other grasswrens. These grasswrens are usually in groups of three to six birds and seem to be gregarious, in the manner of a party of babblers. Observers seem impressed by the rich chestnut and black of the plumage.

Probably the most convenient site for this species is the vicinity of Manning Creek, Mt Barnett Station.

▶ See also pages 193 201 208 *209* 210 211 360–1

507 SILVER-CROWNED FRIARBIRD

Philemon argenticeps

The Silver-crowned Friarbird is common almost throughout the Kimberley Region and occurs across northern Australia to north-eastern Queensland. It inhabits forests, woodlands and mangroves where it feeds mainly on insects caught around flowering trees, some of these taken on the wing. There appear to be considerable movements, both seasonal and nomadic, so that the species may be common in a locality at one time but completely absent in other months. In parts of the Kimberley Region the Silver-crowned Friarbird appears to move to rough sandstone country to breed during the wet season. The abundance of this species, its presence in towns and its noisy behaviour should ensure sightings.

▶ See also pages 175 *209* 211 375

528 WHITE-GAPED HONEYEATER

Lichenostomus unicolor

The White-gaped Honeyeater is a tropical woodland species but prefers situations of dense vegetation, especially where there is a dense understorey along watercourses and river banks. It also inhabits patches of monsoon and vine scrub in gorges, and coastal mangroves.

▶ See also pages 175 197 211 380

528 **WHITE-GAPED HONEYEATER** *Lichenostomus unicolor* Immatures have a yellowish gape.

538 **YELLOW-TINTED HONEYEATER** *Lichenostomus flavescens*

556 BAR-BREASTED HONEYEATER *Ramsayornis fasciatus* The nest is suspended over a lily lagoon.

556 BAR-BREASTED HONEYEATER
Ramsayornis fasciatus

The Bar-breasted Honeyeater is a woodland species with a strong preference for water-edge situations, by streams, lagoons or paperbark swamps. Very often it is not the bird that is noticed first but the large nest which hangs, like flood debris, from a slender branch over water.

When the eucalypts or melaleucas are in flower these honeyeaters may be abundant about the flowers. Their numbers tend to fluctuate as they follow the flowering of trees. Insects also are taken. These birds are distinctive in appearance, both sexes strongly barred across the breast.

▶ See also pages   174 197 208 211 324 387

558 RUFOUS-THROATED HONEYEATER
Conopophila rufogularis

This active honeyeater will usually be seen about eucalypt forests and woodlands, especially along watercourses where it forages at flowering trees for nectar and insects. It appears to be nomadic and seems attracted to flowering bauhinia trees. At Kununurra the species appears more or less sedentary, while at Mount Isa it is present from August to March.

▶ See also pages   175 208 *209* 211 387

562 BANDED HONEYEATER
Certhionyx pectoralis

540 GOLDEN-BACKED HONEYEATER
SUBSPECIES OF BLACK-CHINNED HONEYEATER

Melithreptus gularis laetior

The Golden-backed Honeyeater is the far northern subspecies of the Black-chinned Honeyeater and was previously regarded as a separate species. Whether species or subspecies, it is a distinctive and beautiful bird, of much brighter colours than the south-eastern nominate subspecies.

This is essentially a bird of the treetop canopy which feeds by gleaning insects from foliage and flowers. It is not conspicuous when among the high foliage and would often be missed but for its far-carrying, ringing call, a 'chee-chee, creep-creep-creep-' which, once known, can reveal the presence of the species at a distance of several hundred metres. At a waterhole where birds were being photographed from a hide the approach of this bird was known long before it arrived near the water. At that site the species seemed solitary with just one at a time coming to water, at irregular intervals morning and evening, and seeming shy compared with the much more common Grey-headed Honeyeaters.

▶ See also pages   11 175 185 *209* 211 221 230 233 382

05 GOULDIAN FINCH

Erythrura gouldiae

The Gouldian Finch has declined greatly in numbers and its range has constricted, the greatest losses being to the east and south of the Gulf of Carpentaria. The decline in Queensland has been steady since around the turn of the century but in the Northern Territory and Kimberley Region, since the mid-sixties the decline has been sudden. Counts at some sites have dropped from thousands to hundreds in the 1970s and to tens in recent years. The losses are thought to be due mainly to burning and cattle grazing, with trapping probably also responsible.

The Gouldian Finch is never far from water and is usually seen in open woodland with grassy understorey. In the wet season there is a general movement to the southern parts of its range, which may be the main breeding area. As the southern areas dry out through the winter months the Gouldian Finch moves back to the northern regions. In the breeding season the species may be seen in small flocks, and after breeding in larger flocks in which dull-plumaged birds are common.

The Gouldian Finch feeds in grass and other low vegetation rather than on the ground. It is shy and if disturbed will fly to the tops of nearby trees. Unlike most other birds it seems to enjoy the full heat of the tropical sun, often sunbathing and active during the hottest part of the day.

The birds of a group often gather together in late afternoon, feed together, preen and visit waterholes to drink and bathe. During the wet season these finches are sometimes conspicuous as they acrobatically pursue flying insects, mainly termites.

▶ See also pages 190 198 208 *209* 211 398

593 **CRIMSON FINCH** *Neochmia phaeton*

260 **RED-WINGED PARROT**
Aprosmictus erythropterus

597 **LONG-TAILED FINCH** *Poephila acuticauda*

600 **PICTORELLA MANNIKIN** *Lonchura pectoralis*

BIRD PLACES OF THE KIMBERLEY

DAMPIER PENINSULA

Dampier Peninsula juts northwards
from the Kimberley coast between
Broome and Derby. For the most part
it is flat and scenically unexciting but
gives opportunity for sightings,
especially of mangrove species. Most
of the peninsula is station country,
part is Aboriginal reserve and there is
a nature reserve at Point Coulomb.

The largest patches of mangroves
are at the base of the peninsula and
south-west of Broome, at Crab Creek
and Dampier Creek, in Roebuck Bay.
A site of easy access is the mangrove at
Willie Creek, about 20 km north of
Broome. The Coulomb Point Nature
Reserve contains some of the few
distinct watercourses and some
freshwater swamps. Further reserves
have been proposed farther north at
Cape Bordas and Cygnet Bay, the
former including vine forest and the
latter with tall mangroves. The major
part of the peninsula has pindan scrub
dominated by small acacia trees and
there are some areas of eucalypt forest
and woodland.

One of the common birds of this
coast is the Brown Booby which often
feeds quite close inshore, sometimes
recorded in flocks of up to 60 birds.
The species breeds in colonies,
sometimes numbering thousands of
birds, on offshore islands including the
Lacepede group.

Species of particular interest
recorded on the Dampier Peninsula
include the Great-billed Heron at
Barred Creek, Red-legged Rail (the
only Australian record being in
Broome, 1958), Rose-crowned Fruit-
Dove at the extreme north-east in vine
thickets and mangroves, Kimberley
Flycatcher, Mangrove Golden
Whistler, White-breasted Whistler,
Mangrove Fantail (subspecies of Grey
Fantail), Northern Fantail, Shining
Flycatcher, Dusky Warbler, Yellow
White-eye, Red-headed Honeyeater,
and the Gouldian Finch in the extreme
north.

The Kimberley Flycatcher, a
subspecies endemic to the Kimberley
Region, has been recorded south to
Barred Creek, a few kilometres to the
north of Willie Creek. The Dusky
Warbler has a subspecies endemic to
the Kimberley mangroves, between
King George Sound and Roebuck Bay,
where it is moderately common.

The total birdlist stood at 214
species at the time of a biological
survey in 1983 with the possibility of
additions, especially of migrant
waders. The richness of species seems
due mainly to the diversity of habitat,
especially along the coast, to which
some 63 species were confined.

MANNING GORGE-DRYSDALE RIVER

The area from the King Leopold Range
north to the Drysdale River, including
Barnett, Adcock and Manning gorges,
has a rich birdlife and is more easily
accessible than places farther north.
From here the Gibb River Road can be
followed eastwards through similar
country to Wyndham.

The Drysdale River crossing has a
reputation as a good birding site, with
the Purple-crowned Fairy-wren, now
very scarce in Western Australia, often
sighted in pandanus along the river
banks; a group from the Bird
Observers Club recorded this species
as being plentiful in August 1985.
They also found here the Black
Bittern, Grey Goshawk, Lavender-
flanked form of the Variegated Fairy-
wren, Leaden Flycatcher, White-
bellied Cuckoo-shrike, White-throated
Warbler, Black-tailed Treecreeper,
Bar-breasted, Rufous-throated and
Banded honeyeaters and other more
commonplace species. This part of the
Drysdale should not be confused with
the Drysdale River National Park
which is on the lower reaches of the
river, roadless and for all practical
purposes inaccessible.

The gorges, Barnett, Manning and
others that cut back into the very
rough sandstone ranges, especially to
the west of the 'beef road', have other
birds typical of that habitat. In this
general area the Bird Observers Club
listing included Red-collared and
Varied lorikeets, the Northern Rosella,
Red-winged Parrot, Grey-fronted
Honeyeater, Brolga, Pacific Baza,
Spotted Harrier, Black Falcon,
Peregrine Falcon, Brush Cuckoo,
Barking Owl, Varied Triller, White-
browed Robin, Partridge Pigeon,
White-quilled Rock-Pigeon and, in the
Caroline Ranges, the Black Grasswren.

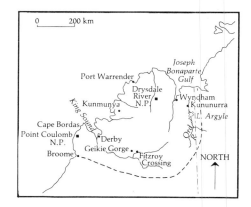

MITCHELL PLATEAU

The Mitchell Plateau as a bird locality covers considerably more than the plateau proper, which is an undulating area of laterite covering an area of about 220 sq. km and with an altitude of about 300–350 m above sea level. On most sides, except parts of the south-eastern approach, the plateau is bordered by steep escarpments, deeply dissected by tributaries of the Mitchell and Lawley rivers. Beyond the relatively level laterite parts the plateau and its escarpments are of sandstone, extremely broken, with deep gorges and landscapes of massive sandstone boulders. On the western side the Mitchell River has cut an immense gorge, headed by huge waterfalls, into this sandstone. To the north and east are steep escarpments overlooking Port Warrender, either as rocky headlands or falling away to bays with mangroves, accessible near Walsh Point but much more extensive at the estuary of the Lawley River.

The climate resembles that of the Top End of the Northern Territory, with a heavy wet season over the months of November or December to February or April, and extending to March or April, giving the bulk of the annual average of almost 1600 mm. This area probably has the heaviest rainfall and the longest growing season for plants than any other part of the Kimberley.

Vegetation is predominantly eucalypt woodlands of varied composition, with many small patches of rainforest-like vine thicket, the largest of these on escarpment slopes overlooking Port Warrender. There are several swamps on the laterite of the plateau, the largest being Airfield Swamp.

A biological survey of the area by the Western Australian Museum recorded a total of 219 species, 82 of these passerines. It was considered that more work along the coast, which is mostly very difficult of access, would add many migrant waders to this list. The number of species here is greater than other surveyed areas of the Kimberley, including the Prince Regent and Drysdale rivers. This is probably because there is a wider variety of habitats, the monsoon or vine thickets being the richest on the Kimberley mainland and surpassed in Western Australia only by those of the Osborne Islands about 40 km to the north.

Because this is the nearest that Western Australia comes to having rainforest, the birds of this habitat, isolated from the main populations of their species farther east, are of considerable interest. They are the

Orange-footed Scrubfowl, Rufous Owl, Rainbow Pitta, Cicadabird, Torresian Imperial-Pigeon, Bar-shouldered Dove, Emerald Dove, Olive-backed Oriole, Yellow Oriole, Figbird, Common Koel, Varied Triller and Little Shrike-thrush.

225 **Bar-shouldered Dove** *Geopelia humeralis*
233 **White-quilled Rock-Pigeon** *Petrophassa albipennis*
344 **Barn Swallow** *Hirundo rustica*
349 **Yellow Wagtail** *Motacilla flava*
375 **Kimberley Flycatcher** *Microeca flavigaster tormenti*
409 **Northern Fantail** *Rhipidura rufiventris*
444 **Black Grasswren** *Amytornis housei*
507 **Silver-crowned Friarbird** *Philemon argenticeps*
540 **Golden-Backed Honeyeater** (subspecies of Black-chinned Honeyeater) *Melithreptus gularis laetior*
558 **Rufous-throated Honeyeater** *Conopophila rufogularis*
605 **Gouldian Finch** — *Erythrura gouldiae*

307 **BARKING OWL** *Ninox connivens*

In the coastal and riverine scrubs are also the Green-backed Warbler, White-browed Robin, Northern Fantail and Leaden Flycatcher.

Of the other habitats, the rugged sandstone areas have the species that attract most excitement. These are the Black Grasswren, White-lined Honeyeater, White-quilled Rock-Pigeon, Sandstone Shrike-thrush and Lavender-flanked Fairy-wren. These can be seen on the walks, very rough and all but trackless, from the plateau down to Mitchell Falls and to Surveyors Pool.

Mangroves here are in large blocks, well developed, with nine species of mangrove trees, some reaching 7–8 m in height; 14 species of birds have been recorded, with the Kimberley Flycatcher and Dusky Warbler of special interest as endemic subspecies.

THE ORD RIVER AREA

The Ord is one of the largest rivers across northern Australia. The construction of the diversion and main dams has created extensive additional wetlands habitat, adding to the already considerable bird fauna of the Ord catchment. In many respects this area is a westerly extension of the Top End birdlife but has also birds unique to the Kimberley Region.

As a birdwatching locality it has the advantages of ease of access and the facilities of the towns of Kununurra and Wyndham. There are immense tracts of wilderness country away from these main centres, some of the scenery spectacular, notably the Bungle Bungle Range to the south, the ranges along the Durack River to the south-west and the huge waterfalls of the King George River to the north-west.

Kununurra, in Western Australia's eastern Kimberley close to the Northern Territory border, is central to an area of excellent birding opportunities. The town was created to service the Ord River irrigation scheme, from which much of the attraction for birds results. The dams and the large areas of irrigated land provide additional habitat and refuge for birds through the dry season, while natural habitats of rivers, rugged ranges and gorges, and coastal mudflats and mangroves at nearby Wyndham, together make this a rewarding locality for birds in a setting often of great scenic beauty.

Within a few hundred metres of Kununurra's motels and caravan park, Lake Kununurra, behind the concrete wall of the diversion dam, has over the years acquired reed-beds and lush fringing vegetation; the birdlist is reported to be close to 200 species. The

irrigated crops attract Magpie Geese, at times in thousands, and the grasslands of the lower Ord are the only Western Australian locality for the Zitting Cisticola, which is reported moderately common here. Many of the wetlands birds of the Alligator rivers area occur here and on the headwaters of nearby Lake Argyle: herons, egrets, spoonbills, Black-necked Storks, Black Bitterns, ibises, spoonbills, whistling-ducks, Radjah Shelducks, Hardheads, Green Pygmy-Geese and Comb-crested Jacanas. This is one of very few Kimberley and indeed Western Australian localities for the Pacific Baza, Grey Goshawk, Red Goshawk, King Quail, Chestnut Rail, White-browed Crake, Common Koel, Channel-billed Cuckoo, Eastern Grass Owl, Barn Swallow, Yellow Wagtail, White-browed Robin, Lemon-bellied and Broad-billed flycatchers, Shining Flycatcher, Rufous Fantail, Tawny Grassbird, Zitting Cisticola, Green-backed Warbler, Yellow Chat, Yellow-rumped and Chestnut-breasted mannikins and Yellow Oriole.

In most instances where these species have been recorded elsewhere in the Kimberley region, it has been in northernmost coastal parts where access is difficult, making the Ord River area the only convenient locality for so many of these species. The Dusky Honeyeater occurs on Northern Territory parts of the Keep River, which crosses into Western Australia, so that this species is predicted to be found here.

Sites for wetland species in addition to Lake Kununurra include Packsaddle Swamp, situated 4–5 km south-west of Kununurra, and Marlgu Lagoon, near Wyndham. Lake Argyle, a huge body of water behind the Ord River Dam, is developing into an outstanding sanctuary for waterbirds, as the vegetation of its shallower backwaters increases. Boat tours of the lake are readily available.

The Ord is set among ranges which create spectacular scenery and contain some of the species typical of that habitat, including the White-quilled Rock-Pigeon, easily seen at Hidden Valley, and the Sandstone Shrike-thrush.

At Wyndham, mangroves are easily accessible but contain numerous large saltwater crocodiles, requiring reasonable caution on the part of mangrove birdwatchers. A much sought-after species is the Kimberley Flycatcher, a Kimberley subspecies here merging with the Lemon-bellied Flycatcher. Also in the mangroves here are the Yellow White-eye, Mangrove Robin, Mangrove Warbler and Mangrove subspecies of Grey Fantail.

KIMBERLEY BIRDWATCH

A birdwalk at Manning Creek, in the north-west Kimberley, will traverse varied habitat and give sightings of a large number of species, with the possibility of several not often recorded.

A greater variety of habitat can be included by beginning well downstream where the road crosses the Barnett River and, following this, the Manning Creek up into the sandstone ranges. But this would be a lengthy walk, especially if stopping to watch birds, so most walkers would probably take it in several segments, perhaps during a stay of two or three days.

The easiest is at the Barnett River crossing where one can wander up or down the sandy river bed. Through most of the dry season a series of pools, often connected by flowing water, lie in the deeper parts of the river bed. The watercourse here is lined with some massive cajuput trees, and clumps of pandanus palms grow along the river bed.

This is a most pleasant place to wander slowly up the river bed, mostly shady and an easy walk, watching the surrounding birdlife, particularly the birds coming in to drink at the pools. In the heat of the day it may be just as rewarding to sit quietly near one of the pools and watch the comings and goings of the birds.

The clumps of pandanus, too, are well worth investigating for they give secure shelter for many small birds, especially the Crimson Finches which are quite abundant along here. These finches stuff their untidy domed nests securely between the serrated-edged leaves of the pandanus.

Finches are the most common of the visitors to these river pools, with, in addition to the Crimson, the Long-tailed, Double-bar, and possibly the Gouldian. Also coming to the water here will be Peaceful and Diamond doves and various honeyeaters, which often flutter across the surface to dip momentarily into the water. Among these are likely to be Bar-breasted Honeyeaters, which suspend their long nests over the waters of streams, lagoons or swamps. The cajuput trees attract and shelter birds also. When

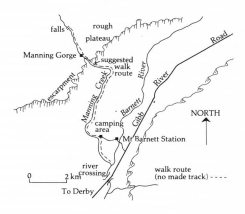

these or other trees are in flower they attract large numbers of honeyeaters. At almost any time of day, in the dry season from around June to August, flowering swamp bloodwoods and orange-flowered *Eucalyptus miniata* and *E. phoenicea* and other trees attract nectar-seeking birds. The honeyeaters include the Blue-faced, Golden-backed (subspecies of Black-chinned), Banded, Rufous-throated, White-gaped, Brown, Bar-breasted, Yellow-tinted and Singing, and the Silver-crowned and Little friarbirds.

Some other birds likely to be seen here are Northern Rosellas, Red-collared Lorikeets and Silver-backed

433 PURPLE-CROWNED FAIRY-WREN
Mulurus coronatus

Butcherbirds. Small pools in the river bed are ideal for watching finches and other birds coming to drink during the heat of the day, among them Masked and Long-tailed finches, the Pictorella Mannikin and, with luck, perhaps Gouldian Finches.

The second part of this walk begins where Manning Creek breaks out of the sandstone ranges; this point is usually easily accessible by car. There are two obvious routes, both worth following if there is time. One is to follow the watercourse downstream, watching for birds of woodland and the quite densely pandanus-fringed watercourse. This would seem to be a likely site for the Purple-crowned Fairy-wren. The pandanus on the water's edge are favoured by the numerous Crimson Finches as nest sites, the bulky domed nests conspicuous but often difficult to reach among the sharply serrated leaves.

The third route is upstream, either beside the river pools in the gorge or along the top of the low range of rough, broken sandstone. Three species are of considerable interest here. The White-quilled Rock-Pigeon is fairly common and nests on ledges of the gorge, and the Sandstone Shrike-thrush may be seen about the gorge and along the range. The species of greatest interest, occasionally seen in the range-top, is the Black Grass-wren.

Where Manning Creek enters the sandstone is a beautiful pool edged with low cliffs. Here are different birds — the Azure Kingfisher, White-quilled Rock-Pigeon, Lavender-flanked Fairy-wren, Great Bowerbird and many other common birds.

Although there are no tracks, it is not too difficult to follow the creek upstream into the gorge. In some places it will be necessary to walk along the top of the cliff where pools reach right to the rock walls. This will give an opportunity to look out for other birds on the top of the range, including the Black Grasswren. Most visitors will walk in only as far as a large pool with waterfall, but it is possible to continue very much farther up into the ranges, keeping within sight of the river for the return.

568 CRIMSON CHAT *Ephthianura tricolor*

WESTERN DESERTS

This region covers a part of Australia into which very few ornithologists, professional or amateur, are able to go to see at first hand the land, vegetation and birdlife. Fortunately some of its greatest assets are to be found at the more accessible margins of the region, and there are very few of its birds that cannot be seen in one of the adjoining and less formidable regions.

The Western Deserts Region cuts across the continent as a great belt of red sand and golden spinifex almost from coast to coast. The red dunes of the desert meet the Indian Ocean between the Kimberley and the Pilbara and extend through the interior to the northern Nullarbor Plain, where the desert continues to the Great Australian Bight. That last southernmost part is not of red dunes and spinifex but limestone with stunted bluebush clumps.

The Western Deserts Region consists of a series of five named deserts which flow one into the other, but each with slight differences of character. From the Indian Ocean to the Great Australian Bight, these are the Great Sandy Desert, the Little Sandy Desert, the Gibson Desert, the Great Victoria Desert and the Nullarbor Plain.

The Great Sandy Desert is the most desert-like, with vast expanses of sand ridges clad in harsh needle-pointed spinifex, almost treeless, and with only a very few watercourses lined with rivergums; there are some localized groves of desert oaks. In a few places the sand dunes are interrupted by low gravelly uplands such as the South Esk Tablelands. There are comparatively few salt lakes or claypans.

The Gibson Desert has a mixture of sand-dune country, red sandplains, clay flats with mulga scrub and spinifex, and ranges: some of those in its eastern parts very beautiful. There are also numerous salt lakes and claypans, usually dry. In parts there is mallee vegetation, some species spectacular in flower. These and other wildflowers, of the trees and shrubs and of the ephemeral ground-covers, appear in magnificent profusion after rain. There are also areas of desert oaks, and casuarinas of surprising size, in places so close together that they form patches of forest. Indeed, to travel from Ayers Rock to Kalgoorlie by the Gibson Desert track during August and September, especially if rain has fallen two or three months earlier, does not give the impression of a desert at all, for much of the country is surprisingly well vegetated.

Farther south again, the Great Victoria Desert is essentially a sand-dune desert but carries across its southern parts vegetation of stunted marble-gum woodland, mallee eucalypts, sheoak, myall, belah and other small trees, forming a belt of woodland habitat. Finally, the elevated plain of the Nullarbor is mostly limestone with low sparse bluebush shrubs, and mallee around its margins.

The woodlands and mallee of the southern parts of the Great Victoria Desert provide a corridor for the continuous distribution of a considerable number of birds between west and east. These birds are found both in the south-western parts of Western Australia and on Eyre Peninsula. Many of them show so little difference between western and eastern populations that they are of the same subspecies. In fact these birds are not separate populations but are linked through the arid woodlands of the Great Victoria Desert and mallee of the northern Nullarbor Plain. The birds concerned are the Purple-crowned Lorikeet, Scarlet-chested Parrot, Jacky Winter, Restless Flycatcher, Gilbert's Whistler, Rufous Treecreeper, Yellow-rumped Pardalote, Grey Currawong and Australian Magpie.

The Western Deserts Region has only one endemic species: the uncommon and secretive Nullarbor Quail-thrush, but has among its parrots the attractive Naretha Parrot, a subspecies of the Blue Bonnet that is found only around the western Nullarbor.

This is a region of beautiful but rare or uncommon parrots. The magnificent Alexandra's Parrot is shared between this region and the adjoining Central Deserts Region. The Western Deserts Region is the centre of occurrence of the Scarlet-chested Parrot, which expands to outer areas in time of abundance. There are also other attractive and widespread parrots here: the Mulga Parrot, Port Lincoln Ringneck and Bourke's Parrot.

Among the small birds, this region is a large and central part of the range of the Rufous-crowned Emu-wren and the Striated Grasswren, both probably quite common, at least locally, but very secretive and both among the most attractive of Australia's small birds.

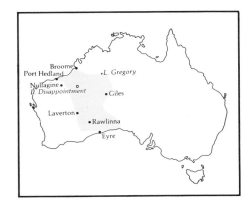

BIRDS OF THE WESTERN DESERTS

160 INLAND DOTTEREL

Peltohyas australis

The Inland Dotterel is a remarkable bird in many respects. It is adapted to the arid conditions of the interior in having large salt glands in the head which enable it to eliminate the salt taken in through eating succulent desert plants that supply its water when no other is available.

During the day the Inland Dotterel will doze or stand about inactively, sometimes in the shade of the sparse low vegetation. It is an inhabitant of inland plains, usually the most sparsely vegetated sites, including gibber plains and claypans.

If approached, the Inland Dotterel will stand immobile or crouch low, and being so well camouflaged in colour and markings it is very difficult to see under most lighting conditions. It is often seen in small flocks, in a very tight group when resting. During the day the Inland Dotterel will occasionally feed on flowers and leaves of any succulent plants close by but becomes much more active at night, feeding on insects.

The nest is a slight natural depression with a certain amount of loose debris around the edge. When approached, the incubating bird rises and, with several quick flicks of the feet, tosses the accumulated debris over the eggs. As it darts away the bird may then perform the broken-wing act to distract the intruder away from the nest. The Inland Dotterel is so still and quiet, and so effectively camouflaged, that it can be missed even when being searched out by birdwatchers who have some idea of its habits and appearance. Its distinctive features are the vertical black stripe through the eye and the black 'V' on the breast.

▶ **See also pages** 138 173 *215* 220 291

263 ALEXANDRA'S PARROT

Polytelis alexandrae

This is one of the most elegantly beautiful of all Australian parrots. Its range covers a vast area of the most arid parts of the western interior though it does not appear to remain long in any one area. Like so many other desert species it is highly nomadic, appearing in a region where rare heavy rain has fallen and where the resultant lush but temporary growth ensures a good season for seed-eating birds. After breeding, the parrots leave with their young as the desert returns to its usual drought condition.

Across such great distances of uninhabited country these parrots must often breed unnoticed. The few records indicate that they sometimes nest in quite large numbers in localities where there is abundant surface water to last through the breeding period and where the spinifex is seeding. There are records of five or more nests in a single tree, though this is probably in an area where trees are sparse.

The few recorded observations on the habits of Alexandra's Parrot date back to the 1890s. Those accounts noted that it fed on the ground, preferring spinifex seed, and seemed very tame.

When perched or feeding on the ground the extremely long-tailed Alexandra's Parrot is unmistakable. In flight at a distance the long tail and swept-back wings give a superficial resemblance to the Cockatiel. Short flights are close to the ground but it will fly high when travelling far. The flight is direct and swift and when landing the birds flutter vertically down to the ground, possibly an approach which prevents damage to the long tail feathers.

Specific habitats favoured appear to be spinifex plains, often far from water, with scattered trees or woodlands of desert oaks, eucalypts or acacias and, when breeding, in the vicinity of eucalypts along waterways.

There have been periodic sightings in the ranges around Alice Springs, perhaps because they would be far more likely to be seen here than in the ranges of the western deserts. In 1932, in casuarina and sand-dune country at the Rawlinson Range, near the Western Australian–Northern Territory border, a flock of at least 100 birds was seen. Alexandra's Parrot was recorded in a Western Australian Wildlife Research Survey over the period 1978–82, being found in the Great Sandy Desert near Well 39, in hummock-grass on sand; when flushed the parrots perched in a clump of desert oaks.

Northern Territory records include Ellery Creek, near Hermannsburg; the Todd River at Alice Springs; the Hugh and Hale rivers; Howells Ponds; Atlee Creek; and Angas Downs Station. In Western Australia, the Rawlinson Ranges; Menzies; Sandstone; Fossil Downs in the southern Kimberley; Tobins Lake on the Canning Stock Route; and Wanjarri Station (now a reserve), near Wiluna.

▶ **See also pages**   213 *215* 219 221 232 315

290 SCARLET-CHESTED PARROT

Neophema splendida

Without doubt the most spectacular of the small parrots, it inhabits remote and arid regions where the usual habitat is of mallee and acacia scrub with a sparse ground-cover of spinifex. Towards the western extremity of its range, in the southern interior of Western Australia, it occurs in arid open woodlands with spinifex and low shrub ground-cover, while across the northern edge of the Nullarbor Plain the habitat is of open casuarina woodlands.

Although generally thought to be rare, the Scarlet-chested Parrot is considered by some authorities to be moderately common across parts of its range and in some places locally common. The fluctuations in sightings seem to indicate that it has periods of abundance followed by comparative rarity. During the periods of abundance the species spreads beyond its usual strongholds and is found in mallee country of the south-eastern interior.

In the Great Victoria Desert the Scarlet-chested Parrot is common on the better vegetated country, in localities where there is a mosaic of patches of marble-gum, mallee and mulga, from which it occasionally irrupts outwards to occupy adjoining arid scrub and dune country.

This parrot tends to be a very infrequent visitor to most places at the extremities of its range so that it is only rarely reported from the far western parts of Victoria, New South Wales and Queensland, while it is an irregular and scarce visitor to the semi-arid parts of the central and southern interior of Western Australia. The western district of South Australia, closer to the core of the Scarlet-chested Parrot's range, has times of comparative abundance and it has also been temporarily common in the far west of its range.

The Scarlet-chested Parrot is most often reported from the arid country along the northern edge of the Nullarbor Plain and farther north in the Great Victoria Desert. Under normal circumstances it is usually seen in isolated pairs during the spring breeding season and in small parties of up to perhaps 20 birds at other times of the year. In times of abundance, flocks of over 100 birds have been reported.

This species, like so many other birds of arid environs, apparently exploits the occasional exceptionally good season by breeding quite rapidly. At such times the nesting in some favoured localities could almost be described as semi-colonial, with many nesting pairs in a small area, in clumps of slightly larger trees where more hollows are available than in the surrounding open country. After the peak of the season the parrots disperse, some to the extremities of the range, and the population gradually declines until the next favourable season.

Scarlet-chested Parrots are very quiet and unobtrusive, sheltering in foliage through the middle of the day in hot weather but otherwise feeding on the ground through much of the day, where they are usually not noticed unless accidentally flushed at close range. These parrots are often quite tame and when feeding may allow a close approach, moving steadily away while continuing to feed, or flying up to a nearby tree for a while before departing for another locality.

Any groups that include the fully coloured males should present no identification problems; the females and immatures are much less distinctive. In flight the Scarlet-chested Parrots keep low, weaving between the trees well below canopy level. The flight, though swift, appears erratic and sometimes fluttering; at takeoff and landing these parrots typically spread the tail sufficiently to show the bright yellow of the outer-tail feathers. The call is a soft twittering chatter, not carrying far enough to attract attention.

Localities in Western Australia are Balladonia, the Eyre Bird Observatory and the Great Victoria Desert. South Australian localities are: occasionally, east to the Murray River mallee district, near Mannum, and also near Swan Reach.

▶ See also pages 164 184 213 220 221 242 321

420 NULLARBOR QUAIL-THRUSH

Cinclosoma alisteri

The one species endemic to this region is the Nullarbor Quail-thrush, confined to the stony limestone plains with scattered low bluebush shrubs. There is some uncertainty as to whether this bird should be a separate species or be merged with either the Cinnamon or Chestnut-breasted quail-thrush as a subspecies.

The Nullarbor Quail-thrush is very tightly tied to its specific habitat, avoiding even the hollow donga depressions of the plains, wherein the vegetation is richer, and not entering the sand-dune vegetation or other habitats encircling the limestone plains. It appears to be uncommon and becoming rare, with a possibility of

extinction. The habitat is now heavily grazed, resulting in loss of protective cover. The Nullarbor Quail-thrush is sometimes seen in small parties; it is extremely shy and wary and is able to move quickly and inconspicuously across the ground well before it is likely to be noticed. The call is a weak, high-pitched whistle.

▶ See also pages 213 220 354–5

156 **Large Sand Plover** *Charadrius leschenaultii*
157 **Oriental Plover** *Charadrius veredus*
160 **Inland Dotterel** *Peltohyas australis*
176 **Black-tailed Godwit** *Limosa limosa*
178 **Red Knot** *Calidris canutus*
179 **Great Knot** *Calidris tenuirostris*
182 **Red-necked Stint** *Calidris ruficollis*
184 **Curlew Sandpiper** *Calidris ferruginea*
263 **Alexandra's Parrot** *Polytelis alexandrae*
283 **Naretha Parrot** (subspecies of Blue Bonnet) *Northiella haematogaster narethae*
290 **Scarlet-chested Parrot** *Neophema splendida*
420 **Nullarbor Quail-thrush** *Cinclosoma alisteri*

442 RUFOUS-CROWNED EMU-WREN
Stipiturus ruficeps

442 RUFOUS-CROWNED EMU-WREN

Stipiturus ruficeps

The Rufous-crowned Emu-wren, one of Australia's smallest birds, is extremely elusive and able to remain out of sight in spinifex clumps even when close at hand. The calls appear to offer the most reliable method of locating this species, the proven technique being to walk briskly through the spinifex, perhaps covering the area in strips 15–25 m apart, and listening attentively for any high-pitched calls.

The sudden appearance of an intruder often seems to be effective in disturbing the birds, so that one or both of the pair will climb into a small shrub and give the typical extremely high and squeaky calls or song. They can then usually be seen, perhaps only for a few seconds, but sometimes much longer; usually they are quick to drop back out of sight into the spinifex ground-cover. It may be possible to flush the birds up in this way several times, but they will usually tire of this and remain in the spinifex.

The calls of the Rufous-crowned Emu-wren have some slight resemblance to the calls of the fairy-wrens but are much higher pitched and weaker. They are similar to the calls of the better-known Southern Emu-wren but, again, are higher, more squeaky, have a sharp-scratchy quality and can be confused with the squeaky sounds of a cricket or other insect that seems common in spinifex country. The

Rufous-crowned Emu-wren's calls appear to be pitched too high to be heard by some people.

Rufous-crowned Emu-wren country is often inhabited also by other wrens, most commonly the White-winged and Variegated fairy-wrens; there is no possibility of mistaking their calls for those of the Rufous-crowned Emu-wren once the higher squeaks of the latter are known.

The usual habitat of the Rufous-crowned Emu-wren is spinifex country with widely scattered taller shrubs and perhaps stunted trees, on sandplain or red sandy loam with stone-littered surface; it probably does not inhabit the more rugged, rocky parts of ranges.

Once the Rufous-crowned Emu-wrens have been located they can often be followed as they bounce from one spinifex clump to another, giving many tantalizing brief glimpses as they go but disappearing every now and then into the needle-leaved clumps where their progress can be followed by the squeaky contact calls. If forced to fly they will flutter low across the spinifex, long tail trailing, before dropping back to cover. But often they will suddenly fall silent and no amount of searching will find them again, such is their ability to conceal themselves, perhaps while continuing to move away under cover.

In a number of searches for these birds in the Pilbara region, it was found that they would call and show themselves only early in the mornings, suddenly becoming silent and vanishing around 8 or 9 am; if the same site was visited later in the day there was never any sign of the birds.

The Rufous-crowned Emu-wren will breed opportunistically whenever conditions are favourable. After a tropical cyclone had dropped flooding rain on North West Cape (WA), late in the summer of 1964, three nests were found and one pair of birds photographed in May. These nests were then newly built or with eggs and located along the spinifex plains of the eastern side of the Cape where the runoff from Cape Range had caused some local flooding. This species has, however, most often been recorded breeding in spring.

Although its habitat is extremely widespread through the Western Deserts Region, the Rufous-crowned Emu-wren appears to have a patchy and localized distribution. But its ability to remain silent and concealed even at sites where it is known to be present would ensure that on many occasions it would be missed even by observers familiar with its calls and habits.

The Mallee Emu-wren, a previously separate species, has now been incorporated into the Rufous-crowned Emu-wren species as a subspecies, although some authorities prefer to retain it as a distinct species. It inhabits spinifex under mallee, to each side of the central part of the Victorian–South Australian border.

While the vast spinifex expanses of the Western Deserts Region occupy a major part of the range of the Rufous-crowned Emu-wren, it is also widespread through much of the Pilbara, the Central Deserts Region and into western Queensland. Localities in Western Australia include North West Cape, Kennedy Range National Park, the Wittenoom area, Warburton and Wiluna. In Queensland, in the Opalton district, about 190 km west of Longreach, it is in mallee-spinifex. Central Australian localities include the MacDonnell Ranges, the Tanami Desert, the south-western fringes of the Barkly Tableland, the western Simpson Desert and the north-west of South Australia.

▶ See also pages 28 138 170 184 213 219 230 232 233 360

447 STRIATED GRASSWREN

Amytornis striatus

Although usually inconspicuous and easily missed, the Striated Grasswren can at times make itself obvious. On one occasion, after several days had been spent searching without success through habitat that seemed suitable, these birds were suddenly in clear view, several metres above the spinifex ground-cover, hopping in agitated manner about the twigs of several open shrubs where they gave a clear view, all the while giving agitated calls and bursts of strong, sweet rippling song.

Evidently this was the boundary of territories; after this brief burst of battle by song the two pairs departed in opposite directions and the area was silent once again, as if the grasswrens did not exist. Only after some searching were they found, concealed and silent, beneath a clump of spinifex. But for the chance encounter at the height of activity, this site would have seemed as devoid of grasswrens as those sites previously searched.

The Striated, like other grasswrens, is skilled in its use of the low dense spinifex cover, hopping between and beneath clumps yet always contriving to be hidden from any observer. Further visits to the site very early in the mornings found the grasswrens rather more vocal at that time, and always located somewhere in the vicinity of the first sighting. When one was seen carrying food it was eventually, over numerous feeding trips during several hours, traced to a nest well hidden in a clump of spinifex.

The skill of these birds in moving unseen through the spinifex to the nest was incredible. But for the subdued snatches of song as they went, perhaps as contact between the pair, and rare glimpses whenever one would cross a bare rock ridge, they could not have been followed. As it was, they managed to keep secret the location of their nest for several hours. When not breeding, the Striated Grasswren is probably quieter and even less conspicuous than when breeding; it would undoubtedly be missed by many birdwatchers.

If a group of these grasswrens is encountered suddenly, they are likely to bounce away in all directions, dropping out of sight to sit motionless under clumps of spinifex. The alarm call is loud, trilled. The flight is similar to that of an emu-wren: fluttering, with long tail streaming behind.

Striated Grasswrens forage in the early morning and late afternoon, bouncing among rocks and spinifex with tail upright and sometimes feeding higher in shrubbery.

The Striated is the most widespread of all the grasswrens, occurring unevenly almost throughout arid parts of Australia. There are several subspecies, which are so distinctively coloured that they have previously been listed as separate species. The nominate subspecies covers most of the range, but with a gradual colour change. The grey-brown upperparts of birds of the south-eastern interior change gradually to red-brown northwards and westwards, becoming almost fiery red on the back in the Western Deserts and Pilbara. Altogether three subspecies are recognized, one for the richly coloured Pilbara population and another for the shorter-tailed population of the mid to northern Flinders Ranges.

Localities include: the Opalton district of western Queensland; a site about 110–150 km south-south-west of Cobar in New South Wales, in mallee and spinifex; the Little Desert, Big Desert, Kulkyne National Park in Victoria; the Flinders Ranges and north-central Eyre Peninsula in South Australia; the Tanami Desert, Ayers Rock area, Illamurta and Hermannsburg area of central Australia; the Hamersley Range and other parts of the Pilbara, and the Great Sandy, Great Victoria and Gibson deserts in Western Australia.

▶ **See also pages** *10* 130 138 155 163 167 171 184 213 219 220 223 230 232 233 361

447 **STRIATED GRASSWREN** *Amytornis striatus*

267 **BUDGERIGAR** *Melopsittacus undulatus*

BIRD PLACES OF THE WESTERN DESERTS

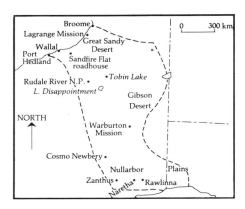

EIGHTY MILE BEACH

The Western Deserts Region extends to the north-west coast between Broome and Port Hedland where the sand ridges of the Great Sandy Desert extend west to the Indian Ocean. This meeting of sand and ocean is revealed on maps as the long, gently curving coastline of the Eighty Mile Beach. Here the treeless and usually waterless expanses of spinifex-covered dunes of the desert are a formidable barrier to many birds, preventing a large number of the birds of the northern Australian woodlands from reaching the south-west.

The Eighty Mile Beach is accessible from the Great Northern Highway at a number of points including Cape Keraudren, Wallal and Mandorah. Here the wide expanse of sand stretches in both directions as far as the eye can see. The large rise and fall of tides in the north-west exposes vast expanses of mud and wet sand as the tide recedes, making this beach Australia's foremost wader site in terms of numbers of birds.

Farther north, just south of Broome, Roebuck Bay also hosts huge numbers of migratory waders and ranks fourth nationally in counts of waders; convenient access to the north side is via Crab Creek, near Broome. Beyond the south-eastern end of the Eighty Mile Beach, the Leslie Saltworks have such large numbers of waders on the evaporation ponds that the aerial counts place that site sixth nationally. Being private property, permission to enter should be obtained at the office of Leslie Salt, Port Hedland.

The use of these sites by such immense numbers of waders is, however, temporary. For the vast majority it is a stopover point en route to the wader areas of south-eastern and south-western Australia. Here they rest and in some areas feed after their long flight from their Northern Hemisphere breeding grounds. The aerial counts therefore show the greatest numbers of waders between August and December as the birds arrive in Australia, and between March and April as the waders which have flown over the deserts from southern Australia again feed and rest before resuming their long journey towards China and northern Russia. The aerial counts of waders have recorded peak numbers in November. The largest wader concentration ever counted in Australia was 564 000, between Broome and Port Hedland, and was made up of 337 000 along the Eighty Mile Beach, 170 000 in Roebuck Bay and 57 000 at the Leslie Saltworks.

Counts of individual species also show some impressive numbers. At Roebuck Bay, there have been an estimated 14 980 Bar-tailed Godwits and 13 500 Great Knots. At Bush Point, on the southern side of Roebuck Bay, there have been an estimated 3000 Large Sand Plovers, 1500 Curlew Sandpipers and 1000 Red-necked Stints. At Leslie Saltworks 20 000 Sharp-tailed Sandpipers have been counted.

These figures are among many being compiled by the RAOU in their Waders' Studies Programme, which included a national count that has built up a picture of Australia's wader population. This shows that about 85 per cent of the total wader population inhabit as few as 20 key areas and that the most common nationally are the Red-necked Stint with a minimum of 260 000 around Australia's coasts in summer and the Great Knot with over 250 000. The wader studies in the north-west have involved a series of expeditions at peak times in both spring and autumn. A large number of volunteers have been involved in netting and banding the many thousands of birds for possible recovery in the Northern Hemisphere or southern Australia, thus building up a picture of migration routes and other information.

482 **CHESTNUT-RUMPED THORNBILL**
Acanthiza uropygialis

196 **WHISKERED TERN** *Chlidonias hybrida*

Also in this area are the Roebuck Plains, a great expanse of treeless, wet grasslands crossed by the Great Northern Highway between Sandfire Roadhouse and Broome. The plains are often flooded in the summer wet season and retain pools and damp areas for much of the year. This is one of the very few Western Australian sites for the scarce Yellow Chat, with scattered flocks of up to 100 birds recorded here. This is also a good area for raptors, usually large numbers of Brown Falcons, kestrels and Black Kites which hunt over the grassy flats. Along the northern edge of the Roebuck Plains a dense belt of melaleuca trees, through which the highway passes, is a site for the Mangrove Warbler.

The mangrove belt along the north-west coast is also worth visiting, the mangroves being very stunted and in isolated patches, with a number of locally distinctive birds, notably the endemic subspecies of the Dusky Warbler. The main mangroves of interest are at the northern end, from Roebuck Bay northwards, and in the south from about the De Grey River around the coast of the Pilbara–Goldfields Region to Carnarvon, with good blocks of mangroves at Cossack, near Roebourne.

BEDOUT ISLAND

This north-west coast has a number of seabird islands of interest, one of the best of these being Bedout Island, 55 international nautical miles north-north-east of Port Hedland. This island is of special interest because it is the most southerly recorded breeding site on the western side of the continent of the Least Frigatebird and the Brown and Masked boobies; it is however rarely visited by ornithologists as access is difficult.

Bedout Island is a low-lying, undulating sandy cay, surrounded by a large expanse of reef exposed at low tide. The breeding birds of the island include the Brown Booby, with estimates of up to 5000 pairs, Masked Booby with about 400 pairs, Least Frigatebird with up to 2000 pairs, and Crested Tern with about 300 pairs. Other birds recorded on the island include the Lesser Crested Tern, Roseate Tern and Common Noddy.

The best time of the year to observe breeding seabirds is around May to July, the boobies nesting from May to September and the Least Frigatebirds about June. Helicopter access is not advisable because of the great number of large birds in the air. The island is a fauna reserve.

GREAT SANDY DESERT

The Great Sandy Desert is a vast expanse of sand-dune and other arid country which after the heavy rains of a summer cyclone can support great numbers of birds but which at other times is extremely inhospitable. Rugged desert sand tracks along the Canning Stock Route and into the Rudall River National Park should be attempted only by well-equipped expeditions. But there are some reasonable tracks along the De Grey and Oakover rivers. Such areas are very attractive after rain but should be avoided in hot dry times and appropriate preparation should be made and every precaution taken before travelling into such remote areas.

The Rudall River National Park, just north of Lake Disappointment, is a trackless wilderness area.

The number of species recorded for the Great Sandy Desert is 126, or for a wider area covering also parts of the Tanami and Gibson deserts, 148 species. Among the more interesting species found were the Black-breasted Buzzard, Black Falcon, Alexandra's Parrot, Pink Cockatoo, Striated Grasswren, Rufous-crowned Emu-wren, Spinifexbird and Black Honeyeater.

There are no bird species endemic to the Great Sandy Desert; Alexandra's Parrot is most nearly so but it extends eastwards into the Central Deserts Region. In the Great Sandy Desert it has been observed at a number of sites, with a record in 1979 of a party of five birds at Tobin Lake, at the eastern end of the Percival Lakes system, a site where this species had been recorded 36 years earlier. In 1943 it was seen at Well 37 along the Canning Stock Route, and large flocks between wells 36 and 37. In 1897 a flock of 20 was seen near Joanna Spring.

177 **BAR-TAILED GODWIT** *Limosa lapponica*

171 **COMMON SANDPIPER** *Tringa hypoleucos*

169 **GREY-TAILED TATTLER** *Tringa brevipes*

243 **GALAH** *Cacatua roseicapilla*

NULLARBOR PLAIN AND QUEEN VICTORIA SPRINGS

For most birdwatchers the Nullarbor Plain has some bird interest mainly because it must be traversed to reach other more attractive places. It does, however, have birdlife of interest, including a rare species endemic to these flat limestone plains: the Nullarbor Quail-thrush. Ornithologists have an interest in the area as a natural barrier, isolating some populations of birds, linking others, and playing a role in the evolution of species.

The Nullarbor Plain is a limestone plateau with a vegetation of low succulent shrubs; trees occur only around the margins. The birds of the north-western Nullarbor were observed during a study of Wedge-tailed Eagles being conducted in 1967–68. In that part of the Nullarbor, north of Naretha, Rawlinna and Haig on the Transcontinental Railway, the vegetation includes thick myall-mulga woodland as well as areas of low shrubs, mainly bluebush.

A total of 91 species was recorded for the area, of which only 28 were sedentary; of the remainder, 15 were nomadic, 29 were irregular visitors to the area and 19 were vagrants. Among the species recorded were the Black-breasted Buzzard, Spotted Harrier, Black Falcon, Australian Hobby, Grey Falcon, Brown Falcon, Malleefowl, Australian Bustard, Inland Dotterel, Australian Pratincole, Pink Cockatoo, Purple-crowned Lorikeet, Regent Parrot, Mulga Parrot, Naretha Parrot (Blue Bonnet), Scarlet-chested Parrot, Gilbert's Whistler, Slender-billed Thornbill, White-fronted Honeyeater, Black Honeyeater, Crimson Chat and Orange Chat.

The Naretha Parrot is interesting because it is a locally endemic subspecies, *narethae*, of the much more widespread Blue Bonnet. On the north-western Nullarbor it was at one time quite common and widespread. This parrot occurs in naturally waterless country and, unlike most seed-eaters, would appear to be able to survive without access to permanent water.

Queen Victoria Springs is a claypan soak in the side of a sand-hill, about 70 km north of Zanthus on the Transcontinental Railway. The size of the pool seems to vary, depending upon rainfall; the sand-hill possibly acts as a reservoir, keeping some water at the bottom of the claypan.

On occasions visitors to the pool have found huge flocks of Budgerigars coming in to drink, with an estimate of as many as 20 000 birds. Other species seen coming to the water have been the Australian Hobby, Purple-crowned Lorikeet, Mulga Parrot, Red-backed Kingfisher, Little Eagle, Peregrine Falcon, Brown Falcon, Chestnut Quail-thrush, White-browed Babbler, Rufous Treecreeper and Spiny-cheeked Honeyeater.

GIBSON DESERT

A track through the Gibson Desert, linking Wiluna and Ayers Rock, has become quite popular. From west to east it passes through Cosmo Newbery, Warburton and then through the central Australian Aboriginal Reserve to Ayers Rock. This desert route should be attempted only by well-prepared travellers, preferably a group with several vehicles, and only during the cooler months of May to September, and preferably within two or three months of good rains if the desert is to be seen at its best.

A survey of the wildlife of existing and proposed reserves in the Western Deserts, in 1975, included studies at a number of sites along and to the north and south of the Warburton Track. Among the birds found were the Wedge-tailed Eagle, Brown Falcon, Australian Bustard, Naretha Parrot (Blue Bonnet), Scarlet-chested Parrot, Red-backed Kingfisher, Cinnamon Quail-thrush, Striated Grasswren, Gilbert's Whistler and Grey-fronted Honeyeater.

564 **PIED HONEYEATER** *Certhionyx variegatus*

A DESERT BIRDWATCH

Birdwatchers must always contend with the fact that they are not only the watcher but also the watched. Unless you are some distance away from the birds, you in turn will be watched as keenly by the birds. Often the behaviour of the birds is in some way altered by the human presence, or in extreme cases they are so disturbed that they depart for other places. Even when the birds remain, their behaviour may be modified by their need to keep a wary eye on this large creature, which they must presume to be a predator, sneaking slowly closer as if stalking.

The effect varies enormously between species. Small bush birds seem to pay little attention to an observer 20 or even 10 m away, waterbirds and waders often become noticeably nervous at distances of 50–100 m, depending upon many factors, such as the extent and nature of their previous experience of humans. The effect of the human observer begins to be noticeable on the larger land-birds such as the pigeons and parrots especially when they are feeding, coming to water, or are involved in nesting activities. They depart from their normal routine, especially their behaviour in the vicinity of a nest, where most birds are very much aware of the presence of an intruder. Most raptors are extremely sensitive to the presence of an observer and their behaviour while being watched bears no resemblance to their usual nest routines. Their attention is fixed entirely upon the intruder and, because their perception is so acute, even the farthest of useful observation distances will often not be tolerated. Reactions vary from species to species but are unlikely to be normal in the presence of a human.

The obvious answer in trying to watch and perhaps photograph natural behaviour lies in the use of concealment. This may take the form of a screen of natural vegetation that, if necessary, can be given greater density with additional foliage, or a hide may be constructed. If the hide has been in place for a week or so rather than a day or two, the birds are more likely to ignore it and behave naturally while being observed or photographed. For raptors and most large birds a full hide of opaque fabric is required, either put in place a small piece at a time or brought up closer in stages.

The desert environment lends itself to the use of a hide, for the normally dry conditions restrict the availability of water to a few sites. Most birds are strongly attracted to water; the seed-eating species, the pigeons and finches, need to drink often and usually go to water several times daily. Most insectivorous and nectar-eating birds like to visit water, even though not of necessity, to drink and often to bathe. The ideal location for a waterhole observation point or hide is a small pool in a drying watercourse, preferably where substantial rain some months earlier has attracted birds to the district and perhaps caused many species to nest, further adding to the bird population. When the watercourses cease to flow, the shallow claypans dry out, the creek-beds are reduced to chains of still pools and the birds must concentrate upon these remaining waters. Ideally there should be no other water within several hundred metres either way along the watercourse. Perhaps a little time spent watching the pool from a distance will give some indication of the extent of its use by birds.

If there is dense shrubbery 5–10 m from the pool, as there often is along watercourses, a full hide may not be needed, simply a piece of canvas or hessian tied to stems and branches as a screen to front and sides, and perhaps overhead. Early mornings and evenings are usually best but there will probably be some birds coming to water throughout the day.

Most of the birds seen will be common birds of the surrounding spinifex or mulga scrub, but the opportunity to see them at such close range and to observe how they behave when not concerned about the presence of humans is always interesting. Often there will be birds all around, at times perhaps up to half a dozen species will be at or near the water's edge, with others calling and fluttering about the trees and foliage near the hide.

Sights may include flocks of Budgerigars, which gather on perches above the water then drop down in large numbers, often landing in shallow water and drinking for just a split second before taking off again.

Honeyeaters are likely to be frequent visitors, the White-plumed, Grey-headed and Golden-backed (subspecies of Black-chinned) honeyeaters drinking from a water's-edge twig if possible and often fluttering over the surface, splashing momentarily into the water then preening on a nearby perch before repeating the process a few times. Flocks of finches are almost certain visitors: in the north-west of this region Zebra Finches, Painted Firetails and perhaps Star Finches.

Among the large birds, visitors may include the Spotted Bowerbird, Grey Shrike-thrush, Mulga Parrot, Bourke's Parrot, Galahs and corellas, Crested Pigeon and Spinifex Pigeon. There is always the possibility that a rare species may arrive, a Scarlet-chested Parrot or Alexandra's Parrot. Quite likely is a party of Emus, standing taller than the hide, and fascinating to see at such close range in the wild.

Excitement may be added if a local raptor finds the creek and its profusion of small birds a rich hunting area. Most likely would be a Collared Sparrowhawk, Australian Goshawk or Australian Hobby. The sparrowhawks will skulk in dense foliage, to dash out in an effort to snatch one of the small birds near the waterhole.

Possibly one of the less common raptors may turn up: a Grey Falcon or a Black Falcon. Almost invariably the arrival of a bird of prey will trigger a ripple of alarm calls from honeyeaters in the area, giving the birdwatcher in the hide a chance to scan the surrounding trees for the cause of the alarm. Because the action often takes place away from the pool, the hide should have ample observation openings on all sides.

103 SPOTTED HARRIER *Circus assimilis*

PILBARA REGION

This region takes in the north-west corner of Western Australia and extends southwards and inland to include the Gascoyne, Murchison and Eastern goldfields. Except for its coastal lowlands, this region is entirely on the great western plateau, an ancient and stable plateau only 400–600 m above sea level, that makes up the western part of the continent.

Near its north-west corner the plateau rises much higher and becomes very rugged. The major ranges are the Hamersley Range, at 1245 m the highest in Western Australia and, nearby, the Chichester and other lesser ranges. These fade away eastwards to the sand-ridged plains of the Great Sandy Desert, and to the south and south-east blend into the extensive and almost flat Yilgarn Peneplain.

Rivers extend well into the western part of this region but flow only after unusually heavy rains. At other times they are no more than sandy or rocky watercourses with occasional pools, their banks lined with large river red-gums. The eastern parts of the region have no rivers, though there are watercourses draining to salt lakes which are especially common throughout the goldfields district.

This is one of the hottest and driest parts of Australia. The predominantly easterly winds in summer normally travel across the interior of eastern and central Australia, gathering heat all the way before finally reaching the Pilbara coast. There are lengthy periods when the maximum temperature remains above 40° and often rises above 45°. Rainfall is sparse, sometimes small amounts resulting from winter cold fronts moving through from the south-west. The most significant rains are from the north.

Summer usually brings several tropical cyclones, in some years half a dozen, usually originating in the Timor Sea and typically either crossing the Kimberley coast or else following the north-west coast. Moving inland, usually north of Shark Bay, the cyclones bring torrential rain to those parts of the interior that they cross.

The avifauna of the Pilbara Region is basically that of the interior of the continent, with birds typical of the whole of arid and semi-arid central Australia predominant. In addition, this Eyrean fauna is enriched by an infusion of species from the south-west Bassian avifauna and from the tropical Torresian avifauna of the Kimberley. But unlike eastern Australia, where woodland and forest habitats extend right down the east coast, there is in the west a major barrier, the Great Sandy Desert, preventing most tropical woodland birds from extending southwards from Kimberley to the Pilbara.

Among the birds that do occur both across tropical northern Australia and in the Pilbara Region are the Pheasant Coucal, Plumed Whistling-Duck, Bar-shouldered Dove, Peaceful Dove, Flock Bronzewing, Brolga, Black-necked Stork, Singing Bushlark, Star Finch and White-breasted Woodswallow. The Pilbara populations of the Star Finch and Blue-winged Kookaburra appear to have been isolated by the Great Sandy Desert, the latter long enough for an endemic subspecies to have evolved.

The coastal mangrove belt has brought some other northern birds southwards into this region, though there is a major break in the mangroves where the Great Sandy Desert meets the ocean. Species found in mangroves across northern Australia and in the Pilbara Region are the Striated Heron, Collared Kingfisher, Beach Thick-knee, Brahminy Kite, Mangrove Robin and Dusky Warbler.

Birds reaching this region from the south include the Malleefowl, Australasian Shoveler, Australian Shelduck, Port Lincoln Ringneck, Spotted (White-browed) Scrubwren, Splendid Fairy-wren and Rufous (Striated) Fieldwren.

The Pilbara Region has a number of endemic subspecies, including a subspecies of the Striated Grasswren, isolated in and around the Hamersley Range and previously known as the Western Grasswren, and the Dusky Warbler with two endemic subspecies isolated in widely spaced mangrove sites.

The reddish form of Striated Heron that occurs here was previously thought to be an endemic subspecies but it has been discovered that the plumage tones vary to match the colour of the mangrove mud, which in this part of the coast is reddish, and are not a true characteristic of the bird. Maximum bird listings during the RAOU Field Atlas survey were 197 species around Carnarvon and 175 species on the coast and islands around Dampier.

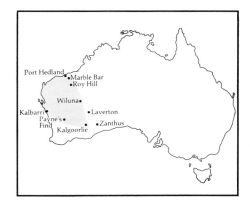

BIRDS OF THE PILBARA REGION

103 SPOTTED HARRIER

Circus assimilis

The Spotted Harrier is one of the more commonly sighted raptors of the almost treeless spinifex plains. It is often seen in the distance, floating slowly, with an occasional leisurely flap of its broad wings, so low that it almost brushes the tops of the spinifex. Occasionally it will drop the 2–3 m to the ground to snatch with long thin legs at some small bird or lizard.

Conditions in the Pilbara seem ideal for the Spotted Harrier. Here the vast, open spaces with the dense low cover of spinifex hold an abundance of small reptiles and, except through long droughts, many small birds, mainly finches and fairy-wrens that shelter and feed among the spinifex. These creatures are vulnerable to a harrier that hunts low and silently, its victim probably not aware of its approach until it is directly overhead.

The spinifex plains of the Pilbara also have tree-lined billabongs and watercourses which are ideal for the nesting harriers. The watercourses are often far from roads, across harsh hummocky spinifex where it is difficult to drive or walk. The Spotted Harrier, unlike the Marsh Harrier, nests in a tree.

It has been suggested that the Spotted Harrier was once a ground-nester like all the other harriers. This change from ground to tree nesting means that the Spotted Harrier is a comparative newcomer to the art of building nests in trees. Their nests, instead of being cupped, are crude, flat platforms from which eggs or young sometimes fall. As well, these harriers tend to build among thin, reed-like branchlets, as if using building techniques more suited to reed-beds.

When young Spotted Harriers have fledged they often perch on the ground rather than in trees, and the adult harriers roost either in trees or on the ground. This behaviour, unusual for an arboreal raptor, suggests ancestral ground-nesting like other harriers.

The advantage of treetop-nesting is presumed to be a lower level of predation. While the Marsh Harrier has security in having its nest site among dense reeds of a swamp, surrounded by water or sometimes hidden in very tall grass or crops, the Spotted Harrier in these arid regions has very little chance of finding such secure wetland nesting sites. Those individuals that began to use densely twiggy tops of eucalypts or perhaps very low, crop-like mallee thickets at first, may have gained an advantage in breeding success compared with those nesting on the comparatively open ground.

There are records of this species nesting in autumn after heavy rains.

▶ **See also pages** 82 137 138 164 183 184 208 220 222 276

162 BANDED STILT

Cladorhynchus leucocephalus

The first breeding colony of the Banded Stilt was not discovered until 114 years after the species was described. Although the Banded Stilt is widespread across southern Australia it has a breeding range almost entirely restricted to the Pilbara Region of Western Australia, mainly in the goldfields district of the southern interior.

The vast, low plateau of these parts has no rivers to the sea but a great many shallow and usually dry salt lakes, some very large. These lakes are filled only by exceptionally heavy rain, as when a summer cyclone curves in across the coast and dumps its rain across part of this region.

When filled, the lakes support immense numbers of brine shrimps. With such abundance of food and secure nest sites on islands of the lakes, the Banded Stilts nest in colonies containing thousands of birds, sometimes hundreds of thousands. The nesting often continues until the lakes dry out, when the adults abandon the site and those chicks still unable to fly. There are records of thousands of chicks wandering from such abandoned colonies, to die or be taken by predators in the surrounding arid scrub.

Only occasionally do the Banded Stilts use a lake several years in succession, undoubtedly choosing whichever of hundreds of lakes has the best combination of waterlevel, food supply and safe colony site. There have been only about 20 colonies recorded since 1904, most across a wide range of this region, from Lake Disappointment near the northern Great Sandy Desert to Esperance on the south coast.

In September 1980, a colony at Lake Barlee, in the south-east of this region, had been abandoned shortly before its discovery, apparently because of falling waterlevel, leaving about 225 000 addled eggs and dead chicks. The colony was estimated to have had 179 000 nests, a total of 600 000 eggs laid and possibly up to 350 000 young surviving to leave the colony.

Other sites on record include Lake Cowan, Nannine, Lake Grace, Lake King, Menzies, Wagga Wagga Lake, Lake Disappointment, Lake Ballard, Lake Marmion, Percival Lake, Lake Goongarrie and Esperance, all in this part of Western Australia, and Lake Callabonna in South Australia.

When these lakes dry out, usually through spring and early summer, the Banded Stilts disperse to coastal wetlands, with large numbers going to the Western Australian and South Australian coasts; at The Coorong in February 1984 there were 70 000.

▶ **See also pages** 33 138 173 183 *231* 244 292

161 **BLACK-WINGED STILT** *Himantopus himantopus*

427 **LITTLE GRASSBIRD** *Megalurus gramineus*

235 **SPINIFEX PIGEON** *Petrophassa plumifera*

catching the eye. At some of the national park lookout points, notably that at the junction of Weano, Hancock and Red gorges, these birds have become tame and fossick about the picnic area, coming within 3–4 m. The delightful bowing display seems to be given quite often. This species is usually associated with spinifex in or near rocky country, within a few minutes' flight of water.

The nomenclature of the Spinifex Pigeon has suffered many changes, from comprising three full species and up to five subspecies, to being a single species without any subspecies. Although there are considerable plumage differences between the rich reddish Pilbara forms (usually subspecies *ferruginea*) and the white-bellied northern and central Australian birds (usually subspecies *leucogaster*), it seems that the change in plumage may be gradual from place to place rather than clearly defined, a clinal progression, so that it may be artificial to recognize subspecies. Whatever the current fashion in names, whether species or subspecies, the various local populations remain sufficiently distinctive in appearance to be of interest to birdwatchers visiting those sites.

▶ **See also pages** 28 175 *179* 183 184 185 198 221 230 233 309

279 **MULGA PARROT** *Psephotus varius*

235 SPINIFEX PIGEON

Petrophassa plumifera

The plump little Spinifex Pigeon will be seen without effort by most birdwatchers visiting the Hamersley Range. It is beautifully patterned in the gold and rust tones of its habitat of red rock and spinifex, and difficult to see unless it is moving. The superb camouflage serves it well on the nest, which is most often found only when one walks to within 2–3 m, the bird then taking fright and bursting into flight with a loud clatter of wings before gliding away.

But usually these birds will be seen in pairs or small flocks feeding on sand or rocky ground between clumps of spinifex, their scurrying movement

284 BOURKE'S PARROT

Neophema bourkii

At one time Bourke's Parrot was considered rare and possibly endangered, to the extent that in 1958 it was included in a listing of endangered species of the world. In about 1950 it was found to be common and widespread around Leonora in the south-east of the Pilbara Region and since then has been widely reported throughout the mulga parts of this and adjoining regions. The species has been found sedentary here but nomadic in some other parts of

419 CINNAMON QUAIL-THRUSH
Cinclosoma cinnamomeum castaneothorax
Top: *Male* Bottom: *Female*

Australia. It is also now moderately common through parts of central Australia to western New South Wales and western Queensland.

Bourke's Parrot is quiet and inconspicuous but if present in reasonable numbers is not likely to be overlooked by anyone with an interest in birds. It is usually seen feeding on the ground, flying up when disturbed, to sit quietly in the foliage.

The best prospect for a sighting is to camp a day or so in the mulga scrub almost anywhere in the area between Shark Bay, Paynes Find, Laverton and Mundiwindi, around August to October. This parrot is often first noticed in flight, when it keeps low, undulating, with bursts of wingbeats interspersed with alternate glides, and often calling, a soft mellow 'chu-wee, chu-wee', and 'chirrup, chirrup'.

▶ See also pages   184 213 221 230 231 *231* 232 320

418 CHESTNUT QUAIL-THRUSH

Cinclosoma castanotum

The Chestnut Quail-thrush is usually found in areas of sandy soil, under acacia scrub or mallee, often where the ground-cover is of spinifex. It is wary, usually keeps well ahead of the observer and, unless suddenly startled, walks rather than flies.

The call is heard at dawn, an often-

repeated soft 'seeep', and occasionally a soft tremulous song, also at dawn, from an elevated perch. It is common in the optimum habitat of dense mallee on sand, preferably with undershrub or spinifex ground-cover. Large areas of this habitat have been cleared for agriculture, with the result that the range of the species has been reduced.

▶ See also pages   130 137 138 162 164 215 220 *229* 354

419 CINNAMON QUAIL-THRUSH

Cinclosoma cinnamomeum

This is a shy bird, typical of quail-thrushes; it runs swiftly to cover or, if pressed too closely, bursts into fast flight, usually for but a short distance, and on alighting immediately runs again, dodging behind cover. It is skilled at using low cover as concealment, and as shade during the heat of the day. When not agitated it will walk, slowly and deliberately. The call is a very high 'see-see-', the alarm a louder 'si-si-si'.

The Cinnamon Quail-thrush inhabits mulga, gidgee or other open arid scrubland, usually on rocky ground.

▶ See also pages   130 164 173 175 215 231 354 355

440 BLACK-AND-WHITE FAIRY-WREN

SUBSPECIES OF WHITE-WINGED FAIRY-WREN

Malurus leucopterus leucopterus

The White-winged Fairy-wren is one of the most widespread and common of small birds of arid and semi-arid parts of Australia, but it was discovered and named at a later date than the Black-and-white Fairy-wren which has a range confined to Dirk Hartog and Barrow islands, off Australia's far north-western coast. The Black-and-white Fairy-wren was discovered in 1818 by zoologists Quoy and Gaimard during French explorer Freycinet's exploration of the Australian coast and was given the species name *leucopterus* in 1824.

The mainland bird, identical but with blue in place of black, was named *leuconotus* in 1865. These remained separate species: the Black-and-white Fairy-wren, *Malurus leucopterus* and, as it was then known, the Blue-and-white Wren, *Malurus leuconotus*. Much later the two were combined as a single species and the appropriate common name of White-winged Fairy-wren applied to that species. As the black-and-white population from Dirk Hartog Island had been first-named, it had to be the nominate subspecies, *Malurus leucopterus leucopterus*, with

the mainland population being the subspecies *Malurus leucopterus leuconotus*.

Fairy-wrens with black-and-white plumage had been found also on Barrow Island, off the Pilbara coast, with differences sufficient to justify a third subspecies, *M. l. edouardii*. The common name of Black-and-white Fairy-wren is used here as the common name for both island subspecies, and, in this context, White-winged Fairy-wren for the mainland population only.

This species, both on the islands and mainland, is an inhabitant of dense low vegetation, spinifex on Barrow Island, saltbush and low hakea scrub on Dirk Hartog, and on the mainland saltbush, spinifex, heath, coastal scrub, mulga and similar acacia scrub. There seem to be no significant differences of behaviour between the three subspecies, though some observers recorded the male Black-and-white Fairy-wren as shy and difficult to call up with squeaky noises. The song is similar to that of the mainland birds: a rapid, undulating, reeling trill, but slightly weaker than that of the mainland birds.

The Black-and-white Fairy-wren is common, the only difficulty in obtaining a sighting being access to the islands; Dirk Hartog is a privately owned grazing property and Barrow Island an oilfield. As there are long-standing rumours of occasional sightings of black-and-white plumaged fairy-wrens on the adjacent mainland, birdwatchers could be on the lookout for significantly darker than usual plumage among White-winged Fairy-wrens in mainland coastal parts of this region.

▶ See also pages   8 170 *229* 230 360

472 DUSKY WARBLER

Gerygone tenebrosa

Along the north-west coast of Western Australia the mangrove belt is fragmented, with several major breaks such as the Eighty Mile Beach where there are no mangroves. These breaks are made more effective because this shoreline is backed by semi-desert country, arid grass and scrublands, largely treeless and unable to provide any connecting corridor of closed-canopy habitat.

One of the west coast mangrove birds whose population is fragmented in this way is the Dusky Warbler, a species endemic to the north-western coast of Western Australia from the north-western Kimberley Region south to Carnarvon. Along this coastline the

435 **SPLENDID FAIRY-WREN** *Malurus splendens*

Dusky Warbler replaces the Large-billed Warbler, from which it differs in having the iris white rather than brick-red, bill more slender and legs black rather than grey.

The nests of Dusky and Large-billed warblers are very different, the former having a domed nest that is short-tailed and compact, the latter having a suspended domed nest with a very long, tapering tail. Fortunately the overlap where both occur is not only small but is in the far northern Kimberley Region where limited access to the coast restricts the number of sites where an identification problem could arise. Over the major part of its range, from Derby southwards, the Large-billed Warbler does not occur.

Within this range the population of the Dusky has been broken into three segments. The nominate form occurs along the western Kimberley coast, the subspecies *whitlocki* along the Pilbara coast from Cape Keraudren south to Cossack and nearby islands, and the third subspecies, *christophori*, around Shark Bay. Each of these has been isolated long enough to have evolved

differences which, though slight, are sufficient to allow them to be recognized as subspecies. The differences are of size and of relative darkness of upper plumage.

The Dusky Warbler is probably sedentary and is seen in pairs or small parties feeding among foliage. It is evidently more common on the seaward than the landward side of the mangroves. In the Kimberley portion of its range it is also to be found in paperbark swamps, patches of monsoon forest in gorges and at the base of cliffs near the coast, especially where these are close to mangroves.

In the Kimberley Region it has been recorded at Port Warrender, Careening Bay, St George Basin, Kunmunya, Point Torment, La Grange and Cape Bossut. The second population, in the Pilbara Region, is recorded from Cape Keraudren, Cossack, Legendre and other islands, and the third population is found around Carnarvon.

▶ **See also pages** 201 210 218 223 228 *229* 231 367

486 SLENDER-BILLED THORNBILL

Acanthiza iredalei

This thornbill is to be found through the southern part of the region and across southern Australia to western Victoria. It shows a preference for localities dominated by samphire and saltbush and was previously known as the Samphire Thornbill. However it does occur in other habitats, including casuarina and banksia heaths of the Murray–Darling Region.

There are three subspecies. The nominate subspecies, which occurs throughout this region, is found about the saline flats around salt lakes and saltpans, mainly inland, but reaching the arid coastal flats between Shark Bay and Carnarvon.

The Slender-billed Thornbill is an uncommon and localized species. Areas of suitable habitat are plentiful throughout the southern half of this region, so that a sighting will require, as a beginning, the searching of the samphire-saltbush flats of salt-lake sites, perhaps combined with a watch for other species of these environs, such as the Orange Chat.

This very plain little bird is usually searching for small insects in the low dense samphire bushes. It is reported to be very shy, the small flocks breaking up and scattering if disturbed. The calls are a rapid series of piercing 'ti-ti-ti-ti' notes.

▶ **See also pages** 130 138 164 220 *229* 231 370

592 **STAR FINCH**
Neochmia ruficauda

459 GREY HONEYEATER

Conopophila whitei

The Grey Honeyeater is widespread across the arid regions of Australia but is not often reported. Until 1981 there had been only 19 published records of the species, eight in the Pilbara Region. The RAOU Field Atlas bird survey of 1977–81 seems to confirm this pattern, with sightings concentrated towards this region, though this could reflect the greater number of observers working this region compared with the adjoining Western Deserts and other regions where it also occurs.

This is a honeyeater of dense mulga scrub, including spinifex country with mulga thickets or scattered mulga trees. Attention may be drawn to this rather plain species by its contact calls, described as high and silvery, or its short, high-pitched jingling song. The calls are also said to have qualities similar to the calls of the western subspecies of the Silvereye.

The bird has been recorded as appearing, in the field, as greyish, unattractive, lacking any remarkable or interesting coloration. In general appearance it is sometimes described as not obviously like a honeyeater, though the bill is slightly downturned. Characteristics noticeable in the field are the grey upperparts, head and breast, whitish underparts, and a showing of white feathers in flight. Some observers comment on a whitish eye-ring, but this may be confined to juveniles.

The Grey Honeyeater seems to have been quite common, in some years at least, in the Yalgoo district. Other sites in this region include the Hamersley Range, Lake Way, Ajana, Day Dawn and Wanjarri. In the Northern Territory it has been seen at Wave Hill, Tanami Range, Frewana, MacDonnell Ranges and surrounds, and Granite Downs; in New South Wales at Wave Hill, and in South Australia at Cordillo Downs.

▶ See also pages   184 231 232 387

592 STAR FINCH

Neochmia ruficauda

The range of the Star Finch has decreased greatly since European settlement and the resultant changes to the habitat, the greatest loss being in eastern Australia. The species remains moderately common in the north-western parts of the Pilbara Region, where it is most likely to be found along watercourses where there is a fringing of lush tall grasses in place of or among the spinifex.

The Star Finch may in good seasons be seen in flocks, usually small, occasionally large, or may be flushed from the grass.

▶ See also pages   221 223 *228* 230 395

152 **Red-kneed Dotterel** *Erythrogonys cinctus*
418 **Chestnut Quail-thrush** *Cinclosoma castanotum*
440 **Black-and-white Fairy-wren** (subspecies of White-winged Fairy-wren) *Malurus leucopterus leucopterus*
472 **Dusky Warbler** *Gerygone tenebrosa*
486 **Slender-billed Thornbill** *Acanthiza iredalei*
500 **Black-tailed Treecreeper** *Climacteris melanura*
539 **White-plumed Honeyeater** *Lichenostomus penicillatus*

BIRD PLACES OF THE PILBARA REGION

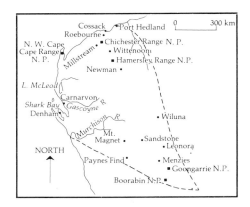

THE HAMERSLEY RANGE

The north-western part of the Pilbara Region is largely taken up by the Chichester Range, along the northern side of the Fortescue River, and the Hamersley Range along the southern side. These ranges, with their diversity of habitat — spinifex slopes, undulating plateau-tops and deep gorges — have a considerable variety of birds. The presence of permanent water in river and gorge pools enables many more bird species, and in greater numbers, to remain in the area at times when the surrounding open mulga and spinifex plains are in drought and have far fewer birds.

The Hamersley Range is spectacular, well worth visiting for its scenery alone, but it provides also a superb backdrop to the birdlife. Appreciation of the awesome gorges seems enriched by the birdlife of their surrounds, without which the magnificent scenery would seem lifeless. The satisfaction of finding the birds, especially rare or localized species, seems all the greater in such magnificent surroundings. During one visit the shadowy depths of Red Gorge were enlivened by the passage of flock after flock of Budgerigars, green specks hurtling upstream, 100 m or more below the cliff-edge yet still well above the dark river pools.

While the high screechings of the Budgerigars, almost lost in the immensity of the chasm, drifted faintly up to the clifftop lookout, the closer, louder calls of a Spotted Bowerbird echoed across the gorge, coming from a native fig clinging to the cliff-face. Closer, on flat red-rock ledges between the scattered clumps of straw-coloured spinifex, an occasional glimpse of movement attracted attention to small dark-red Spinifex Pigeons, crested heads bobbing as they scurried along.

On the spinifex-clad plateau around the gorge other small birds may catch the attention: Grey-headed and White-

327 RED-BACKED KINGFISHER
Halcyon pyrrhopygia
Feathers are fluffed out to capture
warmth of early morning sunlight.

plumed honeyeaters about the red-flowered *Grevillea wickhami* shrubs, flocks of Zebra Finches flying up with twanging calls from the spinifex, woodswallows and Rainbow Bee-eaters hawking insects from dead limbs of the stunted ghost-gums, a pair of Red-browed Pardalotes zipping in and out of their tiny tunnel drilled into a creek-bank. These are all common birds of the Hamersleys. The Hamersley Range National Park has a list of 128 species; the RAOU Field Atlas survey recorded 133 species, 39 breeding, in the Wittenoom area. Among these are some that will require much more time and effort to find.

Scarce and difficult to see are the Black-breasted Buzzard, Grey Falcon, Bourke's Parrot, Barking Owl, Spinifexbird, Rufous-crowned Emu-wren, Striated Grasswren, Slaty-backed Thornbill, Golden-backed Honeyeater (subspecies of the Black-chinned Honeyeater) and Star Finch. Some of these, such as the buzzard and falcon, may be but rare visitors to the area and one would have to be lucky to see them. Others are resident and can be found if sufficient time is put into searching. A few days or a week here would give a significant list of sightings, especially with observation time split between the plateau-tops, the lower gorges and the river flats. The pools of Millstream, on the Fortescue River, and other river pools attract some waterbirds, including grebes, cormorants, egrets and herons, while the flooding of the river flats after heavy rains provides for large breeding colonies of some of these, and for an influx of nomadic ducks and other waterfowl.

SHARK BAY

The birdlife of Shark Bay has been well-studied and documented over a considerable time. Localities of interest for birdlife include Dirk Hartog Island, Peron Peninsula and, north of Carnarvon, Lake McLeod. This is a very arid part of the coast, flat and low-lying. The vegetation is mainly of acacia scrub with thickets of small eucalypts, and there are some mangrove-lined creeks and inlets. The meagre rainfall usually comes in winter but occasionally a tropical cyclone will bring heavy summer rain. There have been about 120 species of birds recorded in the area. About 38 of the mainland birds have not been found on Dirk Hartog Island and 14 of the island's birds not seen on Peron Peninsula.

Two species stand out as being of interest: the Black-and-white Fairy-wren on Dirk Hartog Island and the Thick-billed Grasswren on the mainland. If arrangements can be made to visit the island, the fairy-wren should be found easily enough, as it is common.

The Thick-billed Grasswren occurs in acacia-scrub country, with shrubbery of cottonbush, mulla-mulla and emu bush. The Denham airstrip is a favoured site, fences keeping out the stock which destroy the dense low cover that these birds need. This grasswren is also to be found on Woodleigh Station, in regenerating cottonbush country.

An unusual bird site at the southern end of the inner part of Shark Bay, known as Hamelin Pool, is a small permanent lake of several hectares area, fringed with reed-beds. This water is maintained by an artesian bore and, except for a short while after rain, provides the only freshwater habitat available over a great expanse of country. It has a variety of waterbirds, both of the open water and reed-beds.

Within the deep inlets of Shark Bay a number of islands are used by Wedge-tailed Shearwaters as breeding sites, the main islands being Slope Island with 150 burrows in use, Freycinet Island with 250, and Baudin Island with 100. Other birds using the islands are Bridled Terns, and a colony of about 1000 Pied Cormorants nest on Freycinet Island.

Considerably farther north, between Carnarvon and Shark Bay, Lake McLeod is a very large salt lake with a saltworks operation at its southern end. The lake is of interest because it contains one of only two inland mangrove communities in Western Australia. It also happens to be midway along a 350 km stretch of rocky coast devoid of mangroves and therefore its mangrove species are very isolated. The lake is often largely dry, except for seepage underground from the sea close by, which maintains the mangroves. Freshwater occasionally floods into the lake, when inland rain causes the rivers — the Minilya, Lyndon or Gascoyne — to flow. Surveys of Lake McLeod resulted in a list of 48 species, most being waterfowl and waders attracted to the open waters of the lagoons and the surrounding shallows. There were five birds dependent upon the mangroves, including the Dusky Warbler and Yellow White-eye.

Some of the most pleasant birding in the Gascoyne district is to be found inland from Carnarvon, along the Gascoyne, Lyons and Wooramel rivers. These rivers, in most parts lined with large river red-gums, flow across flat mulga-scrub plains. Here the birding can be both rewarding and pleasant between about May and September, especially if there has been enough rain in the preceding months to spread green across the red earth and fill the creek and river-bed waterholes. A birdlist compiled for Gascoyne Junction totalled 67 species, while the RAOU Field Atlas survey recorded 191 species, 36 breeding, for the Carnarvon to southern Lake McLeod area, the latter including coast, ocean, mangroves, river and mulga-scrub habitats.

The Chiming Wedgebill is one of the most common birds of the Gascoyne and Murchison mulga scrublands. The loud, repetitive chiming calls are one of the most characteristic sounds and almost certain to be heard by any traveller passing through the Gascoyne or Murchison districts. The Chirruping Wedgebill of the south-eastern interior has not only a different song but is

284 BOURKE'S PARROT *Neophema bourkii*

found in more open habitat of low shrubs. It is much less shy, singing from exposed perches rather than from concealment, and is generally more easily observed.

In 1973 a single species, known simply as 'Wedgebill', was divided into two species, the Chiming Wedgebill in central and Western Australia and the Chirruping Wedgebill in the eastern interior. The separation was based on differences of call and behaviour and very slight differences of appearance, evidently now considered insufficient reason, so that these species may once again be combined as a single species.

MURCHISON RIVER

There is also some very rewarding birding about the headwaters of the Murchison River and southwards through Yalgoo and Paynes Find. This is superficially barren-looking country with many low breakaway hills and sparse mulga scrub with scattered stands of gnarled eucalypts.

In early spring this country can be among the very best for abundance of birds, provided there has been some rain during the preceding three or four months. The stony-surfaced red clay becomes transformed at first by the green of the new vegetation, then through August and September it is hidden by massed papery everlasting flowers.

This area, around Yalgoo, Mount Magnet and south to Paynes Find, has a diversity of semi-arid habitat. There are numerous salt lakes with samphire margins, sites for Orange Chat and Slender-billed Thornbill, while Cinnamon Quail-thrush inhabit the stony rises, and the Grey Honeyeater has been recorded breeding.

This is an excellent area for arid-country parrots. Usually abundant here are Port Lincoln Ringnecks and Mulga Parrots, and often Bourke's Parrot also, though it is not as conspicuous as the larger parrots. Small patches of arid woodland, the gnarled and stunted eucalypts full of hollows, attract those birds of the surrounding mulga scrublands that need trees for nesting. Here also will be found Cockatiels, Pied and Black honeyeaters, Red-capped Robins, Variegated Fairy-wrens, countless Galahs, and the occasional Pink Cockatoo.

Around September the mournful and persistent calling of Red-backed Kingfishers can be an almost constant sound, in some places, as they establish their territories. They are late breeders, with young in nest tunnels around November, when this country is becoming hot and dry and most other nesting activity is finished.

Crimson Chats are usually common in the mulga scrub, and Orange Chats around the salt lakes. At almost every campfire can be heard the churring calls of the Owlet Nightjar, and often also of the Southern Boobook. One of the charms of this region is its seemingly endless kilometres of unfenced outback tracks where one

162 BANDED STILTS *Cladorhynchus leucocephalus*

534 **GREY-HEADED HONEYEATER** *Lichenostomus keartlandi*

224 **DIAMOND DOVE** *Geopelia cuneata*

can camp almost anywhere, under a clump of trees or beside a river pool, with no visitors but the birds.

THE EASTERN GOLDFIELDS

The Eastern Goldfields too has the wide empty spaces, but with a different vegetation. Tall, slender salmon gums and areas of sandplain with mallee eucalypts are the more usual vegetation.

Conveniently situated along each side of the Great Eastern Highway between Southern Cross and Coolgardie, Boorabbin National Park has a varied landscape of sandplain with granite outcrops. The birdlist includes Purple-crowned Lorikeet, Mulga Parrot, Regent Parrot, Rufous Treecreeper, Gilbert's Whistler, Crested Bellbird, Shy Heathwren, Redthroat, Southern Whiteface, and the White-eared, White-fronted, Spiny-cheeked and Tawny-crowned honeyeaters.

Farther out towards the western desert, the Kathleen Valley Wildlife Sanctuary, previously Wanjarri Station, between Kalgoorlie and about 100 km south of Wiluna, was the site of the RAOU field outing for 1970.

This site lies at the junction of the mulga and spinifex vegetation zones and has birds typical of each habitat. The landform here is an elevated plain with low scarps or breakaways of laterite, and in places of granite. The sandplain on the flat tops above these scarps carries spinifex, in places with mallee, acacia or other open scrub. Areas of heavier soil have mulga and eremophila scrub. There is one watercourse lined with river red-gums, and salt lakes about 16 km to the south of the site. Rain may fall in summer or winter, ranging between 74 and 449 mm, the heaviest falls resulting from the occasional summer cyclonic depression moving through the interior.

About 111 bird species have been recorded, more than for most other places in the arid zone. Kathleen Valley is situated where southern and northern or north-eastern avifaunas overlap. In this area such species as the Malleefowl, Regent Parrot, Splendid Fairy-wren and Thick-billed Grasswren are close to the northern limits of their range, while another group, including Bourke's Parrot, Alexandra's Parrot, Rufous-crowned Emu-wren, Striated Grasswren, Grey Honeyeater and Spotted Bowerbird, are near their southern limits. Further richness is given by the intermingling of several habitats, mainly of mulga and spinifex-sandplain.

HAMERSLEY BIRDWATCH

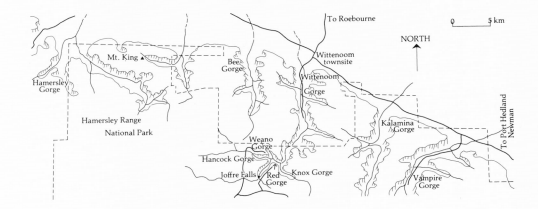

The Hamersley Range is a plateau with its northern edge an impressive escarpment falling to the flat floodplain of the Fortescue River. Along this northern side, the tributaries of the Fortescue that drain the valleys of the plateau have cut huge gorges. These are about a kilometre wide where they meet the lowland plains but become narrow as they cut back deeper into the range. Several are wide enough all the way through to allow for a road, following beside the watercourse, to climb to the plateau-top and the gorge-rim lookouts. A walk, or a drive with occasional stops, along one of these gorges, from plains to plateau, will provide an opportunity to record a large number of birds. There are several suitable gorges close to Wittenoom, including Bee Gorge a few kilometres west, or Yampire about 20 km to the east.

Perhaps a kilometre out from the escarpment the spinifex plains rise gently towards the foot of the range and the stony clay is clad with spinifex and scattered shrubs, a vegetation type that extends all along the foot of the range. This is the habitat of the Rufous-crowned Emu-wren. These incredibly small birds could be located by the simple procedure of walking briskly through the spinifex and listening for their extremely high alarm calls. Along the track towards Bee Gorge they could be found only early in the morning.

Where creek and road enter the broad mouth of the gorge there are often tall anthills scattered about the slopes. These can be inspected for nest tunnels of the Red-backed Kingfisher; it is however a late nester and though the mournful calls may be heard and the birds seen, they probably will not be nesting until the heat of October or November has set in.

Across this wide lower gorge, the creek-bed and flats on either side have scattered river red-gums, some with hollows, providing nesting sites for the Port Lincoln Ringneck and Blue-winged Kookaburra. Although often a noisy bird, with its fiendish laughter, the Blue-winged Kookaburra seems to become secretive and silent in the vicinity of the nest.

The roads or tracks that follow these gorges into the range usually cross and re-cross the creek-bed a number of times. It can be rewarding to find a small pool in a section of creek-bed, where there is no other water within several hundred metres or more, and wait quietly in the shade of a creek-bank rivergum and, from 10–20 m away, watch the birds coming in to drink and bathe; as usual, early morning seems to be the best time.

Visiting such a pool in Wittenoom Gorge were the Spinifex Pigeon, Diamond Dove, Grey Shrike-thrush, Grey-headed Honeyeater, White-plumed Honeyeater, Golden-backed Honeyeater (subspecies of the Black-chinned Honeyeater), Painted Firetail, Zebra Finch and Spotted Bowerbird.

In wandering among the spinifex clumps of the floor of the lower gorge and slopes there is a possibility of flushing a Painted Firetail from the water, or from its nest. They often nest in the big spinifex clumps within 100 m or so of the water. In such situations Painted Firetails can be quite common. The domed nest, set into the top of a spinifex clump, is inconspicuous but becomes obvious once the bird has revealed the site by flying out.

Also on the slopes of the ranges, especially among the largest clumps of spinifex, which can be several metres across and half a metre high, there is every chance of spotting a Spinifexbird. Again, it is easiest to let the bird do the finding. Wander along the clumps of spinifex until the abrupt 'jik, jik' alarm, rather like two stones being struck together, is heard from one of the spinifex clumps.

Parts of the wide lower gorge have scrubby flats between the watercourse and the enclosing cliff walls. Here, rivergums, acacias and other trees and shrubs with undergrowth of smaller shrubbery and spinifex ground-cover form some of the most dense vegetation to be found anywhere through the ranges. In such areas the harsh, grating calls of the Western Bowerbird, the local subspecies of the Spotted Bowerbird, can lead to discovery of his display bower, an 'avenue' type of structure, usually in the shade under dense scrub.

Farther into the ranges these gorges become narrow, the road enclosed between cliffs and in places passing under big, lush-foliaged trees that thrive in the permanent seepage; their dense foliage is sometimes used by Barking Owls as daytime roosting sites.

Where the track finally winds up from the gorge to the tableland the scattered small white-barked eucalypts are frequented by Black-tailed Treecreepers, in pairs or small groups, their sharp, short and typically treecreeper-like calls attracting attention. Areas of *Grevillea wickhami* and other flowering shrubs of the range-top are popular with the abundant Grey-headed Honeyeaters. Here also, where the plateau-top is broken with rough outcroppings, small spinifex-filled valleys and sparsely scattered trees and shrubs, is likely country for the Striated Grasswren. Like so many of the small birds of the spinifex, this grasswren can be extremely difficult to find. This species is probably quite common across the top of the range and has been seen around the Weano Gorge campsite, and above Bee Gorge.

547 **BROWN HONEYEATER** *Lichmera indistincta*

SOUTH WEST

The landscape of the South-West Region is mostly flat. Its major landform is the western edge of the Great Western Plateau, an elevated, gently undulating and ancient land surface that to the east extends far out into the central deserts, to the south-east meets the Great Australian Bight at the cliffs of the Nullarbor coast, and to the west forms the Darling Scarp.

This scarp, the Darling Range, dissected by rivers into numerous and in places steep valleys along its western edge, averages only 300–400 m in height. It has very little effect on climate, which is typically Mediterranean, with cool, wet winter months and warm to hot, dry summers. The period December to April is usually without significant rain, and temperatures are high.

In the extreme south-west corner the annual rainfall is around 1500 mm but fades away rapidly inland and northwards, these parts becoming semi-arid to arid and merging with the central deserts. The south-west corner is completely and effectively cut off from other moderately high rainfall parts of northern and eastern Australia by a great expanse of semi-desert country.

But it is this isolation that has given the South-West Region much of its distinctive flora and fauna. In isolation, in response to local conditions, there has evolved an exceptionally rich flora, for which the region has become renowned.

Unlike the flora, the birdlife of the region has lost rather than gained in total number of species because of its isolation. A great many birds of the humid tropics, which on Australia's eastern coast extend south into Victoria, cannot reach the South West because of the wide desert barrier, which in the Pilbara extends right to the coast. There are some 60 to 65

Kimberley species which do not reach the south-west, but most of these extend far down the east coast of Australia. The South West has fewer habitat types, in particular the rainforest environment is totally absent, and with it the entire list of rainforest birds.

On the other hand, the isolation of the region has led to the evolution of a number of unique endemic species and subspecies. These are mostly related to similar species of south-eastern Australia, which at some time in the past have had a continuous distribution across the continent but were later broken into separate populations by the increasing aridity of the intervening country. In some instances species found in the South-West Region occur also on Eyre Peninsula, the break with the east being caused by arid country at the head of Spencer Gulf. These include the Rufous Treecreeper and Western Yellow Robin.

While most of the South West's endemic birds have evolved differences only to subspecies or species level, the Red-capped Parrot is endemic as a genus. But it is thought that rather than having evolved within the South West, it is a relict species surviving in an area that remains especially favourable, long after its ancestral forms have become extinct elsewhere.

Some western species, considered to be relict populations, have not fared so well. The Noisy Scrub-bird, even more than its eastern near relative the Rufous Scrub-bird, has come close to extinction. The Western Bristlebird is now almost as rare, and the western subspecies of the Rufous Bristlebird, evidently of extremely restricted distribution even in the early days of European settlement, seems now to be extinct.

The largest birdlist for the South-West Region, compiled

589 RED-EARED FIRETAIL *Emblema oculata*

during the RAOU Field Atlas survey, was for the 1° block centred on the coastal plain just south of Perth, where a total of 260 species was recorded. This area probably has the highest list for the region because it has diverse habitats, including ocean and islands, the coast, sandplain heath and banksia woodlands, coastal lakes, swamps and river estuaries and, on the Darling escarpment, wandoo woodlands and jarrah forest; the area is also convenient for metropolitan birdwatchers.

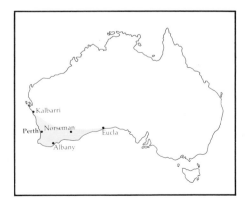

46 RED-TAILED TROPICBIRD *Phaethon rubricauda*

BIRDS OF THE SOUTH WEST

24 FLESHY-FOOTED SHEARWATER

Puffinus carneipes

Islands of the southern coast of Western Australia are the only Australian breeding grounds of the Fleshy-footed Shearwater; in the Pacific, Lord Howe Island and New Zealand are the closest sites.

At the Recherche Archipelago, off the southern coast of Western Australia, near Esperance, this is the common breeding shearwater species; it also breeds on other islands farther west including Breaksea Island, near Albany, and Coffin, Michaelmas, Eclipse, Stanley, Sandy and St Alouarn islands. Many of the colonies have been estimated at over 10 000 birds, and that on Sandy Island at 600 000.

▶ See also pages 239 255

29 LITTLE SHEARWATER

Puffinus assimilis

In Australian waters, the Little Shearwater breeds only on islands of the south-west coasts of the South-West Region, from the Recherche Archipelago near Esperance, to the Houtman Abrolhos Islands offshore from Geraldton. New Zealand and Lord Howe Island are the nearest eastern breeding grounds.

This species is moderately common in the South West, and mainly sedentary, being present around the breeding colony sites some 10 months of the year. However it is not readily seen on the islands for during daylight hours it is either at sea or in the nest burrow, which it begins occupying up to 10 months before laying. Two of the six subspecies occur in Australia, *tunneyi* in the South West, and probably *assimilis* on the east coast.

▶ See also pages   239 244 256

46 RED-TAILED TROPICBIRD

Phaethon rubricauda

The Red-tailed Tropicbird in Australia breeds at two widely separated parts of the coast. The subspecies *roseotincta* breeds on atolls of the Coral Sea and on Raine Island on the Great Barrier Reef near the tip of Cape York Peninsula. A second subspecies, *westralis*, breeds on several islands off the south-west coast of Western Australia. Some of these South-West birds are conveniently located and easily seen.

Until about 1954 a few pairs nested on the Houtman Abrolhos, but this small colony seems to have been abandoned. In 1963 breeding occurred on a tiny islet of almost bare granite, about 1 ha in area, 55 m high and separated from the rocky mainland by a usually turbulent channel about 70 m wide. Sugarloaf Rock, Yallingup, has had a varying number of Red-tailed Tropicbirds breeding, ranging from about four up to about 26 pairs. In some years a few pairs nest on the adjacent mainland, without benefit of the considerable protection given by the difficult access to the islet.

The birds may first be seen in about December or January, when their aerial displays attract attention, being clearly visible from the mainland. The display, usually involving both birds of a pair, lasts from a few seconds up to about five minutes, the birds circling one above the other, holding an almost fixed position over the nest site, the long red tail-streamers swinging downwards.

The nests are generally sited on rock ledges, usually partly protected and shaded. The Tropicbirds can only just shuffle forwards on tiny feet, so must glide in against the wind to land right beside the nest. During the breeding season, usually December–April or May, some birds can often be seen hanging on the wind over the rock, easily recognized by their long red tail-streamers.

▶ See also pages 45 97 262

183 LONG-TOED STINT

Calidris subminuta

The tiny Long-toed Stint breeds in Siberia and migrates to Australia during the southern summer. In most parts of Australia it is a regular but rare to uncommon visitor, most sightings being of only one or two birds. But in Western Australia it is often seen in much greater numbers, mostly in parties of four to 13 birds. It favours the drying margins of shallow freshwater lakes, where it has wide expanses of wet mud, a habitat that is usually available for but a few weeks as the lakes dry out through the rainless mid to late summer months.

Lake Forrestdale, about 25 km south of Perth, is probably the most favourable Australian site for regular sightings of parties of up to 80 birds. Occasionally, irregularly, and under exceptionally favourable local conditions, even larger numbers have been sighted in the Pilbara–Goldfields Region at Carnarvon and Wiluna. However the Lake Forrestdale site, in February–March, is the most convenient and reliable site for sightings of large numbers of the species. During these months the last muddy shallows may be several hundred metres out from the shoreline reed-beds, but the mud layer is thin, the underlying stratum is hard, so that it is possible to approach across the lakebed if these and other waders are far out.

▶ See also pages 197 *239 244 297*

201 ROSEATE TERN

Sterna dougallii

Major breeding colonies of the elegant little Roseate Tern occur along the south-west coast, with the breeding range steadily extending southwards, from the Abrolhos near Geraldton around 1960, to as far south as Carnac Island, south of Perth, by 1978. While most colonies have fewer than 200 birds, as many as 5000 have been recorded breeding at Pelsart Island in the Houtman Abrolhos in 1947, and in November 1982 probably at least 1000. The species occurs also on Australia's eastern coast, with breeding on some islands of the Great Barrier Reef.

▶ See also pages *49 71 81 219 239 244 302*

204 SOOTY TERN *Sterna fuscata*

211 LESSER NODDY

Anous tenuirostris

The islands of the Houtman Abrolhos are the only breeding grounds in the world for the subspecies *melanops* of the Lesser Noddy. Here it is present throughout the year, with nesting occurring through spring and summer. The location and size of colonies has varied greatly over the years. An immense colony on Pelsart Island disappeared soon after 1900, and the second colony on Wooded Island was recorded as declining in 1913. Pelsart colonies were found to be re-established by 1936, with one estimated at 27 000 nests in 1947. Smaller colonies have existed on Morley and perhaps some other islands of the Houtman Abrolhos.

The large colonies of Wooded and Pelsart islands continue, with nests densely packed onto almost every available branch of the stunted mangroves that fringe the shallow lagoons of these islands. The Lesser Noddy can be confused with the

211 LESSER NODDY *Anous tenuirostris*

Common Noddy, but the breeding colonies of the latter occur in different environs, away from mangroves, the nest platforms being built on low saltbush and similar shrubs close to the ground. The Lesser Noddy is smaller and overall darker than the Common Noddy and lacks the well-defined black mark between eye and bill, where it is whitish.

The birds are exceptionally tame at the nests, but advantage should not be taken of this to excessively disturb any of the colonies.

▶ See also pages *244 304*

241 LONG-BILLED BLACK-COCKATOO

Calyptorhynchus baudinii

This species is found only in the South-West Region and is largely confined to heavier forests of jarrah, marri and karri. Also present in the

South-West Region is the White-tailed Black-Cockatoo, the subspecies *latirostris* of the eastern Yellow-tailed Black-Cockatoo. Both have whitish tail and cheek patches. It was previously thought that this local subspecies (*latirostris*) and the Long-billed Black-Cockatoo were both subspecies of a single South-West Region species known as the White-tailed Black-Cockatoo. The common name of White-tailed Black-Cockatoo was, however, retained here for the subspecies *latirostris*.

The two species are distinguished by their bills and habitat preferences. The unique Western Australian Long-billed Black-Cockatoo has an extended fine tip to the bill and occupies the forested south-west corner, while the White-tailed Black-Cockatoo has a heavier bill with a shorter point and inhabits mostly the open sandplain and mallee country farther inland.

269 RED-CAPPED PARROT *Purpureicephalus spurius*

Corellas typically occur in large and noisy flocks, so in the northern part of the range it is a matter of differentiating between the Western Long-billed Corella and the Little Corella, whose range overlaps here, and with which the Long-billed often associates and feeds in mixed flocks. Generally the species inhabits open forests and woodlands, watercourse timbers and treed farmlands. Like the Little Corella, the Long-billed feeds on the ground, taking the seeds of the introduced double gee; it also uses the long point of the bill to dig bulbs and corms from the ground. In these northern areas any corellas will need to be examined closely, for the greatly elongated bill tip seems to be the only useful identifier of this species in the field. In the south of its range, where it seems centred about and not uncommon around Lake Muir (a good sighting area) the Little Corella does not occur, the Long-billed being the sole corella species.

The numbers of Western Long-billed Corella have greatly declined since settlement, having once being common around the Swan River, where it has not been seen in living memory. However, in recent years the trend seems to have been reversed with both populations showing some increase in numbers.

Other localities on record include the Pallinup River, Perup River, Manjimup, Moora and Kalannie.

▶ See also pages   *239* 311

The Long-billed Black-Cockatoo feeds mainly on wood-boring insect larvae, and on blossoms and gumnuts. It is able to pry seed from the large capsules of the marri trees, using the finely elongated bill tip. It seems so dependent upon the marri that its range approximates the distribution of that tree. The White-tailed Black-Cockatoo, on the other hand, feeds largely upon pine seeds and seeds of native trees and shrubs, especially of hakeas, grevilleas, dryandras and banksias of the sandplains.

The two south-western black-cockatoos have contact calls so different that an experienced observer can separate the species on the basis of calls alone, that of the Long-billed being shorter, more guttural, and with less of the attenuated whistling of the White-tailed species.

Habitat is also helpful in separation, the Long-billed preferring marri and marri-karri forests and woodlands, especially when nesting, the White-

tailed occupying drier wandoo and salmon-gum woodlands for nesting, but then moving to open habitats, especially sandplain-woodlands and pine plantations.

▶ See also pages   *239* 242 310–11

245 WESTERN LONG-BILLED CORELLA

Cacatua pastinator

A 'new' endemic species for south-western Australia, formerly listed as a subspecies of the widespread Little Corella. The Western Long-billed Corella occurs in two separate populations, one in the extreme south-west corner, between Boyup Brook, Lake Muir and Frankland, and the second in the northern wheatbelt, from about Mingenew south to Moora, west to the coast, and somewhat inland of these and other nearby wheatbelt towns including Coorow and Carnamah.

269 RED-CAPPED PARROT

Purpureicephalus spurius

The magnificently plumaged Red-capped Parrot is found only in this South-West Region, where its range is determined by the occurrence of the marri or red-gum, a rough-barked forest tree with large, urn-shaped, woody and very hard seed capsules. The bill of the Red-capped Parrot has evolved a lengthened and slender tip, which enables it to pry seed from the marri gumnuts whereas other local parrots, principally the Twenty-eight Parrot (the greener version of the Port Lincoln Ringneck), must chew away the hard wood to get at the seeds.

The Red-capped Parrot remains common in the South West, and may be seen in the suburbs of Perth, the banksia-marri woodlands of the Swan Coastal Plain, the abundant wandoo-marri-jarrah forests of the Darling Range foothills, the wandoo-marri woodlands of the western wheatbelt and the stunted jarrah-marri of the south coast. It is also common in those excellent wader sites, Forrestdale,

Bibra and Thompsons lakes. The species wanders beyond the confines of marri and finds other food, including fruit in orchards. The abundance of this species in easily accessible areas makes a sighting almost certain.

The Red-capped Parrot's bold colour pattern makes recognition easy, except perhaps for very young birds. When in flight, especially flying away, the conspicuous yellow-green rump is distinctive. The call, once known, is unmistakable.

▶ **See also pages** 235 *238* 242 245 317

275 WESTERN ROSELLA

Platycercus icterotis

The Western Rosella is the only rosella in south-western Australia. It is completely isolated from all other species of rosella of eastern and northern Australia.

Although found throughout all but the northern part of the South-West Region, it is uncommon on the Swan Coastal Plain, and while occurring and nesting in the heavy jarrah-karri forests, it is easiest sighted in the more open wandoo woodlands farther inland. The Great Southern district, centred about the wheatbelt towns of Narrogin and Katanning, is a stronghold for the species. Here it may readily be seen in the many small remnant blocks of wandoo woodland, where it usually feeds on the ground, often among casuarina trees.

▶ **See also pages** 242 245 318

340 NOISY SCRUB-BIRD

Atrichornis clamosus

This secretive bird is extremely difficult to sight. Its loud, clear, ringing calls can be heard from more than a kilometre away on a calm day, making location of territories easy when males are calling, especially from May to November. But the calling male can be within a metre or two of the observer's feet and not be sighted, so skilfully does it conceal itself in tall, dense, rushy cover.

Only rarely will there be more than a fleeting glimpse of the scuttling brown shape. Early on cold, clear mornings one may be seen on a perch above the cold, shadowy, damp rushes, perched on a twig of a banksia, taking in the warmth of the first sunlight.

Although the habitat is often given as coastal, the typical habitat in earlier times was in the wetter areas of the south-western jarrah-marri forests, usually where a break of canopy in the

vicinity of stream or swamp allowed prolific low growth of scrub and rush. The present habitat of the remnant population may not have been typical of the species over much of its range. At Two People's Bay it occurs in very dense rushy vegetation under stunted trees along gullies and swamps around Mt Gardner, and in similar but more extensive areas around the swampy

24	**Fleshy-footed Shearwater** *Puffinus carneipes*
29	**Little Shearwater** *Puffinus assimilis*
183	**Long-toed Stint** *Calidris subminuta*
201	**Roseate Tern** *Sterna dougallii*
241	**Long-billed Black-Cockatoo** *Calyptorhynchus baudinii*
245	**Western Long-billed Corella** *Cacatua pastinator*
340	**Noisy Scrub-bird** *Atrichornis clamosus*
453	**Western Bristlebird** *Dasyornis longirostris*

margins of creeks and small coastal lakes. The surrounding low and often dense sandplain-heathland is probably only occasionally used or traversed.

The calls offer the only practical way of locating, though perhaps not even sighting, the bird. As well as being very loud, the notes are clear and ringing, sometimes described as melodious, and, with some variation, building up into a crescendo of sound that at close range verges on being painful on the ears. Mimicry is not normal, though the imitating of some sounds of human origin was reported for at least one bird close by the Two People's Bay buildings.

▶ **See also pages** 116 235 *239* 245 336

370 **WHITE-BREASTED ROBIN**
Eopsaltria georgiana

370 WHITE-BREASTED ROBIN

Eopsaltria georgiana

Most abundant in the luxuriant understorey thickets of the karri forest of the extreme south-west, the White-breasted Robin extends northwards in the denser undergrowth of river valleys through the jarrah forest, to within 30 km of Perth along the Wungong and Canning rivers. A second population occurs near the coast north of Perth, in thickets of coastal wattle.

While the species is generally quiet and inconspicuous it is not shy and is unlikely to be missed by an observer spending some time in the wetter forests of the extreme south-west. Near Perth, it can be seen in dense thickets of creeks around the Wungong and Serpentine dams.

The White-breasted Robin gives a loud, aggressive chatting when its territory is entered, especially when breeding.

▶ **See also pages** 66 242 343

381 CRESTED SHRIKE-TIT

Falcunculus frontatus

The endemic western subspecies of the Crested Shrike-tit is one of the more difficult of the south-western birds to find. Although not rare, it keeps to the upper canopy and limbs, where it is unlikely to be noticed unless it is calling. The call is undulating, with a mournful quality, not loud, but carrying for some distance. Its direction seems difficult to establish unless the bird continues to call, but all too often it will call once or twice then remain silent for some time. Although it occurs in the karri-jarrah forests, the best chances of a sighting seem to be in the wandoo woodlands of the Great Southern district, in forest blocks such as Dryandra, and many smaller bush reserves.

▶ **See also pages** 122 139 148 345–6 365

439 RED-WINGED FAIRY-WREN

Malurus elegans

Possibly a remnant population now confined to Western Australia's extreme south-west corner by climatic changes. The Red-winged Fairy-wren is found only in the heavier karri and southern jarrah forests, where the undergrowth is dense and often damp,

and northwards in the jarrah-wandoo of the Darling Range in the thickets along rivers and creeks. There is a similar extension on the south coast to the east of Albany in swampy creek-side situations. In the karri it occurs throughout the forest; in the more heavily forested damp parts of the Darling Range river valleys it forages in undergrowth up valley slopes hundreds of metres from the stream thickets.

In such situations it seems to favour areas with a profusion of low blackboys, where it often nests where the 'skirt' of dead leaves touches the ground. Areas long unburned, and with abundant leaf-litter, are favoured. The species seems to suffer heavy loss both of nests and habitat even from mild spring burning.

In these dense environs the call is the best locator, and this is distinctive, beginning with several sharp notes, followed by a rattling, uneven trill. The similar Variegated and Blue-breasted Fairy-wrens do not occur in such moist, dense habitats, and overlap only slightly, if at all, along the Red-winged Fairy-wren's easternmost range. The Splendid Fairy-wren is quite distinctive in looks and call.

▶ **See also pages** 160 242 359–60

439 RED-WINGED FAIRY-WREN *Malurus elegans*

453 WESTERN BRISTLEBIRD

Dasyornis longirostris

The Western Bristlebird is a species of very restricted distribution, its habitat evidently greatly reduced by climatic change. Early records were from as far north as the Perth area but it has long been confined to a few small relict populations along the coast east of Albany. This species is found in areas of low dense heath on sandplain, sometimes with intermixed or adjoining damper rushy vegetation. Its decline since settlement is thought to have been caused by the clearing and burning of heathlands. The species appears to be sedentary.

The Western Bristlebird has been closely studied at Two People's Bay, where there are about 100 pairs. Other localities include the sandplain areas of Fitzgerald River National Park and of the Waychinicup River area of the Mt Manypeaks range.

Being a weak or reluctant flier it keeps to the ground beneath the densest of the low shrubbery. But very early in the morning, and again towards sunset, it sings from a higher and usually quite exposed perch, giving the best chance of a clear view.

The song is a beautiful quick lilting 'chip-pee-tee-peetle-pet', quite loud, very clear, and far-carrying in still conditions. This appears to be the male's territorial song, to which the female may respond with a sharp three-noted whistle. The singing bird will drop to cover at the slightest disturbance, so a relatively distant sighting is usually the best that can be expected. After the breeding season the song may not be heard, only an alarm call, a single abrupt, shrill whistle.

▶ See also pages   130 235 *239* 242 245 362

484 WESTERN THORNBILL

Acanthiza inornata

This very plainly plumaged thornbill is entirely confined to the South-West Region where it is an inhabitant of woodlands and forests. It is common on the sandplain-banksia woodlands of the Swan Coastal Plain, in the jarrah forests of the Darling Range, and in remnant woodlands of the wheatbelt.

Although the dullest of the thornbills, and with but a feeble twitter of song, its common occurrence in patches of bushland close to Perth, including Kings Park, make a sighting very likely for any observer spending some time in appropriate habitat. Compared with the similar common local Inland Thornbill, the Western is plainer,

484 WESTERN THORNBILL *Acanthiza inornata*

lacking the rufous rump, and has a short, truncated tail which is never carried uplifted but always straight out from the body.

Except in the breeding season this species may be seen in small parties, often in loose mixed parties with other small birds, foraging for insects among the foliage, at any height, from near ground level to the treetops.

▶ See also pages   242 370

561 WESTERN SPINEBILL

Acanthorhynchus superciliosus

This small honeyeater, entirely confined to the South-West Region, is active, noisy, generally quite conspicuous, and should be found without difficulty. It is likely to be seen wherever there are flowering trees or large wildflowers of copious nectar, especially banksias, bottlebrushes, dryandras, grevilleas and kangaroo-paws. It occurs in most patches of banksia-eucalypt woodlands on the coastal plains close to the city and suburbs of Perth. Along the foothills it is most common where dryandras and calothamnus dominate undergrowth thickets beneath the white-barked wandoos, and at dryandra, calothamnus and grevillea undergrowth in the jarrah forest. The calls are loud, and the birds attract attention by a clapping together of the wings in flight.

▶ See also pages   *11* 245 388

589 RED-EARED FIRETAIL

Emblema oculata

This spectacular finch is confined to the South-West Region, where it occupies diverse habitats. It may be seen within about 30 km of Perth, where rivers such as the Wungong have cut steep valleys through the escarpment. Here it is in undergrowth beneath wandoo and marri, nesting high in foliage clumps. Farther into the main forest block it favours winter-wet paperbark flats towards the headwaters of the rivers, using the dense crowns of paperbarks and banksias as nest sites.

In the extreme south-west corner the Red-eared Firetail is found in karri forest thickets, while along the south coast it may be seen in stunted coastal scrub trimmed by sea winds and salt spray, and nests are necessarily very low.

This firetail is usually in pairs or small parties of three or four, always very quiet and easily overlooked, even when the soft calls are known. It is usually first noticed when accidentally flushed from low heath or forest undergrowth where it feeds upon seeds of native grasses. When likely sites are traversed this finch is likely to be flushed from the ground before it is seen or heard, and it is then that a flash of crimson on the rump may be noticed. It is then likely to perch briefly and call softly several times before departing for some other feeding spot not far distant.

▶ See also pages   235 242 394–5

BIRD PLACES OF THE SOUTH WEST

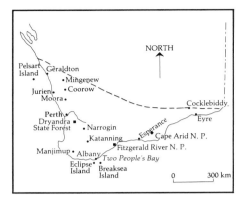

BENGER SWAMP

A large wetland of some 320 ha situated on the Swan Coastal Plain several kilometres west of the South-West Highway at Benger. It has a long-established reputation as one of the outstanding south-west sites for aquatic birds, and a total list of over 100 species of aquatic and land birds. The swamp is now a conservation reserve, to be managed as a waterbird habitat, maintaining a balance between open water areas and reed-beds or other vegetation to provide habitat for the greatest range of species. Many thousands of waterbirds use Benger as a summer drought refuge.

Among the birds of great interest are the rare Freckled Duck, which breeds here. Also on the birdlist are the Great Crested Grebe, Australasian and Little bitterns, Yellow-billed and Royal spoonbills, Pink-eared Duck, Marsh Harrier, Banded Land Rail, Australian and Spotless crakes, Little Stint, Whiskered Tern, Little Grassbird, Marsh Sandpiper, Black-tailed Godwit and Oriental Pratincole.

Many others are common species, some in quite large numbers. The surrounds of the lake have numerous terrestrial birds, including usually the Red-capped Parrot.

DRYANDRA

Dryandra State Forest is situated in the Great Southern, an old-established wheatbelt district centred upon the towns of Narrogin and Katanning. The original vegetation was largely of eucalypt woodland, much of it the white-barked wandoo. Many small blocks of natural vegetation remain, one of the larger being Dryandra State Forest, now managed for flora and fauna conservation rather than timber production.

Dryandra is reached from Perth via the Albany Highway, Wandering and Pumphreys Bridge. Initially the highway passes through the Darling Range jarrah forest, giving opportunities to see several unique Western Australian species. Where the road crosses creeks, as at Sullivans Rocks, 36 km from Armadale, there is opportunity to sight Red-winged Fairy-wrens, Red-eared Firetails and White-breasted Robins in the creekside thickets. Farther south, at 40 to 60 km, paperbark swamps between Mt Randell and Mt Cooke are the habitat of firetails and Red-winged Fairy-wrens. Almost anywhere through this main forest block may be sighted other endemics: the Long-billed Black-Cockatoo, Red-capped Parrot, Western Thornbill, Western Rosella and Twenty-eight Parrot (subspecies of Port Lincoln Ringneck), together with many birds not peculiar to this region.

EYRE BIRD OBSERVATORY

Set among sand dunes at the western end of the Great Australian Bight, south of the Eyre Highway near Cocklebiddy, Eyre Bird Observatory is one of comparatively few southern Western Australian sites with a birdlist exceeding 200 species. The bird observatory utilises the historic stone building of the Eyre Telegraph Station, restored to accommodate the warden and assistant, and visitors. This section of the coast is part of a very large nature reserve.

The birds of Eyre fall into two main groups, as they tend to be seen: those of the ocean and shores and those of the bush. The shorebirds are greatly increased in species and numbers by an influx of migrant waders which peaks during October and November, as the migrants pass through en route to south-eastern Australia. There is a lesser peak during March–May as some return following the same route.

Sightings of special interest include the Oriental Plover, Buff-breasted Sandpiper, Pectoral Sandpiper, Baird's Sandpiper, Northern Phalarope, and many of the more common species.

The numbers of bushland birds also are boosted by influxes from time to time. There appear to be considerable seasonal movements of birds, particularly of honeyeaters, apparently linked with the flowering of the mallee eucalypts. Of special interest among the bush birds is the Southern Scrub-robin, and a sighting of the Scarlet-chested Parrot. Eyre can be reached by bus from Perth or Adelaide, and courses are conducted

on birdlife, banding, photography and other associated subjects. For information contact the Royal Australasian Ornithologists Union, Perth or Melbourne.

FITZGERALD RIVER NATIONAL PARK

The Fitzgerald River National Park has come into prominence comparatively recently as the habitat of three quite rare species of birds: the Ground Parrot, the Western Bristlebird and the Western Whipbird. In addition there are many other birds of interest including the Cape Barren Goose, Southern Emu-wren, Yellow-rumped Pardalote and Red-eared Firetail.

The Ground Parrot has been recorded on heathland country in the north of the park, and more frequently in vacant Crown land adjoining the northern side where the habitat could be destroyed by clearing or burning. These birds are best found by listening for their calls (which are similar to the calls of Tawny-crowned Honeyeaters) before sunrise, and for a period after sunset. In the South-West Region, this species is also found in Cape Arid National Park, east of Esperance.

FORRESTDALE LAKE

The Swan Coastal Plain has a number of lakes which are excellent habitat for waterfowl, waders, and bush birds in the surrounding woodlands. Several are outstanding by any standards, with very large congregations of birds in certain seasons.

At the southern edge of Perth's suburbs, Forrestdale Lake, Bibra Lake and Thompsons Lake are convenient bird sites. Forrestdale in particular has a very rich birdlife until, as usually happens, it dries out completely in mid to late summer. The lake is encircled by reed-beds, with an excellent variety of aquatic birds, particularly at its peak of activity around October and November.

However it is for its impressive assembly of waders that this lake has become renowned. The water is quite shallow and the lakebed almost flat, so that as the water evaporates through the hot dry months from November onwards, mudbanks and islets appear and the water steadily contracts towards the centre. It is to these mudflats being exposed by the receding water that the migrant waders are attracted in huge numbers.

The South-west Waterbird Project surveys of wetlands, conducted by the Royal Australasian Ornithologists

514 **YELLOW-THROATED MINER** *Manorina flavigula*

544 **WHITE-NAPED HONEYEATER** *Melithreptus lunatus*

Union, showed that of 127 wetlands surveyed throughout the South-West Region, Forrestdale had the greatest number of species: 57 out of a possible 115. Species of special interest include the Long-toed Stint, a rare migrant, with greater numbers here than any other site in Australia; also the Little Stint, Little Bittern and Marsh Harrier. At the other extreme are counts of up to 3000 Banded Stilts. The greatest wader population occurs when the water is very shallow, when there can be as many as 20 000 birds on the lake. Thompsons Lake has almost as great a total number of species recorded and is in many respects similar.

WETLANDS OF THE GREAT SOUTHERN DISTRICT

In the Great Southern district, the wheatbelt centred on the towns of Narrogin and Katanning, lakes to the east of Narrogin and to the east and west of Wagin are rich waterbird habitats. Much of this low-lying land is salty, so that most of the lakes are salt and many of the trees dead. Some lakes contain water for only part of the year or only in wet years.

Outstanding among the many lakes are Dumbleyung and Toolibin. The former is salt, and very large, 12 km long by 8 km wide. Most of this wetland consists of open waters, used by resting 'rafts' of ducks and diving birds. At the lake's south-eastern corner the mouth and shallows of the Coblinine River has dead trees and samphire providing a sheltered area. A one-day bird survey, 30 March 1985, counted 25 000 birds on the one-third of the wetlands most used by birds. There have been about 36 species recorded. Included were 10 500 Eurasian Coots, 7000 Grey Teal, 475 White-faced Herons and 76 Great Egrets. Of special interest was the sighting of Freckled and Blue-billed ducks. The large totals establish

Dumbleyung Lake as one of the most important wetlands in the South-West Region.

Among the many other lakes in the district worth visiting, Toolibin Lake is distinctive, being freshwater, the living trees standing in water across most of the lake providing a very sheltered habitat. Unfortunately Toolibin goes dry in summer after low-rainfall winters. The quality of habitat is reflected in the fact that, of south-western wetlands, this lake has the most breeding species, 17 of the 56 waterbirds known to breed in the region. Among these are the Yellow-billed Spoonbill, Hardhead and Musk Duck.

HERDSMANS LAKE

Close to Perth, surrounded by housing and industry, Herdsmans Lake has long been a popular birdwatching site with more than 80 species recorded. Of these, between 20 and 30 species nest on the lake or in its extensive reed-beds. It is one of the few South-West sites where the Little Bittern breeds and one of a small number of Australian wetlands known to be visited by the migrant Little Stint. A bird observatory–visitor centre has been constructed.

HOUTMAN ABROLHOS

For sheer numbers of birds the islands of the Houtman Abrolhos afford the most spectacular sights in the South-West Region. This cluster of low limestone and sand islets, situated about 60 km offshore near Geraldton, has long attracted attention for prolific birdlife. Ornithologists visiting the group have recorded breeding colonies of Crested Terns with over 100 000 pairs, and equally large colonies of Common Noddies and Lesser Noddies.

Other seabirds regularly nesting in colonies large or small include Wedge-tailed and Little shearwaters, Pacific Gulls, Caspian, Roseate, Fairy and Sooty terns. Ospreys and White-bellied Sea-eagles are quite common. Pelsart Island has some of the largest colonies along its 12 km length and some 40 species can be sighted within three or four days. The species list, and more so the list of breeding species, varies considerably throughout the year, with November to January the best for large breeding colonies. The islands are set among extensive reefs, so it would be wise to obtain local expertise on boat access. The islands are a fauna reserve, with a permit required from the Department of Conservation and Land Management.

Other seabird islands farther south, down the west coast, are closer to the mainland and though very tiny, with much smaller bird populations, are of interest. These include Lancelin Island, 0.5 km offshore at Jurien Bay, with colonies of Wedge-tailed Shearwaters and White-faced Storm-Petrels, apparently in very large numbers if the abundance of their burrows indicates actual numbers, as well as smaller numbers of various terns and gulls. The North Fisherman and South Fisherman islands, near Jurien Bay, have a large colony of Bridled Terns.

PEEL INLET

On the Swan Coastal Plain about 60 km south of Perth the almost landlocked Peel Inlet and Harvey Estuary, into which the Serpentine, Murray and Harvey rivers flow, together with nearby Lake Clifton and Lake Preston, are important habitats for birds of the open waters, and for waders. The main gatherings are on the shallows of the eastern and south-eastern sides of Peel Inlet, where a count of total birds in one month was as high as 41 000. The importance of the inlet for waders is shown by a count of 19 000, placing this site fourteenth nationally.

There are various access points for birdwatching. An approach via Yunderup will allow sightings of birds along the channels of the Yunderup Delta before reaching the open water of the inlet.

SWAN RIVER

Although surrounded by housing, the Swan River has many excellent bird sites, especially for waders during the summer months, but also places where the more common of the bushland birds may be seen.

The main areas are the Como Foreshore and Point Waylen (Alfred Cove) on the south side, and Pelican Point (Pt Currie) on the north. Here wide mudflats are exposed at low tide.

The Point Waylen–Alfred Cove area is a nature reserve. The habitats include mudflats at Point Waylen, samphire, low sedge and reeds in Alfred Cove, with some bushland adjoining. The reserve is frequented by about 70–75 species of birds, with sightings of around 500 Red-necked Stints and 200 Curlew Sandpipers. Pelican Point is commonly used by very large numbers in summer as a roost site.

TWO PEOPLE BAY

The rediscovery of the Noisy Scrub-bird at Two People's Bay, on the south coast 40 km east of Albany, led to the creation of a nature reserve for the protection of the habitat. Also at this site are the rare Western Bristlebird and the very restricted Western Whipbird.

Though taking its name from the bay to the north side, the reserve is centred upon the high granite headland of Mt Gardner and extends west along the coast to take in coastal heathlands, sand dunes and several small lakes.

The Noisy Scrub-bird when rediscovered was confined to swamps near the Two People Bay beach and gully thickets of Mt Gardner, but as the protected population has expanded territories have been taken up in dense thickets around Lake Gardner and Moates Lagoon, possibly better localities for a sighting. The Western Bristlebird inhabits dense low heath close by, in the area between the lakes and Mt Gardner.

The third species of special interest here, the Western Whipbird, is yet another brownish-plumaged, long-tailed, secretive bird, and it too has a loud call. It is found in sandplain scrub on the slopes below Mt Gardner. The song, often built up with notes from both male and female, gives the only useful method of initially locating the bird. The call usually begins softly, as if the bird is far away, and builds up in volume until very loud. The song is varied, but not ventriloquial. Although shy, the whipbird is much less difficult to sight than the Noisy Scrub-bird; calls and habitats are extremely useful in separating scrub-bird, bristlebird and whipbird in the field.

DRYANDRA BIRDWATCH

The bird experience suggestion for a visitor to the South West is planned as a trip of one or, if desired, several days, to cover habitats of many of the region's endemic birds and others of considerable interest. The months May to December are suitable, with September to November optimum. Midsummer to autumn is extremely dry and the birdlife very subdued.

Dryandra State Forest is easily traversed on a network of narrow forestry roads which allow an overview by vehicle of large parts in a short time. The landform is mostly gently undulating, with broad, often flat-floored valleys, but some of the comparatively low hilltops having a broken laterite cap. The lower parts generally carry open woodland of white-barked wandoo eucalypts, many old and large, with an abundance of hollows. Usually the forest floor here is very open, but in places with a dense low undergrowth of poison-bush.

On the rises the trees change to pinkish powder-barked wandoo and slender umbrella-crowned brown mallet, while the lateritic ridges carry a profusion of flowering shrubs, mainly dryandra species. There are some small areas of sandplain-heath, and of marri or marri-wandoo woodland.

As the habitat is almost uniformly good for birdlife, and as there are no marked trails or tracks, it is rewarding to wander slowly through almost any part of Dryandra with excellent bird-spotting results. All types of habitat described above can easily be found along the network of dirt roads.

Among the birds of greatest interest will be the South West's endemics. Common here is the Blue-breasted Fairy-wren, occurring almost throughout, usually where there are thickets of low poison-bush undergrowth in wandoo woodland areas. It is the sole species of chestnut-shouldered wren found here.

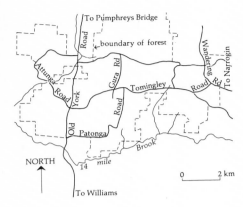

The Rufous Treecreeper, while not endemic to the region, is abundant and conspicuous almost everywhere. The parrots are throughout: the Red-capped, Twenty-eight, Elegant, Western Rosella, occasionally the Regent Parrot and, in some years, large numbers of Purple-crowned Lorikeets when forest trees are in flower.

In some of the patches of mallee around sandplain areas Mallee Fowl occur, and the sandplain areas can usually give sightings of Tawny-crowned Honeyeaters.

A walk around one of the lateritic hilltops gives additional species, mainly honeyeaters on the dryandra scrub. These include the Western Spinebill, New Holland Honeyeater, and the Red and Little wattlebirds. Dryandra's most common honeyeater, the Yellow-plumed, is more a bird of the open woodland areas, and always abundant.

Birds of prey may be sighted almost anywhere. Some breeding species include the Square-tailed Kite, Wedge-tailed Eagle, Brown Goshawk, Collared Sparrowhawk and Brown Falcon.

Birding is usually good throughout the day, except during very warm to hot weather, when early morning is best. The RAOU Field Atlas survey results suggest that up to approximately 170 bird species can be found in this area.

BIRD REFERENCE

This general reference to the birds covers all Australian species with the exception of uncommon vagrants that are of such unusual and irregular occurrence that they could not be considered part of the usual avifauna of any region; there is a supplementary listing of the vagrant species at the back of the book. The basis for the coverage is the main list of the Royal Australian Ornithologists Union's *Atlas of Australian Birds*, but with some recent reclassifications and name changes.

Previous and alternative common names are given for each species, and are included in the index for the assistance of those not familiar with the many changes in bird names in recent years. Also included are the alternative passerine family names recently proposed by C. G. Sibley and H. E. Ahlquist in a DNA based reclassification of Australian birds (*Emu* 85:1–14). The description for each species is of the adult male in breeding plumage; descriptions of female and immature, or migrant species usually seen in non-breeding plumage, are sometimes included.

EMUS

Dromaiidae Family of 1 species
1 in Australia, 1 breeding, 1 endemic

Largest endemic bird; second largest of the world's flightless birds. Related forms extinct in Tasmania and Kangaroo Island. It has many similarities with the cassowaries, perhaps being an early offshoot of cassowary stock which became adapted to more arid regions. Food consists of native fruits, vegetation, and insects taken from the ground.

1 **EMU** *Dromaius novaehollandiae* Adult

1 **EMU** *Dromaius novaehollandiae* Chicks

1 EMU

Dromaius novaehollandiae   Dromaiidae
OTHER NAMES Dwarf Emu

RECOGNITION Huge, to 2 m height; flightless. Only others of similar size are Southern Cassowary (restricted to rainforest) and Ostrich (introduced and restricted to a small area of South Australia). Widespread; most often seen on inland plains; usually in pairs or small parties. The Emu is highly nomadic, except while breeding, moving to regions of recent good rains. Breeding female has deeper blues on head and neck. 1.7 m.

VOICE Deep resonant thudding booming (female), and grunts (male). The young give plaintive, high whistling or peeping sounds.

HABITAT Almost all habitats; arid mulga and spinifex, woodlands, eucalypt forests, alpine and coastal heaths, margins of wetlands, shores; not rainforests.

BREEDING Breeding variable, from March–November. Rough, usually sparse nest of grass, bark and sticks, on ground. Five to 11 granulated, deep-green eggs; 13.5 × 9 cm; brooded by male, which escorts chicks for up to 18 months.

RANGE Throughout mainland; except rainforests and closely settled areas. Highly nomadic.

STATUS Abundant. Endemic.

▶ See also pages
221 *249* 280 283

CASSOWARIES

Casuariidae Family of 3 species
1 in Australia, 1 breeding

Heavily built, flightless birds of tropical rainforests. The casque on the head may be an adaptation for crashing through dense undergrowth, as may be the very coarse wiry plumage. Food consists of fallen rainforest fruits, occasionally dead animals.

2 SOUTHERN CASSOWARY

Casuarius casuarius   Casuariidae
OTHER NAMES Double-wattled Cassowary, Australian Cassowary

RECOGNITION Massive size, up to 2 m tall; black with pale blue on bare skin of face becoming deep purplish-blue down neck; with crimson wattles. Grey horny casque on head. Female tends to be larger, more brightly coloured. The entire plumage of the Southern Cassowary is of glossy, coarse hair-like feathers. Wanders over a large territory in search of fallen fruits, but

remains confined to rainforests of north-eastern Queensland.

VOICE Low rumbling, deep boomings and roaring, rough or harsh coughing; fluffs up feathers and gives a loud hiss on meeting intruders.

HABITAT Tropical rainforest, with preference for stream edges, small clearings; also in cane-fields. Mostly solitary; sometimes in small groups.

BREEDING July–August. Nest is a roughly cleared scrape lined with grass, leaves and fern fronds; deep in rainforest. Three to five large, granulated, light yellow-green eggs; incubated by the male.

RANGE North-eastern Queensland; from Townsville north almost to tip of Cape York Peninsula. Also in New Guinea. Sedentary.

STATUS Common in optimum habitat; elsewhere uncommon.

▶ See also pages
96 97 *249*

GREBES

Podicipedidae Family of 17 species
3 in Australia, 3 breeding, 1 endemic

Extremely well adapted to an aquatic environment, principally freshwater to brackish rather than marine. The legs are placed far back on the body for underwater propulsion, making them very awkward out of water; the feet are not webbed, but have toes with widely flattened paddle-like margins. They fly well, but only at night, avoiding danger by diving. Food consists of aquatic plants and small, water creatures.

3 GREAT CRESTED GREBE

Podiceps cristatus   Podicipedidae
OTHER NAMES Diver, Gaunt, Carr's Goose, Tippet Grebe, Loon

RECOGNITION Breeding plumage: upperparts dark brown; underparts silky white; with prominent chestnut-and-black frill encircling and framing the white face. Pointed black ear-tufts rising above the dark-brown crown; large straight dagger-like bill. In flight has conspicuous white margins to grey wings. Non-breeding plumage: ear-tufts and frill greatly reduced or absent. Female similar. Immatures: grey upperparts; white underparts; no tufts. Swims strongly, long dives. 50 cm.

VOICE Varied calls, most associated with elaborate courtship displays: a far-carrying double-noted advertising call; barking and whirring sounds.

HABITAT Mostly fresh waters of lakes, reservoirs and swamps with large areas of open waters; occasionally on sheltered coastal inlets and bays.

BREEDING November–January. The nest is a large mass of waterweeds; sometimes stabilized with mud; built up from the bottom, or in deeper waters usually anchored to surface or submerged branches or logs. Three to five greenish-white eggs.

RANGE East, south-east, south-west, and Tasmania; interior on large rivers, temporary waters. Almost cosmopolitan species. Nomadic.

STATUS Uncommon; or common locally.

▶ See also pages
123 125 137 *144*
163 174

3 GREAT CRESTED GREBE *Podiceps cristatus*

4 HOARY-HEADED GREBE
Poliocephalus poliocephalus

HOARY-HEADED GREBE

Poliocephalus poliocephalus Podicipedidae

OTHER NAMES Hoary-headed Dabchick, Diver, Tom Pudding

RECOGNITION A small grebe which in breeding plumage has a black head with abundant white streaks, giving a grey-haired appearance. Back and wings grey-brown. Lores and chin black; fore-neck and upper breast light buff; darker down the nape and back of neck. Bill black. Non-breeding plumage: crown and nape dark brown or black; sides of head and throat white; bill pale. Eye is golden (male) or ivory (female). Immatures: like non-breeding adults. 29–30 cm.

VOICE Usually silent, but occasionally gives soft churring sound, and also a quiet squeak when feeding young.

HABITAT Open-water areas of swamps, lakes, reservoirs; occasionally on sheltered bays and inlets; and uncommonly on open farm dams.

BREEDING November–January. Nest is a

*Rockhopper Penguin

*Fiordland Penguin

*Gentoo Penguin

*King Penguin

6

1 **Emu** *Dromaius novaehollandiae*
2 **Southern Cassowary** *Casuarius casuarius*
3 **Great Crested Grebe** *Podiceps cristatus*
4 **Hoary-headed Grebe** *Poliocephalus poliocephalus*
5 **Australasian Grebe** *Tachybaptus novaehollandiae*
6 **Little Penguin** *Eudyptula minor*

*Occasional visitors to Australian waters

floating collection of waterweeds; anchored or attached to reeds or other substantial waterlevel vegetation. Occasionally nests in groups. Three to six pale blue eggs; sitting bird covers eggs when leaving.

RANGE Almost throughout Australia in suitable habitat except Cape York. Nomadic.

STATUS Moderately common. Endemic.

▶ See also pages
163 249

5 AUSTRALASIAN GREBE

Tachybaptus novaehollandiae
                    Podicipedidae

OTHER NAMES White-throated Dabchick, Little Grebe, Australian Dabchick, Red-necked Dabchick

RECOGNITION A very small grebe. Breeding plumage: black head; brownish-black neck and back; patch of yellow skin at gape of bill sloping up towards the yellow eye. Flanks and sides of neck dusky chestnut; underparts silvery grey. Non-breeding and immature plumage is duller overall; paler patch at base of bill. In pairs or small parties; dives frequently, and quickly if disturbed. In non-breeding plumage it may be confused with non-breeding Hoary-headed Grebe. 23–25 cm.

VOICE A rapid shrill chatter, or chitter; sometimes by several birds as if a duet. Alarm call is a single sharp 'tik'.

HABITAT Freshwater swamps and lakes; occasionally on broader open waters in company with Hoary-headed Grebe. Also occurs, uncommonly, on sheltered bays.

BREEDING September–January. Nest is a floating mass of waterweeds and other plant materials; usually anchored to reeds or other vegetation; tends not to nest close to others. Four to six pale blue eggs.

RANGE Throughout Australia in suitable habitat. Also in New Guinea, New Zealand and Eurasia. Nomadic; especially in drier regions.

STATUS Generally common.

▶ See also pages
99 185 249

**Spheniscidae Family of 17 species
11 in Australia, 1 breeding**

So extremely adapted to the marine environment that they are now flightless; the former flying beat of the wings now being underwater flipper propulsion. The legs are short and set far back so they require an upright stance for balance, and have a slow waddling walk. The plumage is dense and oily. Penguins are confined to the Antarctic and adjacent seas. Most feed on small fish, crustaceans. Most are uncommon visitors to Australia.

6 LITTLE PENGUIN

Eudyptula minor   Spheniscidae

OTHER NAMES Fairy Penguin, Little Blue Penguin, Southern Blue Penguin

RECOGNITION A small penguin, with upperparts steely dark blue-grey; trailing edge of flipper and underparts white. Lacks any crest, head plumes or bold facial markings; gradual transition from dark blue-grey of crown and nape to white of throat and breast. Eye silver-grey; bill black; feet pale flesh-coloured. New plumage is bluer, acquires browner tone near moult. This species well known subject of penguin parade, Phillip Island (Vic). 33 cm. The Rockhopper Penguin (*Eudyptes chrysocome*), Gentoo Penguin (*Pygoscelis papua*), King Penguin (*Aptenodyptes patagonica*) and Fiordland Penguin (*Eudyptes pachyrhynchus*) may occasionally occur in Australian waters.

VOICE A sharp 'yap-yap', at sea, and on leaving the breeding or roosting islands just before dawn. In threat and mating displays, loud hoarse braying.

HABITAT Oceans, bays, coasts, coastal islands. Nest burrows used as roosting places by some penguins out of breeding season.

BREEDING July–March. Usually males return to islands first and are soon joined by females; often previous burrow is re-used. The two white eggs are laid July-December; both parents share the five weeks of incubation; chicks remain to about April.

RANGE Southern coasts; from south-western Australia to south-eastern Queensland. Also in New Zealand and Chatham Islands. Dispersive or sedentary.

STATUS Common; locally abundant, especially Bass Strait.

▶ See also pages
45 124 151 249

**Diomedeidae Family of 3 species
1 in Australia, 1 breeding**

Large, long-winged gliding birds, including some known as mollymawks. The exceptionally long thin wings generate optimum lift. These birds are skilled in utilizing the wind energy to conserve their own, diving close to the water to gain speed, being lifted steeply as they rise into the wind, then sweeping round to repeat the cycle. Bills are long and hooked; nostrils tubular; feet webbed. Only the Shy Albatross breeds on the Australian coast.

7 WANDERING ALBATROSS

Diomedea exulans   Diomedeidae

OTHER NAMES Snowy Albatross, White-winged Albatross, Cape Sheep, Man-of-War Bird

RECOGNITION Largest of flying birds, with wingspan to 3.5 m. In flight, undersurfaces are white except for black wingtips. Upperparts white, and a variable extent of uppersurface of wings white, the amount increasing with age. Upperwings almost all black on young birds, extending along centre of wings beyond bend of wing on older birds, until, after about nine years, only flight feathers black. Massive bill, pinkish-tipped yellow; eye brown; feet pale flesh-pink. In flight, wings very straight. Female marked brown on crown. Immatures all brown.

VOICE Hoarse croaks when squabbling for food at sea. On breeding islands, hoarse braying calls; clapping of bill during courtship.

HABITAT Southern oceans.

BREEDING September–February. Breeds on subantarctic islands including Macquarie Island. Nest is a large, shallow bowl of plants and mud, on ground. A single white egg is laid, usually speckled reddish-brown.

RANGE Northern coasts; from vicinity Fremantle (WA) to Whitsunday Island (Qld).

STATUS Common; is usually seen well offshore.

▶ See also pages
123 251 251 252

8 ROYAL ALBATROSS

Diomedea epomophora   Diomedeidae

OTHER NAMES Southern Royal, Northern Royal Albatross (subspecies *sanfordi*)

RECOGNITION Only slightly smaller than the Wandering Albatross, with a wingspan of up to 3.25 m. Two subspecies. Nominate subspecies (Southern Royal): appearance very like old and whitest Wandering Albatross; old birds entirely white except for thin black trailing edge, younger birds more black on upperwing but where white this white extends to leading edge of wing. Subspecies *sanfordi* has uppersurface of wings wholly black. Bill has black cutting edge to upper-mandible.

VOICE A variety of hoarse sounds when feeding or in courting; often braying sounds; bill-clappering.

HABITAT Oceanic; usually sighted near edge of Continental Shelf; not often close inshore. In flight, wings more backswept from carpal joint.

BREEDING September–January; usually only every second year. Southern Royal breeds only in New Zealand region; Northern Royal breeds only on Chatham Islands and in New Zealand. Nest is a large mud bowl on ground. One white egg, often marked pinkish-brown.

RANGE Southern oceans; probably circling pole in westerly windbelt.

STATUS Uncommon within sight of land; more common farther out.

▶ See also page 250

BLACK-BROWED ALBATROSS

Diomedea melanophrys   Diomedeidae

OTHER NAMES Mollymawk, Mollyhawk, Black-browed Mollymawk

RECOGNITION Comparatively robust, short-necked appearance. Body entirely white except that the black of uppersurface of the wings extends unbroken across the back; stumpy tail black above and beneath. Underwing white with broad black leading edge that is wider at the elbow and outwards of carpal joint, black wingtip and narrow black trailing edge. Black eyebrow line, yellow bill. Subspecies *impavida* has dark collar, more black under the wings. Wingspan 2.4 m.

VOICE Cacklings and guttural croakings; at breeding grounds, braying calls and clattering of bill while displaying.

HABITAT Oceans and seas; often relatively close inshore, visible from clifftops; appears to prefer seas of surface water temperature below 18°C.

BREEDING September–May; colonially, on many subantarctic islands including Macquarie Island, Heard Island. Nest of mud and plants. Single, pinkish-white egg, marked dark red-brown. Birds banded on these islands have been recovered on Australian seas.

RANGE Circumpolar; visitor to southern Australia, north to tropics. May–October.

STATUS Most common albatross visiting Australia.

light phase

dark phase

▶ See also pages 123 164

YELLOW-NOSED ALBATROSS

10

Diomedea chlororhynchos   Diomedeidae

OTHER NAMES Yellow-nosed Mollymawk, Carter's Albatross

RECOGNITION Smallest albatross, wingspan around 2 m; white head and body; uppersurface of wings brownish-black, this continuing unbroken across the back. Undersurfaces white, except black wingtip and narrow clear-cut black edging to wings, slightly wider along leading edge than along trailing edge. Long, slender, glossy black bill with yellow strip along the top ridge, and pink-tipped. Cheeks and nape sometimes pearly grey. Immatures have black bills. Length 1 m.

VOICE When squabbling over food, and in courtship displays, a guttural coughing; also bleating cry; a call with bill pointed skywards; bill clapping.

HABITAT Oceanic; but more often inshore waters, along coastlines, in large bays; feeds upon squid, crustaceans, fish.

BREEDING Visitor to eastern Australian coasts May–October; to western coasts April–November. Breeds on northern subantarctic islands of the Atlantic and Indian oceans. Breeds in summer, building a mud nest on the ground. A single white egg, marked with brown.

RANGE Temperate to subtropical seas; southern Australia, from North West Cape (WA) to south-eastern Queensland.

STATUS Common off west coast; less common off east coast.

▶ See also pages
123 164 *257*

SHY ALBATROSS

11

Diomedea cauta   Diomedeidae

OTHER NAMES Mollyhawk, White-capped Albatross, Mollymawk, Molly

RECOGNITION Smaller, but similar in flight and underwing pattern to the Wandering Albatross. Upperwing surface entirely blackish-brown, continuing unbroken across the back; underparts white with very narrow black edging to the leading and trailing edges of wings. Tips of flight feathers and tail black. Head may be all white, or pale grey on cheeks and round neck, with dark eyebrow line, so crown looks white-capped. Bill greyish with yellow tip. Wingspan 2.3 m.

VOICE Hoarse and gurgling or guttural sounds when feeding or squabbling; bill-clapperings and throaty sounds in courtship.

HABITAT Southern seas; some travelling circumpolar. Approaches coast and is sometimes sighted from cliffs; attracted to fishing boats.

BREEDING The only albatross to breed in Australian waters. The local subspecies *cauta* breeds in three colonies on Tasmanian offshore islands. Breeds September–May. Nest is a bowl shape of mud and plants. One large white egg, usually flecked reddish.

RANGE Subspecies *cauta*; coasts southern Australia, southern oceans.

STATUS Common south-east; uncommon elsewhere.

▶ See also pages
123 164 250 *251*

PETRELS, SHEARWATERS

Procellariidae Family of 66 species 40–44 in Australia, 10 breeding, 1 endemic

Small to medium, gliding seabirds which come to land only to breed. Highly adapted to oceanic life, not usually touching Australian coasts except as storm casualties. The bill is surmounted by tubular nostrils, this tube being divided by an internal septum which distinguishes this family from the storm-petrels. Sociable, usually seen in flocks. Most are extensive wanderers across the oceans of the world, returning to southern islands to breed.

SOUTHERN GIANT-PETREL

12

Macronectes giganteus   Procellariidae

OTHER NAMES Giant Fulmar, Sea Goose, Mother Carey's Goose, Vulture of the Seas

RECOGNITION Largest petrel, wingspan around 2 m. Two colour phases. Dark phase: adults (rarely seen in Australia), dark-brown body, merging to grey-mottled neck and white head; wings dark, mottled grey-white along the leading edge. Bill horn-coloured, green-tipped, with nostril tubes extending well along top edge. Immatures much more common on Australian waters; uniform blackish-brown, bill light, head lightens with age. Light phase: white with sparse dark spots; rare in Australia.

VOICE Deep guttural sounds, raucous laughter-like calls. Flies with head low, giving humpbacked appearance; glides best in strong winds.

HABITAT Oceanic; sometimes follows ships; feeds on fish, squid, small birds, crustaceans, floating refuse; sometimes gathers at sewage outlets.

BREEDING Breeds in colonies on Antarctic coasts, and subantarctic islands including Macquarie Island. Nests August–March. Nest is a depression encircled by dead grass. There is a single, large white egg.

RANGE Southern coasts of Australia; north to Pt Cloates (WA), and to south-eastern Queensland on east coast.

STATUS Immatures of dark phase quite common.

▶ See also pages
164 *251*

NORTHERN GIANT-PETREL

13

Macronectes halli   Procellariidae

OTHER NAMES Giant Fulmar, Hall's Giant-Petrel, Stinkpot, Mother Carey's Goose

RECOGNITION Closely resembles the Southern Giant-Petrel. Does not develop any large areas of white plumage, body being sooty grey-brown; head, neck and leading edges of wings speckled and mottled with white; increasingly so with age, especially on the face. There is usually a slight dark mask through the eye. Bill is massive, horn-coloured to pinkish; tip darker pink or orange. Immatures almost uniformly dark. Wingspan 2–2.2 m.

VOICE Deep throaty or guttural sounds, and a laughing series of 'hu-hu-hu-hu-'.

HABITAT Southern oceans. Adult birds not often seen on Australian seas; the dark immatures much more common, but very like immatures of Southern Giant-Petrel.

BREEDING Breeds July–February; on subantarctic islands including Macquarie Island. Tends to arrive off Australian coasts and breed earlier than Southern Giant-Petrel. Nest is also similar, one white egg. Interbreeding of Northern and Southern Giant-Petrels recorded.

RANGE Southern Australian coasts; mid-west coast to south-eastern Queensland.

STATUS Uncommon to rare; not recognized as a separate species until 1966.

▶ See also page
251

CAPE PETREL

14

Daption capense   Procellariidae

OTHER NAMES Black-and-white Petrel, Pied Petrel, Pintado, Cape Fulmar, Cape Prion

RECOGNITION A small, plump-bodied petrel with back, rump and wings conspicuously chequered with large sooty-black spots and patches. Head, nape and back of neck sooty blackish-brown; tail white with broad dark tip. Underparts white, except dark chin and dark margins to underwing. Amount of black on back and upperwing varies. Flight fast and close to the waves, with quick-beating wings; often dives; frequently follows ships. 35–40 cm.

VOICE Birds in feeding flocks at sea give harsh cackling calls. At breeding sites, prolonged whirring 'cooo' sounds.

HABITAT Oceans and seas; probably most often seen well offshore along the edge of the Continental Shelf. Sometimes scavenges close inshore.

BREEDING Breeds in summer, October–April; on Antarctic coast and on subantarctic islands. Nest is a shallow scrape in stone debris, usually situated between boulders, or on a rock ledge; in colonies. One white egg.

RANGE Southern Australian coasts; North West Cape (WA) to south-eastern Queensland, April–May.

STATUS Common; regular visitor.

▶ See also page 251

GREAT-WINGED PETREL

Pterodroma macroptera   Procellariidae

OTHER NAMES Great-winged Fulmar, Long-winged Fulmar, Grey-faced Fulmar, Grey-faced Petrel, Muttonbird

RECOGNITION Entirely blackish-brown or black, with long narrow wings that in flight are curved forward to the bend of the wing then backswept to fine-pointed wingtips. Bill short, deep, black, face pale around base of bill, more distinctly so on New Zealand subspecies *gouldi* (Grey-faced Petrel). Sometimes in flocks; flight swift and powerful, wheeling and swooping. Takes little notice of ships. Diet includes squid. Wingspan 1 m; length 42 cm.

VOICE Squeaky calls, like newly-hatched chicks, often preceded by soft sounds, 'keeoor, kik-kik-kik-'. In courtship, deep braying, possibly from male.

HABITAT Oceanic; mainly frequenting the cool temperate and colder subantarctic waters. Sometimes blown inshore during winter gales.

BREEDING May–November. Breeds subantarctic, New Zealand, south coast islands of Western Australia including Eclipse and Bald islands, some islands of Recherche Archipelago. Nest is depression under bushes, rocks, or in a short burrow. One white egg.

RANGE Southern oceans, coasts of south-western and south-eastern Australia, and Tasmania.

STATUS Moderately common; subspecies *gouldi* an uncommon visitor.

▶ See also pages 46 47

WHITE-HEADED PETREL

Pterodroma lessonii   Procellariidae

OTHER NAME White-headed Fulmar

RECOGNITION A large petrel, white on the head and underside of the body blending to pale grey on the nape and mid-grey on the back. Wings dark grey above and below, with flight feathers near-black; rump and

Broad-billed Prion bill

Lesser Broad-billed Prion bill

Slender-billed Prion bill

20 **Antarctic Prion** *Pachyptila desolata*
21 **Slender-billed Prion** *Pachyptila belcheri*
23 **Streaked Shearwater** *Calonectris leucomelas*
36 **Masked Booby** *Sula dactylatra*
37 **Brown Booby** *Sula leucogaster*
190 **Great Skua** *Stercorarius skua*
191 **Arctic Jaeger** *Stercorarius parasiticus*
192 **Pomarine Jaeger** *Stercorarius pomarinus*

tail pale grey. A dark patch through and just below the eye. Eye brown; bill black; legs flesh-pink. Fast, wheeling flight, showing long, narrow, pointed, very dark wings, in contrast with white head and underbody. Wingspan 1 m.

VOICE Similar to Great-winged Petrel.

HABITAT Oceanic; most sightings being of birds well out to sea, usually at the edge of the Continental Shelf. Feeds mainly upon squid.

BREEDING Breeds in summer on islands, including Kerguelen, in the southern Indian Ocean, and islands of the New Zealand region. A single egg is laid in a grass-lined chamber at the end of a tunnel about 1 m long.

RANGE Southern Australia; to north-west of Western Australia and north of New South Wales.

STATUS Uncommon; usually a winter visitor; either well offshore or beachwashed specimens.

▶ See also page *251*

17 KERGUELEN PETREL

Pterodroma brevirostris   Procellariidae

OTHER NAMES Little Black Petrel, Short-billed Petrel

RECOGNITION Overall dark slaty-grey, with short bill. Face mottled grey; darker about the eyes. The leading edge of the uppersurface of the wings, almost out to the bend of the wing, is finely scalloped with white, looking grey in the distance. In flight has quick wingbeats and keeps high above the waves. Fish and squid appear to be the main food. Wingspan 85 cm.

VOICE Not recorded.

HABITAT Oceanic. Sightings at sea suggest a circumpolar movement, ranging farther north in winter. Most records along coasts are of storm-blown birds.

BREEDING September–March. Breeds on a few subantarctic islands of southern Pacific and southern Indian oceans. Nest is a burrow. One white egg.

RANGE Southern Australian waters; north to Fremantle (WA), and to New South Wales coast.

STATUS In some winters, moderately common off parts of coast.

▶ See also page *251*

18 GOULD'S PETREL

Pterodroma leucoptera   Procellariidae

OTHER NAMES White-winged Petrel, White-winged Fulmar

RECOGNITION Upperparts slaty-black, including the entire uppersurface of the wings and tail; underparts white. A distinctive head pattern: forehead white; crown, eye patch and sides of neck slaty-black. In flight, the white of the underwing is outlined in black; with the dark leading edge curving inwards from the leading edge, approaching the body diagonally. Eye brown; bill black; legs flesh-coloured. Wingspan 71 cm; length 31 cm.

VOICE In flight around the nest colony, a high 'ti-ti-ti-ti-'. At nest, squeaky high 'peee-peee-peee-peeoo', and also low tremulous growl.

HABITAT Oceans, islands.

BREEDING The Australian (nominate) subspecies breeds only at Cabbage Tree Island off Port Stephens (NSW). Present at nest island October–April, breeding in summer. Nest often among rocks, or under fallen palm fronds. One white egg.

RANGE Usually not far from the breeding grounds.

STATUS Rare.

▶ See also pages *113 117*

19 LESSER BROAD-BILLED PRION

Pachyptila salvini   Procellariidae

OTHER NAMES Salvin's Prion, Medium-billed Prion, Marion Island Prion

RECOGNITION A large prion. Upperparts grey; steep high forehead; face white; dark line through eye. The bill is broad, boat-shaped from above, near black, and with the comb-like serrated edge or lamellae visible even with the bill closed. In flight, uppersurface of wings grey, with black leading edge from wingtips to bend of wing, then diagonally across inner-wings forming a wide M. Length 28 cm. The Broad-billed Prion (*Pachyptila vittata*) resembles the Lesser Broad-billed Prion but is larger. Upperparts similarly grey but darker on forehead, crown and nape; prominent white eyebrow. The bill is extremely broad and, when closed, reveals more obviously the comb-like lamellae. It is an infrequent visitor to southern coasts.

VOICE A crooning but rasping call, 'ku-a, ku-a, ku-a kuk', this repeated several times, sometimes with variations.

HABITAT Subantarctic oceans and seas. Although very like the Broad-billed Prion, it is on separate breeding grounds for part of the year.

BREEDING Breeds in southern Indian Ocean on Marion and Crozet islands. Nesting November–March. The single white egg is laid in a burrow. After breeding, these

prions disperse widely, not returning to the breeding grounds until October.

RANGE Southern Australian seas during winter dispersal.

STATUS Common offshore; coastal records are generally of beachwashed birds.

▶ See also page *253*

20 ANTARCTIC PRION

Pachyptila desolata   Procellariidae

OTHER NAMES Dove Prion, Banks's Dove-petrel, Blue Dove-petrel, Snowbird

RECOGNITION Almost identical at sea to the Lesser Broad-billed Prion, but in the hand can be seen to have narrower bill with larger nail at tip, straighter sides, and little of the lamellae exposed when bill is shut. Has a bolder eye-stripe, and less distinct white eyebrow than the other prions. Sides of neck are dusky, as a partial collar, which is not the case with the Slender-billed Prion. 25–30 cm.

VOICE In flight, and from within the burrow, makes a cooing sound expressed as 'kur-u-kur-atcha'.

HABITAT Oceanic. Ranges north between 66° and 35°S; and sometimes north to equator.

BREEDING December–April. Antarctic and subantarctic islands, including Kerguelen, South Orkney, South Georgia, Heard, Auckland, and Macquarie islands. Nest is a burrow, often first through deep snow to reach soil. One white egg.

RANGE Offshore, and beachwashed after storms; south-western and south-eastern Australia.

STATUS One of the most common subantarctic seabirds.

▶ See also page *253*

21 SLENDER-BILLED PRION

Pachyptila belcheri   Procellariidae

OTHER NAMES Narrow-billed Prion, Thin-billed Prion

RECOGNITION Very much like Antarctic, Broad-billed and Lesser Broad-billed Prions, but with much narrower bill, sides of bill straight, and when closed, comb-like lamellae not exposed; broader white eyebrow line; and more white about the face. The dark M-shaped marking across the uppersurface of the wings is less distinct. Said to feed mostly at night, probably taking luminous plankton from the surface. 25 cm.

VOICE Not known.

HABITAT Oceanic. South to the Antarctic pack-ice, and north to about 30°S.

BREEDING Summer months, October–March. Breeds only on Kerguelen, Falkland and Bouvet islands, excavating a burrow in which a single white egg is laid.

RANGE Southern Australian coasts; mostly beachwashed specimens after storms.

STATUS Uncommon on Australian seas; rare on coasts.

▶ See also page 253

FAIRY PRION

Pachyptila turtur   Procellariidae

OTHER NAMES Dove Petrel, Blue Petrel, Fairy Dove-petrel, Short-billed Prion

RECOGNITION The smallest of the prions. Upperparts light blue-grey; face white with grey eye-stripe; tail broadly tipped blackish. Bill comparatively short, narrow, with short, robust hook, separated only narrowly from the nasal tubes. Dark M-pattern across grey of upperwing. Can be distinguished from the Fulmar Prion (*Pachyptila crassirostris*), which also has a very broad black tail-band, by the lighter crown and, usually, more bulbous bill of the latter. The Fulmar Prion is a rare vagrant to Australian waters. 23–28 cm.

VOICE Soft, even, quick cooing sounds, 'kuk-kuk-kooer, kuk-kuk-kooer' a number of times in rapid succession.

HABITAT Oceanic. Feeds on plankton, small crustaceans, and squid; from the surface of the sea; probably mostly at night.

BREEDING The only prion to breed in Australia, with a number of colonies on Bass Strait islands and on islands round the Tasmanian coast; also on islands of southern Indian and Atlantic oceans. Nest is a burrow in soft soil. One white egg.

RANGE Seas and coasts of south-eastern Australia and westwards to south-western Australia.

STATUS Common offshore south-eastern Australia, Eyre Peninsula to south-eastern Queensland, uncommon in Western Australia.

▶ See also pages 45 145

STREAKED SHEARWATER

Calonectris leucomelas   Procellariidae

RECOGNITION The largest of the Australian shearwaters. Upperparts grey-brown, with lighter scalloping; flight feathers and tail darker grey; head white, with dark streaks on the crown; nape dark grey. Underparts white, including white underwing, with dark leading edge, black primaries and secondaries. Tail-tip rounded. In flight, straight-winged; gliding, albatross-like. Single birds, groups, sometimes flocks of up to 70 birds recorded. 50 cm.

VOICE Not recorded.

HABITAT Oceanic. Feeds upon schools of small fish, sometimes in company with terns and other seabirds.

BREEDING Breeds on islands of the north-west Pacific.

RANGE Seas and coasts of northern and north-western Australia.

STATUS Until 1980 considered a rare vagrant; fairly common off northern coasts.

▶ See also page 253

FLESHY-FOOTED SHEARWATER

Puffinus carneipes   Procellariidae

OTHER NAMES Pale-footed Shearwater, Pale-footed Petrel, Flesh-footed Shearwater, Big Muttonbird

RECOGNITION A large shearwater, with blackish-brown plumage overall; heavy straw-coloured or fleshy-pink, black-tipped bill; pale pink legs and feet. Undersurfaces entirely dark brown; tail short, rounded, longer than the trailing feet. In flight, tends to hold wings straight; slow stiff-winged flapping action; often glides near surface. Will form large rafts of birds where food is concentrated, diving from surface; attends fishing boats. 45 cm.

VOICE A loud 'kukee-arrgh', rapidly repeated with rising and diminishing intensity.

HABITAT Oceanic and coastal. Feeds on small fish, crustaceans, squid. These birds spend the southern winter off Japan, Korea and in the north-western Indian Ocean.

BREEDING Coastal islands of south-western Western Australia, New Zealand, Lord Howe Island and South America. Nest is a burrow, with chamber lined with pieces of dry vegetation. The single white egg is laid late November–early December, and birds leave the colonies April–May.

RANGE In Australian waters, the southern coasts; approximately Shark Bay to southern Queensland.

STATUS Common during the warmer months; absent April–September.

▶ See also pages 236 239

WEDGE-TAILED SHEARWATER

Puffinus pacificus   Procellariidae

OTHER NAMES Little Muttonbird, Wedge-tailed Muttonbird, Wedge-tailed Petrel

RECOGNITION Entirely blackish-brown (except that some, especially from Western Australia, have whitish breast), with large wedge-shaped tail. In flight, the tail appears pointed. Even when the tail is not clearly visible, this species can be distinguished by its buoyant drifting flight, on broad wings that are held with the wrists well forward. This species has a much lighter body than the larger shearwaters of southern seas. 43 cm.

VOICE Crooning, wailing sounds, especially at night. The call begins softly, ends with a gasping or gurgling sound: 'ka-whoooo-agh', repeatedly.

HABITAT Oceanic and coastal.

BREEDING October–April. In large and crowded colonies, where the ground becomes honeycombed with burrows; sometimes among rocks, low bushes, or forest canopy. A single white egg is laid. Breeding islands on west and east coasts of Australia.

RANGE West and east coasts; rare or vagrant north and south coasts.

STATUS Common in breeding range.

▶ See also pages 71 82 230 244 257

SOOTY SHEARWATER

Puffinus griseus   Procellariidae

OTHER NAMES Sombre Shearwater, Ghost Bird, King Muttonbird, Sombre Petrel

RECOGNITION Dark brown overall, except underwing linings which are whitish or silvery. This species shares colonies with the Wedge-tailed and Short-tailed shearwaters, from which it can be separated by the light underwing; longer bill; impression of slower flight; slimmer body. Some Sooty species have darker underwings, however, while some Short-tailed shearwaters have light underwings. 46–53 cm.

VOICE A deep even rhythmic sound, lower-pitched and slower than that of the Short-tailed Shearwater.

HABITAT Coasts and oceans. Feeds where small cephalopods are concentrated at the surface. Subantarctic oceans generally. Winters north of equator.

BREEDING November–April. In Australia breeds on a number of islands of the south-east coasts from Little Broughton Island to southern Tasmania. Always breeds in mixed colonies with Wedge-tailed or Short-tailed shearwaters. Nest is a burrow. One white egg.

RANGE South-eastern Australia; vagrant westwards to South Australia and south-west of Western Australia.

STATUS Common in south-east in breeding season. Abundant in New Zealand region.

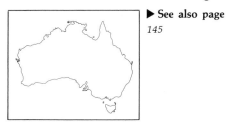

▶ See also page 145

27 SHORT-TAILED SHEARWATER

Puffinus tenuirostris Procellariidae

OTHER NAMES Muttonbird, Bonaparte's Shearwater, Short-tailed Petrel, Seabird

RECOGNITION Plumage is brownish-black overall, with underwings slightly paler. Tail short and rounded. In flight, the feet trail behind the tail-tip; bursts of rapid wingbeats interspersed with short glides. Usually in large flocks, often of huge numbers of birds, which travel well offshore to feed on krill and small squid. The most abundant of Australian shearwaters. About 500 000 chicks are taken annually by the muttonbird industry. 39–43 cm.

VOICE Usually calls from ground or burrow, rarely while in flight; a throaty, rapid 'coo-roo-ra, coo-roo-ra', repeated, rising in tempo and pitch.

HABITAT Coast, islands, oceans. The annual migration takes this species from Australian breeding islands to the north Pacific, returning to colonies late September.

BREEDING November–April. All known breeding colonies are in the Australian region, on islands off coast of New South Wales, Bass Strait, around Tasmania, and South Australia. Nest is a burrow where the nest chamber is lined with grass and leaves. One white egg.

RANGE Coast and seas of southern Australia; south-eastern Queensland to south-west of Western Australia.

STATUS Abundant in south-east; uncommon northern New South Wales and south-eastern Queensland; rare south-west of Western Australia.

▶ See also pages 125 *145* 151 163 255

28 FLUTTERING SHEARWATER

Puffinus gavia Procellariidae

OTHER NAMES Forster's Shearwater, Brown-backed Petrel, Hutton's Shearwater

RECOGNITION Upperparts entirely black or brownish-black; extending downwards on the face to include the eye, and on the sides of the neck to form a partial collar. Underparts white; underwing white except innerparts (axillaries) smudged brown. In flight, alternates between rapid wingbeats

and short glides, keeping close to surface; feet trail slightly behind the tail. Hutton's Shearwater (*Puffinus huttoni*) is almost identical but has browner underwings. 33–37 cm.

VOICE Loud, rapidly repeated 'ka-howo-ooo', the last syllable very soft.

HABITAT Mainly coastal; occasionally the open ocean.

BREEDING August–March, on New Zealand offshore islands, and Chatham Islands. Nest is a burrow in soft soil, lined with dry plant materials and feathers. One white egg. Disperses widely after breeding, reaching Australian waters.

RANGE Mainly south-east coast, and Tasmania.

STATUS Common. Subspecies *huttoni* less common.

▶ See also page 117

29 LITTLE SHEARWATER

Puffinus assimilis Procellariidae

OTHER NAMES Allied Shearwater, Dusky Shearwater, Gould's Shearwater, Gould's Petrel

RECOGNITION A small petrel, with black upperparts, and white underparts. Dark eye is conspicuous in white face. Underwings white narrowly edged black; eye dark brown; bill blackish; legs and feet cobalt-blue with pink tinge to webs. In flight, has plump body silhouette; short fast-beating wings. Often on water, singly or in flocks. Most likely to be confused with Audubon's Shearwater, a possible vagrant to Australian seas. 28 cm.

VOICE Often calls from within the nest burrow; a relatively high-pitched rapid, wheezy 'wah-i-wha-i-wah-oooo', of varied structure and intensity.

HABITAT Coastal; near breeding colony islands most of the year. Some dispersal well out to sea at times. Breeds south and west coasts of Western Australia.

BREEDING Birds return to breeding sites around February, with activity at the colony increasing until egg-laying in June–July; chicks are fledged by late October. Most of the activity is at night, with birds at sea or in burrows during day.

RANGE South-western to south-eastern Australia. Sedentary.

STATUS Moderately common in south-west; uncommon in south-east.

▶ See also pages 236 *239* 244

Oceanitidae Family of 21 species 7 in Australia, 1 breeding

Storm-petrels differ from the closely related true petrels in having shorter wings and longer legs; they are the smallest of the petrels, less than 25 cm in length. The nasal tube is undivided. Storm-petrels typically patter over the waves, the long legs dangling to touch the water as they feed on various surface micro-organisms.

30 WILSON'S STORM-PETREL

Oceanites oceanicus Oceanitidae

OTHER NAMES Mother Carey's Chicken, Flat-clawed Storm-Petrel, Yellow-webbed Storm-Petrel

RECOGNITION Swallow-sized; butterfly-like flight, skipping erratically across the wave-tops. Upperparts brownish-black, except rump which is white. In flight, lighter brown edges to the wing-coverts form a pale diagonal bar on each inner-wing; long yellow webbed legs trail well behind the tail. The near-black tail is slightly forked appearing almost square-cut when fully spread. Back-curved slender wings, brownish beneath. 15–19 cm.

VOICE Calls at the nest, repeated soft nasal 'aaark-aaark'.

HABITAT Oceanic. Wanders far over the globe, from Antarctic and subantarctic to northern Pacific, northern Indian and northern Atlantic oceans.

BREEDING Summer, on Antarctic and subantarctic oceans. The nest is a short burrow, or among boulders. The single white egg is lightly spotted red-brown, more heavily round the broader end.

RANGE All Australian coasts except Queensland and Gulf of Carpentaria.

STATUS One of the most common Antarctic birds; common in north-western Australian seas.

▶ See also page 257

31 WHITE-FACED STORM-PETREL

Pelagodroma marina Oceanitidae

OTHER NAMES White-breasted Storm-Petrel, Frigate-Petrel

RECOGNITION Upperparts are grey-brown; underparts white. The only storm-petrel with a white forehead and face. Broad dark eye-stripe. In flight, white underwings with dark-brown flight feathers; tail dark, square-cut. Legs and webbed feet yellow, trail behind tail. Erratic flight, appearing to dance across the wave-tops, fluttering and dipping to pick up food from the surface; the long legs often dangling into the water. Floats high when over water. 20 cm.

VOICE In breeding colonies, calls are soft repeated 'peoo-peooo-peooo'. The species is a nocturnal visitor to the breeding colonies.

HABITAT Oceanic; coastal islands in breeding season. Out of the breeding season the Australian populations probably migrate into the northern Indian Ocean.

BREEDING The only species of storm-petrel to breed in Australian waters, on many islands around the southern coast from Houtman Abrolhos on west coast to northern New South Wales on the east coast. Nest usually a burrow. One white egg, spotted red-brown.

RANGE In Australia, mid-west coast, southern coasts, to mid-east coast.

STATUS Common in regions of breeding islands.

▶ See also pages
46 47 151 164 244

DIVING-PETRELS

**Pelecanoididae Family of 5 species
2 in Australia, 1 breeding**

A small family of dumpy, short-winged, short-tailed birds that have become highly adapted to underwater 'flight'. They plunge into the waves and use their wings like penguin flippers with up-and-down beating as if flying through the air, then emerge to continue in almost unbroken flight between waves before plunging back into the sea. Their airborne flights are short, with rapidly-beating wings.

COMMON DIVING-PETREL

Pelecanoides urinatrix   Pelecanoididae

OTHER NAMES Smaller Diving-Petrel, Teetee, Diving-Petrel

RECOGNITION Very small, dumpy or tubby bodied; black upperparts; white underparts, underwings silvery. In flight, fast-beating wings, with short glide before plunging into the sea; emerges from water like a flying-fish, for a short bumblebee-like flight before diving again into the waves. It 'flies' through water using its wings as flippers, like a penguin. Often bursts from the water ahead of a boat; on surface, floats low. 20 cm.

VOICE A pleasant and distinctive rising 'ku, ku-aaa'. Other sounds reported at breeding grounds include a nasal 'kerraa-ek', rapid 'ek-ek-ek-'.

HABITAT Oceanic; large bays, inshore

*White-tailed Tropic Bird

waters near breeding grounds. Prey consists mainly of small fish and crustaceans.

BREEDING July–December; on islands of Bass Strait, New Zealand and subantarctic. Nest is a short burrow, in soft soil, under tussock-grass cover or forest canopy. A single white egg. Nocturnal traffic of adults to and from breeding grounds.

RANGE Mainly south-eastern Australia; some beachwashed specimens in the

10 Yellow-nosed Albatross *Diomedea chlororhynchos*
25 Wedge-tailed Shearwater *Puffinus pacificus*
30 Wilson's Storm-Petrel *Oceanites oceanicus*
34 Australasian Gannet *Morus serrator*
37 Brown Booby *Sula leucogaster*
40 Great Cormorant *Phalacrocorax carbo*
44 Great Frigatebird *Fregata minor*

*Occasional visitor to Australian waters

south-west of Western Australia. Mainly sedentary.

STATUS Common in Bass Strait; rare elsewhere.

▶ See also pages
145 151

PELICANS

**Pelecanidae Family of 8 species
1 in Australia, 1 breeding, 1 endemic**

One of the best known of birds, with huge pouched bill, and heavy body carried on short stumpy legs. The group is unusual in having four, rather than the usual three, toes linked by webs. The large gular pouch is bare of feathers, and effectively radiates heat as a cooling mechanism in hot weather. Pelicans fish in shallow waters, often in coordinated flocks, but spend much of their time sunning, preening or sleeping on mudbanks.

33 AUSTRALIAN PELICAN
Pelecanus conspicillatus

---

33 AUSTRALIAN PELICAN

Pelecanus conspicillatus   Pelecanidae
OTHER NAMES Australasian Pelican, Spectacled Pelican

RECOGNITION Very large, black-and-white plumaged bird with massive straight bill. Primaries, shoulders, rump, and tail black, the remainder white; often some grey on the head. Bill and bill-pouch pinkish. In flight, has head drawn back on the breast. Runs across the water to get airborne, then as soon as uplifting air is found, soars on broad flat wings, often to great heights. Often in large flocks, may then fish cooperatively, in formation. 1.5–1.9 m.

VOICE Usually silent; at-most, some grunting sounds, except at breeding grounds where it has a variety of deep resonant sounds, often in display.

HABITAT Almost any large area of sheltered fresh or salt water; coastal or inland, estuaries, lakes, large rivers, temporarily flooded land.

BREEDING All months; dependent upon rainfall in the interior. Usually nests in colonies on islands, sometimes on shrubbery over water. Two to four white eggs; incubation takes 32–35 days; chicks are attended for about 14 weeks.

RANGE Throughout Australia in suitable habitat. Vagrant to New Guinea; accidental in New Zealand and Indonesia. Nomadic.

STATUS Common.

▶ See also pages
136 137 138 173
184

GANNETS, BOOBIES

**Sulidae Family of 9 species
5 in Australia, 4 breeding**

These large-billed seabirds hunt in spectacular vertical dives, from heights of 20 m or more, to take fish well below the surface. The skull has no orthodox nasal opening. Breathing is accomplished via the mouth, which is extended well back beyond the eye, where the protecting bill has a section remaining open. Except when on land to breed, these are birds of the shallower coastal seas, and may sometimes be sighted from headlands.

34 AUSTRALASIAN GANNET

Morus serrator   Sulidae
OTHER NAMES Australian Gannet, Diver, Booby, Solan Goose

RECOGNITION Overall plumage colour white, with golden yellow head, black flight feathers and inner-tail feathers. Has a sleek streamlined shape, with the lines of the straight, evenly-tapering bill blending almost unbroken into the smooth contours of head and body. When fishing, these birds plunge into the sea often from a great height. Immatures: patchy grey-brown and whitish, finely speckled white; develop adult plumage in two years. 82–90 cm.

VOICE Silent at sea, but extremely noisy at the nesting grounds; the usual call being a loud, repeated 'urragh', and other raucous sounds.

HABITAT Oceans, bays. Feeds at sea, coming ashore on islands in the breeding season, and sometimes to rest on steep slopes or calm inshore waters.

BREEDING October–May. There are large breeding colonies on islets around main islands of New Zealand and on a number of sites on Victorian coast, Bass Strait and Tasmanian coast. Nest is a mound of guano and debris. A single white egg is laid.

RANGE Southern Australian coasts; north to about the Tropic of Capricorn on east and west coasts.

STATUS Common; widespread southern coasts in summer; farther north in winter.

▶ See also page
257

35 RED-FOOTED BOOBY

Sula sula   Sulidae
OTHER NAMES Red-footed Gannet, Red-legged Gannet

RECOGNITION Two colour phases, and intermediates. White phase has dominantly white plumage, with a slight yellow tint on head and black flight feathers. Dark phase has grey-brown head and body, with white rump, lower belly and tail. Intermediate phase has light brown on head, neck and breast; remainder of body white; wings brown. All have bright pink or red legs and feet; large straight blue-grey bill, becoming pink at base. Immatures wholly brown. 66–79 cm.

VOICE A harsh 'karr-urrk, karr-urrk' in vicinity of nest; no difference evident between calls of male and female.

HABITAT Oceanic. Found throughout the year near the breeding colonies, moving out to sea in search of fish and squid. Some dispersal after breeding.

BREEDING April–October. This tropical species breeds on islands of Indian, Atlantic and Pacific oceans. Nests in colonies, building a nest of sticks in a low tree or shrub, or sometimes on the ground. One white egg.

RANGE Australian coastal islands; reefs of north-eastern Queensland, north-west of Western Australia.

STATUS Uncommon; localized occurrence.

► See also pages
46 47 97

MASKED BOOBY

Sula dactylatra **Sulidae**

OTHER NAMES Blue-faced Booby, Gannet, White Booby, Masked Gannet

RECOGNITION A large booby, with white plumage except for black flight feathers and tail. The face is black round the base of the bill and surrounding the eye. The massive, straight bill is yellow, darkening to black towards the base. Eye is golden yellow; legs and feet blue-grey or tinged yellow. Female is similar, but with a duller, greenish-yellow bill. Immatures have brown head, flight feathers and tail; remainder mottled brownish-white. 73–86 cm.

VOICE At the nest, the calls of the male are reported to be higher-pitched than those of the female.

HABITAT Oceanic; foraging farther off-shore and venturing farther south than other boobies, taking mainly flying fish and squid.

BREEDING All months; activity peaking in spring, and diminishing during the summer cyclone season. In Australian region, breeds on islands of north-west and north-east coasts. Nest is a scrape on ground; in widely spaced colonies. Two pale blue eggs.

RANGE North-west and north-east Australian coasts.

STATUS Moderately common offshore in breeding range; uncommon inshore.

► See also pages
81 97 218 219 253

BROWN BOOBY

Sula leucogaster **Sulidae**

OTHER NAMES Booby, Brown Gannet

RECOGNITION A smaller booby, with dark-brown plumage on upperparts; and white lower breast, belly, undertail and underwing-coverts; the demarcation between brown and white being sharply defined. In flight, white of underwing encircled by dark brown of wing's leading edge, and flight feathers. Naked skin of face, eye-ring, and throat, blue; bill pale yellow shading to blue at the base. Female: bill and face pale yellow. Immatures have grey underparts. 71–76 cm.

VOICE In the vicinity of the nest a harsh quacking by the female and a higher-pitched hissing sound from the male.

HABITAT Oceanic; often foraging for fish and squid hundreds of kilometres out to sea. Also inshore waters; estuaries, bays, harbours.

BREEDING All months; peak in autumn, reduced activity in summer. In Australian region, breeds on offshore islands, reefs of north-west of Western Australia and eastern Queensland coast. Nest may be a scrape on ground, or often built up with sticks. Two to three pale green eggs.

RANGE Tropical. Northern Australian seas and coasts; north-west of Western Australia to north of New South Wales.

STATUS Common in north; abundant in breeding range.

► See also pages
71 81 97 110 208
218 219 253 257

DARTERS

Anhingidae Family of 2 species
1 in Australia, 1 breeding

The extremely long, snake-like, but kinked neck immediately identifies the darters. These birds are sometimes placed in the cormorant family, an evolutionary offshoot based upon a specialized way of fishing. Like the cormorants, their plumage is not waterproof, and much time is spent with wings outstretched, drying. Unlike the cormorants, the darters have straight, sharp-pointed bills.

DARTER

Anhinga melanogaster **Anhingidae**

OTHER NAMES Snakebird, Diver, Needle-beaked Shag

RECOGNITION A large blackish waterbird, with extremely long, kinked, snake-like neck, and straight needle-point bill. Male is dark grey to glossy black with white stripe through eye and along side of neck; buff streaks on upperwing-coverts; naked skin round eye and on throat yellow; yellowish bill; pinkish-grey feet. Female has grey-brown upperparts; pale grey underparts; and white neck stripe is dark-edged. Immatures like female, no neck stripe. 86–94 cm.

VOICE Metallic clicking sounds; near the nest, various harsh sounds, raucous staccato cacklings, and rattling noises.

HABITAT A variety of wetlands, fresh and salt; including inlets and tidal estuaries, but not open sea; usually rivers, lakes, lagoons, swamps.

BREEDING September–March. Nest is a bulky platform usually lined with leaves, in a tree in water, or on a limb over water,

often in a small colony, and may be used for several years. Four to six white eggs with a slight greenish tinge.

RANGE Africa, Asia, Australasia. Throughout Australia in suitable habitat. Local subspecies extends to New Guinea.

STATUS Moderately common, but patchy.

► See also pages
135 137 161 174
183 185 198

38 DARTER *Anhinga melanogaster*

CORMORANTS, SHAGS

Phalacrocoracidae Family of about
29–33 species
5 in Australia, 5 breeding, 1 endemic

Long-necked birds which dive and swim for fish. The large webbed feet are placed far back on the body for greatest efficiency underwater, but compel an upright stance and shuffling walk. As with darters, the plumage is not waterproof. Tails are short, and the feathers almost spiky; bills are long and straight, with a hooked tip. Both marine and inland waters are utilized.

BLACK-FACED SHAG

Leucocarbo fuscescens **Phalacrocoracidae**

OTHER NAMES Black-faced Cormorant, Black-and-white Shag, White-breasted Shag

RECOGNITION Non-breeding plumage: upperparts black, with the black of the crown reaching down to the eye; underparts white, including lower face, almost up to the eye. Bare skin round base of bill and eye is black; bill dark grey. There is a black bar down the side of the flank to the dark-grey legs. Breeding plumage: a dense cover of white nuptial plumes on back of neck, rump and thighs. Immatures: browner with buff face; brown-blotched underparts. 61–68 cm.

VOICE Usually silent, but in breeding colonies male has loud guttural croaking calls; female gives soft hoarse hissing sounds.

HABITAT Coastal; offshore waters, bays and inlets, islands, rock stacks. Fishing is by diving, the bird staying submerged for half a minute or longer.

BREEDING September–January; in colonies. Breeds on offshore islands of southern Australian coasts, especially Bass Strait, Victoria to South Australia, and south coast of Western Australia. Nest is a mound of seaweed and other plant debris, on rock close to sea. Three to five pale green eggs.

RANGE Southern Australian coasts and seas; south-west corner of Western Australia to south-eastern New South Wales. Sedentary.

STATUS Common in breeding range; otherwise uncommon. Endemic.

▶ See also pages
45 151 156 *157*

40 GREAT CORMORANT

Phalacrocorax carbo Phalacrocoracidae
OTHER NAMES Black Cormorant, Big Black Cormorant, Black Shag, Shag

RECOGNITION Largest of cormorants, with wingspan up to 1.5 m. Non-breeding plumage: entirely black; bare skin of face and throat pouch is deep yellow. Bill grey; legs and feet black. Breeding plumage: black area is more glossy, and shows white lines of nuptial plumes on sides of neck and lower flanks. Immatures: more brownish; duller yellow on face; centre of neck and breast dull white. Flight strong, and direct; in V formation or drawn-out line. 71–90 cm.

VOICE Usually silent; noisy when breeding. Male has loud raucous calls; female makes hoarse hissing sounds, but calls like male after egg-laying.

HABITAT Coastal waters, bays, estuaries, large rivers; also on some of the more extensive freshwater habitats — lakes, rivers, dams, floodwaters.

BREEDING All months; usually spring and autumn, but varies depending upon food supplies. Breeds in large or small colonies on lakes, estuaries. Nest of sticks, in trees or shrubs, sometimes on ground. Three to four limy, pale green eggs.

RANGE Throughout Australia in suitable habitat. Sedentary and nomadic.

STATUS Common; non-breeding and uncommon visitor to far north. Cosmopolitan species.

▶ See also pages
45 161 *257*

41 PIED CORMORANT

Phalacrocorax varius Phalacrocoracidae
OTHER NAMES Yellow-faced Cormorant, Black-and-White Shag, Diver

RECOGNITION A large black-and-white cormorant. Upperparts black; from forehead across crown and nape, to entire back, wings and tail. Underparts white, including the face up to eyebrow level, and back to the sides of the neck. There is a conspicuous patch of orange or deep yellow bare skin down the front of the face between the base of bill and eye. There is a black patch down the flanks, visible when perched. Eye green; bill grey; legs black. 66–80 cm.

VOICE Usually silent except in the breeding colony, when it utters various cackling and croaking sounds, as when arriving at nest.

HABITAT Coastal waters, estuaries, bays, lakes, rivers, mangrove channels. Favours

shallower waters and gently sloping shorelines.

BREEDING Throughout the year, depending upon food supply; usually in autumn in southern Australia. The nest of sticks and marine debris is built in a tree, often a mangrove, occasionally on ground. Three to five white eggs, tinged green.

RANGE Coastal Australian inland waters. Rare in Tasmania. Also in New Zealand. Nomadic or sedentary.

STATUS Common.

▶ See also pages
124 161 173 *191*
199 230 261

42 LITTLE BLACK CORMORANT

Phalacrocorax sulcirostris
                              Phalacrocoracidae
OTHER NAME Little Black Shag

RECOGNITION A small cormorant, with black plumage. Bare skin of face black; bill dark grey. Breeding plumage: white nuptial plumes appear as white flecks, on the side of the head behind the eye, and on the neck. Immatures have brown plumage, with some white patches on the underparts. In flight, has faster wingbeats than the larger Great Cormorant. Flocks work

41 PIED CORMORANT *Phalacrocorax varius*

in unison herding schools of fish. 58–63 cm.

VOICE Generally silent; guttural and ticking sounds at nest, possibly by male alone.

HABITAT Coastal waters, inlets, bays, mangroves; also inland, on fresh waters of lakes and rivers, swamps.

BREEDING Throughout the year; depending upon food supply. Nests in colonies, often with other cormorants, spoonbills, or herons. The nest is a platform of sticks and leaves, over water. Four limy, greenish-white eggs.

RANGE Throughout Australia in suitable habitats; also in Indonesia, New Guinea and New Zealand. Usually sedentary. Nomadic to dry inland regions.

STATUS Common.

▶ See also pages
79 136 161 183 185

LITTLE PIED CORMORANT

Phalacrocorax melanoleucos
Phalacrocoracidae

OTHER NAMES Frilled Shag, Little Black-and-white Cormorant, Little Black-and-white Shag

RECOGNITION Smallest of Australian cormorants. Non-breeding plumage: upperparts black; undersurfaces white; face white to above the eye. Closely resembles Pied Cormorant, but has shorter yellow bill; no yellow on any bare skin areas about face or throat; short crest on forehead; and usually no black mark down flanks to legs. Breeding plumage: crest more noticeable; white tufts on sides of head. Immatures have black flank mark; grey bill. 58–64 cm.

VOICE Usually silent; except in breeding colonies, where it has a short croaking 'uk-uk-uk', and cooing sounds at the nest.

HABITAT Coastal waters, islands, reefs, estuaries; also great variety of inland waters, including small or temporary pools. Singly, to large flocks.

BREEDING At any time of the year; depending upon abundance of food. Nests in colonies, building a platform of sticks in a tree in, or overhanging, water. Seems to prefer a freshwater site. Two to five limy, bluish-white eggs.

RANGE Throughout Australia in suitable habitat. Also occurs in South-East Asia, New Guinea, Solomon Islands and New Zealand. Sedentary or nomadic.

STATUS Common.

▶ See also pages
79 99 136 162 185

42 **LITTLE BLACK CORMORANT** *Phalacrocorax sulcirostris*
43 **LITTLE PIED CORMORANT** *Phalacrocorax melanoleucos*

FRIGATEBIRDS

**Fregatidae Family of 5 species
3 in Australia, 2 breeding**

Large, long-winged, blackish, seabirds, with long straight but hooked-tipped bills, and deeply forked tails. Males have a patch of bare red skin at the throat, which inflates balloon-like in display. The name frigatebird derives from their piratical harassment of other seabirds forcing them to drop or disgorge food. They also snatch food from the surface, but rarely alight on the water.

GREAT FRIGATEBIRD

Fregata minor
Fregatidae

OTHER NAMES Man-of-War Bird, Man-of-War Hawk, Sea Hawk, Frigatebird

RECOGNITION Large, with a wingspan around 2 m. Plumage wholly black, with skin of naked throat patch bright red, and capable of being inflated to balloon-like shape during courtship, otherwise contracted as small red patch. In flight, brown upperwing-coverts form a bar across uppersurface of wings; long wings are bent or cranked back from the wrist. Eye brown; eye-ring black or dark blue. Female has greyish throat; white breast; red eye-ring. 86–100 cm.

VOICE Usually silent; near the nest male has a braying 'wah-ho-ho-o-o', and various rattling or clappering sounds; landing at nest, yelping calls.

HABITAT Tropical and subtropical islands and coasts. Food is obtained on the wing, often by harassing other seabirds; also catches flying fish.

BREEDING January–October; in colonies varying from a few to thousands of birds. In Australia, breeds on Raine and Quoin islands and northern Queensland coast. The nest is a platform of sticks and twigs built on top of a tree or shrub. Two glossy white eggs.

RANGE North and east coasts; approximately Darwin to Sydney; vagrant to Victoria and Western Australia. Sometimes blown to southern coasts by cyclones.

STATUS Uncommon.

▶ See also pages
97 257 262

45 LEAST FRIGATEBIRD

Fregata ariel   Fregatidae

OTHER NAMES Lesser Frigatebird, Man-of-War Bird, Sea Hawk

RECOGNITION Closely resembles the Great Frigatebird, slightly smaller with wingspan just under 2 m. The plumage is entirely blackish except for white patch on each underwing, close to the side of the body. Red throat; deeply forked tail; grey bill; black eye-ring. Female is larger, with white breast and collar, and black throat; no red throat sac; eye-ring red. Immatures have dark-brown upperparts, with light brown wingbars; and whitish head and underparts. 71–82 cm.

VOICE Usually silent; male, near nest, makes grunting and bill-rattling sounds. Fast and agile in the air; pirates some of its food from other seabirds.

HABITAT Tropical and subtropical seas, coastal waters, islands. Although a superb aerialist it cannot walk or swim but snatches prey from beach or sea.

BREEDING May–December. Large breeding colonies occur on islands of Pacific, and smaller colonies on islands and reefs of the north-western and north-eastern Australian coasts. A flat platform of sticks is placed on trees, shrubs, or ground. Two limy, white eggs.

RANGE Northern seas and coasts; North West Cape (WA) to northern New South Wales; vagrant to Victoria.

STATUS Moderately common in north; rare in south of range.

▶ See also pages
47 47 81 97 110
218 219

TROPICBIRDS

**Phaethontidae Family of 3 species
2 in Australia, 1 breeding, 1 vagrant species**

Dominantly white-plumaged, tern-like, but with long tail-streamers. The central pair of tail feathers of mature tropicbirds are greatly elongated, streaming behind in flight. At sea, they fly moderately high, and tend to be attracted to ships. The White-tailed Tropicbird is an occasional visitor to parts of the Australian coast.

46 RED-TAILED TROPICBIRD

Phaethon rubricauda   Phaethontidae

OTHER NAMES Silver Bosunbird, Red-tailed Bosunbird, Bosunbird, Bos'nbird

RECOGNITION Large tropicbird; mostly white, except black marking through eye, black shafts to the primaries, black markings on tertiary and flank feathers; the white sometimes has a slight pink tint. Tail has two very long red central streamers, doubling the total length of the bird; these may not be visible at a distance. Large red or orange bill, rarely yellow. Flies with fluttering wingbeats, diving from considerable heights. 46 cm plus tail 30–50 cm.

VOICE In flight, a rattling or ratchet-like call; at the nest, loud defensive screaming.

HABITAT Oceans, islands and coasts. Usually alone, wandering far over the oceans, feeding on fish and squid, returning annually to breeding grounds.

BREEDING Mainly spring–summer. Birds return to nest sites at beginning of breeding season, and engage in circling display flights. Nest is scrape on ground or sheltered ledge of cliff, under bushes. One light stone-coloured egg, marked brown.

RANGE Most Australian coasts except south, to where it is vagrant. Widespread Indian and Pacific oceans. Dispersive-nomadic.

STATUS Moderately common.

▶ See also pages
45 97 236 *236*

HERONS, EGRETS, BITTERNS

**Ardeidae Family of 64 species
14 in Australia, 14 breeding, 1 endemic**

This family has two major subfamilies, one the herons and egrets, the other the bitterns. All are relatively long-legged, long-necked aquatic birds, with straight dagger-like bills. The bitterns are far less well known, being secretive, usually solitary birds of dense swamp vegetation. The herons and egrets are much more gregarious, and many are colonial breeders. The birds of this family feed upon various small aquatic and terrestrial creatures.

47 GREAT-BILLED HERON

Ardea sumatrana   Ardeidae

OTHER NAMES Giant Heron, Dusky-grey Heron, Alligator-bird

RECOGNITION A very large, heavily-built heron with massive grey-brown bill, and dark grey-brown plumage. Naked skin between bill and eye is yellow; legs dark grey. In breeding season has grey plumes on nape, neck and back. Immatures overall more rust-brown, and lack plumes. Solitary and wary; most likely to be seen standing motionless in shallows of quiet backwaters of swamps, where it preys upon fish, crabs and other aquatic creatures. 1–1.5 m.

VOICE Loud resonant roaring sounds, day or night; has been likened to the bellowing of an angry bull.

HABITAT Tidal mudflats, estuaries, mangrove swamps and mangrove-lined creeks and river banks; usually coastal, sometimes well inland on major rivers.

BREEDING September–March; usually November–January. Nest is usually in a secluded part of a mangrove swamp, a platform of sticks on a limb of a mangrove or other tree, usually no higher than 3 m, occasionally to 12 m. Two pale, dull blue-green eggs.

RANGE North and north-east coasts; Derby (WA) to north of New South Wales. Also in South-East Asia and New Guinea. Sedentary.

STATUS Uncommon to rare.

▶ See also pages
22 22 96 98 188
196 197 198 199
208

---

48 PACIFIC HERON

Ardea pacifica   Ardeidae

OTHER NAMES White-necked Heron, White-necked Crane

RECOGNITION A large heron, with white head and neck; dark grey-black body; black bill and legs. There is a line of dark spots down the centre of the fore-neck; breast and belly are streaked white. In breeding season, long maroon nuptial plumes on the back, and upper breast. Immatures have whites more buff-toned. In flight, large white patches at leading edge of bend of wing; stately flight, long slow wingbeats; holds neck in folded back position. 76–100 cm.

48 PACIFIC HERON *Ardea pacifica*

VOICE A deep harsh rattling croak, and a variety of guttural sounds at the nest.

HABITAT Usually seen in shallow freshwater environs; margins of swamps and rivers, flooded areas, moist paddocks; rarely brackish or salt.

BREEDING Almost any time of the year; depending upon timing of rain in arid regions, and food supplies generally. Nest is a rough platform of sticks in a tree standing in water, or overhanging water. Three to four blue-green eggs.

RANGE Throughout Australia; including arid regions when habitat is suitable. Nomadic or migratory; irruptive.

STATUS Common.   Endemic   breeding species.

▶ **See also pages**
139 *173 185 262*

49 WHITE-FACED HERON
Ardea novaehollandiae

WHITE-FACED HERON

49

Ardea novaehollandiae   Ardeidae

OTHER NAMES Blue Crane, White-fronted Heron

RECOGNITION A common species; as much at home in pools of city and suburban parks, and ditches of busy highways as in secluded wetlands. Plumage overall pale grey, with face and throat white. Grey of wings slightly darker, and on belly paler. In breeding season has long lanceolate pale-grey nuptial plumes on the back, and grey-brown hackles on the breast; legs yellow. Usually flies with neck folded back. Immatures like adults, only slight white on throat. 66-69 cm.

VOICE When startled, a loud croak; and a variety of deep croaking sounds at the nest.

HABITAT Any areas of shallow water or wet ground; swamps, margins of lakes and rivers, mangroves, mudflats, damp grasslands, ponds in parks and gardens.

BREEDING Almost any time of year; varying with region, rainfall and availability of food. Nest is a loose rough platform of sticks in a tree, often well away from water. Three to seven pale blue-green eggs.

RANGE Throughout Australia; including arid areas when habitat is suitable. Also Indonesia, New Guinea and New Zealand. Nomadic.

STATUS Common.

▶ **See also pages**
47 162 165 *165*
244

PIED HERON

50

Ardea picata   Ardeidae

OTHER NAMES Pied Egret, White-headed Egret

RECOGNITION Small; pied plumage, with head, body and wings dark slate-grey; bill and legs yellow. The white of the neck extends upwards on the nape, and on the face almost up to the eyes. At the back of the crown is a crest of backswept black plumes, and long white plumes hang down from the front of the neck. In non-breeding, plumes are reduced. Immatures have no crest; head, neck and underparts whitish. Flies with neck folded back. Singly or in flocks. 43-48 cm.

VOICE In flight, a loud abrupt croaked 'orawk'.

HABITAT Both salt and freshwater coastal swamps, river margins, flooded pastures, mangroves, mudflats, estuaries, sewage ponds.

BREEDING October-April. Nest is a shallow platform of sticks, in a tree standing in water or overhanging water; and usually in company with other herons and egrets. Three to four deep blue-green eggs.

RANGE Northern and north-eastern Australia; Kimberley to north-eastern Queensland. Also Indonesia and New Guinea. Dispersive and nomadic or migratory.

STATUS Common.

▶ **See also pages**
186 197 199

CATTLE EGRET

51

Ardeola ibis   Ardeidae

OTHER NAME Buff-backed Heron

RECOGNITION A small egret, easily distinguished in the breeding season by long orange-buff plumes on head, breast and lower back. These plumes begin to appear

around mid-August, and remnants can be seen into May. Remainder of plumage is white; face and legs red; bill orange, shading to red at base. In non-breeding, plumage entirely white; bill yellow; legs variable. Short stocky appearance; face deep-jowled; hunts actively, in groups or flocks. 49-53 cm.

VOICE Deep and guttural croaks, similar to voice of other egrets, possibly somewhat softer; mostly at the nest.

HABITAT Flooded and moist grasslands, pastures; often feeding among grazing cattle, buffaloes, horses; also margins of swamps.

BREEDING October-April; mostly November-March. In colonies during northern wet season, in trees of swamps or inundated floodplains; often in company with other species of egrets. Nest is a rough platform of sticks. Three to six pale blue eggs.

RANGE Mostly northern and eastern Australia; recorded most regions. Also Europe, Africa and Asia. Expanding range.

STATUS Common north and east; uncommon remainder.

▶ **See also pages**
99 161 *281*

52 GREAT EGRET *Egretta alba*

GREAT EGRET

52

Egretta alba   Ardeidae

OTHER NAMES Large Egret, White Egret, Great White Egret, White Crane

RECOGNITION Tall egret; very long-necked. When it stands with neck outstretched, as it often does when peering into the water ready to jab at a fish or other water creature, the head and neck can be seen to be about one and a half times as long as the body. Plumage entirely white, with long fine plumes over the back in breeding season, when the bill and legs are black; facial skin greenish; eye reddish. Non-breeding: bill, face and eye yellow; legs yellow-brown. 77–90 cm.

VOICE In alarm, a deep rattling croak; various low guttural noises at the nest.

HABITAT Swamps, lakes, mudflats, lagoons, river edges, irrigated pastures, sewage farms, roadside ditches; hunts fish, frogs, invertebrates. Usually solitary, sometimes large flocks in northern Australia in wet season.

BREEDING October–May; other months in good conditions. In colonies, with other waterbirds. Usually fewer than 100 nests, but colonies of 500 nests have been recorded. Nest a platform of sticks in a tree over water. Three to five blue-green eggs.

RANGE Throughout Australia, including interior; wherever habitat suitable. Also Europe, Africa and Asia. Sedentary or nomadic.

STATUS Common.

▶ See also pages
79 *132* 137 161
162 165 183 197
199 244 *263*

53 **LITTLE EGRET** *Egretta garzetta*

53 **LITTLE EGRET**

Egretta garzetta   Ardeidae

OTHER NAMES Lesser Egret, Spotless Egret

RECOGNITION Small, slender, active egret. Plumage entirely white, with long fine plumes from the head, back and breast in the breeding season. Face orange; legs and bill black; the latter having a yellowish base to the lower-mandible. Non-breeding plumage: plumes absent or few; face yellow. Compared with the patient waiting of the other egrets, the Little Egret tends to be more active, dashing back and forth, stabbing into the water. 56 cm.

VOICE An abrupt 'karrrk' when alarmed; bubblings at the nest.

HABITAT Estuaries, tidal mudflats, mangrove and lagoon edges, sewage farms and swamps. Usually solitary; sometimes hunts in company with Sacred Ibis.

BREEDING September–April. Nests colonially, often with other waterbirds. Nest is a sparse platform of sticks, in a tree over

water. Three to five pale blue-green eggs. Colonies of coastal northern Australia tend to be much larger than in southern regions.

RANGE Northern, eastern and coastal Australia, but recorded sparsely most parts of Australia. Widespread Europe, Africa and Asia. Sedentary or nomadic.

STATUS Common in north.

▶ See also pages
79 96 137 161 183
197 199

54 **INTERMEDIATE EGRET** *Egretta intermedia*

54 **INTERMEDIATE EGRET**

Egretta intermedia   Ardeidae

OTHER NAME Plumed Egret

RECOGNITION Like the Great Egret, but smaller; and if neck is outstretched, the length of head and neck together is not significantly greater than the body length; proportionately shorter than for Great Egret. Breeding plumage: long fine plumes from breast and especially from the scapular area of the wings; bill orange to reddish; bare facial area greenish; legs black, red on upper part. Non-breeding plumage: bill and bare facial area yellow; legs black with no red. 62–63 cm.

VOICE A loud croaking alarm call; and various softer low croaking sounds at the nest.

HABITAT Often feeds on wet pastures, semi-flooded grasslands, sometimes among cattle; also mangroves, mudflats, margins of lagoons, rivers.

BREEDING Recorded all months; mainly in northern summer wet season. Nests colonially; often in company with other waterbirds. Nest is a rough platform of sticks, in a tree over water. Three to six pale greenish eggs.

RANGE Northern and eastern Australia; rare vagrant to interior and south-west. Also Africa, southern Asia, Indonesia and New Guinea. Sedentary or nomadic.

STATUS Common in north; uncommon south.

▶ See also pages
79 *102* 137 183

55 **EASTERN REEF EGRET**

Egretta sacra   Ardeidae

OTHER NAMES Eastern Reef Heron, Blue Heron, Sacred Heron, White Heron, Reef Heron

RECOGNITION Two colour phases. Dark phase: overall deep grey plumage except for slight white streak down the front of the throat; facial skin greenish; bill grey; legs yellowish-grey. Light phase: plumage entirely white, with yellow bill. In breeding plumage: both forms develop long plumes on back and breast. Compared with other egrets, legs appear shorter and thicker, and bill longer and heavier. Often crouches, wings half open, while hunting. 61–66 cm.

VOICE When alarmed, a loud hoarse croak; various guttural sounds at the nest. Usually roosts in small open colonies, and maintains a foraging territory.

HABITAT Exposed reefs, beaches and rocky shores, mudflats, islets. Remains coastal, rarely sighted inland from coast. Hunts both day and night.

BREEDING August–April; mainly October–March. Nests in colonies, which are of a loose nature, and with only some of the birds nesting at any one time. The nest is a rough stick platform, in trees, or on a rock ledge. Two to five pale greenish eggs.

RANGE Coastal Australia; vagrant to Victoria and Tasmania. Through Indian and Pacific oceans region. Nomadic or part nomadic.

STATUS Common in north; uncommon south coast.

▶ See also pages
25 47 47 82

56 **STRIATED HERON**

Butorides striatus   Ardeidae

OTHER NAMES Mangrove Heron, Green-backed Heron, Mangrove Bittern, Green-backed Bittern

RECOGNITION A comparatively short-legged, short-necked, dumpy, bittern-like heron. There are five Australian subspecies of slightly varying plumage colours, but these have in common the glossy black crown with nuchal crest; dark upperparts with metallic sheen; fore-neck streaked black and dark brown; bill black; legs yellow. Breeding plumage: legs orange. In eastern Australia subspecies *macrorhynchus* dark-olive back and wings; *rogersi* rufous-cinnamon. 48 cm.

VOICE A scratchy, sneeze-like 'tchew' or 'tchah'. Other calls are a sudden 'hooh', and sounds like those of the Purple Swamp-hen.

HABITAT Tidal estuaries, especially mangroves and associated mudflats, waterways, and sometimes nearby tidal reefs; taking fish and crabs.

BREEDING September–March. Solitary; builds a nest of sticks in a mangrove or other water's-edge tree. Two to four limy, blue-green eggs. Interbreeding of subspecies is reported, however, some subspecies are isolated, and sometimes are listed as species.

RANGE North coast; Shark Bay (WA), to extreme west of Victoria. Widespread South America, Africa, Asia and New Guinea. Sedentary.

STATUS Common north; uncommon south-east.

▶ **See also pages**
22–3 23 98 122 223

RUFOUS NIGHT HERON

Nycticorax caledonicus   Ardeidae

OTHER NAMES Nankeen Crane, Night Heron, Nankeen Night Heron

RECOGNITION A compact, short-necked, large-headed heron. Non-breeding plumage: upperparts rich bright cinnamon; underparts creamy white; crown of head black; bill blackish; eyes and legs yellow. Breeding plumage: two long slender white plumes from crown down across the back. Immatures have very different plumage; buffy, heavily streaked brown and white. During daylight usually roosts in densely foliaged swamp trees; hunting at night. 56–64 cm.

VOICE Mostly silent; at night, and when leaving roosting place for the night's hunting, gives a loud 'kyok'.

HABITAT Swamps, edges of rivers, mangroves, estuaries, dams, flooded pastures. Hunts for small fish, amphibians and other aquatic creatures.

BREEDING August–March. Nests colonially, with colonies of more than 4000 birds recorded. Sites may be more or less permanent, or temporary. Nest is a rough platform of sticks, usually in a tree in water. Two to five pale greenish eggs.

RANGE Throughout Australia in suitable habitats. Pacific islands, South-East Asia. Vagrant to New Zealand. Sedentary or nomadic.

STATUS Common.

▶ **See also pages**
79 99 137 139 161 162 175 185 197 199 265

LITTLE BITTERN

Ixobrychus minutus   Ardeidae

OTHER NAMES Leech Bittern, Minute Bittern, Kaoriki

RECOGNITION A very small bittern. Plumage on crown, back and tail black; hindneck deep red-brown; face and breast cinnamon. The wings are black with a large chestnut or buff patch on the shoulders. Lower breast and flanks white streaked brown; belly and undertail white. Eye yellow, bill greenish-yellow, legs and feet greenish. Female has black replaced by brown. Immatures have chestnut upperparts; light cinnamon underparts; overall heavily streaked brown. 30 cm.

VOICE Male in breeding season has a deep regular croak, repeated regularly and monotonously at intervals of several seconds.

HABITAT Dense reed-beds, and other lush low vegetation of swamps, lakes and rivers; feeds on frogs, small fish, insects.

BREEDING October–December. Reported to nest in small loose colonies at times. The nest is a small loosely constructed platform in reeds, rushes or cumbungi; sometimes in a tree low over water. Four to five white eggs.

RANGE Northern, north-eastern, eastern, south-eastern and south-western Australia. Sedentary; in places nomadic-migratory.

STATUS Uncommon; very secretive. Endemic subspecies of very widespread species.

▶ **See also pages**
34 35 99 137 163 242 244

BLACK BITTERN

Dupetor flavicollis   Ardeidae

OTHER NAMES Yellow-necked Bittern, Yellow-necked Mangrove Bittern, Mangrove Bittern

RECOGNITION Overall sooty black, except for a golden yellow streak down each side of the long neck, and fine white stripes from the throat down the front of the neck to the upper breast. Female dark brown rather than black upperparts, and less prominently streaked underparts. Immatures duller; feathers buff-edged; breast streakings yellow. Extremely secretive, keeping to dense cover most of the time, but occasionally hunting in more exposed

situations. If surprised the bittern may freeze, with bill pointed skywards. 55–66 cm.

VOICE A deep moaning 'cooor' or 'whooo' repeated at regular intervals; also a repetitive 'eh-he, eh-he'.

HABITAT Dense vegetation of swamps, margins of creeks and rivers, moist paperbark woodlands, mangroves, tidal creeks and mudflats.

BREEDING September–January. The nest is a bowl of sticks built in a tree, over water; usually well hidden in dense foliage. Three to five very pale blue to white eggs.

RANGE Northern, eastern and southwestern Australia. Also India, South-East Asia and New Guinea. Probably mainly sedentary, or locally nomadic.

STATUS Moderately common in north; rare in south-east and south-west.

▶ **See also pages**
35 35 208 210

AUSTRALASIAN BITTERN

Botaurus poiciloptilus   Ardeidae

OTHER NAMES Brown Bittern, Australian Brown Bittern, Boomer, Bullbird, Bunyip

RECOGNITION A large heron-like bittern. Overall plumage colour brown; upperparts mottled with yellow ochre and black; underparts buff and ochre, streaked dark brown. Crown dark brown; dark-brown streak down side of neck, forming margins to the white throat. Bare skin of face round eye and base of bill light green or blue-green; legs green. Eye yellow; bill brown, with greenish tone on the lower-mandible. Immatures paler. 66–76 cm.

VOICE Booming or deep braying sound, 'wooomph', repeatedly, loud or softly. In alarm, an abrupt hoarse 'craaak'.

HABITAT Reed-beds, swamps, dense vegetation along rivers, around lakes, wet grass of pastures. Adopts reed-like pose, with bill pointed skywards, if disturbed.

BREEDING July–April; mainly September–March. Breeding seems sometimes loosely colonial, with a group of nests in one locality. The nest is a platform of trampled reeds, usually in a clump of reeds just above water. Four to six olive eggs.

RANGE South-eastern and south-western Australia. Also in New Zealand. Appears to be nomadic.

STATUS Uncommon generally; in places abundant.

▶ **See also pages**
35 35 163 242

57

58

59

60

61 BLACK-NECKED STORK
Xenorhynchus asiaticus

STORKS

Ciconiidae Family of 17 species
1 in Australia, 1 breeding

Large and very tall waterbirds, with long necks and legs. Flight is strong, soaring, with neck and legs extended. Usually solitary, or in pairs, occasionally in larger numbers where concentrations of food occur. Their prey of frogs, small fish, lizards, insects and occasional carrion is taken while wading through shallow water or from wet grassland.

61 **BLACK-NECKED STORK**

Xenorhynchus asiaticus   Ciconiidae
OTHER NAMES Policeman-bird, Jabiru
RECOGNITION Very tall and upright; heavy-billed; superficially black-and-white plumaged. Head and neck have glossy iridescent green sheen over black; black wingstripe and tail; body and remainder of wings white. Eye black (male) or yellow (female); very long, red legs; bill black. Immatures browner, with breast, rump and part of wing buffy-white. Wades in shallows with long strides. In flight, slow-beating wings; neck outstretched; legs trailing. 1.2 m.
VOICE Clappering sounds made with bill; also reported to make dull booming sounds, but this seems uncertain or very infrequent.
HABITAT Swamps, edges of lagoons, river sandbars, mangroves, irrigated and flooded land, nearby savannah-woodlands; solitary, pairs, or family groups.
BREEDING February–September; mainly October–May. Nest is a large flat platform of sticks, rushes and grass; in a living part of a dead tree; usually high above ground and near water. Two to four white eggs.
RANGE Northern and eastern Australia; from North West Cape (WA) to north-eastern New South Wales; vagrant to Victoria. Also India, South-East Asia and New Guinea. Sedentary.
STATUS Common in north; uncommon in east; rare in south-east.

▶ **See also pages**
80 83 122 183 188
188 196 197 198
199 210 223

IBISES, SPOONBILLS

Plataleidae Family of 28 species
5 in Australia, 5 breeding, 2 endemic

Long-legged, long-necked waterbirds, with distinctive long bills. Ibises have slender, downcurved, sickle-shaped bills, and feed with a probing and stabbing action in shallow water or damp grasslands. Spoonbills have a broad flattened spoon-like tip to the bill, and feed in shallow water with side to side sweeping of the bill tip through the water, sifting out small edible organisms. In flight, unlike herons and egrets, the neck is outstretched.

62 **GLOSSY IBIS**

Plegadis falcinellus   Plataleidae
OTHER NAME Black Curlew
RECOGNITION Smallest Australian species of ibis. It appears near-black at a distance. Plumage dark red-brown with metallic, iridescent bronzed and greenish sheen especially on the wings. Bill long, down-curved, sickle-shaped and dark brown; eyes and legs brown. Female similar, bill shorter. Immatures less colourful than adults; have some white streaks on head and neck; bill less strongly curved. In flight, holds neck extended and slightly drooped; legs trailing. 48–61 cm.
VOICE In flight, a grunting 'thu-thu-th-'; in courtship displays has drawn-out harsh croaking 'eh-eh-eh-eh-'.
HABITAT Lake edges, swamps, wet flood-plains and grasslands, mangroves and coastal mudflats; with preference for fresh-water situations.
BREEDING Recorded throughout year; mainly September–May. Breeds in colonies, some quite large, and often with or near other waterbirds. The nests are placed in trees or shrubs over water, or in reeds. Three to six deep blue-green eggs.
RANGE Northern and eastern Australia; vagrant to south-west (WA) and Tasmania. Also Europe, Africa and Asia. Highly nomadic.
STATUS Abundant in far north; generally uncommon.

▶ **See also pages**
137 161 *281*

63 **SACRED IBIS**

Threskiornis aethiopica   Plataleidae
OTHER NAMES Australian White Ibis, Black-necked Ibis, Sicklebird
RECOGNITION Unmistakable as an ibis, on the ground or in flight, by the long sickle-shaped bill. The white plumage, with bare black head and neck, black wingtips and black lacy wing-plumes, identify this species. When the Sacred Ibis is perched, the black plumes of the outer secondary feathers of the wings envelop the tail, giving a black-tailed appearance. Immatures have shorter bill; no wing-plumes; and some black feathers on the head. 68–76 cm.
VOICE A deep croaking 'urk'; also various harsh and grunting sounds, usually when breeding. The Sacred Ibis occurs singly or in flocks of hundreds.
HABITAT A wide variety of wetlands, tidal mudflats, mangroves, estuaries, lagoon and lake edges, floodplains, wet pastures, parks.
BREEDING Variable; mainly September–April. Nests in colonies over water; in densely-foliaged trees, mangroves, in swamp vegetation, on ground of islands; building a platform of sticks and reeds, lined with water-plants. Two to five dull white eggs.
RANGE Throughout Australia generally, except western arid regions. Also in New Guinea and New Zealand. Highly migratory.
STATUS Common; abundant in coastal north, east and south-east; rare in interior.

▶ **See also pages**
34 35 79 136 137
161 174 *198* 264

STRAW-NECKED IBIS

Threskiornis spinicollis   Plataleidae

OTHER NAMES Dry-weather Bird, Farmer's Friend, Letterbird

RECOGNITION Plumage of back, wings and tail glossy black, with metallic green, bluish, and bronze highlights; head and throat without feathers, the bare skin black. Neck white, with pale yellow, straw-like plumes down the front of the lower part of the neck and most prominent against the black of the upper breast. Lower breast, abdomen and undertail white. Bill long, downcurved, black; legs black. Immatures lack plumes; plumage comparatively dull. 59–76 cm.

VOICE In flight, drawn-out grunted 'urrrgh'; in breeding display, loud deep 'orrgh'.

HABITAT Shallow flooded land, wet or moist pastures, and dry grassland where insects are abundant; margins of swamps; very rarely marine wetlands.

BREEDING Recorded most months; usually August–May. Nests in colonies, some huge, estimates of 20 000 birds on record. Nest is a platform of sticks and rushes; over water in paperbarks, in rushes, or on ground. Four to five white eggs.

RANGE Throughout Australia in suitable habitats and conditions. Also in New Guinea. Nomadic or migratory.

STATUS Common; uncommon in arid regions.

▶ See also pages
125 136 *136* 137
161 174

ROYAL SPOONBILL

Platalea regia   Plataleidae

OTHER NAME Black-billed Spoonbill

RECOGNITION Tall, with plumage entirely white; and distinctive bill that is broadened and spoon-shaped towards the tip; bill and legs black. Front half of head from base of bill back to just behind the eyes, including forehead and throat, is black and naked of any feathers; at a distance looks like a continuation of the black bill. Usually a small yellow ochre patch over the red eye. In breeding season, long white plumes from crown and nape. Immatures: some black on flight feathers. 75–80 cm.

VOICE Usually silent; at nest, soft grunting sounds and clapping of the bill.

HABITAT Has preference for large expanses of shallow water, lakes, swamps, coastal and far inland; also tidal mudflats, mangroves.

BREEDING Most of the year; usually August–March. Nests colonially or singly; in company with ibis, cormorants and other waterbirds; usually in trees over water. Two to four dull white eggs, marked brown.

RANGE Northern, western and eastern Australia; vagrant to most of interior. Also in Indonesia, New Guinea and New Zealand. Nomadic.

STATUS Common locally; generally uncommon.

▶ See also pages
83 *102* 122 125
137 161 174 198
199 242

YELLOW-BILLED SPOONBILL

Platalea flavipes   Plataleidae

OTHER NAME Yellow-legged Spoonbill

RECOGNITION Tall; entirely white-plumaged, except for some black tips to the flight feathers. In breeding season has long fine white plumes from the breast, these when new having a slight pink tinge; white plumes from inner-wings. Long, yellow bill, straight, and spoon-shaped towards the tip. No feathers on face, grey with black border. Legs and feet yellow. Immatures have yellowish facial skin with no black border. Neck outstretched in flight. 76–91 cm.

VOICE Usually silent; occasionally soft or feeble reedy grunting, and bill-clapperings.

HABITAT Broad shallow waters, fresh or brackish; with preference for inland rather than coastal localities; claypans and other temporary waters.

BREEDING Recorded most months of year; usually September–April. Seldom in large breeding colonies, but solitary, or small groups with other waterbirds. Nest is a platform of sticks, usually in trees standing in water. Two to three dull white eggs.

RANGE Almost throughout Australia in suitable habitat; vagrant to Tasmania. Nomadic.

STATUS Common in south-east, especially Murray–Darling region; sparse in interior and in Western Australia. Endemic.

▶ See also pages
83 137 161 174
175 185 *196* 198
199 242 244

Anatidae Family of 148 species 23 in Australia, 21 breeding, 10 endemic

Wetlands birds with large flattened bills, webbed feet and dense waterproof plumage. The necks are usually long, the legs short and placed well back on the stout bodies. Size varies greatly, from the 35 cm pygmy geese, to the swans. Habitats are mainly inland waters and coastal estuaries. Feeding methods vary, some using long necks to reach the bottom of shallow waters, or by diving, others by grazing damp pastures.

MAGPIE GOOSE

Anseranas semipalmata   Anatidae

OTHER NAMES Semi-palmated Goose, Wild Goose, Pied Goose, Black-and-white Goose

RECOGNITION A large goose with pied plumage. Head and neck down to upper breast black; body white; upperwings black with white coverts; underwings black with white wing linings. Distinctive black knob on crown of head; tending to be larger on males than females, and larger on older birds. Broad hook-tipped bill and bare, flesh-pink or yellowish-pink facial skin; legs salmon-pink to yellow. Immatures like adults, but white mottled brownish. 71–92 cm.

VOICE Loud resonant honking, given singly or rapidly repeated; may be taken up by many other birds. Call of male is higher-pitched and louder.

HABITAT Open swamp areas, with large expanses of sedges, rushes; also floodplains, both wet and dry, and crops. Feeds on seeds and bulbs.

BREEDING February–July; mainly March–May. Pairs (or often a male mated with two females) trample down rushes to build a bulky platform, where between one and nine creamy white eggs are laid (up to 19 eggs where two females are present).

RANGE Northern and north-eastern Australia; Kimberley to Rockhampton; vagrant south-west, Victoria and Tasmania. Also in New Guinea. Nomadic.

STATUS Abundant in far north (formerly also south-east); rare elsewhere.

▶ See also pages
78 83 99 110 163
195 196 197 199
210 275

WANDERING WHISTLING-DUCK

Dendrocygna arcuata   Anatidae

OTHER NAMES Whistling Tree-Duck, Red Whistler, Diving Whistling-Duck, Water Whistling-Duck

RECOGNITION A large duck of rich red-brown plumage overall; face, front of neck and upper breast tending to a paler cinnamon tone. Crown of head, nape and back of neck brownish-black. Elongated flank plumes off-white with chestnut edges, much less conspicuous than those of Plumed Whistling-Duck. In flight, blackish underwings; cinnamon and chestnut underbody; white undertail; trailing black legs. Immatures similar, duller, paler belly. 55–61 cm.

VOICE Shrill twittering, whistling; especially noisy with almost incessant whistling when flocks are airborne.

HABITAT Lagoons and swamps; preferring deeper waters of more permanent waterways, where aquatic plants and insects are plentiful; flooded grasslands.

BREEDING December–July; mainly January–April, the northern wet season. Nest is a scrape on ground out of reach of rising floodwaters, hidden in tall grass or shrubbery, and lined with grass. Six to 15, usually seven to eight, smooth creamy-white eggs.

RANGE Northern and eastern Australia; Kimberley to north-eastern New South Wales; vagrant to south-east and south-west. Also in Indonesia and New Guinea. Nomadic.

STATUS Common to locally abundant in north; rare in south.

▶ **See also pages**
78 78 99 197

69 PLUMED WHISTLING-DUCK

Dendrocygna eytoni Anatidae

OTHER NAMES Grass Whistle-Duck, Red-legged Whistler, Plumed Tree-Duck

RECOGNITION A tall, long-necked duck, plumaged in various brown tones, and with very prominent long lanceolate, off-white plumes along the flanks. Head and neck greyish-cinnamon; buffy-white about the face and throat. Back grey-brown; sides of breast chestnut barred black; abdomen buff. Bill, legs and feet pink. Immatures like adults, but paler, and with less distinct breast markings. In flight, slow-beating dark wings, much whistling. 41–61 cm.

VOICE Shrill high whistling; as a single note or extended lively twitters. Flocks especially noisy when flushed, or moving out to other locality.

HABITAT During day, large camps on margins of lagoons, swamps, mangrove creeks; at night flying out, often quite long distances, to feed on grasslands.

BREEDING Begins in tropical wet season; usually January–March. Nest is a scrape on the ground, sparsely lined with grass, usually under shelter of a bush or other vegetation, and often far from water. Eight to 14 smooth white eggs.

RANGE Northern and eastern Australia; Kimberley to Riverina (NSW–Vic). Vagrant to New Guinea and New Zealand. Highly nomadic.

STATUS Abundant to common. Endemic breeding species.

▶ **See also pages**
35 78 110 136–7 197 223 267

70 BLACK SWAN

Cygnus atratus Anatidae

RECOGNITION Familiar long-necked swan shape; plumage entirely black except for the white flight feathers, which usually show slightly as a white wingbar on the folded wing, and are very conspicuous in flight. Red bill, with lighter bar near the tip; eye usually white, becoming red during the breeding season; legs and feet black. Female similar, slightly smaller, eye and bill paler. Immatures have all plumage white, mottled grey-brown; black bill. 1.3–1.6 m.

VOICE Occasionally a loud, far-carrying musical bugle may be given on the water, or in flight; in anger, as in defence of nest, a savage hiss.

HABITAT Fresh, brackish or salt waters; gathers in numbers on large bodies of water, especially when moulting; also smaller swamps, inland river pools.

BREEDING Variable; determined by rains and water levels. Nest a very large mass of reeds, waterweeds; semi-floating, anchored among reeds or other vegetation; sometimes very open shallow-lake situations. Four to seven greenish eggs.

RANGE Throughout Australia in suitable habitats. Nomadic, erratic movements.

STATUS Common; ranging abundant to rare. Endemic.

▶ **See also pages**
78 79 136 138 *140* 150 *150* 161

71 FRECKLED DUCK

Stictonetta naevosa Anatidae

OTHER NAMES Canvasback, Oatmeal Duck, Speckled Duck, Diamantina Duck

RECOGNITION At a distance appears almost uniformly dark grey-brown, without obvious or distinctive markings, but in silhouette a slight but distinctive peak to the rear of the crown of head; bill has strongly dished or scooped-out contour to its uppersurface, and on male, red at the base in the breeding season. In closer view, plumage is dark brown, finely freckled buff. Female and immatures paler. In flight looks dark, but paler beneath. 48–59 cm.

VOICE As a contact call, a soft musical piping. Alarm call a flute-like 'wheeooo'. At the nest, in display, loud discordant quacks.

HABITAT Open lakes; heavily vegetated

swamps; favouring wetlands with dense paperbark, lignum or cumbungi; and areas of floodwaters.

BREEDING Recorded most months, dependent upon rainfall, but usually September–December. Nest a well-constructed bowl of interwoven sticks in a thicket of paperbark or lignum, on branches or forks, over or close to water. Five to 14 creamy eggs.

RANGE South-eastern and south-western Australia; extending to interior in suitable habitats. Sedentary, dispersive.

STATUS Scarce. Endemic.

▶ **See also pages**
35 123 137 163 172 174 183 242 244

72 CAPE BARREN GOOSE

Cereopsis novaehollandiae Anatidae

OTHER NAME Pig Goose

RECOGNITION A very large, overall pale grey goose of comparatively small-headed appearance and with stubby triangular bill that is almost concealed by the very prominent greenish-yellow cere. Has rows of large dark spots in lines across the scapulars and wing-coverts; crown of head white; legs pink to dusky deep-red; feet black. In flight, shows dark wingtips and trailing edge, dark undertail-coverts and tail; wingbeats quick, shallow. 75–90 cm.

VOICE On the ground, usually quiet unless alarmed or in display. In flight more vocal; male has higher-pitched, harsh, trumpeted 'ark, ark-ark'.

HABITAT Offshore islands, usually granite; in areas of pasture, tussock-grass or low heathy scrub; often feeds on coastal and island farm pastures.

BREEDING June–January, mainly July–September. Breeds on small islands amid vegetation of tussock-grass or heath; pairs returning to same site annually. Nest is on ground; a large shallow bowl of twigs and grass, lined with down. Three to six white eggs.

RANGE Southern coast of Australia; south of Western Australia to south-eastern Victoria. Locally dispersive.

72 CAPE BARREN GOOSE
Cereopsis novaehollandiae

STATUS Moderately common within the restricted range. Endemic.

▶ See also pages
142 150 151 152
163 164 242 268

73 AUSTRALIAN SHELDUCK

Tadorna tadornoides Anatidae

OTHER NAMES Chestnut-breasted Shelduck, Mountain Duck, Sheldrake

RECOGNITION A large colourful duck. Smallish, black head with green sheen; this black continuing half-way down neck, where it is separated by a narrow white band from the rich cinnamon of lower neck, mantle and breast. Upper body mainly black; belly dark brown; undertail black. White upperwing-coverts form white shoulder-patch; primaries black; outer secondaries deep chestnut; large green speculum. Female has white eye-ring; chestnut breast. 55–72 cm.

VOICE A loud honking; deeper and more grunted from the male, higher and more resonant from the female; 'ong-ank, ong-ank'.

HABITAT Prefers fresh waters or, if on salt-water habitat, will be within easy reach of fresh water. Grazes on green plants on land or in shallow water.

BREEDING July–December. Nest is usually a large hollow of a tree; well lined with down; sometimes well away from water. Occasionally in a hollow of a cliff-face, limestone cavity on coast, or rabbit burrow. Ten to 14 creamy eggs.

RANGE South-western and south-eastern Australia; vagrant north to Kimberley and central Australia. Migratory.

STATUS Moderately common in south; rare in north. Endemic.

▶ See also pages
136 223

74 RADJAH SHELDUCK

Tadorna radjah Anatidae

OTHER NAMES White-headed Shelduck, Burdekin Duck

RECOGNITION Dominantly white plumage, with back, wings and tail very dark chestnut and black; and narrow deep-chestnut breastband which can appear black against the white of breast and abdomen. Flanks and undertail black; primaries black; upperwing-coverts white; speculum glossy green. In flight, undersurfaces are white, with black-tipped wings and tail; dark narrow breastband; on upperparts, the head, neck and upperwing-coverts are white; remainder dark. 50–55 cm.

VOICE Tends to be noisy; the male with loud hoarse whistlings, the female with harsh rattling sounds.

HABITAT Pools and swamps of mangrove-lined tropical lagoons, and adjoining wet floodplains; also paperbark swamps, creeks, tidal mudflats and estuaries.

BREEDING December–June; usually March–April, following northern wet season. Nest is a large tree hollow, in or near water. Six to 12 creamy eggs are laid on bare wood or wood-dust, and thinly covered with down. Brooding by female only.

RANGE Northern and north-eastern Australia; eastern Kimberley to north-eastern New South Wales; coastal and sub-coastal. Also in New Guinea. Nomadic.

STATUS Abundant coastal Northern Territory; generally uncommon.

▶ See also pages
197 199 210

75 PACIFIC BLACK DUCK

Anas superciliosa Anatidae

OTHER NAMES Black Duck, Brown Duck, Wild Duck, Grey Duck

RECOGNITION Body plumage overall dark, dull brown; individual feathers finely pale-edged. Wing speculum iridescent green and purplish, black-outlined. Distinctive head pattern: crown blackish; face and throat buff or buffy-white, with two black stripes from base of bill back through and just beneath eye. Legs and feet yellow-green. In flight, dark body plumage contrasts with white underwing linings, and pale striped face; whistling wingbeats. 47–60 cm.

VOICE Both sexes, drawn-out quacks; female also loud, raucous, descending sequence 'quark-quark-quark-quark'; male hisses and peeps in courtship.

HABITAT Occurs in a great variety of habitats; including swamps, rivers, lakes; prefers deep permanent wetlands, with plentiful aquatic vegetation.

BREEDING Variable; nesting occurring when waterlevels have risen, and aquatic plants are abundant; usually January–April in north; July–October in south. Nest may be in a tree hollow, stump, old nest, or in swamp vegetation. Eight to 10 creamy eggs.

RANGE Throughout Australia, where and when suitable habitat exists. Widespread; to Pacific islands, Indonesia, New Guinea, New Zealand. Nomadic.

STATUS Abundant.

▶ See also pages
78 152 168 185

76 MALLARD

Anas platyrhynchos Anatidae

RECOGNITION Green head and neck, separated from chestnut breast by a white ring round the lower neck. Female and eclipse male like Pacific Black Duck, but paler and without striped face pattern. Hybridizes with the Pacific Black Duck. *Introduced species.* 52–65 cm.

VOICE Male has a quiet, low 'eeeb' or 'kwek'; female a loud quacking.

HABITAT Lakes, dams, ponds, open waters of swamps.

BREEDING June–March. Nest in dense low vegetation or in tree hollow; built of grass, reeds, and lined with down. Eight to 15 dull cream or greenish-cream eggs.

RANGE South-western and south-eastern Australia; parts of east coast and Tasmania. Widespread elsewhere.

STATUS Common. Introduced species.

77 GREY TEAL

Anas gibberifrons Anatidae

OTHER NAMES Slender Teal, Wood Teal

RECOGNITION A small duck, mottled grey-brown overall, without obvious markings except for whitish throat which serves to distinguish it from the female Chestnut Teal. Wing speculum black with iridescent green gloss, with white band above and below. In flight, triangular white patches from armpits out onto underwing-coverts; white stripe along upperwing. Eye bright red. Immatures similar, paler. Typical dabbling duck, upends to feed. 37–44 cm.

VOICE Male has a muted peep, while female gives a loud series of rapidly repeated quacks on a descending scale, often at night.

77 GREY TEAL *Anas gibberifrons*

HABITAT Almost any wetlands; preferring freshwater swamps, lakes, rivers, temporary floodwaters, but also coastal inlets, bays and estuaries.

BREEDING Any time of the year, triggered by rain and increasing waterlevel; response is rapid and eggs may be laid within two weeks of heavy rains. Nests in hollows of trees, on ground, among reeds. Four to 14 creamy eggs.

RANGE Throughout Australia, where and when habitat suitable. Also in New Guinea, New Zealand, and Indonesia. Highly nomadic.

STATUS Abundant.

▶ See also pages
78 125 173 177 244 *269*

78 CHESTNUT TEAL

Anas castanea   Anatidae

OTHER NAMES Black Teal, Mountain Teal, Chestnut-breasted Teal, Red Teal

RECOGNITION Colourful, with back grey-brown; underparts rich chestnut; head deep iridescent green; conspicuous white patch towards rear of flanks. Rump, uppertail and undertail-coverts black. In non-breeding plumage somewhat duller, less sheen to the green of the head, more dull brown intermixed with chestnut of body. Female dark brown, with feathers edged pale brown; crown, rump and tail dark brown; throat buff. In flight, white armpits and wingstripe. 38–45 cm.

VOICE Male gives muted high peep like male Grey Teal; female gives a rapid sequence of quacking; shorter, higher-pitched than that of female Grey Teal.

HABITAT Found on both large and small bodies of water, saline coastal estuaries, bays, as well as freshwater lakes and swamps.

BREEDING September–December; usually October–November. Nest is a scrape in the ground, in long grass, among rushes, in crevices among rocks, or in hollows of trees. Seven to 15 creamy eggs; usually seven to nine. After breeding, flocks gather on open waters.

RANGE Southern Australia, mainly coastal; vagrant to mid-north, inland. Sedentary or nomadic.

STATUS Common parts of south; elsewhere uncommon. Endemic.

▶ See also pages
124 125 269 *281*

79 AUSTRALASIAN SHOVELER

Anas rhynchotis   Anatidae

OTHER NAMES Spoonbill Duck, Shovelbill, Blue-winged Shoveler, Stinker

RECOGNITION A low-floating, dark-headed duck, with low sloping forehead blending to a heavy, broad square-cut, shovel-tipped bill. Male in breeding plumage has head deep grey-blue, vertical white mark between eye and bill; eye bright yellow. Back and rump black, shoulder and wing-coverts blue-grey with several white bars. Underparts chestnut, white patches to rear of flanks. Female and eclipse male, mottled brown upperparts, chestnut underparts. 46–49 cm.

VOICE Usually silent, but occasionally from the male a soft 'took-took', and low grunting; female a soft, husky quack, and chattering sounds in flight.

HABITAT All kinds of wetlands; preferring large undisturbed heavily-vegetated freshwater swamps; but also on open waters, occasionally coastal.

BREEDING August–December in coastal Australia; or almost any time of year in arid areas with flooding rains. Nests on the ground in dense vegetation, sometimes on a stump or hollow of a tree standing in water. Nine to 11 cream eggs, tinged green.

RANGE In Western Australia north to North West Cape; eastern Australia north to Cairns. Nomadic.

STATUS Common parts of south-east; sparse or vagrant to north of range. Endemic subspecies.

▶ See also pages
223 *281*

80 PINK-EARED DUCK

Malacorhynchus membranaceus Anatidae

OTHER NAMES Pink-eyed Duck, Pinkie, Widgeon, Zebra Duck, Whistling Teal

RECOGNITION Upperparts, including crown, back of neck, back and uppersurface of wings brown; tail brown with white band across near the tip; rump white. Underparts white, barred dark brown; these barrings become finer towards the throat and near plain white on the face, where there is a large near-black patch over the eye, and a small, deep pink spot at the ear. In flight, white underwing-coverts barred dark; trailing edge finely edged white. 38–45 cm.

VOICE Unusual for a duck, a musical chirruping sound, both while in flight and on the water; when fighting, it becomes an almost continuous trilling.

HABITAT Mostly on inland waters, usually fresh, but also brackish; swamps, flooded claypans, sometimes coastal inlets. Feeds on shallow, warmish waters.

BREEDING At any time of year that

80 PINK-EARED DUCK
Malacorhynchus membranaceus

floodwaters are high enough, most often spring and autumn. Nest is a rounded mass of down, in which the five to eight creamy or white eggs are hidden, placed in a hollow, or on a stump, above water.

RANGE Throughout Australia, occasionally to Tasmania. Highly nomadic.

STATUS Common; temporarily abundant in some regions. Endemic.

▶ See also pages
125 137 173 185 242

81 HARDHEAD

Aythya australis   Anatidae

OTHER NAMES White-eyed Duck, Copperhead, White-wing, Brownhead, Punkari

RECOGNITION Upperparts brown; head is darker and has a coppery sheen. Lower breast and belly white mottled with brown, undertail-coverts white. White eye conspicuous in dark brown surrounds; bill black with slate-blue band near the tip. In flight, wide translucent white band along the full length of the wing uppersurface; underwings entirely white; white areas on underbody. Female similar but paler; eye brown. Immatures uniformly yellow-brown. 42–58 cm.

VOICE Mostly silent, or rarely heard. Male has a soft wheezy whistle, the female a soft rough sound that is more croak than quack.

HABITAT This species shows a preference for deep permanent freshwater swamps and lakes; also temporary floodwaters through the interior.

BREEDING September–June; mainly October–May. In southern regions it breeds in spring, in arid regions almost any time of the year after heavy rains. Nest, a well-woven cup, is in dense vegetation near or over water. Nine to 12 creamy white eggs.

RANGE Throughout Australia, where and when suitable habitat exists. Also to New Zealand, New Guinea and Pacific region. Nomadic.

STATUS Common in south-east and south-west; irruptive elsewhere.

▶ See also pages
173 185 197 *198*
210 244

MANED DUCK

Chenonetta jubata   Anatidae

OTHER NAMES Maned Goose, Australian Wood Duck, Blue Duck

RECOGNITION Has a goose-like appearance, with upright stance, long neck and short bill. Plumage dominantly soft mid-grey, with head and upper neck dark brown, and short dense blackish-brown mane down from nape onto back of neck. Lower back, tail-coverts and tail black. Grey wings with green speculum. Mottled brown-and-white breast; white belly and underwings; black undertail. Female gingery brown with pale lines above and below eye. 44–50 cm.

VOICE Female has drawn-out, querulous, mournful 'now' or 'quarr', with rising inflection, like 'meow' of a cat; male has a shorter, higher call.

HABITAT Pastures near fresh water, often around farm dams, including lightly timbered grasslands; also by swamps, lakes, occasionally ocean inlets.

BREEDING Recorded most months; usually in spring in south, or after rain in arid regions. The nest is a hollow of a tree, well lined with down, and may be close by, or far from water. Nine to 12 creamy white eggs.

RANGE Throughout Australia, except far north; vagrant to interior. Nomadic.

STATUS Abundant in south-east and south-west; sparse in arid and central north. Endemic.

▶ See also page
173

COTTON PYGMY-GOOSE

Nettapus coromandelianus   Anatidae

OTHER NAMES White Pigmy-Goose, Cotton Teal, White-quilled Pygmy-Goose

RECOGNITION A small duck with large areas of white in the plumage. Forehead and crown dark brown, back and wing-coverts black, face and neck pure white. There is a blackish collar between the white neck and the near-white of the belly; the latter, being very finely barred dark

81 HARDHEAD *Aythya australis*

82 MANED DUCK *Chenonetta jubata*

brown, appears pale grey at a distance. Eye bright red; bill black; legs and feet olive-green. Female more dusky; dark line through eye. In flight, brown underwings. 24–38 cm.

VOICE Female has a soft quack; male a louder 'ca-ca-carrark', several times in succession, usually while in flight.

HABITAT Has a definite preference for the deeper and more permanent lily lagoons and river pools; some farm dams with floating vegetation.

BREEDING In south of range appears to be September–November; in north the wet season, December–March. Nest site is a tree hollow, usually high, over or near water. Eight to 15 pearly-white eggs.

RANGE Coastal eastern Queensland; formerly south to north-eastern New South Wales, where now vagrant. Also in India, South-East Asia, and New Guinea. Nomadic.

STATUS Moderately common; locally common.

▶ See also pages
72 75 110

GREEN PYGMY-GOOSE

Nettapus pulchellus   Anatidae

OTHER NAMES Goose-Teal, Green Goose, Green Goose-Teal, Pygmy-goose

RECOGNITION A small duck, with goose-like appearance in some respects, especially short strong plant-grazing bill. Head, neck, back and wings blackish with strong green gloss. Prominent large white cheek patch, from throat back almost to nape. Underparts white, with a conspicuous dark green or brownish zigzag barred effect to flanks and tail-coverts. Female duller, neck mottled green-white not solid dark green; light eyebrow. 34–38 cm.

VOICE Sharp musical whistles and trills, 'peee-wit', and on a descending scale, 'peee-oo'; also a sharp high 'whit'.

HABITAT In the northern dry season, this species is concentrated upon the deep permanent lily lagoons; in the wet, it spreads over the flooded lowlands.

BREEDING December–March; mainly January–February. The nest is usually in a hollow tree, or on the ground amid swamp vegetation. Eight to 12 smooth, white or creamy-white eggs.

RANGE Tropical northern and north-eastern Australia; western Kimberley to north-eastern New South Wales. Also in Indonesia, New Guinea. Locally nomadic.

STATUS Moderately common, especially far north.

▶ See also pages
187 197 198 199
210

BLUE-BILLED DUCK

Oxyura australis   Anatidae

OTHER NAMES Stiff-tailed Duck, Spine-tailed Duck, Diving Duck, Little Musk Duck

RECOGNITION A compact diving-duck, with rich deep chestnut plumage overall except black head and upper neck; and buffy-white area at centre of belly. Tail black with stiff pointed feather tips, usually beneath the surface except when fanned in display. Bill large, scooped, bright light blue. In eclipse plumage, male is dull brown, finely barred paler; bill dark grey. Female dull brown, finely barred lighter; head dark brown; bill grey. 37–44 cm.

VOICE Usually silent except in display, when male utters rapid low-pitched rattling sounds, and the female a soft low quack.

HABITAT Usually the larger deeper permanent lakes and swamps; on open waters in winter, moving to smaller more densely vegetated swamps to breed.

BREEDING All months recorded, but mainly September–December. The nest is built among reeds or other dense vegetation, usually over water, and often has a canopy of reeds pulled down and interwoven. Five

85 BLUE-BILLED DUCK *Oxyura australis*

to eight rough textured, pale greenish eggs.
RANGE South-east, south-west, and Tasmania; vagrant to interior. Nomadic.
STATUS Moderately common. Endemic.

▶ **See also pages**
125 137 197 244

86 MUSK DUCK

Biziura lobata   Anatidae
OTHER NAMES Diver, Diving Duck, Mould Duck, Mould Goose, Steamer
RECOGNITION A dusky dark-brown duck that floats very low in the water, often semi-submerged. Plumage dark brown, fish-like body and tail. Bill extremely broad, deep, dark grey. Male has large leathery black lobe or flap of skin hanging beneath the bill. Female much smaller, same dark-brown coloration, and without significant lobe beneath the bill. Broad spiny-tipped tail is usually below surface, except in male's splash display. 47–72 cm.
VOICE Silent except in courtship when male kicks jets of water behind to make a deep 'kplonk' sound, uttering almost simultaneously a shrill whistle.
HABITAT Prefers permanent swamps with heavy vegetation, but is often quick to utilize inland floodwaters if deep; occasionally estuaries and coastal bays.
BREEDING May–January; mainly August–November. The male's splash-plonk-whistle display attracts females with which he mates; the female alone then builds a rough, usually hooded nest in dense swamp vegetation. One to three large, dull greenish eggs.
RANGE South-west, south-east, and Tasmania. Sedentary, but dispersive to the interior after rains.
STATUS Common. The genus of one species is endemic to Australia.

▶ **See also pages**
35-6 35 125

OSPREY

Pandionidae Family of 1 species
1 in Australia, 1 breeding

The cosmopolitan Osprey is a fishing hawk which does not seem to have any close relatives among the other birds of prey. Its distinctive characteristics include closable nostrils, a reversible outer toe, and toes that are covered on the underside by spiny projections assisting the gripping of slippery fish. Wings are broad, legs long. It lives mainly on fish, sea snakes, sometimes birds, taken in coastal waters, estuaries, major rivers.

87 OSPREY

Pandion haliaetus   Pandionidae
OTHER NAME Fish Hawk
RECOGNITION Hunts fish along coasts and estuaries, and in this environment is only likely to be confused with the White-bellied Sea-Eagle. The Osprey in flight looks mainly white below; with darker brownish wingtips, wrist patch, and trailing edge; darker breastband. Dark band through eyes, continued down nape; uppersurfaces of body, wings and tail brown. Hunts by diving feet-first, sometimes plunging entirely underwater. Wingspan 1.5 m.
VOICE Drawn-out whistle, plaintive 'pee-eee, pee-eee'. When alarmed, a sharp 'tchip-tchip'.
HABITAT Coasts and islands, mangroves, estuaries, and considerably inland on major rivers.
BREEDING March–December; mainly April–November. Nest is a bulky structure of sticks, seaweed, and often rope and other shore debris, usually placed in a tree. If on the ground, built on a cliff-edge, becoming a massive tower over years of re-use.
RANGE All Australian coasts; inland on major rivers. Cosmopolitan. Probably mostly sedentary.
STATUS Common except in south-east.

▶ **See also pages**
46 80 81 82 83 98
122 162 168 244

KITES, GOSHAWKS, EAGLES, HARRIERS

Accipitridae Family of 217 species
18 in Australia, 17 breeding, 5 endemic

Birds of prey usually with broad fingered wings, except goshawks and sparrowhawks with broad rounded wings, and two species of hovering kites with slender and pointed wings. Tails are variable, as is the feathering of legs. Identification by colour can be difficult, as several species have two colour phases, even giving rise to different common names, and because distinctly different immature plumages may persist for several years.

88 BLACK-SHOULDERED KITE

Elanus notatus   Accipitridae
OTHER NAME Australian Black-shouldered Kite
RECOGNITION White undersurfaces; pale grey upperparts except for white crown. Black shoulders when perched. White beneath, with black patch at bend of wing. Above, black along leading edge to bend of wing. Gull-like in looks and flight. Hovers often when hunting. Similar species is Letter-winged Kite, which in flight has black right along underwing from body to wrist. Female almost identical, slightly darker on the back. Wingspan 90 cm; length 33–38 cm.
VOICE 'Tew', or 'khar', variable sound, musical to harsh; also quiet and plaintive 'chep'. Will swoop to defend, giving a harsh 'kiarr'.
HABITAT Open country, natural grasslands, sparsely wooded plains and farmlands, especially pastures and other grassy areas.
BREEDING Recorded all months, but mainly April–November, probably influenced by abundance of mice or other very small mammals. Nest usually built high in densely leafy part of a tree and often difficult to see.
RANGE Throughout Australia; probably sparse in arid centre; rare Tasmania.
STATUS Moderately common; fluctuating locally. Endemic.

▶ **See also pages**
6 82 161 168 278

89 LETTER-WINGED KITE

Elanus scriptus   Accipitridae
RECOGNITION Very like the much more common Black-shouldered Kite, especially when perched. At close range, larger eyes, owl-like face. The dark mark ahead of eye does not extend behind. In flight, black bar along underwing from flanks to base of primaries forms an elongated letter M (broken at the body). Hunts at night almost exclusively, may be seen at times in flocks, with communal roosting during the day. Wingspan 90 cm; length 35–39 cm.
VOICE Harsh or screaming 'kharr'; high clear alarm call, 'chip, chip'. A slow harsh chatter has also been recorded.

88 **BLACK-SHOULDERED KITE** *Elanus notatus*

HABITAT Grasslands of open plains, normally arid regions, but with occasional irruptions, sometimes extending to coastal areas.

BREEDING Breeding is variable, linked with abundance of prey, especially the native Long-haired Rat; any month, but usually March–September. Nest bulky, often in watercourse trees. Two to five blue-white eggs, heavily marked in browns.

RANGE Most of mainland; breeding mostly south-east interior. Irruptive-nomadic.

STATUS Usually uncommon; occasionally locally common. Endemic.

▶ **See also pages**
136 138 167 168
169 179 183 184

PACIFIC BAZA

Aviceda subcristata　　　Accipitridae

OTHER NAME Crested Hawk

RECOGNITION Australia's only crested hawk. Soars on broad wings that are pale grey beneath, with dark-barred flight feathers. Breast whitish with conspicuous dark bars across, continuing to undertail-coverts. Tail grey, black-tipped. Head and neck blue-grey; rest of upperparts dark grey-brown. Floats slowly through the treetops, snatching small reptiles, large insects from the foliage. At times performs aerial acrobatics. Wingspan 75–85 cm.

VOICE Double-noted whistle, rising then falling, given in flight, as 'wee-choo, wee-choo'; and various softer piping calls.

HABITAT Rainforests, eucalypt forests and woodlands; where large insects such as mantids are taken from foliage, and occasionally tree-frogs, lizards.

BREEDING Variable; usually September–December. Nest is a flimsy, shallow structure of sticks and leaves, lined with green twigs and leaves, and usually 15–30 m above ground. Two to three pale blue-white eggs, sometimes marked with brown.

RANGE Northern, north-eastern and eastern Australia; mainly coastal. Also in New Guinea and other islands to the north. Sedentary.

STATUS Uncommon; locally quite common.

▶ **See also pages**
72 72 82 121 196
197 208 210

BLACK KITE

Milvus migrans　　　Accipitridae

OTHER NAMES Fork-tailed Kite, Kite-Hawk, Kimberley Kite

RECOGNITION In flight, distinctive long tail that usually is forked when partly closed but almost square-cut if fully spread. Lazy flight, often low. Colour mostly dark brown, appears black against sky, especially in distance. Slightly paler about the face. Very gregarious, usually seen in numbers, especially around northern

91 **BLACK KITE** *Milvus migrans*

towns, rubbish dumps, grassfires. Preys on small reptiles, insects, and is also a scavenger. Wingspan 1.1–1.3 m; length 48–56 cm.

VOICE Thin plaintive descending whistling 'kweee-errr'. Also a sharp staccato 'keee-ki-ki-ki-ki-'.

HABITAT Open savannah-woodlands, semi-arid grasslands and scrublands, northern towns, and station yards.

BREEDING Variable; September–November in south; February–May in north of range. Large, rough stick nest in tree forks, usually quite high. Two to three dull white eggs, unmarked or sparsely spotted and streaked purplish-grey and red-brown.

RANGE Most of Australia except heavily forested east and south-east coastal regions, and Tasmania.

STATUS Very abundant through north, to uncommon in south of range.

▶ **See also pages**
82 83 98 136 173
179 184 197 199
199 218

SQUARE-TAILED KITE

Lophoictinia isura　　　Accipitridae

RECOGNITION In flight, tail long, very square-cut; compared with concave V for Black Kite, convex curve for Whistling Kite, and the almost-square but short tail for Black-breasted Buzzard. Floats lazily low across the treetops on long, broad upswept wings; flight feathers barred. Upperparts brown; underwing-coverts are bright light rufous; back brown. At moderate distances the white forehead and face are very distinctive. Wingspan 1.2 m; length 51–55 cm.

VOICE Around nest, a moderately loud yelp, not harsh, but quite pleasant, almost musical. Female on nest gives weak twittering.

HABITAT Open forests, woodlands, heathlands, semi-arid scrublands. Absent from heavy forests and treeless parts of interior.

BREEDING Variable, June–January; mostly September–December. Nest is a quite bulky platform, well-lined with leaves. At two nests photographed by the author, males brought in young of small birds, sometimes with nest. May also take small reptiles.

RANGE Throughout Australia except Tasmania; perhaps only nomadic visits to some regions.

STATUS Scarce; moderately common south-west (WA), Top End (NT) and Queensland. Endemic.

▶ **See also pages**
82 121 *128* 129
130 136 138 *179*
183 245

93 BLACK-BREASTED BUZZARD

Hamirostra melanosternon   Accipitridae
OTHER NAME Black-breasted Kite
RECOGNITION Two colour phases. Dark phase bird looks mainly black in flight, but with white patch towards wingtips; rich buff undertail and undertail-coverts. Light phase has black replaced by brown; white wing patches are less obvious. Soars with large, broad wings upcurved and partly backswept. When perched, note black face and body; rufous nape; rufous-trousered legs. Immatures are brown in place of black. Heavily built, actively predatory. Wingspan 1.5 m.
VOICE Repeated quick yelp; thin whistling scream, and sharp 'chip-chip'. Preys upon rabbits, reptiles, nestling and adult birds.
HABITAT Open woodlands; semi-arid scrublands, especially tree-lined water-courses, northern savannahs; usually absent from more densely forested areas.
BREEDING Variable, any month; mainly May–November. Nest is a large stick structure, lined with green leaves, usually in horizontal fork of a tall tree. Usually two coarse buff-white eggs, boldly blotched with violet and light and dark brown.
RANGE Throughout Australia except east coast, south-east, south-west, and Tasmania. Sedentary.
STATUS Uncommon. Endemic.

▶ See also pages
138 167 168 *169*
173 179 183 184
219 220 230 273

94 BRAHMINY KITE

Haliastur indus   Accipitridae
OTHER NAMES Red-backed Sea-Eagle, Red-backed Kite, White-headed Sea-Eagle
RECOGNITION Distinctive, bright chestnut plumage with contrasting white head, neck and breast. In flight, black wingtips; upswept, broad wings, rounded; white parts conspicuous. Preys upon fish, reptiles, frogs, crustaceans, large insects, and often feeds upon carrion and offal; fish is reported to be the principal food brought in to the nest. Female slightly larger. Immatures brownish, similar to Whistling Kite. Wingspan 1.2 m; length 43–51 cm.
VOICE Drawn-out, high 'pee-ah' and other shrill sounds. The species is quite common around some northern towns, with the calls a familiar sound.
HABITAT Coastal; especially estuaries, tidal mudflats and mangroves, islands, lower reaches of the larger rivers, swamps, harbours, coastal towns.
BREEDING June–September; in mangrove or other coastal or island tree. Nest of sticks; lined with seaweed, leaves, grass, paper and fine sticks; built into a tree fork 10–20 m above the ground. One to three white eggs, finely streaked and spotted purplish browns.

RANGE Coastal north-west, northern and north-eastern Australia. Also to South-East Asia. Mainly sedentary.
STATUS Common; uncommon in south of range.

▶ See also pages
47 47 80 82 83 98
122 223

95 WHISTLING KITE

Haliastur sphenurus   Accipitridae
OTHER NAME Whistling Eagle
RECOGNITION In flight, long rounded tail; body streaked brownish beneath except for darker flight feathers, broken by light patch behind bend of wing. Slow wheeling flight; wingbend held well forward; wingtips back; downcurved, dark primaries swept back, widely fingered. When perched looks nondescript; streaked-mottled brown, lighter beneath. Scavenging habits; gregarious; sometimes in large numbers as at carrion. Wingspan 1.2 m; length 51–59 cm.
VOICE Loud, clear voice, carries far. Drawn-out descending call followed by burst of short, rapid ascending notes. Alarm call a mournful 'kairr'.
HABITAT Woodlands, open forest, semi-arid scrublands, wetlands, estuaries and mangroves.
BREEDING Variable, most months; mainly June–November. Large nest of sticks, becoming quite massive over the years. Usually placed in highest position available. Two to three coarse, bluish-white eggs, marked purplish and red-brown.
RANGE Throughout Australia; vagrant to Bass Strait islands, and Tasmania. Also in New Guinea. Nomadic.
STATUS Abundant in north; has become scarce in south-west.

▶ See also pages
47 83 98 129 173
179 184 273

95 WHISTLING KITE *Haliastur sphenurus*

96 BROWN GOSHAWK *Accipiter fasciatus*

96 BROWN GOSHAWK

Accipiter fasciatus   Accipitridae
OTHER NAMES Australian Goshawk, Chicken Hawk
RECOGNITION Rounded contours in flight; each wing oval-shaped, tail-end rounded. Underparts barred rufous and white, except whitish flight feathers barred dark grey; long tail grey, barred darker. Upperparts brownish to slaty grey; eye and long legs bright golden yellow. Collared Sparrowhawk is very similar, but with pale rufous hind-neck collar and tail more square-cut. The Brown Goshawk is a stealthy yet bold swift predator of birds and small mammals. Wingspan to 1 m; length 41–55 cm.
VOICE High fast chatter; male higher 'kikiki'; female lower-pitched, more drawn-out. Noisy around nest, especially towards intruders.
HABITAT Open forests, woodlands, watercourse trees in mulga and spinifex, farm and roadside timber. Favours localities near water.
BREEDING Recorded most months; mainly August–December. Nest usually a high and quite substantial stick structure, well lined with gum-leaves. Usually three to four smooth, bluish-white eggs; unmarked, or with spots and streaks of lavender and brown.
RANGE Throughout Australia. Also to New Guinea and Pacific islands. Sedentary; in places migratory.
STATUS Common in most regions.

▶ See also pages
64 82 83 123 153
182 184 245 275

COLLARED SPARROWHAWK

Accipiter cirrhocephalus   Accipitridae
OTHER NAME Chicken Hawk

RECOGNITION Closely resembles the more common Brown Goshawk, but smaller (though the female which is larger, is of similar size to the male Brown Goshawk) and of more slender build and outline. Upperparts grey-brown, with distinct pale rufous collar. Underparts barred rufous and white; flight feathers and tail whitish barred darker. Tail-tip square-cut in flight, square to slightly forked when perched. Long, fine, bright yellow legs and eyes. Wingspan 75 cm.

VOICE Fast chatter, more shrill than that of goshawk or kestrel; a very rapid 'ki-ki-ki-ki'; at other times, as at nest, a more drawn-out 'swee-swee-'.

HABITAT Extremely varied; rainforests to arid scrubs. Hunts in swift dashes through foliage to take small birds; often lurks near waterholes.

BREEDING Recorded most months; mainly August–December. Nest usually high, built of fine sticks, and kept well lined with green leaves. Two to four dull bluish-white eggs, sometimes unmarked, or sparsely spotted and blotched red-brown.

RANGE Throughout Australia. Also New Guinea and islands to north. Sedentary.

STATUS Moderately common.

▶ See also pages
82 151 *181 183*
184 221 245 274
325

GREY GOSHAWK

Accipiter novaehollandiae   Accipitridae
OTHER NAMES White Goshawk, White Hawk

RECOGNITION Of similar silhouette but more solidly built and shorter-tailed than the Brown Goshawk. Two distinct colour phases: pure white with red or yellow eyes; or, pale grey upperparts and whitish faintly barred darker underparts, eyes red. Compared with Grey Falcon, wings of the Grey Goshawk have more rounded outline and, when folded, are much shorter than tail. Grey and white phases interbreed. Hunts in powerful fast dashes, taking prey to heron and rabbit size. Wingspan 1 m.

VOICE Like Brown Goshawk, but mellower, slower, 'yuik, yuik, yuik'; in alarm, a rapid 'ki-ki-ki-ki-ki-'.

HABITAT Forests; including rainforests, woodlands, watercourse timber, mangroves, but often hunting out over open areas.

BREEDING Variable, March–December; usually August–December. The nest is a large structure of sticks, lined with green leaves, on a horizontal fork, high in a living tree. Four to five dull bluish-white eggs, sparingly blotched purplish-brown.

RANGE Higher rainfall areas of northern, eastern and south-eastern Australia. Also New Guinea and other northern islands. Sedentary or nomadic.

STATUS Uncommon in most of range.

▶ See also pages
64 *65* 80 82 97
121 123 126 136
152 208 210

RED GOSHAWK

Erythrotriorchis radiatus   Accipitridae
OTHER NAMES Red Buzzard, Red-breasted Buzzard

RECOGNITION In flight, silhouette similar to Brown Goshawk, but larger, slightly longer-winged, shorter-tailed. Upperparts deep rufous, strongly marked dark brown. Face to upper breast white, merging into bright rufous of breast to tail-coverts, which are streaked black, and underwing-coverts. Flight feathers and tail undersurfaces whitish, barred darker; primaries dark-tipped. Eyes and legs yellow. Takes birds to duck size. Wingspan 1.2 m; length 50–60 cm.

VOICE Typical goshawk chatter, loud and harsh; compared with call of Brown Goshawk, said to be slower and less shrill.

HABITAT Open forests and woodlands, tree-lined watercourses. Here the Red Goshawk preys mostly upon lorikeets and other birds, small mammals, reptiles.

BREEDING Recorded March–November; probably mostly August–November. Nest is recorded as being a large, rough structure of sticks, lined with green leaves, usually in a high position. One to three dull white eggs, unmarked or sparingly marked with brown.

RANGE Coastal northern and north-eastern Australia. Sedentary or nomadic.

STATUS Rare. Endemic.

▶ See also pages
82 105 210

WHITE-BELLIED SEA-EAGLE

Haliaeetus leucogaster   Accipitridae
OTHER NAME White-breasted Sea-Eagle

RECOGNITION In flight has distinctively stubby-tailed appearance, appears to be all wings. Boldly patterned underparts; body, tail and wing-coverts snowy-white, in contrast with dark-grey flight feathers; soars with wings steeply upswept. When perched has true eagle appearance of massive build and feathered legs. Head and underparts white; grey back and wings. Immatures brownish, like immature Wedge-tailed Eagle, but with a light patch underwing

---

100 **WHITE-BELLIED SEA-EAGLE**
Haliaeetus leucogaster

and at the base of primaries. Wingspan 2 m; length 70–90 cm.

VOICE Loud and metallic clanking, and deep honking; similar to the call of the Magpie Goose.

HABITAT Coasts and offshore islands, river estuaries, fresh and saline lakes, rivers.

BREEDING April–November; usually June–October. On many parts of the coast builds a massive pile of sticks on a cliff ledge. Where trees are available, often a tall tree over water. Two dull white eggs.

RANGE Round the entire Australian coastline; and far inland on major rivers. Widespread in India, and South-East Asia. Sedentary or nomadic.

STATUS Common on remote parts of the coast.

▶ See also pages
45 80 83 122 123
124 125 129 *131*
138 151 161 162
167 196 *198* 199
244 272

WEDGE-TAILED EAGLE

Aquila audax   Accipitridae
OTHER NAME Eagle Hawk

RECOGNITION Massive black or dark-brown eagle with tail long and tapering to a point or wedge. In flight, slow powerful wingbeats, soars on upcurved wings. Adults over about five years glossy black with tawny nape; younger birds brown, with brown areas becoming darker with age. Soars to great heights, and covers large areas when hunting. The prey includes animals to small wallaby size, but most commonly rabbits, also often carrion. Wingspan 2–2.5 m; length 90–100 cm.

VOICE Piping calls, usually uttered in display flights and near nest, 'psee-eew, psee-eew'; in alarm, a long wheezing scream.

HABITAT Almost all habitats; from heavy forest to very arid and almost treeless plains. Occasionally sighted soaring high over major cities.

BREEDING June–November. The nest, lined with green leaves, is re-used for many years, becoming immense; usually high, but may be very low in arid, mulga scrub country. One to two, rarely three, white eggs, marked in browns.

RANGE Throughout Australia; extending to southern New Guinea. Mainly sedentary.

101 **WEDGE-TAILED EAGLE** *Aquila audax*

STATUS Common, except in closely settled areas.

▶ See also pages
82 129 151 168
179 184 220 245
277

102 ## LITTLE EAGLE

Hieraaetus morphnoides   Accipitridae

OTHER NAME Australian Little Eagle

RECOGNITION Two colour phases; light and dark. In flight, each has light band across wing undersurfaces; in light-phase birds this forms a broad M. Primaries are dark-tipped; tail square-cut; legs fully feathered; short crest on nape. When soaring, wings are held almost flat, tail is fanned; tends to circle tightly. The dipping display flight, usually at considerable height and accompanied by loud calls, often attracts attention to this raptor. Wingspan 1.2 m; length 45–51 cm.

VOICE Three-noted, pleasant, descending call, carries a great distance; once known often gives identification where the species may not have been noticed.

HABITAT Forests and woodlands, farmlands, arid scrublands, watercourse timber in otherwise treeless country; rabbits the main prey, but also birds.

BREEDING August–November. Stick nest, usually high; sometimes uses old nest of another species. Two dull white eggs, unmarked, or sparsely streaked and blotched reddish-brown; incubation takes about 32 days; fledging 50 days.

RANGE Throughout Australia except for Tasmania. Also in New Guinea. Usually sedentary.

STATUS Moderately common. Endemic subspecies.

▶ See also pages
82 *138* 173 *179*
184 220

103 ## SPOTTED HARRIER

Circus assimilis   Accipitridae

OTHER NAMES Jardine's Harrier, Spotted Swamp Hawk, Allied Harrier, Smoke Harrier

RECOGNITION When hunting, floats low on broad, slow-beating wings, sometimes hovers. Primaries widely fingered and dark; otherwise flight feathers beneath whitish, lightly crossbarred; long, pale-grey tail, boldly barred black. Body under-surface and wing-coverts bright chestnut, spotted white. Upperparts smoky blue-grey, spotted white. Distinct chestnut facial disc, edged with a blue-grey ruff. Eyes and long legs yellow. Wingspan

1.2 m; length 50–60 cm.

VOICE High 'kik-kik-kik', not loud, perhaps only around nest. Food call is a loud whistled 'see-eep-'; also a 'kitter-kitter' recorded between adults.

HABITAT Open plains, spinifex and other grasslands; including farmlands, very open woodlands, open sandplain heathlands.

BREEDING Any month in arid regions, but usually May–November. Only harrier species usually nesting in trees. Bulky stick nest is lined with leaves, mostly built in outer foliage where it is inconspicuous. Two to four whitish eggs.

RANGE Throughout Australia; mainly drier mid-north and north-west; vagrant to Tasmania. Also on islands to north. Nomadic.

STATUS Common north and north-west; rare south-east and coastal south-west.

▶ See also pages
82 137 138 164
183 184 208 220
222 224

104 ## MARSH HARRIER

Circus aeruginosus   Accipitridae

OTHER NAMES Swamp Harrier, Swamp Hawk

RECOGNITION A typical harrier in flight; leisurely quartering of low vegetation and water with slow wingbeats, often gliding with wings upswept. Dark brown upperparts, with conspicuous white rump, often visible as the bird banks or circles in low flight. Underparts usually buff, heavily streaked brown, but older males may have grey upperwing and buff to white underparts. When perched, has upright posture and noticeably long, pale yellow legs. Wingspan 1.2 m.

VOICE In breeding, displaying males give high, descending 'keeoo'; a high 'kee-ah' at food transfer; and harsh alarm 'kek-kek'.

HABITAT Wetlands, especially swamps with reed-beds, but may be seen hunting over adjacent open country; rarely very far from water.

BREEDING August–March; usually October–December. Nest typically in reed-bed of a swamp in water 1–1.5 m deep; the base of the bulky platform of reeds extending well into the water. Very shy at the nest.

RANGE Throughout Australia, where there is suitable wetland habitat; rare in arid interior. Also in Europe, Asia and Africa. Sedentary or nomadic.

STATUS Moderately common in wetter coastal regions.

▶ See also pages
82 83 130–1 *130*
137 139 142 151
153 161 163 172
183 224 242 244

FALCONS

Falconidae Family of 61 species
6 in Australia, 6 breeding, 1 endemic

Predators built for swift flight, with smoothly contoured bodies, narrow pointed backswept wings. The Australian species belong to the genus *Falco*. The prey is taken in flight, often in a steep diving stoop, being killed or stunned on impact of the powerful talons; the kill may be completed with the powerful notched bill. Prey for the Australian species ranges from insects to quite large waterfowl.

BLACK FALCON

Falco subniger   Falconidae

RECOGNITION Almost entirely very dark brown; looks black against the sky. At closer range, note paler face and chin; bluish-white cere and eye-ring, and black streak down from eye. Powerful build; short legs, dull grey-white. Flight typically falcon-like: rapid short wingbeats; wings horizontal in glide; very fast and, like Peregrine Falcon, spectacular stoop to take prey. Also hunts small mammals, reptiles on the ground and occasionally feeds at carrion. Wingspan 1 m.

VOICE Harsh scream; more like that of Brown Falcon than Peregrine Falcon. Clear and high-pitched call given during display flight.

HABITAT Semi-arid plains, open dry woodlands, favouring vicinity of watercourses.

BREEDING June–December. Uses old nest of another bird, usually another raptor. Appears not to attempt to repair or re-line the nest, and at times will take over a nest in use, driving off the owners. Two to four creamy eggs, spotted brown.

RANGE Inland Australia, especially western Queensland. Absent from Tasmania. Nomadic or irruptive.

STATUS Uncommon; rare in west of continent and east coast. Endemic.

▶ **See also pages**
136 137 138 139
161 167 168 169
169 173 184 208
219 220 221

PEREGRINE FALCON

Falco peregrinus   Falconidae

OTHER NAMES Duck Hawk, Pigeon Hawk, Black-cheeked Falcon

RECOGNITION Very fast flight, with rapid shallow wingbeats; soars high. Spectacular stoop on half-closed wings to strike its prey; usually ducks, pigeons and parrots, but sometimes even herons larger than the peregrine itself. Boldly marked; head and cheeks blue-black; rest of upperparts deep blue-grey. Underparts white (sometimes

106 PEREGRINE FALCON *Falco peregrinus*,

buff or pale rufous), finely barred black, except for white upper breast. Cere, eye-ring and legs golden yellow. Wingspan to 90 cm.

VOICE Harsh staccato alarm calls, 'kek kek kek', near nest; rising to high pitch as the falcon dives; also various screaming calls.

HABITAT Wide variety, often near wetlands, where waterfowl congregate. In breeding season, near coastal or inland cliffs, gorges, rivers.

BREEDING In tropical north, nests in dry season; in south, August–December. Uses cliff-ledge, large open hollow of a tree (usually dead), or an old nest, usually of the Wedge-tailed Eagle. Two to three creamy eggs, blotched chestnut.

RANGE Throughout Australia. Almost cosmopolitan. Usually sedentary.

STATUS Moderately common in some regions, but generally uncommon.

▶ **See also pages**
8 82 83 129 139
142 145 151 153
153 168 169 183
184 208 220

AUSTRALIAN HOBBY

Falco longipennis   Falconidae

OTHER NAME Little Falcon

RECOGNITION A small falcon, only slightly larger than the Australian Kestrel, but more solidly built. Upperparts dark blue-grey; underparts chestnut, streaked darker; flight feathers and tail whitish, barred darker. Wings long-pointed, backswept from the bend, giving a Swift-like silhouette. Flight always fast. Wings narrower and more backswept than Peregrine Falcon. Much darker, and wings more backswept than Australian Kestrel. Face creamy-white round bold black marking. 83 cm.

VOICE In breeding season, calls similar to those of the Australian Kestrel, a rapid 'kee-kee-kee'; also thin screams and chatterings at nest.

HABITAT Open woodlands, tree-lined watercourses, sometimes open forests, treeless plains, parks and gardens.

BREEDING April–January; earlier in northern Australia than in the south. Usually uses an old nest of another hawk or crow; sometimes in a tree hollow. Nest is usually in a high position, near the top of a live tree, close to water. Two to four creamy eggs, marked brown.

RANGE Throughout Australia. Also in Indonesia and New Guinea. Usually sedentary, possibly partly migratory.

STATUS Uncommon.

▶ **See also pages**
82 83 129 137 139
151 161 173 184
220 221

107 AUSTRALIAN HOBBY *Falco longipennis*

GREY FALCON

Falco hypoleucos   Falconidae

OTHER NAMES Blue Hawk, Smoke Hawk, Smoky Falcon

RECOGNITION In flight, silhouette similar to Peregrine Falcon, slightly more slender-winged. Smoky blue-grey upperparts, darker towards the wingtips. Underparts almost white, with fine dark streaks and lightly barred on flight feathers and tail. Dark streak through eye, and down from front of eye onto white cheek. Eye-ring, cere and legs conspicuously golden-yellow against near-white of plumage. Flight fast, spectacular, peregrine-like stoop. Wingspan 75–100 cm.

VOICE Calls at nest similar to those of the peregrine, 'chak-chak-chak', but not as rapid. At other times quiet and easily overlooked.

HABITAT Semi-arid and desert, open woodland and scrublands, with preference for watercourse and waterhole trees.

BREEDING June–November; mainly August–October. Uses an old nest of another species, often that of a crow; often in a very high position, preferring a creek or waterhole nearby. Two to four buff eggs, finely but densely spotted brown.

RANGE Widespread through dry inland Australia. Recorded in New Guinea. Possibly nomadic.

STATUS Rare. Endemic breeding species.

▶ See also pages
136 167 168–9
169 173 184 185
220 221 230 275

109 **BROWN FALCON** *Falco berigora*

109 BROWN FALCON

Falco berigora Falconidae

OTHER NAMES Brown Hawk, Cackling Hawk

RECOGNITION Dark to mid-brown upperparts; variable underparts dark brown to buff. Distinctive dark facial markings from eye downwards, and from eye, back and down. Rest of face comparatively pale. Undersurface of flight feathers pale. Sometimes hovers, but unsteadily, compared with kestrel. Soars on steeply upswept wings. Often perched on roadside posts and dead trees. Tends to attract attention with display flights accompanied by loud harsh cackling. 40–51 cm.

VOICE Loud harsh call, 'keeahrr'; and hen-like, but much more hoarse, cacklings.

HABITAT Wide diversity of habitat; mainly open country, grasslands, semi-arid scrublands, open woodlands, forest clearings, coastal heaths, farms.

BREEDING Variable, May–January; usually July–December. Often uses old nest of another species, but may build its own, or use a shallow hollow of a tree. Two to five fine textured but not glossy eggs, buff spotted and blotched red-brown.

RANGE Throughout Australia. Also in New Guinea. Sedentary or nomadic.

STATUS Very common.

▶ See also pages
82 83 129 151 153
168 172–3 *180*
184 218 220 245
277

110 AUSTRALIAN KESTREL

Falco cenchroides Falconidae

OTHER NAMES Windhover, Nankeen Kestrel

RECOGNITION Skilful hovering is distinctive; the only other hawk of comparable ability, the Black-shouldered Kite, being very different in colour. Upperparts rufous or pale rufous, with dark flight feathers, and male with blue-grey on crown and nape. Underparts whitish, finely streaked darker. Tail light grey above, whitish and barred beneath, both surfaces with bold black subterminal band; white tail-tip; tail often fanned in hovering. Dark streak down face. Wingspan 70 cm; length 30–35 cm.

VOICE Rapid, excited, shrill 'kee-kee-kee'; fast twitter.

HABITAT Grasslands, open plains, open woodlands, open semi-arid scrublands, coastal heaths; often near cliffs and inland breakaways.

BREEDING June–January; usually August–December. Usually a shallow hollow of a tree, or a cliff-ledge; quite often an old nest of another species. Three to five, rarely six, smooth and slightly glossy eggs, pale buff, spotted and blotched brown.

RANGE Throughout Australia. Also in New Guinea and Indonesia. Sedentary.

STATUS Very common in southern Australia; uncommon in tropical north.

▶ See also pages
82 83 151 173 *174*
184 277

MOUND-BUILDERS

**Megapodiidae Family of 13 species
3 in Australia, 3 breeding, 2 endemic**

Related to the gallinaceous fowls, and retain a fowl-like appearance, with plump bodies, short thick bills, sturdy short legs, powerful feet. Some have fowl-like bare heads and more or less colourful wattles. Incubation of eggs is accomplished by use of warmth other than that generated by the adult bird's body. The eggs are buried in a very large mound of earth and litter, to be incubated by heat of decay, and often also of the sun.

111 ORANGE-FOOTED SCRUBFOWL

Megapodius reinwardt Megapodiidae

OTHER NAMES Jungle Fowl, Scrubfowl, Megapode

RECOGNITION Upperparts dark chestnut-brown; underparts slaty blue-grey, extending round back of neck. Crown of head brown with a short pointed crest; solid legs and large powerful, bright orange feet. Three subspecies with slight variations in the tones of brown and grey. Although a ground-dweller, the scrubfowl is much more inclined to fly than the other Australian megapodes, and when disturbed will often fly up to cover. 40–45 cm.

VOICE Raucous crowing, and loud clucking like protesting domestic fowl. Several birds may combine in a lengthy cacophony; often heard at night.

HABITAT Tropical rainforests, monsoon forests, riverine and vine scrubs, dense vegetation around swamps, and on coast in mangrove-fringed creeks.

BREEDING August–March. Incubates eggs using heat generated by the decaying vegetation in a massive mound of sand and litter. Mounds usually about 5 m wide, 2 m high, but recorded up to 12 m wide and 5 m high. Eggs pale brown.

RANGE Tropical northern Australia; western Kimberley to north-eastern Queensland. Also to New Guinea, Philippines, Java and other islands. Sedentary.

STATUS Common.

▶ See also pages
52 *53* 91 98 209

112 MALLEEFOWL

Leipoa ocellata Megapodiidae

OTHER NAMES Gnow, Lowan, Malleehen

RECOGNITION Larger than domestic fowl, with back, wings and tail barred and intricately patterned with grey, chestnut, white and black. Head and neck light grey-brown blending to whitish from breast to undertail-coverts, and with a conspicuous black streak downwards from front of neck to centre of breast. Small, black bill; legs and feet thickset, grey. Singly, or in pairs; very wary, quiet-moving; if disturbed will freeze, or walk quietly into the scrub. 55–60 cm.

VOICE Male gives a deep, far-carrying territorial booming, and sharp alarm grunt. Female, a harsh, higher-pitched call. Also from pair, low clucks.

HABITAT Usually in dry, inland mallee-eucalypt scrub and open woodland, dry open forest, dry coastal heaths.

BREEDING August–April. Incubator mound constructed of ground litter of dead.leaves, twigs and bark, intermixed with and covered by sand. Early in the spring, heat comes from decomposition, later, from direct sun on the sand.

RANGE Southern Australia; from coastal south-west of Western Australia to interior New South Wales, and north-western Victoria. Locally nomadic.

STATUS Uncommon; rare much of range. Endemic genus.

► See also pages
137 138 139 162
164 220 223 232
245 278–9

AUSTRALIAN BRUSH-TURKEY

Alectura lathami   Megapodiidae

OTHER NAMES Brush-turkey, Scrub Turkey

RECOGNITION Large, turkey-sized; entirely black, with bare skin of head and neck red, and bright yellow collar and wattle round the lower neck. Tail large, black and of unusual vertically flattened shape. Male in breeding plumage has brightest colours; female has smaller neck band, no wattle. The Cape York subspecies *purpureicollis* has pale purplish collar. Brush-turkeys are ground-dwelling birds, but fly up into trees to roost and escape danger. 58–70 cm.

VOICE A deep harsh cluck or grunted 'kyok', and various other more subdued clucking and grunting sounds.

HABITAT Rainforest, mainly coastal and on coastal ranges, and inland into brigalow scrub in Queensland.

BREEDING July–February; mainly August–December. Nest is a large mound of leaf-litter mixed with earth, regularly renewed and turned by the male. Probably about 18–24 white eggs are laid in a season, at intervals of several days.

RANGE North-eastern and eastern Australia; mainly coastal, south to mid-New South Wales. Sedentary.

STATUS Common, but patchy. Endemic genus.

► See also pages
127 *281*

QUAILS, PHEASANTS

**Phasianidae Family of 213 species
3 in Australia, 3 breeding, 1 endemic;
4 introduced**

A large family, including pheasants, quails, jungle fowls, but poorly represented in Australia, where there are more introduced than native species. The quails are dumpy, short-tailed little ground-birds, often reluctant to fly, but when forced, explode upwards on whirring wings before dropping back to cover. The plumage tends to be intricately patterned in rusty-browns and black, creating effective camouflage.

STUBBLE QUAIL

Coturnix pectoralis   Phasianidae

OTHER NAMES Grey Quail, Pectoral Quail

RECOGNITION Upperparts dark grey-brown, with pale buff vermiculations and long pointed creamy-white streaks. Underparts whitish, streaked dark brown mainly on breast and flanks. White streak from base of bill back over centre of crown; wider streaks above each eye to nape; shorter streaks below eye. Male has clearly-defined orange throat-patch; female a white throat. Legs yellowish. Immatures: like female, sparsely spotted on breast. 17–19 cm.

VOICE A clear high 'pip-y-weet' or 'titch-u-wip'; also deep purring sounds that can be quite loud.

HABITAT Grasslands, open grassy woodlands. Since settlement a major habitat has been cereal farmlands. Also in spinifex, saltbush.

BREEDING September–March; usually October–February. Nest is a scrape in the ground, in dense low cover, and lined with a small amount of grass. Seven to 14 eggs, usually seven to eight, buff to pale brown, uniformly spotted and blotched with umber or brown.

RANGE Throughout most of Australia; except parts of far north and arid desert regions. Nomadic.

STATUS Uncommon; but common in optimum habitats. Endemic.

► See also page
281

BROWN QUAIL

Coturnix australis   Phasianidae

OTHER NAMES Swamp Partridge, Partridge Quail, Swamp Quail

RECOGNITION Australia's largest native quail. Upperparts dark brown, heavily pat-terned with intermixed grey, deep chestnut, and black barrings; there is a fine silvery-white central streak to each feather. Underparts cinnamon or buff, closely crossbarred with fine scalloped black flecks. Eye usually red-brown, sometimes yellow; legs and feet dull orange-yellow. Female is larger; more heavily marked black above; paler beneath. Immatures paler. The Swamp Quail (*Coturnix ypsilophora*), formerly listed as a species, is now considered a subspecies of the Brown Quail and is restricted to Tasmania. 17–20 cm.

VOICE A double whistle, short-long, rising in pitch: 'tu-weep' or 'ff-weep', 'be-quick'.

HABITAT Usually rank, moist vegetation; dense grass near forests, swamp and creek edges, irrigated crops, and sometimes on islands devoid of swamps.

BREEDING Variable; breeds when grass is tall, lush and dense; January–May in tropical north; September–December in south. The nest is a small depression in ground, hidden under vegetation; lined with grass and leaves. Seven to 11 whitish eggs, spotted brown.

RANGE Eastern, northern and south-western Australia, and Tasmania. Sedentary; or nomadic inland.

STATUS Common locally in suitable habitat. Endemic.

► See also pages
35 36

KING QUAIL

Coturnix chinensis   Phasianidae

OTHER NAMES Chinese Quail, Chestnut-bellied Quail, Little Swamp Quail

RECOGNITION Very small. Rich chestnut upperparts mottled black and lightly streaked white. Face, breast and flanks slaty blue-grey; belly chestnut. Conspicuous white throat-patch with black border and black chin markings. The short legs are yellow. Female and immatures: upperparts same as male, but underparts are buff barred black, except clearly defined white throat without the black chin-throat markings of the male. Shy, hard to see. 12–13 cm.

VOICE Several high-pitched descending notes; calls day or night. Also clucking sounds, especially by the female.

HABITAT Very dense low cover of damp grasslands; especially swamp edges, moist pastures and crops. Secretive, prefer to squat or run rather than fly.

BREEDING Usually September–April, but recorded most months; evidently some time after rain when cover is most dense. Nest, a small depression in the ground, lined with grass. Four to five, or up to 10, glossy brown eggs, with fine brown spots.

RANGE Coastal northern and eastern Australia. Also in India, China, South-East Asia, and New Guinea. Sedentary.

STATUS Common in suitable habitat.

▶ **See also pages**
96 97 210 *281*

BUTTON-QUAILS

**Turnicidae Family of 16 species
7 in Australia, 7 breeding, 5 endemic**

Also known as bustard-quails or hemipodes, and closely resemble other quails, but are of very different stock. The similarity of general shape results from the similar utilization of terrestrial habitat. One of the anatomical differences is the absence of the fourth toe, which is present on the true quails. There is also the reversal of roles, the female being larger, more active in courtship, while the male incubates the eggs, tends the young.

117 RED-BACKED BUTTON-QUAIL

Turnix maculosa — Turnicidae

OTHER NAMES Red-backed Quail, Black-spotted Quail, Orange-breasted Quail, Red-collared Quail

RECOGNITION Female larger, more colourful. Upperparts grey-brown; intermixed with chestnut on hind-neck, wings and crown; becoming dark grey to black on the lower back. Rich rufous chestnut on sides of neck, face and throat. Underparts buff or pale cinnamon, with black spots along the flanks and on the yellowish wing-coverts. Male duller, smaller, little or no chestnut on the back or neck. Several subspecies of slightly varying colours. Female 16 cm; male 15 cm.

VOICE Male usually silent; female gives quite loud 'oom-oom-oom', a subdued booming sound that is monotonously repeated for lengthy periods.

HABITAT Rank grasses beside watercourses; rainforests, eucalypt woodlands, moist crops, swamp margins.

BREEDING Throughout year; mainly October–July, when insect life is most abundant and grass dense. Nest, a depression lined with grass, tucked under a clump of grass. Two to four glossy, light slate-grey eggs, densely spotted grey and brown.

RANGE Northern and north-eastern Australia, into north-eastern New South Wales. Widespread; to New Guinea and Solomon Islands. Sedentary; or locally nomadic.

STATUS Common in north; rare south of range.

▶ **See also pages**
86 87

118 PAINTED BUTTON-QUAIL

Turnix varia — Turnicidae

OTHER NAMES Butterfly Quail, Speckled Quail, Painted Quail, Varied Quail

RECOGNITION Female larger, more colourful. Upperparts blue-grey, finely streaked white, and with intermixed chestnut and black on the back, wings, hind-neck and crown. Light chestnut on sides of neck and extending back onto the flanks. Face and underparts whitish or pale grey, mottled darker grey and with large creamy-white spots on breast and flanks. Eyes red, legs yellowish. Male has less chestnut round the neck. Female 19 cm; male 16.5 cm.

VOICE The female gives a low booming call, like that of Emu or Common Bronzewing, which is loud for the size of the bird; often at night; male silent.

HABITAT Eucalypt forests and woodlands where there is a layer of twigs and leaf-litter; low shrubbery, mallee, coastal scrub, heaths.

BREEDING All months; usually August–March. Nest is a small depression in the ground, lined with grass and leaves, sometimes partly hooded. The nest-building seems to be done mainly by the male. Four whitish eggs, finely spotted blue and red-brown.

RANGE Eastern, south-eastern, south-western Australia, and Tasmania. Nomadic; movements erratic.

STATUS Uncommon. Endemic.

▶ **See also pages**
136 *281*

119 CHESTNUT-BACKED BUTTON-QUAIL

Turnix castanota — Turnicidae

OTHER NAME Chestnut-backed Quail (Buff-breasted sometimes included)

RECOGNITION Very like Painted Button-quail, but with different range. Female larger, more colourful. Upperparts a lighter sandy or cinnamon tone rather than the blackish-chestnut of the Painted Button-quail; rump and tail plain cinnamon, and may be noticed if the quail is flushed; but it is generally reluctant to fly, and then only a short distance. Male similar; comparatively dull colours. Usually in coveys of six to 20 birds; feeds on insects and grass seeds. Female 18 cm; male 15 cm.

VOICE Low moaning calls, 'oom-oom', apparently a contact-call and given if birds

of a group become scattered.

HABITAT Eucalypt woodland with sparse grassy understorey, including lightly-wooded scrublands, stony ridges; sandstone and laterite in Kimberley.

BREEDING December–June; usually December–March, in wet season when insects are most abundant. Nest is a slight depression in the ground built of grass and leaves, concealed under a shrub or grass; sometimes hooded. White eggs, marked with brown.

RANGE Kimberley and Top End (NT), east to Gulf of Carpentaria.

STATUS Common, at least locally; movements unknown. Endemic.

▶ **See also pages**
188 *189*

120 BUFF-BREASTED BUTTON-QUAIL

Turnix olivei — Turnicidae

OTHER NAME Chestnut-backed Button-quail (if a subspecies of that species)

RECOGNITION Very much like Chestnut-backed Button-quail, and sometimes listed as a subspecies of that species (*Turnix castanota olivei*); but the range is isolated from that species, and probably from that of the similar Painted Button-quail to the south. The female of the Buff-breasted Button-quail is larger, plainer, more uniformly cinnamon-toned, and with more robust bill. Male duller. Female 22 cm; male 17 cm.

VOICE Probably much like that of the Chestnut-backed Button-quail.

HABITAT Woodlands, rainforests, and swamplands where grassy clearings occur.

BREEDING Wet season; about November–June. Nesting similar to Chestnut-backed Button-quail. This species rarely seen, and very little known of its movements.

RANGE Confined to Cape York Peninsula, south to about Cooktown.

STATUS Uncertain; at times locally common. Endemic species or subspecies.

▶ **See also pages**
102 *105*

121 BLACK-BREASTED BUTTON-QUAIL

Turnix melanogaster — Turnicidae

OTHER NAMES Black-breasted Quail, Black-fronted Quail

RECOGNITION Female larger, darker. Upperparts grey-brown, marbled chestnut and black, streaked white. Head and throat black; breast and flanks black with massed large white spots that extend to the greyish underparts. Eye white; legs pale orange to pinkish-brown; bill stout, light brown. Male has much less black about the head. One of the largest of the *Turnix* quails. It seems reluctant to fly, and in flight looks heavy and clumsy. Female 19 cm; male 16.5 cm.

VOICE Female gives a rapid deep booming 'oo-oom, oo-oom'; male when with young utters soft clucking sounds. Male alone incubates and rears young.

HABITAT Tropical and subtropical rainforests, vine scrubs, lantana thickets; in leaf-litter mainly of the drier margins, scrubby clearings.

BREEDING August–March, variable; mainly warmer months. Nest is a shallow depression under cover, lined with grass and leaves; seldom hooded; built by both sexes. Three to four glossy, grey-white eggs, splotched brown, grey and black.

RANGE Eastern coastal Australia; Atherton to north-eastern New South Wales. Probably sedentary.

STATUS Rare. Most of recent reports in south-eastern Queensland. Endemic.

▶ See also pages
72 75 82 121

22

LITTLE BUTTON-QUAIL

Turnix velox   Turnicidae

OTHER NAMES Little Quail, Butterfly Quail, Dotterel Quail

RECOGNITION Small. Upperparts reddish-brown, mottled grey and lightly streaked whitish, and with light streak over centre of crown. Breast and face light cinnamon or buff; throat and remainder of underparts fawny-white. Male less colourful overall, and with a darker scaly pattern to the sides of the neck. In flight, the whitish underparts and white-edged, cinnamon rump should show. Immatures like male, but with dark eyes. Female 14–15 cm; male 13–14 cm.

122 LITTLE BUTTON-QUAIL *Turnix velox*

VOICE A repeated low 'oop-oop' or 'oom-oom', probably by the female when nesting, often at night; also sharp, chipping 'chek-chek' when flushed.

HABITAT Woodlands, grasslands, mulga scrublands, spinifex, saltbush, crops, pastures. Feeds mainly on seeds of grasses, and often in crop stubble.

51 **Cattle Egret** *Ardeola ibis*
62 **Glossy Ibis** *Plegadis falcinellus*
78 **Chestnut Teal** *Anas castanea*
79 **Australasian Shoveler** *Anas rhynchotis*
113 **Australian Brush-turkey** *Alectura lathami*
114 **Stubble Quail** *Coturnix pectoralis*
116 **King Quail** *Coturnix chinensis*
118 **Painted Button-quail** *Turnix varia*
123 **Red-chested Button-quail** *Turnix pyrrhothorax*
149 **Banded Lapwing** *Vanellus tricolor*

BREEDING All months, depending upon local conditions. Nest, a small hollow in or under a clump of grass; lined with grass, and sometimes with a sparse canopy. The male incubates. Four dull white eggs, thickly spotted grey and brown.

RANGE Throughout Australia except for far north and Tasmania. Highly nomadic or part migratory.

STATUS Common; variable; locally abundant to scarce. Endemic.

▶ See also page
281

123 RED-CHESTED BUTTON-QUAIL

Turnix pyrrhothorax   Turnicidae
OTHER NAMES Red-breasted Quail, Yellow Quail, Chestnut-breasted Quail

RECOGNITION Female larger, with brighter colours than the male. Upperparts from crown to tail dark brown, mottled dark grey and streaked light grey. Throat, breast light chestnut or yellowish buff, paler abdomen to undertail. Forehead and face speckled black and white. The male has less extensive cinnamon-buff on the breast, with dark scaly markings down the sides of neck and breast. Bill heavy-looking. Female 15 cm; male 13 cm.

VOICE A rapidly-repeated 'oom-oom-oom' with increasing intensity, by female in breeding season. Also a sharp chatter when flushed.

HABITAT Grasslands, lightly timbered country with long grass, mulga, mallee; pasture and stubble where there is good cover of grass or weeds.

BREEDING All year; usually October–March. The nest is a small depression scratched in the ground at the base of a clump of grass, and usually hooded with woven grass-stems. Four off-white eggs, spotted grey, chestnut and deep brown.

RANGE Northern and eastern Australia, including semi-arid parts of interior. Nomadic.

STATUS Uncommon to rare, but at times locally abundant. Endemic.

▶ See also page
281

Pedionomidae Family of 1 species
1 in Australia, 1 breeding, 1 endemic

The Plains-wanderer is probably closely related to the button-quails, being of similar appearance, with the female larger and more brightly coloured, but it has a hind toe like the true quails. The plumage is like that of the bustards, and its eggs and behaviour have similarities with some waders. The head and bill are somewhat plover-like. It has quite a long neck and legs, and often adopts a very upright posture. The males incubate and care for young.

124 PLAINS-WANDERER

Pedionomus torquatus   Pedionomidae
OTHER NAME Collared Plains-wanderer

RECOGNITION Taller, of more upright stance, and longer neck and legs than the quails. Like button-quails, there is reversed sexual dimorphism. Female larger and more colourful. Crown, back and wings grey-brown, finely barred darker. Neck encircled by a conspicuous wide collar of black, chequered with large white spots. Upper breast rufous or rich buff. Remainder of underparts creamy-white, marked with small dark crescents. Male lacks collar. Female 17 cm; male 15 cm.

VOICE Calls similar to those of button-quails, and said to be a mournful repetitive 'oom', possibly only the female. Male gives a soft 'chuck-chuck'.

HABITAT Grasslands and ungrazed paddocks of inland plains, on areas of open ground. Seldom flies, runs rat-like through grass. Stands tip-toe to watch.

BREEDING August–February; usually September–February. Nest is a scrape beneath a tussock or low bush. Female probably polyandrous; male undertakes most of the incubation and cares for young. Three to four greenish white eggs, marked grey, olive and brown.

RANGE South-eastern Australia, mainly inland; formerly to south-eastern Queensland. Probably nomadic.

STATUS Now rare; reduced range. Endemic family of one species.

▶ See also pages
131 133 *133* 138

Rallidae Family of 132 species
16 in Australia, 14 breeding, 3 endemic

Aquatic birds, long-toed, generally quite long-legged, usually of skulking habits. The rails and crakes are terrestrial, frequenting the wet lush vegetation of the swamp margins; the swamp-hens and coots are equally at home on sheltered waters as in the fringing reed-beds. Although some species travel far on migration, most are reluctant to fly, preferring to escape into vegetation. Plumages are generally sombre, but some have bright bills.

125 BUFF-BANDED RAIL

Rallus philippensis   Rallidae
OTHER NAMES Banded Rail, Banded Landrail, Buff-banded Landrail, Corncrake

RECOGNITION A large and colourful rail. Upperparts olive-brown, softly mottled darker, finely flecked white. Face and nape rich chestnut with very conspicuous white eyebrow line. Chin white, blending to blue-grey on the throat. Remainder of the underparts blue-grey boldly barred black and white except for a chestnut band across the breast. The bill is quite long, slightly downcurved. In flight, long trailing legs, longish neck. 28–33 cm.

VOICE Usually calls at dusk, a creaky or scratchy 'kriik' or 'sswit'. When flushed, a quick loud 'krek', and at the nest, a soft clucking 'kuk-kuk'.

HABITAT Wetlands; especially the lush rank vegetation of the margins of swamps, creeks, swampy woodlands, flooded saltbush and samphire, some islands.

BREEDING Recorded all months; usually September–March. The nest is built of thick grass or reeds pulled down and woven into a deep cup. Five to eight, sometimes 11, rounded eggs, buff to pinkish-white, sparsely blotched and spotted greys and brown.

RANGE Most of Australia except most arid regions. Also New Zealand, migrates across Torres Strait to New Guinea. Nomadic inland.

STATUS Common to uncommon.

▶ See also pages
35 36 82 124 137
242

126 LEWIN'S RAIL

Rallus pectoralis   Rallidae
OTHER NAMES Lewin Water Rail, Water Rail, Slate-breasted Rail

RECOGNITION Almost entirely dark plumaged; upperparts dark brown, flecked black on the crown, streaked black on the back and wings. Long, downcurved, slender bill is pink with black tip. A broad eyebrow strip extending back to the nape is light chestnut; and the lower face to breast is olive-grey; belly to undertail is black with fine white barring. Lateral streaks of white on undertail. Legs pinkish-brown. Immatures overall much duller. 21–23 cm.

VOICE Loud, staccato 'jrik-jrik-jrik', continued, rising louder, then declining, often answered by others. Also sharp alarm call, and grunting near nest.

HABITAT Wetlands; including reedy swamps and creeks, tall lush grass of moist pastures, saltmarshes with samphire cover.

BREEDING August–December. Nest of grass or rushes woven into a cup shape, often with approach ramp and canopy of interlaced stems over. Site chosen usually in reeds or rushes, up to 1 m above water. Four to six cream eggs, marked grey and rust.

RANGE Eastern, south-eastern, south-western Australia, and Tasmania; mainly coastal. Nomadic.

STATUS Uncommon to rare. Endemic subspecies of species also in New Guinea.

▶ See also pages
82 125 *145* 163

127

CHESTNUT RAIL

Eulabeornis castaneoventris   Rallidae

OTHER NAMES Chestnut-breasted Rail, Chestnut-bellied Rail

RECOGNITION Large, swamp-hen-sized; distinctive coloration with extensive chestnut on the body; grey head; large pale-tipped green bill. The grey of the head blends into olive-chestnut upperparts, while the underparts are a dusky chestnut tone. Yellowish-green legs and feet are large and powerful. A shy inhabitant of the mangroves; best seen at low tide when it may emerge to feed on mudflats, otherwise its presence may be detected by the loud call. 50–52 cm.

VOICE A loud, raucous call, repeated regularly. First note like the screech of the Sulphur-crested Cockatoo, then a drumming like that of an Emu.

HABITAT Mangroves along tidal waters. Prefers tall mangrove forest, with dense leaf canopy; occasionally in low scrubby mangroves.

BREEDING September–March. The nest is a large flat platform of sticks usually built on a low sloping mangrove, up to height of about 3 m. Four elongated, pinkish-white eggs, spotted various tones of brown.

RANGE Coastal northern Australia; Kimberley to eastern Cape York. Sedentary.

STATUS Possibly common, but rarely recorded. Endemic species or subspecies.

▶ See also pages
23 *23* 196 197 210

128

RED-NECKED CRAKE

Rallina tricolor   Rallidae

OTHER NAMES Red-necked Rail, Scrub Rail

RECOGNITION Body almost uniformly dull dark olive-brown, but entire head, neck and breast bright chestnut. Abdomen to lower flanks and undertail sooty black with dull buff crossbars; and underside of wings spotted and irregularly barred white. The robust bill is green; eyes red; quite long legs olive. Immatures have dull colours. Tail is repeatedly flicked. Distinctive in appearance, but difficult to sight; crepuscular. 28 cm.

VOICE More likely to be heard than seen in gloomy environs. Usually loud repeated, harsh 'naaak-nak-nak-' for a minute or more; also 'tok-tok-tok-'.

HABITAT Tropical rainforests; preferring very dense wet localities, often swampy parts, watercourses. On Cape York, also on drier rainforest ridges.

BREEDING Wet season, November–April. Nest may be among leaf debris between the buttress roots of a tree, or more substantial and up to 50 cm above ground in sites such as the centre of a small pandanus. Three to five initially glossy white eggs.

RANGE Coastal ranges of north-eastern Queensland; Cape York to Townsville. Some apparently cross Torres Strait to New Guinea. Part migratory.

STATUS Moderately common.

▶ See also pages
86 *86* 98

129

BAILLON'S CRAKE

Porzana pusilla   Rallidae

OTHER NAMES Marsh Crake, Little Crake, Little Water Crake

RECOGNITION Smallest Australian crake. Upperparts ochre or tawny, with black-streaked feathers on crown, back and wing-coverts; primaries dark brown. Face, throat, breast and belly light blue-grey; rest of underparts barred black and white, conspicuous from behind especially whenever the tail is flicked higher showing the barred undertail-coverts. Bill and legs are grey-green to olive-brown; eyes red. Shy, secretive. Immatures paler. 15 cm.

VOICE A harsh 'krek-krek', also a rapid or whirring 'chirr' alarm, and soft whining sound. Calls often reveal presence otherwise unnoticed.

HABITAT Freshwater wetlands, especially the edges of swamp reed-beds; often on floating vegetation; swims, or flies, between cover.

BREEDING September–February, but recorded most months. In dense vegetation, usually in or beside water. A shallow cup of stems and leaves; living vegetation above pulled down to form a canopy. Four to eight glossy olive-brown eggs, streaked darker.

RANGE Eastern, south-eastern, south-western Australia, scattered records in most other regions. Almost worldwide species. Migratory.

STATUS Moderately common in south; uncertain elsewhere.

▶ See also pages
82 *135* 165

130

AUSTRALIAN CRAKE

Porzana fluminea   Rallidae

OTHER NAME Spotted Crake

RECOGNITION Upperparts drab olive-brown, lightly mottled with black and speckled with white. Face, throat and breast dark blue-grey. Lower flanks barred black and white; white undertail-coverts, conspicuous from behind. Conspicuous red eye set in the dark blue-grey of the face. Bill light green, with orange-red at the base of the upper-mandible. Legs and feet olive-green. Immatures comparatively dull colours. 17–20 cm.

VOICE Sharp and harsh 'krik-krik' or 'krek-krek'; also rapid high-pitched chatter.

HABITAT Freshwater and brackish swamps, around edges of reed-beds, where there is dense cover and floating vegetation; also saltmarshes.

BREEDING August–February. Nest is a shallow cup or platform, often with approach ramp; in clump of rushes or grass, usually in shallow water. Three to four, up to six, glossy, pale olive-greenish eggs, spotted grey and brown mainly at larger end.

RANGE Most of Australia is suitable habitat. Erratic nomad to the interior and north-west.

STATUS Moderately common in south-east and south-west; uncertain in interior. Endemic.

▶ See also pages
35 36 82 183 242

131 SPOTLESS CRAKE

Porzana tabuensis   Rallidae

OTHER NAMES Little Swamp-hen, Leaden Crake, Tabuan Crake

RECOGNITION Entirely very dark. Upperparts dark olive-brown; face and underparts dark slaty blue-grey, with throat slightly paler; and some white crossbarring or spotting on the undertail-coverts. Legs and eye bright red in conspicuous contrast against dark plumage. Immatures have whitish throat, otherwise less colourful than adults. When walking these crakes flick tail often. In flight, long legs trail. 20 cm.

VOICE Varied calls, usually a 'Klik-blop-blop-blop' that starts slowly, becoming very rapid as it fades away; also dove-like 'crooo'.

HABITAT Swamps, including coastal, that are densely vegetated with sedges, rushes, mangroves; also on offshore islands, in mangroves, or dry scrub.

BREEDING September–January. Nest is an open shallow cup of reeds and other aquatic plants; in a clump of reeds or other dense cover, often with some canopy over. Four to six cream or pale brown eggs, mottled lavender-grey and chestnut.

RANGE Mainly eastern, south-eastern and south-western Australia; scattered records through the interior. Nomadic.

STATUS Uncommon. Endemic subspecies; species also to Polynesia.

▶ **See also pages**
146 242

132 WHITE-BROWED CRAKE

Poliolimnas cinereus   Rallidae

OTHER NAME White-eyebrowed Water Crake

RECOGNITION Upperparts almost uniformly dark brown, with slight buff or olive edging to the feathers of back and wings. A conspicuous, short white eyebrow extends from base of bill to just above the eye, and a parallel white line close below the eye, angles from white chin almost to nape. The bill is dull yellowish, red towards base of mandible. Legs olive-green; very long and slender toes can support the crake on floating vegetation. Eye red. 20 cm.

VOICE Often many birds will call together towards dusk; nasal, chattered 'cutchee-cutchee'; also 'krek-krek', and soft 'charr-r'.

HABITAT Wetlands, fresh and marine, where there is dense vegetation; includes mangroves, lagoons, swamps. Reputed not to be particularly shy.

BREEDING September–May. Nest a shallow cup of reeds and grasses lined with finer materials, and situated on or near the ground in thick swamp vegetation. Three to six lustrous pale buff or green-tinged eggs, with ochre and brown markings.

RANGE Coastal northern Australia. Some migration across Torres Strait to New Guinea.

STATUS Probably common. May be an endemic subspecies.

▶ **See also pages**
98 188 *193* 197 210

133 BUSH-HEN

Gallinula olivacea   Rallidae

OTHER NAMES Brown Rail, Rufous-vented Rail, Rufous-tailed Crake, Rufous-tailed Moorhen

RECOGNITION Almost uniformly dull plumaged: plain olive-brown upperparts; grey underparts, slightly paler on the throat; belly and undertail-coverts buff. The bill is heavy yet sharply pointed. In the breeding season the bill is olive-green, with orange frontal shield between bill and forehead. Out of the breeding season the bill is dull grey-green, and the shield grey. Female smaller, with very small shield. Immatures duller than adults. 26 cm.

VOICE Very noisy, particularly in breeding season, with harsh shrieking followed by a succession of low grunts; also single 'tok' repeated many times.

HABITAT Heavily vegetated wetlands; including rainforest edges, swampy margins of lagoons, creeks, lantana thickets.

BREEDING October–April. Nests on or near the ground, often in long grass under bushes. The nest, a platform or shallow cup, is further concealed by the vegetation drawn together above it. Six to seven white eggs, with irregular marks of grey and brown.

RANGE North-eastern and central eastern coastal Australia. Probably nomadic.

STATUS Rare or uncommon. Endemic subspecies of species also in New Guinea.

▶ **See also pages**
82 86 87

134 TASMANIAN NATIVE-HEN

Gallinula mortierii   Rallidae

OTHER NAMES Native-hen, Water-hen

RECOGNITION Large, being much larger than the Black-tailed Native-hen of the Australian mainland. Upperparts brown, tinged green; underparts blue-green, with a white patch on the flanks. Bill heavy, dull yellowish; eye red. No white on the undertail area. Almost constantly jerks tail

135 BLACK-TAILED NATIVE-HEN
Gallinula ventralis

up and down. The wings of this bulky bird have become very small, so that it is virtually flightless; but it runs very fast and swims well. Singly or in small parties. 43–45 cm.

VOICE A loud, rasping-squeaky sound, likened to sound of a hacksaw or a saw being sharpened, often from several birds; also high 'kik', grunts.

HABITAT Most inland waters; wetlands, edges of swamps, lakes, streams; where there is protective vegetation; forages out onto nearby grassland, crops.

BREEDING June–January; usually August–November. Nest site in dense vegetation, near water, sometimes in shallow water, or floating attached to reeds. Built as a shallow saucer of grass and reeds. Six to nine buff eggs, with brown blotches and spots.

RANGE Northern and eastern Tasmania, except mountain-rainforest. Introduced to Maria Island. Sedentary.

STATUS Common; probably benefited from clearing. Endemic.

▶ **See also pages**
142 *142* 151 152

135 BLACK-TAILED NATIVE-HEN

Gallinula ventralis   Rallidae

OTHER NAMES Black-tailed Water-hen, Water-hen, Gallinule

RECOGNITION A dark-plumaged, fast-running, gregarious native-hen. Dark olive-brown upperparts, very dark on the head; underparts dark blue-grey. Tail large, laterally-flattened and up-cocked; large white spots along flanks; red legs. There is no white on the black undertail area. The bill is green, with the base of the lower-mandible orange; eye golden. Will fly, in a laborious manner, if hard-pressed. Sometimes arrive in great numbers, then depart as suddenly. 35 cm.

VOICE Usually silent; but will sometimes

give harsh metallic cackling, or single sharp alarm call. Even big companies are noticeably silent.

HABITAT Any inland wetlands; margins of swamps, lakes, rivers, temporarily flooded claypans of the interior, irrigated crops, gardens.

BREEDING At any time of the year, especially in arid areas. Nest is a bowl-shape of sticks and grasses, usually in dense cover. Five to seven pale to dark-green eggs, with spots of lavender-grey, chestnut and brown.

RANGE Throughout Australia; except parts of far north and east coast; vagrant to Tasmania. Highly nomadic.

STATUS Common; variable; rare to abundant. Endemic.

▶ **See also pages**
173 *284*

137 **PURPLE SWAMP-HEN** *Porphyrio porphyrio*

---

136 DUSKY MOORHEN

Gallinula tenebrosa   Rallidae

OTHER NAMES Moorhen, Black Moorhen, Black Gallinule

RECOGNITION Plumage entirely dull black, except for white edges to the undertail-coverts that show more conspicuously whenever the tail is flicked up. The black of the upper plumage has a brown tone on back and scapulars, while the underparts are slaty blue-black. Colourful bill obvious against dark plumage, yellow-tipped with remainder bright red continuing onto the forehead as a red frontal shield. Flies with greenish legs trailing. 35–38 cm.

VOICE An occasional loud and resonant 'kerrk'. Shy in its natural haunts, but often quite tame in city parks.

HABITAT Most inland waters; usually well vegetated freshwater situations, with some open waters, including swamps, reedy lakes and rivers, parks.

BREEDING August–February. Nest is a substantial, slightly dished platform of rushes and grass, usually some overhead vegetation pulled down as a canopy, and placed in reeds or other vegetation, usually in water. Seven to 10 sandy eggs, marked purple-brown.

RANGE Eastern and south-western Australia, and in Tasmania; isolated interior and north-west locations. Sedentary or nomadic.

STATUS Generally common. Endemic subspecies.

▶ **See also pages**
35 37 82 99

137 PURPLE SWAMP-HEN

Porphyrio porphyrio   Rallidae

OTHER NAMES Blue-breasted Swamp-hen, Blue Bald Coot, Eastern Swamp-hen, Western Swamp-hen

RECOGNITION Large and black, with face, neck and breast to upper belly deep violet-blue; massive bill and frontal shield bright red. The subspecies *bellus* of south-western Australia has less violet tone in the blue. Flicks tail when walking or swimming, showing white undertail. Tame on many suburban lakes, otherwise shy, keeps out of sight in the reed-beds, venturing out morning and evening, to open shallows, pastures and lawns. Runs fast, swims infrequently. 46 cm.

VOICE Loud rasping screech or shriek, 'keeeooww'. When disturbed, the swamp-hen flies ponderously with legs trailing. Feeds mainly on tender young reeds.

HABITAT Always near water, usually an inhabitant of swamps and lakes with bulrush or other dense cover, where it clambers among the reeds.

BREEDING Recorded most months; varying according to region. Nest in rushes which it bends over and tramples to form a large dished platform. Three to five, sometimes to eight, buff to pale green eggs, marked with brown and black.

RANGE Most of Australia in suitable habitat, except arid interior (WA and NT). Possibly migrant to New Guinea. Nomadic some areas.

STATUS Common; uncommon in north.

▶ **See also pages**
82 99 *137* 165 183 265

138 EURASIAN COOT

Fulica atra   Rallidae

OTHER NAMES Coot, Australian Coot

RECOGNITION Entirely slaty blue-black, with white forehead shield and bill. No white markings on flanks or undertail. Legs are blue-grey; toes have flattened lobes; eye is red. Coots feed both in the water and on land, gathering and pecking at various kinds of vegetation. They have been observed to dive to depths up to 7 m. Solitary when breeding, otherwise gregarious. Highly nomadic; swift in flight; often travelling long distances, usually at night. 38 cm.

VOICE A single loud and raucous 'kyok' or 'kyik', sometimes repeated rapidly, as 'kik-kowk', 'kok-kowk'.

HABITAT Most possible aquatic habitats; usually freshwater and brackish lakes, swamps, temporary inland waters, sometimes sheltered coastal inlets.

BREEDING Almost any time when conditions are suitable; especially variable in the interior; most commonly August–February. Nest in swamp vegetation, or floating, anchored to reeds. Six to 15 dull white eggs, finely spotted greys and browns.

138 **EURASIAN COOT** *Fulica atra*

RANGE Throughout Australia; including most arid areas after heavy rains. Also in New Guinea. Nomadic.

STATUS Abundant in south-east and south-west; less common in north.

▶ **See also pages**
82 125 131 165
244 *285*

139 BROLGA *Grus rubicundus*

139

CRANES

Gruidae Family of 14 species
2 in Australia, 2 breeding, 1 endemic

Tall and graceful, long-necked and long-legged, bills long, straight, sharp pointed. Plumage includes decorative feathers, mainly about the head. The hind toe is small and set higher than the other three. The often spectacular dancing displays are well known. The Australian species are monogamous, mating for life. Their food, obtained in shallow water, swampy or dry grass-lands, includes small insects, small vertebrates, plant materials.

BROLGA

Grus rubicundus **Gruidae**

OTHER NAMES Australian Crane, Native Companion

RECOGNITION Tall, standing 1–1.25 m, wingspan 2 m. Very long neck and legs. Stately upright posture; moves with delib-erate, elegant fluid motions; including slow powerful wingbeats in flight, and graceful dancing displays. Only likely to be con-fused with the Sarus Crane, but has scarlet only on head (not extending down neck as Sarus), circular grey ear-patch, and loose dark skin dewlap showing under chin. Female smaller. Immatures have pink faces.

VOICE Far-carrying trumpeting calls, given both in flight and on the ground. Often a pair will call in unison; also hoarse croaks.

HABITAT Grasslands, usually near water; often at the edge of billabongs, swamps; ranges out through dry open-wooded grasslands; also moist farmlands.

BREEDING Usually October–April; variable with rainfall; some records most months. Nest is a large mound of vegetation, in shallow water, on a small islet of wetlands, or dry land. One to two cream eggs, lavender and brown spots.

RANGE Northern, eastern and south-eastern Australia, well into interior; also in north-west but not so far inland. Vagrant to New Guinea. Nomadic.

STATUS Common in north; uncommon in south. Endemic.

▶ **See also pages**
72 78 79 83 99
110 122 136 138
163 173 184 208
223

140

SARUS CRANE

Grus antigone **Gruidae**

OTHER NAME Eastern Sarus Crane

RECOGNITION So closely resembles the Brolga in appearance and behaviour that it was not noticed in Australia until 1967 when small parties of the Sarus Crane were recognized among brolgas in north-eastern Queensland. Can be distinguished from the Brolga by the red of the head being more extensive and continuing well down the neck; the lack of the slight pendant dark underchin dewlap; the eye red rather than yellow; and being slightly taller at 1.5 m. Immatures: rufous replaces red on head.

VOICE Like that of Brolga; a whooping, far-reaching trumpeting call given both in flight and on the ground, and in dancing displays.

HABITAT The Sarus Crane occupies habi-tats similar to Brolga, perhaps with more inclination towards irrigated and other artificial wetlands than dry sites.

BREEDING Breeds in the wet season, with nest of similar structure and situation to that of the Brolga. Two whitish eggs, usually spotted brown. The species has now been accepted as a breeding resident of northern Australia.

RANGE Northern Queensland, Top End (NT), and possibly Kimberley (WA). Also South-East Asia and India. Migratory.

STATUS Uncommon, but locally abundant in north-east.

▶ **See also pages**
72 75 99

BUSTARDS

Otididae Family of 23 species
1 in Australia, 1 breeding

Large stately birds of grasslands and other open terrain. The neck is long, legs moderately long, body rather heavy; yet once airborne, after a short takeoff run, their flight is powerful and graceful on broad wings. The bustards are probably polygamous; the female alone incubates, and cares for the young. The plumage is of camouflage colour and pattern.

141

AUSTRALIAN BUSTARD

Ardeotis australis **Otididae**

OTHER NAMES Plains Turkey, Wild Turkey

RECOGNITION Large, up to 1 m tall, solidly built with long (but not slender) neck. Head, neck and underparts white, except black crown; black line back from eye; narrow black breastband; bend of wing patterned black and white. Back and wings brown. Female similar, but dark-brown crown, neck and breast; thin light-grey breastband. Walks in slow stately manner, with head high and bill uplifted. Runs to take off, flies with slow deep beats of broad wings. 76–120 cm.

VOICE Usually silent, but harsh barking croak if alarmed. Males give deep guttural roar during display, with neck-sac dis-tended and tail fanned.

HABITAT Grasslands; including spinifex, open grassy woodlands, mulga and similar open scrublands. Absent or rare in south-east and near settled regions.

BREEDING Recorded all months; usually September–January. Nest is an area of bare ground, or site sheltered by a shrub or tussocks. One to two buff to greenish-buff eggs. Chicks are downy, striped buff and brown; will freeze if alarmed.

RANGE Formerly almost throughout main-land. Also in New Guinea.

STATUS Moderately common through remote regions.

▶ **See also pages**
138 184 220 *287*

141 AUSTRALIAN BUSTARD
Ardeotis australis

Jacanidae Family of 7 species
2 in Australia, 1 breeding, 1 vagrant

Specialized for a life on the floating vegetation of inland waterways, with light bodies, long legs and incredibly long toes. The jacanas are included in the large group of birds generally known as waders. Other characteristics include small spurs on the wings, and the habit of bobbing the head back and forth while walking. The eggs are often wet in the floating nests, but are impervious to water.

COMB-CRESTED JACANA

Irediparra gallinacea   Jacanidae

OTHER NAMES Lily-trotter, Jacana, Lotus-bird

RECOGNITION Small, long-legged bird, with extremely long toes which enable it to walk on floating leaves of waterlilies. Upperparts dark brown and black, with bright pink comb on forehead. Face and fore-neck white, edged buff to golden yellow. Immatures have very small, less colourful comb; white neck. These birds are usually in small parties, searching for insects on floating leaves. Flies with long legs and toes trailing. Length 23 cm; footspan 15 cm.

VOICE Shrill, repeated piping 'pee-pee-pee'; often given while in flight.

HABITAT Deep permanent lagoons where there is a permanent floating mat of lilies and other aquatic plants.

BREEDING Variable, recorded most months; usually October–July. Nest a low flat circle of waterweeds on floating vegetation; or eggs just placed on a large leaf. Three to four glossy, pale brownish eggs, intricately patterned with black.

RANGE Northern Australia, but not western Kimberley; extending down east coast into north-eastern New South Wales. Nomadic.

STATUS Common in north; rare in south of range. Endemic subspecies.

► **See also pages**
80 83 197 199 210

Burhinidae Family of 9 species
2 in Australia, 2 breeding, 1 endemic

A small family of two genera, part of the wader group. Nocturnal and crepuscular in habits. Plover-like in general appearance, but taller, longer in neck and legs; bustard-like in plumage and in having thick legs with small feet with hind toe lacking, and shortish bills. The eyes are large, in keeping with nocturnal habits. When alarmed, do not readily fly, but squat or run. The eggs and young are vigorously defended.

BUSH THICK-KNEE

Burhinus magnirostris   Burhinidae

OTHER NAMES Bush Stone-curlew, Stone Plover, Southern Stone-curlew

RECOGNITION A large, superficially curlew-like, aberrant wader, which makes excellent use of cryptic coloration and is easily overlooked. It has distinctive behaviour when disturbed; it may freeze, prostrate, or walk away with slow deliberate motion. Grey-brown upperparts; buffy-white underparts; strongly streaked darker above, and on breast. Whitish shoulder patch and throat. Dark streak back from eye; white forehead and white through the eye, which is large and yellow. 55–58 cm.

VOICE Usually calls at night; a loud, mournful, wailing 'weer-looo', starting low and rising. May become a chorus of the calls of several birds.

HABITAT Open woodland with short or sparse grass, leaf-litter, open semi-arid mulga and similar scrub; also farmlands, golf courses.

BREEDING Usually August–January, but records for all months. Nests on the ground, making a shallow depression. Two eggs, variable in background colour to match the ground; often brownish-grey blotched with darker brown.

RANGE Most of Australia in suitable habitat; avoids spinifex and forests. Sedentary.

STATUS Abundant parts of north; uncommon to rare in south. Endemic.

► **See also pages**
47 72–3 73 138 184 288

BEACH THICK-KNEE

Burhinus neglectus   Burhinidae

OTHER NAMES Beach Stone-curlew, Large-billed Stone Plover, Reef Thick-knee

RECOGNITION A large, long-legged wader with a massive, heavy-looking bill that is black tipped with yellow towards the upper base portion. Upperparts and breast grey-brown; throat and abdomen white. Dark patch on shoulder, edged below by a white streak, edged above by a shorter white patch. Face marked boldly black and white. There is a broad black band through the eye, white streaks above and below. Flies with wings that are downcurved and white with a black bar. 55–58 cm.

VOICE A mournful 'weer-loo', like the call of the Bush Thick-knee, but higher and harsher.

HABITAT Beaches, reefs, mudflats, mangroves; especially of islands and other undisturbed localities.

BREEDING August–February; mainly October–December. Nest is a slight hollow scratched on a beach, just above high-tide mark, often in among wave-washed debris. One to two creamy-white eggs, blotched olive-brown.

RANGE Coastal northern Australia; from mid-west to mid-east coast. Found through Indo-Australian region. Sedentary.

STATUS Uncommon.

▶ See also pages
47–8 47 80 81 197 223

▶ See also pages
47–8 47 80 81 197 223

PAINTED SNIPE

**Rostratulidae Family of 2 species
1 in Australia, 1 breeding**

Long-billed waders with a superficial resemblance to the true snipe. The plumage is colourful, patterned, with the female the brighter. Sexual roles are reversed; the female establishing and maintaining the territory, the male incubating and caring for the young. The painted snipes appear to be quite closely related to the jacanas.

145 PAINTED SNIPE

Rostratula benghalensis Rostratulidae
RECOGNITION Long bill, distinctly downdrooped and slightly thickened near the tip; conspicuous facial markings. Female larger and more colourful. Grey-bronze to chestnut-bronze hood over head, neck and breast; wings bronzed-green, with distinct white line encircling shoulder, separating wing from hood, then continuing down to join white abdomen. Eye encircled by white, especially behind. Male and immatures darker, buff in place of white. 22–27 cm.

VOICE Usually silent, except alarm call, a loud repeated 'kek-kek-kek'. In display female gives low, softly resonant booming call.

HABITAT Freshwater wetlands, marshy and swampy areas with ground-cover of dense low vegetation, especially samphire.

BREEDING Usually October–April, probably extends most of year. Nest a depression in mud lined with grass and usually surrounded by water and under cover. Four tapered, quite glossy eggs, buff-coloured and heavily splotched with grey, olive and brown.

RANGE Northern, eastern and southeastern Australia; rarely Western Australia; inland but not arid. Nomadic.

STATUS Uncommon to rare. Endemic subspecies of species to southern Asia and Africa.

▶ See also pages
35 37 163 183

OYSTERCATCHERS

**Haematopodidae Family of 6 species
2 in Australia, 2 breeding, 1 endemic**

Moderately large sturdy waders of the marine coasts. Plumage black or pied; bills long, very slightly upturned, quite heavy and laterally flattened, giving strength for leverage when prying open shellfish. Their evolutionary origins are uncertain, but there are affinities with avocets, stilts, and possibly thick-knees.

146 PIED OYSTERCATCHER

Haematopus longirostris Haematopodidae
OTHER NAMES Common Oystercatcher, Black-and-white Oystercatcher, White-breasted Oystercatcher

RECOGNITION A moderately large wader with sharply defined black-and-white plumage; straight stout, bright-red bill and eyes; pink legs. The upperparts including wings, the entire head, neck and upper breast black; remainder of underparts white. In flight, shows conspicuous white wingbar, white rump and uppertail-coverts. Immatures have brownish-black plumage; brown eyes; dusky bill and grey-brown legs. Feeds in tidal zone, prising open small molluscs. 48–52 cm.

VOICE Clear ringing 'kleep-kleep' especially in flight; also rapid piping 'pee-pee-pee', and prolonged high 'kervee-kervee' in display.

HABITAT Ocean coasts; especially sandy beaches, estuaries, islands; rarely on inland waters.

BREEDING August–January in south; May–September in north. Nest is a shallow scrape on a sandy beach just above high-water mark. Has suffered disturbance from people, dogs and vehicles, now endangered in New South Wales. Two to three sandy-grey eggs, marked grey and brown.

RANGE Entire Australian coastline wherever suitable habitat. Almost worldwide. Sedentary.

STATUS Common, but scarce in disturbed localities.

▶ See also pages

147 SOOTY OYSTERCATCHER

Haematopus fuliginosus Haematopodidae
OTHER NAMES Black Oystercatcher, Black Redbill, Redbill

RECOGNITION A quite large, solidly-built wader with entirely black plumage making the bright orange-red bill, scarlet eye and pink legs very conspicuous. In northern Australia Sooty Oystercatchers have a larger pink or red eye-ring. The Sooty-Oystercatcher feeds on a variety of molluscs, including limpets and dogwhelks, and also various crustaceans and polychaete worms. It may be only a rare visitor to the far north due to lack of the preferred coral reefs. 48–51 cm.

VOICE Loud and far-carrying, similar to that of the Pied Oystercatcher.

HABITAT Undisturbed ocean coasts and islands; preferring rocky shores, rocky islands; infrequently estuaries and sandy beaches.

BREEDING Variable, usually September–January. Nest a depression in sand, or hollow among rocks, the latter situation sometimes built up with pebbles, seaweed and shells. Two to three eggs, ground-colour stone or olive, marked with dark brown and purple.

RANGE The entire Australian coastline in suitable habitat. Migratory south-eastern Tasmania.

STATUS Uncommon; rare in the north. Endemic.

▶ See also pages
45 47 48 82 122 124

LAPWINGS, PLOVERS, DOTTERELS

**Charadriidae Family of 65 species
16 in Australia, 7 breeding, 6 endemic**

Plump, moderately long-legged, short-billed waders, found in marine and inland aquatic and dry-land environs. The bills are generally shorter than the length of the head. Plumages are patterned in browns, greys, black and white; some have colourful wattles. The nest and young are strongly defended, with distraction displays, and sometimes actual physical attack upon intruders. When feeding, they typically run, pause, jab at the ground, run again.

MASKED LAPWING

Vanellus miles   Charadriidae

OTHER NAMES Spurwinged Plover, Masked Plover

RECOGNITION Grey-brown on back and wings, otherwise white except for extensive yellow facial wattles; yellow bill and spurs at shoulders; black crown and flight feathers. Subspecies *novaehollandiae* has smaller wattles, larger black cap extending down nape, and bold black mark down each side of breast. Both subspecies aggressive and noisy at nest. Subspecies interbreed. In flight, white underwings with black flight feathers. 35–38 cm.

VOICE Loud 'kek-kek-kek-kek', especially when nest site is approached. Often calls at night.

HABITAT Moist open grasslands, margins of swamps, estuaries. Now very often green pastures, airfields and other man-made environs.

BREEDING July–March. Nest is a shallow scrape on the ground, edged or roughly lined with twigs, pebbles. Four yellowish-olive to brownish-green blotched eggs, spotted with various shades of grey and brown.

RANGE Throughout Australia except from central deserts to west coast. In different localities either sedentary or nomadic.

STATUS Common.

▶ See also pages 77 137 138 149

Vanellus tricolor   Charadriidae

OTHER NAME Banded Plover

RECOGNITION Brown back and wings; white underparts with black band beginning at base of bill, below eye, down sides of neck and widening to form broad and conspicuous breastband. Black crown; white line through eye; small red wattle above base of bill. In flight, white underwing is black-tipped with white bar along upperwing. Flies with quick short wingbeats. Sometimes in large flocks, often small groups; uneasy, restless. 25 cm.

VOICE Higher, more plaintive than Masked Lapwing; a wild, lonely feeling to the nocturnal calls: 'keer-kil-kil-keer-keer'.

HABITAT Open plains, grasslands, bare paddocks; generally drier terrain than Masked Lapwing; only rarely on beaches.

BREEDING Variable; at any time of year when conditions favourable, but usually July–December. Nest a shallow depression with sparse lining. Three to four variable olive-green to olive-brown eggs, marked

grey and dark brown and obviously tapered.

RANGE Throughout Australia except far north and northern deserts. Nomadic.

STATUS Moderately common. Endemic.

▶ See also page 281

GREY PLOVER

Pluvialis squatarola   Charadriidae

OTHER NAMES Grey Sandpiper, Black-bellied Plover (for breeding plumage)

RECOGNITION Plump shape. Non-breeding plumage: grey upperparts, dappled brown; white underparts, lightly dappled grey on the breast. Large dark eye, robust dark bill. In flight, underparts white except black armpits; above white rump, barred tail, white wingbar. Breeding plumage: black chin to lower abdomen (between plumages, patchy appearance). Wary, often solitary, or in small groups. 27–30 cm.

VOICE Plaintive, drawn-out 'pee-oo-ee', usually uttered while in flight.

HABITAT Coasts, islands, estuaries; including tidal reefs, mudflats, saltmarshes; sometimes large inland lakes, swamps.

BREEDING Breeds Northern Hemisphere. Regular migrant to Australia August–April. Stages of breeding plumage sometimes seen August–September and March–April.

RANGE Coastal Australia.

STATUS Common some localities; generally moderately common.

▶ See also pages 98 124 *161*

LESSER GOLDEN PLOVER

Pluvialis dominica   Charadriidae

OTHER NAMES American Golden Plover, Eastern Golden Plover, Pacific Golden Plover

RECOGNITION Non-breeding plumage: upperparts mottled brown and golden-buff; forehead and face of light golden-buff in contrast to the crown which is heavily marked brown, has small brownish marking over ear-coverts. Underparts buffy-white, with breast lightly mottled grey-brown. Breeding plumage: upperparts darker, strongly spangled gold; face and entire undersurfaces black, edged white above the eye and down the side of the neck. 25 cm.

VOICE Usually a whistled 'too-weet', a musical 'tlooee', and scratchy 'kree-kree-kree-'.

HABITAT Varied; includes rocky coasts, mudflats of coasts and estuaries, coastal marshes; favours sites with vegetation in shallow water; pastures.

BREEDING Breeds northern Asia, North America; migrates to Australia during the southern summer. A few birds remain through the winter.

RANGE Throughout Australia, mainly coastal, but inland on suitable habitat.

STATUS Common; abundant some sites. Northern Hemisphere south to New Zealand.

RED-KNEED DOTTEREL

Erythrogonys cinctus   Charadriidae

OTHER NAME Previously *Charadrius cinctus*

RECOGNITION Back, wings olive-brown; underparts white. Head and breast black except for pure white chin-throat patch. Black of lower breast extends to flanks, then blends to chestnut. Deep pink bill, tipped black. In flight, uppersurface of wings has conspicuous wide white trailing edge, white-edged rump and tail. Immatures without black areas. Runs, bobs head with jerky, stop-start action. Solitary, or small parties. 18–19 cm.

VOICE Abrupt, mellow 'chet-chet', usually when taking flight; also musical soft trills.

HABITAT Margins of coastal and inland fresh and brackish waters, with a preference for still and shallow edges of lakes, swamps, claypans, dams.

BREEDING Recorded all months, but usually October–December. Nest is a shallow depression lined with grass, not far from water, often under a bush or by rocks. Four stone-coloured or light brownish eggs, speckled and finely lined with black.

RANGE Almost throughout Australia where suitable habitat exists; vagrant to Tasmania. Nomadic, moves coastwards in summer.

STATUS Fairly common. Endemic.

▶ See also pages 229 295

HOODED PLOVER

Charadrius rubricollis   Charadriidae

OTHER NAME Hooded Dotterel

RECOGNITION Small, chubby shaped. Head entirely black-hooded, including throat and shoulders, broken by white nape band. Remainder of upperparts light grey-brown; underparts white. Black on shoulders may extend down sides of breast. Red bill tipped with black; red eye-ring; legs light pinkish-brown. In flight, white bar along black flight feathers; tail and rump black, edged white. Immatures have brown cap and eyeline; dark bill. 20 cm.

VOICE Short piping calls; also deeper barking sounds.

HABITAT Ocean beaches; and adjoining sand dunes, estuarine mudflats, exposed reefs; also inland salt lakes in Western Australia.

BREEDING Recorded August–March, but usually September–January. Nest a slight depression in sand, on or near beach; may be lined or encircled by small pieces of shell, seaweed and debris. Two to three buff eggs, spotted and blotched lavender and dark brown.

RANGE Coasts of south-eastern Australia; south-western Australian beaches and salt lakes. Sedentary.

STATUS Uncommon; in places fairly common. Endemic.

▶ See also pages
124 *295*

154 MONGOLIAN PLOVER

Charadrius mongolus   Charadriidae

OTHER NAMES Mongolian Sand Plover, Mongolian Dotterel, Lesser Sand Plover

RECOGNITION Non-breeding plumage: dark grey-brown upperparts; white underparts; prominent dark line from bill through eye becoming wider across ear-coverts; broad dark breastband. In flight, narrow white wingbar visible; small edging of white to tail. Breeding plumage: chestnut nape and breast. Looks like a smaller version of Large Sand Plover, but is distinguished by dark grey legs, darker markings about head and relatively lighter bill. 18 cm.

VOICE Clear short 'drrit' or 'drreet'.

HABITAT Coastal mudflats, wide sandy beaches, mangrove mudflats. May be seen singly, or in parties or large flocks. Quick, alert, restless, often runs.

BREEDING Migrant; breeds Northern Hemisphere. Reaches Australia in September, remaining until March–April, some staying till May. More abundant than Large Sand Plover in eastern Australia; less abundant in south-west of Western Australia.

RANGE Australian coastline; occasionally inland. Migratory.

STATUS Common in the north; uncommon in Victoria, Tasmania and south-west Western Australia.

▶ See also pages
73 75 80 98

155 DOUBLE-BANDED PLOVER

Charadrius bicinctus   Charadriidae

OTHER NAMES Double-banded Dotterel, Banded Dotterel

RECOGNITION Non-breeding plumage: dark buff-brown upperparts; white underparts; faintly smudgy brown breastband; indistinct light eyebrow; yellowish or light greenish-grey legs. In flight, white especially at bend of wing, strong edging of white to tail. Breeding plumage: two prominent bands; black across the upper breast, separated by white from wider chestnut lower breastband. Black across the forehead and through eye. Immatures speckled upperparts; single faint band. 18 cm.

VOICE Loud staccato 'pip-pit-pit'; also long trill.

HABITAT Coastal waters; occasionally inland. Beaches, mudflats, brackish and freshwater swamps, margins of lakes and dams, sometimes paddocks.

BREEDING Summer migrant; breeds in New Zealand. Arrives in South Australia in February; leaves by August. Some remain but do not breed. Occurs singly or with other species of waders or in flocks. Breeding plumage seen on arrival and before departure.

RANGE Mainly along coast; eastern and south-eastern Australia; scattered records north to Cairns and west to Fremantle.

STATUS Common in south; uncommon north; rare in Western Australia.

▶ See also pages
117 *149*

156 LARGE SAND PLOVER

Charadrius leschenaultii   Charadriidae

OTHER NAMES Large Sand-Dotterel, Large Dotterel

RECOGNITION Non-breeding plumage: light grey-brown upperparts; white underparts; darker line from bill through eye, broad grey-brown breastband; these colours and patterns lighter and less distinct than for the smaller, similarly patterned Mongolian Plover. Legs pale, varying from light bluish-grey to greenish-grey. Bill black, relatively longer, of heavier appearance. In flight, has distinct wingbar; tail darker towards end, tipped white. 23 cm

VOICE Clear 'chweep-chweep', and trilling sound.

HABITAT Coastal mudflats, wide sandy beaches, mangrove mudflats. Prefers quiet undisturbed localities. May be seen singly or in small groups or flocks.

BREEDING Migrant; breeds in Northern Hemisphere. Reaches Australia in September, remaining until April or May.

RANGE Australian coastline and islands.

STATUS Common in north and Western Australia; uncommon east and south-east; scarce in Tasmania.

▶ See also pages
215 218

157 ORIENTAL PLOVER

Charadrius veredus   Charadriidae

OTHER NAMES Asiatic Dotterel, Eastern Dotterel, Caspian Plover

RECOGNITION Non-breeding plumage: very plain, upperparts grey-brown, lighter buff on neck. Pale buff forehead and eyebrow. Dark brown through the eye; off-white chin; fore-neck blending gradually to darker, sometimes slightly rufous; very indistinct breastband. Slender black bill; long, olive-grey to yellow-grey legs. Flight fast and strong; underwing grey; tail brown, only slightly tipped white. Breeding plumage: broad cinnamon breastband; female has paler breastband. 25 cm.

VOICE Sharp 'chit-chit' or 'chip-chip', and more melodious 'chrreep'.

HABITAT Mainly inland, often far from water, frequently dry bare country. Also ploughed land, tidal mudflats, saltmarshes and salt lakes.

BREEDING Migrant from Northern Hemisphere; present September–March. Small groups or solitary, or flocks in northern Australia. Stands erect, bobs head, often perches on stumps or rocks, generally very wary, often seen with Australian Pratincole.

RANGE Recorded most parts of Australia; mostly northern, coastal and inland.

STATUS Erratic-uncommon visitor to south; common in north.

▶ See also pages
215 242

158 RED-CAPPED PLOVER

Charadrius ruficapillus   Charadriidae

OTHER NAME Red-capped Dotterel

RECOGNITION Soft sandy grey-brown upperparts; white underparts; blending to cinnamon-brown on crown and nape, this extending in black part-way round neck to form a broken collar, and through eye to base of bill. White forehead. Short, black bill and legs. Flight feathers dark grey; thin white bar along top of extended wings. Female: colours much softer, no black. Immatures: like female, and mottled upperparts. Runs swiftly, abrupt stop-start, bobs head. 14–16 cm.

VOICE Plaintive sharp 'tik', once, or rapidly repeating.

HABITAT Water edges, especially sandy or shelly, nearby dunes. Also mudflats, inland salt lakes, sometimes freshwater lakes, swamps.

BREEDING Recorded throughout the year; usually September–March. Nest is a shallow scrape in the sand, usually near water, often beside a small plant or stones. Two pale sandy-green eggs, blotched and spotted lavender-grey and dark brown.

RANGE Throughout Australia; coastal and suitable habitats of interior. Sedentary or nomadic.

STATUS Common.

▶ **See also pages** 80 149

158 RED-CAPPED PLOVER *Charadrius ruficapillus*

159 **BLACK-FRONTED PLOVER** *Charadrius melanops*

---

159 **BLACK-FRONTED PLOVER**

Charadrius melanops Charadriidae

OTHER NAME Black-fronted Dotterel

RECOGNITION Rarely on ocean beaches. Back mottled brown; white underparts. Bold black breastband, much thicker in centre of breast, forming a very conspicuous heavy V. Black on forehead, through eye and down back of neck. Bill orange-scarlet, tipped black; red eye-ring. In flight, underparts white; upperparts dark, with white wingbars; white to tip and outer feathers of tail. Immatures have no black on breast. Flight jerky, dipping. 16 cm.

VOICE Quick 'dip' call, singly or repeatedly; also tinkling and churring sounds, often in courtship flight. Calls and flies at night.

HABITAT Inland watercourses, especially stream sandbars. Also margins of lakes, swamps, farm dams. Sometimes salt lakes, marshes, tidal waterways.

BREEDING Mainly September–January. Nest a shallow scrape in sand or river shingle, sometimes well away from water on bare or leaf-littered ground. Two to four pale greenish or buffy-grey eggs, blotched and lined grey and dark brown.

RANGE Throughout Australia; interior in suitable habitat. Sedentary or nomadic.

STATUS Common; uncommon in Tasmania and arid regions. Endemic.

▶ **See also page** 149

---

160 **INLAND DOTTEREL**

Peltohyas australis Charadriidae

OTHER NAMES Australian Dotterel, Desert Plover

RECOGNITION Inhabits semi-desert country. Cinnamon-buff upperparts mottled blackish brown. Forehead, face and upper breast white or buff-white, with bold black bars down each side of breast joining and extending under the abdomen to form a conspicuous Y; this separates white breast from chestnut abdomen. Black line across crown continues through and below the eye. In flight, buff underwings; dark chestnut belly; white undertail-coverts. 20 cm.

VOICE Usually silent; tends to run then freeze, bobs head. Call has been described as brisk or metallic 'quoick', low 'krroot'.

HABITAT Desert and semi-desert, especially stony areas, bare or with sparse scrub; not necessarily near water.

BREEDING Recorded all months; mainly August–November. Nest a slight scrape on bare ground, sometimes roughly ringed with pebbles and sticks. Two to three creamy, buffy-olive or buffy-brown eggs, spotted and blotched reddish-brown.

RANGE Interior, except sandy deserts; to coast at north-west Nullarbor. Sedentary, or nomadic in north; migratory in south.

STATUS Uncommon. Endemic.

▶ **See also pages** 138 173 214 *215* 220

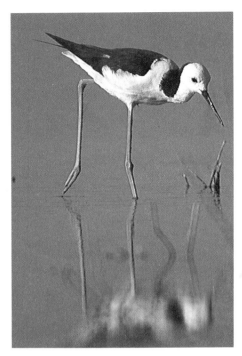

161 BLACK-WINGED STILT
Himantopus himantopus

STILTS, AVOCETS

**Recurvirostridae Family of 6 species
3 in Australia, 3 breeding, 1 endemic**

Medium sized waders with very long legs, long necks, and long straight bills (stilts) or very long upturned bills (avocets). Plumage mainly white, with solid areas of black or brown. Toes are partially or completely webbed. They feed in the shallows of lakes, estuaries, swamps — the avocets often in salt or brackish waters, the stilts tending to fresh waters — taking small crustaceans, molluscs, aquatic insects, some seeds.

BLACK-WINGED STILT

Himantopus himantopus Recurvirostridae

OTHER NAMES Pied Stilt, White-headed Stilt

RECOGNITION Tall; bold black-and-white patterned plumage; very long pink legs. Head and underparts entirely white, with distinctive black patch down back of neck, and black wings. Immatures have grey-brown face, wings and back. Straight, sharp-pointed bill. In pairs or small parties or sometimes flocks of hundreds. In flight, wings are black both above and below; pink legs trail far behind. Wades in shallows to feed, rarely swims. 35–38 cm.

VOICE A sharp yap or yelp, repeated irregularly. Immatures give a plaintive soft whistle.

HABITAT Shallow lakes or swamps, fresh or brackish water; also estuaries, mudflats, salt lakes. Nests in small colonies, to about 50 pairs, rarely 200.

BREEDING Recorded all months; variable, depending on rainfall in drier regions, but

generally August–December in south; January–March in north. Nest near water, on ground; sometimes built up in shallows. Four olive eggs, marked grey and brown.

RANGE Almost throughout Australia in suitable habitat; vagrant in Tasmania. Nomadic.

STATUS Common.

▶ See also pages
224 303

BANDED STILT

Cladorhynchus leucocephalus
Recurvirostridae

OTHER NAME Rottnest Snipe

RECOGNITION Tall; bold black-and-white patterned plumage; long pink legs; but unlike Black-winged Stilt has no black patch to back of neck. Adults have prominent deep chestnut breastband extended centrally under abdomen where it becomes blacker. Long, straight, fine-pointed bill; blackish wings. In flight, very long trailing legs; breastband visible; white panel to trailing edge of upperwing. Immatures no breastband; brownish wings. 36–45 cm.

VOICE A short yelping call or bark; single or double 'yook-yook'.

HABITAT Salt lakes, salt fields; sometimes coastal mudflats, estuaries, shallow freshwater lakes. Very gregarious; wades and swims to feed.

BREEDING Recorded all months; depending on rain in the arid regions. Breeds in colonies, sometimes tens of thousands; only a few remote sites known. Nests on ground, on lake islets and spits. Three to four fawn eggs, marked brown and black.

RANGE Throughout Australia except tropical north; restricted breeding range. Migratory.

STATUS Generally uncommon; locally abundant. Endemic genus.

▶ See also pages
*33 138 173 183
224 231 244*

RED-NECKED AVOCET

Recurvirostra novaehollandiae
Recurvirostridae

OTHER NAMES Avocet, Cobbler's Awl, Cobbler

RECOGNITION Tall, elegant wader, with long finely-pointed upcurved black bill; chestnut head and neck; very long legs. Rest of body white, wings black. Female similar, bill less strongly upturned. In flight, feet trail far behind tail; black

163 RED-NECKED AVOCET
Recurvirostra novaehollandiae

wingtips and two black bars down the back. Immatures are paler, grey on scapulars. Feet are fully webbed. When feeding, wades with bill sweeping side to side. 40–46 cm.

VOICE A sharp yelp, and musical fluty toot given mostly when nesting.

HABITAT Coastal estuaries, tidal mudflats, saltmarshes, salt lakes, swamps, temporary inland waters such as claypans.

BREEDING After good rains in arid regions; otherwise usually August–December. Nests in colonies by water, laying eggs in a shallow hollow in ground, lined with pieces of vegetation. Four olive to buff eggs, spotted and blotched grey, brown and black.

RANGE Throughout most of Australia; sparse in far north. Vagrant to New Zealand. Nomadic.

STATUS Fairly common, especially in interior. Endemic.

▶ See also pages
36 125 173 173

CURLEWS, SANDPIPERS, SNIPES, GODWITS

Scolopacidae Family of 92 species about 43 in Australia, non-breeding migrants

A large family of waders, generally quite long-billed and fairly long-legged. Size varies greatly, from the Eastern Curlew at 60 cm down to the stints at around 14 cm. The length of the bill is greater than the length of the head. The bill is usually straight for probing in sand or mud, but some are slightly upcurved or downcurved. In Australia usually seen in non-breeding plumages, mainly dull greys, grey-brown and white. Often in flocks, sometimes huge.

RUDDY TURNSTONE

Arenaria interpres   Scolopacidae

OTHER NAMES Beachbird, Eastern Turnstone

RECOGNITION A small, thickset wader. Non-breeding plumage: dark brown upper-parts mottled with black and cinnamon, white rump. Dark brownish-black breast patch, with white chin. Breeding plumage: back and crown extensively patterned with rich cinnamon-brown; face intricately pat-terned black, joining into the bold black breastband. Short, black bill looks slightly upturned. Short, orange-coloured legs. In flight, white wing patch; two black tail-bars. 21–25 cm.

VOICE Loud rattling 'kiti-kiti-kiti-', and clear ringing 'keeooo'.

HABITAT Usually exposed reefs and rocky shores, where it forages by probing among shells and seaweed; also mudflats, occasionally shallow inland waters.

BREEDING Summer visitor; breeds in Northern Hemisphere. Arrives in Australia September, departs April. Some individuals overwinter, and may be seen in breeding plumage.

RANGE Coastal Australia; occasionally inland. Migratory.

STATUS Moderately common, but rare in south.

▶ See also pages
47 48 149 150

EASTERN CURLEW

Numenius madagascariensis Scolopacidae

OTHER NAMES Australian Curlew, Sea Curlew

RECOGNITION The largest migrant wader. Extremely long, downcurved bill. Other-wise very plain, overall buff extensively streaked and barred with dark brown, in-cluding rump and underwings. Long, grey legs. In flight, the long bill is conspicuous; wings pointed; flight feathers blackish above. Brown rump distinguishes it from similarly long-billed Whimbrel which has whitish rump. Wary; in solitary or loose parties. 50–60 cm.

VOICE Loud, far-carrying, 'car-lee' or 'cur-lee'; usually when in flight; often calls at night.

HABITAT Coastal; estuaries, mudflats,

---

mangroves, sandspits. Less often fresh and brackish lakes. Some sites have flocks of hundreds of birds.

BREEDING Breeds northern Asia; summer migrant to Australia, September–May.

RANGE All Australian coasts; occasionally inland. Migratory.

STATUS Common in north and south-east; uncommon in South Australia; scarce in south-west of South Australia.

▶ See also pages
117 122 *149* 150

WHIMBREL

Numenius phaeopus   Scolopacidae

OTHER NAME Little Curlew

RECOGNITION Medium to large, with long downcurved bill. Looks a smaller version of Eastern Curlew, almost identical in shape and colour. The bill, though long (7.5 cm), is only half the length of curlew's bill. Plumage buffy, streaked and barred brown, as for curlew, except crown striped. In flight, similar but white rump and lower back, faster wingbeats. Gener-ally tends to be very wary. (Subspecies *hudsonicus*, extremely rare in Australia, has brown rump.) 38–45 cm.

VOICE Calls often; a loud, shrill, melodious rippling or undulating whistle, 'ti-ti-ti-ti-'.

HABITAT Coastal estuaries, beaches, mud-flats, mangroves, reefs, wet paddocks, sewage farms. If in flock, watch for tendency to variable size.

BREEDING Non-breeding migrant from Northern Hemisphere; arrives September, departs by April. Australian birds usually subspecies *variegatus* (white rumped). Some individuals regularly overwinter.

RANGE All Australian coasts, except appar-ently west coast of Tasmania.

STATUS Common far north and east, especially Great Barrier Reef; scarce in Western Australia and Tasmania.

▶ See also pages
73 75 123 149 150

LITTLE CURLEW

Numenius minutus   Scolopacidae

OTHER NAMES Little Whimbrel, Pygmy Curlew

RECOGNITION A miniature curlew, with typical curlew appearance: long down-curved bill which though longer than many other waders, is much shorter than that of Whimbrel and Eastern Curlew; base of bill pink. Upperparts mottled in shades of buff

---

and brown, darker in centre of back than Whimbrel, and with dark streak down centre of crown. Pale brow; chin and abdomen near white. In flight, brown rump; wings upheld on landing. 30–35 cm.

VOICE Harsh 'tchew-tcheew', and higher 'tee-tee-tee'. Wary, and when approached tends to squat before flying, then flushes with excited calls.

HABITAT Often far from water, favouring inland plains, floodplains, edges of swamps and other areas of short grass. Also on mudflats, crops.

BREEDING Summer migrant August–April; breeds in Northern Hemisphere. Little Whimbrels seen on coasts are probably in passage. Large migrating flocks numbering many thousands are sometimes seen in north-west (WA), Top End (NT), north-western Queensland.

RANGE Widespread records, but mainly from northern Australia.

STATUS Abundant far north; rare in south.

▶ See also pages
188–9 *193* 196

WOOD SANDPIPER

Tringa glareola   Scolopacidae

OTHER NAME Upland Plover

RECOGNITION Non-breeding plumage: up-perparts brown with white freckling; dis-tinct white eyebrow and eye-ring; white rump. Bill medium length, straight, black. Breast grey-brown, abdomen white. Breed-ing plumage: upperparts much richer brown, making white spotting more con-spicuous. In flight, the yellow legs extend beyond the tail; shows white rump and black-barred tail. Has a nervous manner, bobs, flicks tail; high zigzag flight when flushed. 20–30 cm.

VOICE Loud rapid whistle, a shrill, excited sound; given also when flushed.

HABITAT Freshwater wetlands; not usually coastal. Favours swampy woodlands and also edges of tidal mudflats, mangroves, saltmarshes, sewage ponds.

BREEDING Migrant to Australia September–April; breeds in Northern Hemisphere. In flooded woodland environs, feeds up to belly in shallow water; sometimes perches. Solitary or small groups.

RANGE Throughout Australia in suitable habitat; including interior.

STATUS Common in north; uncommon south; sparse through the interior.

▶ See also page
295

169 GREY-TAILED TATTLER

Tringa brevipes　　　Scolopacidae

OTHER NAMES Grey-rumped Sandpiper, Asiatic Tattler

RECOGNITION Non-breeding plumage: upperparts delicate greys; white eyebrows, throat and abdomen; grey breast; yellow legs. Very similar to Wandering Tattler, which is very slightly darker, more mottled above. Positive separation of these by length of nasal groove: Grey-tailed Tattler has nasal groove not more than half the bill length; Wandering Tattler has groove two-thirds bill length. Breeding plumage: the Grey-tailed Tattler has finely streaked and barred-brown underparts. 25 cm.

VOICE A clear, flute-like, drawn-out 'tlooeeep'; also thin plaintive piping, 'peee, peeep', and strident 'klee-klee'.

HABITAT Coastal; with preference for exposed rocky shores, reefs. Also tidal mudflats, mangroves.

BREEDING Summer migrant to Australia; breeds in Northern Hemisphere. Seen singly or in small groups. Has uneasy, restless appearance, bobbing and dipping. On landing momentarily holds wings high, showing white underwing with grey armpit area.

RANGE All Australian coasts and islands.

STATUS Common in north; uncommon south.

▶ See also pages
123 150 *219*

170 WANDERING TATTLER

Tringa incana　　　Scolopacidae

RECOGNITION Non-breeding plumage: upperparts soft greys; white eyebrows, throat and abdomen; grey breast; yellow legs. Very like Grey-tailed Tattler, but has darker coloured upperparts. Positive separation of these by length of deep part of nasal groove: Grey-tailed Tattler has groove not more than half the bill length; Wandering Tattler has groove two-thirds bill length. Breeding plumage: the Wandering Tattler is more strongly barred along the underparts. 26–28 cm.

VOICE Distinct from that of Grey-tailed Tattler; a rapid sequence of notes, a rippling trill, becoming faster, yet fading in volume.

HABITAT Similar to those of Grey-tailed Tattler; usually reefs, islands, beaches.

BREEDING Visits Australia September–April; breeds in Northern Hemisphere.

RANGE Probably regular visitor to Great Barrier Reef islands; occasionally to northeast coast.

STATUS Rare.

▶ See also page
295

171 COMMON SANDPIPER

Tringa hypoleucos　　　Scolopacidae

RECOGNITION Non-breeding plumage: upperparts dark olive-brown, finely marked darker; underparts white except indistinct brownish patch down each side of breast. Pale eyebrow line, throat. Behaviour helpful: tends to bob head-tail, a constant teetering activity, perched and walking. In flight, has distinctive pattern of shallow wingbeats, interspersed with glides on down-arched wings; shows white wingbar, and white-edged rump and tail. Sometimes swims. 19.5–21 cm.

VOICE Thin plaintive piping 'twee-twee-twee-'.

HABITAT Coastal and interior; with preference for rocky or muddy edges of streams, rivers, channels of mangroves or saltmarshes, lakes; also beaches.

BREEDING Migrant to Australia July–May; mainly August–March or April. Breeds in Northern Hemisphere. Solitary or in small parties, feeds along the shallows.

RANGE All Australian coasts; salt and freshwater inland habitats.

STATUS Common in north, south-west; uncommon south-east; quite rare Tasmania.

▶ See also pages
98 149 183 *219*

172 GREENSHANK

Tringa nebularia　　　Scolopacidae

OTHER NAME Common Greenshank

RECOGNITION Large wader with dark, slightly upturned bill; long greenish legs. Non-breeding plumage: upperparts pale brownish-grey; very light and streaked on crown and hind-neck. Underparts entirely white. In flight, upperwings dark, particularly flight feathers, outermost of which has a white shaft. Rump and lower back conspicuously white between dark wings; tail crossbarred. Breeding plumage: darker blackish-browns on back and wings. 30–33 cm.

VOICE A ringing, quite strident 'teew-tew-' or 'chew-ee-'; often at night.

HABITAT Coastal, and margins of inland waters; estuaries, mudflats, swamps, lakes, sewage farms.

BREEDING Migrant to Australia August–April; breeds in Northern Hemisphere. Although often solitary or in small parties, flocks of a hundred occasionally to be seen

particularly in northern Australia. Very wary, nervous head-bobbing behaviour.

RANGE All Australian coasts; inland in suitable habitat.

STATUS Moderately common; common in north.

▶ See also pages
98 122 149 150 *153* 183

173 MARSH SANDPIPER

Tringa stagnatilis　　　Scolopacidae

OTHER NAME Little Greenshank

RECOGNITION Like Greenshank, but smaller. Non-breeding plumage: delicate mid-grey on back and wings; lighter buffy-grey on crown and hind-neck; underparts white. Bill black and upturned like Greenshank, but finer. Legs long, like those of stilts; yellow-green, and trail behind tail-tip in flight. Breeding plumage: back darker-mottled. In flight, white of rump and lower back seen to extend wedge-shaped between grey of wings. Flight graceful, swift, weaving. 20–23 cm.

VOICE Sharp call when put to flight; also more drawn-out 'tee-oo'.

HABITAT Prefers freshwater wetlands; not often coastal waters. Swamps, lakes both fresh and brackish, sometimes mangroves, estuaries, mudflats.

BREEDING Migrant August–May; breeds in Northern Hemisphere. Seen singly or in small parties; sometimes large flocks. Feeds actively; often wades to depth of long legs.

RANGE Australian coast, except apparently Great Australian Bight; parts of inland.

STATUS Moderately common in north; uncommon to rare in south-east and Tasmania.

▶ See also pages
122 242 *295*

174 TEREK SANDPIPER

Tringa terek　　　Scolopacidae

RECOGNITION A long, slightly upcurved bill that looks large for the bird, and is black, sometimes yellow, towards the base. Legs not particularly long, yellow to deep orange in colour. Otherwise unremarkable. Non-breeding plumage: soft greyish-brown upperparts blending to white underparts; white forehead; slight dark line through eye. Breeding plumage: brown areas darker. In flight, brown rump; white trailing edge on wings; legs shorter than tail-tip. Dashes about actively, bobs head and jerks tail. 21–25 cm.

VOICE A musical piping trill, variously described as 'weeta-weeta-weeta', or 'terrr-da weet, teer-da-weeta-weet'. Also rapid high 'tee-tee-tee'.

HABITAT Coastal; tidal mudflats, estuaries, shores and reefs, offshore islands, coastal swamps. Only occasionally inland.

BREEDING Migrant to Australia September–May; breeds in Northern Hemisphere. Although most often seen singly or in small groups, flocks of many hundreds have been recorded.

RANGE All Australian coasts, except only vagrant to Tasmania.

STATUS Common in north; uncommon to rare in south.

▶ **See also pages** 122 294

LATHAM'S SNIPE

Gallinago hardwickii   Scolopacidae

OTHER NAMES Japanese Snipe, Australian Snipe, Common Snipe

RECOGNITION Long straight solid-looking bill. Non-breeding plumage: overall buffy, boldly marked with dark brown and black. Dark lines through eye, above and below eye. Breast more lightly flecked brown; flanks whitish, barred. If flushed, bursts upwards in fast, evasive flight; may then show the rufous tail. The pale feather-edgings form lines down the back; also, white belly and underwing. Brown eyes look high-set; short, olive-yellow legs. Well camouflaged and easily overlooked. 24–26 cm. In the Northern Territory and Kimberley, Swinhoe's Snipe (*Gallinago megala*) is more prevalent. Almost identical to Latham's Snipe except that it is slightly paler; broad white tips to tail feathers. Most certain identification by count (and width) of tail feathers which number 20–24 compared with 16–18 for Latham's Snipe, and 24–28 for Pin-tailed Snipe (*Gallinago stenura*).

VOICE Latham's Snipe: loud, harsh, abrupt 'krzek'; has been likened to the sound of sudden tearing of cloth. Swinhoe's Snipe: short abrupt rasping 'shrek'.

HABITAT Dense cover around swamps, thick grass of swampy woodlands and irrigated areas, alpine bogs, dams, mangroves, moist samphire. Feeds by rapid vertical probing action.

BREEDING Migrant to Australia August–April; breeds in Northern Hemisphere. Usually solitary, or scattered parties.

RANGE Latham's Snipe: north-eastern and south-eastern Australia. Swinhoe's Snipe: Cape York to Western Kimberley.

STATUS Uncommon; though common in some favourable localities.

▶ **See also pages** 82 149

151 **Lesser Golden Plover** *Pluvialis dominica*
152 **Red-kneed Dotterel** *Erythrogonys cinctus*
153 **Hooded Plover** *Charadrius rubricollis*
168 **Wood Sandpiper** *Tringa glareola*
170 **Wandering Tattler** *Tringa incana*
173 **Marsh Sandpiper** *Tringa stagnatilis*
174 **Terek Sandpiper** *Tringa terek*
175 **Latham's Snipe** *Gallinago hardwickii*
186 **Broad-billed Sandpiper** *Limicola falcinellus*
187 **Ruff** *Philomachus pugnax*
188 **Oriental Pratincole** *Glareola maldivarum*

176 BLACK-TAILED GODWIT

Limosa limosa — Scolopacidae

RECOGNITION A large wader, with very long, straight bill that is pink towards the base. Non-breeding plumage: upperparts mottled light-and-dark tones of greyish cinnamon-brown; underparts white. In flight, bold patterns on wings and tail. Underwing white, bordered black; upperwing has black flight feathers, with white bar. Rump and basal half of tail white; terminal half of tail black. Breeding plumage: rich russet head, neck and breast. 36–43 cm.

VOICE Recorded as staccato, slightly harsh, 'witta-wit' or 'reeta-reeta-reeta'; also a single quick low 'kuk' when feeding.

HABITAT Coastal, infrequently inland; tidal mudflats and river edges, sandy beaches, brackish swamps, shallows of lakes, reservoirs, sewage farms. Feeds by slow, deep probing.

BREEDING Breeds in Mongolia, eastern Siberia. Migrates to Australia August–March. Some stay through winter. Usually singly, or small groups; occasionally very large flocks; often in company with Bar-tailed Godwit.

RANGE Most of Australian coast; inland in suitable habitat; vagrant in Tasmania.

STATUS Common in north; widespread but uncommon in south.

▶ See also pages
80 122 197 *215*
242

177 BAR-TAILED GODWIT

Limosa lapponica — Scolopacidae

RECOGNITION A large wader, with very long, slightly upcurved bill that is pink towards the base. Non-breeding plumage: upperparts in mottled light-and-dark tones of grey-brown; paler on the neck. Underparts buffy-white. In flight, note white rump; black-and-white barred tail. Breeding plumage: male has back and wings patterned black and buff; remainder cinnamon-chestnut; female has head and body deep buff. Female is larger, longer billed. 38–45 cm.

VOICE Loud and clear 'kew-kew', and soft 'kit-kit-kit'.

HABITAT Coastal, seldom inland; sandy beaches, mudflats, estuaries, coastal marshes. Feeds in shallow water; rams long bill vertically down into mud to feed.

BREEDING Breeds in Siberia and northern Alaska. Migrant to Australia August–April. Singly or small parties, to flocks of thousands. Not extremely shy.

RANGE Most of the Australian coast; infrequently to interior.

STATUS Common, very abundant; flocks of thousands in north.

▶ See also pages
48 *48* 80 122 123
124 149 150 218
219

178 RED KNOT

Calidris canutus — Scolopacidae

OTHER NAMES Knot, Common Knot, Grey-crowned Knot, Lesser Knot

RECOGNITION The name Red Knot is appropriate only for the breeding plumage: largely rust-red, extensively marked on the back with black; rump pale; undertail-coverts white; flanks barred. Non-breeding plumage: upperparts pale grey; under-surfaces near white, lightly speckled round neck and flanks; light streak over eye. Legs short, dull green; bill black, straight-tapered to point. In flight, light, barred rump. Looks squat; often a horizontal, hunched stance. 25 cm.

VOICE A low, guttural or throaty 'knut', 'nuoot' or 'kloot'; a whistling 'too-it-twit'; and soft chattering sounds in flight or when feeding.

HABITAT Usually coastal; keeping to open mudflats and wide sandy shores, salt-marshes, flooded areas. Feeds with rapid probing in shallow water.

BREEDING Breeds in Arctic. Migrant to Australia August–April. Some overwinter; some into breeding plumage. Usually seen in small numbers with other waders, or small close flocks.

RANGE Most Australian coasts; infrequent, but regular, inland.

STATUS Uncommon; except common in north-west; rare in south-east.

▶ See also pages
98 124 149 *215*

179 GREAT KNOT

Calidris tenuirostris — Scolopacidae

OTHER NAME Japanese Knot

RECOGNITION Like Red Knot but larger, with proportionately much longer bill, that becomes noticeably heavier towards the base. Looks thickset; short sturdy legs. Non-breeding plumage: upperparts mid-grey, streaked and patterned with lighter and darker greys; crown streaked grey. Underparts white, grey-spotted on breast and flanks. In flight, rump white; tail dark; faint white wingbar. Breeding plumage: chestnut in upperparts; bold, black scalloped breast-markings. 20–30 cm.

VOICE Usually silent, but recorded as having a double-noted whistle, and other calls similar to those of the Red Knot.

HABITAT Ocean shores; especially tidal mudflats, beaches. Rare inland; much less frequently recorded inland than Red Knot.

BREEDING Breeds in eastern Siberia and Arctic. Migrant to Australia September–March. With other waders, or in tight, sometimes large flocks.

RANGE Most Australian coasts.

STATUS Abundant in parts of northern coastline; rare in south.

▶ See also pages
98 124 *215* 218

180 SHARP-TAILED SANDPIPER

Calidris acuminata — Scolopacidae

OTHER NAMES Asiatic Pectoral Sandpiper, Sharp-tailed Stint

RECOGNITION Non-breeding plumage: upperparts dark grey-brown; scapulars edged light grey. Crown of head rufous with darker streaks; whitish eyebrow and chin. Neck and upper breast greyish-buff with sparse darker streaks, and blending into the white of the rest of the underparts; dark streakings along the flanks. Tail pointed, blackish. In flight, white wingbars, white to each side of rump and tail. Breeding plumage: more rufous; darker markings, especially on flanks. 18–23 cm.

VOICE A sharp, repeated 'wit-wit', usually on taking flight. Also softer and musical twitterings.

HABITAT A variety of coastal and interior wetlands; prefers fresh waters to seashores; tidal mudflats, swamp mudflats, salt-marshes, mangrove edges, fresh and brackish shallow lakes.

BREEDING Migrant to Australia August–April; breeds in Northern Hemisphere. Seen in small or large parties.

RANGE Throughout Australia wherever suitable habitat; including arid interior.

STATUS Abundant; very large counts in passage in north.

▶ See also pages
98 99 124 149 156
157 218 297

181 PECTORAL SANDPIPER

Calidris melanotos — Scolopacidae

RECOGNITION Non-breeding plumage: upperparts dark brown, patterned on the back by buff feather-edgings; crown streaked dark brown. Neck and breast dusky cinnamon, streaked darker in a roughly V-shaped area, pointing down onto white abdomen. Chin and brow whitish; legs yellow. Bill longer than for

Sharp-tailed Sandpiper; slightly down-curved, pale at base. In flight, dark under-wing linings; zigzags up if flushed. Shy; reported sometimes to freeze prostrate. Variable size, 18–24 cm.

VOICE Harsher than Sharp-tailed Sandpiper, and with a reedy quality, 'krik', 'kreek', 'trrrt-trrt' or 'krrrt'.

HABITAT Freshwater wetlands rather than seashores; with a preference for vegetated swamp-margins, flooded pasture and saltmarshes, rather than open mudflats. Feeds on small crustaceans and insects.

BREEDING Migrant to Australia August–April; breeds in Arctic, Siberia and Alaska. Solitary, or intermingling with Sharp-tailed Sandpipers, or in small parties of up to 10 birds.

RANGE Scattered records from widespread areas; all States.

STATUS Rare, but possibly more common than records indicate.

▶ See also pages
98 149 156 *157*
197 242

RED-NECKED STINT

82

Calidris ruficollis   Scolopacidae

OTHER NAMES Little Dunlin, Red-necked Sandpiper

RECOGNITION Very small. Non-breeding plumage; grey-brown upperparts, streaked and mottled darker brown. Eyebrow, forehead, lower face, chin and rest of underparts white. Short black bill; black legs. In flight, conspicuous white wingbar; black on the rump extending as a median line down the tail. Tends to forage above the waterline, finding various small invertebrates. Breeding plumage: back feathers black-centred with chestnut edges; head, neck and breast chestnut. 15 cm.

VOICE A soft 'chit', often when flushed, and high-pitched trills, twitterings, especially when feeding.

HABITAT Coastal; favouring estuaries, tidal mudflats, sandy beaches. Also inland on margins of salt or freshwater lakes, saltpans.

BREEDING Migrant to Australia August–May; breeds in Arctic and Siberia. Many overwinter, generally retaining the non-breeding plumage. Huge numbers of this stint are recorded on some favoured beaches; especially flocks in passage in the north-west.

RANGE Throughout Australia, including inland in suitable habitat.

STATUS Abundant generally; uncommon eastern coastal Queensland.

▶ See also pages
98 124 149 150
161 183 *215* 218
245

183

LONG-TOED STINT

Calidris subminuta   Scolopacidae

RECOGNITION Very small. Non-breeding plumage: dark brown upperparts with back and wing feathers edged lighter; crown streaked. Whitish underparts; wide zone of light grey-brown, with darker flecks, across breast. In flight, snipe-like, zigzagging; long yellow legs trail behind tail-tip. White edged rump, dark-centre strip joining to dark tail. Often in company with Red-necked stints, Sharp-tailed sandpipers. 14.5–16.5 cm; central toe +/− 2.5 cm.

VOICE A quite loud, high 'chree-chree-chree', repeated rapidly, or sometimes as a single call.

HABITAT Both coastal and interior, but rarely ocean shores. Prefers swamps and lakes, whether fresh or brackish, river edges.

BREEDING Migrant to Australia September–April; breeds in Siberia. Once considered extremely rare, but possibly not noticed. Usually in very small numbers, but flocks of up to 92 recorded in some favoured localities in Western Australia.

RANGE Widespread across most parts of Australia.

STATUS Rare, but regular visitor.

▶ See also pages
197 236–7 239
244

184

CURLEW SANDPIPER

Calidris ferruginea   Scolopacidae

OTHER NAME Curlew Stint

RECOGNITION Bill is long, downcurved, black. Non-breeding plumage: upperparts light grey-brown; overall whitish underparts except light brownish tone round the upper breast; light eyebrow line. Breeding plumage: almost entirely rusty or deep chestnut; crown streaked darker; back and wings patterned with black and buff. Pale round base of bill; rump and undertail whitish, sparsely barred. In flight, white wingbar; short, white rump patch; dark tail. 20–21 cm.

VOICE A clear, quite loud, liquid 'chirrup'; also musical twitterings.

HABITAT Both coastal and inland; salt, brackish or fresh waters. Found on mudflats, estuaries, reefs, edges or shallows of lakes, salt fields. Feeds belly-deep in water, probing in the mud.

BREEDING Migrant to Australia September–April; breeds in northern Siberia. Many birds overwinter. Huge numbers, in passage, on north-west beaches in spring and autumn.

RANGE Widespread; most parts of Australia in suitable habitat.

STATUS Abundant in north; uncommon in eastern Queensland.

▶ See also pages
98 99 124 149 150
162 *215* 218 245

185

SANDERLING

Calidris alba   Scolopacidae

RECOGNITION Non-breeding plumage: very pale coloration, with upperparts extremely light silvery-grey. Forehead, eyebrow streak, and entire underparts white. Against this overall white and near-white, the quite large, thick straight bill, the small dark patch at the bend of the wing, the slender line of the folded black primaries and the black legs, are all conspicuous. Breeding plumage: greys replaced by chestnut, and chestnut on breast. In flight, large white wingbar; white rump and tail, with dark centre strip. 18–20 cm.

VOICE Liquid 'twik-twik'; soft querulous 'jerks-jerks-ket'; also a short trill 'twik' or 'jerks'.

HABITAT Coastal; with preference for sandy beaches, but also mudflats, inlets, near reefs; only rarely inland. Feeds where waves gently flow and ebb along flat beaches.

BREEDING Migrant to Australia September–May; breeds in Arctic. Some overwinter, and may acquire breeding plumage.

RANGE Coastal Australia, but patchy distribution; regular to some beaches.

STATUS Generally uncommon; abundant some spots in south-east and south-west.

▶ See also pages
47 48

186

BROAD-BILLED SANDPIPER

Limicola falcinellus   Scolopacidae

RECOGNITION A medium-small sandpiper, with distinctive bill that is long, thicker at the base, quite broad, and downcurved towards the tip. Non-breeding plumage: upperparts grey-brown; crown streaked darker and with two white lines above eye. White underparts, except breast, dusky buff streaked darker. In flight, dark upperparts, narrow white wingbar; white-sided rump. 17–19 cm.

VOICE A clear trilling call 'chri-chri-chreet' or 'trii-trii-trit'; also abrupt single 'treet', and chattering sounds in flight.

HABITAT Coastal; infrequent inland; prefers muddy shores, mudflats, including mangrove-edge mudflats, and also reefs. Occasionally freshwater swamps. Feeds with rapid jabbing action, sometimes with head underwater.

BREEDING Migrant to Australia September–April; breeds in northern Eurasia. Usually single birds or small parties in South Australia. Solitary, or with other waders, or in flocks, especially in north.

RANGE Scattered widespread records; mainly coastal; not Tasmania.

STATUS Rare to uncommon in south; abundant some north-west and north-east localities.

▶ **See also pages**
122 *295*

187 RUFF

Philomachus pugnax   Scolopacidae

OTHER NAMES Reeve for the much smaller female; Ruff for male

RECOGNITION Quite large. Non-breeding plumage: plain, lacks bold markings. Head looks small for size of bird; neck and legs long. Short, black, slightly downcurved bill. Upperparts brownish, with buff edgings to the dark-brown feathers of back and wings, giving scaly look. Head and neck lighter, slightly streaked. Underparts whitish, slightly buffy on the breast. Legs greenish to orange or grey. Breeding plumage: Ruff has great frill, unlikely to be seen in Australia. In flight, white sides to rump. Stands distinctively erect, more hunched when feeding. 23–28 cm.

VOICE Usually silent, may give low 'tuu-wit' when flushed.

HABITAT Inland rather than coast; on freshwater lagoons with vegetated or muddy edges; also saltmarshes, saltponds and sewerage works.

BREEDING Migrant to Australia September–April; breeds northern Europe and Asia. Usually single birds sighted.

RANGE Widespread, scattered records; all States.

STATUS Rare, but apparently regular visitor.

▶ **See also pages**
138 197 *295*

**Glareolidae Family of 16 species
2 in Australia, 1 breeding**

Aberrant waders of plains, often of arid regions. They are long-winged, fork-tailed or square-tailed, with tern or swallow-like flight. They take insects in flight as well as on the ground. Plumage is brownish, with some white. Bills are short and arched. Their legs vary, shortish to quite long.

188 ORIENTAL PRATINCOLE

Glareola maldivarum   Glareolidae

OTHER NAMES Grasshopper-bird, Swallow-Plover

RECOGNITION A slender-bodied, long-legged bird, with long forked tail that is longer than the folded wings. Non-breeding plumage: upperparts olive-brown, darker on wings, and without patterning. Throat buff, edged with black. Underparts buffy-white. Bill and legs short, black. Breeding plumage: buff and black of throat, more clear-cut, brighter. Bill red on base, gape. In flight, swallow-like shape, pointed backswept wings; chestnut underwings; blackish flight feathers; white lower breast-abdomen and rump; and long, white, dark-tipped forked tail. 20–23 cm.

VOICE Noisy in flight, with loud, tern-like 'chet-chet' or 'chick-chick'; also softer calls, 'tooeet-tooeet'.

HABITAT Open plains, usually near water, including claypans, bare ground by riverbanks and swamps. Often hawks insects on the wing.

BREEDING Migrant to Australia August–May; breeds eastern Asia. There seem to be very few overwintering. Singly or pairs in south, flocks of thousands in far north.

RANGE Records from all regions of Australia except Tasmania.

STATUS Common; at times abundant in north, rare and vagrant in south.

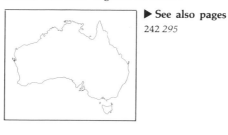

▶ **See also pages**
242 *295*

189 AUSTRALIAN PRATINCOLE

Stiltia isabella   Glareolidae

OTHER NAMES Grasshopper-bird, Australian Courser

RECOGNITION A slender-bodied, long-legged bird, with long pointed wings that when folded come to a long finely-tapered point well beyond the tail-tip. Upright stance on long black legs. Bill short, upper profile downcurved, red on basal half, black-tipped. Colour almost overall cinnamon, except buff underparts with broad chestnut lower-breast band; black flight feathers; black through eye. Flight,

swallow shape; short square tail; white rump. 22–24 cm.

VOICE A plaintive whistle, also described as tern-like, 'tu-whee' or 'quirree-peet'.

HABITAT Open plains; almost always near water, favouring lagoon edges, bare floodplains, gibberplains, claypans. Colours match environs.

BREEDING Nesting recorded all months, but usually October-January. Two to three eggs laid on bare ground, sometimes encircled by pebbles, sticks; colour creamy-white to pinkish-brown, spotted and blotched with grey, dark brown, and black.

RANGE Most of Australia except southwest, extreme south-east coastal and Tasmania. Visitor to New Guinea but doubtful breeding. Nomadic.

STATUS Common. Endemic breeding species.

▶ **See also pages**
133 *133 136* 137
138 173 220 290

**Stercorariidae Family of 5 species
5 in Australia**

Heavily-built seabirds; related to gulls, with similarity of shape, but with mainly dark plumage, heavy hooked bills and elongated, central tail feathers. Their flight is swift and powerful, facilitating their piratical harassment of other seabirds to rob them of their catch; they are also predators and scavengers. Seen at closer range, they have a characteristic sheath covering the base of the upper bill.

190 GREAT SKUA

Stercorarius skua   Stercorariidae

OTHER NAMES Antarctic Skua, Southern Skua, Dark Skua, Sea Hawk, Robber Gull

RECOGNITION Large; wingspan 1.5 m. Uniformly dusky dark brown, with white at base of primaries, in flight making conspicuous white wing patch; short fan-shaped tail. Plumage becomes paler towards the end of the breeding season. Eye brown; bill hooked; and feet black. A viciously predatory species, kills prions, shearwaters, petrels, rats and mice, and steals eggs; bullies others into disgorging catch; often feeds on carrion. Female larger. 63–66 cm.

VOICE Gull-like shrieks; loud crowing calls uttered with outstretched wings, often as duet between male and female, in recognition or challenge.

HABITAT Oceans; often following fishing boats; also bays, harbours, and sometimes ashore, especially where attracted by offal from whaling or fishing.

BREEDING Breeds on subantarctic islands including Macquarie Island. The very similar South Polar Skua (*maccormicki*), a rare vagrant, breeds farther south on Antarctic coasts. Both most often recorded in Australian seas in winter.

RANGE South coast; west coast north to Pilbara; east coast north to Sandy Cape (Qld).

STATUS Fairly common; more common in south-west; with gatherings of up to 50.

▶ See also page *253*

ARCTIC JAEGER

Stercorarius parasiticus   Stercorariidae
OTHER NAMES Arctic Skua, Arctic Gull, Parasitic Jaeger, Parasitic Skua
RECOGNITION Large; wingspan to 1 m. Dark phase uniformly dark blackish-brown, with white shafts to primaries showing in flight. Light phase has upperparts grey-brown with darker-brown cap; pale yellowish collar; underparts whitish. Flies gracefully, buoyantly, with hawk-like action. Tail distinctive, the two central feathers having elongated points extending up to 10 cm (often missing from moulting and immature birds.) Harrying attacks on smaller seabirds. 45–52 cm.

VOICE Usually silent at sea, but may utter squealing 'eeeaarr' during pursuit of other birds, and a single gull-like shriek when alarmed.

HABITAT Oceans and offshore waters during migration; more often seen in bays, inlets, harbours; possibly remaining in one locality through summer.

BREEDING Breeds Arctic regions and northern Europe, wintering on oceans and coasts of Southern Hemisphere; in Australian waters October/November–April. In their breeding grounds they are reported to be strongly territorial, and fiercely defend nest and young.

RANGE Most of Australian coasts, but most often recorded in south-east.

STATUS Moderately common south-east; uncommon to rare elsewhere.

▶ See also page *253*

POMARINE JAEGER

Stercorarius pomarinus   Stercorariidae
OTHER NAMES Pomatorhine Skua, Twist-tailed Skua, Pomarine Skua
RECOGNITION Like Arctic Jaeger, but larger, with unique tail. The central pair of tail feathers protrude 5–10 cm, broaden towards tips, twist across each other (often missing from moulting and immature birds). Looks heavier, has a longer, more solid bill, white bases to primaries more conspicuous from above and below. Immatures: breast mottled buff, brown-and-white underwing. Takes from other seabirds, often feeds on carrion, but also takes fish, molluscs. 48–55 cm.

VOICE Similar to call of Arctic Jaeger, or as a quick harsh 'which-you'.

HABITAT Offshore waters; less often seen in bays and estuaries than the Arctic Jaeger. Like other jaegers and skuas, often follows ships for offal.

BREEDING Breeds north of the Arctic Circle, most wintering on Atlantic coasts, but some reach Antarctic regions. In western Pacific as far south as Tasmania and New Zealand. Most likely to be seen off east coast September–April.

RANGE Probably offshore any part of Australian coastline; usually south-east and west.

STATUS Moderately common offshore east coast; scarce off west coast.

▶ See also page *253*

Laridae Family of 85 species
28 in Australia, 18 breeding, 1 endemic

The Silver Gull is well known, other gulls are larger, but recognizably alike. They are solid-bodied, medium-winged, heavy-billed, with webbed feet. Terns and noddies are of more slender build, with wings proportionately longer, more slender, and bills finer. They typically have black caps, light grey upperparts and white underparts. Both gulls and terns are gregarious, gathering in numbers on favoured marine or inland waters.

SILVER GULL

Larus novaehollandiae   Laridae
OTHER NAMES Seagull, Red-billed Gull, Red-legged Gull, Kitty Gull, Mackerel Gull
RECOGNITION One of the most familiar birds, only likely to be confused with some of the terns. Plumage white shading to delicate silver-grey on back and wings. Scarlet bill, eye-ring and legs. (Legs black-tipped in Western Australia.) In flight, wings tipped black, with subterminal white patches. Sexes alike, except male has slightly heavier bill. Immatures: mottled brown-grey upperparts; legs and bill blackish; after first year, mottled wing-coverts, bill and legs straw-coloured. 40–42 cm.

VOICE Noisy, varied calls; commonly a very harsh, drawn-out, 'kwarrr'; also 'kwark-kwark-kwark'. Immatures: high peevish begging.

HABITAT Coasts and islands, and inland near any large body of water. Forages

193 **SILVER GULL** *Larus novaehollandiae*

often away from water, on ploughed land, sportsgrounds, city rubbish dumps.

BREEDING Differs in various regions, usually within July–January, and has a second autumn breeding in the south-west. Nests in colonies, some very large. Nest is usually a bowl-shape of seaweed, on the ground. Two to four eggs, marked brown and black.

RANGE Throughout Australia in suitable habitat; and to offshore islands.

STATUS Abundant in south; uncommon in north. Subspecies in New Zealand and New Caledonia.

▶ **See also pages** 80 81 82 124 173 175 299–300 *299*

194 PACIFIC GULL

Larus pacificus　　　　　Laridae

OTHER NAMES Mollyhawk, Larger Gull, Jack Gull

RECOGNITION A spectacular, large white gull, with black wings and back; and deep, massive-looking red-tipped orange bill. Black band near tail-tip. Legs and feet yellowish. In flight, wings entirely black above, except for white trailing edge; no white patch on wing. Immatures: overall mottled brown and grey; bill grey with black tip; legs grey-brown. Frequents reefs, shores, taking small squid, fish, shellfish, and smaller seabirds, eggs and young. 58–66 cm.

VOICE A loud abrupt 'ow, ow' and deep, harsh 'kiorr'; various other sounds at nest and feeding.

HABITAT Ocean beaches and offshore islands; only rarely far inland, but at times forages on near-coastal pastures, rubbish dumps.

BREEDING August–November. Single pairs or small loose colonies, sometimes up to 100 birds. Nest is a cup-shaped structure of sticks, seaweed and other debris; on beach, or rocky headland. Two to three grey-brown eggs, marked dark brown.

RANGE Southern Australia; on west coast north to Shark Bay, on east to about Sydney. Adults sedentary; immatures dispersive.

STATUS Common. Endemic.

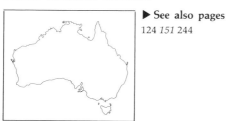

▶ **See also pages** 124 *151* 244

195 KELP GULL

Larus dominicanus　　　　Laridae

OTHER NAMES Dominican Gull, Southern Black-backed Gull

RECOGNITION A large, white gull with black back. Compared with the Pacific Gull this species has a slimmer pale-yellow bill with red spot near the tip of the lower-mandible; and legs more greenish-grey than yellow. At rest, shows white wing patches, which in flight become white windows near the tips of the dark wings, and a broader white trailing edge; usually no black tail-band. Immatures: first year, speckled brown; second to third years, whiter and with darker wings. 53–59 cm.

VOICE A yelping or laughing 'kioh-kioh-kioh-kioh-' at rapidly increasing rate; alternatively as 'yo-yo-yo'. Also nasal 'garr-', harsh 'oo-waaagh'.

HABITAT Coastal seas, offshore islands, beaches, sandspits. This gull has increased greatly in numbers in Australia since first reported about 1939–43.

BREEDING September–December. Breeding sites mainly in south-eastern Tasmania and New South Wales coast. Nests on offshore islands; builds a bulky mound of weed and debris. Two to three eggs, variable size and colour; usually grey-green, heavily speckled browns and black.

RANGE South-east (south-eastern Queensland to Eyre Peninsula); Tasmania; south-west.

STATUS Rare, but locally common; increasing. Widespread in the Southern Hemisphere.

▶ **See also page** *145*

196 WHISKERED TERN

Chlidonias hybrida　　　　Laridae

OTHER NAME Marsh Tern

RECOGNITION Medium-sized tern, with slightly forked tail. Breeding plumage: black crown extends well down on the nape, and is sharply cut off at eye-level by white, whiskered cheeks. Silvery-grey underparts, darkening to blackish abdomen. Back, tail and wings pale grey; wingtips darker. In flight, underwings and undertail-coverts white. Bill and legs red. Non-breeding plumage and immatures: black-streaked crown and face; underparts white; bill and legs black. 25–27 cm.

VOICE A sharp and high-pitched 'kii-it' or 'kittit'; threat calls 'kek-kek-kek'. Excited chattering from roosting or feeding flocks.

HABITAT Most often on inland waters, fresh or salt, including lakes, temporary waters of claypans and salt lakes, commercial salt fields, swamps.

BREEDING September–December. Usually nests in loose colonies; building up a pile of vegetation on lake or swamp islands, or floating in water. Three glossy, pale green to brownish-olive eggs, spotted and blotched with dark brown, and with underlying grey.

RANGE Almost throughout mainland Australia in suitable habitat. Migratory; some

migrate to New Guinea.

STATUS Moderately common. Endemic breeding subspecies.

▶ **See also pages** 173 183 *218* 242

197 WHITE-WINGED TERN

Chlidonias leucoptera　　　Laridae

OTHER NAMES Black Tern, White-tailed Tern, White-winged Sea-swallow

RECOGNITION Breeding plumage not often seen in Australia: body black; white shoulders, rump and tail. Bill and legs red. In flight, underwing white, except wing-linings dark; undertail white. Non-breeding plumage: streaked black crown and nape; dark grey upperwings and tail; white rump; white underparts including tail; blackish bill and legs. Often in moult; black partially replaced by grey or white. Immatures: like non-breeding, but brownish on shoulders. 23–24 cm.

VOICE Usually quiet; but noisy in feeding flocks, with sharp buzzing 'kweek-kweek'. Other calls include harsh 'kek-kek' in threat, rising 'kreeek'.

HABITAT Shallow coastal lakes and swamps whether fresh, brackish or salt; estuaries, salt fields, sewage farms. Takes various insects from water, land.

BREEDING Non-breeding visitor during northern wet season, October–April. Greatest numbers usually seen around January in north. Breeds in swamps of Asia and southern Europe. Sometimes sighted far inland, apparently after tropical cyclones in north.

RANGE Coastal north, north-west, north-east; usually reaching south-west and south-east in small numbers.

STATUS Moderately common in north; usually uncommon to scarce elsewhere.

▶ **See also pages** 183 *301*

198 GULL-BILLED TERN

Gelochelidon nilotica　　　Laridae

OTHER NAME Long-legged Tern

RECOGNITION Quite large tern, with deep or heavy bill giving a distinctly gull-like appearance. Folded wings extend beyond a short and slightly forked tail. Head black-capped from bill onto nape and down to the eyes. Upperparts, including tail, very light grey. Underparts white, flight feathers darker. Immatures: white often streaked with black or brown on the crown and nape; shadowy blackish ear patch; wings speckled brown. 35–43 cm.

VOICE A throaty rasping 'kagh-wuk' and 'chee-aaghr'. Relatively silent except when breeding.

HABITAT Wetlands, fresh or saline, coastal or inland; sometimes far from water; includes lakes, tidal mudflats, beaches, grasslands, ploughed land.

BREEDING Variable following inland rains. Appears in numbers where remote inland lakes are filled, nesting in colonies on spits or islets. Nest varies; may be a simple scrape, or built up. Two to three buff to greenish eggs, blotched umber and lilac.

RANGE Almost throughout Australia in suitable habitat; vagrant to Tasmania. Nomadic.

STATUS Moderately common north; uncommon south. Subspecies of worldwide species.

▶ **See also pages**
98 138 173 183

CASPIAN TERN

Hydroprogne caspia **Laridae**

RECOGNITION Largest tern; wingspan to 1.3 m. Massive scarlet bill 7.5 cm. Breeding plumage: pale grey upperparts with black cap from forehead to nape. The short, slightly-forked tail is white, as are underparts except for the dark tips of the long slender wings. Non-breeding plumage: cap is streaked with white, retaining most black round the eye and nape; bill retains scarlet colour. Immatures: bill orange-red; cap markings shadowy; wings sometimes mottled. 48–56 cm.

VOICE A very deep, loud and harsh 'kaaagh, kraa-ah'; slow 'kuk, kuk'; and quicker, sharper, agitated or aggressive 'kak-kak-kak'.

199 **CASPIAN TERN** *Hydroprogne caspia*

HABITAT Coasts, estuaries, large rivers, tidal mudflats, fresh or brackish lakes. Most common on sea coasts, but occasionally on large lakes of interior.

BREEDING Variable in northern Australia; September–December in south. In small colonies, or singly among other nesting seabirds. Nest a scrape in the sand, with a few pieces of stick or seaweed. One to two, light grey-brown eggs, blotched dark brown or black.

197 **White-winged Tern** *Chlidonias leucoptera*
198 **Gull-billed Tern** *Gelochelidon nilotica*
200 **Common Tern** *Sterna hirundo*
205 **Bridled Tern** *Sterna anaethetus*
209 **Lesser Crested Tern** *Sterna bengalensis*
215 **Rose-crowned Fruit-Dove** *Ptilinopus regina*
226 **Emerald Dove** *Chalcophaps indica*
227 **Common Bronzewing** *Phaps chalcoptera*

RANGE Throughout Australia in suitable habitat. Almost cosmopolitan. Nomadic.

STATUS Moderately common; sparse or sporadic inland.

▶ See also pages
156 175 244

200 COMMON TERN

Sterna hirundo   Laridae

OTHER NAMES Long-winged Tern, Asiatic Common Tern, Black-billed Tern

RECOGNITION Mantle pale grey; rump to tail white. Breeding plumage: a black cap over head; underparts light pearly-grey; throat and lower face white. Non-breeding plumage: as usually seen in Australia, forehead and underparts become white. At rest this tern has wings gently upcurved to a long slender point, at least as long as the tail. Bill black and/or red. In flight, translucent wing patches. 30–38 cm.

VOICE A harsh 'keer, keer, keer', or 'kee-ar, kee-ar'. Other calls include a brisk 'kik-kik-kik-kik-', and a higher, drawn-out 'keee-aaah'.

HABITAT Offshore waters, shallow estuaries, sandbars and mudflats, lower reaches of large rivers, occasionally brackish or fresh coastal lakes.

BREEDING Regular, non-breeding summer visitor, August–April; some birds overwinter. Breeds in Asia, Europe and Africa. Most visiting northern Australia appear to be from northern and eastern Siberia; those reaching south-west are European Common Tern.

RANGE Most parts of Australian coast; most records from east coast.

STATUS Uncommon; locally abundant, especially in north-west on arrival and departure.

▶ See also pages
123 *301*

201 ROSEATE TERN

Sterna dougallii   Laridae

OTHER NAME Graceful Tern

RECOGNITION Breeding plumage: upperparts light silver-grey; white underparts with faint, rosy pink tint to the breast; black cap extending from base of bill to back of neck; rump white. When at rest, the finely elongated tail-streamers extend about 10 cm beyond wingtips. Bill scarlet and/or black; legs red. Non-breeding plumage: forehead white; crown white-streaked; black at nape. Bill black; legs

brown. Immatures: cap streaked white; mantle often mottled brown. 36–40 cm.

VOICE Harsh guttural or rasping 'aaak, aaak,' or 'kaaak'. When driving off intruders, a rattling 'kekekekek-'.

HABITAT Entirely marine: offshore waters and islands, reefs, sandy cays. Feeds on small fish, usually offshore, but in south-west inlet shallows.

BREEDING September–December in east; also February–May in Western Australia. Nests on offshore islands, in colonies, sometimes of thousands, usually far smaller numbers. Nests on sand, rock, or low bush. One to two green-grey eggs, blotched umber and grey.

RANGE Coastal south-western, north-western, northern and north-eastern Australia. Sedentary; dispersive.

STATUS Uncommon; locally abundant, as at Houtman Abrolhos, and in north-west. Endemic subspecies.

▶ See also pages
49 71 81 219 237 239 244

202 WHITE-FRONTED TERN

Sterna striata   Laridae

OTHER NAMES Black-billed Tern, Southern Tern

RECOGNITION A medium-sized tern. Breeding plumage: silvery-grey back and wings; crown and nape black, but forehead white, separating the long, slender, slightly downcurved black bill from the black crown. Tail deeply forked, with long streamers that extend about 2 cm beyond the folded wings. Underparts white, sometimes with a faint rosy wash. Non-breeding plumage: white forehead extends to white-streaked crown; bill black. Immatures: brown-mottled wing-coverts. 38–42 cm.

VOICE A high, whistling 'tsiet, tsiet'; rasping 'kearhk'. A gregarious tern, feeding in flocks, diving for fish, usually well out to sea.

HABITAT Offshore waters; islands, reefs, bays. Large companies at times seen at sea off New South Wales coast. Occasionally accidental inland.

BREEDING Previously thought to breed only in New Zealand. In 1979 a few pairs bred on an island in Bass Strait and subsequently on other islands and reefs. Two to three stone-coloured eggs, marked with grey and umber, are laid on ground.

RANGE Coastal south-eastern Australia, and Tasmania. Most birds seen are immatures from New Zealand.

STATUS Variable: usually uncommon; sometimes large numbers after storms.

▶ See also page
145

203 BLACK-NAPED TERN

Sterna sumatrana   Laridae

RECOGNITION An elegant small tern. Breeding plumage: predominantly white shading to very light grey on back and wings; and with a black line through the eye and downcurved to the back of the neck as a wide black nape patch. Tail near-white, forked, with long streamers. Underparts white, some birds with very faint rosy tint to breast. Bill and legs black. Non-breeding plumage: black of nape indistinct. Immatures: nape brownish, flight feathers grey. 30–35 cm.

VOICE Noisy with sharp yapping 'tsee-chee-chi-chip'.

HABITAT Mainly around coral reefs of tropical and subtropical waters. On Great Barrier Reef, lagoons and outer reefs; occasionally to mainland.

BREEDING August–February; also recorded April and June in Queensland. Breeds in colonies on islands. Two to three creamy-white eggs, spotted black, grey, dark brown and lavender; laid on shingle beach, or in crevice of coral or rock.

RANGE Tropical western Pacific and Indian oceans; north and north-east coasts of Australia.

STATUS Moderately common.

▶ See also pages
47 48–9 81 82 96

204 SOOTY TERN

Sterna fuscata   Laridae

OTHER NAMES Wide-awake, Whalebird, Eggbird

RECOGNITION A medium-sized tern, with upperparts entirely and uniformly sooty black, including the deeply forked tail. Forehead white, extending back as a white eyebrow only as far as the eye on each side. Tail-streamers and leading edge of wing white; underparts white. Bill and legs black. Immatures are the only sooty grey terns with deeply forked tails; mantle mottled paler; wings speckled whitish. 40–46 cm.

VOICE A nasal 'yak-yaaak'. Only vaguely like 'Wide-a-wake', the early seafarers' name for the species. Colonies very noisy.

HABITAT Tropical and subtropical oceans; coming to land only to breed. After nesting, adults disperse across local seas; immatures migrate.

BREEDING Varied, September–November in south; also March–May in north. Usually large, and sometimes huge colonies, off north-east Queensland coast, Kimberley and west coast. Nest a scrape in sand. One off-white egg, spotted and blotched grey and brown.

RANGE West, north and east coasts; and through Indian, Pacific and Atlantic oceans. Subspecies extends to New Guinea and New Caledonia.

STATUS Common.

▶ See also pages
48 49 82 96 97 237 244

BRIDLED TERN

Sterna anaethetus   Laridae

OTHER NAMES Brown-winged Tern, Dog Tern, Smaller Sooty Tern, Panayan Tern

RECOGNITION Resembles the Sooty Tern, but is slightly smaller, and with upperparts dark brown rather than black, underparts very light grey instead of white. White forehead patch extends back each side as a white eyebrow line, well past the eye. Black of crown and nape separated from brown back by a pale collar. Tail very long; tail-streamers and inner feathers white. Immatures have brown crown, streaked white; back barred buff. Swift, graceful flight. 41 cm.

VOICE A staccato 'yep-yep-yep-', rather like Black-winged Stilt or bark of small dog; grating 'krarrh' when fishing. Immature's call like tinkling bell.

HABITAT A bird of open seas, rarely fishing inshore. Occurs across tropical and subtropical waters.

BREEDING September–November in south; March–May in north. Breeds in colonies on small offshore islands of western, north-western, northern and north-eastern Australia. No nest is constructed; single egg laid under rock ledge among boulders, bushes; creamy-white, spotted and blotched browns.

RANGE Australian coasts; from south-west, round north to north-east. Subspecies extends to southern India and Japan. Species circumtropical. Migratory.

STATUS Common.

▶ See also pages
81 82 230 244 301

LITTLE TERN

Sterna albifrons   Laridae

OTHER NAMES White-shafted Ternlet, Sea-swallow, Black-lored Tern

RECOGNITION The smallest Australian tern. Breeding plumage: back, wings and tail light grey with black on outer flight feathers. Black crown and nape, with black line from crown through eye and tapering to a point at the base of the bill, so that lores are black. Underparts white; bill yellow, usually black-tipped; legs and feet cadmium yellow. Non-breeding plumage: grey streaked crown; lores mostly white; bill and legs black. 20–25 cm.

VOICE A short, high, slightly rasping 'kweeik' or 'kreeik'. Also, often while hovering, a rapid 'krik-krik-krik-'.

HABITAT Coastal waters, estuaries, shallow inlets and bays, salt and brackish lakes, salt fields. Feeds mainly on fish taken in plunging dive.

BREEDING Variable; August–December in north, January–March in south; colonies on islands. In south-east, where Little and Fairy terns overlap, some mixed colonies and interbreeding. Nest a scrape in sand. One to three grey or fawn eggs, spotted greys and browns.

RANGE Round northern coastline; approximately Perth to Adelaide. Migratory.

STATUS Common; but beach colonies are endangered in south-east. Endemic subspecies.

▶ See also pages
117 124

FAIRY TERN

Sterna nereis   Laridae

OTHER NAMES Little Sea-swallow, Ternlet, Little Tern, White-faced Ternlet

RECOGNITION Closely resembles Little Tern, but, in breeding plumage: black of cap does not reach farther forward than eye; white forehead extends back only to eye; lores white; bill bright orange rather than yellow, rarely with black tip. Non-breeding plumage: white forehead extends to crown; bill black at tip and base, central part usually dull yellow. (Little Tern in non-breeding, bill black; more black on outer flight feathers.) Short, yellowish legs. 21–27 cm.

VOICE Noisy, with loud 'chiwik, chiwik' or 'krik-krik'; much like call of Little Tern. Also excited high 'ket-ket-ket-ket-'.

HABITAT Coastal waters, usually within sight of land, and rarely inland. Fishes in shallow waters by plunge-diving.

BREEDING August–January. Nests in colonies, on sheltered beaches of islands, shores of inlets and estuaries. Two to three slightly glossy, stone-grey eggs, blotched darker greys and umber; laid on sand.

RANGE North-west, west and south coasts; western Kimberley to eastern Tasmania. Part-migratory.

STATUS Abundant in Western Australia; uncommon south-east. Endemic subspecies.

▶ See also pages
156 156 244

CRESTED TERN

Sterna bergii   Laridae

OTHER NAMES Greater Crested Tern, Bass Strait Tern, Diver, Torres Strait Tern

RECOGNITION Breeding plumage: back and tail grey, wing darker grey above; face (below eye), entire neck and undersurfaces white. Crown and nape black, with feathers of nape forming shaggy low crest. Bill large, lemon-yellow, greenish towards base with white strip across; eye brown; legs black. Non-breeding plumage: crown streaked white, more on forehead. Immatures similar to non-breeding, but with varied amounts of brown and black. 44–48 cm.

VOICE Noisy, especially in colonies. Alarm calls 'wep-wep', and loud rasping 'kirrik'. Also a cawing call given in courtship.

HABITAT Coastal; well out to sea, and extending inland along major rivers. May be seen on islets, bays, inlets, salt or brackish coastal lakes.

BREEDING September–December in south; March–June in north. Nests in colonies, with sites and numbers of breeding birds changing from year to year. One to two glossy, stone-grey eggs, marked grey, brown and black; laid in a slight depression in sand.

RANGE All Australian coasts. Subspecies extends to Malaysia; species widespread in Indian Ocean. Migrates or disperses widely.

STATUS Common.

▶ See also pages
12–13 71 74 81 82 96 97 151 219 244

LESSER CRESTED TERN

Sterna bengalensis   Laridae

OTHER NAME Allied Tern

RECOGNITION Like Crested Tern, but smaller and with bill orange rather than slightly greenish-yellow and, in breeding plumage, little or no white on the forehead. Non-breeding plumage: the bill remains orange or deep cadmium-yellow; the forehead becomes white; the crown white streaked black; and with black through eye onto nape. Some birds breed while still in this plumage. Immatures similar to non-breeding; sooty shoulder and outer-tail feathers. 36–41 cm.

VOICE Like Crested Tern, shriller alarm notes. Flight and foraging habits also similar, often mixes with other terns.

HABITAT Offshore waters, tropical and subtropical; visiting ocean beaches, islands, cays, reefs. Disperses widely from breeding sites.

BREEDING September–December in east and south; March–June in north. Nest is a shallow scrape in sand. Nesting is colonial, on offshore islands, coral cays and sandbanks along the Queensland coast. One whitish egg, marked purplish-brown and grey.

RANGE Northern Australian coasts; approximately Shark Bay (WA), to Stradbroke Island (Qld). Widespread.

STATUS Uncommon; usually found in small colonies.

▶ See also pages
81 82 96 97 219
301

210 COMMON NODDY

Anous stolidus   Laridae

OTHER NAMES Noddy, Greater Noddy, Noddy Tern

RECOGNITION Quite large, wingspan 65 cm. Body, wings and tail entirely sooty, warm black. Forehead and crown silvery-white, blending smoothly through grey to black on the nape, but sharply defined along a line from bill and eye where white forehead meets black of lores. Bill and legs black. In flight, very dark, including long tail with notched tip. At close range this tail and heavier bill help separate from other noddies. Immatures: cap patchy or absent. 38–45 cm.

VOICE A threat or alarm note, harsh 'kaark', or 'kraa', given if disturbed on nest. Also a threatening 'kreeaw', and 'kwok, kwok' calls.

HABITAT Tropical, subtropical seas, especially in the vicinity of islands; with presence of colonies correlating with warmer water temperatures.

BREEDING Variable, but usually September–November and March–May. Nest an untidy mound of dry seaweed, grass, sticks; on ground, or on low shrub. One dull white egg, blotched shades of red-brown, purple, and black.

RANGE Northern Australian coasts; breeding in west, north-west and north-east; vagrant to south-east and south-west. Dispersive or migratory. Widespread.

STATUS Common in north-east, north-west and west; scarce in south.

▶ See also pages
49 49 81 96 97
219 237 244

211 LESSER NODDY

Anous tenuirostris   Laridae

RECOGNITION Like Common Noddy, but smaller (wingspan 63 cm), and with bill much more slender, proportionately longer and almost straight rather than down-curved upper profile. Plumage entirely dark brownish-black; forehead and crown very light grey shading smoothly on both nape and face to the darker tones. In flight, slimmer than Common Noddy; tail more fan-shaped, square-cut, with notched tip. Immatures have whiter cap. Flight moth-like, erratic and buoyant. 30–34 cm.

VOICE A rattling yet soft 'churr' as alarm call at the nest; and almost constant soft purring within rookeries.

HABITAT Tropical and subtropical oceans, islands. Feeds on fish and other sea creatures taken near the surface; sometimes dives through crests of waves.

BREEDING August–January. Only known breeding sites are the Houtman Abrolhos islands (subspecies *melanops*) and the Seychelles (*tenuirostris*). Nests colonially, on platforms of seaweed in low trees. One creamy egg, marked brown.

RANGE Indian Ocean; usually to Australian coast only at Houtman Abrolhos islands.

STATUS Seasonally abundant at Houtman Abrolhos. Endemic breeding subspecies.

▶ See also pages
237 *237* 244

212 BLACK NODDY

Anous minutus   Laridae

OTHER NAME White-capped Noddy

RECOGNITION Size and general appearance similar to Lesser Noddy; face pattern like Common Noddy; with sharp demarcation between white crown and blackish lores and face. Body plumage is darkest of noddies, against which the white cap stands out conspicuously. In flight, tail forked rather than notched. Bill long, slender. Flight buoyant. 33–36 cm.

VOICE A rattling, fast 'krik-krik-krik-krik-krik' in breeding colonies; also louder, staccato, alarm call.

HABITAT Tropical Pacific and Atlantic oceans; vicinity of islands, cays and atolls to nest and roost in non-breeding season. Takes food from surface of sea, and usually hunts in large flocks.

BREEDING August–January. Breeds on islands of eastern Queensland coast, Norfolk Island, and islands of the Coral Sea, some of the colonies very large. Nest an untidy mass of leaves and seaweed, in branches of trees. One creamy-white egg, blotched grey, brown.

RANGE East coast; Torres Strait to north-eastern New South Wales. Widespread. Sedentary.

STATUS Abundant in breeding range; scarce elsewhere.

▶ See also pages
71 73 75 82 97

PIGEONS, DOVES

Columbidae Family of 290 species
25 in Australia, 24 breeding, 14 endemic

All bear unmistakable resemblance to the familiar domestic pigeon, but vary greatly in size and plumage colours. Pastel colours are common, but some have patches of vivid colour, and iridescent sheens, especially on the wings. The flight is powerful and swift, often with noisy clapping takeoff. Legs are short, and bills fairly short, with the nostrils open in a soft basal cere. Calls are soft, and mating displays elegant.

213 BANDED FRUIT-DOVE

Ptilinopus cinctus   Columbidae

OTHER NAMES Black-Banded Fruit-Dove, Banded Pigeon, Black-banded Fruit-Pigeon

RECOGNITION Back, wings and lower breast black, in bold contrast to white of head, neck and upper breast. Rump grey; tail black broadly tipped grey; belly pale grey. Eye red; bill grey-green with yellow tip. Immatures have light grey in place of white, bronze-green replacing black. Flight swift, often whistling sound from wings. Usually singly or small numbers feeding in native figs; well-hidden in dense foliage. 48–51 cm.

VOICE A single loud note, a hoot or coo, of about one second duration, and repeated six or seven times at intervals of four or five seconds.

HABITAT Sandstone escarpment and gorge country; pockets of sandstone rainforest; broadleaf shrubbery of trees, shrubs, some spinifex.

BREEDING Nest not discovered until May 1971. Breeding recorded April–November, usually about July. Nest a very sparse and flimsy, almost flat platform, on horizontal fork of a leafy tree. The single egg is usually visible from below.

RANGE Confined to the western escarpment of Arnhem Land. Sedentary.

STATUS Moderately common within very restricted range. Endemic.

▶ See also pages
189 *189* 196

14 SUPERB FRUIT-DOVE

Ptilinopus superbus   Columbidae

OTHER NAMES Purple-crowned Pigeon, Purple-crowned Fruit-Dove, Superb Fruit-Pigeon

RECOGNITION A superbly colourful small pigeon. Male with forehead and crown rich purple; neck-band vermilion; ear-coverts pale green; and chin white. Remainder of upperparts rich golden and olive greens, mottled black; primaries black. Underparts, throat and breast white, lightly flecked purple; separated from off-white of flanks and belly by a broad purple-black breastband. Female has small purple-blue crown patch, no red on neck, no dark breastband. 22–24 cm.

VOICE A loud and resonant double-noted whoop, as an identity call used to advertise its presence; also softer cooing calls and low quiet murmurings.

HABITAT Tropical and subtropical rainforests and scrubs, but often feeding in fruiting trees of nearby woodlands; also mangroves, lantana thickets.

BREEDING June–February, with most beginning November–December. The nest is a very rough platform of sticks placed in forks of trees or shrubs, on horizontal palm leaves, or in vine thickets, usually below 10 m. One glossy white egg.

RANGE Coastal north-eastern Queensland; Cape York to Rockhampton; vagrant south to Tasmania. Also in New Guinea and Celebes. Nomadic.

STATUS Common in north; uncommon south of Cardwell.

▶ See also pages
52-3 *53* 81 111

15 ROSE-CROWNED FRUIT-DOVE

Ptilinopus regina   Columbidae

OTHER NAMES Red-crowned Pigeon, Red-crowned Fruit-Dove, Pink-cap, Ewing's Fruit-Pigeon

RECOGNITION A small dove, with rich glossy-green back, wings and tail, blending to grey-green on neck, breast, throat and head. A deep rose-pink patch, from forehead onto front of crown, is finely edged yellow. The deep-yellow belly and yellow-tipped tail are distinctive. Bill and legs grey-green; eye orange. Female similar but duller, particularly underparts. Immatures: upperparts, including crown, are green; underparts are green, scalloped - yellow. 20–23 cm.

VOICE Surprisingly loud for size of bird. A series of deep resonant notes, becoming more rapid until merging, 'hook-oo, ook-oo, ook-oo-ook-ookoo'.

HABITAT Rainforests, both tropical and subtropical; also monsoon scrubs, deciduous vine thickets, mangroves, paperbark swamps, wherever fruiting trees.

BREEDING In south-east, October–February; in north, October–March. The nest is a flimsy platform of fine, mostly forked, sticks and vine tendrils. In south, tends to be in dense cover but in north often in more open trees. One white or creamy-white, lustrous egg.

RANGE Coastal north-western (subspecies *ewingii*) and eastern Australia, south to Hunter River. Extends into Indonesia. Nomadic.

STATUS Common, but declining with loss of habitat.

▶ See also pages
81 121 208 *301*

216 WOMPOO FRUIT-DOVE

Ptilinopus magnificus   Columbidae

OTHER NAMES Wompoo Pigeon, Wompoo Fruit-Pigeon, Green Pigeon, Bubbly Mary

RECOGNITION Large, long-tailed. Upperparts dominantly green, blending to pale grey on the head, and with a broken yellow band across the wing. Underparts distinctive, throat, neck and breast deep purple; abdomen to undertail-coverts golden yellow; in flight showing yellow also on underwings. Red bill tipped pale yellow; legs olive-green. Immatures as adults, but purple on breast blotched green. Presence usually revealed by calls, and falling fruit. 35–50 cm.

VOICE Main advertising call is a deep, bubbling, 'wollock-a-wooo'. Often male gives a low-pitched call, and the female answers slightly higher.

HABITAT Lowland rainforest is the optimum habitat, but is present in most tropical and subtropical rainforests; extending to adjacent habitats.

BREEDING August–January. Nest is a small flat platform of sticks and pieces of vine, built on a horizontal fork 2–10 m above ground, and usually so thin that the single egg can be seen from below. Egg is white and lustreless.

RANGE Coastal north-eastern Australia, south to Hunter River district. Sedentary.

STATUS Moderately common in north; scarce in south. Endemic subspecies, species to New Guinea.

▶ See also pages
81 86-7 *87* 98 111 121

217 TORRESIAN IMPERIAL-PIGEON

Ducula spilorrhoa   Columbidae

OTHER NAMES Torres Strait Pigeon, Spice Pigeon, Nutmeg Pigeon

RECOGNITION A large pigeon, with predominantly snowy-white plumage except for the terminal half of the tail and the flight feathers, which are black. The white extends to the underparts but with black spotting on flanks and undertail-coverts. The bill is grey becoming yellow towards the tip; the eye is brown with the surrounding bare skin blue-grey, and legs are blue-grey. In flight, white with dark wingtips. 38–44 cm.

VOICE Usual call is a loud deep 'coo-woo' with the second part stronger, and slightly higher; in bowing displays, a very loud 'coo-hoo-hoo'.

HABITAT Tropical rainforests, monsoon forests, eucalypt woodlands, mangroves on coasts, islands. In Kimberley, only in semi-deciduous vine scrubs. Feeds on the fruits of trees, palms, vines.

BREEDING August–January. Nests in large colonies in mangroves or rainforest canopy, usually on offshore islands. Spectacular massed daily flights to and from mainland to feed. Nest is substantial, often of mangrove twigs. One white egg.

RANGE Northern and north-eastern Australia, western Kimberley to Mackay (Qld). In east, migrates to New Guinea.

STATUS Common in north; reduced by loss of habitat and shooting in south.

▶ See also pages
87 *87* 97 98 196 209

218 TOPKNOT PIGEON

Lopholaimus antarcticus   Columbidae

OTHER NAME Flock Pigeon

RECOGNITION A large, dominantly grey pigeon with backswept crests on forehead and crown. The grey crest of forehead and cere gives an unusual, bulbous-headed appearance, while the crest on the crown is rust-red, extending back over the nape. Round the neck the slate-grey feathers have dark bases, giving a streaked effect. Flight feathers and tail are black, though base and tip of tail are grey. Eye orange with red eye-ring; bill red; feet pinkish. 40–46 cm.

VOICE Usually silent, but occasional low short screech while feeding or fighting, low abrupt squeaks during the bowing display, sometimes a soft coo.

HABITAT Tropical, subtropical and temperate rainforests, extending out to feed and sometimes nest in eucalypt forests where there are fruiting trees.

BREEDING June–December. Few nests have been described, as the Topknot Pigeon appears to build high in densely-foliaged and vine-choked treetops of the rainforest canopy; rarely low or open sites. Nest is flimsy flat platform. One white egg.

RANGE Coastal eastern Australia, Cape York to eastern Victoria; vagrant to Tasmania. Highly nomadic.

STATUS Common in optimum habitat; elsewhere scarce. Endemic genus.

▶ **See also pages**
81 *117* 121 122

219 WHITE-HEADED PIGEON

Columba leucomela   Columbidae

OTHER NAMES Baldy, Baldy Pigeon, White-headed Fruit-Pigeon

RECOGNITION Upperparts, back, wings and tail entirely black with green and purple iridescence. In strong contrast are the white of head, neck and breast which shade to very light grey or buffy-white from lower breast onto flanks, belly and undertail-coverts. Undertail and underwings black. Female similar but greyish, duller. Immatures have grey crown, nape and breast. 38–42 cm.

VOICE Low, mournful, with ventriloquial quality. The advertising call is a deep drawn-out 'oooom-coo', with second note lower; also low repeated 'oom'.

HABITAT Tropical and subtropical rainforests, tropical scrubs, rainforest remnants and regrowth; isolated fruiting trees, including street trees. Usually feeds on fruits of figs and other trees, but also takes grains on the ground.

BREEDING July–March; mainly October–December. Nest is a frail structure of a few twigs and vine tendrils, but occasionally quite substantial. Usually placed in very dense foliage including lawyer-vine tangles. One white egg.

RANGE East coast; Cooktown to Hunter River. Nomadic, follows fruiting of trees.

STATUS Moderately common, apparently increasing. Endemic.

▶ **See also pages**
87–8 87 121

220 SPOTTED TURTLE-DOVE

Streptopelia chinensis   Columbidae

OTHER NAMES Indian Turtle-Dove, Chinese Turtle-Dove, Laceneck, Burmese Turtle-Dove

RECOGNITION A large and long-tailed dove with grey head, and black, white-spotted patch on hind-neck. Remainder of upperparts grey-brown, mottled darker dull browns. Underparts pale cinnamon-grey. Eye pink; bill and legs black. Immatures

plainer; lacking spotted neck-patch. *Introduced species.* 27–31 cm.

VOICE Mellow, drowsy 'coo-coo, croo-ook' and numerous variations.

HABITAT Cities, suburban parks, gardens, some grain-growing rural areas, roadsides and other disturbed habitats; to lesser extent some natural habitats. Feeds on grains and seeds of weeds, usually in small flocks on open ground. The lack of suitable food may be limiting its spread away from settled districts.

BREEDING Throughout year. Nest a frail platform of rootlets, sticks, at heights 1–10 m in dense shrub or tree foliage, or building ledge. Two white eggs, slightly glossy.

RANGE Eastern, south-eastern, south-western Australia, and Tasmania. A native of Asia and South-East Asia.

STATUS Common. In places may be displacing native Bar-shouldered Dove. Introduced species.

221 LAUGHING TURTLE-DOVE

Streptopelia senegalensis   Columbidae

OTHER NAMES Senegal Dove, Laughing Dove, Senegal Turtle-Dove

RECOGNITION Upperparts brown with mauve tint, merging to soft slaty-blue on lower back and wing-coverts. Underparts pale lilac-brown, darkest on the upper breast where dark-based feathers give a black-speckled appearance most conspicuous when the feathers of the neck ·are raised during the bowing display. Also has a display flight, male rising steeply, then dropping in a spiral with wings and tail outspread. Immatures duller; no blue on wings. *Introduced species.* 25 cm.

VOICE Has a bubbling or laughing quality, a series of short notes, at first rising, then falling: 'coo, coo-oo, coo, coo' and variations.

HABITAT Confined to cities, towns, nearby cultivated country; fortunately it seems unable to colonize the natural bush to compete with native species.

BREEDING Throughout the year, mostly September–January. Constructs a frail platform of fine twigs. Two white eggs.

RANGE South-west corner of Western Australia; a native of Africa and southern Asia. Sedentary.

STATUS Common, but patchy distribution, centred on towns. Introduced species.

222 BROWN CUCKOO-DOVE

Macropygia amboinensis   Columbidae

OTHER NAMES Brown Pigeon, Large-tailed Pigeon, Pheasant-tailed Pigeon

RECOGNITION Large and long-tailed, with plumage of overall brownish tones. Upperparts coppery-brown with mauve-green sheen about the neck, lightening to cinnamon on the head, and darker browns on wings and tail. Underparts light cinnamon-buff, with distinct pinkish tinge to the breast; underside of tail dark brown. Female similar, less iridescence on neck, fine black barrings on throat and breast. Immatures chestnut on crown, heavier black barring. 38–43 cm.

VOICE A penetrating three-note call, high-pitched yet mellow; the first part short and low, the second drawn-out, stronger: 'coo, coo-woot'.

HABITAT Principally rainforest, but ranging out into eucalypts where there are outlying fruiting rainforest species, usually along creeks.

BREEDING Most of year, May–March; usually September–January. Nest structures vary from flimsy to quite substantial and well dished on top; built of dry sticks, vine tendrils, bark. Sites include tree-ferns, vine tangles. One dull white egg.

RANGE East coast and coastal ranges; Cape York to eastern Victoria. Also in New Guinea, Sumatra, Philippines. Locally nomadic.

STATUS Common, in remaining habitat.

▶ **See also pages**
53 *53* 81 122

223 PEACEFUL DOVE

Geopelia placida   Columbidae

OTHER NAMES Turtledove, Ground Dove, Zebra Dove, Doodle-doo, Four o'clock

RECOGNITION A tiny dove, with upperparts grey-brown, extensively barred and scalloped black. Head, neck and upper breast blue-grey, closely and heavily barred black; throat white; lower breast white with pinkish tinge; flanks and abdomen creamy-white. Tail grey above, dark brown beneath; outer tail feathers black, tipped white. Eye light blue; bare skin of cere and round eye blue-grey. In flight shows chestnut wing-lining. Immatures paler. 18–23 cm.

VOICE Clear, musical, oft-repeated with three- and four-syllable versions intermixed: 'doodle-doo, doodle-doodle-doo'. Also sharper metallic 'coo-luc'.

HABITAT Grassy woodlands, forest verges near grasslands, margins of rainforests and monsoon forests, tree-lined watercourses in semi-arid regions.

BREEDING Recorded throughout the year, mainly March–April in north; November–January in south. Often two or more broods in season, sometimes from the one nest. The nest is a small rough platform of sticks, in varied sites, 1–12 m height. Two white eggs.

RANGE Throughout Australia, except in south-west, western arid regions, Tasmania. Also Malaysia, Indonesia, and New Guinea. Sedentary or nomadic.

STATUS Common; becoming rare in parts of south-east.

▶ See also pages
40 *40* 211 223

224 DIAMOND DOVE

Geopelia cuneata   Columbidae

OTHER NAMES Little Dove, Little Turtle-Dove, Red-eyed Dove

RECOGNITION A tiny dove, with entire head, neck and breast soft blue grey. Back, wings and tail smoky grey-brown, with wings speckled with white spots or diamonds. The eye and bare eye-ring are red; conspicuous on plain blue-grey of the face; bill light grey; legs and feet pinkish. Although of similar length to Peaceful Dove, it is more slender, longer-tailed and looks smaller. Female similar but duller. Immatures browner, barred; retain white wing spots. 19–21 cm.

VOICE Mournful soft 'coo, coo-oo', the last part dropping in pitch. A second call has five level coo notes. In bowing display, a single sharp note.

HABITAT Lightly-wooded semi-arid and arid grasslands wherever there is water, favouring open mulga scrub and spinifex with scattered trees.

BREEDING Almost any month, most activity following rainfall which in the more arid parts of the range is very erratic; October–November towards south of range. Nest is the usual frail platform of twigs, in widely varied sites. Two white eggs.

RANGE Almost throughout Australia except coastal south-east, south-west, Tasmania. Highly nomadic.

STATUS Common; patchy in occurrence. Endemic.

▶ See also pages
211 *232* 233

225 BAR-SHOULDERED DOVE

Geopelia humeralis   Columbidae

OTHER NAMES Pandanus Pigeon, Scrub Dove, Mangrove Dove, Scrub Pigeon, Kook-a-wuk

RECOGNITION Upperparts mainly brown, barred black: hind-neck and shoulders coppery, with each feather edged black, giving a scalloped effect. Head, face, throat and upper breast light blue-grey; the crown finely scalloped black. Lower breast and belly creamy-white with a light-pink wash. Eye pale yellow; eye-ring grey to red (when breeding); bill blue-grey; legs red. In flight, chestnut underwings; holds head high. Immatures duller; buff eye-ring. 28–31 cm.

VOICE Very vocal, loud calls that have a pleasant rollicking quality, three clear notes, 'cook-a-wook', repeatedly; also loud 'hook-oo, hook-oo'.

HABITAT Woodlands and open forest where there is abundant low cover of shrubs and herbage, near water, edges of monsoon scrubs, mangroves and lantana thickets.

BREEDING Throughout the year, usually March–July in north; November–January in south. The nest of thin sticks is small and very frail; usually quite low in a bush, and on occasions on a clump of grass or rock ledge. Two white, lustrous eggs.

RANGE Northern Australia, mainly coastal; North West Cape (WA) to Bega (NSW). Sedentary.

STATUS Common; particularly in north. Endemic subspecies to New Guinea.

▶ See also pages
209 *209* 223

226 EMERALD DOVE

Chalcophaps indica   Columbidae
OTHER NAMES Green-winged Pigeon, Lilac-mantled Pigeon, Green-winged Dove

RECOGNITION Head, neck, upper back and underparts brown; the upperparts with a russet tone and slight violet or wine-red tint, and the underparts a lighter cinnamon. Wings bright iridescent emerald green on scapulars and innerwing-coverts; brown on primaries, secondaries and underwings. Lower back, rump and tail dark brown; rump crossed by two light-grey bands. White patch at shoulder is small and grey on female. Immatures have dark-barred head and underparts; less green. 25 cm.

VOICE A monotonous, mournful call, consisting of a series of up to 30 long, drawn-out coos, the first being the longest; also other variations.

HABITAT Tropical and subtropical rain-forests, monsoon forests and vine scrubs, particularly the margins; tropical plantations, lantana thickets, mangroves.

BREEDING Throughout the year; mainly October–February in north; September–December farther south. Nest usually a flimsy platform of twigs (sometimes more substantial), on limbs, in vine tangles, on tree-ferns or large epiphytes. Two creamy-white eggs.

RANGE Two races: *longirostris* Kimberley–Northern Territory; *chrysochlora* in the east. Also in New Guinea, South-East Asia. Sedentary or locally nomadic.

STATUS Common.

▶ See also pages
81 121 209 *301*

227 COMMON BRONZEWING

Phaps chalcoptera   Columbidae

OTHER NAMES Scrub Bronzewing, Forest Bronzewing, Squatter, Bronzewing

RECOGNITION A large and plump pigeon; brown on the upperparts, with pale-edged feathers that give a scaly appearance. The secondaries have a conspicuous wing patch of iridescent green and bronze. Distinctive head markings: forehead buff; crown dark brown with dark-brown line through eye to bill; buff line under eye curving down onto neck. Breast pinkish-grey; belly paler. Female: less colourful; grey on forehead and breast. Immatures duller overall. 29–35 cm.

VOICE The advertising and nest call is a long series of deep, resonant and mournful 'oom' sounds; ventriloquial, making its location difficult.

HABITAT Throughout almost all dry-land habitats except dense wet forests. These range from open forest to arid mulga and saltbush if water is near.

BREEDING Throughout the year; peak of activity August–December. Nest sites vary greatly; high horizontal limbs in forests, low shrubs, among rocks on the ground. Nest varies from sparse to quite substantial platform. Two white, oval eggs.

RANGE Throughout Australia in suitable habitat. Nomadic in arid regions.

STATUS Moderately common. Endemic.

▶ See also pages
16 280 *301* 308

228 BRUSH BRONZEWING

Phaps elegans   Columbidae

OTHER NAME Box-poison Pigeon

RECOGNITION Upperparts plain olive-brown, with rich chestnut shoulders, and two bars of iridescent metallic bronze-green and purple across centre of wings. Head distinctive: forehead cinnamon; crown and nape blue-grey; line through eye is black from bill to eye, then chestnut margined white below back to hind-neck; chestnut throat patch. Breast blue-grey; underparts grey. Female and immatures duller; little chestnut on shoulders. 28–30 cm.

VOICE A series of 'oom' sounds, almost incessant when breeding. Call is similar to that of Common Bronzewing but with each 'oom' higher, longer and wider spaced.

HABITAT Dense, low cover, particularly the thick coastal heaths, scrubby undergrowth of forests, mallee thickets.

BREEDING Throughout the year; mainly October–January. Nest like that of Common bronzewing: almost flat platform of sticks; often on the ground under low bush; also in shrubs and trees; in wide variety of situations. Two glossy white eggs.

RANGE South-west of Western Australia; Tasmania; and south-east from Eyre Peninsula to Fraser Island. Sedentary.

STATUS Scarce; only very locally common. Endemic.

▶ See also pages
16 17

229 FLOCK BRONZEWING

Phaps histrionica   Columbidae

OTHER NAMES Flock Pigeon, Harlequin Bronzewing, Harlequin Pigeon

RECOGNITION Upperparts almost entirely coppery red-brown; with flight feathers grey-brown tipped white. Head distinctive: all black but for a conspicuous white patch covering entire front of face back to the eye, including forehead, lores and chin. A white near-circular line from back of eye encircles the ear-coverts. Throat black; upper edge of breast white; breast and belly grey. Female and immatures: black of head replaced by brown; throat grey; breast brown. 28 cm.

VOICE Usually silent. Apparently no advertising call; advertisement in flocks being visual. Murmured contact call in flight, deep coo in display.

HABITAT Open treeless plains, especially the Mitchell grass plains of the Barkly Tableland. Also spinifex, saltbush. Often in the vicinity of stock tanks.

BREEDING Variable, usually mid dry season; March–July in north, and spring in south, when grasses are seeding. Nest is a shallow scrape in the ground, under tussock or low bush; reportedly at times in great numbers. Two white eggs.

RANGE Northern interior; irrupting southeast to north-eastern New South Wales. Highly nomadic.

STATUS Common, but greatly reduced; patchy. Endemic.

▶ See also pages
28 29 175 223

230 CRESTED PIGEON

Ocyphaps lophotes   Columbidae

OTHER NAMES Topknot Pigeon, Crested Bronzewing, Crested Dove

RECOGNITION Distinguished by a dark crest that tapers to a single, long fine vertical point. Crown, back and rump grey. Wings grey-brown with conspicuous black barring, and green-and-purple iridescent wing patch. Underparts grey, with pinkish-bronze sheen to the sides of the breast. Tail long, blackish, tipped lighter. Red eye and surrounding bare skin; pink legs. Flies with bursts of whistling wingbeats, then glides. 30–35 cm.

VOICE Contact call is a soft wavering 'woof-woof'. As an alarm, a quite loud, explosive 'whoop', and a similar call in the bowing courtship display.

HABITAT Open country; woodlands, with scattered trees or bushes, and never very far from water. Also farmlands and other cleared land.

BREEDING At any time after rainfall, but most often September–February. Nest is a thin and flimsy, almost flat platform of twigs on a horizontal fork, up to about 3 m above ground. Two oval, glossy white eggs.

230 CRESTED PIGEON *Ocyphaps lophotes*

RANGE Throughout Australia, except in Tasmania, forested south-east and south-west, north-eastern Queensland, coastal Northern Territory. Range increased by clearing. Sedentary.

STATUS Common. Endemic.

▶ See also pages
136 221

231 SQUATTER PIGEON

Petrophassa scripta   Columbidae

OTHER NAMES Partridge Pigeon, Partridge Bronzewing

RECOGNITION A squat pigeon of dull grey-brown upperparts, with the edges of the feathers paler giving a scaly pattern. Head darker brown with distinctive facial pattern. Face and throat black with white lines through and below the eye, both curving downwards; white patch on throat. Eye-ring usually whitish. Upper breast dull brown; lower breast dark blue-grey; flanks white, extending as stripe up each side of breast. Bill black. 26–31 cm.

VOICE A long drawn-out musical coo. Also when walking through grass an almost continuous low murmured 'oo-poop'. Like calls of Partridge Pigeon.

HABITAT Shows preference for sandy localities in woodland, near permanent water; often river flats, gravelly ridges.

BREEDING All months; peak activity in dry season, May–June. The nest is a scrape under shelter of tussocks or low bushes. The Squatter Pigeon keeps to the ground, running rather than flying, perching only after being flushed.

RANGE Eastern Queensland and north of New South Wales; coast and inland in suitable habitat. Locally nomadic.

STATUS Common in north; reduced to rare in south. Endemic.

▶ See also pages
74 75 110 121 309

232 PARTRIDGE PIGEON

Petrophassa smithii   Columbidae

OTHER NAMES Bare-eyed Pigeon, Red-eyed Squatter, Partridge Bronzewing

RECOGNITION Upperparts including the head, dull uniform brown without major distinguishing markings except a wide strip of brilliant-scarlet bare skin from bill through the eye to ear-coverts, narrowly edged white above and below; white throat patch. The subspecies *blaauwi* has the bare orbital skin deep-yellow instead of scarlet. Breast pinkish-brown prominently edged white, and with a small central patch of scaly black marks. Bill black and heavy. 25–28 cm.

VOICE A long drawn-out musical coo. When in long grass, an almost incessant low, murmured 'oo-poop', very like calls of Squatter Pigeon.

HABITAT Tropical tall open forests and woodlands of the heavier rainfall, near-coastal north; open ground near water.

BREEDING Most of the year, with a peak around the middle of the dry season. At this time in the north the protective grass cover is still abundant, seeds have matured. Nest is a scrape, usually in grass. Two white, lustrous eggs.

RANGE North coast of Kimberley and Northern Territory. Sedentary, or locally nomadic.

STATUS Now uncommon; remains common in a few localities. Endemic.

► See also pages
189–90 *193* 208

233 WHITE-QUILLED ROCK-PIGEON

Petrophassa albipennis   Columbidae
OTHER NAME Rock Pigeon

RECOGNITION Almost entirely deep red-brown, with centre of each feather shaded grey producing a lightly scalloped appearance. Crown of head grey-brown mottled darker; blackish line through eye. A large white wing-patch conspicuous in flight; at rest may show as a white streak. This white patch may be reduced or missing in east of range. Body colour also varies, darkest in northern Kimberley. Lives among rocks; flies with loud whistling whirr of wings. 27–31 cm.

VOICE Probably indistinguishable from the calls of the Chestnut-quilled Rock-Pigeon: usually a clear 'coo-carook'.

HABITAT Similar to that of the Chestnut-quilled Rock-Pigeon: sandstone plateaus deeply dissected into broken escarpments and gorges, interspersed with woodland.

BREEDING Recorded throughout the year, probably most active at the end of the wet and early in the dry season. Nest is of similar construction to that of the Chestnut-quilled Rock-Pigeon, possibly in more open location. Two white eggs.

RANGE Kimberley (WA) to west of Top End (NT). Sedentary.

STATUS Common in suitable habitat. Endemic.

► See also pages
187 198 201 202
208 *209* 210 211

234 CHESTNUT-QUILLED ROCK-PIGEON

Petrophassa rufipennis   Columbidae
OTHER NAMES Rock Pigeon, Red-quilled Rock-Pigeon

RECOGNITION A large, long-tailed pigeon which looks heavy-bodied, short-legged and almost reptilian, standing with body in horizontal posture, wings drooped and tail depressed. In flight, it has a partridge-like wing action. Almost entirely dark dusky brown; with head, face and neck speckled light grey; and remainder of upperparts mottled browns. A dark line from bill through eye. Primaries are mostly chestnut; sometimes visible as a narrow streak. 30–32 cm.

VOICE The usual call is a loud clear and musical 'coo-carook', expressed in Aboriginal name 'Kukarook'. Sudden alarm results in a single sharp coo.

HABITAT Sandstone escarpments and gorges, with scattered trees and shrubs, ground cover of spinifex, and many small plant species; adjoining woodland.

BREEDING Few nests located; indications are that breeding occurs throughout the year, but mainly late wet to early dry season. The nest is a substantial platform of sticks, leaves and spinifex; built in a rock crevice. Two white eggs.

RANGE Western Arnhem Land (NT). Sedentary.

STATUS Common within very restricted range. Endemic.

► See also pages
189 190 196 198

235 SPINIFEX PIGEON

Petrophassa plumifera   Columbidae
OTHER NAMES Plumed Pigeon, Red-plumed Pigeon, Ground Dove

RECOGNITION A plump, erect-standing, small pigeon, with plumage mostly bright cinnamon including the erect finely-tapered crest. Conspicuous facial markings: bright red bare skin in broad band round eye, edged black above and below. Broad white band across lower face; wide black neckband. Wings scalloped red-brown and barred grey and black. Subspecies *plumifera* has white lower breast; northwest subspecies *ferruginea* is entirely cinnamon beneath. 20–22 cm.

VOICE A deep, soft, 'cu-wooo' with second part drawn-out and rising. May be repeated 'coo-woo, coo-woo, coo-wooo', the final note loud.

HABITAT Spinifex on or near rocky ranges, gorges; in some places occur where there is grass other than spinifex. Only found near permanent water.

BREEDING Breeds throughout the year, with greater nesting activity after rain, however some individuals will nest in drought conditions. Nest is a scrape in the ground, sheltered by grass, bush or rock. Two white, smooth eggs.

RANGE Central Australia to Kimberley; subspecies *ferruginea* in north-west. Sedentary.

STATUS Common in suitable habitat. Endemic.

► See also pages
28 175 *179* 183
184 185 198 221
226 *226* 230 233

236 WONGA PIGEON

Leucosarcia melanoleuca   Columbidae
OTHER NAME Wonga-Wonga

RECOGNITION A large pigeon; upperparts slaty blue-grey, shading through grey on crown and face to white on forehead and chin. The grey of the upperparts extends downwards onto the breast; broken by prominent white lines extending upwards from the white belly in a large V-shape, to sides of neck. Across the white of the remainder of the underparts are large black spots. 36–38 cm.

VOICE As an advertising call, a single loud clear and quite high-pitched 'coo-coo-' or 'wonk-a', repeated monotonously; in alarm, a sharp cluck.

HABITAT Rainforests; usually where forest is tall with relatively open floor. Also in nearby eucalypt forest where there is scrubby undergrowth. Feeds on fallen fruits on forest floor, morning and evening.

BREEDING Throughout the year, mainly spring and summer. Nests tend to be in open situations, often in adjoining eucalypt forest; usually on horizontal forks; sometimes in vine tangles. Two white eggs.

RANGE East coast of Australia; approximately Rockhampton (Qld) to Gippsland. Sedentary.

STATUS Scarce, but common locally. Endemic genus.

► See also pages
53 *53* 123

COCKATOOS, LORIKEETS, PARROTS

Psittacidae Family of 340 species
53 in Australia, 53 breeding, 45 endemic
Members of the parrot family are unmistakable, with short, deep, strongly hooked bill, prominent cere, toes arranged two forward and two backwards, and short legs. Their bright colours, adaptability as cage birds, and ability of some species to mimic human speech, has made this one of the best-known of bird families. The

feet and bill have exceptional versatility; the feet have hand-like usefulness, and the bills are used for gripping in climbing.

237 PALM COCKATOO

Probosciger aterrimus   Cacatuidae

OTHER NAMES Great Palm Cockatoo, Cape York Cockatoo, Great Black-Cockatoo, Black Macaw

RECOGNITION Large; black with dark-grey highlighting in strong light; head looks disproportionately large with very tall erectile black crest; massive dark-grey bill; and large patch of bare crimson facial skin. Female has smaller bill and colourful facial patch. Immatures similar to adults but with the feathers of underparts and underwing-coverts edged pale yellow; and lighter-coloured bill. Usually seen perched in tall rainforest trees. 56–64 cm.

VOICE Contact call, in flight: landing, and gathered with others, is double whistle, low/high; in alarm: a harsh screech. Also mournful wailing cries.

HABITAT Tropical rainforests and nearby savannah-woodland of eucalypts and melaleucas; feeds in woodland; escapes midday heat in the shady rainforest.

BREEDING August–February. Nest is a large hollow in a treetrunk; usually a eucalypt in woodland. The bottom of the hollow is lined with splintered twigs, possibly allowing wet-season water to drain. Single white egg.

RANGE Cape York, mainly coastal; south to Archer River and Princess Charlotte Bay. Also in New Guinea and Aru Islands. Sedentary.

STATUS Common within restricted range.

▶ See also pages
102-3 *105*

238 RED-TAILED BLACK-COCKATOO

Calyptorhynchus magnificus   Cacatuidae

OTHER NAMES Banksian Cockatoo, Banks's Black-Cockatoo, Great-billed Cockatoo

RECOGNITION Large; black, with massive, rounded, helmet-like crest extending well forward of the bill. Tail has scarlet panels, visible from beneath; fanned tail, on takeoff or landing, is spectacularly colourful, fiery translucent with the sun behind. Female has yellow tail-band, becoming orange towards tip, and barred black; yellow spots to head, sides of neck and shoulders; underparts barred yellow; bill pale horn. Immatures like female. 50–60 cm.

VOICE Contact call, often given in flight, is a harsh, sharp, metallic-squeaky 'kree'. Alarm call, a harsh rolling 'kreiaagh'.

HABITAT Woodlands and open forests, scrublands and grasslands with lines of trees along watercourses. Often in casuarinas, brown stringybark, bulloak.

BREEDING In south-west of Western Australia has two distinct periods of egg-laying, March–April and July–October; in Queensland, May–September; and in Northern Territory, March–July. Nest is in a hollow limb or treetrunk, usually high. A single white egg on wood-dust of hollow.

RANGE Northern, north-eastern, central, north-western and south-western Australia; small isolated population in south-east. Nomadic to migratory.

STATUS Common in the north, west, and centre; scarce in south-east. Endemic.

▶ See also pages
185 *192*

239 GLOSSY BLACK-COCKATOO

Calyptorhynchus lathami   Cacatuidae

OTHER NAMES Latham's Cockatoo, Leach's Black-Cockatoo, Casuarina Cockatoo

RECOGNITION Upperparts black; brownish-black on head and underparts; slight sheen on primaries. Very like Red-tailed Black-Cockatoo, but slightly smaller, and without prominent crest. Tail has smaller red panels. Bill and legs grey. Female usually has extensive patchy yellow markings on sides of head and neck. Tail-band red, barred black, sometimes marked yellow; underparts flecked yellow. Immatures like female; yellow spots on wings; little yellow to head. 46–50 cm.

VOICE Distinctly different from Red-Tailed Black-Cockatoo: contact call is a soft, drawn-out almost whining 'taarrr, taarrr'. Alarm call is abrupt, harsh.

HABITAT Forests of coast, drier inland scrub; usually among casuarinas of forests or drier woodlands and ridges, these trees being a dominant food source.

BREEDING March–August; eggs usually April–June. Nest is a hollow limb or large hollow in the trunk, often in an isolated dead tree, 15–25 m above ground. A single white egg is laid on the natural wood-dust of the bottom of the hollow.

RANGE South-eastern Australia; Eungella south to eastern Victoria; isolated population on Kangaroo Island (SA). Sedentary.

STATUS Uncommon; localized and reduced. Endemic.

▶ See also pages
65 121 122 137

240 YELLOW-TAILED BLACK-COCKATOO

Calyptorhynchus funereus   Cacatuidae

OTHER NAMES Funereal Cockatoo, White-tailed Black-Cockatoo (WA subspecies)

RECOGNITION Large, brownish-black cockatoo, with pale yellow tail-band spotted black, and rounded pale-yellow patches on ear-coverts. The feathers of the neck and underparts are margined yellow, giving a yellow-scalloped, or possibly barred, effect. Eye-ring pink; upper-mandible of bill, dark grey. Female similar but tail-band more heavily spotted; yellow ear patch larger and lighter; eye-ring and bill light grey. Immatures similar to adult female. 62–69 cm.

VOICE Contact call, usually in flight, extremely loud, harsh and wailing 'wyeeela'; alarm call is abrupt, harsh screech. Grinding noises while feeding.

HABITAT Heavy forests including rainforests; also open forests, woodlands including alpine, coastal heaths, trees of farmlands, pine plantations.

BREEDING Variable: August–November in Western Australia; July–January in south-east; March–August in Queensland; April–July in far north. Nest is a tree hollow, usually high. One to two white eggs. Gathers in large flocks after breeding, attracting attention with loud calls.

RANGE East, south-east and south-west; not far inland. South-west subspecies has white in place of yellow. Nomadic.

STATUS Common. Endemic.

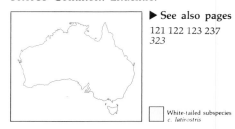

▶ See also pages
121 122 123 237
323

White-tailed subspecies
c. latirostris

241 LONG-BILLED BLACK-COCKATOO

Calyptorhynchus baudinii   Cacatuidae

OTHER NAMES Baudin's Black-Cockatoo, Carnaby's Cockatoo

RECOGNITION Very much like the Yellow-tailed Black-Cockatoo, but slightly smaller, browner and with white replacing all yellow in the plumage of male, female and immatures. The name White-tailed Black-Cockatoo has been used for all Western Australian black-cockatoos, which all have white in the tail. This Western Australian population is now divided between two species, the Long-billed Black-Cockatoo and the Yellow-tailed Black-Cockatoo. The western subspecies of the latter will still be known locally as the White-tailed Black-Cockatoo. The Long-billed Black-Cockatoo is distinguished by the very much elongated tip to the bill. 53–59 cm.

VOICE Compared with White-tailed Black-Cockatoo (western subspecies of the Yellow-tailed Black-Cockatoo), more guttural, less prolonged, with less of the wailing and whistling sounds.

HABITAT Forests of extreme south-west.

BREEDING August–December. Uses a tree hollow as nest. One to two white eggs.

RANGE South-west corner of Western Australia. Nomadic.

STATUS Uncommon. Endemic species or subspecies.

▶ **See also pages** 237–8 *239* 242

GANG-GANG COCKATOO

Callocephalon fimbriatum　　Cacatuidae

OTHER NAMES Red-crowned Cockatoo, Helmeted Cockatoo

RECOGNITION Plumage overall grey, lightly scalloped and barred light grey, except head and finely filamentous crest, entirely brilliant scarlet. Feathers of belly and undertail-coverts edged dull orange-buff; bill horn-coloured; legs dark grey. Female has grey head and crest; the feathers of underparts more heavily edged red and buff. Immatures like female but underside of tail heavily barred light grey; immature males have touches of red to head and crest. 30–33 cm.

VOICE Unique rasping screech, with both growling and squeaky elements; like the sound of a door with very rusty hinges. Soft growling while feeding.

HABITAT Eucalypt forests; dispersing into more open country in autumn and winter. In pairs in breeding season, at other times flocks of up to 60 birds.

BREEDING October–January. Nests high, and is reported to show a preference for hollows in living trees near water. Three white eggs. The young males show increasing amounts of red on head and crest over the first three years.

RANGE South-eastern Australia; from about the Hunter River to western Victoria; vagrant to Tasmania. Nomadic or part migratory.

STATUS Moderately common. Endemic genus.

▶ **See also pages** 113–14 *117* 122 123

243 GALAH

Cacatua roseicapilla　　Cacatuidae

OTHER NAMES Rose-breasted Cockatoo, Goulie

RECOGNITION One of Australia's best-known and widespread birds, plumaged entirely in tints and shades of pink and grey. Crown and crest light pink; back, wings and tail silvery soft grey; remainder of plumage deep pink. Male has dark-brown eye; female, pink within dark red eye-ring. Subspecies *assimilis* has light grey eye-ring; deeper pink on crest; lighter greys. Large flocks are spectacular, twisting and turning to show alternately grey then pink. 36 cm.

VOICE The usual call, often given in flight, is a high scratchy-metallic double screech. When disturbed or alarmed, particularly near nest, a harsh screech.

HABITAT A great variety of habitats. The galah is characteristically a bird of dry inland plains, but has expanded with clearing of coastal forests.

BREEDING July–December. Nest is a large hollow, in a living or dead tree. The bottom of the nest hollow is well lined with gum-leaves. Two to five white eggs. When young in the nest are being fed, they give constant harsh, wheezy sounds.

RANGE All except wet coastal; *assimilis* in central and Western Australia. Sedentary or locally nomadic.

STATUS Abundant. Endemic genus.

▶ **See also pages** 129 134 173 220 221 231

244 LONG-BILLED CORELLA

Cacatua tenuirostris　　Cacatuidae

OTHER NAMES White Cockatoo, Slender-billed Cockatoo, Dampier Cockatoo

RECOGNITION Superficially resembles the more widespread Little Corella and has similarly insignificant crest; but is slightly larger, and upper-mandible of bill has extremely elongated point. The white plumage has overall slight pink tint and the deep pink patch across forehead and lores is more extensive than on the Little Corella; a patchy deep pink bar across the throat. Wide, bare, blue-grey eye-ring. (Former south-west subspecies now full species.) 35–41 cm.

VOICE Contact call, usually in flight, a peculiar double-noted wavering and querulous falsetto 'carr-up'. Frequent harsh screech 'war-aaak'.

HABITAT Trees bordering watercourses, open forests, woodlands, sparsely timbered grasslands, farmlands; seldom far from water.

BREEDING August–November. Nests in a hollow limb or the trunk, usually of a living tree, near water. Sites tend to be high and inaccessible. Two to three white, oval

eggs, laid on the decayed wood-dust of the floor of the hollow.

RANGE South-east of South Australia, western Victoria, south-western New South Wales. Sedentary or locally nomadic.

STATUS Uncommon; declined as result of grazing. Endemic.

▶ **See also pages** *133* 137

245 WESTERN LONG-BILLED CORELLA

Cacatua pastinator　　Cacatuidae

OTHER NAME Long-billed Corella

RECOGNITION Closely resembles the other Corella species, and probably most conveniently distinguished from the Long-billed Corella of south-eastern Australia by the widely separated range, and from the Little Corella, which also occurs in Western Australia, by the greatly elongated tip to the upper-mandible of its bill.

VOICE Similar to that of the other Corella species.

HABITAT Forests, woodlands or farmlands with trees.

BREEDING August–November. The nest is a hollow of a large tree. Eggs similar to those of the other corellas.

RANGE South-west and mid-west coast of Western Australia. Sedentary.

STATUS Uncommon; locally moderately common. Endemic.

▶ **See also pages** 238 *239*

246 LITTLE CORELLA

Cacatua sanguinea　　Cacatuidae

OTHER NAMES Bare-eyed Cockatoo, Short-billed Cockatoo, Blood-stained Cockatoo

RECOGNITION Plumage overall white, with a suffusion cf pink to the bases of the feathers of the crown and most noticeable as a pink smudge on the lores; short, white crest. Bare blue-grey eye-ring, more extensive beneath eye. Bill short, horn-coloured; legs grey. Differs from Long-billed Corella in its much shorter bill; no pink bar across throat and less on face; has much pink to bases of these feathers, but it is usually hidden. 35–39 cm.

VOICE Noisy, particularly in the usual large flocks; often heard before coming into sight; quavering contact call; varied raucous screeches.

HABITAT Mulga and similar arid scrublands, spinifex, usually along tree-lined watercourses; tropical and arid woodlands, mallee, mangroves, farms.

BREEDING May–October, but variable within this period; usually August–October. Uses a hollow of any reasonably large tree available, including baobabs, and mangroves in northern Australia; holes in cliffs and, in north-west, in tall termite mounds. Three to four white eggs.

RANGE Throughout Australia, except wet east, south-east, coastal south-west, Tasmania and waterless deserts. Also in southern New Guinea. Sedentary and nomadic.

STATUS Abundant.

▶ See also pages
129 *171* 184 238
311–12

247 PINK COCKATOO

Cacatua leadbeateri   Cacatuidae

OTHER NAMES Wee Juggler, Chockalock, Major Mitchell, Leadbeater's Cockatoo

RECOGNITION Almost entirely plumaged in delicate tints of pink; and with a crest that is near-white when folded, but when raised to its full radiating fan-shape reveals bands of pink, scarlet and yellow. Upperparts mostly white, with just the faintest trace of pink; remainder of plumage pale salmon-pink except crest; deeper pink on forehead and on undersurfaces of wings and tail. Male has brown eye; female has red eye, and more yellow in crest. 33–36 cm.

VOICE Usual contact call, often given in flight, is a thin, undulating and almost musical screech; also gives harsher screeches when alarmed.

HABITAT Sparsely timbered grasslands, mulga, native pine on sand ridges, casuarinas on rocky ridges, mallee, inland watercourse gums, drier farmlands.

BREEDING August–December. Nests in a hollow of living or dead tree, with some preference evidently shown for a site near water. Two to four eggs, laid on the wood-dust of the hollow. Out of breeding season may be in flocks; usually small.

RANGE Widespread through inland and drier coastal regions. Sedentary, but occasionally nomadic.

STATUS Uncommon. Endemic.

▶ See also pages
1 134 *134* 137 138
139 164 184 185
219 220 231

248 SULPHUR-CRESTED COCKATOO

Cacatua galerita   Cacatuidae

OTHER NAME White Cockatoo

RECOGNITION Entirely white, with tall, forward-curving, plain sulphur–yellow crest; white of face, underwings and undertail lightly tinted yellow. The naked eye-ring is white or tinged blue; the bill grey-black; legs dark grey. Sexes alike, except male has dark-brown eye; female usually red-brown eye. Raises the crest after alighting. 45–51 cm.

VOICE Usual contact call, often given in flight, is a raucous and harsh screech; and when alarmed, a series of abrupt screeches.

HABITAT Usually near rivers or other watercourses, in a wide diversity of vegetation; eucalypt forests and woodlands, rainforests, mangroves, farmlands. In pairs, small parties or flocks of hundreds of birds, usually feeding on ground, but also in fruiting trees.

BREEDING August–January in south; May–September in north. Usually a hollow of a tree, or sometimes a cliff, that is high and inaccessible. Two, rarely three, eggs are laid on the wood-dust of the hollow; both sexes share the incubation.

RANGE Northern and eastern Australia, and Tasmania; introduced to south-west. Also in New Guinea. Mostly sedentary.

STATUS Common; locally abundant. Endemic subspecies.

▶ See also pages
74 129 198 283

249 ECLECTUS PARROT

Eclectus roratus   Psittacidae

OTHER NAMES Red-sided Parrot, Rocky River Parrot

RECOGNITION Brilliant colours; female more colourful. Male entirely bright green, except for large orange-yellow bill, and scarlet flanks which may be almost or entirely hidden by wings. Uplifted wings show scarlet flanks and underwing-coverts. Bend of wing, primaries and outer-tail feathers deep blue. Female: almost overall deep scarlet; darker on back and wings. Violet-blue in broad band across breast, on collar, shoulders and wing-linings. 40–43 cm.

VOICE As a contact call; a harsh screech, 'krraaark, krraaark', and 'kaa, kaa'. While feeding; wailing, whistling and metallic clucking (by female).

HABITAT Rainforests, gallery forests; at times open woodlands, possibly in passage between patches of rainforest. Feeds on nectar, seeds, berries.

BREEDING October–January; mainly November–December. Nest is usually a hollow in the trunk of a tall tree; usually at edge of rainforest or rainforest clearing; always high and inaccessible, 15–25 m. Two white

eggs; numerous adults attend many of the nests.

RANGE North-east of Cape York; Pascoe River, Iron Range, McIlwraith Range. Also in New Guinea and Indonesia. Sedentary.

STATUS Common in very limited range. Endemic subspecies.

▶ See also pages
7 101 103 *105* 111
312

250 RED-CHEEKED PARROT

Geoffroyus geoffroyi   Psittacidae

OTHER NAMES Geoffroy's Parrot, Pink-cheeked Parrot

RECOGNITION A small, short-tailed parrot, dominantly rich green in colour; upperparts deeper green; underparts and tail lighter yellow-green. Crown and nape violet-blue; remainder of head entirely bright red, including forehead, lores, cheeks, ear-coverts and throat. Underwing bright blue. Bill is red on upper-mandible, grey on lower-mandible. Female has entire head olive-brown; bill grey-brown. Immatures same as female; head greener; and some males with touch of red. 22 cm.

VOICE The usual contact call is a sharp metallic 'hank-ank-ank-ank-ank', in quick succession, usually in flight. Also various chatterings and screeches.

HABITAT Almost entirely confined to tropical rainforests, particularly near watercourses; occasionally adjoining woodland. In New Guinea, also in mangroves.

BREEDING Probably usually September–December. Nest is a hollow of tree or palm, at least on some occasions hollowed out by the birds themselves from the soft heartwood of a rainforest tree. Two to three white, rounded eggs, laid on wood debris.

RANGE Eastern coastal Cape York. Locally nomadic following fruiting trees. Also in New Guinea and Indonesia.

STATUS Locally common.

▶ See also pages
101 103 *109* 111

251 RAINBOW LORIKEET

Trichoglossus haematodus   Loriidae

OTHER NAMES Red-collared Lorikeet, Blue Mountain Parrot, Rainbow Lory

RECOGNITION A large and very brightly coloured lorikeet, with head streaky-blue; bill bright orange-red; and red breast mottled with yellow. Upperparts green with yellow-green nape. Underparts:

251 RAINBOW LORIKEET
Trichoglossus haematodus

centre of abdomen deep blue; trousered legs green; underwings with linings red and narrow yellow wingbar. Swift direct flight with short rapid wingbeats. 26–32 cm.

VOICE A sharp screech, repeated several times, is usual contact call; while feeding, shrill chattering; and while resting, soft twitterings.

HABITAT A wide variety; including rainforests, eucalypt forests and woodlands, coastal heaths, farms and gardens, mangroves and monsoon forests in the north. Conspicuous and noisy. Flocks feed with much screeching and chattering, upon nectar, insects and fruits.

BREEDING Usually August–January. Nest is a hollow in a eucalypt or melaleuca. Two to three white eggs. The male spends considerable time in the nest hollow, but does not appear to assist with brooding; he does share feeding of young.

RANGE Eastern Australia; Cape York–Eyre Peninsula, mainly on coast; farther inland in Queensland. Also in New Guinea, Indonesia and south-west Pacific area. Nomadic.

STATUS Abundant.

▶ **See also pages**
103 202

252 RED-COLLARED LORIKEET

Trichoglossus rubritorquis   Loriidae
OTHER NAME Orange-naped Lorikeet

RECOGNITION Very much like the Rainbow Lorikeet, but with orange instead of green band round the nape of the neck, and greenish-black on belly in place of blue. The breast is orange rather than the orange-red of the Rainbow Lorikeet. At various times treated as subspecies of the Rainbow Lorikeet, or as full separate

species. The breeding ranges of the two species appear effectively separated by the almost treeless grasslands south of the Gulf of Carpentaria. 27–31 cm.

VOICE A sharp screech, rolling like that of the Rainbow Lorikeet. Most often calls while in flight, which is swift, noisy.

HABITAT Tropical woodlands, eucalypt-melaleuca woodlands, mangroves. Will travel long distances following the flowering of trees in various districts.

BREEDING August–May; usually October–January. The nest is a hollow in a tree. Two to three white eggs. This is one of the most common of the parrots of the Top End of the Northern Territory, but less abundant in the Kimberley.

RANGE Northern Australia; from Broome (WA) to about Normanton (Qld). Widespread through northern islands. Nomadic.

STATUS Common. Endemic subspecies.

▶ **See also pages**
196 197 *200* 202 208 211

253 SCALY-BREASTED LORIKEET

Trichoglossus chlorolepidotus   Loriidae
OTHER NAMES Green Keet, Green Lorikeet, Green-and-Gold Lorikeet, Greenie

RECOGNITION Almost entirely green, including entirely green head, but with feathers of back of neck, throat and breast yellow, broadly edged green, giving a scaly appearance; more extensively yellow along the flanks, and undertail-coverts. A touch of orange-red to base of outer-tail feathers, and sometimes to sides of breast. In flight, conspicuous orange-red underwing-coverts. Eye orange; bill coral-red. Immatures, bill and eye brownish. 23 cm.

VOICE Calls similar to those of the Rainbow Lorikeet, but higher-pitched and sharper. Hybridization between the species has been recorded in the wild.

HABITAT Occupies habitats similar to Rainbow Lorikeet, and mixed flocks occur. Although inconspicuous in colour, attracts attention with incessant noise.

BREEDING May–February; usually August–January in south. There are indications that an early flowering of eucalypts or early heavy rain results in earlier breeding. Nest is in a hollow, usually high. Two to three oval, white eggs.

RANGE Eastern Australia; Cape York, south to Illawarra (NSW). Nomadic.

STATUS Common; abundant many districts. Endemic.

▶ **See also page**
76

254 VARIED LORIKEET

Psitteuteles versicolor   Loriidae
OTHER NAMES Red-crowned Lorikeet, Red-capped Lorikeet, Varied Lory

RECOGNITION A small, dominantly green lorikeet, with forehead and crown deep red; ear patch yellow; naked eye-ring white, giving a prominently spectacled appearance. There is a tint of blue about the neck, and a touch of mauve-pink to the upper breast. The feathers of the plumage have yellow shafts, which give a finely yellow-streaked appearance, with more yellow on underparts. Bill coral-red; legs grey-green. Immatures are dull; crown mostly green; bill brown. 18 cm.

VOICE In flight, almost incessant contact call is high-pitched, not very loud screech; much shrill chattering while feeding.

HABITAT Tropical lowlands wherever there are flowering trees, but most common in forests; tending to favour watercourse paperbarks and eucalypts.

BREEDING Throughout the year, but usually in the tropical dry season, April–August. Nests in a hollow, with preference for trees near water. Both birds prepare the hollow, sometimes providing a bed of leaves. Two to four white eggs.

RANGE North-western and northern Australia; western Kimberley to north-western Queensland–Cape York. Nomadic.

STATUS Common. Endemic.

▶ **See also pages**
40 175 *193* 208

255 MUSK LORIKEET

Glossopsitta concinna   Loriidae
OTHER NAMES Red-crowned Lorikeet, Red-eared Lorikeet, Musk Lory, Green Keet

RECOGNITION A moderately large lorikeet, plumaged almost entirely in bright green; slightly lighter and more yellowish on the underparts, including the yellow-green underwing-coverts; nape and mantle bronzed brown. Across the head, a broad band of brilliant red, including forehead and back through lores and eyes to ear-coverts; crown blue-green. Bill black with red tip; eye orange. Female similar, but dull blue on crown. Immatures have dull reds, brown-black bills. 22 cm.

VOICE Contact call, usually given in flight, is a shrill metallic screech. While the flock is feeding, a constant noisy chattering.

HABITAT Wherever there are flowering trees, but less commonly in heavy forests of mountains. Preference for woodlands, watercourses and farm trees.

BREEDING August–January. A hollow of a tree, usually high; the birds become very excited when the site is approached. Two to three white eggs. These lorikeets feed on fruits, nectar, seeds and insects; sometimes in orchards and grain crops.

RANGE South-eastern Australia, approximately Rockhampton to Eyre Peninsula; and Tasmania. Nomadic.

STATUS Generally common, but patchy. Endemic.

▶ **See also pages**
156–7 *157* 163

156–7 *157* 163

256 PURPLE-CROWNED LORIKEET

Glossopsitta porphyrocephala   Loriidae

OTHER NAMES Zit Parrot, Blue-crowned Lorikeet, Porphyry-crowned Lorikeet

RECOGNITION A very small and slender, light-green lorikeet, with pale blue breast and abdomen, and distinctive head markings: crown deep purple; forehead, lores and ear-coverts vermilion. Bend of wing bright blue; underwing-coverts crimson, sometimes visible as a flash of crimson as it dashes overhead. Bill black; eye brown; legs grey. Immatures without, or with only a trace of purple on the crown. Leaf-sized and difficult to sight in foliage. 15–17 cm.

VOICE The contact call, given almost continuously in flight, is a sharp high 'zit'. From flock passing over, rapid 'zit, zit-zit-'; quieter feeding.

HABITAT Found in most eucalypt forests and woodlands where there are trees flowering, especially drier woodlands and mallee; in south-west often in karri forest.

BREEDING August–December. Nests in a small hollow, in limb or trunk of a eucalypt. Sometimes nests in flocks, with almost every available hollow occupied through site, probably a locality with abundant flowering trees. Three to four white, rounded eggs.

RANGE South-west of Western Australia; south-east from Eyre Peninsula to southern New South Wales; vagrant north to Queensland. Highly nomadic.

STATUS Moderately common. Endemic.

▶ **See also pages**
138 *156* 157–8
163 213 220 232
245

138 *156* 157–8 163 213 220 232 245

257 LITTLE LORIKEET

Glossopsitta pusilla   Loriidae

OTHER NAMES Red-faced Lorilet, Jerryang, Little Keet, Green Keet

RECOGNITION Very small; general plumage light green; yellower on underparts; bronzed on nape and mantle. Face, entirely surrounding the black bill, is bright red; including forehead, lores and throat. Primaries dark green, underwing-coverts

yellow-green. Immatures have dull reds, browner bills. Swift weaving flight, bullet-like; showing yellowish underwings. Occurs in small parties or large flocks; leaf-sized, hard to sight feeding among foliage. 15 cm.

VOICE Very high thin screeching, 'zeeit-zeit-', higher than that of the Musk Lorikeet, more a thin metallic screeching compared with Purple-crowned Lorikeet.

HABITAT Forests and woodlands wherever there are flowering trees; heavy forests of coastal ranges; more often open country with isolated stands of trees.

BREEDING August–January; but as early as May in north. Nest is a small hollow, usually quite high. Both birds clean out the hollow to prepare for laying, but apparently only female broods, sitting very tightly, fed by male. Three to five white eggs.

RANGE Eastern and south-eastern Australia; approximately Cairns to south-east of South Australia; also Tasmania. Nomadic.

STATUS Fairly common; but uncommon in south of range. Endemic.

▶ **See also pages**
136 *323*

136 *323*

258 DOUBLE-EYED FIG-PARROT

Psittaculirostris diophthalma   Loriidae

OTHER NAMES Blue-faced Fig-Parrot, Red-browed Fig-Parrot, Marshall's Fig-Parrot, Coxen's Fig-Parrot, Lorilet

RECOGNITION Tiny, the smallest Australian parrot. Overall bright leaf-green; darker on upperparts; yellow-green underparts; primaries blue. Very short tail gives stumpy and unbalanced appearance. Large, pale grey bill with dark tip. Three subspecies: *marshalli*, red forehead continuous with red lores and red of cheeks (yellowish on female); *macleayana*, smaller red patches separated by blue lores; *coxeni*, forehead mainly blue. Females less red. 13–15 cm.

VOICE A thin, sharp, penetrating squeak repeated several times, often in flight, 'zeit-zeit-'; also a more attenuated screeching, only in flight.

HABITAT Rainforests, and nearby swamp woodlands, savannah-woodlands, thick vegetation and scrubs along watercourses; gardens and plantations in northern Queensland. Feeds on native figs, nectar and certain fungi from bark.

BREEDING August–October. Uses a small hollow of a rainforest tree, usually one that has been hollowed from soft decayed wood by the birds themselves. Two white, rounded eggs.

RANGE Separate subspecies: Cape York; Atherton region; and south-eastern Queensland to north-eastern New South Wales. Also in New Guinea. Nomadic.

STATUS Uncommon; rare in south. Endemic subspecies.

▶ **See also pages**
88–9 97 98 114

88–9 97 98 114

259 AUSTRALIAN KING-PARROT

Alisterus scapularis   Polytelitidae

OTHER NAMES King Lory, Red Lory, Blood Rosella, Scarlet-and-Green Rosella

RECOGNITION A large parrot with spectacularly coloured plumage: back and wings viridian green; head and entire underparts scarlet, without other markings. There is a pale-green marking across the wings, and the lower back, rump and uppertail-coverts are blue. Flight and tail feathers black, underwing-coverts blue-green. Bill with upper-mandible red tipped black, and lower-mandible entirely black. Female and immatures mostly green with red belly; grey bill. 42–43 cm.

VOICE The contact call, usually in flight, a series of scratchy brassy 'carrak, carrak'; in alarm, a harsh metallic screech. Soft whistles from male.

HABITAT Forests, including rainforests and heavier, wetter, eucalypt forests; also coastal woodlands, denser scrubs along streams, adjoining woodlands.

BREEDING September–January. Nest is a hollow in treetrunk or limb; it has a high entrance but nest chamber is usually well down in the trunk. There is an elaborate courtship display involving both male and female. Three to five white eggs.

RANGE Coast and coastal ranges of eastern Australia, Cooktown to southern Victoria. Dispersive.

STATUS Moderately common. Two subspecies of an endemic species.

▶ **See also pages**
117 122 *122* 123
136

117 122 *122* 123 136

260 RED-WINGED PARROT

Aprosmictus erythropterus   Polytelitidae

OTHER NAMES Crimson-winged Parrot, Red-winged Lory, Crimson-winged Lory

RECOGNITION Conspicuously colourful, with body almost entirely bright yellow-green; back and shoulders black; wing-coverts crimson. Lower back, shading to pale blue on rump. Uppertail-coverts greenish-yellow, tail dark-green tipped yellow. Eye red; bill coral-red. Female almost entirely green; yellowish on underparts, with line of red across outermost wing-coverts; and lower back pale blue. Unique flight, with deep, erratic-looking wingbeats. 30–32 cm.

VOICE A sharp, rapid, metallic sound, often in flight as a contact call, 'chillink, chillink'; in alarm, high rapid screeches; when feeding, soft chattering.

HABITAT Woodlands, especially tropical savannah-woodlands; also open forests, timbered watercourses in drier regions, acacia, casuarina, mangroves.

BREEDING April–February; usually April–August in north, August–February in south of range. Nest is in a hollow, usually deep, of limb or treetrunk; nest chamber is near ground level though the entrance may be at 5–20 m height. Three to six white eggs.

RANGE Northern and eastern Australia; Kimberley to northern inland New South Wales. Also in New Guinea. Sedentary-dispersive.

STATUS Common. Two subspecies, northern and eastern.

▶ See also pages
40 *41* 136 137 207 208

SUPERB PARROT

Polytelis swainsonii   Polytelitidae

OTHER NAMES Barraband Parrot, Scarlet-breasted Parrot

RECOGNITION Slender; long-tailed; green-plumaged, with forehead and throat yellow, and scarlet crescent across throat. Crown blue-green; bend of wing and primaries dull blue; tail green above, black beneath. Eye yellow; bill usually coral-red. Female green on the entire head and upperparts, with only a touch of blue to cheeks and throat; tail black beneath; outer feathers edged pink. Immatures like female, but with eye brown. Swift graceful flight. 40 cm.

VOICE Contact call, most often given in flight, is a rolling and somewhat grating 'currack-currack'; similar but less harsh than call of Regent Parrot.

HABITAT Almost restricted to the river-edge strip of black-box and red-gum, and adjoining woodlands of yellow-box, bimble-box, white-gum; irrigated areas.

BREEDING September–December. Nest is in a hollow of a tree, often a river-edge gum. A favourite site is in a horizontal hollow spout extending out high over the water. Four to six white, rounded eggs, incubated solely by the female.

RANGE Inland eastern New South Wales; along parts of Murrimbidgee, Lachlan and Murray rivers. Partly nomadic.

STATUS Common locally. Endemic.

▶ See also pages
129 133 134 137

REGENT PARROT

Polytelis anthopeplus   Polytelitidae

OTHER NAMES Rock Pebbler, Rock Peplar, Smoker, Black-tailed Parakeet

RECOGNITION Head and underparts rich cadmium yellow, with a touch of olive to crown and nape. Mantle, back and scapulars blackish olive-green; shoulder yellow; a band of red across the wing between yellow of shoulder and blue-black of flight feathers. Tail long, slender, blue-black. Bill coral-red; eye brown. Female dull olive-yellow where male is yellow; less red on wing; outer-tail feathers margined and tipped pink. South-west subspecies duller, greener. 40 cm.

VOICE Contact call is a prolonged rolling and harsh 'currruk-currrak', usually given while in flight. Soft sounds while perched.

HABITAT In the east, eucalypt woodland and adjacent mallee along the Murray River; in south-west, open woodland, wheatbelt-woodland remnants, mallee.

BREEDING August–May; usually September–December. Nest in a hollow, usually quite high, in a large eucalypt, but where the hollow continues far down in the treetrunk, often almost to ground level. Four, occasionally six, white eggs.

RANGE Two populations: inland south-eastern Australia, and south-west. Locally nomadic.

STATUS Locally common. Endemic.

▶ See also pages
137 139 *139* 220 232 245

ALEXANDRA'S PARROT

Polytelis alexandrae   Polytelitidae

OTHER NAMES Princess Parrot, Spinifex Parrot, Rose-throated Parrot

RECOGNITION A slender parrot with extremely long tail, more than half total length of bird. Upperparts overall soft olive-green, with head light grey-blue becoming brighter pale blue on crown and nape; throat rose-pink; shoulders bright lime-green; rump sky-blue; tail blue-green. Breast soft light blue-grey; thighs and lower flanks pink; undertail-coverts pink. Eye orange; bill pink. Female and immatures similar, but colours softer, tail shorter. 45 cm; tail 34 cm.

VOICE Soft contact call like that of the Budgerigar, and loud harsh crackling notes, 'kee-ark-curruk'.

HABITAT Spinifex plains, often far from water; stands of casuarinas on arid sandplains, mulga and other acacia scrublands.

BREEDING September–January. Sometimes a few pairs nest in the one locality forming small breeding colonies; up to 10 nests have been found in the one large tree. Uses a hollow, with four to six eggs laid on the decayed wood-dust.

RANGE The western-interior arid regions. Highly nomadic; irregular.

STATUS Rare. Endemic species and genus.

▶ See also pages
213 214 *215* 219 221 232

COCKATIEL

Nymphicus hollandicus   Polytelitidae

OTHER NAMES Weero, Quarrion, Crested Parrot, Cockatoo-Parrot

RECOGNITION The only parrot, as distinct from cockatoos, with a tall slender crest. General colour light grey, underparts

264 **COCKATIEL** *Nymphicus hollandicus*

paler. Distinctive markings are the pale yellow over the crest, forehead, throat and most of the face; and an orange patch on ear-coverts. There is a broad conspicuous white band across the folded wings. Central tail-feathers elongated; outer feathers barred yellow. Female and immatures duller; grey replacing most of yellow. 30–33 cm.

VOICE Contact call, usually while in flight, is a melodious, prolonged 'quarreel-quarreel-quarreel', each ending with an upward inflection.

HABITAT Most types of open drier country; semi-arid woodlands, mulga and similar arid scrub, spinifex, tree-lined watercourses, drier farmlands.

BREEDING Variable, very dependent upon rainfall; often taking place in autumn following late summer cyclones, particularly in north-west; in south, spring. Often selects a large hollow of a dead tree or dead limb. Four to seven white eggs.

RANGE Throughout inland Australia; to coast in drier regions. Highly nomadic.

STATUS Overall quite common. Endemic species and genus.

▶ **See also pages**
129 136 214 231
315

265 GROUND PARROT

Pezoporus wallicus   Platycercidae

OTHER NAMES Swamp Parrot, Button-grass Parrot

RECOGNITION A long-tailed, terrestrial parrot, with bright yellow-green plumage overall; strongly streaked and barred with black and yellow; more yellow on underparts. Central feathers of tail green barred yellow, and outer feathers yellow barred black. Narrow red bar across the forehead. Eye dull yellow; bill grey-brown. Immatures: no red on forehead; heavier black markings about head and breast. In flight, note long barred tail. 30 cm.

VOICE Calls quite regularly at dawn and dusk for 30–40 minutes: a high thin clear and bell-like sequence of three or four notes, 'tee-tee-tee-teee'.

HABITAT Heaths, where there is dense low ground cover, often swampy. In Tasmania, sub-alpine button-grass. Requires a high density of small seeding plants.

BREEDING September–December. The nest is situated in dense low vegetation well concealed at the base of tussock or low bush. A slight hollow in the ground is lined with stalks and leaves; may be built up in wet areas. Three to four white eggs.

RANGE Coastal heaths; south-eastern Australia north to Fraser Island; south-west. Mainly sedentary.

STATUS Scarce or rare most of range. Endemic.

▶ **See also pages**
15 16 *17* 123 124
126 142 152 242

266 NIGHT PARROT

Geopsittacus occidentalis   Platycercidae

OTHER NAMES Spinifex Parrot, Night Parakeet

RECOGNITION A small, dumpy, ground-dwelling parrot resembling the Ground Parrot, but with much shorter tail, no red on forehead, different range and habitat. Olive-green plumage overall, becoming greenish-yellow on the belly and undertail. Crown, back, wings and breast streaked and mottled black; outer tail-feathers yellow barred black. Hides by day in spinifex; if flushed flies low, then drops back into the spinifex; drinks late at night. 24 cm.

VOICE Recorded as uttering several short sharp notes while in flight, a squeak when flushed, and a low whistle when coming in to water at night.

HABITAT Closely associated with spinifex, especially on rocky breakaway country, but also recorded from samphire bushes of salt-lake country.

BREEDING Breeding habits little known. Nest recorded as being in a spinifex clump, or low dense samphire bush, enclosed with pieces of spinifex, and approached through a tunnel of spinifex. Four white eggs.

RANGE Scattered records from arid parts of all States. Probably nomadic.

STATUS Extremely rare. Endemic.

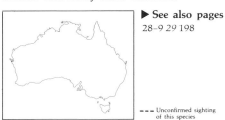

▶ **See also pages**
28-9 *29* 198

- - - Unconfirmed sighting of this species

267 BUDGERIGAR

Melopsittacus undulatus   Platycercidae

OTHER NAMES Budgerygah, Shell Parrot, Warbling Grass-Parakeet, Zebra Parrot

RECOGNITION A familiar, small, slender parrot which in the wild has only dominantly green-and-yellow plumage. Back of crown, sides of nape, upper back and wings cinnamon-brown, closely barred black and yellow, becoming boldly scalloped on the wings; flight feathers dark-green edged yellow. Forehead, lores, fore-part of cheeks, and throat yellow; cere blue. Female similar, but cere brown in breeding season. Immatures duller; barred forehead. 17–20 cm.

VOICE Contact call, in flight and when flocks settle, a pleasant musical chirrup; also sharp short screeches, and soft conversational chatterings.

267 BUDGERIGAR *Melopsittacus undulatus*

HABITAT Grassland plains, especially spinifex; open mulga, especially watercourse trees.

BREEDING August–January in south, June–September in north, but will respond to rain at any time; in a good season a pair will raise several broods in succession. Nest is a small hollow of a tree, low mulga, stump, or post. Four to six white eggs.

RANGE Throughout inland Australia, and to drier parts of coast. Highly nomadic.

STATUS Abundant. Endemic species and genus.

▶ **See also pages**
129 136 173 177
184 198 *217* 220
221 230 315 316
316

268 SWIFT PARROT

Lathamus discolor   Platycercidae

OTHER NAMES Red-faced Parakeet, Swift-flying Parakeet, Red-shouldered Parakeet

RECOGNITION A slender small parrot with dominantly green plumage; upperparts mostly bright viridian; underparts lighter, yellower. Forehead and chin-throat vermilion; lores and edges of throat-patch yellow; crown blue; ear-coverts lightly-washed turquoise. There are patches of vermilion on the bend of the wing, lesser wing-coverts, and tertials if seen from behind or above. Tail finely pointed, red-brown. In flight, red underwing and undertail-coverts. 25 cm.

VOICE A high metallic 'klink-klink', a tinkling sound that is mellow or piping rather than harsh; repeated quickly. Also subdued chatterings.

HABITAT Both wet and dry types of eucalypt forest, grassy woodlands, parks and gardens; usually in small flocks feeding on nectar, pollen and lerp.

BREEDING September–December. Gregarious tendency is retained when breeding, several nests often being in one tree. The nest is a small hollow, frequently high. Three to five white eggs. Apparently only the female broods.

RANGE Known only to breed in Tasmania. In February–April most move to south-east on mainland. Nomadic and migratory.

STATUS Common in Tasmania. Endemic species and genus.

▶ **See also pages**
142–3 *145* 150
151 152 156

269

RED-CAPPED PARROT

Purpureicephalus spurius   Platycercidae

OTHER NAMES King Parrot, Western King Parrot, Hookbill, Pileated Parrot

RECOGNITION Colourful to extent of being described as gaudy. A well-plumaged male is impressive, seeming more so in natural surrounds. Rich, bold, solid areas of colour: the entire top of the head deep crimson, rest of head including cheeks yellow with a green tinge; breast and belly deep blue-violet; thighs and undertail-coverts bright red. Back, wings and uppertail green; rump yellow. Bill grey, tip elongated. Female and immatures, colours much less intense. 36 cm.

VOICE A rolling, grating, almost rattling 'kchurrrink', often repeated several times; and softer conversational versions; occasional sharp harsh screeches.

HABITAT Forests and woodlands, including heavier forests, mainly marri open forests, woodlands, farmlands with marri trees; also south-west heathlands.

BREEDING August–December. Nest is in a hollow of treetrunk or limb, usually high. The bark at the hollow entrance is usually considerably chewed. Four to seven eggs. Female broods throughout; male calls female from hollow and feeds her in a nearby tree.

RANGE South-west; roughly coinciding with distribution of marri eucalypt forests. Sedentary.

STATUS Common. Endemic species and genus.

▶ **See also pages**
235 238–9 *238*
242 245

270

GREEN ROSELLA

Platycercus caledonicus   Platycercidae

OTHER NAMES Tasmanian Rosella, Tasman

Parrot, Green Parrot, Tussock Parrot, Yellow-bellied Parrot

RECOGNITION Confined to Tasmania and Bass Strait islands. Head and underparts rich yellow, with red frontal band and lores; and large cobalt-blue throat-patch extending well up onto the cheeks. Nape, back and wings dark olive-green, heavily mottled grey-black, and with blue along shoulder and edges of flight feathers. Tail blue-green, edged with light blue. Female smaller, and slightly softer colours. Immatures lack much of the yellow, plumage dull. 32–36 cm.

VOICE Usual call, often in flight, a loud metallic 'kussick, kussick'. Has a far-carrying, piping double-noted whistle, and various lower whistles.

HABITAT Usually the heavier eucalypt forests, but also visits rainforests, woodlands, lightly timbered farmlands, heathlands.

BREEDING September–January. Nest is a hollow of a tree, usually a living eucalypt. Four to five white eggs, laid on wood debris of the hollow. The female alone broods, leaving the hollow in the mornings to feed with, and be fed by the male.

RANGE Tasmania, Flinders Island, King Island, Kent Group. Sedentary.

STATUS Common in Tasmania and most of islands. Species endemic to Tasmania.

▶ **See also pages**
141 142 143 *145*
151 152

271

CRIMSON ROSELLA

Platycercus elegans   Platycercidae

OTHER NAMES Yellow Rosella, Adelaide Rosella, Mountain Lowry, Murrumbidgee Lowry

RECOGNITION A spectacular species, incorporating as subspecies the former separate Adelaide and Yellow rosellas. The nominate subspecies *elegans* is almost entirely crimson, with violet-blue cheek patches, shoulders and tail; back heavily mottled black. The Adelaide Rosella, subspecies *adelaidae*, has varying amounts of orange replacing crimson, while the Yellow Rosella, subspecies *flaveolus*, has yellow replacing almost all red except forehead. Females greener. 32–36 cm.

VOICE Contact call a piping whistle on an ascending scale; when alarmed gives shrill metallic screeches. Yellow Rosella's call possibly slightly higher.

HABITAT Crimson Rosella: rainforests, wet eucalypt forests, woodlands, including alpine. Adelaide Rosella: forests, woodlands, mallee. Yellow Rosella: river red-gum environs.

BREEDING September–February. Nest is a hollow of a tree; in case of Yellow Rosella often a river-edge tree, or one standing in water. The female alone breeds the five to eight white eggs; leaves the nest briefly in the mornings to be fed by, and feed

with, the male.

RANGE Crimson Rosella: north-eastern Queensland, south-eastern Australia; Adelaide and Yellow Rosellas: south-eastern Australia. Sedentary.

STATUS Common. Subspecies of endemic species.

▶ **See also pages**
114 124 127 136
138 155 158 164

272

EASTERN ROSELLA

Platycercus eximius   Platycercidae

OTHER NAMES Rosehill Parakeet, Common Rosella, Red-headed Rosella, White-cheeked Rosella

RECOGNITION A very brightly coloured rosella, with bright red head and upper breast; white cheek patches; underparts mostly yellow. Feathers of back and wings black edged yellow-green; rump and uppertail-coverts light green. Wing-coverts, bend of wing and flight feathers blue. Tail blue-green, outer feathers tipped white. Eye brown; bill light grey. Female, red less extensive; colours duller. Immatures like female; greener. 30–34 cm.

VOICE In flight, a brisk high 'chink-chink' or 'clink-clink'; contact call a whistle of about three ascending notes. When alarmed, a shrill screech.

HABITAT Open forests and woodlands with nearby grasslands, farmland and roadside trees, parks and gardens.

BREEDING September–January; sometimes April–May. Nest is a hollow in a living or dead tree, sometimes in a stump, fence-post or log on the ground, and, on rare occasions, holes in the ground. Four to nine white, rounded eggs.

RANGE South-eastern Australia, and Tasmania; south-eastern Queensland to Adelaide. Sedentary.

STATUS Common. Endemic. Closely related to Pale-headed Rosella.

▶ **See also pages**
41 *41* 136 318

273

PALE-HEADED ROSELLA

Platycercus adscitus   Platycercidae

OTHER NAMES Moreton Bay Rosella, Blue Rosella, Blue-cheeked Rosella, White-headed Rosella, Mealy Rosella

RECOGNITION Separated from all other Australian parrots by the white or very pale yellow head. Cheek patches white just beneath the eye, light violet-blue towards the throat. Feathers of back and wings black, margined pale or dusky yellow; shoulders and outer edges of primaries blue. Tail feathers deep green-blue, with the outer feathers tipped white. Upper breast yellow, merging to light violet-blue on the abdomen; undertail-coverts red. Immatures duller. 28–32 cm.

VOICE Call similar to Eastern Rosella but deeper; in flight, several quick notes; when perched, a whistle of three ascending notes; in alarm, a sharp screech.

HABITAT Grassy woodlands, open grassy scrubs, timber belts along watercourses; coastal heaths, paperbark woodlands, margins of rainforests.

BREEDING September–December in south; February–June in north. Nest is a hollow in a tree, with some preference reported for a tree near water. Two to four eggs are laid on the wood-dust of the hollow. Only the female broods; incubation takes about 22 days.

RANGE North-eastern Australia; Cape York south into north-eastern New South Wales. Sedentary.

STATUS Common. Endemic species of two to four subspecies.

▶ **See also pages**
74 75 80 121 387

274 NORTHERN ROSELLA

Platycercus venustus   Platycercidae

OTHER NAMES Brown's Rosella, Brown's Parakeet, Smutty Rosella

RECOGNITION Plumage largely dusky pale yellow; black on the head; heavily marked black on the back. The head is entirely black, except for white cheek patches, shading to light violet-blue towards the throat; there is often red showing through black of crown. Tail, shoulders and flight feathers blue; remainder of wings and back black, broadly edged yellow. Rump and underparts yellow, with fine black edgings, looking scaly; undertail-coverts red. 28–32 cm.

VOICE A high, metallic, double 'trin-see, trin-see, trin-see', with some resemblance to call of Eastern Rosella. When in tree-tops, soft chatterings.

HABITAT Savannah-woodlands where either eucalypts or paperbarks dominate; timber along watercourses in scrub country; occasionally mangroves, gardens.

BREEDING June–August. Nesting generally similar to Eastern Rosella. Shows a preference for a tree standing near water. Two to four rounded, white eggs are laid on wood-dust in hollow. Young remain in nest about five weeks after hatching.

RANGE Northern Australia; approximately Derby to far north-western Queensland. Sedentary.

STATUS Locally common; generally quite uncommon. Endemic.

▶ **See also pages**
174 190 *193* 197 208 211

275 WESTERN ROSELLA

Platycercus icterotis   Platycercidae

OTHER NAMES Stanley Rosella, Stanley Parakeet, Yellow-cheeked Parrot, Yellow-cheeked Rosella

RECOGNITION Head and entire underparts red; large yellow cheek patches. The only rosella in south-west. Feathers of mantle and back are black, edged dark green, or red and green, or red and buff, depending upon race and age. Upperwing-coverts, underwing-coverts and flight feathers deep blue. Rump and tail-coverts green; central tail-feathers bronzed-green; outer feathers blue edged white. Female: green upper-parts; green suffused through red and yellow areas. 26 cm.

VOICE Melodious, a softly whistled 'ching-ching-ching'. Generally a quiet and inconspicuous species, feeds on the ground and in trees.

HABITAT Woodlands and forests, especially in casuarinas, wandoo woodlands, south-west farmlands. Occurs and nests in jarrah forest.

BREEDING September–December. A small hollow is chosen as nest site, often in a wandoo. The male calls the female from the nest to feed her in a nearby tree. The male (and later the pair) feeds quite close by, often on the ground. Three to seven white eggs.

RANGE South-west; north to Moora, east to Norseman. Sedentary.

STATUS Moderately common. Endemic.

▶ **See also pages**
239 242 245 *432*

276 MALLEE RINGNECK

Barnardius barnardi   Platycercidae

OTHER NAMES Mallee Parrot, Barnard's Parakeet, Cloncurry Parrot, Ringneck

RECOGNITION Moderately large, long-tailed. Plumage dominantly green, with yellow collar round the nape. Head blue-green, with dull red frontal band; mantle dark blue-grey; shoulders turquoise and yellow; bright blue on flight feathers; rump green; tail green and blue; outer feathers edged white. Underparts light green; irregular yellow-orange breastband. The Cloncurry Parrot (subspecies *macgilli-*

vrayi) is paler, has yellow belly, and no red on forehead. 34 cm.

VOICE Flight or contact call is a high ring-ing 'kling-kling-kling-'; in alarm, a harsh metallic shriek; when feeding in trees, subdued chatterings.

HABITAT Drier inland open forests, wood-lands, mallee and native-pine country, river red-gums and other timber along watercourses, farmlands.

BREEDING May–January; mainly August–September, considerably influenced by rain in drier regions. In good seasons two broods may be raised; in drought many birds will not breed at all. Usual clutch four to six rounded, white eggs, brooded by female.

RANGE Inland eastern Australia. Cloncurry Parrot at north-western Queensland part of range. Sedentary.

STATUS Common. Endemic species of three subspecies.

▶ **See also pages**
58 *59* 129 136 137 139 158 175

277 PORT LINCOLN RINGNECK

Barnardius zonarius   Platycercidae

OTHER NAMES Western Ringneck, Banded Parrot, Twenty-eight Parrot

RECOGNITION A large, long-tailed parrot, with dominantly green plumage and black head; conspicuous bright yellow collar across hind-neck. Deep blue-violet of lower cheeks blends into the black of the head. Remainder of upperparts green; yellow-green on outer-wing coverts; deep blue on the primaries. Underparts green, with broad yellow breastband. The Twenty-eight Parrot, subspecies *semitor-quatus*, has red forehead patch; little or no yellow on breast. 37 cm.

VOICE In flight, a ringing 'kling-kling-kling'; subspecies *semitorquartus* has 'twenty-eight' call. When disturbed, a high whistle, repeated evenly.

HABITAT Extremely varied: woodlands, semi-arid and arid mulga, spinifex, mallee, wheatbelt. Subspecies *semitorquatus*: forests, heavy and open; woodlands.

BREEDING June–January; usually July–October. In northern arid regions this species is an opportunistic breeder, nesting after good rains. Pairs choosing nest hollows become very excited, with much noisy chattering. Four to seven white eggs.

RANGE West of Flinders Range (SA); north to Tanami (NT); north into Pilbara (WA). Sedentary.

STATUS Common. Endemic species of three subspecies.

► See also pages
158 *158* 213 223
231 233 238 242

RED-RUMPED PARROT

Psephotus haematonotus   Platycercidae

OTHER NAMES Red-backed Parrot, Red-Rump, Grass Parrot, Ground Parrot

RECOGNITION Dominantly green, including the head and neck which are bright emerald green without any markings. Back grey-green; wings lightly washed turquoise; bend of wing and flight feathers blue. Lower back to rump orange-red, conspicuous in flight. Tail blue-green, with outer feathers edged white. Upper breast light emerald-green merging to yellow on the belly. Female dull olive-green in place of greens; no red to lower back; belly white. 25–28 cm.

VOICE Contact call in flight is a cheery two-syllable, uplifting whistle, 'chee-chlip chee-chlip'; also, from treetop perch, a pleasant warbling song.

HABITAT Open environs, rarely far from water; open grassy woodlands, watercourse trees of open grassy plains, open mallee, paddocks, sports fields.

BREEDING August–December; and in arid parts of range, from May, after early rains. Nest is a hollow of a living or dead tree, often near water; occasionally a stump or fence-post. Many of the nest sites are lost to sparrows. Four to seven white eggs.

RANGE Inland south-eastern Australia. With clearing has expanded range towards south-east coast. Sedentary.

STATUS Moderately common. Endemic species of two subspecies.

► See also pages
41 *41* 129 136

MULGA PARROT

Psephotus varius   Platycercidae

OTHER NAMES Many-coloured Parrot, Many-coloured Parakeet, Varied Parrot

RECOGNITION Slender, long-tailed parrot, with mostly bright emerald-green plumage, and small patches of bright colour giving the many-coloured effect. These include deep yellow patches on forehead, shoulders and undertail-coverts; red patch on the crown and rump; orange-red on abdomen and thighs; blue on bend of wing and primaries. Female brownish-green; no reddish-tones on the underparts, but with dull rust-red on nape and shoulder. Has an undulating flight, skimming close to the ground. 25–30 cm.

VOICE Distinctive flight call, a briskly whistled 'swit-swit-swit'.

HABITAT Semi-arid mulga and myall scrub with sparsely scattered eucalypts, mainly along watercourses; also in mallee, saltbush, drier farmlands.

BREEDING July–December. Nest is a hollow; usually at 2–5 m height on taller trees of watercourses, but in some arid regions, close to ground in very stunted trees. In north of range, breeds almost any month after rain. Four to six white eggs.

RANGE Australian interior; drier coastal, but not northern arid areas. Sedentary; part-nomadic.

STATUS Common. Endemic.

► See also pages
139 162 *170* 183
185 213 220 221
226 231 232

GOLDEN-SHOULDERED PARROT

Psephotus chrysopterygius   Platycercidae

OTHER NAMES Anthill Parrot, Golden-winged Parrot

RECOGNITION Crown and nape black; back and wings brown; golden patch on shoulders. Face, sides of neck, throat and breast turquoise. There is a small pale-yellow forehead patch; and the lower abdomen, thighs and undertail-coverts are red. Female dull yellowish-green, with bronzed tone to the crown and nape; breast greenish-yellow merging to pale blue on the abdomen; undertail-coverts grey-green with traces of red. Young males show dark crown. 27 cm.

VOICE In flight, the normal contact call is a pleasant drawn-out whistle, repeated several times, 'fweep-fweep, few-eeep'.

HABITAT Usually in eucalypt or paperbark woodland with extensive grassy flats and abundant tall termite mounds; have also been recorded in mangroves.

BREEDING May–January. The nest is a tunnel drilled into a termite mound to a depth of about 40 cm, where it is enlarged to form a nest chamber. A mound rising from swampy ground seems preferred. Four to six white, rounded eggs.

RANGE Confined to central parts of Cape York Peninsula. Sedentary.

STATUS Scarce. Endemic.

► See also pages
101 103 *105* 110

HOODED PARROT

Psephotus dissimilis   Platycercidae

OTHER NAMES Anthill Parrot, Black-hooded Parrot

RECOGNITION Resembles the Golden-shouldered Parrot; the two are sometimes regarded as subspecies of a single species. The two species occupy different ranges, so can easily be differentiated. Male has more extensive black hood coming down below the eyes and to the base of the bill; and larger golden shoulder patches. Female has forehead and face pale blue; undertail-coverts reddish. Immatures duller. 25–26 cm.

VOICE Contact call is a sharp, metallic 'chissink-chissink'. Has also a variety of mellow whistling calls.

HABITAT Open, dry, grassy woodlands, spinifex with scattered trees; often rocky country; usually where there are termite mounds, and near water.

BREEDING May–January. The nest is a tunnel drilled into a tall termite mound. Four to six white, rounded eggs. The female alone broods, incubation lasting about 23 days. The young remain with parents to form small family parties. In flocks of up to 100 after breeding.

RANGE Top End (NT). Sedentary.

STATUS Generally uncommon; common in a few localities. Endemic.

► See also pages
189 190–1 196
198

PARADISE PARROT

Psephotus pulcherrimus   Platycercidae

OTHER NAMES Beautiful Parrot, Scarlet-shouldered Parrot, Soldier Parrot

RECOGNITION No confirmed sighting since 1927 (though various later unconfirmed sightings), so seems very likely to be extinct. One of the most beautiful of small parrots. Crown and nape black, but not down to eyes; forehead scarlet. Back and wings brown, with intense scarlet on shoulders, abdomen and undertail-coverts. Face bright emerald; neck, breast and flanks turquoise. Female is paler; face and breast buff; underparts pale blue; rump turquoise. 27–30 cm.

VOICE Recorded as being a series of soft, melodious whistle-like notes repeated three or four times. Alarm call was sharp, metallic.

HABITAT Eucalypt woodlands, especially grassy valleys with termitaria. Burning of grasslands for green stock-feed may have altered this habitat.

BREEDING Recorded in September, December and March. Nest was a tunnel drilled into termite mound, occasionally a hole in a creek-bank, or tree hollow. No lining was used, the four or five white eggs being laid on the earth of the chamber.

RANGE Inland south-eastern Queensland and into northern inland New South Wales. Sedentary.

STATUS Extremely rare; probably extinct. Endemic.

▶ See also pages 74 75

See also pages 74 75

283 BLUE BONNET

Northiella haematogaster   Platycercidae

OTHER NAMES Red-vented Blue Bonnet, Crimson-bellied Parrot, Bulloak Parrot

RECOGNITION Upperparts, including head, neck, back and wings pale olive-brown; deep blue of forehead, cheeks and throat completely encircling the bill. Wings are distinctively coloured; differing for each of several subspecies. Nominate race has deep blue on bend of wing and flight feathers; yellow-ochre shoulder; and red-brown patch at centre of the yellow underparts. Subspecies *haematorrhous* has green and dark red on shoulder; red patch extending to undertail-coverts. The Naretha Parrot has at various times been listed as a separate species, but is now generally accepted as another subspecies (*narethae*) of the Blue Bonnet. The forehead is turquoise instead of blue; cheeks deep blue; and the red of the underparts is confined to the undertail-coverts. 35 cm.

VOICE In flight, an abrupt, harsh 'chack, chack-chack'. The same call is used when alarmed, but more rapidly. Occasionally a high piping whistle.

HABITAT Open grassy woodlands, grasslands and arid scrublands with sparse trees along watercourses. Favours areas of sheoaks, native pine, sandalwood.

BREEDING July–December; possibly varied by timing of rainfall in arid regions. Uses a hollow of a tree, sometimes close to the ground in arid mulga scrubs. Usual clutch is four to seven white eggs. Young remain with parents in family parties.

RANGE Subspecies *haematogaster* and *haematorrhous*: interior south-eastern Australia; subspecies *narethae*: almost entirely confined to Nullarbor (WA-SA). Sedentary or locally nomadic.

STATUS Uncommon. Endemic.

▶ See also pages 133 213 220

☐ Naretha

☐ Blue Bonnet

See also pages 133 213 220

284 BOURKE'S PARROT

Neophema bourkii   Platycercidae

OTHER NAMES Pink-breasted Parrot, Night Parrot, Bourke Grass-Parakeet, Sundown Parrot

RECOGNITION Upperparts mostly soft grey-brown; darker on the wings where the feathers are edged whitish. There is a small patch of blue on the forehead; crown and hind-neck tinged dark pink; area round eyes white. Feathers of neck and upper breast brownish edged pink, merging to a stronger and more uniform pink across the entire lower breast and abdomen; undertail-coverts light blue. Female: subdued colours; no blue on forehead. 18–22 cm.

VOICE Contact call, usually given while in flight, is a pleasant mellow 'chuweeep'; while perched, a high chirruping. Alarm call is sharp, metallic.

HABITAT Mulga (*acacia*) scrublands, arid open eucalypt woodlands. In pairs or small parties, coming to drink in semi-darkness, morning and night.

BREEDING August–December, but variable, depending upon rainfall in central and northern parts of range. Nest is a small hollow, often in gums along inland watercourses; sometimes a hole low down in a mulga shrub. Three to six white eggs.

RANGE Southern interior; north-western New South Wales, south-western Queensland to mid-west coast Western Australia. Nomadic.

STATUS Moderately common. Endemic.

▶ See also pages 184 213 221 226–7 230 231 *231* 232

See also pages 184 213 221 226–7 230 231 231 232

285 BLUE-WINGED PARROT

Neophema chrysostoma   Platycercidae

OTHER NAMES Blue-banded Grass Parrot, Blue-banded Grass-Parakeet, Hobart Ground Parrot

RECOGNITION Upperparts dull olive-green; yellowish about the face particularly round the lores and eyes; and with a deep blue band across the forehead extending back to touch the eye. Entire shoulder area deep ultramarine-blue becoming darker blue-black on the flight feathers. Throat and upper breast olive-green, blending to yellow across the remainder of the underparts; tail blue-green above, yellow beneath. Female has softer, greener coloration. 20–23 cm.

VOICE The usual call while in flight is a pleasant tinkling sound. In alarm, sharp high-pitched calls. Soft twitterings while feeding and at nest.

HABITAT Varied habitats; from forested valleys to open grassy woodlands, grasslands, mallee, arid acacia scrublands, saltbush plains, heaths, dunes.

BREEDING October–January. Nest site is variable, with a tendency in Tasmania to

choose a high hollow of a tall tree, but in Victoria often in a low site such as a stump, fence-post or log. Four to six white, rounded eggs.

RANGE South-eastern Australia to east of South Australia, and south-western Queensland; and Tasmania. Migratory across Bass Strait.

STATUS Common in south of range. Endemic.

▶ See also page 117

See also page 117

286 ELEGANT PARROT

Neophema elegans   Platycercidae

OTHER NAMES Elegant Grass Parrot, Grass-Parakeet, Elegant Grass-Parakeet

RECOGNITION A small, green-and-yellow parrot that could be confused with Blue-winged Parrot in south-eastern Australia. The Elegant Parrot is yellower overall, with much less blue on wings. Upperparts olive-yellow; yellowish rump and yellow outer tail and tail-tips noticeable in flight. Underparts yellow; greener on upper breast. Brighter yellow on the face, particularly about lores and eyes, with blue frontal band carried back above and slightly behind eye. Female duller. 21 cm.

VOICE In flight, a single sharp 'tsiit'; often first sign of species; when flushed, they fly up with tinkling twitterings.

HABITAT Open woodlands, mallee, acacia scrublands, wheatbelt farmlands; also present in south-west and breeds in the heavier jarrah forest.

BREEDING August–December. Nest is a small hollow of a eucalypt; may be high in forest environs, quite low in smaller inland trees. Four to five white eggs. Female alone broods, sitting tightly. Young acquire adult plumage within three to four months.

RANGE South-west of Western Australia, south-east of South Australia, western Victoria, south-western New South Wales. Partly nomadic.

STATUS Moderately common. Endemic.

▶ See also pages 158–9 *159* 245

See also pages 158–9 159 245

287 ROCK PARROT

Neophema petrophila   Platycercidae

OTHER NAMES Rock Grass Parrot, Rock Elegant Parrot

RECOGNITION Upperparts, including head and wings, dull brownish-olive. Pale blue on forehead, lores, round the eyes and base of the bill, with a narrow band of darker blue across the light blue of the forehead. Throat and breast dull olive-grey; abdomen and remainder of underparts yellow. Bend of wing light blue; outer webs of primaries and underwing-coverts dark blue. Tail blue; outer feathers edged and tipped yellow. Female duller. 22 cm.

VOICE In flight, a high penetrating, plaintive 'tsit-tseet-tseet' repeated often. When flushed, flying up, a rapid 'tsit-tsit-tsit-'.

HABITAT Coastal: especially rocky islets, among granite or limestone boulders; where on mainland: dune vegetation, coastal swamplands, grasslands.

BREEDING August–October; often two broods. The nest is on the ground, usually under a slab of rock, or hole in limestone; often so close to sea that the nest site is wet by spray in windy weather. Four to five white eggs.

RANGE Shark Bay (WA) to Robe (SA), except Great Australian Bight; rarely far from sea. Mostly sedentary.

STATUS Common. Endemic.

▶ See also pages
158 159 162

88 ORANGE-BELLIED PARROT

Neophema chrysogaster   Platycercidae
OTHER NAMES Orange-breasted Parrot, Orange-breasted Grass-Parakeet, Orange-bellied Grass-Parakeet

RECOGNITION Upperparts, from crown to tail and wings bright, deep grass-green. Face, throat and breast lighter yellow-green, blending to orange in centre of the belly; with remainder of underparts, including flanks, undertail-coverts, and underside of tail bright yellow. Face, about lores and bill, yellowish; with bright blue forehead band carried back only as far as the eyes. Bend of wing and flight feathers deep blue. Female duller. 20–21 cm.

VOICE Contact call, while in flight, is a tinkling sound. In alarm, a fast buzzing chatter.

HABITAT Coastal; though less closely tied to coast than Rock Parrot, and found in greater variety of habitat, including grasslands, button-grass.

BREEDING Probably November–December. Nests recorded have been in hollows of trees, but may nest on ground among rocks of islands. Four to six white eggs are laid; little is known about behaviour at the nest.

RANGE Western Tasmania, to coastal mainland between Coorong (SA) and Gippsland. Migratory.

STATUS Rare; greatly reduced from earlier levels. Endemic.

▶ See also pages
125 126 142 143
145 *145* 152 163

289 TURQUOISE PARROT

Neophema pulchella   Platycercidae
OTHER NAMES Red-shouldered Parakeet, Chestnut-shouldered Parakeet, Turquoisine Parrot

RECOGNITION A colourful, small slender parrot; grass-green upperparts; underparts from upper breast to undertail entirely yellow. Front of head bright turquoise, including forehead, face and throat. Wing-coverts turquoise, blending to deep blue along bend of wing and on flight feathers; with innerwing-coverts of shoulder chestnut-red. Female: without chestnut shoulder; paler turquoise on face; lores yellow; breast greenish. Immatures duller. 19–21 cm.

VOICE In flight, a soft yet quite penetrating double-syllable tinkling whistle; like call of Blue-winged Parrot but higher. Also single high whistle.

HABITAT Open grassy eucalypt woodlands; especially the margins of clearings and lightly timbered ridges of farmlands, lines of trees along watercourses.

BREEDING August–December. Nest is a hollow of a tree, often dead; and frequently in a stump, log or weathered hollow fence-post. The four to five white eggs are laid in the unlined hollow. Only the female broods, sitting very tightly.

RANGE Eastern Australia: south-eastern Queensland to north-eastern Victoria, inland to mid-western New South Wales. Partly nomadic.

STATUS Generally uncommon; endemic.

▶ See also pages
121 134–5 *135*
136 137

290 SCARLET-CHESTED PARROT

Neophema splendida   Platycercidae
OTHER NAMES Scarlet-breasted Parrot, Scarlet-chested Grass-Parakeet

RECOGNITION One of Australia's most spectacularly colourful parrots. Head entirely brilliant blue; centre of chest scarlet; remainder of underparts deep yellow. Upperparts, from nape to upper surface of tail, bright green; this colour extending round to the sides of breast and flanks to meet crimson and yellow of underparts. Wing-coverts light blue, bend of wing and underwing dark blue. Female: less blue on face; breast green. Immatures duller. 17–21 cm.

VOICE A soft, feeble twittering which does not carry far. Usually seen in pairs or small flocks; quiet and inconspicuous.

HABITAT Arid acacia and mallee scrub, usually with spinifex; clumps of sparse and stunted trees; saltbush and parakeelya country. Feeds on the ground.

BREEDING August–January; considerably influenced by timing of rain and subsequent seeding of grasses and other food plants. Nest is a hollow of a mulga or small eucalypt. The three to five white eggs are laid on wood-dust of hollow.

RANGE Dry interior of southern Australia, reaching southern parts of Northern Territory. Highly nomadic.

STATUS Generally scarce; locally common. Endemic.

▶ See also pages
164 184 213
214–15 *215* 220
221 242

CUCKOOS AND COUCALS

**Cuculidae Family of 128 species
13 in Australia, 12 breeding**

A family with two main subdivisions, both represented in Australia: the parasitic cuckoos, and the coucals which build nests and tend their young. The birds of this family are slender, long-tailed, short-legged, and with outer toe reversible and able to grip from behind. The bill is short, and sometimes slightly downcurved. Plumage is generally in greys and browns, sometimes with iridescent sheen, often barred beneath. Many are migratory.

291 ORIENTAL CUCKOO

Cuculus saturatus   Cuculidae
OTHER NAMES Himalayan Cuckoo, Blyth's Cuckoo, Hawk-cuckoo

RECOGNITION A large cuckoo, with dove-grey upperparts; paler on the head. Tail dark grey, white spotted. Underparts, from chin to upper breast light grey; breast and belly buffy-white, boldly barred dark brown; eye brown with whitish outer, and yellow eye-ring; feet yellowish. Underwing-coverts white, barred grey-brown. Falcon-like flight; sleek shape; powerful action of long-pointed wings. Immatures: upperparts barred cinnamon and brown; underparts barred to chin. 28–33 cm.

VOICE Usually quiet; but varied calls include an even-pitched, piercing 'pi-pi-pi-', like kestrel; and a harsh 'gaak-gak-', like dollarbird.

HABITAT Rainforests, eucalypt forests and woodland, watercourse thickets, monsoon forests, paperbark swamps and, in passage, mangroves and coral cays.

BREEDING Breeding not recorded for Australia. Migrant from China, Siberia and Japan; wintering southern Asia to Australia; usually present November–May. Often solitary or small parties, shy and not easily approached.

RANGE Northern and north-eastern Australia; south to north-eastern New South Wales; mainly coastal.

STATUS Uncommon in north; rare in south of range.

▶ See also pages
323 339

292 PALLID CUCKOO

Cuculus pallidus   Cuculidae

OTHER NAMES Brainfever-bird, Rainbird, Grasshopper Hawk, Scale-bird

RECOGNITION A large, long and slender cuckoo, predominantly grey. Upperparts dark grey; inner web of flight feathers barred white; small white patches on edge of shoulder and nape; tail darker and prominently notched white. Face and underparts almost uniformly pale grey, except indistinct dark line through the eye; yellow eye-ring. Female has mottled chestnut on the upperparts. Immatures: upperparts heavily mottled browns; breast mottled buff and brown. 28–33 cm.

VOICE A monotonously repeated sequence of notes, on a rising scale; evenly spaced, and with a plaintive, though not unpleasant quality.

HABITAT Woodlands, open forests, semiarid scrublands, mangroves and most other open habitats; least often observed in rainforests.

BREEDING Variable; usually September–March. Eggs laid singly in open, cup nests of various other species, especially honeyeaters, but also cuckoo-shrikes, woodswallows and flycatchers. Egg vari-

able colour, usually pinkish, spotted darker.

RANGE Throughout Australia. Migrant, especially in south; winter vagrant to New Guinea.

STATUS Common.   Endemic breeding species.

293 BRUSH CUCKOO

Cuculus variolosus   Cuculidae

OTHER NAME Square-tailed Cuckoo

RECOGNITION A small, plain cuckoo, with head and nape pale blue-grey; remainder of upperparts, including tail, brownish with a slight bronze-green sheen. Wing slightly darker brown, with small white patch at the bend. Tail tipped white; in fresh plumage shows fine white edge markings that are lost as the feather margins become worn. Face and throat light grey, merging to the pale cinnamon underparts. Immatures heavily mottled buff and dark brown. 22–24 cm.

VOICE A far-carrying, high, but descending sequence of four to eight drawn-out plaintive notes, 'feww-feww-'. Displaying males give noisy, excited variations.

HABITAT Eucalypt forests, woodlands, rainforests, monsoon forests, mangroves. Reaches the alpine areas of south-east in summer. Usually solitary, unobtrusive.

BREEDING Variable, recorded most months; September–December in south. Hosts include various red-breasted and yellow-breasted robins, flycatchers, honeyeaters; less often domed nests of warblers, wrens. Whitish egg, lightly spotted brown.

RANGE Northern and eastern Australia; mainly coast and ranges. Migrant, September to February–April. Extends to New Guinea, the Solomon Islands, Indonesia and Malaysia.

STATUS Common.

▶ See also pages
122 208 *323*

294 CHESTNUT-BREASTED CUCKOO

Cuculus castaneiventris   Cuculidae

RECOGNITION Rare, and usually confined to Cape York Peninsula. Upperparts glossy dark blue-grey; tail blue-black tipped white and edge-notched in light grey. Underparts, from chin to undertail, entirely deep rufous or light chestnut. Eye brown; eye-ring and legs yellow. In flight, pale wingbar. Immatures: upperparts mottled brown and grey; buff underparts, not barred. Tends to keep to the forest canopy, but at times drops to ground to feed. 23–24 cm.

VOICE Similar to that of Fan-tailed Cuckoo; an even trilling, and a single whistle.

HABITAT Usually in rainforest, but will forage well out into adjoining eucalypt woodlands; also monsoon scrubs, riverine forests, possibly mangroves.

BREEDING The only records are from the Claudie River, Cape York Peninsula. Sightings in that district have been throughout the year, so the species has a small resident population on eastern Cape York Peninsula.

RANGE North-east of Cape York Peninsula, south to Bloomfield River. Probable migrant from New Guinea.

STATUS Uncommon. A New Guinea species, with an outlier population in Australia.

▶ See also pages
98 103–4 *107* 111

295 FAN-TAILED CUCKOO

Cuculus pyrrhophanus   Cuculidae

OTHER NAME Ash-tailed Cuckoo

RECOGNITION Upperparts dark, shining blue-grey, blending to brown on wings; darker blue-black on the long, 15 cm tail. Tail feathers notched white along their outer webs, giving conspicuous white-rippled margins; undertail broadly notched white, appearing boldly black-and-white barred. Underparts are entirely cinnamon; lighter on undertail-coverts. Eye brown; eye-ring yellow. Female has duller underparts. Immatures have mottled brown upperparts, grey and brown underparts. 26 cm.

VOICE A rapid descending trill, 'pee-ee-ee-ee-ew', repeated four or five times; and a single whistle. Calls have a mournful quality.

292 PALLID CUCKOO *Cuculus pallidus*

HABITAT Mainly a forest bird: rainforests, eucalypt forests; but also in woodlands including alpine, mallee, inland scrubs, heaths, mangroves.

BREEDING Variable; August–December in south. Usually selects a domed nest, of thornbill or wren, in which to deposit egg. White or mauve-white egg, finely speckled and blotched brown and purple, more heavily round the larger end.

RANGE North-eastern, eastern, south-eastern and south-western Australia, and Tasmania; inland but not usually in arid regions. Sedentary or part migratory.

STATUS Common. Endemic breeding subspecies.

▶ **See also pages** 153 174

96

BLACK-EARED CUCKOO

Chrysococcyx osculans   Cuculidae

RECOGNITION Upperparts dull grey-brown with slight coppery sheen. Wings and tail darker; tail white-tipped. Facial pattern distinctive, with dark line from base of bill through the eye becoming wider over ear-coverts and curving down side of neck. This black is edged above by a similar-shaped white eyebrow line, and below by off-white of chin. Throat, breast and underwing buff to cinnamon. Immatures: ear-patch brownish; underparts pale grey. 19–20 cm.

VOICE A descending, mournful 'peeeeer, peeeeer', often repeated several times; or in display, an excited 'pee-a-wit, pee-a-weer', repeatedly.

HABITAT Drier inland scrubs and woodlands; mulga, mallee, spinifex, samphire, paperbark woodlands, watercourse thickets of arid regions.

BREEDING August–January in the south; variable following rains in arid regions and in north. Uses various hosts' nests including Redthroat and Speckled Warbler. Host species tend to have red-brown eggs. Black-eared Cuckoo's egg is small, uniformly chocolate-brown.

RANGE Throughout Australia, except forested south-west, south-east, parts of east coast, and Tasmania. Migratory to New Guinea and Aru Islands.

STATUS Rare to uncommon. Endemic breeding species.

▶ **See also pages** 136 137

297

HORSFIELD'S BRONZE-CUCKOO

Chrysococcyx basalis   Cuculidae

OTHER NAMES Rufous-tailed Bronze-Cuckoo, Narrow-billed Bronze-Cuckoo

RECOGNITION Dull, grey-brown plumage. The brown of the upperparts has a metallic, coppery-bronze and greenish sheen overall, in good light. Breast off-white, with dull brown crossbars, often broken at

240 **Yellow-tailed Black-Cockatoo** *Calyptorhynchus funereus*
257 **Little Lorikeet** *Glossopsitta pusilla*
291 **Oriental Cuckoo** *Cuculus saturatus*
293 **Brush Cuckoo** *Cuculus variolosus*
295 **Fan-tailed Cuckoo** *Cuculus pyrrhophanus*
296 **Black-eared Cuckoo** *Chrysococcyx osculans*
299 **Little Bronze-Cuckoo** *Chrysococcyx malayanus*
302 **Channel-billed Cuckoo** *Scythrops novaehollandiae*
303 **Pheasant Coucal** *Centropus phasianinus*

centre. Eye dark, with brown line through eye to ear-coverts and side of neck; dull white eyebrow, cheek-line and throat. Outer-tail feathers bright rufous towards the base, not always visible in field. Female has grey eye. Immatures are dull; crossbars indistinct. 17 cm.

VOICE A long, drawn-out, plaintive whistle, beginning high and sliding down the scale, 'tseeeeoo, tseeeeoo'; repeated persistently from a high perch.

HABITAT Open forests, forest margins and clearings, woodlands, mallee, mulga, spinifex, saltbush, samphire, mangroves, farmlands, parklands.

BREEDING August–December. Uses host species with domed nests, especially the *Malurus* wrens, but also thornbills and warblers; and sometimes cup nests of robins and honeyeaters. Pinkish-white egg, finely spotted and speckled red-brown.

RANGE Almost throughout Australia. Breeding migrant to southern Australia; many overwinter. Some migrate to northern islands.

STATUS Common. Endemic breeding species.

297 HORSFIELD'S BRONZE-CUCKOO
Chrysococcyx basalis

298 **SHINING BRONZE-CUCKOO**

Chrysococcyx lucidus   Cuculidae

OTHER NAMES Greenback, Golden Bronze-Cuckoo, Broad-billed Bronze-Cuckoo

RECOGNITION Resident subspecies *plagosus*: crown and nape purplish-bronze; back, wings and tail bright iridescent bronze-green; underparts white, with bold bronze-brown crossbars, unbroken centrally; finer crossbars to chin and face. Nominate subspecies more uniform bronze-green over entire upperparts; greener barring of underparts; more conspicuous white scalloping of forehead. Immatures: *plagosus*, greyer upperparts; crossbars absent, incom-

plete or shadowy. 14–16 cm.

VOICE Repeated high-pitched whistles each ending with an upwards inflection, 'fweeit-fweeit-fweeit'; and often ending with downwards 'pee-uww'.

HABITAT Eucalypt forests, woodlands, rainforests, adjoining open country. Singly or in pairs; usually inconspicuous; takes caterpillars and other insects.

BREEDING Present August–April. Usually chooses small domed nests in which to lay eggs. Over 60 host species recorded, including thornbills and fairy-wrens. Also occasionally uses open cup nests. Egg uniformly olive-green to bronze-brown.

RANGE South-west (migrates to Indonesia); east and south-east, and Tasmania (migrates to New Guinea).

STATUS Race *plagosus*, common; *lucidus* rare, to east coast from New Zealand.

▶ See also pages 64–5 65

299 **LITTLE BRONZE-CUCKOO**

Chrysococcyx malayanus   Cuculidae

OTHER NAME Malay Bronze-Cuckoo

RECOGNITION Closely resembles Shining Bronze-Cuckoo, but smaller, and with crown and nape dark, bronzed blue-green, distinct from lighter back and wings. Underparts white, completely barred coppery-bronze. Face mainly white, with dark ear-patch; bright red eye and surrounding eye-ring (male), or brown eye with tan eye-ring (female). Outer-tail feathers with bold black and white bars; rufous on inner, tipped white. Immatures: dull, bars indistinct. 15 cm.

VOICE A high downwards trill, with tremulous and insect-like quality; also a four-noted 'chu-chu-chu-chu'.

HABITAT Edges of rainforests and monsoon forests, paperbark woodlands, swamp-woodlands, mangroves. Usually alone or in pairs; occasional small parties.

BREEDING October–February. Host species include Large-billed and White-throated warblers, and Bar-breasted Honeyeater. Egg, olive-green to olive-brown. There are two subspecies, and some migratory movements on east coast, and across Torres Strait.

RANGE Northern and north-eastern Australia, mainly coastal; on east coast, south to north-east of New South Wales.

STATUS Common, at least in north. Subspecies *minutillus* apparently endemic.

▶ See also pages 96 323

300 **GOULD'S BRONZE-CUCKOO**

Chrysococcyx russatus   Cuculidae

OTHER NAMES Rufous-throated Bronze-Cuckoo, Rufous, Rufous-breasted Bronze-Cuckoo

RECOGNITION Like Little Bronze-Cuckoo, but with much rufous in plumage. Upperparts with distinct rufous wash to the bronze-greens; flight feathers usually with rufous margins; tail feathers deep rufous. Underparts off-white, barred dark bronze; but only indistinctly on the breast where partly obscured by a wide rufous-grey breastband. Male has red eye and eye-ring; female has brown eye, tan eye-ring. Immatures are duller; underparts dull white. 15 cm.

VOICE Like that of Little Bronze-Cuckoo; high downwards trill, with tremulous insect-like quality; also a four-noted 'chu-chu-chu-chu'.

HABITAT Tropical rainforests, mangroves, open forests, woodlands, swamp-woodlands. Feeds on insects, especially caterpillars.

BREEDING October–February. Hosts usually *Gerygone* warblers, some 10 species of foster-parents recorded. Egg olive-green to olive-brown. At least some individuals of this species appear to cross Torres Strait to New Guinea.

RANGE Coastal Queensland, south to about Yeppoon. Migratory in south of range. Also in New Guinea and other northern islands.

STATUS Common in north-eastern Queensland.

▶ See also page 107

301 **COMMON KOEL**

Eudynamis scolopacea   Cuculidae

OTHER NAMES Indian Koel, Black Cuckoo, Flinders' Cuckoo, Cooee, Rainbird

RECOGNITION Large, long rounded tail; overall glossy blue-black plumage; bright red eyes. Bill and feet greyish. Female has head black, remainder of upper plumage brown, barred and spotted white; underparts creamy-white, lightly barred brown; throat chestnut; white stripe through eye; eye red. Immatures like female; eye paler; broad pale eyebrow line. Tend to keep to shelter of dense foliage; males bolder. Sometimes in groups, feeding in fruiting trees. 39–46 cm.

VOICE Usually silent, but become noisy in breeding season, with shrieking calls from males, 'kooeel', and 'koo-ka-eeooee'; often at night.

HABITAT Rainforests, eucalypt forests and woodlands, particularly along streams. Also stands of leafy trees of farms, parklands, streets, gardens.

BREEDING September–March, variable; depending upon rains, and breeding of host species. Hosts include crows, currawongs, Australian Magpie, friarbirds, Australian Magpie-lark. Egg is salmon-pink, marbled grey and red-brown.

RANGE Northern and eastern Australia; winters in Indonesia, New Guinea and other islands.

STATUS Common along coast; uncommon inland.

▶ **See also pages**
75 196 209 210

302 CHANNEL-BILLED CUCKOO

Scythrops novaehollandiae　　Cuculidae

OTHER NAMES Stormbird, Rainbird, Giant Cuckoo, Storm Cuckoo, Hornbill, Toucan

RECOGNITION Very large; grey, with massive curved pale grey-brown bill which has a deep groove along the upper-mandible. Head, face, and neck to breast, pale grey. Back and wings darker grey, with black tips to the feathers. Tail long; uppertail grey, with black subterminal band; white tail-tip, barred beneath. Remainder of underparts white, barred dark brown, especially on flanks. Eye and eye-ring red. In flight, shows long tail, strong hawk-like wingbeats. 60 cm.

VOICE A loud raucous 'kawwk-awk-awk-', quickening and dropping in pitch; often uttered in flight, attracting attention to the bird, and also at night.

HABITAT Open forests and woodlands; especially along watercourses, rainforest streams, swamp-woodlands; where native figs are most abundant.

BREEDING The Channel-billed Cuckoo winters on northern islands; arrives in Australia August–September; breeding and remaining until April–May. Lays in nests of Pied Currawong, Collared Sparrowhawk, Australian Magpie. Egg buffy, blotched with browns.

RANGE Coastal north-west; almost throughout Queensland; north-eastern New South Wales, south to about Sydney.

STATUS Common on north-east coast; elsewhere uncommon.

▶ **See also pages**
210 *323*

303 PHEASANT COUCAL

Centropus phasianinus　　Cuculidae

OTHER NAMES Coucal, Swamp Pheasant, Swamp Cuckoo, North-west Pheasant

RECOGNITION Very large; dark-plumaged; long-tailed; pheasant-like. Breeding plumage: head, body and tail black; wings chestnut, intricately streaked and barred buff and brown. The shafts of the black feathers of head and body are highly glossy, giving a streaked appearance. Tail mostly black, barred grey; curved bill black; eye red. Non-breeding plumage: black of body replaced by brown, heavily streaked pale buff. Female larger. Immatures are pale; eyes brown. 60–80 cm.

VOICE A deep, liquid 'coooop-coop-coop-coop-oop-oop'; starting slow, loud and distinct; quickening, and descending to a gurgling or bubbling sound.

HABITAT Rank and often moist undergrowth around swamps, wet heaths, grassy woodlands and forests, mangrove edges, pandanus, lantana thickets, sugarcane.

BREEDING Variable, August–March. Builds own nest, on or near ground, in grass clump or other dense low vegetation. Nest is an open saucer-shape usually with some vegetation pulled over as a hood. Two to five dull white eggs.

RANGE North-western, northern and eastern Australia, mostly coastal. Also in New Guinea. Sedentary.

STATUS Common in wetter regions.

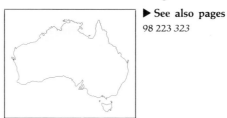

▶ **See also pages**
98 223 *323*

HAWK OWLS

**Strigidae Family of 123 species
5 in Australia, 4 breeding, 1 endemic**

Nocturnal, moderately small to large, and powerful, the owls of this family are somewhat more hawk-like in appearance than the barn owls. There is not the single large facial disc, but smaller dark discs about each eye; iris often yellow. Bills are strong, hooked; talons powerful. In Australian species the body plumage is generally boldly barred or prominently marked with chevrons.

304 RUFOUS OWL

Ninox rufa　　Strigidae

RECOGNITION Overall rufous tone. Usually only in rainforests. Upperparts closely barred buff and dark rufous-brown. Underparts are finely cross-barred buff and rufous; tail with broad bars. Eyes and feet yellow. Female smaller. Immatures: head and underparts white, and distinct dark eye-patches. A large species, northern subspecies *rufa* approaching Powerful Owl in size, take prey to size of brush-turkey, flying foxes. 44–51 cm.

VOICE A slow soft 'woo-hoo', the second note shorter; like the call of the Powerful Owl but not as far-carrying.

HABITAT Tropical closed forests: rainforest, monsoon and vine scrubs; also swamp-woodlands, sometimes mangroves.

BREEDING July–October. A tree hollow, usually high. Two to three white eggs. Nests 3–4 km apart, foraging territories 400–800 ha (Ingham). Habits little known. There are accounts of attacks upon both goannas and humans climbing to nests.

RANGE Two populations: Kimberley to Top End (NT), and north-eastern Queensland to Cape York. Also in New Guinea and Aru Islands. Sedentary.

STATUS Rare or uncommon.

▶ **See also pages**
87 89 97 196 209

305 POWERFUL OWL

Ninox strenua　　Strigidae

OTHER NAMES Eagle Owl, Great Scrub Owl

RECOGNITION Very large, piercing yellow eyes; powerful feet dull yellow. Upperparts dark grey-brown, streaked white on the crown, remainder barred light grey. Underparts buffy-white, boldly marked with dark grey-brown. Legs feathered to the ankle. Male larger than female. Immatures paler, more heavily barred white on the back; underparts white, only very lightly streaked grey; face white with very prominent dark eye-patches, a masked appearance. 55 cm.

VOICE A deep slow double hoot, 'whoo-hoo', or 'woof-woof', often between male and female, with call of female apparently the shorter higher sound.

HABITAT Coastal and mountain scrubs and woodlands, especially densely vegetated deep gullied terrain; territories are large, pairs 3–10 km apart.

BREEDING April–September; usually August–September. Nest a hollow in limb or trunk of a large forest tree, usually high, 15–40 m above ground. Courting begins April–May, and the white eggs are laid in May–June.

RANGE Coastal eastern and south-eastern Australia; not Tasmania. Sedentary.

STATUS Uncommon. Endemic.

▶ **See also pages**
65 *65* 80 82 121
123 136

306 SOUTHERN BOOBOOK

Ninox novaeseelandiae   Strigidae

OTHER NAMES Northern Boobook-Owl, Mopoke

RECOGNITION Small; brown upperparts; white underparts heavily streaked brown. Distinctive dark brown goggle-like patches round and back from each eye, otherwise face whitish. Variable, darker brown in coastal north-eastern Queensland, paler grey in north-western Australia and arid regions. Eyes dark except in Tasmania, where yellow. Probably Australia's most common owl, whose presence is usually made known by the familiar call. Female larger, darker, 30–36 cm.

VOICE Probably the best-known nocturnal sound of the Australian bush, a double-noted 'boo-book', repeated for lengthy periods; male's call quicker.

HABITAT Forests and woodlands, almost treeless plains, suburban parks, gardens.

BREEDING August–December; usually September–November. A tree hollow, where two to three white eggs are laid on decayed wood dust.

RANGE Throughout Australia. Also in New Guinea, Timor and New Zealand. Sedentary or nomadic or part migratory.

STATUS Common.

▶ See also pages
82 137 *180* 231

307 BARKING OWL

Ninox connivens   Strigidae

OTHER NAME Winking Owl

RECOGNITION Superficially resembles the Boobook, but is much larger, longer-bodied and has a more upright posture. Large bright yellow eyes. Head dark brown; off-white round and between the eyes. Upperparts dark brown, white spots across the wings. Underparts white with extensive streaking of rusty-brown or grey-brown. Male larger than female. Generally roost during the day in pairs in dense foliage. 38–45 cm.

VOICE A double-noted dog-bark 'woof-woof, woof-woof', beginning softly, increasing very loud. Sometimes sounds like a baby screaming.

HABITAT Open forests, woodlands, trees along watercourses and in gorges, especially rivergums and paperbarks of semi-arid mulga and spinifex country.

BREEDING June–November, usually August–October. A large tree hollow, often high. Two or three white eggs laid on wood debris. May sometimes be seen roosting in dense foliage in area of nest, in company with large young of last nesting.

RANGE Most of Australia; absent from Tasmania and most arid treeless regions. Also in New Guinea. Sedentary.

STATUS Uncommon in south; more common in north.

▶ See also pages
82 126 208 *210*
230 233

BARN OWLS

**Tytonidae Family of 10 species
5 in Australia, 5 breeding, 1 endemic**

Upright, and long-legged. The large dark eyes are rigidly set in a facial disc with ruff-like edges, more or less heart-shaped, encompassing the entire facial area. The plumage, soft in all owls, is exceptionally so in the barn owl family, enabling silent wingbeats. The neck, though hidden beneath the deep plumage, is sufficiently flexible to allow the head to be turned as much as 270 degrees.

308 BARN OWL

Tyto alba   Tytonidae

OTHER NAMES Delicate Owl, Screech Owl, White Owl

RECOGNITION Very light colour and upright posture. Long lower legs are unfeathered and trail just behind tail in flight. Upperparts softly mottled fawn and grey, lightly marked with black, white-tipped spots. Underparts white, sparsely dark-flecked. In flight, especially in a beam of light at night, looks ghostly pure-white. Face white, with heart-shaped disc finely outlined in dark brown; small black eyes. Flushes easily from hollows during the day. 35 cm.

VOICE A thin rasping, wavering screech, uttered both in flight, and when perched, 'skeeeairr, skeeeairr'. Especially noisy early in breeding cycle.

HABITAT Most habitats except heavy and closed forests; usually open woodlands, grasslands and farmlands with scattered trees, but also treeless.

BREEDING All months; usually April–October. Uses a deep hollow of a treetrunk, often a dead limb or tree; sometimes a cliff-ledge or cave. Three to six white eggs. Breeds in response to abundant food.

RANGE Throughout Australia. Australian subspecies to Solomon Islands. Nomadic, perhaps seasonally; irruptive.

STATUS Common. Cosmopolitan species.

▶ See also pages
29 80 82 137 163
327 396

309 MASKED OWL

Tyto novaehollandiae   Tytonidae

OTHER NAMES Cave Owl, Chestnut-faced Owl, Maw-faced Owl, Tasmanian Masked Owl

RECOGNITION Like Barn Owl, but larger, much more solid and powerful build, overall darker, fully feathered, thicker legs. Colour variable, males mostly paler with underparts almost as light as Barn Owl, especially in northern and north-western Australia. Upperparts mottled dark brown, light cinnamon-brown, grey, and silvery speckled. Facial disc and underparts usually buff or pale cinnamon tone, disc encircled dark brown, darker toned towards the eyes. 35–50 cm.

VOICE Drawn-out, unpleasant rasping screech, louder than Barn Owl; apparently not often heard.

HABITAT Forests, woodlands, small patches of trees on cleared land and inland watercourses. Subspecies *troughtoni* roosts, nests, in caves of Nullarbor.

BREEDING All months, variable; mainly May–October. On debris at the bottom of a high, deep treetrunk hollow, or on sand of a cave ledge. Two to three white eggs; the incubation period is about 35 days.

RANGE Throughout Australia except most arid regions. Also in New Guinea and Indonesia. Sedentary.

STATUS Common in Tasmania (larger, darker subspecies *castanops*); elsewhere scarce.

▶ See also pages
82 121 *331*

310 EASTERN GRASS OWL

Tyto longimembris   Tytonidae

OTHER NAME Grass Owl

RECOGNITION Very like Barn Owl, but ground-dwelling, roosting and nesting in tall grass or other habitat vegetation. (Barn Owl sometimes roosts in grass.) Compared with the Barn Owl, underparts pale cinnamon, buff, sometimes off-white, and this may be noticed as the bird flies up. Female larger. When flushed, flies up with very long legs trailing well behind tail-tip. Darker wingtips in flight. 33–36 cm.

VOICE Barn Owl screech, though softer; also quavery whistle; cricket-like chirpings reported.

HABITAT Grasslands, especially semi-inundated. Swampy heaths, cane-grass, lignum and other low swamp-margin or floodplain vegetation.

BREEDING All months, variable; related to prey abundance. Nest a trampled-down platform of grass in or under dense grass clumps, generally with approach path or tunnel through the grass. Four to six white eggs.

RANGE Northern and eastern Australia, and parts of interior. Also occurs in Asia and Africa. Nomadic.

STATUS Rare; locally common temporarily.

► See also pages
29 *29* 175 196 210

311 SOOTY OWL

Tyto tenebricosa   Tytonidae

OTHER NAME Dusky Barn Owl

RECOGNITION Inhabits rainforests and similar closed environments, which the Barn Owl usually avoids. Dusky or sooty-grey; upperparts darker; underparts pale with dark-grey mottling and barring. Facial disc distinctly heart-shaped, pale grey outlined in black, and darker round comparatively large eyes, making them seem even larger. Legs only sparsely feathered, tail stumpy. Build, particularly the feet, more solid, powerful. Female larger. 33–37 cm. The Lesser Sooty Owl (*Tyto multipunctata*) was previously a subspecies of the Sooty Owl, but now is considered a separate species. It is found only in north-eastern Queensland rainforests.

VOICE A descending screech with a whistle-like quality, carries far through forest. Also various cricket-like sounds, sometimes as a duet.

HABITAT Closed forests, including rainforests from tropical to temperate; wet eucalypt forests in dense, closed-canopy parts, especially fern gullies.

BREEDING Following the wet season, January–July; usually May–July. Nest in a hollow, often very high. One to two white eggs. Incubation is reported to be a lengthy six weeks, and young remain in the nest a further three months.

RANGE Coastal south-eastern Australia. Lesser Sooty Owl in the rainforest coastal strip, Townsville to Cooktown. Also in New Guinea. Sedentary.

STATUS Uncommon; is probably often overlooked.

► See also pages
53 82 97 121

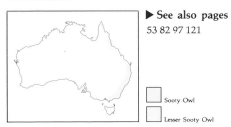

Podargidae Family of 12 species
3 in Australia, 3 breeding, 1 endemic

Moderately small to quite large nocturnal birds with massively wide bills, small weak feet, large rounded wings and long tails. They have only a superficially owl-like appearance, and are probably aberrant nightjars. Frogmouths use the wide bill to take insects and other small nocturnal creatures from the ground. Plumage is mottled greys, browns and buff; bark-like colours that hide the bird in its broken-branch pose, by day.

312 **TAWNY FROGMOUTH**
Podargus strigoides
Cryptic pose by day, alert at night

312 TAWNY FROGMOUTH

Podargus strigoides   Podargidae

OTHER NAMES Mopoke, Morepork, Night Hawk, Tawny-shouldered Frogmouth

RECOGNITION A large nocturnal bird which during daylight hours mimics a broken limb. Plumage overall grey or grey-brown, intricately streaked and mottled lighter and darker greys, and often with tawny-browns above. Colour variable, from greys without any brown tone, to a colour phase with greys replaced by tawny-brown. Bill distinctive, very broad, deep, hooked, surrounded by bristles. Eyes large, bright yellow. 33–47 cm.

VOICE A low yet far-carrying, 'wooom, wooom, wooom', difficult to locate, may be repeated for lengthy periods, particularly in breeding season.

HABITAT Wherever there are trees; eucalypt forests, woodlands, mallee, mulga scrub, interior watercourse timber, rainforest clearings.

BREEDING August–December. Nest a flimsy, loose and almost flat, platform of sticks lined with a few leaves, on a horizontal fork usually 5–10 m above ground. Sitting bird will adopt broken branch pose. Two white eggs.

RANGE Throughout Australia in suitable habitat. Sedentary.

STATUS Common. Endemic species; variable, at present two subspecies.

► See also pages
75 198 328

313 PAPUAN FROGMOUTH

Podargus papuensis   Podargidae

OTHER NAMES Plumed Frogmouth, Large Frogmouth, Great Papuan Frogmouth

RECOGNITION Largest Australian frogmouth, has long and pointed tail, red eyes, otherwise resembles Tawny Frogmouth in having two colour phases. Dark form has upperparts mottled, streaked tawny-brown, grey, white and black; buff bar at shoulder. Underparts grey-buff, marbled or spotted white, streaked darker, and often with black markings down each side of the breast. Grey form lacks brown and buff tones. Plumage more marbled, not as streaked as Tawny Frogmouth. 45–58 cm.

VOICE A long series of deep 'oom' notes similar to those of the Tawny Frogmouth; also a more rapid, deep and descending 'hoo-hoo-hoo-hoo-'.

HABITAT Eucalypt forests and woodlands, rainforest margins, dense vegetation along watercourses and swamps, mangroves.

BREEDING September–February; mainly October–December. Nest a sparse platform of sticks, on a horizontal fork, deep vertical fork, or in the hollowed end of a large limb. Nests recorded as close as 100 m intervals in mangroves. One to two white eggs.

RANGE North-eastern Queensland. Two subspecies: *rogersi* Cape York; *baileyi* Atherton. Also in New Guinea and Aru Islands. Sedentary or nomadic.

STATUS Common in north of range; uncommon south of Cooktown.

▶ See also pages
89 *89* 97 110

314 MARBLED FROGMOUTH

Podargus ocellatus Podargidae

OTHER NAME Plumed Frogmouth

RECOGNITION Similar to Tawny Frogmouth, but smaller. Plumage variable, but has a marbled rather than streaked appearance, with white spots and blotches; white markings about the shoulders more noticeable than for other frogmouths. Indistinct buff eyebrow and wingbar. Eyes orange. Brown form: mottled browns, grey, and buff upperparts; and buff marbled off-white underparts. Grey form lacks browns. Plumed Frogmouth has plumes over bill. 33–38 cm.

VOICE A soft, repetitive, monotonous 'oom-oom, oom-oom' or 'koo-loo, koo-loo'.

HABITAT Confined to tropical rainforests and vine scrubs; usually in vicinity of streams. Roosts in dense foliage and hunts large insects.

BREEDING Few records; apparently around October. Nest is usual frogmouth flimsy platform of sticks, pieces of vines, on branch of a tree, usually in thick scrub. One to three white eggs.

RANGE Nominate subspecies: Cape York Peninsula; *plumiferus*, south-eastern Queensland to north-eastern New South Wales. Sedentary.

STATUS Scarce. An endemic subspecies (includes as subspecies, former Plumed species).

▶ See also pages
53 54 74–5

OWLET-NIGHTJARS

Aegothelidae Family of 8 species
1 in Australia, 1 breeding

Very small, like miniature owls, but with long tails. The plumage is soft, not only in its delicate grey or grey-brown colours, but in texture, giving a silent flight like the softly fluttering flight of a large moth. Eyes are very large, forward-facing, their size exaggerated by encircling dark markings. The small but broad bill is almost hidden in the surrounding feathers and is surrounded by prominent bristles.

315 AUSTRALIAN OWLET-NIGHTJAR

Aegotheles cristatus Aegothelidae

OTHER NAMES Little Owlet-nightjar, Fairy Owl, Crested Owlet-nightjar, Moth Owl, Goatsucker

RECOGNITION Superficially like a miniature owl. Large head; large dark eyes; short very broad bill; long tail; and, compared with an owl, small weak feet. Plumage moth-like in softness; flight also moth-like, erratic or fluttering, totally silent. Colour variable, usually overall grey, finely mottled, barred. Flight feathers and tail heavily barred darker grey. Dark marks through eye to crown, across nape. Inland, northern forms: pale rufous replaces grey. 20–24 cm.

VOICE A peculiar and distinctive 'chirrr-churrr', the first part high, the second lower, quite loud, carries on still nights; also calls during day.

HABITAT Open forests, woodlands, mallee, and in arid regions of dominantly mulga, spinifex and sandplain; in timber along watercourses.

BREEDING July–December; usually September–November. Uses a narrow deep hollow of treetrunk or limb, occasionally a cliff-face hole. Three to four white eggs. If flushed from nest or roosting hollow will quickly vanish into another nearby hollow.

RANGE Throughout Australia in suitable habitat. Also occurs in New Guinea. Apparently sedentary.

STATUS Moderately common.

▶ See also pages
138 231

NIGHTJARS

Caprimulgidae Family of 67 species
3 in Australia, 3 breeding

Nocturnal birds with plumage beautifully patterned in the colours and visual textures of the leaf-litter of the forest floor, in grey, creamy white, chestnut, buff. By day they sit motionless, extremely difficult to see on the forest floor, eyes closed to slits. At dusk they hawk for insects, flying gracefully on long pointed wings. Eyes are large, set in rather flat heads. Bills are short and wide-gaped, tails are long, legs short, feet tiny.

316 WHITE-THROATED NIGHTJAR

Caprimulgus mystacalis Caprimulgidae

OTHER NAMES Fern Owl, Laughing Owl, Moth Hawk, Night Hawk

RECOGNITION A large dark nightjar. Upperparts black, beautifully mottled grey and brown, particularly on shoulders, inner-wing, and tail. Face and throat dusky black with a conspicuous white crescent each side of throat. Breast dull-black mottled grey, blending on remainder of underparts to dark brown and rufous barring. Small white spots on flight feathers; no white on tail. Immatures mottled red-brown, black. Roosts on ground among leaf-litter. 33–35 cm.

VOICE A weird, laughing call, starting low, rising and increasing tempo, 'koook, kook-kook-ook-ok-ok-', ending as a rapid chuckling.

HABITAT Forests and woodlands of coastal ranges, usually dry ridges with little undergrowth, but abundant twig and leaf-litter; also wallum, heath.

BREEDING October–February. The single egg, laid on leaf-litter, is cryptically coloured, greenish-yellow spotted and blotched dark browns. Both sexes share incubation; the bird's trust in its camouflage permits a very close approach.

RANGE East coast; Cape York to Otway Range. Migratory, particularly in south.

315 AUSTRALIAN OWLET-NIGHTJAR *Aegotheles cristatus*

STATUS Moderately common. Endemic breeding subspecies, reaching New Guinea.

▶ See also pages
65 *65*

SPOTTED NIGHTJAR

Caprimulgus guttatus Caprimulgidae

RECOGNITION Upperparts mottled greys, cinnamon, beautifully and intricately patterned with streaks and specklings of black and white. Conspicuous large white spots on wing primaries in flight, form a white wingbar; no white on tail. Throat and breast mottled black and cinnamon, with a single broad white band across throat, remainder of underparts cinnamon, barred black. In spot or headlights, note red eyes, white wing patches. Immatures browner. 29–33 cm.

VOICE A strange, bubbling call on an ascending scale, sometimes during the day, 'tok-tok-tok-gobble-gobble-gobble'.

HABITAT Drier eucalypt forests and woodlands, mallee, mulga, spinifex; often stony sites, roosting on ground, often in unshaded heat of the sun.

BREEDING April–October in south; October–December in north. A single pale green to creamy egg, spotted grey-brown, purplish-red, and black, is laid on the ground. Breeding pairs seem to occupy territories of 1–2 ha.

RANGE Throughout Australia, except on wetter east and south-east coast and in Tasmania. Migratory.

STATUS Common. Endemic breeding species; non-breeding to northern islands.

▶ See also pages
136 139 *331*

LARGE-TAILED NIGHTJAR

Caprimulgus macrurus Caprimulgidae

OTHER NAMES Axe-bird, Carpenter-bird, White-tailed Nightjar, Hammer-bird

RECOGNITION Very much like the Spotted Nightjar, particularly in flight. Has white on corners of tail, and on wing primaries; underneath lower half of the tail is entirely white. Upperparts greyish, with less of brown tones than Spotted Nightjar. Has band of buff spots across the closed wings. Throat and breast brownish-grey, with large white throatband; rest of underparts buff-grey barred darker. Immatures more rufous on wings. Length 26 cm; tail 14 cm.

VOICE Distinctive; a loud, monotonously repeated 'chop-chop-chop-', likened to chopping of wood, deep croaking of a

large frog.

HABITAT Unlike the Spotted species (drier habitats) the Large-tailed Nightjar favours parts of rainforests, tropical scrubs, woodlands, mangroves, with open leafy floor.

BREEDING August–November. Two creamy or light pinkish eggs, with cloudy markings of lilac-grey and brown, laid on the ground. Reputed to shift eggs if disturbed. It has been estimated that a pair hunts over area of about 50 ha.

RANGE Northern and north-eastern Australia, mostly coastal. Species widespread, to southern Asia. Sedentary.

STATUS Common in north and north-east; patchy south of Ingham.

▶ See also pages
104 *104*

SWIFTS, SWIFTLETS

Apodidae Family of 76 species
6 in Australia, 1 breeding

Highly adapted for an almost entirely aerial life, with very long swept-back wings making them probably the fastest of birds. Some species remain constantly airborne, drinking in flight by snatching water from the surface of lakes, copulating and even sleeping while in flight, coming to land only to nest. Stubby bills open to wide-gaping mouths for scooping up insects in flight; feet are tiny; tails are variable, often forked or spine-tipped.

WHITE-RUMPED SWIFTLET

Collocalia spodiopygia Apodidae

OTHER NAMES Grey Swiftlet, Grey-rumped Swiftlet, Mothbird, Chillagoe Swiftlet

RECOGNITION Almost uniformly grey-brown; wings and tail glossy grey-black. Rump whitish, and underparts grey-brown; tail slightly forked; bill and feet black. When perched, the folded wings extend well behind the tail. Swiftlets take insects on the wing, hawking over forest canopy with swift erratic bat-like flight. Although the bill is tiny the gape is large for the bird, to take flying insects. In flight entire day except at nest. 11 cm.

VOICE In flight, high-pitched cheeping. In nesting caves, gives bursts of sharp, clicking sounds, using the echoes in navigating the dark chambers.

HABITAT Aerial; except when roosting or at nest; usually over forest canopy, clearings, beaches, in vicinity of gorges, caves, boulder outcrops.

BREEDING September–February. Nests in colonies in caves; the small cup nest of

grass, mosses and feathers being bound together and adhered to the rock with dried saliva. A single white egg. Incubation and care of young, by both parents.

RANGE North-eastern Queensland, coast and ranges, hilly-rocky islands; south to Eungella.

STATUS Common. Disperse from cave vicinity after breeding. Endemic subspecies.

▶ See also pages
81 87 89

WHITE-THROATED NEEDLETAIL

Hirundapus caudacutus Apodidae

OTHER NAMES Spine-tailed Swift, Needle-tailed Swift, Stormbird

RECOGNITION A large swift with wingspan of 50 cm; one of the world's fastest birds. Upperparts sooty black with slight blue-green sheen except for grey-brown on centre of back; breast and belly brownish-black. White across forehead, on throat, and undertail-coverts. In flight, long slender backswept wings; white undertail. At rest, wings extend 5–8 cm beyond the short, square-cut tail, which has needle-like tips to the feather shafts. 19–21 cm.

VOICE Rapid, high-pitched twitterings, possibly contact calls between birds in flight, when in parties or large flocks; often before thunderstorms.

HABITAT Aerial; may be seen over almost any landscape, including cities; tend to favour skies above timbered ranges, tree-top height and upwards.

BREEDING Breeds in Asia, migrates to Australia October–April; coming via Torres Strait in large flocks; often fly very high, and out of sight; there are but few records of roosting while in Australia.

RANGE Northern and eastern Australia, northern Kimberley to Spencer Gulf (SA); and Tasmania. Also in Asia.

STATUS Common in east; rare across the north.

▶ See also pages
330 *331*

FORK-TAILED SWIFT

Apus pacificus Apodidae

OTHER NAMES White-rumped Swift, Pacific White-rumped Swift, Australian Swift

RECOGNITION A large dark swift; wingspan 40–43 cm. Plumage overall warm black, rump white and visible from sides as saddle-shaped white patch; whitish throat.

Wings very long, back-curved; tail long, deeply forked. These swifts appear in sometimes huge flocks; often preceding or during stormy weather. In flight, more erratic and bat-like than the White-throated Needletail. Remains almost constantly airborne, rarely seen to alight in Australia. Attracted to fires. 18 cm.

VOICE Shrill twitterings, and also high-pitched thin screaming calls, 'skreeee'.

HABITAT Aerial; generally over open landscapes, sometimes cities. Usually at great heights; occasionally, as when taking winged termites, very low.

BREEDING Breeds in Asia, in clusters of nests on rock faces; non-breeding migrant to Australia October–May. From northern Australia the swifts move to Western Australia and South Australia, where they are more common than the White-throated Needletail; occasional mass movements to south-eastern Australia.

RANGE Throughout Australia, usually to Tasmania; dependent upon weather systems. Also in New Guinea; vagrant to New Zealand.

STATUS Common, but usually uncommon in south-east.

▶ See also page 331

KINGFISHERS

**Alcedinidae Family of 87 species
11 in Australia, 10 breeding, 2 endemic**

Although ranging from very small to large, and with diversely coloured plumage, the members of this family are easily recognizable. Their bodies are plump; heads large with long, heavy, straight bills; legs very short and feet small. The posture is upright as they sit motionless on a vantage point ready to plunge to ground or water to take their prey of small mammals, fish, reptiles, insects. Flight is swift, direct; usually low for short distances.

322   AZURE KINGFISHER

Ceyx azurea   Alcedinidae

OTHER NAMES Blue Kingfisher, Creek Kingfisher, River Kingfisher, Water Kingfisher

RECOGNITION Small; frequents water's edge. Rich deep glossy blue upperparts, with flight feathers black, and buff or rufous patch each side of neck. Throat pale buff, merging to rufous or deep cinnamon from breast to undertail-coverts. Bill black; legs and feet bright orange-red. Immatures: dull upperparts; paler underparts. Darting

324 **LAUGHING KOOKABURRA** *Dacelo novaeguineae*

flight along streams, skimming the water surface; perches low over water, taking aquatic creatures in plunging dive. 17–19 cm.

VOICE A high drawn-out squeak, 'peee-peee', usually as it dashes across the water; when perched, it is quiet, staring intently into the water.

HABITAT Both fresh and marine; tree-lined rivers, creeks, mangroves, well-vegetated estuaries, swamps, lakes.

BREEDING December–April in the north; September–December in the south. Nest a tunnel excavated in a bank of earth, usually at the water's edge, and towards the top of the bank. Usually six rounded, lustrous, white eggs. Often two broods in a season.

RANGE Northern and eastern Australia including Tasmania, inland to extent of stream habitat. Also in New Guinea.

STATUS Quite common in north; uncommon elsewhere.

▶ See also pages 84 89 124 174 198 199 211

323   LITTLE KINGFISHER

Ceyx pusilla   Alcedinidae

RECOGNITION Australia's smallest kingfisher; much smaller than Azure Kingfisher, and very much smaller than Sacred Kingfisher. Upperparts glossy rich royal blue, sometimes tinged turquoise on the crown, with a small white spot on each side of forehead and neck. Underparts from chin to undertail-coverts pure white, except that blue of the shoulders extends to the sides of the breast. Legs and feet black. Flies low across water; hunts by plunging into water from perch. 11–13 cm.

VOICE Shrill whistle, like that of Azure Kingfisher, but higher-pitched, usually given in flight; unobtrusive, and, but for call, would often go unnoticed.

HABITAT Along streams of tropical rainforests and monsoon scrubs, mangrove-lined creeks and billabongs, tropical paperbark swamps, tidal mangrove creeks.

BREEDING October–March; the northern wet season. Nest is a chamber at the end of a tunnel into a creek-bank or low termite mound. Five to six glossy white eggs. Both sexes participate in drilling out the nest tunnel.

RANGE Two separate subspecies: coastal Northern Territory, and north-eastern

Queensland coast and ranges. Probably sedentary.

STATUS Moderately common. Endemic subspecies.

▶ **See also pages**
87 89 98 110 196 197 198

24 LAUGHING KOOKABURRA

Dacelo novaeguineae   Alcedinidae

OTHER NAMES Giant Kingfisher, Laughing Kingfisher, Jackass, Bushman's Clock

RECOGNITION A very large, predominantly brown-and-white kingfisher. Back and wings dark brown; pale sky-blue mottled patch on wings. Tail barred rufous and black, and edged white. Head and breast off-white, with brown patch on the crown, and broad brown line through the eye becoming a broad ear-patch. Males often have some blue-green on rump; females more buff about the head. Immatures: shorter darker bill. Lifts tail on landing. 41–47 cm.

VOICE Rollicking and boisterous laughter, beginning with low chuckling 'kook-kook-kook', then switching to louder 'kook-kook-kaak-kaak-kaak-ka-ka-ka'.

HABITAT Woodlands, open forests, inland timbered watercourses, farmlands. Family groups, breeding pair and up to four auxiliaries occupy territories.

BREEDING September–May; usually September–January. Nest is a hollow of a tree-trunk or limb, sometimes a hole in a termite nest, at heights up to 20 m. One to four rounded, white eggs, laid on wood-debris of hollow.

RANGE Eastern Australia, from north-eastern Queensland to Eyre Peninsula; and Tasmania. Introduced to south-western Australia. Sedentary.

STATUS Common. Endemic.

▶ **See also pages**
143 330

25 BLUE-WINGED KOOKABURRA

Dacelo leachii   Alcedinidae

OTHER NAMES Howling Jackass, Barking Jackass, Nor-West Kookaburra, Leach's Kookaburra

RECOGNITION A very large kingfisher, with off-white head streaked brown. Back brown, with large patch of blue across the shoulder. Male has rump pale blue; tail deep blue barred darker blue; female has tail red-brown, with darker brown barring. The whitish eye contributes to this kookaburra's distinctive appearance. In flight,

pale wing patch; blue rump; pale head. Usually much more wary and secretive than Laughing Kookaburra. 40–44 cm.

VOICE A harsh, raucous cacophony of sound, begun by one bird giving a 'klok-klok-' with others joining, developing into a bedlam of barking squawks.

HABITAT Mostly in tropical and subtropical woodlands. In arid north-western Australia occurs along tree-lined watercourses;

309 **Masked Owl** *Tyto novaehollandiae*
317 **Spotted Nightjar** *Caprimulgus guttatus*
320 **White-throated Needletail** *Hirundapus caudacutus*
321 **Fork-tailed Swift** *Apus pacificus*
333 **Dollarbird** *Eurystomus orientalis*
345 **Welcome Swallow** *Hirundo neoxena*
346 **Tree Martin** *Cecropis nigricans*
351 **White-bellied Cuckoo-shrike** *Coracina papuensis*
353 **Cicadabird** *Coracina tenuirostris*

in Kimberley, in monsoon vine scrubs.

BREEDING September–January. The nest is usually in an arboreal termite nest, or hollow of a tree. Three to four white, rounded eggs. Family parties occupy territories, with the breeding pair being assisted by other members of the group.

RANGE Northern Australia; approximately Shark Bay in west to Brisbane in east. Also in New Guinea. Seasonally nomadic.

STATUS Common north; uncommon in south of range.

▶ **See also pages**
82 175 197 223 233

326 FOREST KINGFISHER

Halcyon macleayii   Alcedinidae

OTHER NAMES Macleay's Kingfisher, Blue Kingfisher, Bush Kingfisher

RECOGNITION A kingfisher of boldly contrasting deep-blue and white coloration. Upperparts blue: a brilliant deep royal blue on head, wings and tail; a lighter turquoise on back and rump. Underparts and forehead spot pure white, unlike buffy tone of underparts of Sacred Kingfisher. On the male this white extends round the neck as a broad white collar, while female has blue nape. Feet grey to black. Immatures: duller; whites finely scalloped darker. 19–23 cm.

VOICE A harsh or scratchy high 'treek-treek-' or 'kree-kree-kree'; also high, repeated whistle. Calls mainly in breeding season.

HABITAT Usually not far from water, woodlands, edges and clearings of eucalypt and rainforests, paperbark and watercourse forests, mangroves.

BREEDING September–January. Drills into an arboreal termite nest or uses a hollow, 2–5 m above ground. Four to six glossy white eggs are laid in an unlined chamber. In south of range, arrives September–October to breed; some birds winter in New Guinea.

RANGE Top End (NT), and Cape York to Sydney. Also in New Guinea.

STATUS Common in north; uncommon migrant to south of range.

▶ **See also page**
80

328 SACRED KINGFISHER *Halcyon sancta* Flying out of the nest hollow

327 RED-BACKED KINGFISHER

Halcyon pyrrhopygia   Alcedinidae

OTHER NAME Golden Kingfisher

RECOGNITION Upperparts turquoise-blue, streaked white on crown, becoming light azure blue on the shoulders. Lower back and rump cinnamon-rufous. Underparts, from chin to undertail-coverts, white or greyish-white, continued round neck as a collar, and to face round base of bill and eyebrow. From the front of eye, a broad black band extends back to the nape. Female: duller colours; back and wings more uniformly greenish-blue. 20–24 cm.

VOICE In breeding season, drawn-out, mournful low-pitched call, repeated monotonously, unlike other kingfishers, and Sacred Kingfisher, which often shares habitat.

HABITAT Most inland habitats, often far from water; spinifex with scattered trees, mulga scrub, dry open woodlands, tree-lined watercourses.

BREEDING August–February; usually September–December. Nest is a tunnel drilled into a termite mound, sometimes an arboreal termite nest, or into an earth bank, old mineshaft, or earth clinging to roots of a fallen tree. Four to five white, rounded eggs.

RANGE Throughout Australia, except in wetter forested south-east, south-west and Cape York. Migratory.

STATUS Generally uncommon; common in parts of north-west. Endemic.

▶ **See also pages**
136 138 164 173 183 184 220 230 231

328 SACRED KINGFISHER

Halcyon sancta   Alcedinidae

OTHER NAMES Green Kingfisher, Wood Kingfisher, New Zealand Kingfisher

RECOGNITION Upperparts turquoise; bright turquoise-blue on lower back and rump; deeper blue on shoulder and tail. Underparts and collar whitish, variable, in winter plumage becoming buff on the breast, this fading almost to white by late summer. There is a broad black band from base of bill through eye to nape of neck, and a pale buff to cinnamon-buff spot in front of each eye. Female: larger; duller and greener, especially tail. 20–23 cm.

VOICE An even 'kik-kik-kik-kik' in spring and early summer repeated with monotonous regularity; also, near nest, a higher, drawn-out 'keer-keer-keer-'.

HABITAT Woodlands, open forests, often well away from water, also margins of lakes and swamps, shores, mangroves (see also Collared Kingfisher).

BREEDING September–March, usually October–January. Nest site is usually a small hollow in treetrunk or limb, or drilled into a termite nest in a tree, occasionally into an earth bank. Three to five glossy white eggs.

RANGE Throughout Australia in suitable habitat; absent in most arid regions. Also to northern islands and New Zealand.

STATUS Common; regular migrant.

▶ **See also pages**
23 330 333

COLLARED KINGFISHER

Halcyon chloris   Alcedinidae

OTHER NAMES Black-masked Kingfisher, Mangrove Kingfisher

RECOGNITION Very much like the marginally smaller Sacred Kingfisher, which also occurs in mangroves. Note longer, heavier bill, which is often carried slightly open. Colour generally as for Sacred Kingfisher, but darker on crown and back, and white on underparts and broad collar, though some individuals may have a slight touch of buff to the smaller forehead spot and sides of the breast. Female duller. Immatures: whites finely barred darker. 25–29 cm.

VOICE A double-noted 'kek-kik', repeated several times; slower, more deliberate, harsher and louder than call of the Sacred Kingfisher. Also high 'keeer . . .'.

HABITAT Coastal mangroves, in estuaries, bays, creeks; also to adjacent mudflats, woodlands. In regions outside Australia, lives in more habitat types.

BREEDING September–January or March. Nest is a tunnel drilled into an arboreal termite nest, terrestrial termite mound, earth bank, or in a hollow of a tree; sometimes quite high. Two to three glossy white eggs, almost spherical.

RANGE Coastal Australia; from Shark Bay (WA) to north of New South Wales. Species in Africa and India. Sedentary.

STATUS Common. Endemic subspecies.

▶ **See also pages**
23 *23* 98 110 223
332

YELLOW-BILLED KINGFISHER

Syma torotoro   Alcedinidae

OTHER NAMES Saw-billed Kingfisher, Lesser Yellow-billed Kingfisher

RECOGNITION Only Australian kingfisher with bright cadmium-yellow bill. The plumage also is unique, with head, neck and breast an orange-yellow tone similar to that of the bill; becoming a deeper cinnamon-rufous on the crown of the male; fading on the abdomen to a creamy-buff. Wings and back dark olive-green; flight feathers black; rump turquoise; tail cobalt-blue encircled black; black hindneck crescent. Female: black on crown. 18–21 cm.

VOICE A loud, clear trilling whistle, usually on ascending scale, often quite prolonged; frequent in breeding season, at other times usually silent.

HABITAT Tropical rainforests and scrubs, edges of adjoining woodlands. Keeps to lower levels of, and is concealed by, vegetation.

BREEDING August–January; usually October–December. Nest is a chamber at end of a tunnel drilled into a termite nest, or in a hollow of a tree, at heights up to 15 m.

Three white, rounded eggs.

RANGE Eastern side of Cape York; south to Princess Charlotte Bay. Species in New Guinea, other northern islands. Sedentary.

STATUS Common within range. Endemic subspecies.

▶ **See also pages**
7 101 104 *107* 111

BUFF-BREASTED PARADISE-KINGFISHER

Tanysiptera sylvia   Alcedinidae

OTHER NAMES Racquet-tailed Kingfisher, White-tailed Kingfisher, Long-tailed Kingfisher

RECOGNITION An extremely beautiful species unique among Australian kingfishers for its two very elongated, stiff white tail plumes. These make up 18–25 cm of the bird's total 30–35 cm length. This kingfisher's colourful plumage is unmistakable; bill bright coral-red, crown royal blue, underparts entirely rich rufous-ochre. Centre of back and rump white; legs red. Usually shy, keeping to high canopy, more observable when establishing territories.

VOICE A trilling high 'whee-whee-whee' for long periods when breeding; also an ascending, regular, 'chop-chop-chop-', sometimes repeated many times.

HABITAT Confined to lowland rainforests, to an altitude of about 600 m, where there is a high canopy, and a relatively open forest floor.

BREEDING November–March. Nest is a tunnel drilled into a termite mound on the forest floor, usually 35–50 cm above ground. The nest chamber is left unlined. Usually three to four white, rounded eggs are laid.

RANGE Coastal north-eastern Queensland; Cape York almost to Townsville. Species in New Guinea. Migratory.

STATUS Locally common. Endemic breeding subspecies.

▶ **See also pages**
87 90 97 98

BEE-EATERS

Meropidae Family of 24 species
1 in Australia, 1 breeding

Colourful, active, with acrobatic flight in pursuit of insects. Bodies slender; bills moderately long and downcurved. Tails quite long with central pair of feathers narrow and longer; wings slender, pointed. Legs are very short and feet small and slender with forward toes fused together. Plumages are colourful, usually predominantly green with patches of red, blue and yellow. Food consists of flying insects, including some bees, taken in flight.

RAINBOW BEE-EATER

Merops ornatus   Meropidae

OTHER NAMES Rainbowbird, Gold-digger, Gold-miner, Spinetail, Kingfisher

RECOGNITION Australia's only species of bee-eater. Colourful, noisy, actively twists and turns in pursuit of flying insects, showing orange underwings. This bird is generally well known. Mostly bright green, with golden-bronze crown and throat. Long, sharp, slightly downcurved black bill, the line of which continues as a bold black eye-stripe, with a second black stripe across the throat. Central two tail feathers extended, spine-like; shorter on female. 23 cm.

VOICE A high, rolling, persistent yet pleasant 'pirrr-pirrr-pirrr-', usually given in flight, attracts attention to the wheeling and diving bird.

HABITAT Open country, including forest clearings, and usually where there is loamy soil suitable for the excavation of the nest tunnel.

BREEDING September–November in south; September–October and May–July in north. This species is a regular breeding migrant to southern Australia, arriving September–October and departing March–April after breeding. Nest is a tunnel into a bank or flat ground. Three to seven white eggs.

332 **RAINBOW BEE-EATER** *Merops ornatus*

RANGE Almost throughout mainland Australia in suitable open habitat. Migrates to New Guinea and other northern islands.

STATUS Common.

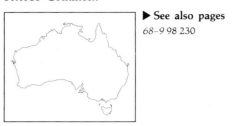

▶ **See also pages**
68–9 98 230

▶ **See also pages**
196 331

▶ **See also pages**
101 104–5 107

ROLLERS

Coraciidae Family of 17 species
1 in Australia, 1 breeding

Robust, colourful birds which are named for their tumbling and rolling display flights. They are of medium size, with large heads, short necks, short wide bills, very short legs and small weak feet. Tails are long, often forked and with the outermost feathers greatly extended on some species. Plumage colours include both bright and darker colours. Most species are noisy, conspicuous and aggressive. Nests are in hollows of trees.

333 DOLLARBIRD

Eurystomus orientalis   Coraciidae

OTHER NAMES Broad-billed Roller, Roller, Starbird

RECOGNITION Quite large and dumpy; large-headed appearance; overall greenish plumage, blending to brown on head; broad red bill; small red feet. The wings are green, with blue-black flight feathers. Back and underparts olive; a deep violet-blue patch on the brownish throat; tail dark blue. In flight, conspicuous large bluish-white spot (silver dollar) on underside of dark-blue underwing; swooping, looping or rolling flight. 28–30 cm.

VOICE A loud rasping 'kaak-kaak-kak-kak-ak-akakak', becoming more rapid, usually while in flight. Especially noisy during courtship, September–November.

HABITAT Margins of rainforests, and dense riverside vegetation, tropical woodlands, clearings and regrowth areas of forests, wooded farmlands, suburbs.

BREEDING October–January. Uses a hollow of a tree, usually high. Three to five oval, glossy white eggs are laid on the wood-dust of the hollow. The nest territory is vigorously defended. Breeds in Australia; winters in New Guinea.

RANGE Northern and eastern Australia; infrequently to semi-arid interior. Non-breeding visitor to northern islands. Migratory.

STATUS Common. Endemic subspecies.

PITTAS

Pittidae Family of 28 species
4 in Australia, 3 breeding, 1 endemic
Sibley-Ahlquist: Family Pittidae

Small, very brightly coloured, plump-bodied, with very short tails and short wings; relatively large, robust legs and feet. Pittas are secretive inhabitants of tropical and subtropical rainforests, monsoon scrubs and mangroves; much more frequently heard than seen. They feed on the forest floor, finding insects and snails among litter, but readily fly up if alarmed, or to call from high perches. Nests are bulky, domed, on or near the ground.

334 RED-BELLIED PITTA

Pitta erythrogaster   Pittidae

OTHER NAMES Blue-breasted Pitta, Macklot's Pitta

RECOGNITION A spectacularly colourful pitta. Head very dark brown, becoming dull dark red on the nape; dark green-blue on the back; purplish-blue on the shoulders, rump and tail. Underparts, throat black; wide bright blue breastband, separated by a thin black band from vivid scarlet of belly, flanks and undertail-coverts. Flight feathers black, with concealed white central wing patch. Usually on ground, but often calls from trees. 17–19 cm.

VOICE A mournful whistle, of four notes, with last two notes drawn-out: 'quor-a, quorr-aa', or 'kar-a, kaar-raa', perhaps a slightly rasping quality.

HABITAT Tropical rainforests, monsoon scrubs, low dense closed-canopy scrub, where it seeks ground-dwelling invertebrates among the leaf-litter.

BREEDING October–January. Nest is placed in a tangle of vines, in the hollowed top of a stump, or between buttress roots of a tree; a substantial domed structure of sticks, leaves. Three to four pale buff eggs, marked purple-brown and blue-grey.

RANGE East coast; Cape York south to McIlwraith Range. Migrant; present October–April. Subspecies also in New Guinea.

STATUS Uncommon.

335 NOISY PITTA

Pitta versicolor   Pittidae

OTHER NAMES Anvilbird, Dragoonbird, Painted Thrush, Buff-breasted Pitta

RECOGNITION Best-known pitta; loud call a common sound of eastern rainforests. Colourful: crown deep chestnut; face, nape and throat black; back and wings olive-green becoming a brighter turquoise-green on the shoulders. Breast, flanks and belly bright mustard-yellow or rich buff; undertail-coverts deep pink. Tail very short, black with dark-green tip. Flight feathers black, with concealed white bar. Forages actively in leaf-litter of forest floor. 18–20 cm.

VOICE A strong call, carries far through the forest; well described by the words 'walk to work', the last uplifting. Also, a single mournful note.

HABITAT Rainforests, from sea level to 1500 m altitude, and in some places extending into adjoining wet eucalypt forests, woodlands, mangroves.

BREEDING October–January, and sometimes August–March. Nest domed, of bulky loose construction using sticks, fronds, leaves, bark, lined with plant fibres, feathers, with ramp to the side entrance. Three to five white eggs, spotted greys and browns.

RANGE Eastern Australia; coast and nearby ranges. Some Cape York birds winter in New Guinea. Migratory, mostly locally.

STATUS Moderately common.

▶ **See also pages**
53 54 81 105 111
121 127

336 RAINBOW PITTA

Pitta iris   Pittidae

OTHER NAME Black-breasted Pitta

RECOGNITION Underparts entirely black except vent and undertail-coverts bright scarlet. Head and neck also black except for a red-brown streak on each side of the crown. Back and wings bright olive-green, with a patch of glossy light blue on each shoulder and on the rump. The only other pitta to occur within the range of this species is the Blue-winged Pitta (*Pitta moluccensis*), a very rare vagrant, which has a whitish throat.

VOICE A loud, clear deep whistle of two or three notes, similar to call of the Noisy

Pitta, a drawn-out 'want a whip', more often in breeding season.

HABITAT Patches of rainforests or monsoon forests (jungles), vine-scrub thickets, riverine forests, bamboo thickets, usually swampy; also mangroves.

BREEDING December–March. The nest is usually a large domed structure, but sometimes lacking part or most of hood. Construction is of quite large sticks, leaves; on ground, or up to 3 m above. Three to four creamy eggs, with grey and sepia blotches.

RANGE Coastal north-western Kimberley and north of Top End (NT). Probably sedentary.

STATUS Moderately common. Endemic.

► **See also pages**
7 81 191 *193* 196
197 209

► **See also pages**
7 81 191 *193* 196
197 209

LYREBIRDS

**Menuridae Family of 2 species
2 in Australia, endemic family
Sibley-Ahlquist: Family Menuridae,
Subfamily Menurinae**

A unique and famous Australian family of very large songbirds with extremely long, lyre-shaped tails. The two species both inhabit dense wet forests, where they scratch among litter with powerful feet. Males perform displays, accompanied by superb powerful song, on prepared mounds or scrapes on the forest floor. Origins are uncertain; their closest allies, on biochemical evidence, appear to be the bowerbirds and birds of paradise.

337 ALBERT'S LYREBIRD

Menura alberti   Menuridae

OTHER NAMES Northern Lyrebird, Prince Albert's Lyrebird

RECOGNITION Resembles the well-known Superb Lyrebird, but is smaller, and of richer, darker chestnut coloration, except the breast and abdomen which are buffy-grey; undertail-coverts chestnut. The long tail of the male lacks the wide lyre-shaped outer feathers of the Superb Lyrebird. The tail is made up of 14 lacy filamentary feathers, and two longer, dark ribbon-like plumes that cross near their tips. Female and immatures: shorter tails. 75–90 cm.

VOICE Male has a powerful, far-carrying song, with mellow and ringing notes, mimicry; alarm call a high shriek. Female also mimics.

HABITAT Rainforest, or mixed eucalypt forest and rainforest where there is dense low cover, sometimes lantana. Feeds on

insects, snails, earthworms.

BREEDING A winter breeder, usually June–August. Nest is tucked between buttress roots or boulders. It is a bulky domed structure of sticks, bark, fronds; lined with feathers, many rufous. One purple-brown egg, marked black.

RANGE Very restricted; south-eastern Queensland, north-eastern New South Wales. Sedentary.

STATUS Generally scarce; locally quite common. Endemic.

► **See also pages**
114–15 *117* 120
121

► **See also pages**
114–15 *117* 120
121

338 SUPERB LYREBIRD

Menura novaehollandiae   Menuridae

OTHER NAMES Lyrebird, Lyretail, Native Pheasant, Queen Victoria's Lyrebird

RECOGNITION Plain, dark, grey-brown upperparts; coppery on the wings; rufous about the throat; pale grey-brown underparts. Tail of male long and trailing, or, in display, widely fanned, lyre-like. The tail consists of two outer lyrates that are dark above, silvery below with rufous notch-markings; between these are 12 fine lacy silvery feathers, and two long slender plumes. Tail of female shorter (though still very long), of 14 simple brown feathers. 85 cm–1 m.

VOICE The call or alarm is a loud shriek. In full song can be heard from afar, a long-continued succession of rich clear notes, including mimicry.

HABITAT On the Australian mainland it inhabits rainforest and eucalypt forest; in Tasmania, where it is introduced, is established in rainforest.

BREEDING May–October; but usually June–July. The nest is a large dome of sticks, ferns and moss, lined with feathers. May be built on ground, rock ledge, stump or crown of a tree-fern. The single egg is purplish-brown, marked blackish.

RANGE Coastal south-eastern Australia; Dandenong (Vic), to south-eastern Queensland. Sedentary.

STATUS Common. Endemic species of endemic family.

► **See also pages**
115 *117* 118 121
122 123 124 126

► **See also pages**
115 *117* 118 121
122 123 124 126

SCRUB-BIRDS

**Atrichornithidae Family of 2 species
2 in Australia, endemic family
Sibley-Ahlquist: Family Menuridae,
Subfamily Atrichornithinae**

Thought to be a primitive family now bordering upon extinction, the two species occupying widely separated pockets of suitable habitat. On anatomical grounds they have been considered to be closest to the lyrebirds. Both are small and plump; with moderately long tails that are sometimes cocked upwards; large powerful legs and feet; short rounded wings; dominantly brown and rufous plumage, and exceptionally loud calls.

339 RUFOUS SCRUB-BIRD

Atrichornis rufescens   Atrichornithidae

OTHER NAMES Mockingbird, Mousebird, Mysterybird

RECOGNITION Extremely difficult to sight, keeping on or very close to the ground beneath dense cover. Upperparts, including the long tail, rufous-brown with fine black barring. Throat whitish, with some blackish mottling down the centre onto the breast; rest of underparts buff, becoming rufous towards rear of flanks and undertail-coverts. Female lacks black on the breast, which is more buffy-yellow; even more secretive than the male. 16–19 cm.

VOICE Extremely powerful, usually a rhythmic ringing 'chip-chip-chip-', beginning slowly, accelerating. In alarm, a scolding 'churr-' and 'zzit'.

HABITAT Rainforest and adjacent eucalypt forest where undergrowth is most dense, moist; especially where breaks in canopy allow lush low-level growth.

BREEDING September–November. The nest is of globular shape, with side entrance; built of interlaced broad grasses, fern fronds, dry leaves, and lined with a hard cardboard-like layer of wood-pulp. Two pale pink eggs, lightly spotted brownish.

RANGE Restricted; south-eastern Queensland, and north-eastern New South Wales; now on uplands only. Sedentary.

STATUS Rare, but moderately common in optimum sites. Endemic.

► **See also pages**
9 52 116 *116* 120
121 127 235 336

► **See also pages**
9 52 116 *116* 120
121 127 235 336

340 **NOISY SCRUB-BIRD**

Atrichornis clamosus Atrichornithidae

OTHER NAME Western Scrub-bird

RECOGNITION Like the Rufous Scrub-bird, it is extremely elusive, keeping beneath dense rushy cover. Upperparts dark brown; throat and breast dull white; undertail-coverts buffy-yellow. Upper breast black, extending upwards in the centre to divide the white of the throat into the two side streaks. The tail is long; wings stubby, rounded; eye dark brown. Female: smaller, without black on breast or throat; silent and seldom seen except at nest. 22–25 cm.

VOICE Exceptionally powerful, penetrating call; notes clear, often melodious, a ringing 'chip' or 'cheap', rising to crescendo. Mimicry doubtful or unusual.

HABITAT Dense low scrub, rushes, sawgrass of swamp and stream margins of wetter jarrah-marri; now only known in coastal gullies, swamp and lake edges.

BREEDING May–September. Nest is large, dome-shaped, built of rushes, and some leaves and twigs; usually well hidden in rushes, or in tangle of low shrubbery. The lining is a plaster of decayed rushes. The one egg is buff, marked orange-brown.

RANGE Known only from one small area of the south coast of Western Australia. Sedentary.

STATUS Generally very rare; common within reserves. Endemic.

▶ See also pages
116 235 239–40
239 245

346 **TREE MARTIN** *Cecropis nigricans*

LARKS

Alaudidae Family of 75 species
2 in Australia, 2 breeding,
1 introduced
Sibley-Ahlquist: Family Alaudidae

Small songbirds of grassland and savannah-woodland environs; principally ground birds, with camouflage plumage of browns, greys and blackish tones, sometimes with richer colours that show only in flight. The soaring display flights are conspicuous, with outpourings of loud rich song. The larks have crown feathers that can be raised in a low rounded crest. Bills are short and stout; legs quite long; and the hind toes very long.

341 **SINGING BUSHLARK**

Mirafra javanica Alaudidae

OTHER NAMES Australian Skylark, Brown Skylark, Brown Fieldlark, Horsfield's Bushlark

RECOGNITION Plumage colour variable, but patterns are consistent. Upperparts brownish, varying sandy to blackish-brown, and broadly mottled or streaked darker; the paler edges of the wing feathers form a strong pattern. Underparts fawn to pale rufous; breast speckled or streaked brown. In flight, shows rufous wing-patch, and white-edged tail. In breeding season performs song flights, rising high to hover while singing loudly. 12–15 cm.

VOICE A rich and varied song; in flight or from elevated perch. Song is interwoven with shrill trilling and rich melodious sounds, including mimicry.

HABITAT Open country, including tussock grassland, crops, open woodlands and scrublands with grassy ground-cover, saltbush plains.

BREEDING All months; usually September–December. Nest well concealed among tussocks, often set in a slight depression in the ground; cup-shaped, usually hooded. Two to four dull white eggs, finely speckled grey, lavender and brown.

RANGE Throughout Australia except south-west, western interior, and tip of Cape York Peninsula. Also in New Guinea and Asia. Nomadic or migratory.

STATUS Generally uncommon, but common locally.

▶ See also pages
29–30 29 223

342 **SKYLARK**

Alauda arvensis Alaudidae

OTHER NAMES Common Skylark, English Skylark

RECOGNITION Similar but larger and overall paler than the Singing Bushlark. Upperparts pale brown, with strong black, central streaks to the feathers, giving a mottled appearance. On the side of face is a distinctive fawn eyebrow line that extends back and curves down to encircle a brown ear-patch. Feathers of crown often raised as a low rounded crest. Underparts buff, with upper breast streaked brown. Tail moderately long, forked, edged white. *Introduced species*. 17–19 cm.

VOICE A clear and very attractive song, musical, high-pitched, lengthy outpourings of rich sound, often in steep upwards flight; also a 'chirrup'.

HABITAT Open country, including pastures and other short-grassed areas, heathlands, swamp margins; sometimes seashores and coastal dunes.

BREEDING August–February; mainly September–December. The cup-shaped nest of dry grass is tucked into a small depression in the ground under cover of a clump of grass. Three to five dull white eggs, densely speckled and blotched brown.

RANGE South-eastern Australia, including Tasmania. Native to Eurasia, Africa. Nomadic or partially migratory.

STATUS Common in south-east. Introduced species.

▶ See also page
118

SWALLOWS, MARTINS

Hirundinidae Family of 75 species
6 in Australia, 4 breeding, 1 endemic
Sibley-Ahlquist: Family Hirundinidae

Small songbirds well adapted for hawking insects. Bodies are slender, streamlined; wings long, pointed, backswept; tails often forked. Although resembling swifts they are not closely related, nor as perfectly adapted to aerial life. The names 'swallow' and 'martin' are more or less synonymous. Plumages are mainly blackish above, white beneath, with variation in reddish and white patches. Bills are small, wide-gaped; feet very small.

WHITE-BACKED SWALLOW

Cheramoeca leucosternum Hirundinidae
OTHER NAMES Black-and-white Swallow, White-breasted Swallow, White-capped Swallow

RECOGNITION Has a cleanly clear-cut black-and-white appearance. Plumage entirely black except for white crown, throat and upper back. The top of the white crown-patch and the nape are mottled brown. Tail deeply forked. Bill black; eye dark brown. Usually in small groups hawking over open areas, with fluttering, irregular flight. Sun catches brightly upon white of back and throat. Takes insects in flight. 12–15 cm.

VOICE In flight, a short sharp 'chip' or 'jk-jk'; also has an attractive twittering song.

HABITAT Open areas, mainly inland but coastal in drier regions; usually where sandy or loamy soils. Open woodlands and scrublands, heathlands.

BREEDING Recorded most months; usually June–December. The only Australian swallow to burrow into ground. May nest singly or colonially; in sandy or soft loamy banks. Builds sparse nest of grass, leaves, in tunnel. Four to six white eggs.

RANGE Throughout Australia except Top End (NT) and north-eastern Queensland. Locally nomadic.

STATUS Common; sparse towards the north. Endemic species and genus.

▶ See also pages
136 138 173 *174*
183

BARN SWALLOW

Hirundo rustica Hirundinidae
OTHER NAMES European Swallow, Chimney Swallow

RECOGNITION Resembles the Welcome Swallow, but with a black breastband separating the chestnut of the throat from the white of the remainder of the underparts. Upperparts glossy blue-black; tail deeply forked. 16–17 cm.

VOICE Weak, pleasant twittering and soft warbling sounds.

HABITAT Open country, near water. In towns often perches on overhead wires.

BREEDING Breeds in Northern Hemisphere; spends the non-breeding northern winter months in South-East Asia, with some individuals and small flocks, occasionally larger flocks to 300 birds, reaching Australia; often with other swallows, swifts.

RANGE In Australia, regular visitor Kimberley to north-eastern Queensland; vagrant to south-east. Also in Europe and Asia.

STATUS Generally scarce; occasionally locally common.

▶ See also pages
202 *209* 210

WELCOME SWALLOW

Hirundo neoxena Hirundinidae
OTHER NAMES Australian Swallow, House Swallow, Swallow

RECOGNITION The well-known swallow of verandahs and sheds. Upperparts black with metallic blue sheen; flight feathers and tail brownish-black. Forehead, face and throat light chestnut or tan, merging to dull white on breast, belly and undertail-coverts. Tail deeply forked, with a row of white spots near ends of inner-tail feathers. In flight, upperparts entirely blackish; underwings brown; no black under body, which is dull white, with chestnut throat. 15 cm.

VOICE In flight, a 'chek', and a high-pitched 'tseet' alarm. While perched, soft twittering and warbling notes are strung together as a song.

HABITAT Almost universal except heavily forested and very arid environs. Now often uses man-made structures for perching, roosting.

BREEDING Recorded all months; mainly June–January. In natural environs uses ledges of caves, cavities of trees; now often beams of verandas, bridges, for feather-lined cup nest of mud. Two to five white eggs, spotted red-brown and lavender.

RANGE Southern and eastern Australia; vagrant to north. Self-introduced to New Zealand. Migratory, at least partially.

STATUS Common in south; sparse in north. Endemic.

▶ See also pages
142 202 *331*

TREE MARTIN

Cecropis nigricans Hirundinidae
OTHER NAMES Tree-swallow, Australian Tree-martin

RECOGNITION Upperparts black with a strong blue sheen, except for a small chestnut patch on the forehead, and dull white rump. The black of the crown extends down onto the cheeks, giving a black-headed appearance. Throat grey; rest of underparts dull white. Tail only slightly forked, black. Immatures: browner, streaked light brown on the breast. Flight erratic, with quick, clipped wingbeats. Sometimes gathers in large companies. 12–14 cm.

VOICE A sound described as a dry little 'drrrt-drrrt' and various animated twittering sounds.

HABITAT Prefers a situation not far from water, sometimes in arid areas. Usually in open country with trees; large companies may roost in reed-beds.

BREEDING July–January, but recorded all other months. Uses small hollows in limbs and trunks of trees; big dead trees may hold dozens of nests. The hollow is lined with grass and leaves. Three to five pinkish-white eggs, speckled pinkish-brown.

RANGE Throughout Australia in suitable habitat. Also in New Guinea and other islands to the north. Partially migratory.

STATUS Very common.

▶ See also pages
142 202 *331* 336

FAIRY MARTIN

Cecropis ariel Hirundinidae
OTHER NAMES Cliff Swallow, Land Swallow, Bottle Swallow, Retort Swallow

RECOGNITION Similar to the Tree Martin, but with crown rust-red instead of black; cleaner white on rump and underparts. Back and scapulars black with blue sheen; wings and tail brownish-black; underparts white; eye dark brown; bill and legs black. When in flight can be hard to separate from Tree Martin unless colour of upperparts can be seen. Usually in companies, hawking insects over water, often tipping the surface. 13 cm.

VOICE High-pitched twitterings, or churring high 'drrt-drrt'; voice similar but higher-pitched than Tree Martin.

HABITAT Open country, often near water, and in breeding season at suitable breeding sites, shallow caves, overhanging creek-banks, treetrunks.

BREEDING July–December, but recorded all months. The Fairy Martin is the only Australian bird with bottle-shaped mud nest, built up of small pellets. Nests of colony usually densely packed. Four to five white eggs, finely freckled reddish-brown.

RANGE Throughout Australia, but rare in Cape York, south-western Australia, and Tasmania; migrant to south August–April.

STATUS Common throughout main range. Endemic.

▶ See also pages
173 *175* 202

PIPITS, WAGTAILS

Motacillidae Family of 54 species
5 in Australia, 1 breeding
Sibley-Ahlquist: Family Ploceidae,
Subfamily Motacillinae

A large and ubiquitous family that is very poorly represented in Australia. Pipits are ground-dwelling birds with longish bills and legs, and the habit of teetering the rear of the body up and down. They are more noticeable in the breeding season, when they make display flights and call from perches. The wagtails are non-breeding visitors or rare vagrants to Australia. Their identification in non-breeding plumage can be difficult.

348 RICHARD'S PIPIT

Anthus novaeseelandiae   Motacillidae
OTHER NAMES Indian Pipit, New Zealand Pipit, Australian Pipit, Groundlark

RECOGNITION Upperparts mottled brown and buff; underparts buffy-white or off-white; fawn along flanks, and breast which is streaked darker brown. Distinctive facial markings are the pale buff eyebrow line, and the fine dark lines from the base of the bill, down the sides of the throat, and just under the eye. Bill slender, pale brown; legs long and pale pinkish-brown. White-edged tail constantly, restlessly teetered up and down. 17–19 cm.

VOICE Call is shrill or thin 'tsweep', and cheery 'chirrup'. Courting male has song flight, undulating upwards with quavering notes.

HABITAT Grasslands, clearings, grassy woodlands, open semi-arid scrublands and gibber plains, beaches and hind-dunes, grassy roadsides.

BREEDING Recorded most months; usually August–December. Nest is a deep cup built into a depression in the ground under the shelter of a clump of grass or rock. Three to four buffy-white to pale brown eggs, spotted and clouded with grey and browns.

RANGE Throughout Australia. Widespread Europe, Africa, Asia, New Zealand. Usually sedentary, but partially migratory or nomadic.

STATUS Common; locally abundant.

▶ See also pages
141 151 174 179

349 YELLOW WAGTAIL

Motacilla flava   Motacillidae
OTHER NAME Barnard's Wagtail

RECOGNITION Pipit-like, but with longer tail; restless bobbing. Two subspecies reach Australia, and are similar. Upperparts grey-brown, underparts buff, pale eyebrow line. Wing feathers dark brown edged buff to off-white. Tail quite long, black, edged white. In breeding plumage, upperparts olive-green, underparts bright light yellow, white or pale yellow eyebrow line; crown and face olive or grey. Females: duller. Immatures: browner, with underparts whitish. 17–19 cm.

VOICE A shrill, slurred 'zweep, zweep'; song is a brief trilling 'tsip-tsip, tip-tip-tsipsip'. Invariably calls before taking flight.

HABITAT Wet and damp areas, margins of swamps, drains, moist pastures and ploughed lands, irrigated crops, bore drains.

BREEDING Non-breeding visitor to Australia; usually November–February, but occasional records for other months, including June, April.

RANGE Most sightings in Kimberley, Top End (NT). Quite regular visitor to far north; rare vagrant to south-east and south-west. Also in Europe, Africa, Asia, Indonesia, New Guinea.

STATUS Scarce.

▶ See also pages
202 *209* 210

CUCKOO-SHRIKES, TRILLERS

Campephagidae Family of 72 species
7 in Australia, 7 breeding, 1 endemic
Sibley-Ahlquist: Family Corvidae,
Subfamily Corvinae, Tribe Oriolini

Not related to cuckoos or shrikes, but named for the general resemblance in body shape and flight to some cuckoos, and for the shrike-like bills. These arboreal, insectivorous birds have long pointed wings and long graduated tails. Plumages are usually in soft greys and browns, some barred beneath. Most shuffle the wings after alighting. The trillers are smaller, with crisp black-and-white plumage, and superb sustained song.

350 BLACK-FACED CUCKOO-SHRIKE

Coracina novaehollandiae Campephagidae
OTHER NAMES Blue Jay, Bluebird, Cherry Hawk, Shufflewing, Summerbird, Grey Jay

RECOGNITION A familiar bird throughout Australia. Overall plumage colour light blue-grey (very light neutral grey, coastal Western Australia); whitish underparts. Clearly-defined black forehead, face and throat. Flight feathers black, edged pale grey. Immatures: black face reduced to

350 **BLACK-FACED CUCKOO-SHRIKE** *Coracina novaehollandiae*

broad black line through the eye; when very young have finely barred forehead, breast. Species has undulating flight, and habit of repeatedly refolding wings after landing. 30–35 cm.

VOICE Usual call a musical churring, and a 'chereer-chereer', often while wing-shuffling, courting and perched; also a harsh 'skiair'.

HABITAT A great variety of country, but usually quite open; woodlands and scrublands, open forests, farmlands, parks and gardens.

BREEDING Recorded most months, but usually August–January. Nest is small for size of bird; neatly blended onto a horizontal limb or fork; built of grasses, bound with webs. Two to three greenish to brownish eggs, marked with greys and browns.

RANGE Throughout Australia in suitable habitat. Also in New Guinea and other northern islands. Partially migratory.

STATUS Very common.

▶ See also pages
142 *338*

WHITE-BELLIED CUCKOO-SHRIKE

Coracina papuensis　　Campephagidae

OTHER NAMES Little Cuckoo-shrike, White-breasted Cuckoo-shrike, Papuan Cuckoo-shrike

RECOGNITION Plumage dominantly pale grey; white underparts (subspecies *hypoleuca*), or with breast darker grey, size larger (subspecies *robusta*). Black facial mark on lores, from base of black bill back to include eye. A dark form of the subspecies *robusta* has head, neck and upper breast dusky black to a variable extent. Flight feathers blackish, light-edged; tail black, tipped white, slightly forked. Immatures: head and underparts mottled grey and brown. 26–28 cm.

VOICE Peevish 'kisseek, kisseek', or 'quizeek', often while in flight; also various churring sounds, 'que-urrk-quee-urrk'.

HABITAT Found in a wide variety of vegetation types; rainforests and eucalypt forests, open woodlands, mangroves, plantations.

BREEDING Usually August–January; recorded July–March. Nest is a shallow saucer of grass and other fine materials, bound with webs, blended inconspicuously into a high horizontal fork. Two to three greenish eggs, with grey and brown markings.

RANGE Northern, eastern, south-eastern Australia; not in Tasmania or arid interior. Also in New Guinea and other northern islands. Locally nomadic.

STATUS Common in north; less common in south.

▶ See also pages
208 *331*

352　YELLOW-EYED CUCKOO-SHRIKE

Coracina lineata　　Campephagidae

OTHER NAMES Swainson's Cuckoo-shrike, Barred Cuckoo-shrike

RECOGNITION A small cuckoo-shrike with distinctive and cuckoo-like appearance. Plumage dark grey except for underparts, from breast to undertail-coverts, narrowly but conspicuously crossbarred black and white. Face dark; bill and lores black, with bright yellow eye. Wing quills black-edged; legs black. Similar to Oriental Cuckoo, but with longer tail, bolder barring, yellow legs and eye-ring. 24–29 cm.

VOICE A quite pleasant sound with quality likened to mouth-organ brassy or nasal tones, often in flight, 'aww-loo-ak', 'aw-ak'; also single 'whaan'.

HABITAT Both rainforest and eucalypt forest, including areas of regrowth, woodlands, swamp-woodlands, plantations, gardens. Feeds on insects and fruits.

BREEDING Usually October–February, but recorded September–April. Although very sociable, colonial nesting has not been reported. Nest in a high position; a shallow saucer of fine materials, bound with webs. Two whitish eggs, spotted grey, olive, brown.

RANGE North-eastern Australia; Cape York to north-eastern New South Wales. Also in New Guinea and other northern islands. Sedentary; often locally nomadic.

STATUS Generally uncommon; scarce in New South Wales.

▶ See also pages
90 *93*

353　CICADABIRD

Coracina tenuirostris　　Campephagidae

OTHER NAMES Jardine Triller, Caterpillar-eater, Jardine Caterpillar-eater

RECOGNITION A small, almost overall dark slaty blue-grey cuckoo-shrike, with black on the face from base of bill to ear-coverts. Wing-coverts and flight feathers black, edged slate-grey; underwing-coverts blue-grey. Tail has two central feathers blue-grey tipped black, the rest black with lighter tips; slightly forked. Female and immatures: grey-brown upperparts; creamy-buff underparts with broken brown barrings to sides of neck, breast; pale eye-brow. 24–27 cm.

VOICE Usually silent, male noisy in breed-ing season with sounds like a cicada, a harsh, often-repeated staccato buzzing; various other calls.

HABITAT In northern Australia, in rain-forest strips along creeks, mangroves, paperbark and eucalypt woodlands; in the south-east, in eucalypt forests and woodlands.

BREEDING October–April; records August–June. Nest is blended into a horizontal fork; built of fine twigs, casuarina 'leaves', bark; bound with webs, decorated with lichens. One pale blue-grey to grey-green egg, marked in grey, lavender, brown.

RANGE Northern and eastern Australia, mainly coastal. Also in New Guinea, south-west Pacific, Celebes. Migratory to south-east about October–March.

STATUS Uncommon; localized.

▶ See also pages
209 *331*

354　GROUND CUCKOO-SHRIKE

Coracina maxima　　Campephagidae

OTHER NAMES Ground Graculus, Ground Jay, Long-tailed Jay

RECOGNITION The largest of the cuckoo-shrikes, and the only species adapted for feeding mainly on the ground; relatively long-legged, slender-bodied. Head, upper back, throat and upper breast light silvery grey; darker from lores to ear-coverts. The wings and the slightly forked tail are black. Lower breast, belly, flanks, and rump white finely barred black; undertail-coverts and underwing pale silvery grey. Immatures: upperparts also barred. 33–36 cm.

VOICE In flight, a far-carrying 'pee-ew, pee-ew', and metallic, ringing 'chill-chill, chillink, chillink'.

HABITAT Open eucalypt woodland, semi-arid woodland, open mallee, mulga, native pine, spinifex. Often feeding on ground in pairs, small parties.

BREEDING August–November; recorded July–February. Nest is a shallow bowl of grasses, plant-down, wool and other fine materials, bound with webs, blended into a horizontal fork. Two to three pale olive eggs, plain, or marked red-brown and black.

RANGE Throughout inland Australia and to drier parts of coast. Nomadic.

STATUS Generally uncommon. Endemic.

▶ See also pages
137 *180 183*

WHITE-WINGED TRILLER

355

Lalage sueurii   Campephagidae

OTHER NAMES Jardine Caterpillar-eater, White-shouldered Caterpillar-eater, Peewee Lark

RECOGNITION Smaller and more lively, but retaining a likeness to the larger species of cuckoo-shrikes. Male in breeding plumage has a clear-cut black-and-white plumage pattern; upperparts black, undersurfaces white. On the head the black just includes the eyes, leaving lower face, chin, and sides of neck white. Conspicuous white shoulders and edges to feathers of wing-coverts. Non-breeding plumage: upperparts brown. Female and immatures similar; buff markings on head, wings. 18 cm.

VOICE In breeding, male has loud spirited territorial song; in flight, from high perches and from nest, an attractive, ringing and varied trilling.

HABITAT Open country, including eucalypt woodlands, arid woodlands, mulga and mallee scrublands, spinifex, heath-woodlands, farmlands.

BREEDING September–February; but recorded most months. Nest is cup-shaped, appears small for the bird; blended onto a horizontal branch or fork; built of fine grasses, rootlets, bark, bound with webs. Two to three green eggs, streaked and blotched brown.

RANGE Throughout Australia in suitable habitat; vagrant to Tasmania. Summer migrant to south. Also in New Guinea, Sunda Islands, Java, Celebes.

STATUS Common.

▶ See also pages
41 *41* 173

VARIED TRILLER

356

Lalage leucomela   Campephagidae

OTHER NAMES Pied Triller, White-browed Triller, White-browed Caterpillar-eater

RECOGNITION A small species resembling White-winged Triller, but with much less white on shoulders, and a conspicuous white eyebrow line. Upperparts glossy black; rump grey; tail black, tipped white. Wings black with prominent white bars. Between white of face and eyebrow is a bold black line through eye. Underparts white, finely barred, with slight cinnamon wash, deeper on undertail-coverts. Female and immatures: dark brown upperparts; barred underparts. 18–20 cm.

VOICE Usual call is a distinctive churring trill, 'drr-eea, drr-eea', or 'brr-eer, bre-eer', repeatedly, with others taking up the call.

HABITAT Rainforest both tropical and subtropical, eucalypt forest and woodland, paperbark woodland and mangroves near rainforest.

BREEDING Usually September–December; recorded August–March. The nest is a very

small and shallow cup, blended into a fork, bound with webs, decorated with bark and lichens. The single egg is pale greenish, speckled chestnut and grey.

RANGE Northern and eastern Australia, mainly coastal; Kimberley to north-eastern New South Wales. Also in New Guinea and adjacent islands. Sedentary.

STATUS Common in north; sparse in New South Wales.

▶ See also pages
75 79 208 209

BULBULS

**Pycnonotidae Family of 109 species
1 in Australia, introduced
Sibley-Ahlquist: Family Pycnonotidae**

Small to medium-sized birds; noisy, gregarious and inquisitive; plumage of mostly plain colours, often dark about the head, which is sometimes crested. They have readily adapted to man's environment of cities, parks and gardens. Of the many species only one has become established in Australia.

RED-WHISKERED BULBUL

357

Pycnonotus jocosus   Pycnonotidae

RECOGNITION Head black with a pointed crest; cheeks and throat white with a fine, black dividing line between. Back and wings olive-brown to grey-brown; breast and belly grey-buff; undertail-coverts and a small patch behind the eye red. Tail blackish with white tips. *Introduced species.* 20 cm.

VOICE Melodic chirps and whistles.

HABITAT Urban areas and generally near human habitation, bush disturbed by man, gardens and orchards.

BREEDING July–March. The nest is a rough untidy cup of bark, leaves, twigs, rootlets, at heights to 3 m in dense vegetation. Two to four whitish eggs, marked reddish or purplish-brown.

RANGE Coastal New South Wales. Native to India, China, South-East Asia.

STATUS Common around Sydney. Introduced species.

FLYCATCHERS

**Muscicapidae Family of 400 species
54–56 in Australia, 53 breeding,
26 endemic
Sibley-Ahlquist: Family Corvidae,
Subfamilies Pachycephalinae and
Monarchinae**

A large assemblage of small to medium-sized insectivorous birds that is sometimes divided into a number of families, at other times into sub-families. Included are thrushes, robins, flycatchers, shrike-tits, whistlers, shrike-thrushes, and fantails, sometimes with others here listed as families. These birds have in common that many take insects on the wing, many are fine songsters, some have spotted juveniles.

AUSTRALIAN GROUND-THRUSH

358

Zoothera lunulata   Muscicapidae

OTHER NAMES Scaly Thrush, Mountain Thrush, Speckled Thrush, White's Thrush, Spotted Ground Thrush

RECOGNITION A large thrush with upperparts grey-brown to golden brown; whitish underparts except throat and upper breast which are light brown. Body feathers are heavily dark-edged, giving a scaly appearance; very conspicuous on white underparts as dark crescents. Tail dark brown with buff tip. White eye-ring and lores; bill black. Shows prominent light and dark bars along wing underside. Usually hunts quietly among leaf-litter. 25–29 cm.

VOICE Rarely heard; consists of two clear notes, which may continue as a weak but tuneful song. Heard usually at dawn, or in gloomy weather.

HABITAT Dense forest, where there is a moist leaf-litter layer; rainforest and eucalypt forest, woodlands, usually in shady gullies, sometimes gardens.

BREEDING Usually August–December; recorded July–March. Nest is a large cup-shaped structure, of bark strips, leaves, rootlets, decorated on the outside with green moss; in fork, or on a stump. Two to three pale green eggs, blotched red-brown.

RANGE Eastern and south-eastern Australia; mainly coast and ranges. Also in eastern Europe, Asia, Siberia, New Guinea. Sedentary or dispersive.

STATUS Common.

▶ See also pages
65 *65* 116 121 139
141 341

RUSSET-TAILED GROUND-THRUSH

Zoothera heinei   Muscicapidae

OTHER NAME Heine's Thrush

RECOGNITION Slightly smaller than Australian Ground-Thrush; more rufous especially on the rump and tail. The scaly markings are fainter, scarcely visible on the rump. Tail shorter, with a larger patch of white at the tip.

VOICE A double-noted whistle, 'theea-thooa'.

HABITAT Lowland forests, below 775 m altitude.

BREEDING Usually July–November; recorded June–December. Pale green or greenish-blue eggs, flecked grey and chestnut, slightly smaller than those of the Australian Ground-Thrush.

RANGE Mid-central New South Wales to north-eastern Queensland.

STATUS Common. Endemic.

▶ See also pages
65 116 *117* 121

NORTHERN SCRUB-ROBIN

Drymodes superciliaris   Muscicapidae

OTHER NAMES Papuan Scrub-robin, Eastern Scrub-robin

RECOGNITION A bird of unusual and distinctive appearance. Upperparts cinnamon brown; crown darker; rump rufous; tail dark brown with outer feathers rufous tipped white. Wings black, with two pale buff bars across the shoulders, and white edges to central tail feathers. Most distinctive feature is a bold black bar vertically through the eye, conspicuous on the fawn-white face. Underparts whitish; buff tone to breast and flanks. Long legs buff. 22 cm.

VOICE A drawn-out whistle, thin or piercing, often preceded by harsh scolding sounds. Some calls like those of the Southern Scrub-robin.

HABITAT Tropical rainforests and vine scrubs, where it feeds on insects and land snails among the leaf-litter; hops and bounces over forest floor.

BREEDING October–January. Nest is a shallow depression in the ground, usually at the foot of a shrub or tree, and lined with sticks, dead leaves, vine tendrils and bark fibres. Two white or pale grey eggs, blotched with grey and umber.

RANGE Cape York Peninsula, and Roper River area of Northern Territory. Sedentary.

STATUS Common locally in Cape York; status uncertain in Northern Territory. Endemic subspecies.

▶ See also pages
105 *107* 363

SOUTHERN SCRUB-ROBIN

Drymodes brunneopygia   Muscicapidae

OTHER NAMES Mallee Scrub-robin, Pale Scrub-robin

RECOGNITION A grey-brown bird, with a long tail that is often carried partly raised. Rump and tail rufous-brown; breast and flanks pale brown; undertail-coverts buff. On the face, slight but distinctive markings: whitish eye-ring, lores and chin, with a short indistinct vertical black bar through the eye. Two dull white wingbars, and some white along the primaries. Usually hopping among leaf-litter, or singing from a perch. When the scrub-robin lands it flicks its wings, lifts the tail. 23 cm.

VOICE Loud, far-carrying, musical calls, while perched on a bare stick or other vantage point, 'chip-pip-eree', or 'whip-whip, paree'; also scolding.

HABITAT Mallee, acacia scrub, broombush, heathlands and sandplains.

BREEDING July–October in west, September–January in east. Nest a shallow cup of bark and fine twigs, rimmed with sticks; on ground among twigs and leaf-litter, often by a bush or mallee. Usually one grey-green egg, spotted and blotched brown.

RANGE Two populations: south-western Australia; mallee of south-eastern Australia. Sedentary.

STATUS Uncommon. Endemic.

▶ See also pages
58 *59* 130 137 139
162 242

ROSE ROBIN

Petroica rosea   Muscicapidae

OTHER NAME Rose-breasted Robin

RECOGNITION Small, dark grey upperparts, becoming grey-brown on wings and tail, and extending beneath to chin and throat; small white forehead spot. Breast a deep rose pink, not extending to the abdomen. Remainder of underparts white. Outer-tail feathers white (Pink Robin has no white on tail). Female has white on tail, but buff forehead, two buff-white wingbars; underparts pale grey sometimes with touch of pink. Immatures like female. Unobtrusive, trusting, inquisitive. 10–12 cm.

VOICE A high-pitched trilling song, a weak but pleasant series of ticking sounds; harsher and louder when agitated.

HABITAT Rainforests, both subtropical and temperate, wet eucalypt forests, especially densely vegetated fern gullies.

BREEDING September–February. In north nests in higher-altitude rainforests; in south in heavy forests down to sea level. Nest a small deep cup of moss, softly lined, and camouflaged with lichens. Two to three pale greenish eggs, speckled brown, purple.

RANGE South-eastern Australia; forested coast, ranges. Dispersive or partially migratory.

STATUS Moderately common. Endemic.

▶ See also pages
80 *119* 123 124
126 127 139

PINK ROBIN

Petroica rodinogaster   Muscicapidae

OTHER NAMES Magenta-breasted Robin, Pink-breasted Robin

RECOGNITION Upperparts entirely sooty dark grey, looking dull black in shadowy forest lighting, and without any white on wings or tail; there is usually a very small white forehead spot. Throat dark grey; breast pink with magenta or violet tone extending, paler, to belly. Female: upperparts rich brown; darker on wings and tail; two conspicuous buff wingbars; no white on the tail. Underparts fawn; greyer on breast. Immatures similar to female. 12–13 cm.

VOICE Both sexes give a sharp 'tik-tik' like the snapping of a dry twig; may become a rapid sharp, scolding chatter. Male has low plaintive warble.

HABITAT Temperate rainforests, where adults, or at least the adult males, seem to remain, while brown birds disperse to open woodlands, farmlands.

BREEDING September–January; in densely vegetated rainforest gullies. Nest is a neat cup of moss bound with webs, decorated with pale green lichens, placed in a leafy shrub or tree-fern. Three to four white eggs, tinted green, speckled grey, brown.

RANGE Southern Victoria, Tasmania, Bass Strait islands. Dispersive or migratory.

STATUS Uncommon on mainland Australia; common in Tasmania. Endemic.

▶ See also pages
124 139 141 146
147 151 152 153

FLAME ROBIN

Petroica phoenicea   Muscicapidae

OTHER NAMES Robin Redbreast, Flame-breasted Robin, Bank Robin

RECOGNITION Slate-grey upperparts; white

spot on forehead; broad irregular white stripe down the wing; white outer-tail feathers. Underparts look almost entirely light flame red, from throat to centre of abdomen; more extensive than for any of the other red- or pink-breasted robins. The chin is grey; the lower abdomen and undertail white. Female: brown upperparts; darker wings, tail. Immatures similar to female; buff markings. 13 cm.

VOICE Male has a pleasant, faint high-pitched song, that continues on in lilting manner. Also a faint repeated ticking call.

HABITAT Forests, woodlands, of coast and ranges during breeding season; disperses for autumn and winter to open grasslands, farmlands.

BREEDING August–February; usually September–January; the later dates in alpine areas. Nest may be tucked behind a projecting piece of bark, into a hollow of a tree, crevice in rock, in creek-bank, or among tree roots. Three to four pale greenish eggs, spotted lilac, chestnut.

RANGE South-eastern Australia. Dispersive, and possible migration across Bass Strait.

STATUS Common. Endemic.

▶ See also pages
66 122 123 136
142 *148* 151 153

364 FLAME ROBIN *Petroica phoenicea*

365 SCARLET ROBIN

Petroica multicolor   Muscicapidae

OTHER NAMES Robin Redbreast, Scarlet-breasted Robin, White-capped Robin

RECOGNITION Generally common, well known. Upperparts, including head, throat, back, wings and tail are jet black, not brown-black or dark grey; and with very conspicuous broad white wingbar and forehead patch. (Most alike is the Flame Robin, greyer upperparts and flame red right up onto the throat.) Female is distinctive, grey where male is black, and with breast pink; white forehead spot; white wingbars and outer tail. Immatures similar to female; no pink. 12–14 cm.

VOICE Male has a pleasant musical trill, beginning with several short ticking sounds followed by an undulating sequence of higher notes.

HABITAT Forests and woodlands, usually of relatively open understorey, and often on ranges, foothills. After breeding, disperses to more open lowlands.

BREEDING July–January; often several broods. Nest an open cup of grass, bark, bound with webs; softly lined, and camouflaged with lichens. Situation and height variable. Three to four dull white eggs, heavily marked blue-grey, purple-brown.

RANGE South-eastern and south-western Australia, including Tasmania. Species to Solomon Islands, Fiji and Norfolk Island. Sedentary.

STATUS Moderately common. Endemic subspecies.

▶ See also pages
64 66

366 RED-CAPPED ROBIN

Petroica goodenovii   Muscicapidae

OTHER NAME Redhead

RECOGNITION A small robin, with large bright red cap over forehead and front of crown. Broad white wingstripe, and white-edged tail, otherwise upperparts dull warm black. Female pale brown upperparts; slightly darker on wings and tail; white wingstripe; white outer-tail feathers; whitish underparts, with grey-buff on the breast. Rusty-red forehead patch; whitish eye-ring. Immatures like female, no red on forehead; males slight pink on breast. 11–12 cm.

VOICE Distinctive ticking trill, a characteristic sound of the interior; two ticks, then faster: 'dit-dit-dirrr-it'. Also slow ticking, both sexes.

HABITAT Drier regions; typically a bird of arid and semi-arid scrublands, mulga, mallee, native pine, open woodland, sandplains, wheatbelt farmlands.

BREEDING July–December; in drier regions, almost any time after rain. Nest is a neat cup of grass, bark, with small pieces of bark and lichens attached. Two to four pale blue-green or grey-green eggs, heavily marked purplish-brown.

RANGE Throughout Australia except extreme south-east, tropical north, and Tasmania. Dispersive in non-breeding season.

STATUS Common. Endemic.

▶ See also pages
58 *58* 231 *246–7*

367 HOODED ROBIN

Melanodryas cucullata   Muscicapidae

OTHER NAMES Black Robin, Black-and-White Robin, Pied Robin

RECOGNITION Among robins, the male is distinctive, with a black hood over the entire head, neck, extending in a V onto the breast, and across the entire back, wings, tail. White on the wing usually shows as two white bars, the upper bar from the shoulder, when wing is folded. Outer-tail feathers white on the basal half. Most alike is Pied Honeyeater, which has longer, and downcurved bill. Female has black replaced by grey-brown; grey throat. 14–17 cm.

VOICE Usually quiet; in breeding season at least, a call with the first note sharp, followed by a series of mellow and slightly descending notes.

HABITAT Dry habitats, open woodlands, inland scrubs including mallee, acacia scrub, occasionally clearings of heavier forests.

BREEDING July–December in south; March–April in north, variable after rain in the interior. Nest a solid cup of bark, grass, bound with webs; placed in a fork, hollow, or crevice of shrub or tree. Two to three pale greenish eggs, brownish on larger end.

RANGE Throughout Australia except north-eastern Queensland, Tasmania. Sedentary or locally nomadic.

STATUS Moderately common. Endemic.

▶ See also pages
123 136 146 *184*

368 DUSKY ROBIN

Melanodryas vittata   Muscicapidae

OTHER NAMES Stump Robin, Wood Robin, Dozey Robin, Sad Robin

RECOGNITION A very plainly plumaged robin; olive-brown upperparts, wings darker and with small patches of white in the centre and at the edge of the shoulder. Tail darker brown, edged buffy-white. Underparts dull white, tinted olive-buff on throat, sides of breast, and on flanks. Female plainer. Immatures: streaked upperparts, mottled darker underparts. This robin consistently chooses areas of stumps, fallen logs, where it sits motionless, scanning the ground. 16.5 cm.

VOICE A quite strong and far-carrying low double whistle, repeated often and more lively in spring, 'choowee-chooweer'; also various subdued notes.

HABITAT Forest edges, woodlands, particularly with stumps, fallen timber; clearings, fence-lines. When it flies, the Dusky Robin shows white on outer wings.

BREEDING July–December. Nest is tucked into a cavity of a stump, side of a treetrunk, behind detached bark, or fork.

Construction is of grasses, rootlets, bark. Three to four greenish eggs, brownish and brown-spotted at the larger end.

RANGE Confined to Tasmania and Bass Strait islands. Sedentary.

STATUS Common. Endemic.

▶ See also pages
142 146 *147* 151 152

369 MANGROVE ROBIN

Eopsaltria pulverulenta   Muscicapidae
OTHER NAMES Ashy Robin, White-tailed Robin, Mangrove Shrike-Robin

RECOGNITION Slaty or metallic dark grey upperparts, shading to darker grey-brown on the wings. Rump and tail blackish, with white on the base of the outer feathers. Underparts whitish, with a touch of smoky grey on the breast. Dark grey of the head and white of throat and chin meet in a sharply defined line from base of bill passing just below the eye. Immatures: mottled brown upperparts. In flight, white panels each side of spread tail. 14–16 cm.

VOICE A clear, plaintive, drawn-out two-note contact call, seems distant; also a repetitive 'chit'. Male sometimes gives attractive, varied song.

HABITAT Mangroves of coasts, estuaries, tidal creeks, favouring the thickets along the edges; hunts often for invertebrates exposed at low tide.

BREEDING July–March; usually September–January. The nest is a small shallow cup of fine bark strips bound with spiders' webs, with long strips of bark hung from the outside, in a mangrove fork. Two to three greenish eggs, spotted lilac and brown.

RANGE Coastal northern Australia; approximately Exmouth to Burdekin River. Also to New Guinea. Sedentary.

STATUS Quite common, but patchy within mangrove habitat.

▶ See also pages
23 *23* 110 196 199 210 223

370 WHITE-BREASTED ROBIN

Eopsaltria georgiana   Muscicapidae
OTHER NAMES White-bellied Robin, White-breasted Shrike-Robin

RECOGNITION Typical robin outline, and habits of upward tail-flicks, clinging sideways on treetrunks while hunting. Looks like a yellow robin without any yellow, which is replaced by white. Upperparts dark sooty grey to blue-grey, with a white

371 EASTERN YELLOW ROBIN *Eopsaltria australis*

wing-mark that becomes a wingstripe in flight. Tip of outer tail white. Immatures have some brownish spotting, particularly on head, shoulders and breast. Evolved from yellow robins. 16 cm.

VOICE A mellow or liquid 'cheeop'; a loud 'zhip'; and a harsh 'chit-chit-chrr' in alarm or aggression.

HABITAT Dense undergrowth mainly of karri forests; moist valleys and along streams of jarrah forest; a second population north of Perth, dense coastal scrub.

BREEDING July–January, often several broods. Nest quite large, deep cup-shaped, with pieces of bark hanging round the exterior, usually unlined, and placed in a shrub, in dense undergrowth. Two olive to greenish eggs, spotted brown.

RANGE Extreme south-western corner of Western Australia, and lower west coast of Western Australia. Sedentary.

STATUS Common in optimum habitat.

▶ See also pages
66 240 *240* 242

371 EASTERN YELLOW ROBIN

Eopsaltria australis   Muscicapidae
OTHER NAMES Southern Yellow Robin, Northern Yellow Robin, Yellow Bob, Bark Robin

RECOGNITION Formerly divided into two separate species, Southern Yellow and Northern Yellow robins. Slate-grey upperparts, with olive tone to rump. Chin and throat white, rest of underparts entirely bright clear yellow. Tail grey-brown, tipped dull white. Subspecies *chrysorrhoa* (Northern Yellow Robin) has bright yellow rump and uppertail-coverts. Immatures duller. A quiet, confiding bird, perches sideways on trunks while hunting. In flight, pale wingbar. 15–17 cm.

VOICE A succession of piping notes, often continuous, monotonous. Short quick 'chop-chop' call; harsh scoldings; drawn-out high whistlings.

HABITAT Forests and woodlands, including rainforested slopes of ranges, mallee, and acacia scrub.

BREEDING June–February; usually August–December. Nest is a neatly constructed, well hidden cup of bark bound with webs, lined with grass, leaves, camouflaged with pieces of bark, lichens, moss. Two to three blue-green eggs, spotted browns.

RANGE North-eastern, eastern, and south-eastern Australia; inland on western slopes of Great Dividing Range. Sedentary.

STATUS Common. Endemic.

▶ **See also pages**
80 118 124 *343* 345

372 WESTERN YELLOW ROBIN

Eopsaltria griseogularis   Muscicapidae

OTHER NAME Grey-breasted Robin

RECOGNITION Closely resembles Eastern Yellow Robin, but has white throat and light grey upper breast. Upperparts grey, with a touch of brown on wings and tail. A faint white, double wingbar shows in flight. Lower breast and abdomen yellow. Rump yellow in south-west of Western Australia (nominate subspecies) and olive in south-east of Western Australia and Eyre Peninsula (subspecies *rosinae*). Immatures duller. Perches on low twigs and sides of treetrunks, to hunt on ground. 15–16 cm.

VOICE Repeated, plaintive piping notes. Harsh low scolding, when disturbed, and if nest locality is approached, 'chit-charr', 'charr'.

HABITAT Almost all vegetation types within its range; dry eucalypt forest, mallee, acacia scrub, especially open woodlands with a low scrub undergrowth.

BREEDING July–January; especially October–December. Nest is a neat cup of bark strips, bound with webs, lined with dry leaves, camouflaged with strips of bark hung vertically round the outside. Two buff or olive eggs, blotched reddish-brown.

RANGE South-west of Western Australia; west coast of South Australia, mainly Eyre Peninsula. Sedentary.

STATUS Moderately common. Endemic.

▶ **See also pages**
155 164 *164* 235

373 YELLOW-LEGGED FLYCATCHER

Microeca griseoceps   Muscicapidae

OTHER NAMES Yellow-footed Flycatcher, Little Yellow Robin, Little Yellow Flycatcher

RECOGNITION Found only near tip of Cape York Peninsula. A small, plain, robin-like bird, but keeps more to the upper levels, taking insects in air and from foliage. Grey on head and nape; olive back and scapulars; wings and tail browner; face light grey-brown. Chin and throat white; upper breast buff, blending to lemon yellow over

remainder of underparts. Legs and feet yellow; bill wide and flattened towards base. Has habit of cocking tail; very active. 11–12 cm.

VOICE A low, fine, piping 'tziit-tziit-tziit', given almost constantly while feeding, and occasional melodious trills. Also a repeated, loud clear whistle.

HABITAT Tropical rainforests, especially where rainforest meets open woodland, and there are dense entangled masses of vines and other vegetation.

BREEDING The nest was not observed until 1977. It was a small cup, at 10.5 m on edge of rainforest. Wider at base than rim, built of fine black rootlets, decorated with lichen, bark. Two pale blue eggs, speckled dark brown, grey.

RANGE North of Cape York; as far south as Claudie River, west coast at Weipa. Also in New Guinea.

STATUS Uncommon or scarce; locally moderately common.

▶ **See also pages**
105–6 *107* 192

374 LEMON-BELLIED FLYCATCHER

Microeca flavigaster   Muscicapidae

OTHER NAMES Yellow-bellied Flycatcher, Lemon-breasted Flycatcher

RECOGNITION A small, robin-like bird, but more active, darting about the foliage in pursuit of insects. Upperparts olive, with wings and tail darker. Throat white, merging to pale olive across the breast, then to light lemon yellow for the remainder of underparts. Legs dark grey; bill short, broad. Immatures: brown upperparts; mottled paler. Similar species is Yellow-legged Flycatcher, which has grey head, yellow legs and feet. 12–14 cm.

VOICE A very pleasant song, a clear, varied, rising and falling sequence of notes, such as 'chew-chew, swee-so-wee-chew'; seems to mimic other birds.

HABITAT Margins of rainforests, monsoon forests, riverine forests and river-edge thickets, sometimes extending to eucalypt woodlands, mangroves.

BREEDING August–March; usually September–January. The nest is a tiny, shallow cup of bark lined with soft bark and grass; blended into a horizontal fork, often on a limb overhanging water, quite high. One pale blue egg, spotted purplish-red.

RANGE Top End (NT), and north-eastern Queensland. Also in New Guinea.

STATUS Moderately common.

▶ **See also pages**
190 191–2 197 198 199 201 202 210

375 KIMBERLEY FLYCATCHER

Microeca flavigaster tormenti
Muscicapidae

OTHER NAME Brown-tailed Flycatcher

RECOGNITION A small flycatcher; now considered a subspecies of, and very closely resembling, the Lemon-bellied Flycatcher, but with tail brown; back yellowish-olive; underparts pale grey with belly almost white. This subspecies is reputed to be shy, keeping to thick mangrove and other swamp vegetation, where there are records of it feeding on tiny crabs and other very small marine life, and insects around mangrove roots and debris. 13 cm.

VOICE Like Lemon-bellied Flycatcher, evidently louder; has been described as a prolonged, musical, 'peter-peter', or as 'quitchup-quitchup'.

HABITAT Found usually in the densest parts of coastal mangroves where these are subject to tidal flooding; adjacent flooded paperbark swamps.

BREEDING Dates uncertain. The only breeding record is from Napier Broome Bay, where eggs were collected in 1909. This nest was of bark, covered with small pieces of leaf. One pale blue-grey egg, spotted purple-grey, chestnut.

RANGE Western Kimberley coast; Dampier Archipelago to Napier Broome Bay. Probably sedentary.

STATUS Uncommon. Endemic.

▶ **See also pages**
192 201 202 208 *209* 210

376 JACKY WINTER

Microeca leucophaea   Muscicapidae

OTHER NAMES Brown Flycatcher, Peter-Peter

RECOGNITION A plain but widespread and familiar small flycatcher. Upperparts grey-brown; tail darker with conspicuous white edges and outer tips. Underparts whitish; greyish-buff across the breast. Indistinct whitish eyebrow; bill short, quite wide. Immatures streaked. Very active, dashing out from a perch on post, stump, dead branch or fence-wire to take insects in flight or on the ground. Hovers, showing white tail-edges. 12–14 cm.

VOICE A clear, far-carrying, varied and musical 'peeter-peeter', or 'jacky-winter', given from perch or in flight. More musical, varied, in spring.

HABITAT Open woodlands, mallee, timbered watercourses in arid regions, heathlands, edges and clearings of eucalypt forests, farmlands.

BREEDING July–February; usually August–December. Nest is one of smallest; a frail low saucer of grass, bound with webs and decorated with lichens, tucked into a horizontal fork of an exposed dead limb. Two pale green eggs, spotted browns.

RANGE Most of Australia in suitable habitat; not in Tasmania. Also in New Guinea. Sedentary.

STATUS Common in optimum habitat.

▶ **See also pages**
41 42 80 213 373

PALE-YELLOW ROBIN

Tregellasia capito   Muscicapidae

OTHER NAMES Pale Robin, Large-headed Robin, Rufous-lored Robin

RECOGNITION Superficially similar to the Eastern Yellow Robin, but with breast a paler and slightly greenish-tinted yellow. Upperparts olive, with grey on the nape. A distinctive face pattern, with whitish patch round the base of bill and back to the eye, emphasized by the sharply adjoining grey of the forehead (the northern Queensland subspecies has buff lores patches). Rump is olive-green; legs orange-yellow. Immatures brown, mottled rufous. 13 cm.

VOICE A monotonous and mournful series of whistles, and a single 'peep' or 'chee', louder and repetitive as dawn call. Harsh scolding 'churr'.

HABITAT Rainforests, tropical and subtropical, especially thick vegetation along creeks, lawyer-vine thickets; also adjoining dense wet eucalypt forest.

BREEDING July–January. Nest is a neat deep cup of fine bark strips, grass, dry leaves, bound with webs, decorated outside with moss, bark, lichens. Site is a vertical fork often of a lawyer vine. Two pale green eggs, marked chestnut.

RANGE Two populations and subspecies: north-eastern Queensland, and south-eastern Queensland to north-eastern New South Wales. Sedentary.

STATUS Common in northern Queensland; uncommon in south. Endemic.

▶ **See also pages**
53 54 *54* 55 97
121 127

WHITE-FACED ROBIN

Tregellasia leucops   Muscicapidae

OTHER NAMES Fly-Robin, White-throated Robin, White-faced Yellow Robin

RECOGNITION A small, yellow robin with unique facial pattern; has a confined range. Crown of head dark grey shading to black towards forehead and round the white face, making a black encircling border. The pure white face patch extends from base of bill and under chin, back to join the white eye-ring. Remainder of upperparts

olive grey-green; underparts yellow, olive on breast; legs pale yellow. Immatures cinnamon-brown; paler underparts. 12–12.5 cm.

VOICE Some sounds reported similar to those of the Pale-yellow Robin. There is a musical song breeding season, and a harsh 'chee-chee-chee'.

HABITAT Confined to gloomy, heavily timbered rainforests and vine scrubs. Confiding or tame in behaviour, perches on sides of trunks, hunts on ground.

BREEDING Probably July–January. Nest is usually built on lawyer vine or small sapling, of bark and lawyer-vine fibre, bound with webs, and disguised outside with moss and bark. Two blue-green eggs, speckled chestnut and dull red.

RANGE Cape York, south to Rocky River. Also in New Guinea. Sedentary.

STATUS Moderately common.

▶ **See also pages**
101 106 *107* 111

WHITE-BROWED ROBIN

Poecilodryas superciliosa   Muscicapidae

OTHER NAMES Buff-sided Robin, Buff-sided Flycatcher, Buff-sided Shrike-Robin

RECOGNITION Upperparts a very dark brown, particularly the head and sides of the face, which may appear black in shadowy lighting and in contrast with the long, wide, clearly defined and conspicuous white eyebrow line and the white chin and throat. Underparts white, greyish on breast. (Subspecies *cerviniventris* Buff-sided Robin, has buff flanks and undertail-coverts.) White bar across centre of wing; white-tipped secondaries and tail. 14–17 cm.

VOICE A clear loud piping whistle, 'teet-toe-eee toe-eee', repeated three or four times. Contact call of soft, drawn-out whistles; alarm chatter.

HABITAT In north-eastern Queensland rainforests, coastal scrub and watercourse vegetation; north-west subspecies, monsoon forests, pandanus along streams, mangroves, wet woodlands.

BREEDING July–March. Builds a shallow cup-shaped nest of dry grass and plant stems, usually camouflaged with pieces of bark and moss; on a horizontal fork at 1–3 m height. Two greenish eggs, spotted chestnut and purplish-brown.

RANGE Two populations: Kimberley–Top End (NT), and north-eastern Queensland. Sedentary.

STATUS Uncommon, patchy; now scarce in Kimberley. Endemic.

▶ **See also pages**
109 174 198 199
208 210

GREY-HEADED ROBIN

Poecilodryas albispecularis   Muscicapidae

OTHER NAMES Ashy-fronted Robin, Fly-Robin

RECOGNITION A large and robust-looking robin; crown and nape dark grey; back and wings olive-brown; rump tawny, becoming chestnut on base of tail. Underparts, throat white, extending back as a line under the eye. Remainder of the underparts whitish, washed tawny on flanks. Dark line from base of bill to eye, widening behind eye as dark ear-coverts. White mark on wing. Legs look long, pinkish-brown. Immatures blotched brown, white. 16–18 cm.

VOICE A long, loud clear whistle, followed by three lower, shorter notes, given continuously, monotonously; all months. Also low chatterings.

HABITAT Rainforests above approximately 240 m altitude; often at margins of rainforest clearings, where it clings to treetrunks, hunts on ground.

BREEDING August–January. Nest is a neat cup of rootlets, dry leaves, bound with webs, camouflaged with mosses and lichens; usually placed on a horizontal or sloping section of a spiny lawyer vine. One to two creamy eggs, marked grey, brown.

RANGE North-eastern Queensland; on ranges, Cooktown to Townsville. Also in New Guinea. Sedentary.

STATUS Common within restricted range.

▶ **See also pages**
85 90 *90* 97

CRESTED SHRIKE-TIT

Falcunculus frontatus   Muscicapidae

OTHER NAMES Eastern Shrike-tit, Western Shrike-tit, Northern Shrike-tit, Bark Tit, Crested Tit

RECOGNITION A black-crested head and bold plumage pattern make this species distinctive. Head and throat black; prominent crest; robust black bill giving big-headed appearance. Two broad white streaks, one from eye up to crest and back to nape, a second below eye; small white patch over the bill. Back olive; wings and tail dark grey. Underparts yellow. South-western subspecies – white abdomen; northern subspecies – smaller, yellower. Female: olive throat. 15–19 cm.

VOICE A mournful, drawn-out, undulating

mellow whistle, usually repeated several times, with increasing volume; also a low chuckling sound.

HABITAT Eucalypt forests, woodlands, rivergums, wandoo forests and woodlands of south-western Australia, coastal banksia and tea-tree, native pine.

BREEDING Usually August–January, but recorded from July–March. The deep, cup nest is built round slender vertical twigs at the very top of a sapling or tree, almost invariably high. Two to three white eggs, with olive, grey and brown markings.

RANGE Three subspecies: south-eastern Australia, south-western Australia, and Top End (NT)–Kimberley. Sedentary.

STATUS Uncommon to rare. Endemic.

▶ **See also pages**
122 139 148 240 *365*

382 OLIVE WHISTLER

Pachycephala olivacea   Muscicapidae
OTHER NAMES Olive Thickhead, Whipbird, Mysterybird, Olivaceous Whistler

RECOGNITION A large whistler of sombre plumage. Back, wings and tail rich olive-brown; head slate-grey. Throat white with dark, broken barrings, separated from the buffy-brown underparts by a grey or grey-buff breastband. Northern subspecies (*mcphersoniana*) has lighter grey head. Female paler; crown olive-brown like back; throat without barrings; breastband indistinct; paler lower-mandible. Feeds near ground, but elusive. 20–22 cm.

VOICE Powerful, yet ethereal quality. Territorial call, 'cho-cho'. In south-eastern Queensland, 'pee-oo' with first part downwards, the second low.

HABITAT In north, mainly in rainforest, especially *Nothofagus* and eucalypt forests; farther south, in eucalypt forests, tea-tree thickets.

BREEDING Usually September–December; recorded August–February. Nest is a large, loosely built cup of twigs, bark, leaves, lined with fine grass and rootlets; in a tree or shrub, bracken, sword-grass. Two to three pale buff eggs, spotted grey, brown.

RANGE South-eastern Australia, coast and ranges; south-eastern Queensland to Tasmania. Sedentary or dispersive.

STATUS Uncommon; rare on parts of range. Endemic.

▶ **See also pages**
121 123 124 127 146 *147* 151 152 163

383 RED-LORED WHISTLER

Pachycephala rufogularis   Muscicapidae
OTHER NAMES Rufous-throated Thickhead, Buff-breasted Whistler, Red-throated Whistler

RECOGNITION Upperparts grey-brown or olive-grey; wings and tail darker olive-grey, edged buff. Lores, throat, upper breast, belly and vent cinnamon, richest about the face and throat, blending to grey on breast and flanks. Eye red-brown; bill black. Female paler grey and cinnamon. Immatures like female, but lores dull white; underparts dark-streaked. Species tends to be shy and elusive, but attracts attention by calls. 19–22 cm.

VOICE Recognizable as the call of a whistler, but with a wistful, sweet, haunting quality, usually a loud clear whistle followed by a soft low note.

HABITAT Restricted to a narrow range of vegetation: mallee with broombush and native pine, and mallee with low ground-cover, in undisturbed areas.

BREEDING Usually September–November, recorded August–January. The nest is a substantial cup of bark, dry leaves, twigs, lined with grasses; in tops of spinifex clumps, low shrubs. Two to three pale buff eggs, marked umber and lavender.

RANGE Mallee region; east of South Australia, north-western Victoria, south-eastern New South Wales. Probably sedentary.

STATUS Rare; sensitive to interference to habitat. Endemic.

▶ **See also pages**
129 *133* 135 137 138

384 GILBERT'S WHISTLER

Pachycephala inornata   Muscicapidae
OTHER NAMES Black-lored Whistler, Red-throated Whistler, Gilbert's Thickhead

RECOGNITION Plumage grey or brownish-grey; slightly darker on head, wings and tail; light buffy-grey on lower breast and abdomen; buffy-white on the undertail coverts. Throat and upper breast rufous or chestnut, lores and round eyes black. Female is almost uniformly plain grey; slightly lighter underparts and sometimes with dark streak on breast or touch of buff to breast and undertail-coverts. Shy and inconspicuous except in breeding season. 19–20 cm.

VOICE Song rich, resonant, far-carrying, 'chong-chong-chong-', rising in pitch; also 'joey-joey-', rising. Often plaintive, drawn-out whistles.

HABITAT Mallee, and eucalypt woodland of the drier regions, mallee-spinifex, mulga scrub, partly cleared country.

BREEDING Usually September–December; recorded August–February. Nest site may be a fork of a shrub or stunted tree, vine

tangle or mistletoe clump. It is a cup of bark strips, fine twigs, grass. Two to three buffy-white eggs, spotted lilac, brown, black.

RANGE Inland southern Australia, and to dry parts of south coast. Sedentary.

STATUS Uncommon; in places common in optimum habitat. Endemic.

▶ **See also pages**
59 *59* 137 138 139 164 213 220 232

385 GOLDEN WHISTLER

Pachycephala pectoralis   Muscicapidae
OTHER NAMES White-throated Whistler, White-throated Thickhead, Thunderbird, Whipbird

RECOGNITION Bold and colourful plumage. Head black, this continued across the upper breast to form a narrow black band between white throat and rich golden yellow underparts. The yellow of the breast continues round the nape as a golden collar between black of head and olive-green of back. Wings black, feathers edged yellow-green; tail blackish. Female grey-brown, washed olive in north-eastern Australia; underparts light grey, pale wing-coverts line. 16–18 cm.

VOICE Loud calls often ending in ringing whipcrack note. In spring, male's 'whit-whit-whit-whittle' is almost incessant; also other softer calls.

HABITAT The heavier forests and other semi-closed environs: rainforests, eucalypt forests, woodland thickets, dense inland mallee, brigalow, mangroves.

BREEDING Usually August–January, but recorded most of year. Nest is a small neat cup of fine rootlets, grasses; placed in an upright fork of a dense shrub or low to

385 GOLDEN WHISTLER
Pachycephala pectoralis

medium tree. Two to three white to pinkish eggs, marked grey, red, browns.

RANGE Eastern, southern and southwestern Australia and Tasmania, mainly coastal. Also in Indonesia, Solomon Islands, Fiji, New Guinea. Sedentary, some inland dispersion.

STATUS Common.

▶ See also pages
24 122 124 151
346

386 MANGROVE GOLDEN WHISTLER

Pachycephala melanura   Muscicapidae
OTHER NAMES Robust Whistler, Black-tailed Thickhead, Black-tailed Whistler

RECOGNITION Very closely resembles the widespread Golden Whistler, but with some important differences of plumage and range of habitats. Male slightly smaller; plumage almost identical to that of male Golden Whistler. Yellows are deeper orange-yellow, extending round neck in wider collar, and onto rump; tail shorter, blacker. The bill is longer, slightly hooked. Females are olive on wings; underparts variable, grey washed yellow, to bright pale yellow. 15–17 cm.

VOICE Like that of Golden Whistler; as the latter may occur in mangroves, call and habitat are insufficient identifiers where ranges overlap in north-eastern Australia.

HABITAT Mangroves, and rarely in adjacent rainforest. The distribution round the north coast is broken by habitat gaps, giving eastern and western subspecies.

BREEDING Usually October–December; recorded August–February. Nest is built into an upright fork of a mangrove or associated coastal tree. It is an open cup shape of grasses, rootlets. Two to three white to buff eggs, spotted red-brown.

RANGE Coastal northern Australia; Exmouth Gulf (WA) to mid-Queensland coast. Species to New Guinea, Java, Pacific. Sedentary.

STATUS Moderately common. Endemic subspecies.

▶ See also pages
23 24 98 192 196
208

387 GREY WHISTLER

Pachycephala simplex   Muscicapidae
OTHER NAMES Brown Whistler, Brown Thickhead, Grey-headed Whistler

RECOGNITION Two subspecies. Nominate subspecies (Brown Whistler), Northern Territory: upperparts grey-brown; slightly greyer head; browner wings; slight buff eyebrow. Underparts fawn-white with pale grey-buff band across faintly streaked upper breast; small white margin at bend of wing. Subspecies *griseiceps* (Grey Whistler), of north-eastern Queensland: head grey; back and wings olive-grey; throat buff-white; upper breast buffy-olive merging to pale-yellow underparts. Bill long, slightly hooked. Female paler underparts. 15 cm.

VOICE Usually a double whistle, often extended with four or five loud clear whistles. Song of Brown Whistler rich, melodious, less of a whipcrack.

HABITAT Grey Whistler: rainforests, mangroves, paperbark swamps. Brown Whistler: monsoon forests, swamp woodlands, mangroves, open woodlands.

BREEDING Usually September–January; recorded all months. Nest is an open cup of rootlets, vine tendrils, dead leaves, loosely bound with webs, and placed in tree fork or vine tangle; often high. Two buff-white eggs, spotted umber, lavender.

RANGE Grey Whistler: coastal north-eastern Queensland. Brown Whistler: coastal Top End (NT). Also in New Guinea and other northern islands. Sedentary.

STATUS Probably moderately common.

▶ See also pages
189 192 196

388 RUFOUS WHISTLER
Pachycephala rufiventris

388 RUFOUS WHISTLER

Pachycephala rufiventris   Muscicapidae
OTHER NAMES Coachwhip-bird, Echong, Thunderbird, Rufous-breasted Thickhead

RECOGNITION Upperparts grey; wings and tail brownish-black. From the bill, a broad black line extends back through eye, then curving down as a black breastband between white throat and rufous underparts. Eye red-brown; bill black; legs grey-brown. Female: upperparts grey-brown, with a touch of olive, and darker on wings and tail; throat white, merging into pale buff breast and abdomen, the underparts dark-streaked. Six Australian subspecies. 16–17 cm.

VOICE Powerful, rich, varied. At times a series of ringing 'ee-chong' calls, or a seemingly endless, rapid 'joey-joey-joey-', or other varied notes.

HABITAT Open forests, woodlands, generally less closed than that preferred by Golden Whistler; extending inland in mallee, mulga, heath.

BREEDING Usually August–February; recorded all months. Nest is an open cup of grass, fine twigs; more fragile than that of Golden Whistler; placed in a foliaged part of tree or shrub. Two to four pale to dark olive eggs, marked in red-browns.

RANGE Throughout Australia in suitable habitat; vagrant to Tasmania. Also in New Caledonia, New Guinea and adjacent islands. Nomadic or migratory.

STATUS Common.

▶ See also pages
122

389 WHITE-BREASTED WHISTLER

Pachycephala lanioides   Muscicapidae
OTHER NAMES Torres Strait Thickhead, White-bellied Thickhead, White-bellied Whistler

RECOGNITION Head entirely black, down to include eye, and back to nape; the black extending down onto the breast as a very broad band separating white of throat from creamy or light buffy-white of underparts. Nape edged rufous; this following round lower edge of black breastband. Wings black, edged grey; tail black. Bill robust, hooked. Female grey-brown or olive-grey upperparts; fawny-white underparts; darker on breast, and streaked brown. 19–21 cm.

VOICE Described as a series of four to five strong deep whistles, or at other times an outpouring of rich mellow notes. Alarm call sharp, harsh.

HABITAT Population is broken into three subspecies, inhabiting separated sections of mangroves round northern coastline; occasionally into adjacent rainforest.

BREEDING Usually March–November; recorded all months. Nest is a sparse cup of twigs and rootlets, lined with finer materials; built into an upright fork of a mangrove. Two buffy or pale olive eggs, spotted umber and lavender.

RANGE North coast, in suitable habitat; Carnarvon (WA) to Norman River (Qld). Sedentary.

STATUS Moderately common. Endemic.

▶ See also pages
23 59 192 196 208

390 LITTLE SHRIKE-THRUSH

Colluricincla megarhyncha Muscicapidae

OTHER NAMES Rufous Shrike-thrush, Red Thrush, Rufous Thrush

RECOGNITION A small shrike-thrush of almost overall rufous tone, having rufous-brown to olive-brown upperparts; slightly grey on head and back, buff on face, off-white throat. Underparts cinnamon, lightly streaked brown. Seven Australian subspecies described: those in eastern Australia more olive upperparts; bill pinkish-brown; in north-west light brown upperparts, whitish lores, bill blackish. A bird of the middle and upper forest canopy, but sometimes forages in leaf-litter. 17–19 cm.

VOICE Various mellow piping whistles, lower-pitched than Grey Shrike-thrush; commonly 'too-eee, wot-wot-wot'; in alarm, sharp calls, wheezy sounds.

HABITAT Damp areas: usually rainforests, mangroves, dense vegetation along watercourses, paperbark swamps; extending to adjacent eucalypt woodlands.

BREEDING Usually September–February; recorded August–March. Nest is smaller than that of Grey Shrike-thrush; quite deep, of leaves, rootlets, bark strips, webs; in fork of a small tree or sapling. White eggs, marked lilac and brown.

RANGE Coastal northern and eastern Australia; northern Kimberley to north-eastern New South Wales. Also in Celebes, New Guinea, other northern islands. Sedentary.

STATUS Uncommon.

▶ See also pages
90 192 209 *365*

391 BOWER'S SHRIKE-THRUSH

Colluricincla boweri Muscicapidae

OTHER NAMES Bower Shrike-thrush, Bower Thrush, Stripe-breasted Shrike-thrush

RECOGNITION A shrike-thrush of distinctive appearance, somewhat short-tailed, large-headed. Head and back blue-grey;

wings and tail grey-brown; lores pale grey; throat buff; remainder of underparts deeper rich olive-buff with dark streaks from chin to breast. Eye red-brown; bill large, black. Immatures browner, duller, more heavily streaked. Of shrike-thrushes, only similar species is the Little Shrike-thrush (smaller, less streaked, pinkish-brown bill). 19–21 cm.

VOICE Quieter than other shrike-thrushes. Calls deeper, richer than that of the Little Shrike-thrush; song is varied, melodious. In alarm or anger, harsh gratings.

HABITAT Mountain rainforests, usually above 500 m altitude, sometimes down to 250 m; may move down to some suitable areas of lowland rainforest in winter.

BREEDING September–October to January–February. Nest is a loose open cup of leaves and bark strips, lined with fine rootlets; built onto a lawyer vine or other vine tangle, or fork of a small tree. Two to three off-white eggs, freckled grey and brown.

RANGE North-eastern Queensland, highlands; from near Cooktown, south almost to Townsville. Sedentary.

STATUS Moderately common within restricted range. Endemic.

▶ See also pages
85 90 *93 97*

392 SANDSTONE SHRIKE-THRUSH

Colluricincla woodwardi Muscicapidae

OTHER NAMES Red-bellied Shrike-thrush, Woodward's Shrike-thrush, Rock Thrush, Brown-breasted Shrike-thrush

RECOGNITION Head greyish, merging to olive-brown back, wings and tail. Face and lores buffy-white; underparts cinnamon with a slight wash of grey across the upper breast; throat and breast very lightly streaked brown. Bill blue-grey; eye red-brown. Subspecies *assimilis*, of Kimberley region, slightly larger; throat whiter; underparts deeper cinnamon. Immatures: wings darker; underparts lighter. Similar to Little Shrike-thrush; usually different habitat. 25–26 cm.

VOICE Clear loud notes, often echoed and accentuated within rock-walled gorges, richer than song of Little Shrike-thrush.

HABITAT Gorges and breakaways of sandstone ranges, cliffs of coasts and islands. Feeds upon spiders, grasshoppers, small vertebrates.

BREEDING Usually November–March. The nest is a rough cup built mainly of reddish roots of spinifex, strips of bark, and hidden in a crevice, hole or under an overhanging cliff. Two to three white eggs, marked grey, brown and blackish.

RANGE Kimberley (WA), Top End (NT). Sedentary.

STATUS Moderately common in suitable habitat. Endemic.

▶ See also pages
174 *189* 192 196
197 198 210 211

393 GREY SHRIKE-THRUSH

Colluricincla harmonica Muscicapidae

OTHER NAMES Native Thrush, Western Shrike-thrush, Brown Shrike-thrush, Native Shrike-thrush

RECOGNITION Nominate subspecies in south-eastern Australia: grey upperparts, with brown on the back; white lores and underparts. In north-western Australia this subspecies (Brown Shrike-thrush) is more uniformly grey-brown above, buffy beneath. In central Australia and Western Australia, south of Kimberley (Western Shrike-thrush), grey upperparts; lores pale grey; underparts buff, becoming cinnamon-buff towards undertail-coverts. With both subspecies, female greyer on lores. Immatures: slightly streaked breast. 22–27 cm.

VOICE Rich and powerful voice, especially during the breeding season. The notes are varied, melodious, with mellow or liquid quality.

HABITAT Woodlands, forests usually open; mallee, mulga and other inland scrubs, vegetation belts along rivers of the interior.

BREEDING August–December. The nest is a large bowl of bark strips, grass, rootlets; placed in a fork among dense foliage, or in the hollow top of a stump, shallow hollow of a tree, or similar. Two to four white eggs, finely speckled brown and grey.

RANGE Throughout Australia, including Tasmania, except sandy deserts. Also in New Guinea. Sedentary.

STATUS Common.

▶ See also pages
153 192 221 233
349

394 CRESTED BELLBIRD

Oreoica gutturalis Muscicapidae

OTHER NAMES Bellbird, Panpanpanella, Bunbundalui

RECOGNITION Upperparts brown; more grey on nape and crown where there is an erectile black crest, that is often folded to show as a black stripe from forehead to nape. A black line extends downwards from black of crown through the eye and widens to form a broad black band between white of the throat and light buff of underparts. Tail grey-brown; eye orange; bill black. Female lacks crest; has black crown stripe; no breastband; throat and face grey. 22 cm.

393 GREY SHRIKE-THRUSH *Colluricincla harmonica*

VOICE Male call like ringing of a metal cow-bell, a regular rhythmic 'pan-pan, panella', in mellow notes, ventriloquial.

HABITAT Eucalypt woodlands, scrubs of inland and drier parts of coast, including mallee, mulga, saltbush, heath; usually keeps to densest shrubbery.

BREEDING Usually September–February; recorded all months. Nest is a quite large and solidly constructed cup of sticks, bark, grass; placed in a thick vertical fork, or hollowed stump. Three to four white eggs, marked grey, red-brown, black.

RANGE Throughout interior and drier coastal areas of Australia. Sedentary.

STATUS Common through most of range. Endemic.

▶ **See also pages**
175 179 *182* 183
232 392

395 YELLOW-BREASTED BOATBILL

Machaerirhynchus flaviventer
Muscicapidae
OTHER NAMES Yellow-breasted Flycatcher, Boat-billed Flycatcher, Wherrybill

RECOGNITION A flycatcher of unique appearance, having a large, very wide flattened bill, slender from side view, but from above or below, shaped like broad prow of a boat. Plumage colourful. Upperparts blackish with olive-green tone; two bold white shoulder bars; tail broadly tipped white. Head black with long, bold yellow eyebrow line; throat white; rest of underparts bright yellow. Female has dark olive upperparts; dull yellow and barred underparts. 11–12 cm.

VOICE Male's song is soft, insect-like, three or four short notes ending in trill, 'wit, wit, wit-zeewit'; also repeated 'chip, chip, chip'.

HABITAT Confined to rainforest, rarely emerging even to the margins. Feeds in the upper and middle-level canopy, snapping up many insects in flight.

BREEDING Usually September–March; recorded August–April. Nest is a shallow saucer of vine tendrils and fine plant stems, bound with webs; usually placed among screening leaves, in a slender horizontal fork. Two white eggs, marked reddish.

RANGE North-eastern Queensland; tip of Cape York Peninsula south to Ingham. Species also in New Guinea. Sedentary.

STATUS Common in range. Endemic.

▶ **See also pages**
90 *93* 97 98 111

396 BLACK-FACED MONARCH

Monarcha melanopsis   **Muscicapidae**
OTHER NAMES Pearly-winged Flycatcher, Black-faced Flycatcher

RECOGNITION A large flycatcher, with upperparts pale blue-grey; darker on wings and tail. Head entirely pale blue-grey except for a black face patch from forehead to throat, but not including eye; this grey extends down to include the upper breast. Remainder of underparts a rich rufous. Immatures lack black on face. Singly or in pairs taking insects from foliage and in flight; sedate and slow-moving compared with many of the small flycatchers. 17–19 cm.

VOICE The whistled calls are rich and clear, varied, often a sequence as 'why-you, whichye-oo', the 'which' drawn-out, rising, almost whipcrack.

HABITAT Rainforests and eucalypt forests; feeding in and around denser middle and lower levels of vegetation.

BREEDING October–January; recorded September–February. The nest is a deep neat cup built into a fork in a dense, usually gloomy part of the forest; bound with webs, camouflaged with moss. Two to three white eggs, spotted greys, red-browns.

RANGE Eastern Australia; from Cape York almost to Melbourne. Also in New Guinea. Partially migratory.

STATUS Common in north of range; uncommon in south.

▶ **See also pages**
81 97 98 *121* 122
124 127 350

397 BLACK-WINGED MONARCH

Monarcha frater   **Muscicapidae**
OTHER NAMES Pearly Flycatcher, Black-winged Flycatcher

RECOGNITION Very much like the more widespread and much better known Black-faced Monarch. Upper plumage lighter, more lustrous or pearly, though this is relative and often difficult to determine in gloomy situations. Wings and tail black, in strong contrast to the pearly grey neck and back, whereas the Black-faced Monarch has wings and tail only slightly darker than the back. Facial pattern and rufous underparts as Black-faced Monarch. 18–19 cm.

VOICE Similar to that of the Black-faced Monarch, of which this species was considered to be a subspecies.

HABITAT Rainforest, and adjoining eucalypt woodlands. On Cape York these species occur together.

BREEDING November–February; recorded October–April. The nest is neat, deep, goblet-shaped; built of paperbark strips bound with webs, and lined with finer plant fibre. It is placed in an upright fork.

Three off-white eggs, dotted red-brown, purple.

RANGE In Australia, confined to eastern Cape York, south to Claudie River. Migrant to New Guinea.

STATUS Probably uncommon. Widespread in highlands of New Guinea.

▶ **See also pages**
53 55 111

398 SPECTACLED MONARCH

Monarcha trivirgatus Muscicapidae

OTHER NAMES Black-fronted Flycatcher, White-bellied Flycatcher, Spectacled Flycatcher

RECOGNITION Some resemblance to the Black-faced Monarch, but darker slaty-grey upperparts, the black facial patch extends back to include the eye; belly and undertail-coverts are white. There is no grey on upper breast, where the deep buff or rufous continues right up to the black facial mask and along flanks, leaving remainder of underparts white; outer tail tipped white. 15–16 cm.

VOICE A clear 'zwe-eet, zwe-eet, zwe-eet' with each syllable uplifting; also a weak, squeaky, warbling song, and harsh or scratchy scoldings.

HABITAT Usually in rainforests, but also in mangroves; often remote from rainforest; also dense and gloomier gullies of adjacent eucalypt forests.

BREEDING Usually September–January; recorded August–March. A deep neat cup is built into a vertical fork of tree or vine tangle, at 1–6 m height; exterior decorated with lichens, greenish spider egg-cases. Two whitish eggs, freckled red-browns.

RANGE Coastal eastern Australia; Cape York to mid-eastern New South Wales. Also in New Guinea, Timor, Moluccas. Partially migratory.

STATUS Uncommon, but locally common.

▶ **See also pages**
81 97 98 121 *365*

399 WHITE-EARED MONARCH

Monarcha leucotis Muscicapidae

OTHER NAME White-eared Flycatcher

RECOGNITION A small flycatcher with very distinctively patterned black, white and grey plumage. Upperparts black with white eyebrow; large white ear patch and small white spot on lores; white throat; white wingbars and white rump; outer-tail feathers white-tipped. The white of the throat is separated from pale grey of the rest of underparts by a narrow black band. Female is slightly duller. Usually seen fluttering about the foliage of the upper canopy. 14–15 cm.

VOICE Much typical flycatcher chattering, and a cuckoo-like rising and falling whistle, 'eee-cheeuw'; sometimes a musical three-note whistled tune.

HABITAT Eucalypt forest along the fringes of rainforest, creeks, and in rainforest clearings; also occasionally in mangroves.

BREEDING Usually nests September–January. The nest is deeply cup-shaped; built of bark strips, grasses and moss bound with webs; decorated with spider-egg cocoons, usually high in forest canopy. Two whitish eggs, spotted red-brown.

RANGE Coastal eastern Queensland south to north-eastern New South Wales. Partially migratory or locally nomadic.

STATUS Generally uncommon to rare; locally common. Endemic.

▶ **See also pages**
65 66 121

400 FRILLED MONARCH

Arses telescopthalmus Muscicapidae

OTHER NAMES Frilled Flycatcher, Frill-necked Flycatcher, White-lored Flycatcher

RECOGNITION One of two similar species with black-and-white plumage and pale blue eye-ring. Separation of this and Pied Monarch is simplified by separate ranges. Frilled Monarch has head black but nape and neck white with erectile frill, the white continuing round neck in broad collar to join with all-white underparts. Back, wings and tail black, with white scapulars forming a large white crescent across the back. Female: chin white; lores grey. 14–17 cm.

VOICE Short, soft, high whistling notes like song of Pied Monarch but softer. In New Guinea, has been described as having trilled song; harsh scolding sounds.

HABITAT Rainforest with eucalypt forest adjacent, chiefly in middle-level vegetation where it seeks insects in crevices and tree foliage.

BREEDING October–January. Nest is a small suspended cup of fine tendrils and twigs, bound with webs; of thin construction, decorated outside with lichens; usually among vines; often high. Two pale pink eggs, freckled darker.

RANGE Tip of Cape York Peninsula, south to McIlwraith Range. Also in New Guinea, Aru Islands. Sedentary.

STATUS Moderately common within restricted range.

▶ **See also pages**
90 106 *107* 111

401 PIED MONARCH

Arses kaupi Muscicapidae

OTHER NAMES Black-breasted Flycatcher, Pied Flycatcher, Kaup's Flycatcher

RECOGNITION Black-and-white plumage; body white, with clearly defined areas of black. Head black, but back of neck white with erectile frill. Black of back continued round upper breast as a broad band completely encircling the body. Elongated scapulars form a white crescent shape across shoulders and back; otherwise wings, back and tail black. Pale blue eye-ring; eye brown; bill blue-grey. Female: black of head meets black of back. 16 cm.

VOICE Soft, high whistling notes, a series of 10 or more, lasting for three or four seconds; also buzzing sounds, and a typical flycatcher creaking.

HABITAT Rainforests, vine scrubs, palm scrubs, usually near water, and often extending to adjoining woodlands. Feeds like a treecreeper, on bark.

BREEDING Usually October–January. The small neat but thin cup is slung between vines or slender twigs. It is built of fine materials, bound with webs, and decorated externally with lichens. Two pinkish-white eggs, spotted grey, brown.

RANGE Coastal north-eastern Queensland; from Cooktown south to Townsville. Sedentary.

STATUS Moderately common in optimum habitat. Endemic.

▶ **See also pages**
85 90 93 97 106

402 BROAD-BILLED FLYCATCHER

Myiagra ruficollis Muscicapidae

RECOGNITION Upperparts glossy blue-grey, including wings; slightly darker on the head which has a slight crest to the rear of the crown. Tail grey; outer feathers edged white. Throat and upper breast orange-rufous, blending to white on the rest of the underparts. Bill broad, blue-black. Male is similar to the female Satin Flycatcher, but smaller, slightly darker. Female duller and paler than male, like female Leaden Flycatcher, but grey eye-to-forehead. 15 cm.

VOICE A harsh 'shweek' call, and song described as similar to song of the Leaden Flycatcher, a whistling 'too-whee' or 'hrr-inny, hrr-inny', far-carrying.

HABITAT Mainly mangroves, paperbark woodland, monsoon forests around swamps, riverside vegetation, swampy and occasionally coastal woodland.

BREEDING October–January or March. Nest is a cup of bark strips and plant tendrils, lined with finer materials, bound with webs, decorated outside with lichens. It is often in a mangrove, over water. Two to three whitish eggs, spotted grey, dark brown.

RANGE Coastal north; western Kimberley to north-eastern Cape York. Also in New Guinea and Indonesia. Sedentary.

STATUS Common.

▶ See also pages
23 24 110 196 210

LEADEN FLYCATCHER

Myiagra rubecula   Muscicapidae

OTHER NAMES Blue Flycatcher, Frogbird

RECOGNITION A restless, active bird that attracts attention by its calls as it darts about the treetop foliage. Glossy blue-grey upperparts, including entire head, throat, upper breast, wings, tail; remainder of underparts white. There is a small erectile crest usually showing as a slight peaked top to head. Bill blue-grey; eye brown; legs black. Female: browner upperparts, with throat and upper breast cinnamon-buff. 14–16 cm.

VOICE A loud, repeated, whistled 'too-whit, too-whoo' or 'see-hear, see-hear', rising and falling, far-carrying; also harsh rattling, buzzing noises.

HABITAT Eucalypt forests, dense river- and creek-margin vegetation, mangroves; and in the north, also in eucalypt woodlands during wet season.

BREEDING September–February; recorded August–April. Nest is a neat cup of fine strips of bark, bound and blended onto the limb with webs; decorated with thin flakes of bark; at heights 3–25 m. Two to three white eggs, spotted grey-violet, brown.

RANGE Northern and eastern Australia; coastal, subcoastal. Also in New Guinea and other northern islands. Sedentary in north; migrant to south.

STATUS Common in north; less common elsewhere.

▶ See also pages
24 198 199 208
210 350 *365*

404

SATIN FLYCATCHER

Myiagra cyanoleuca   Muscicapidae

OTHER NAMES Shining Flycatcher, Satin Sparrow

RECOGNITION Upperparts glossy blue-black, including wings, tail, upper breast and head, which is peaked to a slight crest at the rear of the crown. Underparts pure white, sharply defined and in strong contrast to the dark upperparts. Compared with Leaden Flycatcher, has blacker upperparts; black farther down on the breast. Female: dark blue-grey upperparts; throat light chestnut; underparts white; darker, more slaty, than female Leaden Flycatcher. Immatures like female. 15–17 cm.

VOICE Like Leaden Flycatcher, but louder, more strident. Calls include rattling, wheezing, rasping sounds; song a strident 'wu-chee, wu-chee', or 'choo-ee-'.

HABITAT During breeding season, the densely vegetated gullies of forests, but during migration found in varied habitats, including woodlands, mangroves.

BREEDING Usually October–January; recorded September–March. The nest is a neat cup of strips of bark, green bark, moss, bound with webs; often on a dead branch, and usually with some screening foliage. Two to three dull white eggs, marked brown, grey.

RANGE Eastern Australia; Cape York to Tasmania and south-east of South Australia. Also in New Guinea; vagrant to New Zealand. Migratory.

STATUS Uncommon.

▶ See also pages
65 66 123 139 142
151

405

SHINING FLYCATCHER

Myiagra alecto   Muscicapidae

OTHER NAMES Shining Monarch Flycatcher, Glossy Flycatcher, Satin Sparrow

RECOGNITION Male entirely black with a glossy blue or green iridescence. Crown of head peaked in a slight crown; bill blue-black to blue-grey; eye red-brown. Female very different: crown and nape glossy black, as for male; remainder of upperparts chestnut; underparts white. Immatures like female, duller. A very lively flycatcher, fluttering through the dense vegetation, darting after flying insects, or taking small creatures from mangrove mud. 17–19 cm.

VOICE A variety of calls, from clear pleasant whistles to harsh grating and croaking. The song, in clear musical notes, is a 'toowhit-too-toowhit'.

HABITAT Rainforest along streams, mangroves, monsoon forest around pools or swamps, paperbark swamps, pandanus; rarely in eucalypt forests.

BREEDING September–March, but recorded August–May. Nest a deep, compact, well-

---

woven cup of strips of bark, bound with webs; decorated with flakes of bark and spiders' egg-cases; usually over water. Two to three greenish eggs, speckled grey, lavender, brown.

RANGE Pilbara (WA) to south-eastern New South Wales. Also in New Guinea, other northern islands. Apparently sedentary.

STATUS Moderately common; scarce in south.

▶ See also pages
75 79 80 98 111
208 210

406

RESTLESS FLYCATCHER

Myiagra inquieta   Muscicapidae

OTHER NAMES Scissors Grinder, Crested Wagtail, Razor Grinder, Dishlick

RECOGNITION Black upperparts, with a strong metallic-blue iridescence, including all of the slightly crested head to just below the eyes; on flight feathers and tail the black has a dull brownish tone rather than the blue gloss of the head and back. Chin to sides of neck, and entire underparts white, often with faint yellow wash to the breast. Bill quite long, robust. Immatures lack blue gloss; have dull white on scapulars. Restlessly active, noisy. 17–21 cm.

VOICE Various grinding calls, some suggesting the sound of a metal blade against a grindstone; a clear whistled, repeated 'tooee' or 'joey-joey'.

HABITAT Mainly an inland bird, open eucalypt woodland, mallee, clearings in eucalypt forest, often near water; drier scrubs in autumn and winter.

BREEDING Usually August–March; recorded July–May. The nest is a neat cup, blended onto a dead or exposed horizontal branch, at heights of 1–20 m; sometimes over water. Three to four dull white to buff eggs, marked lavender, greys and browns.

RANGE Northern, eastern and south-western Australia, absent Tasmania. Also in southern New Guinea. Partially migratory or dispersive.

STATUS Moderately common.

▶ See also pages
41–2 *41* 213

407

RUFOUS FANTAIL

Rhipidura rufifrons   Muscicapidae

OTHER NAMES Rufous-fronted Fantail, Red Fantail, Rufous Flycatcher, Wood Fantail

RECOGNITION Upperparts grey-brown, including head and wings; forehead orange-rufous, this colour extending back as an eyebrow streak. Tail is long, often widely fanned, with rump and base bright orange-rufous. Outer tail blackish, tipped white. Throat white, separated from belly by a breastband that is almost black where it meets the white throat in a sharply defined line, then, below, merges into the pale fawn of the remainder of underparts. 16–17 cm.

VOICE Usual call a single 'chip'; in flight similar double, sharp notes. Song is a squeaky thin descending sequence, higher-pitched than that of Grey Fantail.

HABITAT In the south-east, eucalypt forests; in north, rainforests and mangroves. Prefers damp, dense sites. On migration, occasionally open country, suburbs.

BREEDING Usually October–February; recorded September–April. Nest is a neat small cup with long tail or stem; like that of Grey Fantail but slightly larger; built of fine bark and grasses, densely felted with webs. Two to three pale stone to buff eggs, speckled grey, brown.

RANGE Coastal northern and eastern Australia; Kimberley to south-east of South Australia, absent from Tasmania. Migrant to south-east in summer. Also in New Guinea, Indonesia.

STATUS Moderately common.

▶ See also pages
81 97 98 *100* 111
122 127 139 199
210

408 GREY FANTAIL

Rhipidura fuliginosa   Muscicapidae

OTHER NAMES Cranky Fan, Dusky Fantail, Mad Fan, White-fronted Fantail

RECOGNITION Tail long, often fanned; a restlessly active bird, fluttering up to catch insects, swinging widespread tail side to side. Upperparts dark grey, with small

408 GREY FANTAIL *Rhipidura fuliginosa*

white eyebrow and ear marks; two fine white wingbars; tail has white outer margins, large white tips; variable, one subspecies has extensive white on tail. Large white throat-patch separated from pale fawn underparts by dark grey breastband. Numerous subspecies: birds from south-east darker. 14–17 cm.

VOICE Call a frequent 'check' or 'dek'; in breeding season has a squeaky or tinny song, melodious, ascending to final very high notes.

HABITAT Eucalypt forests and woodlands, inland tree-lined watercourses. Some in specialized habitats: *phasiana* (subspecies or species) in mangroves.

BREEDING June–March; varies from north to south of Australia. Nest is a neat cup with long tail beneath; built of fine bark, grass, closely bound with webs to a felted consistency; on thin twig of shrub, tree. Two to four fawn eggs, spotted grey, rufous.

RANGE Throughout Australia in suitable habitat. Also in New Zealand, New Guinea and other northern islands. Some populations migratory.

STATUS Common.

▶ See also pages
202 208

409 NORTHERN FANTAIL

Rhipidura rufiventris   Muscicapidae

OTHER NAMES Banded Fantail, Red-vented Fantail, White-throated Fantail

RECOGNITION Very closely resembles the well-known Grey Fantail, but has only one small, white facial marking, the eyebrow line, lacking the white ear-mark. The head looks larger, and the bill is longer, giving a more flycatcher-like appearance than other fantails. Tail slightly shorter, white-tipped and white-edged, but not white-shafted. Breastband wider, grey streaked white. Behaviour more subdued than Grey Fantail, seldom fanning tail; flight not as erratic. Often in mixed flocks, and takes much of prey in flight. 17–18 cm.

VOICE Generally quieter than Grey Fantail. Call a deeper 'chunk, chunk', which becomes fast when bird is disturbed. Song is very high, tinkling, musical.

HABITAT Rainforests and monsoon forests, riverine vegetation, swamp woodlands, mangroves.

BREEDING Usually August–January, but recorded July–March. The nest is the usual fantail wineglass shape, of fine bark strips and grass felted with webs; built on a slender twig. Two to three cream eggs, spotted blue-grey and dull brown.

RANGE Northern Australia; Broome (WA) to about Mackay (Qld). Also in New Guinea and numerous other northern islands. Sedentary.

STATUS Moderately common.

▶ See also pages
111 198 199 202
208 *209* 210 409

410 WILLIE WAGTAIL

Rhipidura leucophrys   Muscicapidae

OTHER NAMES Black-and-white Flycatcher, Shepherd's Companion, Black-and-white Fantail

RECOGNITION A larger fantail, swings long tail energetically side to side. Upperparts, including wings, tail, head and throat, glossy black; in bold sharp contrast against the entirely white underparts. Seems constantly active, flitting about restlessly, at one moment snapping insects from the air, the next bouncing across the ground after small terrestrial prey; often perches on livestock. Defends nest fearlessly, even against eagles. 19–21 cm.

VOICE Call a sharp metallic rattling, often in alarm or anger. Song is high, spirited, musical sequence, 'sweet-pretty creature', often at night.

HABITAT Open country: woodlands, farmlands, spinifex woodlands, almost treeless plains, mulga and other arid scrubs, mangroves; avoids heavy forests.

BREEDING Usually July–January, but recorded nesting all months. Nest is a neat cup of fine strips of bark, grass, matted with webs to a felt consistency; often built on a limb low over water. Two to four creamy eggs, spotted browns, greys.

RANGE Throughout Australia except heavy forest; vagrant Bass Strait islands, Tasmania. Also in New Guinea and other northern islands.

STATUS Common. Local seasonal movements.

▶ See also pages
204

410 WILLIE WAGTAIL *Rhipidura leucophrys*

CHOWCHILLAS, WHIPBIRDS, WEDGEBILLS

**Orthonychidae Family of 11 species
9 in Australia, 9 breeding, 9 endemic
Sibley-Ahlquist: Family Orthonychidae**

Four genera of long-tailed, ground or near ground-dwelling songbirds that are secretive in habits, yet many have powerful voices, rich loud calls and song. Some are crested, and most have plumage strongly patterned in rich camouflage colours. Their habitats are diverse, some being inhabitants of rainforests, some of semi-desert, but within those environs, many keep to scrubby thickets or dense undergrowth.

411 LOGRUNNER

Orthonyx temminckii   Orthonychidae

OTHER NAMES Southern Logrunner, Spine-tailed Logrunner, Spine-tailed Chowchilla

RECOGNITION A colourful small bird of the forest floor, where its colours blend with the autumn tones of the leaf-litter. Upperparts from crown to tail-coverts rufous, streaked and mottled black, lightly on crown, heavily on back. Wings black, crossed by three prominent vertical black bars. Tail blackish. Throat and breast white, edged with a bold black line each side. Female has throat orange. Immatures mottled brown. 17–20 cm.

VOICE Loud, distinctive and resonant. Song is an excited rapid sequence, 'be-queek, be-queek, bequeek-bequeek-'; if disturbed, an excited 'weet-weet-'.

HABITAT Rainforest, where the floor is relatively open, but with abundant litter of leaves, logs, and some low vegetation of ferns, vines, lantana.

BREEDING March–November. Nest large for size of bird; domed, with side entrance and approach ramp; built of large sticks, leaves, moss on top; looks like heap of debris; on ground, between buttress roots, rocks. Two large, white eggs.

RANGE Eastern Australia; from Bunya Range (Qld) to Illawarra district (NSW). Sedentary.

STATUS Common in north; scarce in south. Endemic.

► **See also pages**
52 116–17 *117*
121 122 127

412 CHOWCHILLA

Orthonyx spaldingii   Orthonychidae

OTHER NAMES Northern Logrunner, Black-headed Logrunner, Northern Chowchilla

RECOGNITION Upperparts glossy blackish-brown, appearing black in gloomy light, blacker on head; conspicuous white eye-ring. Tail and wings entirely blackish-brown; tail feathers inconspicuously spine-tipped. Throat, breast and belly white. Eye brown; bill and legs black. Female: throat and upper breast cinnamon-orange. Immatures: mottled browns and cinnamon. In small family groups, scratching among leaf-litter of forest floor. 26–29 cm.

VOICE At dawn, one of noisiest of birds with ringing 'chow-chilla, chow-chilla-chow-chow-chook-chook'; relatively quiet through rest of day.

HABITAT Tropical rainforests, mostly in highland regions, extending down to lower slopes of ranges that carry upland rainforests.

BREEDING April–November, but may occur any time of year, usually avoiding wet months. Nest is a bulky, domed structure of large sticks, mosses; piled against vine or fern clump, or on a stump or epiphytic fern. Has a single white egg.

RANGE Restricted to north-eastern Queensland; Cooktown south to Mt Spec near Townsville. Sedentary.

STATUS Common in range. Endemic.

► **See also pages**
53 90–1 *91* 97

413 EASTERN WHIPBIRD

Psophodes olivaceus   Orthonychidae

OTHER NAMES Coachwhip-bird, Whipbird, Stockwhip-bird

RECOGNITION Very long-tailed, crested. Back and wings dark olive-green; head and crest black; tail dark olive tipped white. Face and throat black with a large white patch each side of throat, joining at chin. Breast black; abdomen light grey. Female slightly smaller; throat mottled whitish. Immatures dull olive-brown; wings and tail greener; lack white throat. Spends much of time hopping across ground under thickets; noisy but hard to sight. 22–30 cm.

VOICE An extremely loud whipcrack call, given by male, and so instantly answered by female's softer 'choo-choo' that all seems the call of one bird.

HABITAT Rainforest and eucalypt forest, favouring gullies with dense cover. Also occurs in denser heaths, areas of lantana thickets.

BREEDING July–October, but recorded June–December. The nest is a shallow, bulky cup shape; loosely constructed of long twigs, bracken, lined with fine rootlets; placed in dense undergrowth. Two pale blue eggs, marked lilac and black.

RANGE Eastern Australia; approximately Cooktown to Melbourne, coast and ranges. Sedentary.

STATUS Common. Endemic species of two subspecies.

► **See also pages**
81 117–18 *118*
159

414 WESTERN WHIPBIRD

Psophodes nigrogularis   Orthonychidae

OTHER NAMES Black-throated Whipbird, Mallee Whipbird

RECOGNITION Very long-tailed, slightly crested. Upperparts olive-green, including head and crest, back and wings; white-tipped tail. Throat black, separated from olive of face by a white stripe extending back and down from base of bill. Underparts greyish-olive; sometimes paler or white in centre of belly (subspecies *leucogaster*). Very secretive, rarely observed, keeping low, running beneath ground-cover; in flight shows white-tipped tail. 20–25 cm.

VOICE Song very different from that of the Eastern Whipbird, lacking the powerful whipcrack: four scratchy notes, repeatedly, female adding further three notes.

HABITAT Mallee and heath, including mallee and spinifex on dunes, dry eucalypt and mallee, tea-tree and broombush; in Western Australia, open mallee, banksia-heath.

BREEDING June or July, to November or December. Nest is a substantial cup of fine twigs, strips of bark and grass; usually very well concealed in a dense low bush. Two pale blue eggs, with fine spots and lines of black, browns and grey.

RANGE South coast of Western Australia, Eyre Peninsula, Kangaroo Island, and South Australian–Victorian mallee. Sedentary.

STATUS Rare. Endemic.

► **See also pages**
138 155 *157*
159–60 162 164
242 245

415 CHIRRUPING WEDGEBILL

Psophodes cristatus   Orthonychidae

OTHER NAMES Wheelbarrow-bird, Crested Wedgebill, Chimesbird, Kitty-lintol

RECOGNITION Conspicuous crest, long-tailed. Dull pale brown upperparts, including head, crest, back; slightly darker on wings and tail. Wings have central flight feathers edged white; tail rounded, with outer feathers broadly tipped white. Underparts pale grey; bill short, wedge-shaped in profile. The Chirruping Wedgebill is comparatively bold, gregarious. 20–22 cm.

VOICE Lacks the sadly beautiful chiming quality of song of the Chiming Wedgebill;

like chirruping of Budgerigar, often in duet with female.

HABITAT Low, open semi-arid scrubs; saltbush, bluebush, acacia, spinifex, where it is quite easily observed, not being as shy as the Chiming Wedgebill.

BREEDING Most months except mid-summer; breeding greatly influenced by rain in semi-arid interior. Nest a shallow, sparse open structure of twigs, grass; hidden in a dense bush. Two to three pale blue eggs, sparsely spotted grey and black.

RANGE South-east interior, west of New South Wales, south-eastern Queensland, eastern South Australia, north-western Victoria. Sedentary.

STATUS Locally common. Endemic.

► **See also pages**
130 231

416 CHIMING WEDGEBILL

Psophodes occidentalis   Orthonychidae

OTHER NAMES Wheelbarrow-bird, Crested Wedgebill, Chimesbird, Kitty-lintol

RECOGNITION Almost identical to Chirruping Wedgebill: crested, long-tailed. Dull brown upperparts, including head, crest, back; slightly darker wings; tail. Wings have central flight feathers edged white; tail rounded, with outer feathers broadly tipped white. Underparts pale grey. This western species has faint darker streaks on breast. Bill short, wedge-shaped. Much more shy than Chirruping Wedgebill, contriving always to remain well concealed, hard to sight. 20–22 cm.

VOICE One of the characteristic songs of the western interior, in clear, chiming, sad notes, 'pipity-boo', the last note much lower; repetitive.

HABITAT Mulga scrublands, scrub along watercourses in spinifex country, mallee, mallee-broombush country. Apparently feeds on seeds and insects.

BREEDING Most months except mid-summer; breeding greatly influenced by rain in semi-arid interior. Nest a shallow, sparse open structure of twigs, grass; hidden in a dense bush. Two to three pale blue eggs, sparsely spotted grey and black.

RANGE Arid western regions; mid-western Australian coast to southern parts of Northern Territory, north-west of South Australia. Probably locally nomadic.

STATUS Common. Endemic.

► **See also pages**
59 *61* 179 184 231 353

417 SPOTTED QUAIL-THRUSH

Cinclosoma punctatum   Orthonychidae

OTHER NAMES Spotted Babbling-thrush, Ground-bird, Spotted Ground-bird

RECOGNITION Overall brownish plumage, heavily spotted. Upperparts olive-brown, heavily mottled black; shoulder-patch black, spotted white; wing-quills grey; innerwing-quills chestnut and black. Head distinctively patterned. Bold long white eyebrow line; face, chin and throat black, with conspicuous white patch each side of black throat. Breast grey with black band. Belly white; flanks buff, spotted black. Female paler; yellow ochre throat-patches. 25–28 cm.

VOICE As a contact call a high drawn-out 'see-eep'; song of male, from a high perch, an even series of soft, flute-like notes. Harsh chatter in alarm.

HABITAT Eucalypt forest, favouring high-lands, sunny slopes, but extending down to sea level where there is an understorey of low shrubs, grasses.

BREEDING July–February. The nest is built into a depression in the ground; loosely lined with bark, grass and leaves to form a rough, cup shape. It is usually sheltered by a treetrunk or rock. Two to three white eggs, spotted purple and umber.

RANGE South-eastern Australia, ranges and coast; south-eastern Queensland to south-east of South Australia, and Tasmania. Sedentary or nomadic.

STATUS Uncommon; locally common. Endemic.

► **See also pages**
65 66 121 122 136 162

418 CHESTNUT QUAIL-THRUSH

Cinclosoma castanotum   Orthonychidae

OTHER NAMES Chestnut-backed Quail-thrush, Copperback, Chestnut Ground-bird

RECOGNITION Large; overall dark plumage. Upperparts olive-brown; deep chestnut across the lower back and rump. Shoulder-patch black, spotted white; wings patterned chestnut, rufous, black. Head boldly patterned. Face, throat and breast black, with long bold white line at eyebrow level and across each side of throat. Belly white, edged black. Inland forms brighter chestnut upperparts. Female grey on throat and breast; upperparts duller and greyer. 23–25 cm.

VOICE Contact call high-pitched, an almost inaudible 'se-eep', often heard at dawn. The song is a softly tremulous sound, from high perch, at dawn.

HABITAT A wide range of habitats: mulga, mallee, native-pine scrubs, often with spinifex, and usually with sandy soils; tea-tree of drier coasts.

BREEDING July–February; usually August–

December. The nest is built into a small hollow against a mallee, fallen branch, clump of grass; neatly formed of bark, grass. Two to three white eggs, spotted shades of lavender and brown.

RANGE Across drier and usually inland parts of southern Australia. Sedentary or nomadic.

STATUS Generally uncommon. Endemic.

► **See also pages**
130 137 138 162 164 215 220 227 229

419 CINNAMON QUAIL-THRUSH

Cinclosoma cinnamomeum Orthonychidae

OTHER NAMES Western Quail-thrush, Black-vented Ground-thrush, Chestnut-breasted Quail-thrush

RECOGNITION Wide-ranging and variable species; western subspecies *marginatum* sometimes treated as full species. Upperparts plain, pale to rich cinnamon; black shoulder-patch with white spotting. Head darker brown; face and throat black with long, bold white streaks at eyebrow and along sides of throat. Buff to cinnamon across breast, along flanks; black lower breastband; belly white edged black. Female: buff throat; grey-buff breast with no black band. 18–24 cm.

VOICE Contact calls and song, insect-like, far-carrying; some notes very high and almost inaudible: 'see-eee-eee' and 'seee-wit'; sharper alarm notes.

HABITAT Mulga and other acacia scrub, saltbush and spinifex on stony ground, gibberstone country; generally appears to avoid sandy country.

BREEDING All months, rain dependent; mostly August–September. Nest of bark strips, leaves; built into a shallow depression usually under shelter of a low bush; often has apron of leaves, bark. Two to three pale grey eggs, marked grey, brown.

RANGE Across arid inland Australia. Sedentary; possibly locally nomadic.

STATUS Moderately common. Endemic.

► **See also pages**
130 164 173 175 215 227 227 231 355

420 NULLARBOR QUAIL-THRUSH

Cinclosoma alisteri   Orthonychidae

OTHER NAME Black-breasted Groundbird

RECOGNITION This species, which is confined to the Nullarbor, is usually treated as a separate species. Upperparts rich rufous-cinnamon except shoulders which are black with white spots, and outer-tail feathers black tipped white. Face, throat and breast black, continued back as broken black line between cinnamon flanks and white belly; black of breast without any upper breastband of white or cinnamon. Female: face grey-brown; breast grey. 18–21 cm.

VOICE Probably like that of Cinnamon Quail-thrush, very high-pitched, possibly weaker.

HABITAT Confined to those saltbush plains of the Nullarbor where bluebush also occurs; avoids the more richly vegetated dongas, and sandy country.

BREEDING Breeds regularly August–September, but sometimes other months. Nest like that of Cinnamon Quail-thrush, of dry grass; in depression, by a rock, clump of grass, low bush. Two to three creamy eggs, spotted greys and browns.

RANGE Nullarbor; Naretha (WA) to Ooldea (SA). Probably locally nomadic.

STATUS Uncommon; patchy and localized. Endemic.

▶ See also pages
213 215 *215* 220

421 **GREY-CROWNED BABBLER** *Pomatostomus temporalis*

BABBLERS

**Timaliidae Family of 255 species
4 in Australia, 4 breeding, 3 endemic
Sibley-Ahlquist: Family
Pomatostomidae**

Sturdy medium-sized songbirds of extremely gregarious nature, living in communal groups, sharing many of the nest-building and nest attendance duties, and roosting together in the large domed nests. Noisy; much loud chattering within the group. Bills are quite long, robust, downcurved; tails long; plumage dominantly browns and greys with prominent white eyebrows and tail-tips. Feeding is principally on the ground.

GREY-CROWNED BABBLER

Pomatostomus temporalis   Timaliidae
OTHER NAMES Catbird, Apostlebird, Happy Family, Twelve Apostles, Jumper

RECOGNITION Upperparts dark grey-brown, becoming darker on wings; blackish on tail, which is white-tipped. Crown pale grey, this the only babbler without dark crown; very broad buffy-white eyebrows extend back to nape. Grey streak through eye, broadening to merge into grey-brown of body. Throat white, blending to pale grey or rufous on upper breast; rufous to dark grey on underparts. In flight, chestnut

wing-patch. Bill long, black, downcurved. 25–29 cm.

VOICE Churring and cat-like sounds, and loud call in which female gives a 'yaa-' and male follows on with '-ahoo'; also 'chunk' and louder 'pee-oo'.

HABITAT Open forests, scrubby woodlands, acacia scrublands, farmlands; avoids the sandy semi-desert country and wetter country.

BREEDING July–February; recorded June–March. Nest is a bulky, globular structure with side entrance; built of large sticks; well lined with fine grasses, fur; 1–10 m high, conspicuous. Two to six light brown eggs, marked purple-brown and black.

RANGE Most of Australia except south-west, southern interior, and Tasmania. Species in New Guinea. Sedentary.

STATUS Moderately common. Endemic subspecies.

▶ See also pages
183 356

WHITE-BROWED BABBLER

Pomatostomus superciliosus   Timaliidae
OTHER NAMES Twelve Apostles, Stickbird, Jumper, Apostlebird, Catbird

RECOGNITION A plain babbler; upperparts grey-brown; dark brown on the crown,

wings and rump. Long tail blackish-brown, tipped white on all but the central pair of feathers. Wide dark brown stripe from base of bill through eye, between conspicuous long white eyebrow and white of throat. This white of throat and breast merge into grey-brown on lower breast; belly and undertail dark grey-brown. Bill long, thin, downcurved. Immatures: shorter bill. 18–20 cm.

VOICE Greatly varied: cat-like miaowings, repeated 'tuk-tuk-' when foraging; louder 'weet-weet-weet-weeow' as contact call; excited chatter if disturbed.

HABITAT Scrubby open woodlands, occasionally open forests, mulga and mallee, native-pine scrubs. Feeds on insects and seeds from leaf-litter.

BREEDING July–December; recorded from June–February. Groups of three to 15 babblers live together; breed communally. Nest is a large domed structure of sticks; lined with grass, feathers. Two to five grey-brown eggs, with fine, dark brown lines.

RANGE Southern Australia except wetter coastal south-east, south-west and Tasmania. Sedentary.

STATUS Common. Endemic species of several, possibly four, subspecies.

▶ See also pages
41 42 135 220 356

HALL'S BABBLER

Pomatostomus hallii   Timaliidae

OTHER NAMES White-breasted Babbler, White-throated Babbler

RECOGNITION Similar to the White-browed Babbler but darker, with bolder contrast between sooty dark browns, and whites. Crown almost sooty black; eyebrow lines wider, white. White of throat cut off sharply at upper breast, as a bib, rather than blending gradually into darker tones of lower breast and abdomen. Through the eye, a broad dark stripe which appears black between white of eyebrow and throat. Tail blackish, broadly tipped white; bill long, black. 23–24 cm.

VOICE Calls reported to be more like those of Grey-crowned than White-browed Babbler: thin or squeaky chatterings, chucklings, and growlings.

HABITAT Mulga and other acacia scrubs, usually where there is grassy ground-cover; also in nearly treeless spinifex country, semi-arid open woodlands.

BREEDING September–December; recorded August–May. Nest is a dome-shaped structure, somewhat smaller and neater than that of White-browed Babbler, and usually placed in an acacia bush 2–10 m above ground. Eggs like those of White-browed.

RANGE Restricted, eastern interior; south-western Queensland to north-west of New South Wales. Sedentary.

STATUS Locally common, in optimum habitat. Endemic.

▶ See also pages *133* *135*

CHESTNUT-CROWNED BABBLER

Pomatostomus ruficeps   Timaliidae

OTHER NAMES Chestnut-crowned Chatterer, Chatterer, Red-capped Babbler

RECOGNITION Upperparts and broad band through eye are dark grey-brown; in bold, neat contrast to thin white eyebrow streak, and sharply defined large white patch over throat and lower breast; two white wingbars and rich chestnut crown separate this species from other babblers. Flanks dark brown; tail blackish-brown tipped white. Eye brown; legs grey; bill downcurved, black above, grey beneath. Immatures duller; brown-tinged eyebrow. 21–23 cm.

VOICE Noisy, penetrating slightly plaintive flock call 'wee-chee-cheee-'. Territorial song is strident yet melodious. In alarm, excited 'chak-a-chak-'.

HABITAT Mallee and open woodlands especially where dominated by native pine, acacia scrublands, saltbush plains, and similar dry habitats.

BREEDING July–February; recorded June–March. Nest is a bulky, domed structure of large sticks; well lined with bark, plant-

down and wool; usually placed quite high; old nests often reused. Three to five grey-brown eggs, streaked brown.

RANGE South-eastern Australian interior; south-western Queensland, western New South Wales, north-western Victoria, east of South Australia. Sedentary.

STATUS Moderately common; varying scarce to locally common. Endemic.

▶ See also page *133*

OLD WORLD WARBLERS

Sylviidae Family of 400 species
8 in Australia, 8 breeding, 3 endemic
Sibley-Ahlquist: Family Sylviidae,
Subfamily Sylviinae, Tribe Sylviini

A large widespread family of songbirds, the genera included varying according to current opinion. At present includes small songbirds of grasslands and reed-beds. Plumages are brownish, some heavily streaked; tails moderately long, pointed. Some have powerful voices and rich songs, some with aerial display flights. The two species of songlarks are not related to the true larks, but were so named for their lark-like song-flights.

CLAMOROUS REED-WARBLER

Acrocephalus stentoreus   Sylviidae

OTHER NAMES Reed-lark, Water Sparrow, Australian Reed-Warbler, Swamp Tit

RECOGNITION Upperparts plain light olive-brown; darker on the crown, wings and tail; faint buffy-white eyebrow. Face pale buff; slightly darker through the eye. Throat dull white; flanks cinnamon-buff; remainder of underparts buffy-white. Bill brown, paler beneath; legs blackish-brown. The presence of this species in any reed-bed is invariably advertised by its singing, which is not only clamorous, but also delightfully, richly musical. 15–17 cm.

VOICE A common call is a short sharp 'chut, chut'; the full song of the breeding season is a rich, powerful 'twitchy-twitchy-quarty-quarty-quarty'.

HABITAT Wetlands: bulrush reed-beds of lakes, swamps, river edges, parks and gardens; also cumbungi, bamboos, lantana or tall crops close by water.

BREEDING September–February. The nest is a very deep cup of strips of reed and other swamp plants woven round adjacent reed stems, and warmly lined with fine materials. Three to four eggs; variable, pale blue to buff, spotted greys, dark browns.

RANGE Throughout Australia in suitable habitat. Also in New Guinea, South-East Asia, Africa. Migratory, at least partially.

STATUS Common.

▶ See also pages *37* *37* *384*

TAWNY GRASSBIRD

Megalurus timoriensis   Sylviidae

OTHER NAMES Tawny Marshbird, Rufous-capped Grassbird, Rufous-capped Grass-Warbler

RECOGNITION Usually keeps to dense cover, giving few opportunities for even a brief glimpse. Upperparts cinnamon-rufous; streaked black in very heavy longitudinal lines on the back, with black rufous-edged feathers of wings continuing this streaked effect. Forehead, crown and nape light cinnamon, not streaked; pale buff eyebrow. Face and underparts fawny-white. Will sometimes climb above rushes on a taller stem to watch observer. 19 cm.

VOICE In breeding season male makes display flights over territory, to hover like Rufous Songlark while singing a spirited, loud 'ch-ch-chzzzlik-lik'.

HABITAT Bulrush and adjoining lush wet grass, wet heaths, cane-grass, cumbungi swamps, moist tall crops such as sugarcane and corn.

BREEDING August–April. The nest is deeply cup-shaped, narrowed in at the rim; built of grass, lined with finer grasses; placed near ground in grass clump or other dense vegetation. Three pinkish eggs, speckled grey, purplish-brown.

RANGE Northern and eastern Australia, mainly coastal; Derby to Sydney. Also in New Guinea and Philippines. Nomadic.

STATUS Uncommon; locally common.

▶ See also pages *76* *79* *210*

LITTLE GRASSBIRD

Megalurus gramineus   Sylviidae

OTHER NAMES Little Marshbird, Striated Grassbird, Little Reedbird

RECOGNITION Secretive; seldom sighted though common. Upperparts entirely grey-brown; wings darker and greyer; less rufous than Tawny Grassbird, and heavily streaked brownish-black from forehead to rump. The crown has a more tawny tone, and there is a slightly paler eyebrow. Underparts dull buff; lightly streaked and spotted on throat and breast. The long

427 LITTLE GRASSBIRD *Megalurus gramineus*

pointed brown tail is often carried partly cocked. In flight, rump tawny. 14 cm.

VOICE Call is often the only indication of presence: a mournful whistle 'tu-peeeee-peeee', the first low and short, then high and drawn-out.

HABITAT Rushes, lignum swamps, cumbungi, bore-drain vegetation, and sometimes tidal situations including mangroves, samphire, saltmarshes.

BREEDING August–January; recorded July–May. The nest is a deep cup of strips of reeds, grass, well lined with feathers; often semi-domed; woven round reed stems or in a dense low shrub. Three to five pink-tinged eggs, speckled purplish-red.

RANGE Mainly south-western and south-eastern Australia, Tasmania; sparsely to Northern Territory, north-eastern Queensland, north-west of Western Australia. Also, rarely, in New Guinea. Nomadic, especially in arid regions.

STATUS Common.

▶ See also pages
76 225 242 366

428 SPINIFEXBIRD

Eremiornis carteri   Sylviidae
OTHER NAMES Desertbird, Carter's Desertbird
RECOGNITION Upperparts plain, light grey-brown to cinnamon-brown, with slightly more definite rufous tone to the crown, and with buff eyebrow. The darker brown, buff-tipped tail is about as long as combined head-and-body; usually carried in drooped position, but quite often cocked upwards. Underparts buffy-white. Eye

brown; bill black above, paler beneath; legs grey. Rarely out of cover of spinifex except quick hopping or low flight between clumps. 14–16 cm.

VOICE Presence usually revealed by alarm call coming from spinifex, an abrupt 'juk-juk'. Song a clear loud 'je-swee-ah-voo', and regular 'cheerit'.

HABITAT Spinifex; favouring areas of taller clumps, especially where small watercourses and gullies encourage a more lush growth of the spinifex.

BREEDING Usually August–November, but at other times of year after good rains. The nest is a deep cup of fine grasses, usually very well concealed, deep in a clump of spinifex. Two pinkish-white eggs, finely speckled lilac and red-brown.

RANGE Northern arid regions; coastal north-western Australia through Northern Territory to western Queensland. Sedentary.

STATUS Uncommon; locally common. Endemic.

▶ See also pages
28 *29* 30–1 175
219 230

429 ZITTING CISTICOLA

Cisticola juncidis   Sylviidae
OTHER NAMES Streaked Cisticola, Fantail Cisticola, Fantail Warbler, Fantail Grass-Warbler
RECOGNITION Breeding plumage: very like non-breeding plumage of Golden-headed Cisticola. Upperparts cinnamon; lightly streaked black on crown and nape, heavily streaked on back and wings, more heavily than the Golden-headed Cisticola; rump more rufous. Tail dark brown tipped white. Eyebrow, lower face and entire underparts buffy-white. Non-breeding plumage: upperparts more heavily streaked, particularly on nape and rump. Female more heavily streaked on crown. Immatures duller. 10 cm.

VOICE Call is series of chattered notes. Male has persistent 'zitting' song, an insect-like, monotonous 'zit-zit-zit-'; female much quieter.

HABITAT Grassy swamps, localities permanently damp but not seasonally deeply flooded; greater inclination to saline sites than the Golden-headed Cisticola.

BREEDING Usually December–March with wet season. Nest is of oval-domed shape, in grass, of grass-blades drawn together and secured with spiders' webs; entrance on side near top; lined with plant-down. Three to four pale blue eggs, marked red-brown.

RANGE Northern and north-eastern Australia, coastal. Also to South-East Asia, southern Europe. Probably sedentary, at least in Northern Territory.

STATUS Uncommon; probably locally common.

▶ See also pages
192 *193* 210

430 GOLDEN-HEADED CISTICOLA

Cisticola exilis   Sylviidae
OTHER NAMES Barleybird, Golden-headed Fantail-Warbler, Cornbird, Tailorbird
RECOGNITION Male, breeding plumage: upperparts cinnamon, heavily streaked black on back and wings; head richer golden-buff, not streaked; rump deep cinnamon; tail short, dark brown tipped light buff; underparts buff-white. Non-breeding plumage male and female: crown also dark-streaked; tail noticeably longer. Very like male Zitting Cisticola, which is slightly less golden, and has whiter tail-tips; differences of call, nest, habitat. 9–11 cm.

VOICE In spring and summer, almost incessant buzzing calls, with display flights. The call is a persistent 'bzzz-zzt, pil-lek'; also chatters, scolds.

HABITAT Wetlands, usually in lowland swamps, wet grass and rank herbage edges of swamps, rivers, irrigated crops and pastures, tussock grasslands, samphire.

BREEDING September–March. Nest is small domed structure; unique in Australia in that living leaves are stitched together with web, over much of exterior to conceal and strengthen. Three to four bright blue eggs, spotted and blotched red-brown.

RANGE North-western, northern, north-eastern, eastern and south-eastern Australia, rarely northern Tasmania. Probably sedentary.

STATUS Common. Widespread from New Guinea through South-East Asia to India, southern China.

▶ See also pages
30 31 138 192

431 RUFOUS SONGLARK

Cinclorhamphus mathewsi   Sylviidae
OTHER NAMES Rufous-rumped Songlark, Rufous Singing Lark, Skylark
RECOGNITION Upperparts streaky brown except rump and uppertail-coverts which are plain rufous or tawny, showing well as the bird flutters away. Head slightly greyer, with pale fawn eyebrow, lower face, and throat; tail darker brown. Underparts a dull buff; breast slightly dusky or lightly spotted. Female slightly smaller. Immatures paler, with indistinct spotting to front of neck and breast. Often in small parties; inconspicuous except in breeding season. 17–19 cm.

VOICE Extremely vocal when breeding; often a ringing, almost whipcrack 'whitcher', or in joyous full song a repeated ringing 'awitchy-weedle-witch'.

HABITAT Open grassland plains, open grassy woodlands, grassy mulga scrubs, spinifex, farmlands.

BREEDING August–February. The nest is well concealed; a deep grass cup built into a depression; usually under overhanging grass or by a log. Male is polygamous, usually preoccupied with territorial song. Three to four white eggs, speckled reddish.

RANGE Almost throughout Australia except Tasmania and, perhaps, upper Cape York.

STATUS Moderately common. Migrant to south in summer; to north for winter. Endemic.

▶ See also pages
173 356

431 **RUFOUS SONGLARK** *Cinclorhamphus mathewsi*

432 BROWN SONGLARK

Cinclorhamphus cruralis   Sylviidae

OTHER NAMES Harvestbird, Black-breasted Songlark, Australian Skylark

RECOGNITION Overall dark cinnamon-brown, streaked on back and wings with darker brown and buff, and dusky chocolate-brown from chin to belly; tail long, dark brown, with pointed feather tips, and typically carried cocked upwards. In breeding season attracts attention by song-flight, lifting from ground in full song, rising steeply on fast-beating wings, to glide with wings upswept. Female much smaller, paler; breast dull white, streaked darker. 19–25 cm.

VOICE Male's song loud and persistent, rhythmic, with penetrating high scratchy and lower metallic sounds; a reeling 'skitscot-a-wheeler' pattern.

HABITAT Open grassland plains; open woodlands and scrublands with grassy ground-cover; sparse low shrub country such as saltbush, bluebush, farmlands.

BREEDING Usually September–February, but in drier regions at any time of year after good rains. The nest is a deep, open cup of grasses, well hidden in a clump of grass or other dense ground-cover. Three to four white eggs, speckled red-brown.

RANGE Throughout Australia in suitable habitat except Tasmania; absent or rare far north. Nomadic and migratory.

STATUS Moderately common. Endemic.

▶ See also pages
29 31

FAIRY-WRENS

**Maluridae Family of 26 species
18 in Australia, 18 breeding, 18 endemic
Sibley-Ahlquist: Family Maluridae,
Subfamilies Malurinae,
Amytornithinae**

Also known as 'Australian Warblers'. A family of small insectivorous birds with long tails characteristically carried cocked upwards except in flight when trailing behind. Many species have bright colours, but mainly confined to males in breeding plumage. The fairy-wrens are often in family parties, with subordinate non-breeding members assisting the breeding pair. Also in this family are the distinctive, elusive emu-wrens, and the grasswrens.

433 PURPLE-CROWNED FAIRY-WREN

Malurus coronatus   Maluridae

OTHER NAMES Lilac-crowned Wren, Lilac-crowned Fairy-wren, Purple-crowned Wren

RECOGNITION Unique in having purple crown with black centre; broad black line through face and round nape. Back light brown; underparts buff; tail blue. Female light brown upperparts; buff underparts; chestnut patch through eye from base of bill to ear-coverts; tail blue. Eastern population (subspecies *macgillivrayi*): male darker upperparts; female has blue-grey tone on crown and nape. Larger than other fairy-wrens. 16 cm.

VOICE Loud chattered 'cheepa-cheeepa', stronger than most other fairy-wrens, used constantly between members of the foraging family group.

HABITAT Near water, fresh or tidal; in coarse cane-grass, reeds in water, pandanus, sometimes mangroves.

BREEDING During and after wet season, November–June. A bulky nest of paperbark or cane-grass, and placed low in cane-grass clump or pandanus near water. Three white eggs, speckled dark brown.

RANGE Two subspecies in Kimberley and south of Gulf of Carpentaria. Sedentary.

STATUS Uncommon; eastern subspecies endangered. Endemic.

▶ See also pages
174 187 197 198
201 *203* 204 208
211 *211*

434 SUPERB FAIRY-WREN

Malurus cyaneus   Maluridae

OTHER NAMES Superb Blue Wren, Fairy Wren, Mormon Wren

RECOGNITION Dull white underparts separate this from the Black-backed Fairy-wren, which has blue underparts. Distinguished from the Variegated Fairy-wren by the absence of chestnut on the shoulders. Female plain grey-brown; reddish-tinged about the lores and round eyes; tail brown. Male in eclipse is like female, but blue on the tail. Usually in pairs or family parties, foraging for insects in the undergrowth. 13 cm.

VOICE Series of high notes leading into strong brisk trill. Members of a group maintain contact with sharp 'prip'; in alarm, a high 'seeee'.

HABITAT Dense undergrowth of woodlands, open forests, parks, gardens, rainforest margins, riverside vegetation, swamp cane-grass.

BREEDING Nest is a domed, grass construction; in dense shrubbery usually within 1 m of the ground, occasionally to 5 m. Three to five pinkish-white eggs with reddish-brown spots, heavier about the larger end.

RANGE South-eastern Australia. Sedentary.

STATUS Common. Endemic species in Tasmania and endemic mainland subspecies.

▶ See also pages
121 123 153 170

435 SPLENDID FAIRY-WREN

Malurus splendens   Maluridae

OTHER NAMES Splendid Wren, Turquoise Fairy-wren, Banded Wren, Black-backed Fairy-wren

RECOGNITION Male is entirely blue and black, the deep blues glossy, iridescent, violet-tinged, brilliant in full sunlight (in case of south-west nominate subspecies). Turquoise Fairy-wren (subspecies *callainus*): male lighter, less violet blue, black band across lower back; Black-backed Fairy-wren (subspecies *melanotus*) has narrower breastband, paler ear-coverts. Distribution and habitats mostly separate. Females grey-brown; touch of blue on tail; pale grey underparts; pale chestnut lores. 13 cm.

VOICE A rich reeling trill, quite powerful for the size of the bird. Also high piping call, serving as contact within the group. Loud alarm trill.

HABITAT Subspecies *splendens* in forest and woodland scrub undergrowth; *callainus* in drier mulga-mallee-saltbush; *melanotus* in arid mallee-mulga-spinifex.

BREEDING Nest is domed; in low scrub usually ½–1½ m above ground; built of grass, lined with soft plant-down and feathers; side entrance. Three to four white eggs, finely spotted reddish-brown. Often nest is attended by family party.

RANGE South-western Australia through central Australia, and South Australia to western Queensland, New South Wales, and Victoria. Sedentary.

STATUS Common. Endemic.

▶ See also pages
137 185 223 *228* 232 240

436 VARIEGATED FAIRY-WREN

Malurus lamberti   Maluridae

OTHER NAMES Purple-backed Fairy-wren, Lavender-flanked Fairy-wren, Lambert's Fairy-wren, Variegated Wren

RECOGNITION A widespread species with a number of subspecies which have been listed as separate species. Member of chestnut-shouldered group; throat and breast black; crown blue or violet-blue; ear-covert patch usually paler. Range separate from the other black-breasted species, the Red-winged Fairy-wren. Subspecies *dulcis* and *rogersi*, Lavender-flanked Fairy-wren, have lilac flanks; subspecies *assimilis*, Purple-backed Fairy-wren, has purplish mantle and crown. 12–14 cm.

VOICE A high-pitched reeling call, typical fairy-wren sound.

HABITAT Varied. Nominate subspecies confined to forested eastern slopes of Great Dividing Range; *assimilis* semi-arid inland; *dulcis* and *rogersi* tropical.

BREEDING Variable: mainly wet season in tropical north; following any substantial rains in arid northern interior; September–December in south of range. Nest is domed, built into low dense vegetation. Two to four white eggs, speckled red-purple.

RANGE Most of Australia except south-west, south-east, Tasmania and Cape York. Sedentary.

STATUS Common. Endemic species of four subspecies, five if *amabilis* is included.

▶ See also pages
70 80 91 122 137
160 185 192 193
198 216 231 240
358 360

437 LOVELY FAIRY-WREN

Malurus amabilis   Maluridae

OTHER NAMES Purple-breasted Fairy-wren, Lovely Wren

RECOGNITION A very distinctive member of the chestnut-shouldered group, sometimes listed as a subspecies of the Variegated Fairy-wren. Male has light bright blue crown; this same blue extending down, surrounding the eye and forming a large ear-covert patch. Breast black; shoulder-patches chestnut. Female is exceptional among fairy wrens for the large amount of blue in plumage, on forehead, crown, nape, ear-coverts and tail; white round the eyes. 14 cm.

VOICE A thin high reeling trill, probably very close to that of the Variegated Fairy-wren.

HABITAT Margins of rainforests, dense vegetation and grass along creeks, paperbark thickets, edges of mangrove swamps.

BREEDING September–December. Spherical dome-shaped nest is situated close to the ground in dense cover; built of dry grass, dead leaves, and sometimes lightly bound

with webs, it has a side entrance. Three white eggs, sparsely speckled reddish.

RANGE Confined to north-eastern Queensland; Cape York and south almost to Townsville. Sedentary.

STATUS Moderately common. Endemic.

▶ See also pages
91 *93* 96 98 111

438 BLUE-BREASTED FAIRY-WREN

Malurus pulcherrimus   Maluridae

OTHER NAMES Blue-breasted Wren, Purple-breasted Fairy-warbler, Purple-breasted Fairy-wren

RECOGNITION Breast distinctly blue in good light, compared with black for Variegated Fairy-wren, and extremely dark blue for Red-winged Fairy-wren. Crown is more violet than Red-winged. Female similar to Variegated. Best separated from Red-winged by largely exclusive range, and preference for drier woodland habitat.

VOICE Usual fairy-wren trill, stronger than that of Red-winged Fairy-wren.

HABITAT Open forest, woodland and mallee in Western Australia; also swampy areas in South Australian part of range.

BREEDING September–December; possibly at other times after good rains. Nest is a quite substantial domed structure of grasses, usually 30 cm–1 m up in a small bush. Three white eggs, finely spotted red-brown mainly round larger end.

RANGE Southern Western Australia and Eyre Peninsula (SA). Sedentary.

STATUS Moderately common. Endemic.

▶ See also pages
160 *160* 164 240
245

439 RED-WINGED FAIRY-WREN

Malurus elegans   Maluridae

OTHER NAMES Red-winged Wren, Elegant Wren, Elegant Fairy-wren, Marsh Wren

RECOGNITION Habitat and call together provide easiest recognition. Keeps to wettest parts of the south-western corner, usually in dense undergrowth and damp margins of creeks and swamps. Similar Blue-breasted and Variegated fairy-wrens keep to drier woodland and heath habitats to north and east. Breast very deep blue, often looks black. Mantle and cheeks lighter silvery-blue; white across back. Female very similar to Variegated and Blue-breasted fairy-wrens. 14–15 cm.

VOICE Begins with several high squeaks before tenuous high reeling song.

HABITAT Karri forest, wetter parts of jarrah forest; along south coast, swampy heath and paperbark.

BREEDING September–January. Nest bulkier than most other fairy-wrens, includes partly decayed leaves making structure weak. Low in dense undergrowth, often where a grasstree skirt brushes ground. Three to four white eggs, marked red-brown.

RANGE South-western corner of Western Australia. Sedentary.

STATUS Common only in optimum habitat. Endemic.

▶ See also pages
160 240 *240* 242

440 WHITE-WINGED FAIRY-WREN

Malurus leucopterus   Maluridae

OTHER NAMES Blue-and-white Wren; includes Black-and-white Wren

RECOGNITION Entirely cobalt blue, brilliant in full sunlight except wings white (mainland subspecies *leuconotus*). On Barrow and Dirk Hartog islands (north-western Australia), blue replaced by black, though tail still blue (nominate subspecies). Female almost uniformly pale brown except underparts; outer-tail feathers dull white; slight blue-grey to tail. Male in eclipse similar to female but often with a few blue or black feathers in the plumage. 13 cm.

VOICE Typical fairy-wren, reeling song, but undulating, long sustained, very rapid sewing-machine sound.

HABITAT Mostly semi-arid treeless areas, saltbush, samphire, spinifex, sparse mulga scrub, low coastal heath and scrub on north-west coast (WA).

BREEDING July–December, but in any month after good rain; autumn breeding common in north-west after summer cyclones. Three to four white eggs, with fine purple-red marks.

RANGE Throughout semi-arid and arid Australia. Sedentary; some local wandering of family parties after breeding.

STATUS Common. Endemic.

▶ See also pages
130 137 169–70
172 185 216 227

441 RED-BACKED FAIRY-WREN

Malurus melanocephalus   Maluridae

OTHER NAMES Black-headed Wren, Red-backed Wren

RECOGNITION The only red-and-black wren. Male unmistakable when in breeding plumage, body almost entirely black or brownish-black, with deep crimson to fiery-orange saddle across the back; wings deep brown; tail black. Male has spectacular display, when red of the back is fluffed out, like a ball of fire. Female grey-brown, including brown tail; legs and bill pale brown tinged pink; has no reddish eye-ring. Immatures similar to female. 12–14 cm.

VOICE Usual reeling, fairy-wren song, stronger than the song of the Variegated Fairy-wren.

HABITAT Tropical woodlands and grasslands, particularly dense swamp-edge vegetation, lantana and other thickets, gardens, northern spinifex scrublands.

BREEDING June–February. Nest is the usual wren type, globular with side entrance, neat and compact, of grass or bark; placed in grass or low shrub. After breeding, in flocks or family parties. Three to four white eggs, spotted reddish.

RANGE North-west (subspecies *cruentatus*), and east coast (nominate subspecies). Sedentary or locally nomadic.

STATUS Common. Endemic.

▶ See also pages
76 98 122 *194* 204

442 RUFOUS-CROWNED EMU-WREN

Stipiturus ruficeps   Maluridae

OTHER NAME Mallee Emu-wren (subspecies *mallee*)

RECOGNITION Extremely small, with very long fine tail. Bright rufous, streaked with black on upperparts, conspicuous light blue throat-patch. Female bright, light rufous, with touch of blue on face and ear-coverts. Keeps to dense cover, usually spinifex, and best seen when it comes up into a shrub, which it tends to do when disturbed, giving squeaky alarm calls. Subspecies *mallee* darker upperparts; crown more heavily streaked. 12–14.5 cm.

VOICE Extremely high version of fairy-wren calls, easily mistaken for squeaking of an insect, and probably inaudible to some people.

HABITAT Arid; spinifex on sand-flats with scattered shrubs, spinifex on ranges. Subspecies *mallee* inhabits spinifex under scattered mallee.

BREEDING Subspecies *ruficeps* often after good rain; subspecies *mallee* possibly only spring breeder, September–December. Nest built into top of spinifex clump, not under clump, visible yet inconspicuous. Two to three white eggs, speckled in browns.

RANGE North-west coast to western Queensland. Subspecies *mallee*, Murray River mallee, in south-eastern Australia.

STATUS Probably common but not often sighted. Endemic.

▶ See also pages
28 138 170 184
213 216 *216* 219
230 232 233

443 SOUTHERN EMU-WREN

Stipiturus malachurus   Maluridae

OTHER NAME Button-grass Wren

RECOGNITION Extremely small, exceptionally long, fine tail. Rufous, with darker streakings on upperparts, including crown of head; bright lavender-blue throat-patch. Tail made up of six fine, almost transparent, filamentous feathers almost twice as long as the head-plus-body. These tail feathers superficially resemble emu feathers. Female without blues. Flies slowly, long tail trailing. 16–17 cm; tail 10–11 cm.

VOICE Wren-like, much higher pitched, yet quite strong; serves as a convenient way of locating these birds when they keep low in dense cover.

HABITAT In eastern Australia: swampy heaths, sedges, alpine heaths, button-grass; in South Australia and Western Australia: coastal heaths on sandplain.

BREEDING August–December. Nest domed; well concealed in dense low vegetation; built of grass, bark fibres, well lined. Two to four white eggs, sparsely spotted dull red. Breeds in pairs rather than groups; later in small family parties.

RANGE Mainly coastal; south-eastern Queensland to Eyre Peninsula, Tasmania, south-western Australia. Sedentary.

STATUS Uncommon in most of range; common south coast (WA). Endemic.

▶ See also pages
122 124 126 *146*
152 155 162 163
164 216 242

444 BLACK GRASSWREN

Amytornis housei   Maluridae

RECOGNITION Head, back, underparts, and tail black; finely streaked white on head and back; conspicuously streaked white from chin to breast. No other Australian bird with this coloration. Lower back and rump deep chestnut. Female light chestnut underparts. Immatures dark with faint white streaks. Usually in small parties, hopping among tumbled boulders. Will become quite inquisitive and perch conspicuously, but vanish into crevices and spinifex if alarmed. 22 cm.

VOICE Like song of fairy-wrens, but louder, harsher, sustained. The alarm call is a sharp ticking, interspersed with harsh, grating scoldings.

HABITAT Rugged   sandstone   terrain,

spinifex between boulders, scattered small trees. The plumage matches red-brown-black tones of weathered sandstone.

BREEDING No nest records; probably breeds in the wet season. The nest is bulky, dome-shaped; built into the top of a clump of spinifex; measures 20 cm high, 15 cm wide; side entrance.

RANGE North-western Kimberley. Sedentary.

STATUS Not often observed; common in suitable habitat. Endemic.

▶ See also pages
193 201 204–5
208 *209* 210 211

WHITE-THROATED GRASSWREN

Amytornis woodwardi   Maluridae

OTHER NAME Spinifex Grasswren

RECOGNITION Upperparts black, streaked white; tail black. Throat white; black breastband; abdomen rusty. Only likely overlap with another *Amytornis* is to east, with Carpentarian Grasswren (*A. dorotheae*), which is similar, but smaller, and lacks black breastband and paler brownish tail. Usually in small groups or family parties; shy and evasive; usually running rapidly among rocks and spinifex. If forced to fly, keeps low, drops quickly to cover. 20–22 cm.

VOICE Rich and varied song, with rising and falling series of trills. Alarm and contact call a strong sharp 'trrrit'.

HABITAT Rugged sandstone of escarpments, especially where gravelly ledges carry spinifex clumps and scattered low shrubs; boulders of river gorges.

BREEDING Wet season, December–March. Domed nest of grass, leaves, sometimes paperbark, built into the top of a spinifex clump. Two whitish eggs, speckled red-brown and sepia in a band round the broad end.

RANGE Confined to western Arnhem Land (NT).

STATUS Probably common in optimum habitat. Endemic.

▶ See also pages
189 192–3 196
197 198

CARPENTARIAN GRASSWREN

Amytornis dorotheae   Maluridae

OTHER NAMES Dorothy's Grasswren, Lesser White-throated Grasswren, Red-winged Grasswren

RECOGNITION Confined to a very restricted area in north-east of Northern Territory, possibly adjoining Queensland and probably not overlapping range of any other grasswren. Similar to, but smaller than the White-throated Grasswren of Arnhem Land. Has similar white throat and breast, but this white continues to the upper abdomen without any interrupting band of black streakings; upperparts lighter, chestnut-brown replacing black and dark brown. Similar facial pattern. 17–18 cm.

VOICE Like that of White-throated Grasswren. Loud and musical song by male; buzzing alarm call; quiet cricket-like contact calls.

HABITAT Rough sandstone ridges and gullies with spinifex. Keeps close to the rocks, bouncing across boulders and into the protecting cavities.

BREEDING October–March. Bulky, domed nest of grass and spinifex seed-stems, lined with soft leaves, and built into the top of a clump of spinifex. Two to three white to pale pinkish eggs, fine markings of mauve and red-brown.

RANGE Very restricted; extreme north-eastern corner of Northern Territory; possibly north-western Queensland.

STATUS Probably rare; secretive, difficult to observe. Endemic.

▶ See also pages
193–4 *193* 197

STRIATED GRASSWREN

Amytornis striatus   Maluridae

OTHER NAMES Black-cheeked Grasswren, Spinifex Wren, Rufous Grasswren

RECOGNITION Bold black moustache-like mark below eye. Upperparts bright chestnut (Rufous Grasswren in WA) to dull brown (in SA), extensively streaked white and black; chin and throat white. Only similar species are in tropics; this species in more arid environment. Female rufous on flanks. May attract attention by song in breeding season, otherwise very difficult to locate, keeps out of sight among spinifex clumps. 15–18 cm.

VOICE Similar to that of fairy-wrens but clearer and more musical; squeaky alarm notes, high-pitched trill, 'tsseec'.

HABITAT Spinifex; on rough ranges (Rufous Grasswren, in north-west) to sandplains and dunes with spinifex and scattered mallee.

BREEDING Recorded throughout year; following good rains in arid regions. Substantial domed structure of spinifex leaves, grass stems, and bark; built into top of spinifex clump, but inconspicuous. Two to three white eggs, speckled grey-brown.

RANGE Pilbara (WA) through centre to western Queensland, New South Wales, and Victoria. Sedentary.

STATUS Probably common in parts of range. Endemic.

▶ See also pages
10 130 138 155
163 167 171 184
213 216–17 *217*
219 220 223 230
232 233

EYREAN GRASSWREN

Amytornis goyderi   Maluridae

OTHER NAME Goyder's Grasswren

RECOGNITION Small, fairy-wren size; very restricted range. Upperparts including the crown and nape cinnamon, strongly streaked white. Tail and wings dull brown. Face black, but streaked so much with white that this area appears greyish at a distance. Underparts white, lightly washed rufous on the flanks. The solid-looking bill and long, strong legs are grey. Whisker mark very indistinct; no black line through eye. 18–20 cm.

VOICE Reported to be rich and loud, with silvery cadences, pips and trills; also high calls, 'seep seep', upwards 'zzrrt. . .'.

HABITAT Desert dunes with clumps of cane-grass, especially in the vicinity of waterholes.

BREEDING Apparently variable, as with most arid-country birds. Nests reported August–September. Nest globular, side opening near the top, placed close to the ground in a dense cane-grass clump. Two off-white eggs, marked brown and grey.

RANGE Northern Lake Eyre to Simpson Desert region. Locally nomadic.

STATUS Assumed rare; possibly common some localities, in good seasons. Endemic.

▶ See also pages
167 *169* 170

GREY GRASSWREN

Amytornis barbatus   Maluridae

RECOGNITION Very distinctive facial markings. Face white with a bold black line through the eye; black throat-cheek markings. Black crown is streaked white, blending to cinnamon-brown on back, wings and tail; the white streaks edged black increasingly on wings and tail. Underparts white, with fine black flecks on the breast; flanks buff. Tends to fly more readily than other grasswrens, perhaps more observable. 17–19 cm.

VOICE Full song not described; calls are prolonged twitterings of high-pitched sounds.

HABITAT Floodplain beds of cane-grass and lignum bushes, where there are tall dense clumps with little intervening open space.

BREEDING Recorded July; probably June–October; variable according to rainfall. Domed nest in cane-grass or lignum bush,

30 cm–1 m from the ground, grass lined with finer and softer materials. Two white eggs, speckled with brown.

RANGE Very restricted range: Goyder's Lagoon (north-west of South Australia), Bulloo Overflow (south-eastern Queensland–north-western New South Wales). Nomadic.

STATUS Uncommon. Endemic.

▶ See also pages
167 *169* 170 175

450 THICK-BILLED GRASSWREN

Amytornis textilis   Maluridae

OTHER NAME Western Grasswren

RECOGNITION Dull cinnamon-brown upperparts are streaked white, mixed with black streakings on forehead and cheeks; stout conical black bill. Underparts are similar, slightly lighter, pale cinnamon finely streaked white. Overall effect is a very uniform bird without bold contrasts or strong facial markings. Very secretive; seldom flies; keeps tail erect. Seeks insects and seeds under cover of low vegetation. 16–18 cm.

VOICE High-pitched, musical, clear silvery song; also high-pitched alarm calls, abrupt, ventriloquial effect.

HABITAT Sandplains, depressions in gibberstone plains, in areas of low dense vegetation, saltbush, cottonbush, canegrass, bluebush, stunted heath.

BREEDING Variable, any time of year after good rain; less often in winter. Nest usually domed or hooded, sometimes hood reduced or absent; made of grass, fine roots, bark; sparsely lined. Two to three whitish eggs, marked grey and rust.

RANGE Three populations; one in southwestern Australia, two in central and south-eastern Australia. Sedentary.

STATUS Probably uncommon; often overlooked. Endemic.

▶ See also pages
155 163 164 167
169 170-1 178
184 230 232

451 DUSKY GRASSWREN

Amytornis purnelli   Maluridae

OTHER NAMES Buff-throated Grasswren, Thin-billed Grasswren

RECOGNITION Almost uniformly dusky brown; the darkest of the central Australian grasswrens. Upperparts entirely dark brown; finely streaked white on head and back, fawn on the wings. Underparts light cinnamon finely streaked white. No distinct facial markings. Most closely resembles Thick-billed Grasswren, which inhabits plains rather than rocky ranges. Female has a chestnut tone to the flanks. 16–17 cm.

VOICE Pleasant, high, wren-like, reeling song; loud, abrupt and harsh alarm call.

HABITAT Rocky ranges with spinifex and scattered shrubs; bounces over rocks and takes refuge in crevices.

BREEDING Recorded February–December; probably any time of year after good rains, but usually in spring. Domed or partly hooded nest; usually built into the top of a clump of spinifex. Two to four off-white eggs spotted with grey and red-brown.

RANGE Central Australia, in ranges. Sedentary.

STATUS Common in suitable habitat, but elusive. Endemic.

▶ See also pages
167 178 *179* 183
184 185

BRISTLEBIRDS, SCRUBWRENS, WARBLERS, THORNBILLS

**Acanthizidae Family of 59 species
41 in Australia, 41 breeding, 35 endemic
Sibley-Ahlquist: Family Acanthizidae,
Subfamilies Dasyornithinae and
Acanthizinae**

A large family of smallish and generally dull-plumaged species, mostly insectivores of ground and foliage. There is great diversity, and considerable difference of taxonomic opinion. They have small thin-pointed bills with basal bristles; all build domed nests, with the female alone incubating. Habitats within the family vary greatly, from rainforests to semi-desert. Some species are very abundant, others rare.

452 EASTERN BRISTLEBIRD

Dasyornis brachypterus   Acanthizidae

OTHER NAME Brown Bristlebird

RECOGNITION Extremely difficult to sight, more often heard than seen; the piercing melodious song a convenient locator and identifier. Upperparts olive-brown, blending to reddish-brown on crown, wings and rump. Underparts light grey, with faint scaly pattern in brown on the breast. Very long tail, accounts for half total length of the bird; often cocked, wren-like, partly fanned; wings short, rounded. Flights short, low. 20–22 cm.

VOICE Song loud, penetrating, varied, yet sweetly melodious, with some whipcrack effect to the ending. Also abrupt, harsh calls.

HABITAT Lush vegetation of wet heaths, swamp margins, dense coastal and stream-edge thickets, mountain heaths.

BREEDING July–December. The domed nest is well concealed near the ground in grass, litter, swamp sword-grass or low shrub; built of sticks, bark, grasses, and lined with paperbark, decomposed leaves. Two buff eggs, finely marked brown.

RANGE Coastal eastern Australia; scattered isolated populations. Sedentary.

STATUS Quite rare; localized. Endemic.

▶ See also pages
17 *17* 123 124

453 WESTERN BRISTLEBIRD

Dasyornis longirostris   Acanthizidae

OTHER NAMES Brown Bristlebird, Long-billed Bristlebird

RECOGNITION Resembles Eastern Bristlebird, but with shorter tail, longer bill. Crown, nape and mantle blackish-brown, distinctly dappled light grey. Face grey, with paler eyebrow line and throat. Back dark brown, blending to chestnut on the rump; wings rich brown. Underparts brownish-grey, the feathers having darker feather tips giving a scalloped appearance; brownish along the flanks. Tail dark brown. Eye red-brown; bill dark brown; legs grey-brown. 17 cm.

VOICE Call is a shrill abrupt whistled 'zeip'; song of male a musical 'chip-pee-tee-peedle-pet', answered by female with call like 'quick more beer'.

HABITAT Dense low heath, coastal thickets and scrub, long grass and swampy reed-bed margins.

BREEDING July–December. The nest is a large globular structure of coarse grass and lined with finer grass. It is well hidden close to the ground in a dense banksia or other small shrub. Two dull white eggs, marked browns and greys.

RANGE Formerly south-west of Western Australia north to Perth; now only Two Peoples Bay to Fitzgerald River.

STATUS Rare; greatly reduced range. Endemic.

▶ See also pages
130 235 *239* 241
242 245

454 RUFOUS BRISTLEBIRD

Dasyornis broadbenti   Acanthizidae

RECOGNITION Upperparts are olive-grey, blending to rich rufous on crown, nape, ear-coverts, wings and long tail. The rufous of crown and face more distinct on birds from east of range than those of west. Whitish lores extending to eye-ring. Throat whitish, blending to pale grey, with darker scalloped markings on the breast, and to grey-brown over remainder of underparts. Eye red-brown; legs and bill dark brown. Usually on ground, often raises and spreads tail. 24–27 cm.

VOICE Clear squeaky, penetrating, rising, ending almost whipcrack, final notes often repeated by female: 'chip-chip-chip, chewee-chewee'; sharp alarm.

HABITAT Coastal heaths, except in Otway Range where it penetrates inland in dense vegetation along streams, extending to densely vegetated gardens.

BREEDING July–December, peak of egg-laying October–November. Nest is a large domed structure of rushes, grass, rootlets, lined with finer grasses; built into rushes or a dense low shrub. Two pale pink eggs, freckled red and purple-grey.

RANGE South-east of South Australia, south-western Victoria, formerly south-west of Western Australia. Sedentary.

STATUS Uncommon; locally common, but restricted range. Endemic.

▶ **See also pages**
17–18 *17* 121 126 163

455 PILOTBIRD

Pycnoptilus floccosus   Acanthizidae
OTHER NAME Guinea-a-week

RECOGNITION Small, plump, terrestrial; upperparts brown with cinnamon wash. Forehead, face and throat cinnamon, extending to breast where lightly patterned with darker scaly markings. Remainder of underparts olive-brown blending to whitish on belly and rufous-cinnamon on undertail-coverts; tail brown, quite long, often uplifted, partly fanned. Usually on ground foraging in leaf-litter. Flight weak, preferring to run beneath undergrowth. 17–18 cm.

VOICE Male has a penetrating, silvery, double-noted 'guinea-a-week', given most often in the breeding season; female answers with softer version.

HABITAT Forests, usually in wet gullies; in eastern Victoria extends to slopes under tall forest with dense undergrowth. Also rainforests and snow-gum woodlands.

BREEDING July–January; usually September–December. The nest is a bulky, untidy globular mass of bark, dead leaves, rootlets; placed on or near ground, by a log, bank, against a fern, among litter. Two brown eggs, marked blackish-brown.

RANGE South-eastern New South Wales, eastern Victoria. Some movement to higher altitudes in summer.

STATUS Common. Endemic.

▶ **See also pages**
118 *119* 122 123 124 126

456 ROCK WARBLER

Origma solitaria   Acanthizidae
OTHER NAMES Cavebird, Sandstone Robin, Origma Cataract-bird, Rock Robin

RECOGNITION Upperparts dark brown with rufous wash to the rump. Cinnamon wash to forehead, lores and round the eyes; throat whitish, breast and remainder of underparts rich rufous. Bill black or dark brown; legs grey-brown; eye red-brown. Immatures: throat tawny. Very restless, with almost constant side-to-side flicking of tail; bounces actively over boulders, often vanishing into crevices. Some resemblance to scrubwrens. 13–14 cm.

VOICE A repetitive, shrill and melancholy 'good-bye', sometimes shorter, higher. Also a penetrating quick 'pink', and harsh rasping scoldings.

HABITAT Principally a bird of rough, forested sandstone country, but also extending into adjacent limestone country; usually along rocky watercourses.

BREEDING July–January; usually August–December. The nest is globular, with side entry; built of bark strips, grass, moss, bound with webs, and suspended from overhanging rock of cave, mineshaft. Three white eggs, rarely fine black specks.

RANGE Confined to central eastern coastal New South Wales. Sedentary.

STATUS Moderately common. Endemic.

▶ **See also pages**
118 *119* 122

457 AUSTRALIAN FERNWREN

Crateroscelis gutturalis   Acanthizidae
OTHER NAMES Southern Fernwren, Collared Fernwren, Fernwren

RECOGNITION Upperparts, including wings and tail, deep olive-brown; darker on the head. Distinctive facial pattern: long white eyebrow line, white throat-patch extending back as a broad line to each side of neck, and bordered beneath by a black bib across the lower throat. Remainder of underparts paler olive-brown. Bill black, quite long; eye dark red-brown. Female may have slightly less distinct facial pattern. Immatures: underparts all olive-brown. 13 cm.

VOICE A very high, penetrating whistle,

similar to that of Northern Scrub-robin. Also a scolding chatter, like that of scrubwrens.

HABITAT Rainforest above 600 m altitude, usually among ferny undergrowth of densely gloomy situations.

BREEDING June–February. The dome-shaped nest is built of fern stems, dry leaves, rootlets, mosses and lichens, with hooded side entrance; well hidden among ferns; often under an overhanging bank. Two white eggs, finely spotted reddish.

RANGE Confined to highlands, Cooktown to Mt Spec near Townsville (Qld). Sedentary.

STATUS Locally quite common. Endemic.

▶ **See also pages**
85 91 *93* 97

458 ATHERTON SCRUBWREN

Sericornis keri   Acanthizidae
OTHER NAME Bellenden-Ker Scrubwren

RECOGNITION Upperparts are rich olive-brown; slightly paler on eyebrow and lower face. Throat buff, this lighter tone extending down the centre of the breast to the belly; remainder of underparts darker olive-buff. Tail reddish-brown. Generally resembles the Large-billed Scrubwren, but slightly larger, longer-legged, darker on crown and face; keeps more to ground and lower levels. 14 cm.

VOICE Usual scrubwren chattering and scoldings, very much like local subspecies of White-browed Scrubwren; probably similar song also.

HABITAT Rainforest, and rainforest margins; largely terrestrial, foraging among leaf-litter for snails and insects.

BREEDING About November. The nest is a globular structure, on or very close to the ground; built of fibrous, dry plant materials, dead leaves, and lined with feathers. Two eggs, white or tinted purplish-brown, speckled dark brown.

RANGE Confined to Atherton Tableland, above 600 m. Sedentary.

STATUS Uncommon. Endemic.

▶ **See also pages**
85 91–2 *93* 97

459 LARGE-BILLED SCRUBWREN

Sericornis magnirostris   Acanthizidae

RECOGNITION Upperparts are plain olive-brown, more red-brown on head and rump; tail brown, edged brighter. Lacks conspicuous distinguishing markings; face buffy with rufous wash, forehead scalloped buff. Throat buff, and remainder of under-parts light buff with yellowish wash. Eye dark red-brown, prominent against surrounding light buffy tones. Bill long, seems slightly uptilted. Active about upper foliage, rarely descending near forest floor. 12–13 cm.

VOICE Typical scrubwren calls, but slightly softer than most, a high and penetrating repeated 'chew' or 'cheer'; also twitterings while feeding.

HABITAT Rainforest and wet eucalypt forest, mainly along the eastern slopes of the Great Dividing Range, at higher altitudes in the north.

BREEDING June–February; usually July–January. The oval nest with side entrance is constructed of plant stems, rootlets, dry leaf remnants, moss; lined with feathers. Three to four white to pale purplish-brown eggs, freckled darker brown.

RANGE Coastal eastern Australia; vicinity of Cooktown, south almost to Melbourne. Sedentary.

STATUS Moderately common in north; uncommon south. Endemic.

▶ See also pages
53 55 92 121 126

460 **YELLOW-THROATED SCRUBWREN**

Sericornis citreogularis   Acanthizidae
OTHER NAMES Devilbird, Blacknest-bird

RECOGNITION The most brightly coloured of scrubwrens; bold facial markings. Upperparts dark olive-brown; dark brown on crown, rump, tail. Wing quills dark grey, with primaries edged yellow. Forehead black, and a bold wide black mask from bill back across eye to ear-coverts; bordered above by a conspicuous white-and-yellow eyebrow, below by yellow throat and upper breast. Sides of breast and flanks buffy; belly whitish. Female: black replaced by brown. 12–14 cm.

VOICE Commonly a very harsh loud chatter; contact call a sharp ticking. The song of clear and melodious notes includes elements of mimicry.

HABITAT Rainforest and wet eucalypt forest, keeping to the understorey of the gloomiest parts; often along gullies by water.

BREEDING August–March. Nest is unique, very large, domed; usually suspended out in open and conspicuous; blackish in colour from inclusion of fine black rootlets; hooded side entrance. Three pale brownish eggs, with several dark bands.

RANGE Two populations: north-eastern Queensland; and south-eastern Queensland–eastern New South Wales. Sedentary.

STATUS Common. Endemic.

▶ See also pages
121 122 *122* 127

461 **TROPICAL SCRUBWREN**

Sericornis beccarii   Acanthizidae
OTHER NAMES Little Scrubwren, Beccari's Scrubwren

RECOGNITION Similar to the widespread White-browed Scrubwren, but with eyebrow line narrow, broken, comparatively inconspicuous, and dark mask is reduced to blackish lores patch; eye scarlet to vermilion instead of yellow. Shoulder area dark, with two small white wingbars. Upperparts olive-brown; throat white with faint dark streaks; rest of underparts buffy grey-white. Subspecies *dubius* is plainer with less distinct markings. 11 cm.

VOICE Harsh rasping notes in alarm, and often while feeding; song is a musical warble likened to that of the Large-billed Warbler.

HABITAT Confined to rainforests, monsoon forests, riverine forests and similar closed-canopy scrubs, in lower and middle levels.

BREEDING October–December. The domed nest is built into vegetation and debris close to the ground; constructed of bark fibres, grass, vine tendrils, and skeletons of leaves. Two to three white eggs, tinted reddish-brown, finely spotted in browns.

RANGE Cape York, south to about Cooktown, mainly on east side. Also in New Guinea. Sedentary.

STATUS Common; confined to rivers on western Cape York.

▶ See also pages
106 *109* 111

462 **WHITE-BROWED SCRUBWREN**

Sericornis frontalis   Acanthizidae
OTHER NAMES White-fronted Scrubwren, Buff-breasted Scrubwren, Cartwheel-bird, Spotted Scrubwren

RECOGNITION Widespread, several subspecies. Upperparts dark olive-brown to dark cinnamon-brown; darker on head and wings; shoulders black with two small white bars; tail red-brown with darker subterminal band. Face strongly marked: bold white eyebrow line; broad blackish band from base of bill through lores and eye, to ear-coverts in some subspecies. Bold white stripe well below eye; throat and breast white; belly buffy to dull yellow. Subspecies *maculatus* is Spotted Scrubwren. 11–14 cm.

VOICE Harsh scoldings and rasping sounds, usually in alarm or warning. Song is softer,

more musical 'tsi-tsi', 'tseer-tseer' and 'seet-you, seet-you'.

HABITAT Found in dense undergrowth of eucalypt forests, woodlands, mallee and heathlands, mangroves, saltmarshes; favouring areas of twig- and leaf-litter.

BREEDING July–January. The large domed nest is loosely and untidily built, using bark, leaves, fine roots, twigs, lined with feathers; well hidden among debris in dense low undergrowth. Two to three dull white eggs, speckled browns.

RANGE Eastern, south-eastern and south-western Australian coasts, Tasmania; inland but not arid interior. Sedentary.

STATUS Common. Endemic.

▶ See also pages
118 124 141 147
223 363 *365*

463 **SCRUBTIT**

Sericornis magnus   Acanthizidae
OTHER NAMES Fern-weaver, White-breasted Scrubtit, Mountain Wren

RECOGNITION Upperparts grey-brown, with rufous tone to back, crown, nape; dark brown tail has a broad black subterminal band and white tip. Face white with pale grey patch from lores to ear-coverts, but whitish about the dark brown eye; throat white; remainder of underparts pale grey or pale grey-buff. Shoulders dark grey with white flecks. Bill relatively long, black; legs pink-brown. Shy and inconspicuous, keeping to lower levels of forest. 11 cm.

VOICE Song is a pleasant, whistled 'too-whee-too', like that of the Tasmanian subspecies of White-browed Scrubwren or Brown Thornbill.

HABITAT Rainforest and eucalypt forest, in dense wet situations especially the fern-gullies; also in tea-tree scrub on King Island.

BREEDING September–January. The nest is domed, with a slightly hooded side entrance; built of ferns, grasses, moss, lined with bark strips, fine rootlets, down from fern stems, feathers; placed close to ground. Three to four white eggs, speckled red-brown.

RANGE Confined to Tasmania and King Island. Sedentary.

STATUS Moderately common. Endemic.

▶ See also pages
141 142 146-7
147 151 152 153

CHESTNUT-RUMPED HEATHWREN

Sericornis pyrrhopygius Acanthizidae
OTHER NAME Chestnut-rumped Hylacola
RECOGNITION Attracts attention by rich, varied song. Olive-brown upperparts; whitish underparts, streaked grey-brown. Prominent white eyebrow line; bright chestnut rump; pale chestnut undertail-coverts; dark brown tail with black subterminal band, white tips, carried cocked, wren-like, but comparatively short. Female duller. Immatures buff on eyebrow; buff underparts, unstreaked. Will sing from a twig above surrounding vegetation, but quick to dive for cover. 14 cm.
VOICE Begins softly, the song increasing in volume, melodious, has been likened to the song of a canary; includes notes of other species.
HABITAT Varied, wet coastal and mountain heaths, dense undergrowth of forests and woodlands, drier scrubs and inland heaths.
BREEDING June–November. Domed nest of dry grass-stems, rootlets, bark strips; in thick cover on or close to the ground. Three to four buff to salmon pink eggs, freckled and blotched dark brown.
RANGE South-eastern Australia, excluding Tasmania; isolated population in Adelaide region. Sedentary.
STATUS Uncommon. Endemic.

▶ See also pages
118 *119* 121 122
126 139

SHY HEATHWREN

Sericornis cautus Acanthizidae
OTHER NAMES Shy Groundwren, Western Groundwren, Shy Hylacola, Mallee Heathwren
RECOGNITION Upperparts olive-brown, with fiery chestnut rump; tail grey-brown, with outer feathers tipped white. Compared with the Chestnut-rumped Heathwren, has a white patch on shoulder, and a more prominent white eyebrow; underparts whiter with bolder black streakings. Bounces across ground, with tail held erect; has a reputation for being shy, but probably no more so than the Chestnut-rumped. Female duller. 12–14 cm.
VOICE Song is most often given early mornings in spring, a persistent, rich sweet 'chee-chee, chick-a-dee' from high perch; sharp calls if disturbed.
HABITAT Mallee and open woodland with dense low undergrowth. In south-west of Western Australia, sandplain-heathland, banksia woodland, coastal thickets.
BREEDING July–December; mainly August–October. Nest domed, in a depression in the ground; among low undergrowth or debris at the base of a bush, or sometimes in the open, but hard to see. Two to three

olive-grey eggs, marked darker.
RANGE Southern drier parts of Western Australia, South Australia, north-western Victoria, central and south-west of New South Wales. Sedentary.
STATUS Uncommon. Endemic.

381 **Crested Shrike-tit** *Falcunculus frontatus*
390 **Little Shrike-thrush** *Colluricincla megarhyncha*
398 **Spectacled Monarch** *Monarcha trivirgatus*
403 **Leaden Flycatcher** *Myiagra rubecula*
462 **White-browed Scrubwren** *Sericornis frontalis*
468 **Speckled Warbler** *Sericornis sagittatus*
469 **Weebill** *Smicrornis brevirostris*
470 **Brown Warbler** *Gerygone mouki*
479 **Brown Thornbill** *Acanthiza pusilla*
493 **Varied Sittella** *Daphoenositta chrysoptera*

▶ See also pages
59 60 130 137 139
162 232

466 REDTHROAT

Sericornis brunneus   Acanthizidae

OTHER NAME Red-throated Scrubwren

RECOGNITION A very small plain grey bird; darker on the crown; whitish on the lores; throat light chestnut. The female is even plainer, having the throat colour replaced by pale grey. In flight, large tail, dark with prominent white tips except central pair of feathers. An inconspicuous bird except in the breeding season, when the male's beautiful song may draw attention. 12 cm.

VOICE Song is varied, musical, mimics other species; has been compared with the song of the canary, or subdued song of the reed-warbler.

HABITAT Semi-arid and arid inland scrubs; mulga, mallee, saltbush, bluebush, lignum.

BREEDING Variable following good rain in north and north-west of range, otherwise usually August–December. Domed nest, in low shrub, tree hollow, constructed of bark strips, twigs, dried grasses; well lined. Three to four olive-brown eggs, marked darker brown.

RANGE From arid north-western Australia through central Australia to western Queensland, New South Wales, north-western Victoria. Sedentary.

STATUS Uncommon. Endemic.

▶ See also pages
59 60 130 232 323

467 STRIATED FIELDWREN

Sericornis fuliginosus   Acanthizidae

OTHER NAMES Fieldwren, Calamanthus

RECOGNITION Wren-like in that the tail, though comparatively short, is carried cocked upwards. Upperparts dull olive-green or olive-brown heavily streaked black; underparts buff to pale yellow streaked black. Prominent white eyebrow, usually becoming orange towards the bill. Little Grassbird is similar in appearance and with some overlap of habitat and range, but tail seldom cocked. Compare also heathwrens, grasswrens. 12–14 cm.

VOICE Spirited and pleasant song, beginning with sharp notes, then a sustained succession described as 'rich buoyant', 'liquid'.

HABITAT Varied: damp coastal heathlands, dunes, wet button-grass plains, moorland, swamp margins; inland, spinifex, saltbush, sparse low scrub.

BREEDING Throughout the year, after rain in arid regions, but usually July–December, especially in south. Nest domed, of coarse grass; on or close to ground in dense cover. Three to four buff to brown eggs, spotted darker browns.

RANGE South-eastern Australia (subspecies *fuliginosus*); central to Western Australia (*campestris*). Sedentary.

STATUS Locally common; generally uncommon. Endemic.

▶ See also pages
17 18–19 124 150
152 162 163 223

468 SPECKLED WARBLER

Sericornis sagittatus   Acanthizidae

OTHER NAMES Blood-tit, Little Fieldlark, Little Fieldwren, Speckled Jack

RECOGNITION Upperparts grey or grey-brown, mottled and streaked darker, with blackish streak along each side of the dark brown, finely white-streaked crown. Tail dusky brown, white-tipped. Eyebrow, lores, round eye, and underparts creamy white, boldly streaked black from chin to undertail. Eye brown; bill grey-brown; legs blue-grey. Female has chestnut streak in eyebrow. Immatures: head duller patterned. 12–13 cm.

VOICE Song, though subdued, is musical, like that of warblers; often includes mimicry. Also has a harsh chatter.

HABITAT Open forests, woodlands with grassy understorey, often on the stony ridges or gully slopes; most often reported from along the Great Dividing Range.

BREEDING September–March. Nest is dome-shaped structure with hooded side entry; built of grasses and bark strips, well lined with feathers; placed in a small hollow concealed under grass, debris, roots. Three to four reddish-brown eggs.

RANGE Eastern Australia, mostly inland; mid-eastern Queensland to western Victoria. Sedentary.

STATUS Moderately common. Localized. Endemic.

▶ See also pages
136 323 *365*

469 WEEBILL

Smicrornis brevirostris   Acanthizidae

OTHER NAMES Brown Weebill, Yellow Weebill, Short-billed Tree-tit, Short-billed Scrub-tit

RECOGNITION Very small, and with bill so stubby that it looks small even on so tiny a bird. Upperparts variable; dull brownish-olive to quite bright greenish-yellow, especially lower back and rump. Buff or off-white stripe, back from the forehead as a light eyebrow. Wings brown, with flight feathers edged pale olive-yellow. Tail pale brownish, with dark band and pale tips. Underparts creamy-buff, slightly streaked on upper breast. Eye pale yellow. 8–9 cm.

VOICE A lively, high-pitched, clear and far-carrying sequence of calls, as 'weebit-weebeet', and 'willy-wee, willy-weebit', repeated several times.

HABITAT A wide variety of habitats; forages in foliage of trees generally, from drier coastal forests and woodlands, to trees and arid scrubs of interior.

BREEDING August–February in southern Australia; October–May in north; variable in arid parts. Nest is a small sphere with side entrance, of grass, stems, soft plant-down; bound with webs, and suspended in foliage. Two to three whitish eggs, finely speckled brown.

RANGE Mainland Australia except most arid or treeless areas. Sedentary.

STATUS Common; often abundant. Endemic.

▶ See also page
365

470 BROWN WARBLER

Gerygone mouki   Acanthizidae

OTHER NAMES Brown Gerygone, Brown Flyeater, Brown Bush-warbler, Citronbird

RECOGNITION Upperparts rich warm olive-brown. Distinct light grey eyebrow line and grey face. The lores and immediately behind the eye are dark grey; and there is a slight and indistinct whitish eye-ring. Flight feathers grey-brown; tail with broad blackish subterminal band and large white spots near the tips of each feather, most noticeable in flight. Underparts creamy white, blending to pale grey on breast and throat. Eye deep red; bill and legs blackish. 9–11 cm.

VOICE Unlike other fairy-warblers, being an almost incessant brisk cheery 'which-is-it', or 'diddle-diddle-dit'.

HABITAT Regions of heavy vegetation, including rainforests, watercourse scrubs, occasionally mangroves.

BREEDING September–February, sometimes two broods in year. The nest is large for so small a bird; suspended, domed, with long tail; constructed of bark, bound with webs, and decorated with lichens. Three whitish eggs, speckled red-brown.

RANGE Eastern Australia, mainly coastal; Cooktown south to Gippsland. Locally nomadic.

STATUS Moderately common. Endemic.

▶ See also page
365

LARGE-BILLED WARBLER

Gerygone magnirostris   Acanthizidae

OTHER NAMES Brown-breasted Flyeater, Large-billed Gerygone, Large-billed Flyeater

RECOGNITION Upperparts grey-brown to olive-brown. Unlike other brownish warblers, no whitish eyebrow, but does have a slight and indistinct pale buff spot on the forehead, and a very fine faint white eye-ring; head otherwise plain. Flight feathers and tail grey-brown, the latter with broad dark band and without white tips. Underparts white, with a slight cinnamon wash to the breast and flanks. Eye red-brown; bill comparatively large, heavy. 10–11 cm.

VOICE A descending, reeling series of notes, rich and sweet, often repeatedly, given by both sexes. Also soft chattered contact calls.

HABITAT Mangroves, adjoining patches of rainforest, river and stream-edge vegetation, paperbark swamps and flooded eucalypt woodlands.

BREEDING August–April; usually September–March. The nest is of elongated domed shape, with hooded side entrance; resembles hanging flood-debris. It is usually over water, often close to a wasp nest. Two to three white eggs, speckled red-brown.

RANGE Coastal northern Australia; from north-western Kimberley to Mackay (Qld). Also in New Guinea and adjacent islands. Sedentary.

STATUS Common.

▶ See also pages
79 92 98 228 324
364

DUSKY WARBLER

Gerygone tenebrosa   Acanthizidae

OTHER NAMES Dusky Gerygone, Dusky Flyeater

RECOGNITION Very plain plumaged; upperparts grey-brown, with slight rufous wash mainly towards the rump. Small buffy-white spot on forehead; slight white line from bill towards eye; very faint indistinct light eye-ring. Flight feathers and tail grey-brown; the latter with very slight bar. Underparts pale dusky grey. Only warbler with such pale eyes, whitish or straw-coloured. Immatures: more buff to underparts; eye browner. 11–12 cm.

VOICE Soft and plaintive descending trills,

like those of the Large-billed Warbler, but weaker. Also soft chatterings and tickings.

HABITAT Mangroves, especially the denser areas of larger mangroves, but also extending to adjoining swamplands, gorge and creek scrubs.

BREEDING Usually October–March. The domed nest is built of bark strips bound with webs. It is quite compact, with small tail, and slightly hooded side entrance; suspended in mangroves. Two white eggs, spotted red-brown.

RANGE Coastal north-western Australia; Derby south to Shark Bay. Sedentary.

STATUS Moderately common. Endemic.

▶ See also pages
201 208 210 218
223 227–8 229
231

MANGROVE WARBLER

Gerygone laevigaster   Acanthizidae

OTHER NAMES Mangrove Gerygone, Buff-breasted Warbler, Mangrove Flyeater

RECOGNITION Upperparts ashy grey, with a slight brown wash mainly to the wings; flight feathers and tail darker grey-brown. The tail blends towards black in its lower half, with a large white spot to the tip of each feather. There is a bold white eyebrow line that extends forward to the bill; in strong contrast to the dark grey lores. Eye deep red; bill and legs black. Immatures: lack white eyebrow, have faint striations on upper breast. 10–11 cm.

VOICE A sustained pleasant high, silvery warbling, a series of falling notes, the sequences varied and repeated; like call of White-throated Warbler.

HABITAT Mangroves, extending in parts of its range into adjoining rainforest, riverside vegetation, paperbark woodlands and acacia thickets.

BREEDING July–April; some nesting most months in far north. The nest is a compact but elongated dome shape, with slight tail, and hooded side entrance; suspended, usually over water. Three white eggs, tinged pink, speckled red-brown.

RANGE Coastal northern Australia, western Kimberley to north-eastern New South Wales. Also in southern New Guinea. Sedentary.

STATUS Common.

▶ See also pages
23 24 196 199 210
218

WESTERN WARBLER

Gerygone fusca   Acanthizidae

OTHER NAMES Western Gerygone, White-tailed Warbler, Inland Warbler, Sleepy Dick

RECOGNITION Upperparts grey with slight brown wash to back and wings. There is an indistinct white eyebrow, merging into a faint thin white eye-ring; lores dark grey. The flight feathers are darker brownish-grey, usually edged light grey. Tail dark grey-brown with two broad white bars across all but the central feathers, near the base of the tail, and towards the tip. Throat and breast pale grey; belly dull white. Immatures: underparts with yellow tint. 10–11 cm.

VOICE A high thin silvery, but tenuous, sequence of notes, rising and falling, then

474 WESTERN WARBLER *Gerygone fusca*

ending before the tune seems completed.

HABITAT Open eucalypt forests, woodlands, mallee, acacia scrublands; avoids wetter coastal regions.

BREEDING August–February; usually September–December. The nest is neat, small, domed; with side entrance, and a slender tail beneath; built of grass and bark. It is hung among foliage at heights to 10 m. Two to three pinkish-white eggs, marked brown.

RANGE Throughout Australia except most arid deserts and wetter coasts. Partially migratory.

STATUS Generally uncommon; common south-western Australia. Endemic.

▶ See also pages
123 367

475 GREEN-BACKED WARBLER

Gerygone chloronota   Acanthizidae

OTHER NAMES Green-backed Gerygone, Green-backed Flyeater

RECOGNITION Head, including face, mid-grey, blending to olive-green on the back and wings. Flight feathers dark grey-green edged paler green. Tail dark brownish-grey, with an indistinct darker subterminal band on the outer feathers. Underparts white, with a faint wash of grey on the throat and of buff or lemon on the flanks. Eye deep red; bill black; legs slaty-grey. Immatures duller; eye browner. 9–10 cm.

VOICE Recognizably like other warblers but higher-pitched than most; a fast twittering series of whistled notes repeated often, with little variation.

HABITAT Tropical eucalypt forests, favouring dense vegetation near water; and in monsoon forests, paperbark swamps, bamboo thickets, and mangroves.

BREEDING September–April; mainly November–March. The nest is a rounded compact dome shape, with short tail and deep hood over the side entrance; built of grass and bark strips; suspended in foliage. Two to three white eggs, speckled red-brown.

RANGE Northern Australia from north-western Kimberley to eastern Arnhem Land. Also in New Guinea and adjacent islands. Sedentary.

STATUS Common.

▶ See also pages
189 194 198 210

476 FAIRY WARBLER

Gerygone palpebrosa   Acanthizidae

OTHER NAMES Fairy Gerygone, Black-throated Warbler, Fairy Flyeater

RECOGNITION One of the more colourful of the warblers, with distinctive head markings. Upperparts, including head, back and wings, olive-brown to olive-green, becoming blackish on chin or chin and throat. There is a small white spot on each side of the forehead, and a bold white streak from base of bill downwards below eye. Breast and belly pale lemon. Eye red; bill black. Female: throat and lower face off-white. Immatures: throat yellowish. 10–12 cm.

VOICE A lively, undulating reeling series of high notes, at any time of day or year; resembling but weaker than song of the White-throated Warbler.

HABITAT Rainforests and margins, mangroves, especially along the shore side, and often into gardens adjoining these habitats.

BREEDING Through most of the year; usually October–March. The nest is of spherical shape, with slender tail and deeply hooded side entrance; built of bark fibres and grass; usually suspended over water, near wasp's nest. Two to three white eggs, speckled brown.

RANGE North-eastern Australia; Cape York to Rockhampton, mainly coastal. Also in New Guinea and Aru Islands. Sedentary.

STATUS Moderately common.

▶ See also pages
76 79

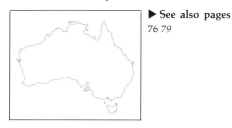

477 WHITE-THROATED WARBLER

Gerygone olivacea   Acanthizidae

OTHER NAMES White-throated Gerygone, White-throated Flyeater, Bush Warbler, Bush Canary

RECOGNITION A colourful warbler, with upperparts grey-brown; throat white, and remainder of underparts entirely yellow. The flight feathers are darker grey-brown edged light grey, and the tail blackish with the outer feathers white near the base and tips. Some northern forms lack white tail-tips. There is an indistinct small white spot to either side of the forehead. Eye red; bill dark brown; legs grey. Immatures: yellowish throat. 10–11 cm.

VOICE Loud and far-carrying, often heard though bird unsighted. A clear silvery thread of notes cascading downwards, then rising before fading away.

HABITAT Eucalypt woodlands and open forests, farmlands and gardens with trees, regrowth, watercourse and roadside trees.

BREEDING July–February; usually September–January. The globular nest of bark fibres and grass has a hooded side entrance and wispy tail. It is suspended among foliage at heights up to 15 m. Two to three white eggs, heavily spotted purplish-red.

RANGE Northern and eastern Australia; Broome to Adelaide. Migratory in south-east. Sedentary in north. Also in south-east New Guinea.

STATUS Moderately common.

▶ See also pages
41 42 162 208 *324 367*

478 MOUNTAIN THORNBILL

Acanthiza katherina   Acanthizidae

RECOGNITION Upperparts olive-grey to olive-brown, becoming tawny on the uppertail-coverts. The forehead is scalloped with buff. Flight feathers darker grey-brown, edged olive; tail feathers dark grey-brown. Face mottled light grey, blending on throat and breast to dull white or buffy-white and streaked grey. Remainder of underparts off-white to pale greenish-yellow. The whitish eye helps separate this species from Brown Thornbill. 10 cm.

VOICE A single note followed by a descending trill; also a series of about five descending whistled notes.

HABITAT Confined to upland rainforests above 450 m altitude, where it gleans insects from the foliage canopy.

BREEDING August–March; usually September–January. The domed nest is large for so small a bird, suspended from its roof; built of vine fibres, covered with mosses. Two whitish eggs, finely speckled brown, encircled grey-brown at larger end.

RANGE Confined to the Atherton Region. Sedentary.

STATUS Moderately common. Endemic.

▶ See also pages
85 92 *93* 97

479 BROWN THORNBILL

Acanthiza pusilla   Acanthizidae

OTHER NAMES Brown-rumped Thornbill, Brown-rumped Tit, Tit-warbler, Scrub Thornbill

RECOGNITION Upperparts brown, with a dull olive tone to the back and wings, and a cinnamon tone to the rump and base of tail. The forehead is scalloped buff and rufous; the face, throat and breast pale grey, flecked and streaked grey, more heavily on the breast. Remainder of underparts dull white, with a touch of buff or olive-buff to the flanks. Tail tawny brown, with a dark grey bar near the pale tip. Eye red; bill black; legs pale brown. 10 cm.

VOICE Varied, some notes squeaky, some quite deep. Has a pleasant brief warble, and skilfully mimics other birds. Alarm call is a harsh loud churring.

HABITAT Most vegetation types, including rainforests, eucalypt forests and woodlands, coastal dune vegetation, mangroves, parks and gardens.

BREEDING June–January; usually September–December. The domed nest is hidden among dense vegetation and debris on or near the ground. It is built of bark, pieces of bracken, grass, loosely bound with webs. Two to four whitish eggs, speckled dull red.

RANGE Eastern Australia and Tasmania; north to Proserpine, west to Adelaide. Locally nomadic.

STATUS Common. Endemic.

▶ See also pages
80 92 122 147 150
153 164 364 *365*

480 INLAND THORNBILL *Acanthiza apicalis*

480 INLAND THORNBILL

Acanthiza apicalis   Acanthizidae

OTHER NAMES Broad-tailed Thornbill, Red-rumped Thornbill, Tanami Thornbill

RECOGNITION Upperparts are light olive-brown; reddish rump. Tail rufous near base, grading outwards to dark brown, and with white tips; often cocked up. Head brown with whitish scallopings to forehead; face pale grey flecked dark grey. Throat and breast buffy-white with dark streakings; rest of underparts off-white to very pale grey, with a slight buff wash to the flanks. Eye deep red; bill black; legs dark brown. Subspecies of interior and north-west, paler. It is anticipated that the Inland Thornbill will be made a subspecies of the Brown Thornbill. 10–11 cm.

VOICE Generally like that of the Brown Thornbill, with pleasant lively and variable territorial song; also high 'see-see' calls, and mimicry.

HABITAT Eucalypt woodlands, mallee, mulga and other acacia scrublands; often near water, mangroves. In south-western Australia, also in heavy wet eucalypt forest.

BREEDING July–January; usually August–December. The small domed nest, like that of fairy-wrens, is built of bark strips and dry grasses, lightly bound with webs, and placed quite low in foliage. Three whitish eggs, speckled red-brown.

RANGE Mainland Australia except wetter north-west, north, east and south-east coasts. Sedentary.

STATUS Common. Endemic.

▶ See also page
241

481 TASMANIAN THORNBILL

Acanthiza ewingii   Acanthizidae

OTHER NAMES Ewing's Thornbill, Browntail, Ewing's Tit

RECOGNITION Very closely resembles the Brown Thornbill, which also occurs in Tasmania, but has only faint scallopings on a chestnut-tinted forehead, and the bill is shorter. The plumage of the upperparts is pale olive-brown, becoming more rufous on the rump and tail, the latter with a blackish subterminal band and pale tip. Face, throat and breast light grey, dappled and streaked darker, remainder of underparts off-white. Eye dark red; bill black; legs brown. 10 cm.

VOICE Contact call a high to thin 'tsirp-tsirp', repeated several times. The song is a pleasant warbling, with drawn-out high notes.

HABITAT Wet eucalypt forests, temperate rainforests, wet gullies of dry eucalypt forests, tea-tree swamps.

BREEDING August–January; usually September–December. The spherical nest, with hooded side entrance, is built of bark strips, grass and moss, bound with webs, placed in outer foliage at 2–5 m height. Three to four pale pink eggs, lightly speckled red-brown.

RANGE Confined to Tasmania, King Island and Furneaux Group. Locally nomadic.

STATUS Common. Endemic.

▶ See also pages
141 142 147 *147*
150 151 152

482 CHESTNUT-RUMPED THORNBILL

Acanthiza uropygialis   Acanthizidae

OTHER NAMES Chestnut-tailed Thornbill, Chestnut-tailed Tit

RECOGNITION A very plain thornbill except for the conspicuous chestnut rump. Upperparts grey with brownish tone to wings and forehead, the latter area with feathers edged white giving a scalloped appearance. Face and entire underparts very pale grey, with lores and ear-coverts mottled darker. Basal one-third of the tail chestnut, remainder black lightly tipped white. Rump colour conspicuous in flight. Eye off-white; bill and legs black. 10 cm.

VOICE Contact call a thin 'tsee-tsee', and squeaky chatterings within flocks; song a rambling, but lively and quite musical high twittering.

HABITAT Eucalypt woodlands, mulga and other acacia scrublands, mallee, open saltbush, bluebush and lignum country, grasslands with sparse timber.

BREEDING June–January; usually August–December. The nest is usually built into a hollow of a tree, stump or fence-post. It is of domed shape, of bark and grass, well lined with fur and feathers. Two to four whitish eggs, finely speckled red and brown.

RANGE Throughout mainland Australia except tropical north, wet east, south-east, south-west. Sedentary.

STATUS Common. Endemic.

▶ See also pages
60 136 137 178
184 *218*

483 SLATY-BACKED THORNBILL

Acanthiza robustirostris Acanthizidae

OTHER NAMES Large-billed Tit, Robust-billed Thornbill, Thick-billed Tit

RECOGNITION Upperparts, including the entire head, uniformly slaty blue-grey, becoming only slightly paler grey on the throat and upper breast, and blending to a brownish-grey on the wings. Forehead finely streaked darker. Rump and base of tail cinnamon or light chestnut; remainder of tail blackish with pale tip. On the underparts the grey of the breast merges to white on the abdomen. Eye deep red-brown; bill and legs black. 9–10 cm.

VOICE Song is a high twittering, and a louder 'wee-pu-chew' repeatedly. Other calls include a soft 'seep-seec' contact, and harsh 'tree-it' in alarm.

HABITAT Acacia scrublands with spinifex, particularly areas of tall mulga, favouring foothills of ranges where runoff increases the vegetation density.

BREEDING Variable with rainfall; usually August–November. The domed nest of dry grasses and strips of bark is warmly lined with fur and feathers, and placed in a low shrub. Three white to pale pink eggs, sparsely speckled reddish.

RANGE The western interior, east to south-western Queensland. Possibly seasonally nomadic.

STATUS Moderately common in west; sparse in east of range. Endemic.

▶ **See also pages**
59 60 173 230

484 WESTERN THORNBILL

Acanthiza inornata Acanthizidae

OTHER NAMES Bark Tit, Plain-coloured Tit, Master's Tit

RECOGNITION The least colourful of the thornbills; upperparts grey-brown, blending to olive-brown on the rump; wings dusky brown. Forehead and face light brown, lightly scalloped and flecked darker brown. Tail brown, darkening to blackish towards the tip, and with pale brown tip. Underparts entirely pale grey-buff, without any streakings. Eye off-white. Bill dark grey-brown; legs dark grey. Immatures even duller than adult; plain forehead, face. 10–11 cm.

VOICE A rapid high twittering, not loud, and with a tinkling quality. May mimic other birds.

HABITAT Woodlands, open eucalypt forests, sandplain heath-woodlands, coastal scrubs, remnant vegetation of roadsides, farmlands.

BREEDING August–December. The nest, dome-shaped with side entrance, is well hidden, often in a narrow crevice-like fork of a casuarina, behind a slab of bark, or in the dry skirt of a grasstree. Three pinkish eggs, speckled red and brown.

RANGE Restricted to south-western Australia; Hill River south-east to Fitzgerald River. Sedentary.

STATUS Common. Endemic.

▶ **See also pages**
241 *241* 242

485 BUFF-RUMPED THORNBILL

Acanthiza reguloides Acanthizidae

OTHER NAMES Bark-tit, Varied Thornbill, Buff-tailed Thornbill

RECOGNITION Upperparts are plain, dusky olive-grey, with rusty tint and darker brown scalloping to the forehead. Face and ear-coverts dull white, finely speckled brown. Rump yellowish-buff, noticeable in flight. Wings brown; tail yellowish-buff at base, then dark brown with fawn tip. Eye very pale yellow; bill and legs dark brown. Immatures duller. The northern subspecies *squamata*, Varied Thornbill: greener upperparts, brighter yellow underparts and rump. 11 cm.

VOICE Varied soft contact calls; song an animated musical tinkling, more metallic than call of Yellow-rumped Thornbill: 'pit-pit-pit, pitta-pitta-'.

HABITAT Open eucalypt forest and woodland, usually with grassy understorey, orchards; northern subspecies in forest margins, occasionally rainforests.

BREEDING August–December. The nest is untidy, of roughly domed shape with side entrance; built of bark, dry leaves, grass; placed close to ground among debris or under bark, in crevice. Three to five whitish eggs, lightly speckled reddish, lilac.

RANGE Eastern Australia; Atherton Tableland, south and west to southern Flinders Range. Sedentary.

STATUS Common. Endemic.

▶ **See also pages**
65 67

486 SLENDER-BILLED THORNBILL

Acanthiza iredalei Acanthizidae

OTHER NAMES Samphire Thornbill, Dark Thornbill

RECOGNITION Upperparts dusky olive-grey to pale brownish-grey; darker on the forehead where pale feather tips give a scalloped effect. Wings brownish-grey; rump buff to olive-buff. Face and entire underparts pale creamy-buff. Tail brownish-black, tipped brown. Eye creamy white; bill black; legs dark grey. 10 cm.

VOICE A rapid succession of piercing 'tsi-tsi-tsi' notes.

HABITAT Over most of its range, saltbush and samphire flats, mainly inland but coastal around Shark Bay, Nullarbor; heath in Murray–Darling area.

BREEDING July–November. The nest is small, globular, with a side entrance, of grasses, bark strips, plant-down, bound with webs, and built into the top of a low shrub. Three white eggs, finely speckled reddish-brown.

RANGE Southern interior; South Australia to mid-Western Australian coast, south-east of South Australia, south-western Victoria.

STATUS Local and uncommon. Sedentary. Endemic.

▶ **See also pages**
130 138 164 220
228 229 231

487 YELLOW-RUMPED THORNBILL

Acanthiza chrysorrhoa Acanthizidae

OTHER NAMES Yellow-tailed Tit, Tomtit, Yellow-tailed Thornbill, Chigaree

RECOGNITION Generally a well-known, distinctively plumaged thornbill, with bright yellow rump that is very conspicuous in flight. Upperparts dusky olive-grey, shading to grey on crown and black on forehead, where white tips to feathers give a white-spotted forehead and front of crown. Face, including ear-coverts, pale grey flecked darker; underparts off-white, washed buff on flanks. Wings dark brown; tail yellow at base, then black. Eye fawny. 11 cm.

VOICE A lively, fast tinkling chatter, descending, and then rapidly repeated several times. In flight, an abrupt 'zip'; also various softer calls.

HABITAT Open eucalypt forests and woodlands, remnant timber of farmlands and roadsides, parks, gardens, favouring margins where trees adjoin grassland.

BREEDING June–December. The nest is massive for so small a bird; an untidy mass of grass and other fibres. The nest chamber is low, with a hooded side entrance and false nest on top; in outer foliage. Three to four pale pinkish eggs, speckled red-brown.

RANGE Throughout Australian mainland and Tasmania except far north and most arid areas. Sedentary.

STATUS Abundant. Endemic.

▶ **See also pages**
61 *371*

487 YELLOW-RUMPED THORNBILL *Acanthiza chrysorrhoa*

488 YELLOW THORNBILL

Acanthiza nana   Acanthizidae

OTHER NAMES Yellow-breasted Thornbill, Little Thornbill, Yellow-breasted Tomtit

RECOGNITION Upperparts olive-grey to olive-green, blending to ochre on forehead; flight feathers olive-brown, each edged pale yellow. No streakings on forehead or crown, but with whitish streaks on the dark grey ear-coverts; buff over eye. Tail olive-brown, with blackish subterminal band. Underparts entirely pale bright yellow, with olive-green wash to flanks and slightly deeper yellow ochre to throat. Inland populations paler. Eye brown. 10 cm.

VOICE Lively and brisk 'tiz-tiz', and 'chidid-tiz-tiz', repeatedly.

HABITAT Eucalypt forests and woodlands, regrowth; also dry scrubs including brigalow, acacia thickets, mangroves. In northern Queensland, highlands only.

BREEDING August–January; usually September–December. The spherical domed nest of fine grass stems and bark strips is bound with webs, often decorated with green moss, lichen; in outer foliage at 3–12 m. Two to four white eggs, marked browns and lilac.

RANGE Eastern Australia including sub-interior, and Atherton district. Sedentary.

STATUS Common but patchy or perhaps locally nomadic. Endemic.

▶ See also pages
133

489 STRIATED THORNBILL

Acanthiza lineata   Acanthizidae

OTHER NAMES Stripe-crowned Thornbill, Striated Tit, Striped Tit

RECOGNITION Upperparts olive, blending to olive-brown on upper back; chestnut crown has distinctive narrow white streakings. There is an indistinct paler eyebrow line. Ear-coverts and face white, streaked dark grey. Wings olive; tail olive-brown with black subterminal band. Underparts off-white, becoming yellow-tinted on abdomen; buffy to olive on flanks, and with throat and upper breast streaked grey. Eye light brown; bill black; legs brown. 10 cm.

VOICE Call is a lively 'zit, zit-zit', or 'tiziz-tiziz', insect-like. The song is a fast, high-pitched trill, usually given in spring only.

HABITAT Eucalypt forests, woodlands; also rainforests, mangroves, parks, gardens.

BREEDING July–December. The nest is domed, oval in shape, with a side entrance; built of fine bark strips, grass, bound with webs, often decorated with moss; suspended in foliage at 3–10 m. Two to four pinkish-white eggs, freckled reddish-brown.

RANGE South-eastern Australia; west to Mt Lofty Ranges, north into south-eastern Queensland. Sedentary.

STATUS Common in localized areas of suitable habitat. Endemic.

▶ See also pages
119 155 164

490 SOUTHERN WHITEFACE

Aphelocephala leucopsis   Acanthizidae

OTHER NAMES Eastern Whiteface, Western Whiteface, Chestnut-bellied Whiteface, Tomtit

RECOGNITION Upperparts are light grey-brown, flight feathers darker brown. Face distinctive with white patch on each side of the forehead extending diagonally down and back through lores to just beneath the eye. The rear edge of this white is edged black across forehead and down through the eye. Tail dusky brown tipped white. Underparts off-white to pale fawn, with flanks tinged fawny to chestnut. Eye cream; bill black; legs brownish grey. 10–12 cm.

VOICE In flight, contact call a brisk 'wit, witta-wit', otherwise an almost continuous 'tik, tik-tik' or 'tweet-tweeter', in flight or foraging.

HABITAT Mulga and similar acacia scrublands, savannah-woodlands, grasslands including spinifex with scattered trees, mallee, drier farmlands.

BREEDING June–January; usually August–November. The nest is domed, with side entrance, made of grass, bark; built into a hollow of tree, stump, fence-post, crevice between branches, or in large stick nests. Two to five dull white eggs, speckled brown, red.

RANGE Southern interior, and to drier parts of western, southern and eastern coasts. Sedentary.

STATUS Locally common; patchy. Endemic.

▶ See also pages
60–1 *60* 171 232
372

491 CHESTNUT-BREASTED WHITEFACE

Aphelocephala pectoralis   Acanthizidae

OTHER NAME Chestnut-breasted Tit

RECOGNITION Crown of head grey, blending on the back to rufous-brown; wings brown; tail dark brown with light tip. Forehead white, with fine black line down the centre to the bill; the white continues down through the lores to the face, and edged black. Underparts white, with a broad pale chestnut band across the breast, and patches of chestnut down the flanks. Eye white; bill black; legs dark brown. Immatures: paler breastband. 10 cm.

VOICE Similar to Banded Whiteface, but weaker; a silvery tinkling trill, plaintive. In flight, twitterings.

HABITAT Gibber plains, especially stony rises with sparsely scattered small shrubs.

BREEDING Dates unknown. A nest found, described as a bulky, untidy sphere with side entrance; built of dead twigs, lined with wool, feathers, and placed in a *kochia* bush at 30 cm height. Three pale pink eggs, marked purplish-grey.

RANGE North-east of South Australia. Probably nomadic.

STATUS Rare. Endemic.

▶ **See also pages**
169 171

492 BANDED WHITEFACE

Aphelocephala nigricincta   Acanthizidae

OTHER NAMES Black-banded Whiteface, Black-banded Squeaker

RECOGNITION In general appearance like the Southern Whiteface, but with a narrow black breastband. Upper back chestnut, becoming darker on lower back and rump; crown brownish-grey. Forehead and front of face white, continuous with white underparts; this white is edged black round its rear margin. Underparts white except for the black breastband and light cinnamon markings along the flanks. Eye off-white; bill and legs blackish. 11 cm.

VOICE The call is a tinkling twittering, often while in flight; has also a plaintive 'peee-peee-'.

HABITAT Spinifex; usually with scattered mulga or similar scrub, on sandhill country; also saltbush-spinifex plains with sparse mulga.

BREEDING Throughout the year depending on rainfall. The nest is a loose, untidy sphere with hooded side entrance; built of dark twigs, placed in a low shrub. Three to four dull white to pale brown eggs, densely speckled red and brown.

RANGE Arid interior; north-west of Western Australia through Northern Territory, South Australia to south-western Queensland. Nomadic, probably locally.

STATUS Moderately common. Endemic.

▶ **See also pages**
59 61 171 183 371

**Neosittidae Family of 1 species
1 in Australia, 1 endemic
Sibley-Ahlquist: Family Corvidae,
Subfamily Pachycephalinae, Tribe
Neosittini**

Previously listed as five distinct species and now considered as one species of five geographical subspecies. The Varied Sittella is a small insectivore of treetrunks and branches, usually seen in noisy, family parties. They are thought to have evolved independently of the widespread, somewhat similar, nuthatch family. Large powerful feet enable them to work down the treetrunks, probing the bark with their slightly upturned bills.

493 VARIED SITTELLA

Daphoenositta chrysoptera   Neosittidae

OTHER NAMES Black-capped Sittella, White-headed Sittella, Orange-winged Sittella, Striated Sittella

RECOGNITION Five subspecies, formerly listed as separate species. In common species it is distinguished by its up-tilted yellow bill, stumpy tail, mainly dark upperparts, usually white underparts, and foraging behaviour. Crown of head usually black except subspecies White-headed Sittella; wings with white bar (northern subspecies) or cinnamon bar (southern) that is conspicuous in flight. Spirals down limbs and treetrunks in search of insects in crevices. 12–13 cm.

VOICE In flight, loud almost incessant high 'seewit-seewit' or 'chippa-chip, chippa-chip-', by all in flock; similar but less noisy while foraging.

HABITAT Eucalypt woodlands and forests, mallee, acacia scrubs, watercourse trees, parks and gardens.

BREEDING July–February; usually August–December. The nest is built into a vertical fork of a tree, blended to the branches and well camouflaged with flakes of bark; very difficult to detect. Three pale blue-grey eggs, marked black, olive, brown.

RANGE Throughout mainland Australia except some desert areas. Locally nomadic.

STATUS Moderately common. Endemic.

▶ **See also pages**
141 148 *365*

**Climacteridae Family of 6 species
6 in Australia, 6 breeding, 6 endemic
Sibley-Ahlquist: Family Climacteridae**

Small, robust insectivorous birds of the treetrunks and branches. Trees are worked in ascending pattern, the strong feet enabling them to spiral up the trunks, and even hop along the underside of limbs. Plumages are dominantly brown, varying bright cinnamon to blackish, often streaked on the underbody. Nests are built into hollows of trees. Habitats vary from wet coastal forests to arid inland scrubs.

494 WHITE-THROATED TREECREEPER

Cormobates leucophaea   Climacteridae

OTHER NAME Little Treecreeper

RECOGNITION Dark olive-brown upperparts; rump and tail grey-brown, with a black subterminal tail-band. Prominent white throat area, not sharply defined but blending gradually into darker surrounding areas, including buff-tinted breast and abdomen. Sides of breast and flanks grey with dark-edged white streaks. Female has orange spot between throat and ear-coverts. Immatures: chestnut rump; light streaks on upperparts. In flight, shows fawn wingbar. 16–17 cm.

VOICE Whistling notes, rising and falling, piercing, repeated for long periods. Also single long whistle with upwards lift.

HABITAT Rainforests, both tropical and temperate; wet eucalypt forests, coastal banksia-heathlands. Inland, drier woodlands, mallee, brigalow.

BREEDING August–January. Nest is in a tree hollow, a loose collection of bark, fur and feathers. Two to four white eggs, usually three; marked with purplish-brown and reddish-brown, rounded spots mainly at the larger end.

RANGE Eastern and south-eastern Australia, not to semi-arid interior. Sedentary.

STATUS Common. Endemic; close to some New Guinea species.

▶ **See also pages**
71 80 92 97 *119*
136 373

495 LITTLE TREECREEPER

Cormobates leucophaea minor
                         Climacteridae

OTHER NAME White-throated Treecreeper (subspecies of)

RECOGNITION First described as a species, later included within the White-throated

Treecreeper as a subspecies, and in 1975 reinstated as a full species. This bird is distinguished from the main population of the White-throated Treecreeper in its considerably smaller size; darker plumage with white of throat greatly reduced and the upper breast deep grey-buff. Remainder of underparts buff, streaked white and black. 14 cm.

VOICE Like that of the White-throated Treecreeper.

HABITAT Rainforests and edges of rainforests of mountainous country, where recorded as feeding upon, or among epiphytic mosses, probably seeking insects.

BREEDING As for the White-throated Treecreeper.

RANGE North-eastern Queensland, around Atherton Region; also an isolated population at Eungella.

STATUS Uncertain. Endemic.

▶ **See also pages** *92* 97

496 RED-BROWED TREECREEPER

Climacteris erythrops   Climacteridae
OTHER NAME Red-Eyebrowed Treecreeper
RECOGNITION Mostly dark dull brown, with red-brown eyebrow and eye-ring, rump and uppertail-coverts grey. Chin and throat white. Breast and belly grey, streaked white and rust; undertail-coverts dull white, marked black. Eye hazel; bill and legs black. Female: brighter more conspicuous reddish eyebrow and breast streaks. Immatures have grey instead of rusty brow; underparts unstreaked. In flight shows buffy-grey wingbar. 14–15 cm.

VOICE The call is rapid and high-pitched, harsh, infrequent. There is also a sustained song of sweet, silvery trilling.

HABITAT Temperate rainforests and eucalypt forests, in wetter areas, usually in ranges; tends to forage in the upper levels of the forests.

BREEDING August–January. The nest is in a hollow, usually in a vertical trunk or limb, which is lined with bark-shreds, fur. Two to three very pale pink eggs, with fine spottings of red and reddish-purple.

RANGE South-eastern Australia, coast and ranges; south-eastern Queensland almost to Melbourne. Sedentary.

STATUS Uncommon. Endemic.

▶ **See also pages** *119* 121

497 WHITE-BROWED TREECREEPER

Climacteris affinis   Climacteridae
OTHER NAME White-eyebrowed Treecreeper
RECOGNITION Upperparts grey-brown; eyebrow streak whitish and quite prominent, ear-coverts lightly streaked black. Rump and tail grey in east; brownish in west of range. Throat white; breast and belly streaked brown or blackish; and tinged ochre on lower belly. Eye brown; bill black; legs brown. Female: thin reddish line above the white eyebrow; feathers of upper breast edged rust. Immatures: underparts plainer. 14–15 cm.

VOICE Usual treecreeper calls, sharp shrill 'peep, peep', and harsh scolding. Song is a weak tinkling, like that of Jacky Winter or pardalotes.

HABITAT Arid and semi-arid scrubs, mainly mulga but also saltbush, native pine and desert-oak woodlands.

BREEDING Nest is in a hollow of a treetrunk or stump, usually quite low, lined with bark strips, fur, feathers. Two to three pale pink eggs speckled over most of surface with red and purplish-brown.

RANGE Most of southern interior, to coast in mid-west. Sedentary.

STATUS Common. Endemic.

▶ **See also pages** *59* 61 130

498 BROWN TREECREEPER

Climacteris picumnus   Climacteridae
OTHER NAMES Black Treecreeper, Woodpecker
RECOGNITION Upperparts dull grey-brown; greyer on crown and nape. Buff eyebrow and face; dark line through eye; broad black tail-band; and in flight, buff wingband. Throat buff; upper breast pale grey with cluster of fine black streaks in centre of upper breast; remainder of underparts streaked dull white and brown; undertail-coverts white barred blackish. Eye dark brown; bill black; legs grey. Female: breast lightly rufous-streaked. 17–18 cm.

VOICE Repeated or single sharp, ringing 'spink, spink, –', if in a long sequence slightly dropping in pitch and frequency; also scoldings.

HABITAT Eucalypt woodlands, dry forests, timber along inland watercourses, dry scrublands.

BREEDING June–January. The nest of grass, fur and feathers is placed in a hollow of a limb or trunk, sometimes in a stump or fence-post. Two to three pale pink eggs, streaked and speckled red and purple.

RANGE Eastern Australia; Cape York–south-eastern Victoria, west to Channel Country (Qld). Sedentary.

STATUS Common in optimum habitat. Endemic.

▶ **See also pages** *41* 42 92

499 RUFOUS TREECREEPER

Climacteris rufa   Climacteridae
OTHER NAME Woodpecker
RECOGNITION Plumage overall cinnamon-rufous tone. Upperparts grey-brown; grey on crown and nape; broad blackish bar across near tip of tail, all but central pair of feathers. Face cinnamon-rufous, extending to throat; breast pale grey with patch of black and buff streakings in centre; rest of underparts light cinnamon-rufous. Eye red-brown; bill black; legs blackish. In flight, rufous wingbar. Female has centre of breast streaked buff only. 15–17 cm.

VOICE Call is a steadily repeated shrill penetrating 'peep' on a level pitch; also gives churring scoldings.

HABITAT Forests and woodlands, from wet heavy karri, through the drier jarrah forest belt and open wandoo woodlands to semi-arid woodland and mallee.

BREEDING September–December. Nest is in a hollow of treetrunk or spout, sometimes in a low stump or rarely in a log on the ground. The lining is of grasses, fur and feathers. Two to three white eggs, speckled and blotched purplish and red-brown.

RANGE South-western Australia, through Great Victoria Desert to Eyre Peninsula. Sedentary.

STATUS Common in suitable habitat. Endemic.

▶ **See also pages** *154* 160 164 213 220 232 235 245

500 BLACK-TAILED TREECREEPER

Climacteris melanura   Climacteridae
OTHER NAMES Chestnut-bellied Treecreeper, Allied Treecreeper
RECOGNITION Very dark plumaged, almost overall sooty or blackish-brown; near black on upperparts; dark brown underparts. Throat and upper breast streaked black and white; ear-coverts very finely streaked white; lacks any light eyebrow. A large patch of concealed buff or cinnamon in the wing shows as a bold wingbar in flight. Eye dark brown; bill and legs black. Female has throat white, with chestnut streakings on upper breast. 16–20 cm.

VOICE The call is loud, clear, high, almost strident, rapid 'pee, pee-pee-pee-pee-pee, pee, pee'.

HABITAT Woodland with grassy under-storey, mulga scrublands, inland timbered watercourses, open eucalypt forests.

BREEDING August–January. A nest of grass, lined with feathers, is built into a hollow limb or trunk of a tree, height limited by trees of habitat, usually 5–10 m. Two to three pinkish-white eggs, finely but densely speckled purple and red.

RANGE North-western and northern Australia; Carnarvon (WA) to north-western Queensland. Sedentary.

STATUS Common. Includes former separate species *wellsi* of north-western Australia. Endemic.

▶ **See also pages**
175 198 208 *229*
233

HONEYEATERS

**Meliphagidae Family of 173 species
67 in Australia, 67 breeding, 49 endemic
Sibley-Ahlquist: Family Meliphagidae**

Small to medium songbirds specialized to varying degree for feeding upon the nectar of flowering plants. For this their principal anatomical adaptation is a brush-tipped tongue, and a slender bill that is shortish to very long, often downcurved. They are important pollinators of many co-adapted flowering plants. Insects are also taken from flowers, foliage, or in flight; nestlings of some species are fed mostly upon insects.

501   ### RED WATTLEBIRD

Anthochaera carunculata   Meliphagidae
OTHER NAMES Barkingbird, Gilly-wattler, Great-wattled Honeyeater

RECOGNITION Largest honeyeater of mainland Australia; long-tailed, and with conspicuous, fleshy red wattles hanging at each side of neck. Plumage of upperparts dark grey-brown, boldly streaked dull buffy-white; flight and tail feathers edged and tipped dull white; dull white patch on cheek below red eye. The red wattles lengthen and deepen in colour with age. Female: shorter tail; overall slightly smaller. Immatures plainer, lack red wattle. 33–36 cm.

VOICE A harsh coughing cackle, single or repeated several times, 'yaka-yak', or 'cookey-cook'. The alarm call is a single 'kook'.

HABITAT Found in a wide variety of vegetation, from eucalypt forests and woodlands to mallee and coastal scrubs, heaths, parks, gardens.

503 **LITTLE WATTLEBIRD** *Anthochaera chrysoptera*

BREEDING July–February; usually August–December. The nest is a rough bowl of grass and fine twigs, built into forks of shrub or tree at heights usually within 2–15 m. Two to three eggs, pinkish-buff to salmon pink, spotted red-brown or purplish-red.

RANGE Southern mainland Australia; south-west of Western Australia to south-eastern Queensland. Occasionally to New Zealand. At least partially migratory.

STATUS Common.

▶ **See also pages**
66 67 148 245 375

502   ### YELLOW WATTLEBIRD

Anthochaera paradoxa   Meliphagidae
OTHER NAMES Great-wattled Honeyeater, Long-wattle Bird, Tasmanian Wattlebird

RECOGNITION Australia's largest honeyeater. Upperparts dark grey to dusky grey-brown, streaked buffy-white on back and shoulder; crown and nape streaked black. Flight feathers edged light grey; primaries tipped white. The long tail is grey-black, tipped white. Eyebrow dull white; face and chin closely streaked whitish. Long pendulous yellow wattles at sides of neck. Underparts grey streaked blackish; centre of lower breast and abdomen yellow. 37–48 cm.

VOICE Harsh discordant coughings and guttural gurglings, usually a loud 'kuk-qwok', or 'ku-kuk-kwok', interspersed with various gurglings and croakings.

HABITAT Eucalypt forests, woodlands, heaths near coasts, banksia scrubs, mountain shrubbery and sub-alpine forests, orchards, gardens.

BREEDING July–January. Nest is a rough but substantial bowl of twigs, bark, and leaves, lined with grass, feathers, sometimes fur or wool; usually in an upright fork of shrub or small tree. Two to three salmon eggs, marked greys, red-brown.

RANGE Tasmania and King Island. Some seasonal or nomadic movements.

STATUS Common east and central Tasmania; elsewhere uncommon. Endemic to Tasmania.

▶ **See also pages**
142 147–8 *147*
150 151 152

LITTLE WATTLEBIRD

503

Anthochaera chrysoptera **Meliphagidae**

OTHER NAMES Biddyquock, Cookaycock, Brush Wattlebird, Mock Wattlebird

RECOGNITION Resembles well-known Red Wattlebird in its long-tailed and slender shape, and harsh calls, but is smaller, and has no wattles. Plumage is overall grey-brown; darker on the head; finely streaked white on upperparts and much more heavily on undersurfaces; lacks any yellow tint to belly. Face from base of bill, in a broad band below eye to sides of neck, is heavily streaked silvery-white. In flight, rufous patch in wings. 27–31 cm.

VOICE Calls similar to Red Wattlebird, but also some more squeaky notes; common calls are 'yekop, yekop' and 'cookay-cook', harsh 'squarrk'.

HABITAT Eucalypt forests, woodlands, heathlands, favouring scrubby areas, where there are banksias and other flowering trees and shrubs.

BREEDING Recorded throughout year, and appears influenced by flowering of trees. Nest is a rough bowl of twigs, well lined with shredded bark and plant-down, 1–10 m high in tree or shrub. One to two salmon pink eggs, spotted red-browns.

RANGE South-eastern and south-western Australia, including Tasmania. Partially nomadic or migratory.

STATUS Common. Endemic.

▶ **See also pages**
122 155 164 245 *374*

SPINY-CHEEKED HONEYEATER

504

Acanthagenys rufogularis **Meliphagidae**

OTHER NAME Spring-cheeked Honeyeater

RECOGNITION A large honeyeater with distinctive bill, pink with dark tip. Upperparts grey-brown, streaked darker, except rump which is pale grey. The pink of bill is continued on a small patch of bare skin between bill and eye. Cheek feathers spiny, bristle-like, white, in a broad band. Throat and upper breast yellowish-buff to pinkish-buff, remainder of underparts dull white streaked grey-brown; tail blackish-brown, tipped white. 23–26 cm.

VOICE The song is distinctive, far-carrying, with pleasantly musical notes, 'widit, widit, peer-peer, peer-peer-'; has varied other calls.

HABITAT Dry eucalypt woodlands, mulga and other semi-arid scrublands, saltbush and samphire, spinifex with scattered shrubs, drier heathlands.

BREEDING July–January in south; irregularly at almost any time of year after good rains in drier northern-inland regions. Nest is a deep, thin but quite strong cup, suspended from its rim. Two to three buffy-white eggs, marked grey and brown.

RANGE Almost throughout inland Australia, absent from wetter and forested regions. Sedentary in south; nomadic in dry parts of north.

STATUS Common. Endemic.

STRIPED HONEYEATER

505

Plectorhyncha lanceolata **Meliphagidae**

OTHER NAME Lanceolated Honeyeater

RECOGNITION A medium-sized honeyeater of overall greyish plumage, with the head and nape heavily streaked black and white. There is a heavier blackish stripe from beneath the eye back onto the sides of the neck, separating the striped head from the whitish underparts. Back and wings grey, streaked darker grey-brown. The white of the undersurfaces is faintly streaked grey. Eye brown; bill and legs blue-grey. Immatures less clearly marked. 21–23 cm.

VOICE Tuneful and cheery, rolling, rising and falling, of mellow notes, variations: 'cher-cher-cherry-cherry-chip-chip', 'free-wheat-peeler-peeler'.

HABITAT Usually the drier scrubs and woodlands; mallee, casuarina, mulga, native pine; on east coast, banksia, tea-tree, paperbarks.

BREEDING July–March; mainly August–January. Nest is a deep suspended cup of grass, fine rootlets, felted with plant-down, wool, and bound with webs; usually in outer foliage, at 1–10 m. Three to four pinkish-white eggs, finely speckled grey, red.

RANGE Eastern Australia, mainly sub-interior; also mid-east coast. Nomadic inland.

STATUS Moderately common. Endemic.

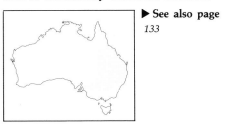

▶ **See also page**
133

HELMETED FRIARBIRD

506

Philemon buceroides **Meliphagidae**

OTHER NAMES Includes Melville Island and Sandstone friarbirds

RECOGNITION A large, plain grey-brown honeyeater, slightly darker on the upperparts. Throat, crown and nape with a silvery sheen; tufted or frilled on the nape. From the base of the bill, encircling eye and back to ear, the side of the face is bare black skin, and the heavy, curved black bill is surmounted by a black knob that extends back onto the forehead. Male has

scarlet eye; female orange eye. Immatures: no knob; face grey. 30–37 cm.

VOICE A cacophony of strange clanking sounds, varied. Among calls are a metallic 'chillank-chillank', repetitive 'chlank-chlank-chlank'.

HABITAT Forests, including rainforests, woodlands, mangroves, coastal scrub and heathlands; often in flowering trees of parks, gardens.

BREEDING August–April; usually September–February. Nest is a loosely constructed, bulky cup of bark strips, twigs, vine tendrils; lined, and slung from a horizontal fork amid foliage, usually quite high. Two to four pinkish eggs, marked greys and browns.

RANGE Coastal north-eastern Queensland; Melville Island and Sandstone subspecies in Top End (NT). Extends to New Guinea and adjacent islands. Seasonally nomadic.

STATUS Common.

▶ **See also pages**
79 98 196

SILVER-CROWNED FRIARBIRD

507

Philemon argenticeps **Meliphagidae**

RECOGNITION A small friarbird with face black; appearing encircled by the silvery-white of forehead, crown, nape and throat. The upper-mandible of the black bill carries a prominent black knob. Back, shoulders and rump grey-brown; flight feathers and tail darker brown. Chin, throat and upper breast silvery-white; remainder of underparts buffy-white. Eye red-brown; legs slate-grey. Immatures: silver less distinct; knob small. 27–31 cm.

VOICE Metallic clankings, not as loud as those of Helmeted Friarbird, described as 'more-tobacco-uh, more-'; also many and varied nasal and cat-like sounds.

HABITAT Eucalypt forests and woodlands, usually those with grassy understorey; acacia scrublands, watercourse vegetation, mangroves, gardens.

BREEDING September–March. Nest is a bowl of bark fibres, grass; bound with webs; suspended by rim from twigs, usually amid outer foliage 1–12 m above ground. Two to three pale salmon pink eggs, sparsely spotted browns and slaty-grey.

RANGE Northern Australia; western Kimberley to north-eastern Queensland. Local seasonal movements.

STATUS Moderately common. Endemic.

▶ **See also pages**
175 205 *209* 211

508 NOISY FRIARBIRD

Philemon corniculatus   Meliphagidae

OTHER NAMES Knobby-nose, Leatherhead, Four O'Clock, Poor-soldier

RECOGNITION A large honeyeater with head and upper neck mostly unfeathered; the bare skin dull black, making the red eye conspicuous. The black of the head merges into a similarly black, long and heavy downcurved bill, which is surmounted by an abrupt black knob. Plumage on fore-neck and upper breast is silvery-white, the feathers long, lanceolate; rest of underparts grey-buff. Back, wings and tail grey-brown; tail white-tipped. Immatures: lack knob. 32–35 cm.

VOICE Many strange harsh, often raucous sounds, commonly a loud 'yacob', or 'four-o-clock'; also clear ringing calls, and brassy screech.

HABITAT Open eucalypt forest and woodland, avoiding dense vegetation; watercourse trees in open country, swamp-woodlands, some inland scrubs, parks.

BREEDING Usually August–February. A large, deep cup of strips of bark, grass, wool and plant-down, is situated in concealing outer foliage; usually within 2–15 m of ground. Two to four pinkish-buff eggs, spotted and blotched slaty-grey, chestnut.

RANGE Eastern Australia; Cape York to southern Victoria, well inland. Migratory south; nomadic north. Also occurs in southern New Guinea.

STATUS Common.

▶ See also pages
122 *383*

509 LITTLE FRIARBIRD

Philemon citreogularis   Meliphagidae

OTHER NAMES Yellow-throated Friarbird, Little Leatherhead

RECOGNITION The smallest of the friarbirds, without any knob on the bill. Upperparts grey-brown; paler on nape and rump, darker on flight feathers. The bare facial skin typical of friarbirds is reduced to a patch of blue-grey skin under the eye, extending from the base of the bill and widening towards the neck. Breast light grey, streaked silvery-white; remainder of underparts white. Immatures: chin, throat, possibly upper breast, tinted yellow. 25–29 cm.

VOICE Raucous and quite loud, but more mellow than the large friarbirds, including a 'rackety-crook-shank', a liquid 'ar-coo', and 'chewip, chewip-'.

HABITAT Open eucalypt forests, woodlands, often along the watercourses; swamp-woodlands, mangroves; extending to drier scrubs when in flower, gardens.

BREEDING August–March. The nest is a deep cup of bark, grass, rootlets, bound with webs; lined with fine rootlets, grasses, and suspended from twigs of the drooping outer foliage. Two to four variable salmon eggs, marked purplish, chestnut.

RANGE Northern and eastern Australia; western Kimberley to Victoria. Partly migratory and nomadic. Also in New Guinea and adjacent islands.

STATUS Common.

▶ See also pages
175 211 *383*

510 REGENT HONEYEATER

Xanthomyza phrygia   Meliphagidae

OTHER NAMES Embroidered Honeyeater, Flying Coachman, Warty-faced Honeyeater

RECOGNITION Plumage dominantly black, with embroidered or lace-like netted pattern in white and yellow. Head and neck plain black except for an area of bare, warty yellow skin round the eye. Back and breast black, heavily scalloped in creamy white and yellow. Wing and tail feathers boldly and prominently edged golden yellow. Eye red-brown; bill black; legs dark grey-brown. In flight, the yellow of wings and tail conspicuous. Immatures duller. 20–23 cm.

VOICE Distinctive bell-like calls, mostly heard when breeding, usually a metallic 'clink-clink-clink-'. Has also various more mellow, liquid calls.

HABITAT Open eucalypt forests, woodlands, timbered watercourses, coastal heathlands, mallee, farmland and roadside tree-belts, parks and gardens.

BREEDING August–January. The nest is a substantial, deep cup of bark strips bound with webs, lined with finer bark shreds and dry grass, and usually built into a thick fork. Two to three salmon eggs, finely spotted violet-grey and red.

RANGE South-eastern Australia; approximately Rockhampton (Qld), to south-east of South Australia. Nomadic.

STATUS Common, but of patchy, irregular occurrence. Endemic.

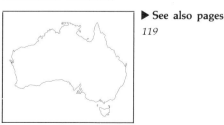

▶ See also pages
119

511 BLUE-FACED HONEYEATER

Entomyzon cyanotis   Meliphagidae

OTHER NAMES White-quilled Honeyeater, Banana-bird, Blue-eye, Pandanus-bird

RECOGNITION An unmistakable species,
with large oval patch of bare blue skin round each eye and extending well back towards the nape. Remainder of head black except for a small band of white across nape, and a white streak from the base of the lower-mandible back across the lower face and side of the neck to join the white of breast, abdomen and undertail-coverts. Black bib from chin to upper breast. Upperparts olive; tail tipped white. 30–32 cm.

VOICE A loud, querulous 'ki-owt' or 'que-it'; also strong monotonous piping notes, and softer calls, chatterings.

HABITAT Eucalypt woodlands, often along watercourses; also edges of rainforests, pandanus, swamp-woodlands, banana plantations, parks and gardens.

BREEDING June–January; usually August–November. Often re-lines a nest from magpie-larks, babblers, miners, friarbirds or apostlebirds, or sometimes builds a typical honeyeater, suspended cup nest. Two to three pinkish eggs, marked greys and chestnut.

RANGE Northern and eastern Australia; from western Kimberley to south-east of South Australia. Also in southern New Guinea. Nomadic–migratory.

STATUS Common in coastal north; less common in south-east.

▶ See also pages
122 197 198 211 *383*

512 BELL MINER

Manorina melanophrys   Meliphagidae

OTHER NAMES Bellbird, Bell Mynah

RECOGNITION Upperparts entirely olive-green, darker on the crown and wings. Bill deep cadmium-yellow, relatively heavy for a honeyeater; small orange patch of skin behind the eye. Lores dull yellow; a small black patch at front of forehead, and a black streak from base of bill back across the lower cheek. Underparts olive-green, paler than upperparts. Eye dark brown; legs cadmium-yellow. In noisy colonies, aggressive. 18–19 cm.

VOICE A metallic 'tink-tink', usually by the many birds of a colony, giving an almost incessant tinkling through the forest; also harsh scolding.

HABITAT Eucalypt forests and woodlands, especially gullies and other wet areas where there is heavy undergrowth; also densely vegetated suburbs.

BREEDING April–February; mainly July–January. The nest is a loosely woven cup of grass, very fine twigs, bark fibres, bound with webs; suspended by the rim, at heights 1–5 m. One to three white to pale pink eggs, spotted purplish-brown.

RANGE South-eastern Australia, mainly coastal; south-eastern Queensland to southern Victoria. Sedentary.

STATUS Common; locally very abundant. Endemic.

▶ See also page
119

NOISY MINER

Manorina melanocephala   Meliphagidae

OTHER NAMES Cherry-eater, Soldierbird, Mickey Miner, Garrulous Honeyeater

RECOGNITION Most of upperparts, including rump, grey; browner on wings where there is a slight olive wash to edges of flight feathers. Crown black, this extending down over the face and ear-coverts to sides of throat, but not including lores and forehead, which are white. A small triangle of bare skin behind the eye is yellow, conspicuous in the black mask; bill deep yellow. Throat and breast light grey; remainder of underparts white. 24–27 cm.

VOICE Very noisy with penetrating 'kwee-kwee-kwee'. Several alarm calls include a strident 'pee-pee-' taken up by all within hearing.

HABITAT Open eucalypt forests, woodlands, trees along inland watercourses, banksia and paperbark woodlands, farms, parks and gardens.

BREEDING Recorded all months; usually June–January. Nest is an open cup, which may be so thin that eggs can be seen from below; placed in outer foliage, 2–20 m above ground. Two to four buff to deep pink eggs, marked blue-grey, chestnut.

RANGE Eastern Australia; north-eastern Queensland to south-east of South Australia, central and eastern Tasmania. Sedentary.

STATUS Common locally. Endemic.

▶ See also pages
135 380 *383*

YELLOW-THROATED MINER

Manorina flavigula   Meliphagidae

OTHER NAMES Dusky Miner, Mickey Miner, White-rumped Miner, Yellow Miner

RECOGNITION Upperparts are grey-brown; crown grey; rump white; wings grey-brown with a wash of olive; forehead washed yellow. A small area of bare skin just behind the eye is deep yellow; both this and the eye are surrounded by a blackish patch that extends back, fading to grey towards the ear-coverts. The yellow of the gape extends back as a line below the eye. Underparts pale grey with slight yellow tint to sides of neck and chin. 25–28 cm.

VOICE Noisy, calls similar but higher than Noisy Miner, most often a strident 'kee-kee-' or 'tew-tew-'; whistled pre-dawn

514 YELLOW-THROATED MINER
Manorina flavigula

song, cat-like scoldings.

HABITAT The drier woodlands, mallee, mulga scrublands, drier types of heaths and banksia–heaths, timbered watercourses of interior, farmlands.

BREEDING Recorded throughout the year; usually July–January. The nest is a bulky, open cup; often including wool as well as grass and twigs in the construction. Two to five pinkish-buff to salmon eggs, marked red, purplish-brown.

RANGE Most drier areas; main exceptions Cape York, south-east coast, Tasmania. Sedentary or locally nomadic.

STATUS Common to abundant. Endemic.

▶ See also pages
135 136 175 *243*

BLACK-EARED MINER

Manorina melanotis   Meliphagidae

OTHER NAME Dusky Miner

RECOGNITION Upperparts grey, including crown and rump; wings and tail darker grey-brown with a yellow wash; tail not white-tipped. Eye margined round its rear edge by a small patch of deep golden yellow bare skin, this set very conspicuously in a large black facial mask that extends from the base of the golden yellow bill and round the eye, back onto the ear-coverts. Underparts light grey, mottled darker on breast; near white on belly. 24–26 cm.

VOICE Calls are reported to be very much like those of the Noisy and Yellow-throated miners with varied harsh and loud complaining sounds.

HABITAT Most often recorded in mallee, thus usually separated in habitat from the Noisy Miner, but not from Yellow-throated Miner.

BREEDING June–January; usually September–November. Nest is recorded as being similar to the nests of other miners. Two to four reddish-buff eggs, densely covered with fine spotting of red-brown.

RANGE A restricted area at junction of Victoria, New South Wales, and South Australia. Sedentary.

STATUS Generally uncommon; locally common. Endemic.

▶ See also pages
129 *133* 135 138

MACLEAY'S HONEYEATER

Xanthotis macleayana   Meliphagidae

OTHER NAMES Yellow-streaked Honeyeater, Buff-striped Honeyeater, Mottle-plumaged Honeyeater

RECOGNITION Plumage is overall grey-brown, heavily mottled and streaked dark brown; with orange-yellow on the mantle, creamy white on the shoulders. Head black-capped, and conspicuous area of bare orange-buff skin round the eye and back to the ear. Sides of neck, chin and throat grey; breast dark grey, streaked orange-yellow; remainder of underparts light grey, mottled and streaked darker grey-brown. Eye dark brown; bill black and legs black. 18–21 cm.

VOICE A quiet species, but has a single 'chip' call, and a five-note 'to-whit, too-wheee, twit'.

HABITAT Rainforest and nearby wetter eucalypt forest, swamp-woodlands, creek-edge scrub, orchards and gardens.

BREEDING September–March; usually October–December. The nest is a deep cup of palm fibres, bark shreds, leaf skeletons, spider cocoons and webs; suspended from rim in foliage canopy, usually quite high. Two pinkish eggs, spotted grey, chestnut.

RANGE North-eastern Queensland; Cooktown south almost to Townsville, coast, ranges. Sedentary.

STATUS Moderately common. Species endemic to north-eastern Queensland.

▶ See also pages
85 92 97 *99*

517 TAWNY-BREASTED HONEYEATER

Xanthotis flaviventer   Meliphagidae
OTHER NAMES Streaked Honeyeater, Streak-naped Honeyeater, Buff-breasted Honeyeater

RECOGNITION Upperparts are dark olive-brown; darker on the head. Wings and tail dark olive-brown, with feathers edged yellow ochre. A small patch of bare skin behind the eye is pinkish-yellow; there is a yellow line from base of bill, below eye back to ear-coverts, and a very small yellow tuft behind the ear-coverts. Sides of neck and throat grey, merging to lightly streaked tawny-brown on remainder of underparts. Eye dark brown; bill black. 18–22 cm.

VOICE A loud strong whistle, described as 'which-witch-is-which', and also a varied whistled song.

HABITAT Rainforests, mangroves, eucalypt woodlands, heathlands. Usually keeps near the canopy, and most readily observed where the canopy is low.

BREEDING October–April; usually November–March. The nest is a cup of bark strips and fibres; suspended from the rim among the foliage of a leafy shrub or tree. Two pinkish-white eggs with fine grey and purplish-red spots.

RANGE Cape York; south usually only to Watson and Rocky rivers. Also in New Guinea and adjacent islands. Sedentary.

STATUS Common to uncommon.

▶ See also pages
106 *109*

518 LEWIN'S HONEYEATER

Meliphaga lewinii   Meliphagidae
OTHER NAMES Yellow-eared Honeyeater, Banana-bird, Orange-bird, White-lug

RECOGNITION Upperparts dark olive-green; greenish-black on the head, extending down to lores and about the eye. Pale yellow streak back from base of bill to the bottom edge of the eye, and a pale yellow crescent on ear-coverts. Underparts olive-grey, indistinctly streaked. Bill black; legs brownish. Very aggressive towards each other and other species. Often feed by spiralling up treetrunks, like treecreepers, pecking insects from the bark. 19–21 cm.

VOICE A rapid loud high-pitched chatter. Also a single drawn-out loud and peevish 'tchewww'.

HABITAT Rainforests and eucalypt forests, less often woodlands; of both coast and ranges. Also some sub-inland scrubs, heaths, mangroves.

BREEDING July–March; usually September–February. Nest is cup-shaped; built of bark and palm fibres, grass, rootlets, sometimes leaves, lined with fine grass, plant-down; suspended among foliage. Two to three white eggs, spotted purplish-red.

RANGE Coastal eastern Australia; Cooktown (Qld), to south-eastern Victoria. Locally nomadic.

STATUS Common. Endemic.

▶ See also pages
55 *55* 92 97 126

519 YELLOW-SPOTTED HONEYEATER

Meliphaga notata   Meliphagidae
OTHER NAMES Lesser Lewin Honeyeater, Yellow-spot Honeyeater

RECOGNITION Very much like Lewin's Honeyeater, but slightly smaller. Upperparts brighter yellow-green, less streaked; face dark olive-brown rather than blackish. Bright yellow line back from base of bill beneath eye, rounded rather than crescent-shaped yellow ear-patch. Underparts a paler, yellowish-grey, lightly streaked. Eye grey-brown; bill black; legs grey-brown. Like the Lewin's Honeyeater, this species is inquisitive, bold and aggressive. 17–19 cm.

VOICE Various calls, including a single-note 'chip-'; has a petulant 'tchu-chua', and a rattle like Lewin's Honeyeater, but softer; also scolding notes.

HABITAT Rainforests, mangroves, flowering trees in nearby woodlands, lantana thickets: principally a lowland species.

BREEDING August–April; usually September–February. The nest is a delicate suspended cup of fine bark and palm fibres; bound with webs, lined with plant-down, and decorated with pale green lichens. Two white eggs, spotted dark red or purple.

RANGE North-eastern Queensland; eastern Cape York, coast and ranges south to Townsville. Sedentary.

STATUS Common. Endemic.

▶ See also pages
52 92 *99*

520 GRACEFUL HONEYEATER

Meliphaga gracilis   Meliphagidae
OTHER NAMES Grey-breasted Honeyeater, Lesser Yellow-spotted Honeyeater

RECOGNITION Closely resembles Yellow-spotted Honeyeater: smaller, with slightly paler and yellower upperparts; underparts grey, less streaked. Face only slightly darkened about the lores and eye, much less than for Lewin's Honeyeater and noticeably less than for the Yellow-spotted. Yellow streak back from base of bill is much thinner, inconspicuous beneath eye; yellow ear-patch rounded. Bill slightly more slender. Quieter, active but unobtrusive. 14–16 cm.

VOICE A short sharp 'plick', 'click', 'tick', or 'tuck'; also said to have a thin whistle, rarely heard.

HABITAT Usually in rainforests, extending to nearby eucalypt forest and woodland, dense stream-vegetation, mostly but not exclusively lowlands.

BREEDING September–March; usually October–February. The nest is a delicate small suspended cup of grass and moss, bound with webs, heavily camouflaged with moss and lichens. Two pale to deep salmon eggs, spotted purple-grey and chestnut.

RANGE North-eastern Queensland; Cape York, and east coast south to Ingham. Also New Guinea and Aru Islands. Sedentary.

STATUS Moderately common.

▶ See also pages
55 92 97 *99*

521 WHITE-LINED HONEYEATER

Meliphaga albilineata   Meliphagidae
OTHER NAME White-striped Honeyeater

RECOGNITION Upperparts dark grey-brown with olive tint; wings and tail darker grey-brown with feathers edged yellow. Head darker grey with fine white from base of bill curving under the eye, then widening as a white tuft over the ear-coverts. Underparts dull white, lightly mottled or streaked grey-brown on the breast. Eye dull white; bill black; feet dark grey. Usually a solitary species, but at times may form loose feeding flocks. 18–20 cm.

VOICE A series of strong clear whistles, the first rising, the second undulating, the third and loudest rising wildly before falling away.

HABITAT Rainforest or monsoon forest, river-edge vegetation, in sandstone gorges and beneath escarpments, nearby woodlands, swamp-woodlands.

BREEDING Probably August–February. Nest is a deep cup of fine strands of creepers, bound with webs, lined with finer plant fibres; built into the outer foliage of a shrub or tree at 1–5 m height. Eggs undescribed.

RANGE Northern Kimberley, and sandstone areas of Top End (NT). Sedentary.

STATUS Locally common. Endemic.

▶ See also pages
189 194–5 196 210

522 YELLOW-FACED HONEYEATER

Lichenostomus chrysops Meliphagidae
OTHER NAMES Chickup, Quitchup, Love-bird, Yellow-gaped Honeyeater

RECOGNITION Upperparts are olive-brown. Conspicuous yellow face-streak back from the bill, surrounds the lower half of eye, and extends back, wider, onto ear-coverts, bordered above and below by black. Sides of breast buffy; rest of underparts grey. Eye blue-grey; bill black; legs brown. Immatures duller. An active honeyeater, hawking for insects about the outer foliage and flowering trees, but also feeding in low heath and scrub. 16–18 cm.

VOICE Varied; usually a brisk cheerful 'chickup'. In the breeding season, a descending, ringing 'calip-calip-calip-'.

HABITAT Eucalypt forests and woodlands, heaths including alpine, coastal scrubs and mangroves, parks, gardens, orchards.

BREEDING July–March; usually October–January. The nest is a small neat cup of bark and fine grass bound with webs, sometimes decorated with moss or lichen; placed in outer foliage of shrub or tree. Two to three light pinkish eggs, marked greys, red.

RANGE Eastern and south-eastern Australia, mainly coastal; Atherton Tableland to Adelaide. Partially migratory in the south.

STATUS Common. Endemic.

▶ See also pages
112 122 136

523 BRIDLED HONEYEATER

Lichenostomus frenatus Meliphagidae
OTHER NAME Mountain Honeyeater

RECOGNITION Upperparts dark brown; blackish-brown on forehead, face, throat. Base of bill deep yellow, this colour extending back in a thin streak beneath the eye, then curving up behind to join a fan-shaped white patch. A finer yellow line from the chin encircles the black ear-covert area; dull yellow patch at side of throat. Underparts grey-brown, mottled lighter. Wing and tail feathers brown, edged yellow. Eye grey; bill tip and legs black. 18–22 cm.

VOICE Noisy, with clear and melodious calls, of descending whistles, 'wee-are', and 'wa-chi-ta, wa-chi-ta'; also a harsh 'chaarrgh'.

HABITAT Rainforests, wetter eucalypt forests, woodlands, especially along streams, and swampy areas, at altitudes above 450 m; lower areas in winter.

BREEDING August–April; usually September–January. The nest is cup-shaped; suspended in leafy part of tree or vine; usually at moderate height. Vine tendrils, fine twigs, and ferns are used in the structure. Two white eggs, spotted grey, brown.

RANGE Restricted to Atherton Region. Probably sedentary.

STATUS Common. Endemic.

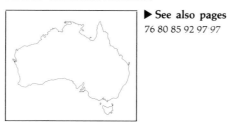

▶ See also pages
76 80 85 92 97 97

524 EUNGELLA HONEYEATER

Lichenostomus hindwoodi Meliphagidae

RECOGNITION Until 1977 it was thought that the Bridled Honeyeater extended south to Eungella; it was then discovered to be a new species, slightly smaller, and with different facial markings. Overall sooty grey, with underparts streaked lighter grey. Distinctive head markings, consisting of a dark facial patch, pale bridle stripe below and behind the eye, white and yellow ear-covert plumes; bill black; legs blue-grey. Female slightly smaller. Immatures show rufous on the crown. 16–18 cm.

VOICE Differs from call of Bridled Honeyeater being more complex and varied, a whistled 'pee-pee-pip-pip-pip-' becoming slower.

HABITAT Highland rainforest, above 900 m altitude, possibly lower.

BREEDING Nest and eggs unknown.

RANGE Clarke Range, central Queensland coast.

STATUS Common within restricted range.

▶ See also pages
71 76 79 80 81

525 SINGING HONEYEATER

Lichenostomus virescens Meliphagidae
OTHER NAMES Forrest's Honeyeater, Grey Peter, Large-striped Honeyeater, Black-faced Honeyeater

RECOGNITION A medium-sized honeyeater with upperparts grey-brown; darker on the wings and tail where the quills are edged yellowish; tends to be paler overall in drier regions. There is a broad black band through the eye extending back to curve down on the side of neck; this bordered at its lower edge by a thinner, shorter yellow line, ending in a broad whitish patch. Underparts light grey; buffy on throat; grey-streaked on breast. 18–22 cm.

VOICE Melodious and drawn-out call, especially at dawn. Contact calls are a scratchy 'shreee', rattling 'prrit-prrit-'; alarm a rapid 'crik, crik-krikkrik'.

HABITAT A wide variety; woodlands, heathlands, mulga, mallee, spinifex with scattered scrub, stunted mangroves along Western Australian coast.

BREEDING Recorded all months; rain influenced in arid regions, otherwise usually August–February. The nest is a frail cup woven of grass, matted with webs, slung by rim in dense foliage. Two to three pinkish-buff eggs, marked brown.

RANGE Almost throughout Australia except Tasmania, and north, east and south-east coasts. Sedentary.

STATUS Common. Endemic.

▶ See also pages
131 136 175 211

526 VARIED HONEYEATER

Lichenostomus versicolor Meliphagidae

RECOGNITION Upperparts are olive-brown, with feathers of wings and tail edged yellow. There is a blackish-brown streak through the eye and back down the side of the neck; from the base of the bill a yellow streak passes below the eye to end with a white patch on the ear-coverts. Chin and throat slightly paler yellow, extending, streaked brown, to breast and abdomen. Eye grey-brown; bill black; legs grey. Immatures: underparts not streaked. 19–21 cm.

VOICE Noisy, with very loud rollicking calls, suggested by phrases such as 'which way, which way you go'; not unlike calls of Singing and Mangrove honeyeaters.

HABITAT Usually in mangroves, extending to other coastal scrubs, nearby woodlands, gardens of coastal towns.

BREEDING April–December. Builds a thin, flimsy cup nest of fine rootlets, bark fibres, bound with webs; attached to a horizontal fork of a mangrove or other coastal tree. Two to three pale pink eggs, lightly speckled red-brown.

RANGE Coastal north-eastern Queensland; tip of Cape York Peninsula south to Ingham. Also in southern New Guinea and adjacent islands. Sedentary.

STATUS Moderately common.

▶ See also pages
93 *99*

527 MANGROVE HONEYEATER

Lichenostomus fasciogularis Meliphagidae
OTHER NAMES Scaly-throated Honeyeater, Fasciated Honeyeater, Island Honeyeater

RECOGNITION Upperparts are dark grey, browner on wings; flight and tail feathers are slightly edged deep yellow. There is a bold black line from base of bill through eye, above a broad pale yellow line that extends back from base of bill, fading to white towards ear-coverts, then turning down side of neck in a wide white band, almost to shoulders. Throat yellowish, with a dark brown scaly or barred pattern. Breast grey; belly whitish streaked grey. 18–20 cm.

VOICE A strong, resonant and tuneful singer, with distinctive calls. The usual songs are musical, flute-like 'wook-ee-wooo' and 'whit-oo-wee-oo'.

HABITAT Principally a bird of the mangroves, but visiting flowering trees of nearby eucalypt woodlands, and may sometimes be seen in coastal towns.

BREEDING Usually August–January; but also March–May in northern Queensland. The nest is usually in a mangrove tree, sometimes within 1 m of high-tide level; cup-shaped; made of grass and webs; suspended at rim. Two pinkish-buff eggs, spotted red-brown.

RANGE Mid-east coast; Townsville–northern Queensland to north-eastern New South Wales. Sedentary.

STATUS Common in north of range; uncommon to rare in south. Endemic.

▶ **See also pages** 23 25 98

528 WHITE-GAPED HONEYEATER

Lichenostomus unicolor   Meliphagidae
OTHER NAMES River Honeyeater, Uniform-coloured Honeyeater, Erect-tailed Honeyeater

RECOGNITION Upperparts dark grey, paler on rump. Wings and tail brownish-grey, with quills lightly edged greenish-yellow. Face darker grey about the lores and eye, with a small triangular creamy white or yellowish patch at the gape between bill and eye. Underparts slightly paler grey, often with a slight yellowish wash to the breast. Eye grey; bill black; legs grey. Immatures: stronger yellow tints to gape and feather edgings. 18–20 cm.

VOICE Loud rollicking calls, commonly 'whit-a-whee', and 'whit-whit, awhit-wit, awhit-wit'; some calls likened to those of Noisy Miner.

HABITAT Eucalypt woodlands, favouring situations near water and areas of denser understorey, often in monsoon forests of gorges; also in mangroves.

BREEDING September–May; usually October–March. The cup-shaped nest of bark strips, fine grass, rootlets, bound with webs, is suspended in foliage of a leafy tree or shrub. Two pinkish-white eggs, freckled and blotched red and purple.

RANGE Northern Australia; Kimberley to north-eastern Queensland. Sedentary.

STATUS Uncommon. Endemic.

▶ **See also pages** 175 197 205 *205* 211

529 YELLOW HONEYEATER

Lichenostomus flavus   Meliphagidae

RECOGNITION Upperparts bright yellow-green; underparts yellow. Wings and tail are a darker grey-brown, with the feathers edged buff. There is a darker brownish line through the eye, and indistinct lighter yellow streaks above and below the eye. Bill black or dark brown; eye light brown; legs grey. Immatures: colours comparatively dull; bill paler. An active, bold and inquisitive species, sometimes in flocks feeding noisily in flowering trees. 16–19 cm.

VOICE Loud clear cheerful whistling, quite piercing, 'whee-whee', or long 'wheee-up, wheee-up'; also a metallic 'whek-whek' or 'tut-tut-'.

HABITAT Eucalypt forests and woodlands, often along rivers, and at edges of rainforest; usually below 450 m altitude. Also swamp-woodlands, mangroves.

BREEDING Usually October–March. Nest is a shallow cup of palm and bark fibres, grass, bound with webs; softly lined with finer plant fibres; suspended by the rim in leafy foliage. Two white to pink eggs, spotted grey, chestnut.

RANGE North-eastern Queensland; Cape York and south almost to Rockhampton. Possibly locally nomadic.

STATUS Moderately common. Endemic.

▶ **See also pages** 76 79

530 WHITE-EARED HONEYEATER

Lichenostomus leucotis   Meliphagidae
OTHER NAME New Norcia Honeyeater

RECOGNITION Upperparts deep olive-green; crown grey streaked black. Face, including lores, and round eye, black; this extending to sides of neck, chin, throat and upper breast; surrounding a very conspicuous white ear-patch. Wings and tail olive-brown. Underparts yellowish-olive to olive-grey. Eye light brown; bill and legs black. The female has less black on the breast. Immatures: duller; crown olive-grey. In flight, wings make 'flop-flop' sound. 20–25 cm.

VOICE Varied loud ringing calls, 'chock-up', 'cherrywheat', 'cherup', 'cherry-bob', 'chittagong'; also a rapid succession of 'chock-chock-chock-'.

HABITAT Heathlands, patches of heath in forests, woodlands, mallee, brigalow, tea-tree thickets; and, in south-eastern Australia, in wet eucalypt forests.

BREEDING July–April; usually August–December. The cup nest, suspended by the rim from twigs of a shrub or low undergrowth, is built of grass, bark shreds, bound with webs, lined with fur or hair. Two to three white eggs, spotted red-brown.

RANGE Widespread eastern, south-eastern and south-western Australia; extending well inland. Partially locally nomadic, some altitudinal migration in south-east.

STATUS Common.

▶ **See also pages** 80 136 163 *163* 232

531 YELLOW-THROATED HONEYEATER

Lichenostomus flavicollis   Meliphagidae
OTHER NAMES Linnet, Green Dick

RECOGNITION Upperparts olive-green, with feathers of wings and tail edged brighter yellow-green. Head, sides of neck, and upper breast dark grey, making conspicuous a large, bright yellow patch on chin and throat. There is a small yellow tuft on the ear-coverts. Beneath, the dark grey of the upper breast merges to mid-grey on lower breast then to olive-grey on remainder of underparts. Eye deep red; bill black; legs grey. Immatures paler. 19–21 cm.

VOICE A loud resonant call, 'tonk, tonk, tonk-', 'tchook, tchook-', usually repeated four to five times. When breeding, a soft warbled song at dawn, dusk.

HABITAT Eucalypt forests, heaths, woodlands; feeds largely upon insects, mostly taken from the bark; but very attracted to cider-gums in autumn.

BREEDING July–January. The deep cup of bark and grass is lined with fur, wool or feathers, usually low in shrubbery, occasionally to 10 m in tree foliage. Two to three pale pinkish-buff eggs, finely flecked and spotted grey and chestnut.

RANGE Confined to Tasmania, King Island and Furneaux Group. Sedentary.

STATUS Common. Endemic.

▶ **See also pages** 142 *147* 148 150 151 152 153

YELLOW-TUFTED HONEYEATER

Lichenostomus melanops   Meliphagidae
OTHER NAMES Golden-tufted Honeyeater, Helmeted Honeyeater, Yellow Whiskers, Black-faced Honeyeater

RECOGNITION Four subspecies; the most brightly coloured being the rare Helmeted Honeyeater. Back, wings and tail olive-grey; wing and tail feathers browner and edged yellow; forehead golden, slightly tufted (Helmeted), shading to slightly duller crown and nape. Bold black line from bill through eye widening over ear-coverts and ending with a bright yellow tuft. Lower face, chin and throat yellow, blending to the streaked greyish breast; yellow-grey underparts. Immatures are greener. 18–23 cm.

VOICE Contact call a sharp 'jik' or 'yip', lengthened to 'jor-jor-jor-jiri-jiri'; also 'tchurr-tchurr-tchurr'. Alarm call harsher.

HABITAT Eucalypt forests and woodlands, coastal heaths, dry inland woodlands, mallee, native pine, brigalow. Helmeted Honeyeater in forest pockets along creeks.

BREEDING July–April; usually August–December. Nest is a deep cup of grass and bark fibres, bound with webs, suspended by rim in shrub, or low in tree foliage or vine tangle. Two to three white to buff eggs, spotted violet-grey and chestnut.

RANGE South-eastern Australia; south-eastern Queensland to south-western Victoria. Inland subspecies tend to be nomadic.

STATUS Uncommon; locally common. Helmeted Honeyeater is rare and restricted. Endemic.

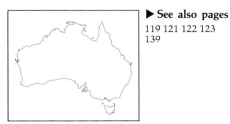

▶ See also pages
119 121 122 123 139

PURPLE-GAPED HONEYEATER

Lichenostomus cratitius   Meliphagidae
OTHER NAMES Lilac-wattled Honeyeater, Wattle-cheeked Honeyeater

RECOGNITION Upperparts are olive-green; yellow-green on wings; grey on the head. From the base of the bill a blackish band widens to include lores and eye; over the ear-coverts area the band becomes broader, lightens to mid-grey, and ends with a small yellow ear tuft. The blackish eye-band is edged beneath by a broad yellow streak. There is an inconspicuous lilac line of bare skin along the gape. Underparts grey with yellowish wash. Immatures: gape yellow. 16–17 cm.

VOICE Varied, including a harsh single quick 'chuck', and a loud whip-like whistle, in flight a sharp 'twit-twit'; also a soft parrot-like warble.

HABITAT Mallee and associated semi-arid woodlands, open grassy woodlands and trees along inland watercourses.

BREEDING August–December. The nest of grass and bark strips, bound with webs, is slung by the rim among foliage; usually quite low. Two white eggs, with a pinkish tinge, with speckling of reddish-brown.

RANGE Drier south of Western Australia, southern South Australia, south-western New South Wales, north-western Victoria. Highly nomadic.

STATUS Generally uncommon; at times locally abundant. Endemic.

▶ See also pages
130 139 155 *157* 160–1

GREY-HEADED HONEYEATER

Lichenostomus keartlandi   Meliphagidae
OTHER NAME Keartland's Honeyeater

RECOGNITION Upperparts are sandy grey-brown; pale grey on the head. A dark grey or blackish band back from base of bill across eye and broader over ear, edged at the rear, towards the side of the neck, by a deep yellow tuft or plume. Underparts entirely pale lemon yellow, streaked slightly darker on throat and breast. Eye brown; bill black; legs brown. Immatures duller; yellow gape. Usually in pairs or parties, active about flowering vegetation. 15–16 cm.

VOICE Usually 'cheetoit, cheetoit', or 'kwoit, kwoit'. Variations are 'chip-chip-chip', 'chickowee'; in flight, 'check-check'. Alarm is rapid trill.

HABITAT Arid country, favouring rocky ranges with spinifex and sparse scrub and trees, especially near watercourse pools; also mulga, dry woodlands.

BREEDING Almost any time of year after good rains; usually July–December. The nest is a small cup of fine strips of bark, bound with webs, lined with plant-down; in foliage usually of a low shrub. Two whitish eggs, marked red-browns.

RANGE Northern interior, to coast in north-west. Probably only locally nomadic.

STATUS Common; locally abundant. Endemic.

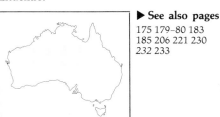

▶ See also pages
175 179–80 183 185 206 221 230 232 233

YELLOW-PLUMED HONEYEATER

Lichenostomus ornatus   Meliphagidae
OTHER NAMES Mallee Honeyeater, Graceful Honeyeater

RECOGNITION Upperparts are grey-brown; olive-green on wings, tail and head, darker about the eye. There is a faint yellow line back from the gape below the eye, and a small blackish mark on the ear-coverts, adjoining a conspicuous yellow plume. Underparts dull white, boldly streaked grey or grey-brown. Eye brown; bill black; legs brown. Immatures duller. Very active and aggressive, noisy, often in parties, taking insects, or around flowering trees. 15–18 cm.

VOICE Noisy, cheerful calls. Contact is a loud 'cho-cho-hik'; more common call 'chickowee' or 'chickwididee'; male has song-flight. Often scolds harshly.

HABITAT Eucalypt woodlands, mallee, acacia scrublands. Near coast, banksia woodlands, heathlands, occasional to semi-arid scrubs, watercourse trees.

BREEDING Usually August–December. The nest is a small cup of grasses and other fine plant fibres, bound with webs; suspended by the rim in foliage of a tree or shrub, 1–10 m height. Two to three salmon-pink eggs, finely speckled red-brown.

RANGE Inland south-east, to coast in South Australia; south-west of Western Australia. Nomadic or migratory.

STATUS Common. Endemic.

▶ See also pages
130 137 *162* 171 245

GREY-FRONTED HONEYEATER

Lichenostomus plumulus   Meliphagidae
OTHER NAMES Yellow-fronted Honeyeater, Plumed Honeyeater

RECOGNITION Upperparts are olive-brown, darker on the head. There is a large, bright yellow plume each side of the neck, edged above with a black streak across the ear-coverts. Underparts pale buff-grey, streaked darker on the breast. Eye dark brown; bill black; legs dark brown. Immatures yellowish at the base of the bill; underparts more strongly streaked. Usually solitary, but sometimes in numbers on flowering trees; reported to be wary. 13–16 cm.

VOICE Loud and sharp, 'it-wit, wit, wit, wit', or 'it-wirt, wirt, wirt'; other calls recorded include a sharp 'boink' of alarm, and 'sw-ee-et'.

HABITAT Mallee, acacia scrub, eucalypt woodlands, sparse scrub on rough hills, and scrub along watercourses. Inland, often in mallee–spinifex.

BREEDING Usually August–January. The nest is a small neat cup of fine grass, bark strips, bound with webs, decorated with spiders' egg-cases, lined with plant-down, and suspended among foliage. Two pale pinkish eggs, spotted red-brown.

RANGE Widespread through the interior, and to drier coasts. Sedentary.

STATUS Moderately common; patchy. Endemic.

▶ See also pages
169 171 175 197
198 208 220

537 FUSCOUS HONEYEATER

Lichenostomus fuscus Meliphagidae

RECOGNITION Overall dull olive-brown; tinged olive on the wings and tail; underparts pale grey-brown. Head brownish, slightly darker through the eye, leading back to a small, black-edged plume at the side of the neck. Bill black, often with pronounced yellow gape; eye brown, usually with fine yellow eye-ring. The yellow of gape and eye-ring seems to be characteristic of immatures and non-breeding birds, while those of breeding birds are black. 15–16 cm.

VOICE Locally variable, loud and clear, often a single 'chip', fast ascending or descending trill, and 'arig-arig, a-taw-taw'.

HABITAT Eucalypt forests and woodlands, occasionally to mallee and heath near coast, rivergums, brigalow, margins of rainforests, gardens.

BREEDING July–March; usually August–January. Nest is a small neat cup of bark strips, grass, bound with webs; lined with plant-down, often also hair, wool; hung in outer foliage at 1–20 m. Two to three buffy eggs, lightly spotted red-brown, lilac.

RANGE Eastern Australia; Cooktown south to south-east of South Australia. Migratory in south.

STATUS Generally common; sparse in South Australia. Endemic.

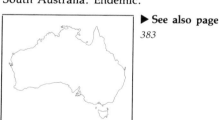

▶ See also page
383

538 YELLOW-TINTED HONEYEATER

Lichenostomus flavescens Meliphagidae
OTHER NAMES Yellowish Honeyeater, Pale-yellow Honeyeater

RECOGNITION Upperparts are pale yellow-brown; wings and tail brown, with feathers edged yellowish. Face uniform pale yellow except for a small yellow plume at the side of the neck, edged above by a short black line across the ear; the yellow plume, set against overall yellowish plumage, is inconspicuous. Underparts very pale yellowish-grey. Eye brown; bill and legs black. Immatures paler; bill brownish. Often in parties around flowering trees. 14–16 cm.

VOICE Contact call a sharp descending 'tew-tew-' or 'jer-jer-'. Song is high, clear 'porra-chew, porra-chew-chew, chi-porra-chew, chew-chew-chew'.

HABITAT Rainforest (monsoon scrubs), eucalypt forests along tropical rivers, woodlands in Kimberley, occasionally mangroves.

BREEDING July–February; usually August–December. The nest is a cup of bark and grass, bound with webs, often decorated with spiders' egg-sacs; lined with finer grass; suspended by rim in shrub or tree. Two pink-buff eggs, marked red-brown.

RANGE Northern Australia; Kimberley, Top End (NT), Queensland mainly northwest. Also in southern New Guinea. Sedentary.

STATUS Common.

▶ See also pages
175 197 *205* 211

539 WHITE-PLUMED HONEYEATER

Lichenostomus penicillatus Meliphagidae
OTHER NAMES Chickowee, Greenie, Linnet, Native Canary, Ringeye

RECOGNITION Upperparts very light grey-brown with strong yellow tint on rump and wing-coverts; wing and tail feathers edged yellow. Head yellow; narrow black-edged white plume at side of neck. Underparts buffy-white. In eastern and south-eastern Australia the rich yellows of the plumage of birds of the north and west are replaced by dull olive tones. Eye dark brown; bill black; legs brown. Immatures duller; bill yellow-brown. Conspicuously active and noisy. 15–16 cm.

VOICE Usually a brisk loud 'chick-o-wee' and varied other chatterings; aggressive scoldings; rapid strident alarm trill.

HABITAT Keeps to localities with large eucalypts. Inland, favours rivergums along watercourses, and nearby mallee; nearer coasts, woodlands, gardens.

BREEDING Throughout the year, rainfall-dependent in arid regions; usually July–January. The nest is a small, deep, neat, frail cup, of grass, fine bark strips, rootlets. Two to three pinkish to buff eggs, spotted chestnut, lilac.

RANGE Almost throughout Australian interior, and to coast in north-west, southeast. Sedentary; nomadic in arid regions.

STATUS Common. Endemic.

▶ See also pages
175 220 *229* 230
233

540 BLACK-CHINNED HONEYEATER

Melithreptus gularis Meliphagidae
OTHER NAMES Black-throated Honeyeater, Golden-backed Honeyeater

RECOGNITION Back and rump olive; tail and wings brown. Head black with crescent of bare blue skin over the eye, and white band round the black nape. There is a blackish patch under the chin; underparts dull white. Eye dark brown; bill black and stout; legs brown. The subspecies *laetior*, Golden-backed Honeyeater, has back and rump deep golden; underparts buffy-white; bare skin over eye greenish-yellow. Immatures: head brownish. 15–16 cm.

VOICE Call is a sharp, harsh 'tshirp'. Song is a somewhat grating 'prrrp, prrp, ch-ch-cheer'. Golden-backed Honeyeater: ringing 'chi-chi-chrinny-chrinny'.

HABITAT Woodlands of eucalypts, paper-barks, acacia scrublands, spinifex country especially watercourse trees; ironbark forests.

BREEDING Throughout year, rainfall dependent in north-west and other dry regions; usually April–December. Nest is of fine bark shreds, grass, wool, bound with webs, and slung in drooping outer foliage. One to two pinkish eggs, spotted rich browns.

RANGE Northern, eastern and south-eastern Australia. Sedentary; probably nomadic in drier areas.

STATUS Moderately common. Endemic.

▶ See also pages
139 148 162 163
175 185 206 221
230 233 382

541 STRONG-BILLED HONEYEATER

Melithreptus validirostris Meliphagidae
OTHER NAMES Black-capped Honeyeater, Black-cap, Barkbird

RECOGNITION Upperparts grey-brown; becoming olive-brown on wing-coverts, lower back, rump and tail; and yellow-green towards the black nape. Head and nape black, with bold white band round the back of the head, and blue crescent over the eye. Throat white, greyish at the centre, and with the white extending right to the base of the bill. Remainder of underparts mid-grey. Immatures duller; brown head. The only Tasmanian honeyeater with white nape-band. 17 cm.

VOICE A sharp 'cheep-cheep', sometimes run together in a rapid staccato 'cheep-cheepcheep-'. The alarm call is a harsh 'churrr'.

HABITAT Eucalypt forests; usually wet forests with heavy undergrowth, but moving to drier forests in winter; often forages on bark like a treecreeper.

BREEDING August–April; usually September–February. Nest is deep cup, woven of bark fibres, grass; often including fur, hair and wool; suspended from rim in outer foliage of tree or sapling. Two to three pinkish-buff eggs, spotted red-brown, grey.

RANGE Confined to Tasmania; King Island and Furneaux Group in Bass Strait. Sedentary.

STATUS Common. Endemic.

▶ See also pages
141 142 *147* 148
150 151 152 153

BROWN-HEADED HONEYEATER

Melithreptus brevirostris   Meliphagidae
OTHER NAME Short-billed Honeyeater

RECOGNITION Back olive-green; browner on wings and tail. Crown of head brown; face blackish-brown. The band round the nape is creamy or buffy-white rather than white; and the small crescent of bare skin over the eye is pale cream to pale orange. Underparts, including chin, pale buffy-white to very light grey. Eye brown; bill blackish; legs brown. Immatures duller. Often in flocks, and frequently seeks insects on bark, like a sittella. 12–13 cm.

VOICE While feeding and in flight, a loud repetitive 'chip' or 'chick'. The song is a rapid series: 'chip, chip, chip-chip-chip-chipchip, chip, chip'.

HABITAT Eucalypt forests, woodlands, mallee; reaching coast where there is relatively dry open woodland or heath; also in mallee, coastal tea-tree.

BREEDING July–February; usually August–December. The nest is a deep cup, slung in outer foliage or at the top of a sapling; construction is usually of bark shreds, grass, hair; often fur-lined. Two to three pinkish eggs, spotted and lined chestnut.

RANGE Eastern, south-eastern and southwestern Australia, with a break at Nullarbor. Locally nomadic.

STATUS Common. Endemic.

WHITE-THROATED HONEYEATER

Melithreptus albogularis   Meliphagidae
OTHER NAMES White-chinned Honeyeater, Grey Honeyeater

RECOGNITION Upperparts are olive-green; browner on wings and tail where feathers are edged yellow. Head black with white band round nape; this black extending down to just below the eye, leaving lower face, chin, throat and rest of underparts white. Crescent of bare skin over eye is

pale blue. Eye red-brown; bill black; legs fleshy-brown. Immatures brown on head: nape-band indistinct; back duller. Forages mainly in upper foliage. 13–14 cm.

VOICE While foraging, as a contact call, a repeated 't-tee, t-tee' or 'pii-pii-'; often a peevish 'tseep'. Song is a ringing 'chick-chick, chick-'.

HABITAT Eucalypt forests, woodlands, paperbark woodlands, tree-lined water-

508 **Noisy Friarbird** *Philemon corniculatus*
509 **Little Friarbird** *Philemon citreogularis*
511 **Blue-faced Honeyeater** *Entomyzon cyanotis*
513 **Noisy Miner** *Manorina melanocephala*
537 **Fuscous Honeyeater** *Lichenostomus fuscus*
542 **Brown-headed Honeyeater** *Melithreptus brevirostris*
553 **White-fronted Honeyeater** *Phylidonyris albifrons*
567 **Scarlet Honeyeater** *Myzomela sanguinolenta*
587 **Red-browed Firetail** *Emblema temporalis*
595 **Double-barred Finch** *Poephila bichenovii*
601 **Chestnut-breasted Mannikin** *Lonchura castaneothorax*

courses; uncommonly rainforests; occasionally mangroves.

BREEDING Recorded throughout year, but usually July–December. Nest is a small cup of bark strips, bound with webs, lined with finer fibres; slung from twigs usually in outer foliage. Two buff to pink eggs, speckled mauve and chestnut.

RANGE Northern and eastern Australia, Broome (WA) to north-east of New South Wales. Also in southern New Guinea. Locally nomadic.

STATUS Common.

544 WHITE-NAPED HONEYEATER

Melithreptus lunatus   Meliphagidae

OTHER NAMES Black-capped Honeyeater, Black-cap, Lunulated Honeyeater

RECOGNITION Upperparts rich olive-green, including secondaries, back, rump and tail. Head, nape, face down to bill, and shoulder crescent black, with a thin white nape-band, but not reaching round to the eye on each side; the crescent of bare skin over the eye is orange. Underparts white. Western Australian subspecies have whitish or pale greenish crescents over the eye. Eye brown; bill black; legs light brown. Immatures: upperparts greyer; eye skin dull white. 13–14 cm.

VOICE A scratchy or grating 'sherp-sherp', and frequent cheeping 'tsit, tsit'; also mellow 'tseeuw-tseeuw'. Alarm is rapid 'tew-tew-tew'.

HABITAT Eucalypt forests and woodlands, with a liking for smooth-barked eucalypts in south-east, jarrah forests in south-west. Takes insects from foliage, and nectar.

BREEDING July–March; usually August–December. The nest is a small, neat cup, suspended by the rim in a horizontal fork in outer foliage, 5–20 m high; built from bark, grass, bound with webs. Two to three pinkish-buff eggs, spotted grey and rufous.

RANGE Eastern and south-eastern Australia; mainly coastal; south-west of Western Australia. Migratory in parts of range.

STATUS Common. Endemic.

▶ See also pages
77 175

545 BLACK-HEADED HONEYEATER

Melithreptus affinis   Meliphagidae

OTHER NAMES Black-cap Honeyeater, King Island Honeyeater

RECOGNITION Back, wing-coverts and rump olive-brown; wings and tail grey-brown. Head black, this extending down to include the chin and throat. There is a thin line of black from the nape down each side of the neck to fade out on the sides of the breast. Does not have a white nape-band. The crescent of white skin over the eye is greenish-white. Remainder of underparts white. Eye dark brown; bill black; legs fawny. Immatures: head brown; throat yellowish. 13–14 cm.

VOICE A high-pitched whistle, which may be as a double note or as a rapid rising series of notes; other calls similar to those of White-naped Honeyeater.

HABITAT Usually in the drier eucalypt forests and woodlands, only rarely recorded from wet forests. Also coastal heaths, orchards and gardens.

BREEDING August–March; usually September–December. The deep cup-shaped nest is suspended among the outer leaves of tree or sapling, at 5–20 m height; built from bark fibres, wool, moss. Two to three pale pink eggs, spotted lilac-grey, red-brown.

RANGE Confined to Tasmania; rare wetter western parts. Sedentary to locally nomadic.

STATUS Common. Endemic.

▶ See also pages
142 *147* 148 150
152 153

546 GREEN-BACKED HONEYEATER

Glycichaera fallax   Meliphagidae

OTHER NAMES Buff-backed Honeyeater, White-eyed Honeyeater

RECOGNITION Upperparts dull olive-grey; slightly browner on the wings; and blackish-brown on the tail. Underparts light olive-buff to pale greenish-yellow; almost white on throat. Bill quite long, slender and slightly downcurved. The iris of the eye is grey-white, and the narrow eye-ring is of whitish feathers. Otherwise lacking obvious identifying markings, and nondescript; very restricted range, habitat. 11–12 cm.

VOICE Contact calls weak twitterings; also while feeding. Often an occasional single 'peep', insect-like; louder and harsher if scolding.

HABITAT Primarily an inhabitant of rainforests, where it appears to feed in upper canopy; also visits trees of adjoining eucalypt woodland.

BREEDING Probably about August–January. Nest not recorded.

RANGE Eastern tip of Cape York Peninsula; vicinity of Iron Range. Also in New

Guinea, Aru and other northern islands. Sedentary.

STATUS Fairly common.

▶ See also pages
106–7 *109* 111

547 BROWN HONEYEATER

Lichmera indistincta   Meliphagidae

OTHER NAMES Brown's Honeyeater, Least Honeyeater

RECOGNITION A slender, small, plain honeyeater. Upperparts grey-brown, with flight and tail feathers edged yellow. Bill long, slender, downcurved, black. There is a small yellow or silvery-white patch immediately to the rear of the eye. Gape yellowish, but becoming black in the breeding season. Underparts very light grey with a slight creamy or buffy wash. Eye and legs grey to grey-brown. Immatures lack eye-marking; yellower gape and plumage. 13–15 cm.

VOICE Powerful, varied and attractive song, similar to Clamorous Reed-warbler, 'swit-swit, quarty-quarty-quarty'; in pre-dawn chorus, a single-noted call.

HABITAT Extremely varied, including rain-forests and heavier wet eucalypt forests, dry forests, woodlands, mangroves, semi-arid inland scrubs, gardens.

BREEDING June–March; usually August–November; rainfall-dependent inland. The nest is a small, neat cup, suspended by the rim in the outer foliage of tree or shrub, at heights 0.5–7 m. Two to three white eggs, finely speckled reddish-brown.

RANGE Throughout Australia except south-east, Tasmania and most arid deserts. Also in New Guinea, Lesser Sunda and Aru islands. Partially nomadic.

STATUS Common.

▶ See also pages
107 175 211 *234*
385 387

548 WHITE-STREAKED HONEYEATER

Trichodere cockerelli   Meliphagidae

OTHER NAMES Brush-throated Honeyeater, Cockerell's Honeyeater

RECOGNITION Upperparts are grey-brown; darkest on the crown. Wing and tail feathers strongly edged yellow. Sides of face dark grey, with an indistinct yellow line on the side of the throat and a long yellow ear tuft. Underparts off-white, with dark grey streakings from the throat down onto the breast. Bill black, quite long, heavy and downcurved; eye red-brown; legs blue-grey. Female: eye brown. Immatures: eye brown; plumage duller. 14–16 cm.

VOICE Very vocal, with a frequent scolding 'churr'; also a pleasant sweet four-noted whistle similar to some calls of Brown Honeyeater.

HABITAT Heathlands, eucalypt woodlands with dense understorey; sometimes mangroves; rainforest scrubs along rivers.

BREEDING December–July; usually January–May. The nest is a deep, frail cup of fine rootlets, grasses, bound with webs; suspended in a fork of a shrub or small tree, and often in a paperbark over water.

RANGE North-eastern Queensland; eastern Cape York, usually only south to Archer River. Locally nomadic.

STATUS Common. Endemic.

▶ **See also pages**
107 *109*

549 PAINTED HONEYEATER

Grantiella picta   Meliphagidae
OTHER NAME Georgie

RECOGNITION A bold, showy plumage pattern; upperparts, including head, back, wings and tail, black except for conspicuous yellow panels in the wings and tail, where the feathers are yellow-margined; there is a small white ear patch. Underparts white; usually with small blackish spots along the sides of the neck, breast and flanks. Bill fleshy pink, tipped brown; legs dark grey. Female: brownish-grey upperparts; a few spots below. 15–16 cm.

VOICE Strong calls and song, especially when breeding, often a melodious 'georgie-ie, george-ie', double noted 'taw-tee, taw-tee', and 'pretty-pretty'.

HABITAT Open eucalypt forests, woodlands, watercourse timber, mallee; especially localities where mistletoe, upon which it feeds, is common.

BREEDING October–March. The frail cup-shaped nest of fine rootlets, plant fibres, bound with webs, is so flimsy that the eggs can be seen from below; it is placed in the outer foliage. Two to three salmon eggs, spotted red-brown and lilac.

RANGE Eastern Australia; Top End (NT) to Victoria, mainly inland. Migratory to nomadic.

STATUS Generally scarce; locally common. Endemic.

▶ **See also page**
133

551 NEW HOLLAND HONEYEATER *Phylidonyris novaehollandiae*

550 CRESCENT HONEYEATER

Phylidonyris pyrrhoptera   Meliphagidae
OTHER NAMES Horseshoe Honeyeater, Egypt, Chinawing, Tasmanian Honeyeater

RECOGNITION Plumage mostly very dark grey. Bright yellow wing and outer-tail panels. White throat and breast with black crescent across the upper breast, broken by white in centre; flanks grey. There is a white eyebrow line. Bill quite long and downcurved, black; eye red; legs dark grey. Female: plumage olive-brown; crescent less distinct; wing and tail panels dull olive-yellow. Immatures duller; crescent absent. 15–16 cm.

VOICE Loud high-pitched 'ee-gypt, ee-gypt' or 'eejik-eejik', usually confined to spring and summer, with a short sharp 'jik' in other months.

HABITAT Wet eucalypt forests, rainforests, coastal heaths, alpine woodlands; uncommonly mallee.

BREEDING July–April; usually August–January. The nest is a substantial deep cup of bark strips, bound with webs; lined with softer bark, fine grasses, plant-down, hair; placed in low shrub. Three pale pink eggs, spotted reds, browns.

RANGE South-eastern Australia, Tasmania; isolated population Mt Lofty Ranges. Migratory.

STATUS Common in Tasmania; locally common on mainland. Endemic.

▶ **See also pages**
123 124 142 *147*
151 153 155 164

551 NEW HOLLAND HONEYEATER

Phylidonyris novaehollandiae
                    Meliphagidae
OTHER NAMES Fuchsia-bird, White-bearded Honeyeater, White-eyed Honeyeater, Yellow-winged Honeyeater

RECOGNITION Plumage heavily streaked black and white; upperparts being black with white streaks, underparts white with black streaks. Head black with distinctive and prominent white streaks at eyebrows, sides of throat, and at ear tufts. There is a spiky-looking white-streaked beard area at the centre of the throat. Wings have a conspicuous yellow panel where the flight feathers are edged yellow; tail feathers edged yellow. Eye white. 17–18 cm.

VOICE Noisy, often with an aggressive-

552 WHITE-CHEEKED HONEYEATER *Phylidonyris nigra*

sounding rapid harsh chatter, and commonly a sharp short 'jik'. The alarm call is a high piping whistle.

HABITAT Heathlands, especially areas of banksia scrub, eucalypt forests and woodlands in dense undergrowth; extending in places to mallee country.

BREEDING March–November; usually May–October, often linked with local flowering. Nest is a solidly constructed, deep cup of bark strips, grass; well lined with soft plant-down; placed low in dense foliage. One to three pinkish-buff eggs, spotted chestnut.

RANGE Southern Australia and Tasmania, mainly coastal. Partially nomadic.

STATUS Common. Endemic.

▶ **See also pages**
122 124 155 164
245 *385*

552 WHITE-CHEEKED HONEYEATER

Phylidonyris nigra   Meliphagidae

OTHER NAME Moustached Honeyeater

RECOGNITION Very closely resembles the more common New Holland Honeyeater, but has a single, much larger, white cheek patch, and brown rather than white eye. The white eyebrow line extends farther forward towards the forehead, and the bill appears heavier. Plumage overall darker; blacker on upperparts; streaked on the body as the New Holland Honeyeater, and with conspicuous, deep golden yellow panels on wings and sides of tail. Bill and legs black. 17–18 cm.

VOICE Commonly a yapping sound, as

'chak-a-chak'; also a more squeaky 'chip-chew, chippy-chew'; and in song-flight, 'twee-ee-twee-ee-twee-'.

HABITAT Eucalypt woodland, creek-side undergrowth, coastal heaths, sedge swamps; wet heathlands and drier sandplain heaths in Western Australia; rainforest edges.

BREEDING March–October; usually April–May and August–September. The nest is a substantial cup of strips of bark, grass, rootlets; well lined with soft plant-down, and placed low in dense shrubbery. One to three pinkish-buff eggs, spotted light chestnut.

RANGE Eastern Australia, mainly coastal; south-western Australia. Locally nomadic or migratory.

STATUS Moderately common; locally scarce to common. Endemic.

▶ **See also pages**
97 122

553 WHITE-FRONTED HONEYEATER

Phylidonyris albifrons   Meliphagidae

RECOGNITION A honeyeater of unusual appearance, resulting from a broad white mask across the forehead and extending back to encircle each eye. There is a narrower white streak from the base of the bill downwards across the lower face, and a small red spot of bare skin just behind the eye. Remainder of head, throat and breast black; back dark brown; streaked whitish. Flight feathers edged pale yellow; underparts white. 17–18 cm.

VOICE Varied, metallic; some notes musical, others harsh, including phrases such as 'per-peetoo-weet', and 'quark-peter-peter-peter'.

HABITAT Mulga and other semi-arid scrublands, mallee, heathlands, drier eucalypt woodlands; mainly inland, but extending to drier parts of the coast.

BREEDING Usually August–February, but responding to rain to breed at other times. The nest is a cup of bark shreds and grass, bound with webs; placed in low vegetation. Two to three buffy-white to reddish-buff eggs, spotted grey and chestnut.

RANGE Most of Australian interior to coasts in south and west. Locally nomadic.

STATUS Common; locally abundant with flowering of vegetation. Endemic.

▶ **See also pages**
220 232 *383* 386

554 TAWNY-CROWNED HONEYEATER

Phylidonyris melanops   Meliphagidae

OTHER NAME Fulvous-fronted Honeyeater

RECOGNITION A small honeyeater with upperparts grey-brown, streaked darker brown. Crown of head creamy white to tawny, edged each side by a white eyebrow line. There is a blackish-brown line from the base of the bill back through the eye, then down each side of the white breast as a brown crescent. Underparts white, except underwing pale salmon. Eye brown; bill black; legs grey. Immatures: yellowish on throat; lacks tawny crown. Recent research suggests that the generic name of *Glyciphila* may be more appropriate for this species. 15–18 cm.

VOICE A pleasant flute-like call, with a sad wistful quality; often given by male in high song-flight, or from an exposed perch.

HABITAT Low vegetation of heathlands, sandplains, mallee country, banksia woodlands, eucalypt woodlands and forests in open areas, button-grass plains.

BREEDING July–March; usually September–November. The nest is a deep cup of bark strips and grass, lined with whitish plant-down, sometimes wool, and usually well hidden very close to the ground. One to three whitish eggs, blotched chestnut.

RANGE South-western and south-eastern Australia, mainly coastal, Tasmania. Nomadic or dispersive.

STATUS Uncommon; locally common. Endemic.

▶ **See also pages**
18 19 122 124 150
152 163 232 242
245

BROWN-BACKED HONEYEATER

555

Ramsayornis modestus   Meliphagidae
OTHER NAMES Unadorned Honeyeater,
Modest Honeyeater

RECOGNITION A plain honeyeater; upperparts dull brown; darker and greyer on
wings and tail. A small white streak immediately below the eye is underlined
black. Underparts creamy white with
indistinct grey-brown scalloping on the
breast and faint darker streakings on abdomen and flanks. Eye red-brown; bill
pinkish-brown, long and downcurved; legs
red-brown. Immatures: breast more
streaked; rufous tone to rump. 10–12 cm.

VOICE The usual song is a chattered and
lively 'shee-shee-shee-', and a sharp rapidly
repeated 'chit-chit-'; in flight, short 'nick-
nick-' calls.

HABITAT Mangroves, dense watercourse
vegetation, swampy paperbark woodlands; extending to open woodlands where
trees are flowering.

BREEDING August–March. The nest is a
domed structure, of vertically elongated
shape; suspended from the top; commonly
in outer foliage of a paperbark 1–3 m
above water. Two to three dull white eggs,
usually finely dotted purplish black.

RANGE North-eastern Queensland; Cape
York south to Townsville. Also in New
Guinea and adjacent islands. Migratory;
possibly to New Guinea.

STATUS Moderately common.

▶ **See also pages**
93 98 99

BAR-BREASTED HONEYEATER

556

Ramsayornis fasciatus   Meliphagidae
OTHER NAMES White-breasted Honeyeater,
Fasciated Honeyeater

RECOGNITION Distinctively patterned with
bold black bars across the breast, often in
scalloped pattern. Upperparts brown, with
fine black-and-white scalloping on the
crown. Face and ear-coverts dull white;
separated from the white throat by a fine
black line extending back and downwards
from the base of the bill. Belly dull white,
streaked blackish. Eye orange-brown; bill
brown; legs brown. Immatures: forehead
and breast streaked brown. 13–15 cm.

VOICE A pleasant rapid chattering piping
sound, likened to the call of the Pale-
headed Rosella; also a softer 'zzzt' or
'mew'.

HABITAT Vegetation along tropical watercourses, and adjacent woodland,
paperbark swamps, swamp-woodlands, especially among flowering trees.

BREEDING Probably most months. The nest
is a very elongated domed shape; large,
solidly constructed largely of paperbark,
and suspended from twigs; usually over-

hanging water. Two to three white eggs,
finely spotted red-brown.

RANGE Across tropical northern Australia;
western Kimberley to eastern Queensland.
Sedentary.

STATUS Common, especially in Kimberley
Region. Endemic.

▶ **See also pages**
174 197 206 *206*
208 211 324

RUFOUS-BANDED HONEYEATER

557

Conopophila albogularis   Meliphagidae
OTHER NAMES Rufous-breasted Honeyeater,
Red-breasted Honeyeater, White-throated
Honeyeater

RECOGNITION Upperparts dull red-brown
blending to grey on the head, and with
golden edging to outer webs of flight
feathers and tail. Underparts white, with a
broad rufous breastband. Eye grey-brown;
bill dark grey-brown; legs slate-grey. Immatures: rufous breastband incomplete,
absent, or appearing as a faint rufous wash
across the white undersurface. 11–13 cm.

VOICE Contact or alarm call is a quick
'zzit'; song, a thin high sequence of notes,
similar but more squeaky than that of the
Brown Honeyeater.

HABITAT Swampy woodlands, paperbark
swamps, creek and riverine vegetation,
monsoon forests; extending out to nearby
woodlands, open forests.

BREEDING September–April. The nest is a
deep, purse-shaped cup of fine strips of
paperbark, bound with webs, lined with
fine grass; suspended at the rim from the
outer foliage; often over water. Two to
three white eggs, spotted red-brown.

RANGE Top End (NT), and Cape York.
Also in New Guinea and Aru Islands.
Nomadic.

STATUS Moderately common, but fluctuating numbers.

▶ **See also pages**
189 195

RUFOUS-THROATED HONEYEATER

558

Conopophila rufogularis   Meliphagidae
OTHER NAME Red-throated Honeyeater

RECOGNITION Upperparts grey-brown, becoming darker and browner on back,
wings and tail, and with the outer edges of
the flight and tail feathers edged yellow.
The lower face, from the base of the bill
back onto the ear-coverts is pale grey.
Chin and centre of throat deep rufous or
rust-red, meeting the grey or grey-brown
of the breast, this then fading gradually to

dull white on the belly; flanks washed rufous. Immatures: throat white; crown
browner. 12–14 cm.

VOICE Has a chattering call, which may be
harsh, scratchy or peevish, or more sweet-
toned. The alarm call is a sharp 'zit-zit'.

HABITAT Eucalypt forests and woodlands,
especially along watercourses; also swamp-
woodlands, mangroves; foraging out to
drier woodlands, scrublands.

BREEDING September–April; usually October–March variable. The nest is a deep
cup, of delicate construction of fine strips
of paperbark and fine grass, bound with
webs; suspended in the outer foliage. Two
to three whitish eggs, spotted reddish.

RANGE Northern and north-eastern Australia; Broome (WA) to Noosa (Qld).
Usually nomadic.

STATUS Common in north; sparse on east
coast. Endemic.

▶ **See also pages**
175 206 208 *209*
211

GREY HONEYEATER

559

Conopophila whitei   Meliphagidae
OTHER NAMES Inconspicuous Honeyeater,
White's Honeyeater

RECOGNITION A very plain species; upperparts light grey, blending to darker grey-
brown on the wings and tail. There is a
slight tint of olive-yellow on the flight
feathers, and the tail is tipped white. The
face is a slightly darker grey, and there is
a very indistinct light grey eye-ring. Underparts dull white, with a pale grey wash to
the breast. Eye brown; bill stubby for a
honeyeater, dark grey. Immatures: yellowish wash on the cheeks, throat. 11–12 cm.

VOICE A rapid series of high-pitched, sibi-
lant notes, with some similarity to the call
of the Silvereye.

HABITAT Mulga and similar acacia
scrublands, including spinifex country with
scattered trees and shrubs; the presence of
mistletoe may be important.

BREEDING Few records, but probably
around August–November and influenced
by rainfall. The nest is a frail cup of fine
plant fibres bound with webs; suspended
quite low in the outer foliage. Two white
eggs spotted chestnut and grey.

RANGE The western interior; central Australia almost to mid-west coast Western
Australia.

STATUS Moderately common Hamersley
Range; elsewhere rare. Endemic.

▶ **See also pages**
184 229 *229* 231
232

560 EASTERN SPINEBILL

Acanthorhynchus tenuirostris
Meliphagidae

OTHER NAMES Hummingbird, Cobbler's Awl

RECOGNITION There are only two spinebills, both with extremely long fine, downcurved bills and with similar colours, though not patterns, of plumage. Wide separation in distribution. The Eastern Spinebill is grey-brown on back; grey-black on wings; black on head and tail. The black of the face continues as a crescent down each side of, and almost encircling, the white breast, which has brown throat-patch. Female and immatures: dull colours. 12–16 cm.

VOICE A clear shrill piping whistle, often prolonged; may be loud and brisk, or a softer 'chee-chee-'. In breeding, rapid four-noted call.

HABITAT Eucalypt forests, woodlands, rainforests, coastal heaths and scrubs, parks and gardens particularly with tubular-flowered plants.

BREEDING August–March, mainly October–January. The nest is a very small deep cup, of grasses, bark and mosses, bound with webs, well lined with feathers; attached by the rim, in foliage, 1–5 m. Two to three buff eggs, spotted chestnut, brown.

RANGE Eastern Australia, approximately Atherton to Adelaide; coast and ranges.

STATUS Common. Winter migrant to parts of north; nomadic to south. Endemic.

▶ See also pages
119 122 136 153 155

561 WESTERN SPINEBILL

Acanthorhynchus superciliosus
Meliphagidae

OTHER NAME Spinebill

RECOGNITION Male has upperparts grey; almost black on head and tail, with a bright light chestnut collar which completely encircles the neck and broadens in front to make the entire chin, throat and upper breast rich chestnut. There are conspicuous white streaks above and below the eye, and as a border below the chestnut breast, where a second breastband is black. Bill long, downcurved; white outer-tail. Female and immatures: dull, plain. Has erratic flight, with noisy clapping of wings. 15 cm.

VOICE A high, clear, ringing 'kachip, kloeep-kleep-kleep-', last notes descending. Softer sounds at nest, as when male arrives with insect.

HABITAT Forests and woodlands, where it favours more open parts with thickets of banksia and dryandra; also sandplain heaths, low coastal scrub.

BREEDING July–February; usually September–December. Nest a neat, small, deep cup of bark, and finer plant fibres, bound with webs, warmly lined with feathers; 1–4 m up, often in prickly dryandra shrub. One or two whitish eggs, spotted chestnut, brown.

RANGE South-western Australia.

STATUS Common. Endemic.

▶ See also pages
11 241 245

562 BANDED HONEYEATER

Certhionyx pectoralis
Meliphagidae

RECOGNITION A small black-and-white honeyeater. Upperparts black, including crown, wings and tail, except the nape freckled grey; the lower back grey; the rump and uppertail-coverts white. The black of the head extends down the sides of the face just far enough to include the eye. Underparts white except for a narrow black breastband. Immatures: much browner on upperparts; buff underparts, breastband brown; yellow on face, chin. 12–14 cm.

VOICE A clear ringing cheerful song, a sequence of descending notes; has been likened to call of Yellow-bellied Sunbird. Also has a finch-like 'tweet-' or 'week-'.

HABITAT Tropical eucalypt open woodlands with grassy understorey, swamp-woodlands, watercourse vegetation, flowering trees in drier woodlands.

BREEDING August–June; usually October–April. The nest is a very small, flimsy, open cup of fine bark strips, grass, bound with webs; suspended by the rim in a horizontal fork, at heights 1–6 m. Two creamy white eggs, speckled buff.

RANGE Northern Australia, western Kimberley to northern Queensland. Highly nomadic.

STATUS Common; abundant locally with flowering of trees. Endemic.

▶ See also pages
174 175 197 206 208 211

563 BLACK HONEYEATER

Certhionyx niger
Meliphagidae

RECOGNITION Not entirely black as the name would suggest, but black and white. Upperparts all black, including the entire head, wings and tail. Underparts white except for a black stripe extending from the black of the throat down the centre of the breast to the belly. Bill quite long, downcurved; eye dark brown. Female and immatures: upperparts grey-brown; darker on wings and tail; short pale eyebrow; underparts white; mottled brown on breast. 10–12 cm.

VOICE A thin clear high 'seeep' or 'see-seee', given from an exposed high perch, or at each downwards dip of the undulating song-flight.

HABITAT Mulga and similar arid acacia scrublands; spinifex country with scattered low trees or shrubs; open mallee and sparse semi-arid woodlands.

BREEDING Recorded breeding throughout the year; influenced by rainfall, but mostly October–December. The nest is a frail, shallow cup of grass, twigs and rootlets, bound with webs, usually low. Two to three buff eggs, spotted purplish-grey and olive.

RANGE Most of Australian interior, to coast in north-western Australia. Nomadic or migratory.

STATUS Uncommon; locally common. Endemic.

▶ See also pages
59 61 137 173 175 219 220 231

564 PIED HONEYEATER

Certhionyx variegatus
Meliphagidae

OTHER NAME Western Pied Honeyeater

RECOGNITION Upperparts black, including the head, back, wings and tail, except for a conspicuous white shoulder and wingbar; white rump and white panel on each side of the tail. The black of the head extends down to include the throat and upper breast; remainder of underparts white. There is a small spot of bare blue-grey skin beneath the eye. Female and immatures: upperparts grey-brown; wing feathers edged buff; breast grey-brown; belly off-white. 14–18 cm.

VOICE The song-flight of the male during the breeding season attracts attention with a drawn-out 'tee, tee, teee- teeee-'.

HABITAT Mulga and similar dry acacia scrublands, mallee, spinifex and semi-arid eucalypt woodlands.

BREEDING Influenced by rainfall, probably almost any month of the year, but usually August–February. The nest is a small cup of fine twigs, grasses; bound with webs; built in a dense low shrub. Two to four eggs, marked grey and brown.

RANGE Most of Australian interior, and to west coast. Nomadic.

STATUS Common; abundant locally in good seasons. Endemic.

▶ See also pages
177 184 220 231 342

565 DUSKY HONEYEATER

Myzomela obscura   Meliphagidae

RECOGNITION Upperparts are dominantly brown; dusky in the Northern Territory, but with a brighter coppery red tone in eastern Queensland, especially on forehead and throat. Wings and tail darker, blackish. Underparts paler grey-brown, with a dark patch at the throat. Eye dark brown; bill black; legs grey-brown. In pairs or parties, very aggressive, active, often inquisitive; usually in upper levels of flowering trees, seeking nectar and insects. 12–14 cm.

VOICE High squeakings, including excited rapid 'tsee-tsee-tsee', a soft pleasant trill, and a dawn song as 'tip, tip-eeee-chip'.

HABITAT Rainforests, dense vegetation along watercourses, mangroves, swamp-woodlands, and adjacent woodlands near the coast.

BREEDING July–February; usually September–January. The nest is a cup of fine rootlets, vine tendrils; bound with webs and slung by the rim in a slender horizontal fork of the outer foliage, often high. Two white eggs, speckled greys and reds.

RANGE Top End (NT); Cape York south to Noosa Heads. Also in New Guinea and adjacent islands. Nomadic.

STATUS Common in north; less common in south.

▶ See also pages
76–7 79 198 210

566 RED-HEADED HONEYEATER

Myzomela erythrocephala   Meliphagidae

OTHER NAMES Bloodbird, Mangrove Redhead, Myzomela

RECOGNITION A spectacular and distinctive honeyeater, with head, lower back and rump glossy scarlet. The remainder of the upperparts are blackish-brown, this extending to the breast; and there is a small blackish patch across the lores. Belly brownish-grey; underwing-coverts white. The bill is long, down-curved, black. Female and immatures: upperparts and breast grey-brown, with a touch of red to the forehead and throat; remainder of underparts off-white. 11–13 cm.

VOICE Male has a repetitive, tinkling metallic song, a high cheep or squeak, and a harsh whistle; the female a high squeak.

HABITAT Predominantly mangroves and adjoining tropical scrubs; often extending to swamp-woodlands and watercourse vegetation in search of flowers.

BREEDING Recorded most months; usually March–May and September–December. The small cup of bark fibres is bound with webs and attached by the rim among thin, leafy twigs of a mangrove over water. Two to three white eggs, spotted and blotched reddish.

RANGE Northern coastal Australia; western Kimberley to north-eastern Cape York. Also occurs Lesser Sunda islands to New Guinea. Nomadic, usually locally.

STATUS Common.

▶ See also pages
23 25 77 110 196 199 208

567 SCARLET HONEYEATER

Myzomela sanguinolenta   Meliphagidae

OTHER NAMES Sanguineous Honeyeater, Bloodbird, Hummingbird, Crimson Honeyeater

RECOGNITION Head, back, rump, throat and upper breast light glossy scarlet. Wings and tail black; lores and round eye black. On the lower breast the scarlet becomes mottled to blend with the light grey of the abdomen. Eye dark brown; bill quite long; downcurved, black. Female: upperparts brownish; throat and breast paler brown; remainder of underparts dull white. There is a slight reddish wash to the chin. Immatures: as for female; males increasing in red. 10–11 cm.

VOICE Male has a song of silvery tinkling notes, beginning very high, falling and fading away. Also short, clear tinkling notes; sharp squeaks.

HABITAT Eucalypt woodlands, forests, heaths, coastal scrubs, swamp-woodlands, rainforests; both on coastal lowlands and highlands.

BREEDING July–March; usually August–January. The small, frail cup of fine bark fibres and grass, is bound at the rim to a slender horizontal fork, in outer foliage at heights of 1–12 m. Two to three white eggs, marked in yellow-browns, greys.

RANGE Eastern Australia, coast and ranges; north-eastern Queensland to south-eastern Victoria. Also on some islands to north. Seasonally nomadic.

STATUS Moderately common; scarce south of Sydney.

▶ See also pages
77 80 122 *383*

CHATS

**Ephthianuridae Family of 5 species
5 in Australia, 5 breeding, endemic family
Sibley-Ahlquist: Family Meliphagidae**

Small, mainly ground-dwelling birds, with males brightly coloured or boldly patterned; females somewhat duller. They walk and run rather than hop, with an accompanying back and forth movement of head and neck. Chats are gregarious, often in family parties; highly nomadic, sometimes irrupting in great numbers in regions where not usually seen. Habitats vary; one species usually in marshy situations, some desert inhabitants, some in varied open situations.

568 CRIMSON CHAT

Ephthianura tricolor   Ephthianuridae

OTHER NAMES Tricoloured Chat, Saltbush Canary, Crimson-breasted Nun

RECOGNITION Spectacular scarlet, black and white plumage. Upperparts brownish-black, with crown and rump scarlet; wing feathers black, edged buffy-white. Throat white; rest of underparts scarlet. Bill moderately long, downcurved, black; eye bright light yellow; legs slate-grey. Female and immatures: upperparts brown, with the rump crimson, but of lighter hue than on the male. Underparts whitish; pale crimson on the breast. 10–12 cm.

VOICE The contact call, given frequently, is a high-pitched, even, drawn-out 'seeee-'; in flight, it draws attention with a brisk 'chek-chek'.

HABITAT Open plains, typically open mulga country with a sparse ground-cover of small plants; also saltbush, spinifex, open mallee, drier farmlands.

BREEDING Throughout the year; very responsive to rain. The nest is a small, deep cup usually well concealed close to the ground in a low shrub or tussock. Three to four white eggs, spotted reddish-purple and grey.

RANGE Throughout Australian interior, and to semi-arid parts of coast. Nomadic.

STATUS Common, but irruptive; varying scarce to abundant. Endemic.

▶ See also pages
136 137 171 173 175 177 180 183 *212 220 231*

569 ORANGE CHAT

Ephthianura aurifrons   Ephthianuridae

OTHER NAMES Saltbush Canary, Orange-fronted Chat, Orange-fronted Nun

RECOGNITION A spectacularly colourful species. Body deep golden yellow, with a more intense orange tone to the crown and breast. Face and throat black. Wings blackish, with feathers broadly edged pale yellow or buff; tail feathers blackish tipped white. Eye red-brown; bill and legs black. Female and immatures: upperparts grey-brown, with rump pale yellow; underparts pale yellow; no black on the face. Feeds on ground, often perches conspicuously on low shrubs. 10–12 cm.

VOICE In flight, a mellow 'chee-chee-chee'.

HABITAT Open plains of low sparse semi-arid vegetation, usually of saltbush, bluebush, the samphire margins of salt lakes and claypans.

BREEDING Very responsive to good rains at almost any time of the year, most commonly August–November. The solid, deep cup-shaped nest of fine twigs, grass, rootlets, is sited close to the ground. Three to four white eggs, spotted sepia and brown.

RANGE Throughout Australian interior, to coast in north-west. Highly nomadic.

STATUS Generally scarce; locally temporarily common. Endemic.

▶ See also pages
137 171 *171* 173
175 184 220 228
231

570 YELLOW CHAT

Ephthianura crocea   Ephthianuridae

OTHER NAMES Yellow-breasted Chat, Bush Chat, Yellow-breasted Nun

RECOGNITION Upperparts olive-yellow to olive-grey; wing and tail feathers black, edged pale greenish-yellow or buff; forehead, face and rump yellow. Underparts yellow except for a black breastband. Eye pale yellow or yellowish-grey; bill and legs dark grey. Female: without the black breastband; yellows paler; eye whitish. Immatures: grey-brown upperparts; white underparts with yellow wash to face, breast and rump. 11–12 cm.

VOICE Calls described include a short, attractive three-note call, and a metallic 'tang' like the call of the White-fronted Chat.

HABITAT Swampy flats and marshes near water, including bore drains; also on tidal samphire flats, grassy and reedy floodplains, dry lake-beds.

BREEDING Recorded most months; usually October–January. The nest is a small cup of dried, herbaceous plant stems, lined with fine grasses; built into a low bush or grass clump. Three white eggs, spotted and blotched olive and dark red-brown.

RANGE Northern and eastern-central Australia, in isolated populations. Nomadic.

STATUS Scarce; occasionally locally common. Endemic.

▶ See also pages
169 171–2 196
210 218

571 WHITE-FRONTED CHAT

Ephthianura albifrons   Ephthianuridae

OTHER NAMES Baldyhead, Banded Tintack, Nun, Tintack, Tang, White-faced Chat

RECOGNITION Bold black-and-white plumage pattern. Nape and back dark grey; wings, tail and crown black. Face and entire underparts white except for a conspicuous black breastband. The black of the crown encircles face as a clear-cut black border, and extends down each side of the neck, continuous with the breastband. Eye orange to white; bill and legs black. Female: lighter grey-brown upperparts; thinner breastband. Immatures: breastband faint. 12–14 cm.

VOICE A short metallic 'tang', usually as the contact call.

HABITAT Prefers damp heathy localities, including swamp margins, coastal banksia and tea-tree heath, but also dry heaths, samphire, saltbush plains.

BREEDING June–March; usually November–January. The nest is a small cup of thin stalks and twigs, lined with fine grass; placed in a low shrub or other low dense ground-cover. Two to four white eggs, spotted grey, reddish-brown and black.

RANGE Southern Australia; north to Shark Bay (WA), extreme south-eastern Queensland. Nomadic.

STATUS Common; locally variable scarce to abundant. Endemic.

▶ See also pages
19 *19*

572 GIBBERBIRD

Ashbyia lovensis   Ephthianuridae

OTHER NAMES Desert Chat, Gibber Chat

RECOGNITION Upperparts overall mottled light sandy grey-buff, blending softly to pale grey on the crown, and slightly darker grey-brown on the wings. Tail dark grey-brown, tipped white. Forehead, eyebrow, lores, face and entire underparts bright light yellow, slightly suffused with grey on the breast. Eye pale yellow or white; bill and legs dark grey. Female and immatures: duller. In flight, shows sandy yellow-edged rump; dark tail. 12–13 cm.

VOICE In song-flight, 'wheet-wheet-wheet'. Possibly as a contact call, a musical chatter. The alarm call is a series of piercing high notes.

HABITAT Gibberstone plains, where the ground is stony and very sparsely vegetated, sometimes found on flats between dunes, and bare saltbush flats.

BREEDING At any time after good rains; usually June–December. The nest, of fine twigs and grass, is built into a small depression scratched into the ground, often under shelter of bush or tussock. Two to four white eggs, spotted olive, brown.

RANGE Eastern interior; drainage basin of Lake Eyre and adjoining. Nomadic.

STATUS Uncommon; has possibly increased in abundance. Endemic.

▶ See also pages
169 172 173 175

SUNBIRDS

Nectariniidae Family of 118 species
1 in Australia, 1 breeding
Sibley-Ahlquist: Family Nectariniidae,
Subfamily Nectariniinae, Tribe
Nectariniini

Small, hummingbird-like nectar-eating birds of the tropics. They are considered to have affinities with the flowerpeckers. Bills are long, slender, downcurved; tongues tubular; insects are taken with the nectar. The flight is quick, and they often hover briefly when feeding at flowers. Both sexes may have colourful plumage, but the males the more colourful, often partly iridescent. Behaviour is very active, often aggressive; calls sharp.

573 YELLOW-BELLIED SUNBIRD

Nectarinia jugularis   Nectariniidae

OTHER NAMES Yellow-breasted Sunbird, Olive-backed Sunbird

RECOGNITION Upperparts are olive-green, blending to brown on the flight feathers, which are edged olive. Throat and upper breast deep iridescent metallic blue-black, remainder of underparts bright deep yellow. Bill long, slender, strongly downcurved; eye dark brown; bill, legs black. Female: lacks blue-black throat; entire underparts lemon yellow; and a yellow eyebrow line. Immatures: as female, duller; males with black line down throat. 10–12 cm.

VOICE High-pitched, excited 'tzit-tzit-tzit-', and occasionally a trill of descending notes.

HABITAT Rainforests, including its margins, regrowth, plantations, gardens and other clearings in rainforest; also mangroves, watercourse vegetation.

BREEDING All months; usually October–January. The nest is a very elongated domed structure with an extended tail, of plant fibres, leaves, webs, cocoons; suspended from twig or building. Two grey-green eggs, blotched brown.

RANGE Coastal north-eastern Queensland; from west coast of Cape York to Gladstone. Also in New Guinea and adjacent islands, South-East Asia, south-eastern China. Sedentary.

STATUS Common.

▶ See also pages
77 81 82 96 388

573 YELLOW-BELLIED SUNBIRD
Nectarinia jugularis

FLOWERPECKERS

Dicaeidae Family of 58 species
1 in Australia, 1 breeding
Sibley-Ahlquist: Family Nectariniidae,
Subfamily Nectariniinae,
Tribe Dicaeini

Small, brightly coloured birds with the majority of species in South-East Asia. Bills and tails are short. The sole Australian species belongs to a genus of about 36 species. Members of the genus are mainly berry feeders, with young usually at least partially fed on insects.

574   MISTLETOEBIRD

Dicaeum hirundinaceum   Dicaeidae
OTHER NAMES Australian Flowerpecker, Mistletoe Flowerpecker, Australian Flower-swallow

RECOGNITION Upperparts entirely black with an iridescent metallic blue sheen; throat, upper breast and undertail-coverts scarlet; lower breast and abdomen white with a conspicuous black streak down the centre. Eye brown; bill and legs black. Female: upperparts grey; darker on the wings and tail; underparts greyish-white, with a pink wash to the undertail-coverts. Immatures: similar to female, but with bill tinged pink. 10–11 cm.

VOICE Loud and spirited, often revealing the bird's presence. Song of male is a clear 'kinzey-kinzey-', and 'wita-perwita-perwita'; also some mimicry.

HABITAT All habitats where mistletoe occurs, dense wet forests of coastal ranges, mangroves, woodlands, mallee; and arid mulga and spinifex country.

BREEDING September–April; usually October–December. The nest is neat, pear-shaped; of soft, felted construction, mainly of plant-down matted with webs; and suspended from a slender twig of the outer foliage, at heights 1–15 m. Three to four white eggs.

RANGE Throughout mainland Australia, absent from Tasmania. Also in New Guinea, other islands. Locally nomadic.

STATUS Common wherever mistletoe is abundant.

▶ See also pages
98 182

PARDALOTES

Pardalotidae Family of 5 species
5 in Australia, 5 breeding, endemic family
Sibley-Ahlquist: Family Acanthizidae, Subfamily Pardalotinae

Tiny colourful birds, formerly placed in the flowerpecker family but, on more recent evidence, now a full family; their affinities appear closer to thornbills and honeyeaters. Appearance is quite distinctive, all extremely small, looking compact with very short bills and tails. Plumage is colourful, tends to be spotted or lined with white. Insects are taken from foliage and flowers. Nests are built in holes of trees or ground.

575   SPOTTED PARDALOTE

Pardalotus punctatus   Pardalotidae
OTHER NAMES Diamondbird, Bank-diamond, Headache-bird, Spotted Diamondbird

RECOGNITION Tiny, appearing diamond-studded, with white spots. Crown, forehead, wings and tail black, with many clearly defined white spots. Back and shoulders grey-brown, with less distinct buff spots; sides of face and neck grey, finely barred black; buff eyebrow line. Rump bright chestnut; throat and undertail-coverts rich yellow; remainder of underparts buff. Female: similar plumage pattern but less intense colours; throat creamy white. 8–9 cm.

VOICE A high-pitched, piping, slow, 'sleep-may-bee', almost incessant in breeding season; softer 'pee-too'. Subdued chatter defending nest territory.

HABITAT Eucalypt forests and woodlands; mainly wetter coastal areas, but extending inland along rivergums, and reaching fringes of mallee.

BREEDING August–March; usually September–December. The nest is dome-shaped; made of bark strips and grass; built as a lining to a chamber at the end of a tunnel, drilled 40–60 cm into the upper part of a loamy bank or similar site. Three to five white eggs.

RANGE South-western, eastern and south-eastern Australia, Tasmania. Seasonally dispersive or nomadic.

STATUS Common in south; scarce in north of range. Endemic.

▶ See also pages
2–3 61 67 67 136
148 153

576   YELLOW-RUMPED PARDALOTE

Pardalotus xanthopygus   Pardalotidae
OTHER NAMES Golden-rumped Pardalote, Fawn-eyed Diamondbird, Yellow-tailed Pardalote

RECOGNITION Similar to Spotted Pardalote, but with rump bright golden yellow rather than chestnut. Unless the rump can be sighted, or the different call heard, this species could easily be confused with the Spotted Pardalote. The two species are closely related and interbreed in areas of contact, but where distribution overlaps, the Spotted Pardalote tends to keep to forest or woodland, and the Yellow-rumped Pardalote to the mallee vegetation. 9–10 cm.

VOICE Heard close at hand, 'chnk, weee-weee', the first part softest, the second high-pitched, and the last falling slightly.

HABITAT Usually confined to mallee, but at times encountered in adjoining eucalypt woodland.

BREEDING July–February; usually September–January. The nest is a domed lining to the spherical chamber, excavated at the end of the nest tunnel, which is usually drilled into flat ground. Three to six white eggs.

RANGE South-east of Western Australia, south of South Australia, south-west of

New South Wales, north-west of Victoria. Locally nomadic.

STATUS Common in mallee. Endemic.

▶ **See also pages**
59 61 213 242

59 61 213 242

577 ## FORTY-SPOTTED PARDALOTE

Pardalotus quadragintus   Pardalotidae

OTHER NAMES Diamondbird, Tasmanian Diamondbird, Many-spotted Pardalote

RECOGNITION Overall a comparatively dull-plumaged pardalote. Upperparts olive-green; yellower about the face, blending gradually to light greyish underparts, and yellowish undertail-coverts. Wings black, each with about 20 clear white spots. Tail black with a white tip. Bill exceptionally short and stubby, black; eye dark brown; legs pinkish-brown. Immatures: yellow of face and undertail paler. Usually high in foliage of tall trees. 10 cm.

VOICE Usually a soft, nasal monotone 'whi-whi' or 'whi-ooo'. The male in the breeding season has a 'twint' territorial call.

HABITAT Forests and woodlands, with preference for those dominated by the manna-gum, and localities undisturbed by human activities.

BREEDING April–January; usually September–January. The nest site is a hollow of branch or treetrunk, to 20 m above ground; occasionally an earthen bank. The hollow is lined with bark fibres to form a domed or cup-shaped nest. Three to five white eggs.

RANGE Confined to south-eastern Tasmania. Local dispersion after breeding.

STATUS Rare; declining and in danger of extinction. Endemic.

▶ **See also pages**
142 147 148–9 150 152

142 147 148–9 150 152

578 ## RED-BROWED PARDALOTE

Pardalotus rubricatus   Pardalotidae

OTHER NAME Fawn-eyed Pardalote

RECOGNITION Upperparts light fawny-brown except crown of head black with white spots; wings dark brown with flight feathers edged golden; tail dark brown. The prominent, large eyebrow streak is golden-buff, with a deep orange to red spot towards the forehead. Underparts buffy-white with a patch of pale yellow at the centre of the breast. Eye pale yellow; bill dark above and pale below; legs grey.

Immatures duller; mottled on crown. 10–12 cm.

VOICE A series of five notes, like the call of the Crested Bellbird; usually two notes slow and rising, three higher and quicker.

HABITAT Woodlands of eucalypts and paperbarks; including watercourse gums in more arid areas.

BREEDING Recorded all months; usually July–January. The globular nest of strips of bark and grass is built as a lining to a chamber at the end of a tunnel drilled 50–70 cm into a bank. Two to three white eggs.

RANGE Arid and semi-arid Australia except southern interior. Sedentary.

STATUS Moderately common; scarce in east of range. Endemic.

▶ **See also pages**
174 230

174 230

579 ## STRIATED PARDALOTE

Pardalotus striatus   Pardalotidae

OTHER NAMES Eastern Striated Pardalote, Black-headed Pardalote, Yellow-tipped Pardalote, Red-tipped Pardalote, Stripe-crowned Pardalote

RECOGNITION Upperparts are olive-grey; crown black, streaked white except for subspecies Black-headed Pardalote which has plain black crown. Wings black with yellow spot near shoulder and narrow white wingstripe (nominate subspecies Yellow-tipped Pardalote), or reddish spot and narrow wingstripe (Eastern Striated Pardalote), or reddish spot and broad white wingstripe (Striated or Black-headed pardalotes). All with broad white eyebrow; yellow or orange at front. Underparts buff. 10–11 cm.

VOICE Repetitive sharp double 'pick-wick' or 'be-quick', and a triple 'pick-it-up'. Also has a long even trill, and a soft 'cheoo-oo'.

HABITAT Eucalypt forests, woodlands, mallee, watercourse gums; Striated and Black-headed pardalotes also in mulga; Black-headed also in rainforests, mangroves.

BREEDING Recorded June–March; usually August–January. The nest is cup- or dome-shaped; made of grass, bark, rootlets; built into a hollow of a tree, or a tunnel into an earthen bank. Three to five white eggs.

RANGE Subspecies of Striated Pardalote together cover Australia; nominate subspecies confined to Tasmania. Migratory movements in some regions.

STATUS Common. Endemic.

▶ **See also pages**
43 43 153

43 43 153

**Zosteropidae Family of 80 species
3 in Australia, 3 breeding, 1 endemic
Sibley-Ahlquist: Family Zosteropidae**

Small, dominantly light bright green to yellow-green, most with distinctive white eye-rings of fine silver-white feathers. Bills are small and fine; tongues are brush-tipped, as nectar forms part of the diet. Out of the breeding season white-eyes form wandering, often large, flocks. Voices are high-pitched, songs very high, almost scratchy, but musical. The family is widespread through southern Asia and Africa.

580 ## PALE WHITE-EYE

Zosterops citrinella   Zosteropidae

OTHER NAME Pale Silvereye

RECOGNITION Upperparts pale olive-green; yellower on head, rump. Forehead, throat and undertail-coverts bright light yellow; breast and belly off-white. White eye-ring; eye dark brown; bill black; longer and more robust than usual for Australian white-eyes. 12 cm.

VOICE Not recorded.

HABITAT Wooded and forested islands, where it inhabits shrubby thickets.

BREEDING Recorded June and December. The nest is cup-shaped; made of dry leaf-skeletons and grass, bound with webs; the exterior covered with thin pieces of paperbark; suspended within a slender fork in outer foliage. Two to four pale green eggs.

RANGE Islands off east coast, Cape York and Torres Strait. Also on Lesser Sunda islands. Probably locally nomadic.

STATUS Possibly quite common.

▶ **See also pages**
107 109 393

107 109 393

581 ## YELLOW WHITE-EYE

Zosterops lutea   Zosteropidae

OTHER NAMES Yellow Silvereye, Gulliver's White-eye

RECOGNITION Upperparts are uniformly yellowish-green or olive-yellow; forehead and underparts brighter yellow; white eye-ring. Eye brown; bill blue-grey; legs brownish-grey. Colours blend well with the yellowish-green of mangrove foliage. There are two subspecies: *lutea*, east of Wyndham (WA); and *balstoni* to the west; the latter has slightly duller colours, with upperparts greyer. 10–11 cm.

VOICE Call is typical of white-eye, but described as lower, more nasal and metallic than of Silvereye; song louder, pleasant, includes mimicry.

HABITAT Usually in mangroves, but not confined to this habitat, moving out to forage in adjoining monsoon scrub, river-edge vegetation, or coastal scrub.

BREEDING June–March; usually September–January. The nest is a small, neatly woven cup of soft grasses; bound with webs, and lined with finer grasses and rootlets. It is usually suspended in the outer foliage of a mangrove. Three to four pale blue eggs.

RANGE Coastal north-western and northern Australia; Shark Bay (WA) to western Cape York. Nomadic.

STATUS Common; numbers fluctuate in some localities. Endemic.

▶ **See also pages**
23 25 208 210 231

582 **SILVEREYE** *Zosterops lateralis*

582 SILVEREYE

Zosterops lateralis   Zosteropidae

OTHER NAMES Grey-breasted Silvereye or White-eye, Eastern Silvereye or White-eye, Western Silvereye or White-eye, Greenie

RECOGNITION A group or complex of subspecies formerly listed as distinct species. Although varying in colours of back (greyish or greenish); and underparts (uniformly olive, grey or yellow-throated, buff or chestnut-flanked); and other variations, the Silvereye is distinguished by a conspicuous white eye-ring. Only along north-western and northern coasts is there possible confusion with the Yellow White-eye, in or near mangroves; or the Pale White-eye on north-eastern islands. 10–12 cm.

VOICE Contact call, a drawn-out, high peevish note. Male has a very attractive warbling, territorial song; various other calls, sometimes mimics.

HABITAT Eucalypt forests, woodlands, heathlands, mallee, mangroves and most other vegetation types except semi-arid and desert.

BREEDING July–April; usually August–February; often several broods. The small cup-shaped nest of fine grass, rootlets, webs, is usually suspended from slender twigs in dense foliage of shrub or vine tangle. Two to four blue or blue-green eggs.

RANGE Eastern, southern and south-western Australia; Cape York to Pt Cloates

(WA). Also south-western Pacific islands, New Zealand. Partially migratory.

STATUS Common; often very abundant.

▶ **See also pages**
107 130 229 387

TRUE FINCHES

**Fringillidae Family of 440 species
2 in Australia, introduced
Sibley-Ahlquist: Family Fringillidae**

Family represented in Australia only by two introduced species, the European Goldfinch and the European Greenfinch.

583 EUROPEAN GOLDFINCH

Carduelis carduelis   Fringillidae

RECOGNITION Very colourful, with brown body. Face bright red, back to the eye; a white stripe extends just behind the eye to the throat; crown of head black, this extending down the side of the head behind the white. Female has less red on the face. *Introduced species.* 13 cm.

VOICE A mellow 'tu-leep' and sharper 'tsi-tsi-tsi'.

HABITAT Around towns and settlements; confined to areas where exotic plants have largely replaced native species.

BREEDING August–February. A neat cup of twigs, rootlets, grass; 1–10 m high in shrub or tree. Four to six pale blue eggs.

RANGE South-eastern Australia, including Tasmania. Widespread in Asia, Europe, Africa.

STATUS Common. Introduced species.

584 EUROPEAN GREENFINCH

Carduelis chloris   Fringillidae

RECOGNITION Olive-green upperparts; yellowish underparts. Wings dark grey with conspicuous yellow panel. Tail blackish, slightly forked and yellow on sides. Bill heavy, ivory coloured. Female duller. *Introduced species.* 15 cm.

VOICE A variety of canary-like trills and chirpings.

HABITAT Urban areas, parks, gardens,

roadsides, farmland verges and other disturbed land.

BREEDING September–February. The cup nest is built of twigs and lined with fine materials, and placed in dense foliage, usually an introduced species of shrub. Four to six pale green-blue eggs, spotted red-brown, violet.

RANGE South-eastern Australia, including Tasmania. Also in Europe, western Asia, northern Africa.

STATUS Common, but patchy. Introduced species.

OLD WORLD SPARROWS

**Passeridae Family of 37 species
2 in Australia, introduced
Sibley-Ahlquist: Family Ploceidae,
Subfamily Passerinae**

Family represented in Australia only by two introduced species, the House Sparrow and the Tree Sparrow.

585 HOUSE SPARROW

Passer domesticus   Passeridae

RECOGNITION Nape, ear-coverts, back and wings chestnut, with back and wings marked black and white. Crown grey; chin, throat and bib black; rest of underparts and cheeks white. *Introduced species.* 15 cm.

VOICE Harsh chatterings, and frequent 'cheerup'.

HABITAT Towns, farmlands; especially where dead trees provide nest hollows.

BREEDING July–April. A bulky, untidy domed nest of grass and lined with feathers; in a tree hollow, opening in a building, mud nest. Four to six dull white eggs, finely spotted brown and grey.

RANGE Throughout Australia except Western Australia. Widespread in Eurasia, Africa, India.

STATUS Abundant. Introduced species.

586 TREE SPARROW

Passer montanus   Passeridae

RECOGNITION Like the House Sparrow, but with a small spot of black in the middle of the large white cheek patch, and throat. *Introduced species.* 14 cm.

VOICE A soft 'tek, tek' in flight, or metallic 'chic'.

HABITAT Towns and outer suburban areas; not as far out into country areas as House Sparrow.

BREEDING Nest like that of House Sparrow, slightly smaller.

RANGE South-eastern mainland Australia. Native to Europe, Asia, South-East Asia.

STATUS Moderately common. Introduced species.

GRASSFINCHES, MANNIKINS AND ALLIES

**Ploceidae Family of 120 species
22 in Australia, 22 breeding, 14
endemic, 2 introduced
Sibley-Ahlquist: Family Ploceidae,
Subfamily Estrildinae**

Two Australian subfamilies. The Australian grassfinches are highly sociable, in large flocks especially after the breeding season. Males of some genera perform courtship displays with long pieces of grass gripped in the bill. Nests are large, domed, mostly of grass, sometimes with long entrance spouts. The second subfamily, true weaver-finches, is represented by two introduced species, probably aviary escapes.

587 RED-BROWED FIRETAIL

Emblema temporalis   Ploceidae

OTHER NAMES Sydney Waxbill, Redbill

RECOGNITION Upperparts soft olive-green; broad scarlet line through and above eye, from scarlet-sided bill; rump scarlet. Undersurfaces pale grey. Immatures duller greens; bill dark; no red eyebrow. Well adapted to urban environment, commonly seen in parks and gardens. 11–12 cm.

VOICE Very high-pitched, drawn-out 'seee'; song of variations of similar notes.

HABITAT Undergrowth of forests, woodlands, heaths and coastal scrubs, farmlands, parks and gardens.

BREEDING September–November in the south of range; January–April in north.

Nest large horizontal bottle-shaped, roughly constructed but well lined; sometimes with entrance spout; usually placed low in dense shrubbery. Four to six white eggs.

RANGE Eastern and south-eastern Australia, not interior; introduced near Perth. Locally nomadic after breeding.

STATUS Common. Endemic genus.

▶ **See also pages**
97 136 155 *383*

588 BEAUTIFUL FIRETAIL

Emblema bella   Ploceidae

OTHER NAME Firetail Finch

RECOGNITION Almost entirely dull olive-brown except undersurfaces, which are black finely crossbarred white. A black mask from base of bill to eye; bill and rump crimson; eye-ring light blue. Crimson rump conspicuous when birds are flushed in good light. Female has less black down centre of abdomen. Immatures have black bills; overall dull colours. Similar to Red-eared Firetail but widely separated range. Quiet, easily overlooked. 11–12 cm.

VOICE A mournful, single 'wee-ee'; also descending series of notes, and clear calls described as 'pee-oo, pee-oo'.

HABITAT Prefers damp situations and dense low vegetation. Coastal heaths, woodland undergrowth, tussock moors.

BREEDING September–January. Nest bulky, horizontal bottle-shape with long entrance spout. Constructed of long green grass stems, lined with finer grass, plant-down, feathers; built into dense foliage of shrub or tree. Five to eight white eggs.

RANGE South-eastern Australia, mainly coastal; and Tasmania. Sedentary.

STATUS Uncommon; locally common. Endemic.

▶ **See also pages**
122 126 *147* 152

589 RED-EARED FIRETAIL

Emblema oculata   Ploceidae

OTHER NAMES Red-eared Finch, Red-eared Firetail Finch

RECOGNITION Almost entirely dull olive-brown except undersurfaces which are black, finely barred and scalloped white. A black mask from base of bill to eye; bill crimson. Crimson ear-coverts; crimson rump and base of tail, conspicuous if bird flushed is in good light. White eye-ring.

Immatures: black bills; lack black mask, red ear-patch. Shy, inconspicuous; often noticed when flushed from ground. 11–12 cm.

VOICE Not loud, usually heard when bird is close. Call, a mournful, attenuated 'weeee', or 'wol-yee'; also very low, soft sounds near the nest.

HABITAT Mostly in jarrah forest, in dense undergrowth along creeks and rivers, especially paperbark swamps; on south coast, in scrubby heath.

BREEDING September–January; usually October–November. Very large, oval nest of long grasses, usually green; long entrance spout; often high, well hidden in foliage. Paperbark and banksia trees often used. Four to six white eggs.

RANGE South-western corner of Western Australia, high-rainfall forest belt and south-coast strip. Sedentary.

STATUS Uncommon, but probably secure. Endemic.

▶ See also pages
235 241 242

590 PAINTED FIRETAIL

Emblema picta   Ploceidae

OTHER NAMES Mountain Finch, Painted Finch, Emblema

RECOGNITION Brown upperparts. Chin crimson; otherwise entirely black underparts with distinctive scarlet streak or patch at centre of breast; and flanks boldly spotted white. Face and rump scarlet; black bill tipped crimson, very pointed for a finch. Range and habitat distinct from all other firetails. Female much less red on face, throat and breast. Immatures dull, very little red. Feeds on ground in spinifex; often in flocks, noisy. 11 cm.

VOICE Presence often announced by loud harsh 'chek-chek', before birds are sighted; similar call repeated rapidly if flushed.

HABITAT Usually inhabits rocky spinifex country, especially gorges where there are pools; sometimes sandplain spinifex.

BREEDING Breeds any time of year after good rain. Nest usually built into the top of a spinifex clump, where it is visible but inconspicuous. It is substantially constructed, and has an entrance platform. Three to five white eggs.

RANGE Central Australia; coastal only in arid north-west. Nomadic.

STATUS Common; present in numbers in good seasons. Endemic.

▶ See also pages
31 *31* 184 221 233

591 DIAMOND FIRETAIL

Emblema guttata   Ploceidae

OTHER NAMES Diamond Sparrow, Spotted-sided Finch

RECOGNITION A solid-looking finch; pale grey on head; brown on back and wings. Underparts white except for a wide black breastband; then black down the flanks, where boldly spotted white. Bill and rump crimson; lores black. Female has narrower breastband. Immatures browner; still with crimson rump, but with black bill, and only faint suggestion of breastband. Feeds on ground, and when flushed, flies up with crimson rump conspicuous. 11 cm.

VOICE Long drawn-out plaintive whistle, 'tooeee'.

HABITAT Open forests, woodlands, grasslands, open mallee, farmlands, parks and gardens.

BREEDING August–January; mainly October–December. Nest horizontally bottle-shaped; built of long-stemmed green grasses, well lined; placed in dense foliage of shrub or tree, usually 2–3 m but sometimes higher. Five to nine white eggs.

RANGE South-eastern Australia; approximately south-eastern Queensland to Eyre Peninsula, and inland. Sedentary.

STATUS Uncommon; patchy. Endemic.

▶ See also page
157

592 STAR FINCH

Neochmia ruficauda   Ploceidae

OTHER NAMES Red-faced Finch, Rufous-tailed Finch

RECOGNITION Upperparts are olive-green; green blending to yellow underparts; white undertail-coverts; conspicuous bright crimson face, forehead, chin and bill. Tail and uppertail-coverts dark red. White spots to face, breast, flanks and uppertail-coverts. Female has smaller area of red on face and is less bright overall. Immatures without red on head or bill; overall dull. Subspecies *clarescens* (north-western and northern Australia) has brighter, yellower breast. 10–12 cm.

VOICE High 'seet'; quicker, softer 'tsit'.

HABITAT Prefers lush green vegetation. Tall grass, along watercourses especially in drier inland areas. Rushy margins of swamps, moist green crops.

BREEDING December–May in the north, or after rain in semi-arid regions. Nest resembles the upright domed wren-nest shape; built of green and dry grasses, softly lined with feathers; placed in low dense vegetation. Three to seven eggs.

RANGE North-western and northern Australia (subspecies *clarescens*); mid-east coast (nominate subspecies).

STATUS Uncommon; abundant in parts of north-west. Endemic.

▶ See also pages
221 223 *228* 229 230

593 CRIMSON FINCH

Neochmia phaeton   Ploceidae

OTHER NAMES Blood Finch, White-bellied Crimson Finch

RECOGNITION Male almost entirely deep crimson becoming brownish or olive toned on back, wings and tail. Black undertail-coverts and abdomen centre. Tail very long and pointed. A few white spots along the flanks. Female: breast greyish olive or fawn; back browner. Immatures: brown with touch of crimson to wings, rump and tail. White-bellied Crimson Finch (subspecies *evangelinae*) has white centre strip from lower breast to undertail-coverts. 12–14 cm.

VOICE A high, piercing 'chee-chee-chee'; sharp, short 'chit' alarm call. Tinkling, flock contact calls when flushed.

HABITAT Usually waterside vegetation of pandanus and cane-grass. Tall, lush rank grass of damp roadsides, clearings, crops.

BREEDING September–May; variable according to rainfall. Nest bulky, rough flat oval, without entrance spout but usually with landing platform. Built mainly of coarse grass; varied sites, often a pandanus. Five to eight white eggs.

RANGE Kimberley to north-western Queensland; White-bellied Crimson Finch, Cape York to Queensland east coast. Also in New Guinea. Usually sedentary.

STATUS Common.

▶ See also pages
174 197 *207* 211

594 ZEBRA FINCH

Poephila guttata   Ploceidae

OTHER NAME Chestnut-eared Finch

RECOGNITION Grey head with bright orange ear-patch; bold black-and-white lines vertically down from eye; orange-red bill; orange flanks white-spotted. The white rump and white-barred black tail are very conspicuous in flight. Female is without orange plumage; retains bill colour and eye stripe. Immatures like female but with black bills. Seen in pairs, to huge flocks especially when coming to water. Noisy; undulating flight; feeds on ground. 9–10 cm.

VOICE Loud nasal twang, 'tiaar'; abrupt 'tet-tet', especially from flocks in flight. Softer and musical trills.

HABITAT A bird of drier inland regions, but never very far from water. Spinifex, mulga, grassland, open grassy woodland, saltbush, saltmarsh, farms.

BREEDING Any time and throughout the year; dependent upon rain, especially in arid regions. Rough, domed nest of grass and small twigs with soft lining; in bush, tree, hollow, or under larger nest. Three to seven white eggs.

RANGE Almost throughout Australia except heavier rainfall forested areas and Tasmania. Nomadic in arid regions.

STATUS Common to abundant. Endemic subspecies.

▶ **See also pages**
136 177 *179* 221
230 233

595 DOUBLE-BARRED FINCH

Poephila bichenovii   Ploceidae
OTHER NAMES Banded Finch, Black-ringed Finch, Owl-faced Finch

RECOGNITION Face and undersurfaces from chin to lower abdomen white, with two conspicuous narrow black bands across. A black edging from forehead round the face (and continuing to form the neck-band) gives an appearance reminiscent of the Barn Owl's facial disc. Upperparts dark grey-brown; black on wings and tail. Wings white-spotted; rump white (black on subspecies *annulosa*). Immatures duller; bars indistinct. Feeds mainly on the ground. 10–11 cm.

VOICE Drawn-out 'teeaat-teeaat'; lower, quicker 'tat-tat', similar in quality to Zebra Finch but stronger.

HABITAT Varied; dry grassy woodlands, open forests, grassy dry scrublands and farmlands, gardens.

BREEDING In north, December–March; inland variable, after rain. Nest smallish, rough, horizontal bottle-shaped. Site varied; shrub, tree, hollow, into structure of a larger nest, or recess of a building. Four to eight white eggs.

RANGE Northern and eastern Australia; subspecies *annulosa*, west of Gulf of Carpentaria. Sedentary.

STATUS Common. Endemic.

▶ **See also pages**
211 *383*

596 MASKED FINCH

Poephila personata   Ploceidae
OTHER NAME White-eared Finch

RECOGNITION Face and chin black, so that the bright yellow bill is encircled by a black mask. The black tail is pointed and quite long. Between the pale buffy-cinnamon of the abdomen and the white of the tail-coverts, the rear flanks are black. The subspecies *leucotis* (from Cape York Peninsula) has white from ear-coverts blending into upper breast. Immatures: bill black; no mask; duller colour. Often in large flocks, especially at water. Feeds on ground. When perched has noticeable tail-flick habit. 13–14 cm.

VOICE Loud 'tiat', like Zebra Finch call; softer 'twat-twat', and chatterings in flocks.

HABITAT Grasslands and open grassy woodlands, never far from water.

BREEDING September–July; mainly March–May after wet. Bulky, elongated-domed nest; usually low, often on ground; may have an entrance platform with pieces of charcoal on it or in the nest. Four to six white eggs.

RANGE Two populations: Kimberley-north-eastern Queensland and on Cape York Peninsula. Sedentary.

STATUS Moderately common. Endemic.

▶ **See also pages**
174 *194* 197 211

597 LONG-TAILED FINCH

Poephila acuticauda   Ploceidae
OTHER NAMES Black-heart Finch, Heck's Finch

RECOGNITION Head pale blue-grey; body and wings soft-toned pale cinnamon. Large black patch on throat and upper breast; black tail tapers to a very long fine point. Bill yellow in Kimberley, grading to orange in north-western Queensland. Black-throated Finch is a similar species but has a different range and shorter tail. Immatures: shorter tail; dark bill. Bobs head after landing. In pairs or flocks. Feeds in grass, will sometimes take flying insects. 15–17 cm.

VOICE Drawn-out clear whistle, probably higher-pitched than that of the Black-throated Finch; a rapid 'chek-chek' or 'chee-chee'.

HABITAT Tropical open grasslands with scattered eucalypts or pandanus; usually not far from permanent water.

BREEDING December–March; wet season. Large domed, horizontal-oval nest with an entrance spout; built of coarse grasses, softly lined and often containing pieces of charcoal; may be quite high. Usually five to eight white eggs.

RANGE Kimberley to Top End (NT) to

north-eastern Queensland. Sedentary.
STATUS Common. Endemic.

▶ **See also pages**
207 211

598 BLACK-THROATED FINCH

Poephila cincta   Ploceidae
OTHER NAMES Black-tailed Finch, Parson Finch

RECOGNITION Black throat-patch and bill; short black tail; black band across lower abdomen. Very similar to the Long-tailed Finch but different range; also great difference in tail length and bill colour. Rump may be black on Cape York (subspecies *atropygialis*) or white for more southerly birds (subspecies *cincta*). Typically bobs head up and down after landing and, with grass stem in bill, during courtship display. 10 cm.

VOICE Mournful, drawn-out whistle; short calls variously described as 'weet-weet', 'beck-beck', or 'tet-tet'; also a quiet musical song.

HABITAT Open grassy woodlands and grassy plains, usually not far from watercourses.

BREEDING January–May (wet) in north; September–January in south. Domed, long, oval-shaped nest with entrance spout; built of dry grass and creeper stems, lined with finer grass, feathers and plant-down. Five to nine white eggs.

RANGE North-eastern Australia; from Cape York to north-eastern New South Wales. Sedentary.

STATUS Common, but of patchy occurrence. Endemic.

▶ **See also pages**
77 79 175

599 PLUM-HEADED FINCH

Aidemosyne modesta   Ploceidae
OTHER NAMES Diadem Finch, Plum-capped Finch, Diadem

RECOGNITION Without bright colours, but with quite distinctive brown-and-white barring of almost the entire underparts. Small but unusual plum-coloured (deep reddish-purple) patches on forehead and under chin. Upperparts brown; white-spotted on wings; white-barred in rump; tail black; white-tipped on outer feathers. Female has smaller plum patch; fine white line over eye. Immatures little or no plum head patch. 10–11 cm.

VOICE High-pitched, drawn-out 'ting' or

'teep'; also song or trill extremely high-pitched.

HABITAT Grasslands, favouring tall grass; also riverside and swamp-edge reeds, shrubs, cumbungi.

BREEDING August–May; varies but mainly September–January. Domed nest without entrance tunnel; built mostly of green grass, sometimes lined with feathers; placed low. Four to seven white eggs.

RANGE Eastern Australia, mainly inland; approximately Atherton south to Canberra. Probably nomadic.

STATUS Uncommon; abundant locally. Endemic genus.

▶ **See also pages** 77 79

600 PICTORELLA MANNIKIN

Lonchura pectoralis   Ploceidae

OTHER NAME White-breasted Finch

RECOGNITION Black face and throat; white and some black scallop markings on breast. Rest of underparts plain and an unusual pinkish-fawn tone; upperparts grey. Female dull brownish-black on face; more black in breast scalloping. Immatures: grey-brown; dark bills. In flocks in non-breeding season, sometimes with Yellow-rumped and Chestnut-breasted mannikins. Feeds both on tall grass and on the ground, and takes flying insects. 11 cm.

VOICE A single, quite loud 'tleep', especially from flocks in flight.

HABITAT Open grassy woodlands, sometimes spinifex, especially tall grass near watercourses.

BREEDING November–May; usually January–April. Bulky, rough, domed nest without entrance spout; constructed of grass, some small twigs, lined; usually placed low, sometimes in grass or spinifex clump.

RANGE Northern Australia, Kimberley, Top End (NT), north-western Queensland. Nomadic.

STATUS Uncommon; common in some localities. Endemic.

▶ **See also pages** 175 208 211

601 CHESTNUT-BREASTED MANNIKIN

Lonchura castaneothorax   Ploceidae

OTHER NAMES Chestnut Finch, Barleybird, Bullfinch

RECOGNITION Black face and chin; light chestnut breast, separated from white

abdomen by a black band; undertail-coverts black. Crown grey-brown; back and wings cinnamon-brown; rump and tail pale bright cinnamon; bill blue-grey. Female paler. Immatures: light olive-brown upperparts; buffy underparts; darker bill. Gathers into large flocks out of breeding season, including many immature birds. Feeds on grass and on ground, takes flying insects. 10 cm.

VOICE Clear 'teet'; when a flock takes off sounds like tinkling bell. Also from the male, a faint, high-pitched wheezing song.

HABITAT Usually near water or damp places; grasslands, swamp edges, damp heaths, mangroves, cane-fields and other moist grassy crops.

BREEDING In the wet season in the coastal north, or at any time of the year after good rains. Nest spherical, with hooded, side entrance; built in long grass, reeds, low shrub. Five to six, sometimes eight, white eggs.

RANGE Northern and eastern Australia, but not far into interior. Also in New Guinea. Nomadic.

STATUS Common, especially in east.

▶ **See also pages** 98 193 195 210 383

602 YELLOW-RUMPED MANNIKIN

Lonchura flaviprymna   Ploceidae

OTHER NAME White-headed Finch

RECOGNITION A pale finch, whitish-buff on the head blending to creamy-buff and fawny-pale yellow on breast and abdomen. Wings contrasting brown; undertail-coverts black. Reported to interbreed with the Chestnut-breasted Mannikin to produce intermediate forms. Immatures: very like those of the Chestnut-breasted species. 10 cm.

VOICE Clear 'teet', like Chestnut-breasted Mannikin.

HABITAT Usually near water or damp places; grasslands, swamp edges; generally sharing same habitat as Chestnut-breasted Mannikin.

BREEDING Recorded December–April. Nest and eggs similar to those of the Chestnut-breasted Mannikin.

RANGE North-eastern Kimberley, Top End (NT). Nomadic.

STATUS Uncommon except some irrigated areas. Endemic.

▶ **See also pages** 193 195 210

603 NUTMEG MANNIKIN

Lonchura punctulata   Ploceidae

OTHER NAMES Space Finch, Ricebird

RECOGNITION Brown upperparts; brown throat; the rest of the underparts from breast to tail white, scalloped brown; bill blue-grey. Immatures: paler brown upperparts; unmarked pale brownish-yellow underparts. Associates and hybridizes with the Chestnut-breasted Mannikin. *Introduced species.* 11–12 cm.

VOICE Contact call, a high 'keee'; also sharp, quick 'treet-treet'.

HABITAT Grasslands, preferring wetter areas, usually disturbed land; tall grass of roadsides, green crops of moist farmlands, urban areas.

BREEDING September–February; variable, some nesting most months. Nest built largely of green grasses, making a bulky, bottle-shape. Placed in tree or shrub, from almost ground level to 10 m; often in colony. Five to seven white eggs.

RANGE Eastern coastal Australia. Native of India to Philippines. Introduced species, probably displacing native finches.

STATUS Now locally common.

604 BLUE-FACED FINCH

Erythrura trichroa   Ploceidae

OTHER NAMES Tricoloured Parrot-finch, Green-backed Finch

RECOGNITION Very distinctive colour, totally unlike any other Australian finch: almost entirely bright leaf-green except for blue face and forehead; black or brown tail edged scarlet; bill black; legs buff. Recorded only from ranges of north-eastern Queensland. Female: less blue, duller. Immatures are dull green, without blue face. In New Guinea, occurs in flocks. 11–12 cm.

VOICE Call described as high-pitched 'tseet-tseet'.

HABITAT Edges and clearings of rainforests of ranges, mangrove swamps.

BREEDING Wet season. Few records for Australia. Nest an inverted pear-shape, with a side entrance. Materials unusual for a finch: rainforest mosses, lawyer-vine strands. White eggs; uncertain number.

RANGE Mossman to Innisfail, Atherton Tableland, possibly Cape York, Lloyd and Double islands. Also in New Guinea and other islands to the north. Sedentary or migratory.

STATUS Rare; few records.

▶ See also pages
93–4 97 99

605 GOULDIAN FINCH

Erythrura gouldiae   Ploceidae

OTHER NAMES Rainbow Finch, Painted Finch, Purple-breasted Finch

RECOGNITION Very brightly coloured combination of green, purple, yellow, blue, white, black, sometimes red. Three colour phases, with the black-headed form outnumbering the red-headed by three-to-one, and the golden-headed very rare. Female duller. Immatures grey and olive tones. The three forms occur intermixed throughout the range. Generally feeds in shrubs, grass, rarely on ground; takes flying insects in wet season. Active in hottest hours. 14 cm.

VOICE Sharp 'seit-seit' alarm call; softer 'ssit' contact call.

HABITAT Grassy woodlands, not far from water; watercourse vegetation. In the wet season, extends to wider range of habitats, including spinifex.

BREEDING November–April; mainly December–March. Nest rough, globular, often quite high. If in a tree hollow or termite mound there may be very little if any structure; the eggs being laid on debris floor of the hollow. Four to eight white eggs.

RANGE Kimberley, Top End (NT), north-western Queensland, west side of Cape York Peninsula.

STATUS Rare; common few localities; once common. Endemic genus.

▶ See also pages
190 198 207 208
209 211

STARLINGS, MYNAHS

Sturnidae Family of 110 species
3 in Australia, 3 breeding, 2 introduced
Sibley-Ahlquist: Family Sturnidae,
Subfamily Sturninae, Tribe Sturnini

Medium-sized; dark, often iridescent black, with brightly coloured eyes; sharply pointed straight bills; large and sturdy legs and feet. They tend to be very local and aggressive; nomadic or migratory; and very adaptable, readily colonizing naturally or by introduction. They are also highly greg-

arious, often nesting in large colonies, which is the case with the single species native to Australia, the Metallic Starling.

606 METALLIC STARLING

Aplonis metallica   Sturnidae

OTHER NAMES Shining Starling, Glossy Starling, Whirlwind-bird

RECOGNITION Plumage entirely glossy black with iridescent purplish and greenish-bronze sheen; eye bright red; tail long and pointed. The feathers round the neck are longer, pointed, forming shaggy hackles. Bill and legs blackish. Immatures: duller brownish, with underparts whitish streaked and mottled darker. Highly sociable, in large noisy flocks. Feeds on fruits of rainforest trees, insects, and nectar. 22–24 cm.

VOICE Nasal and wheezing chatterings; also a canary-like song.

HABITAT Tropical rainforests, nearby coastal woodlands and scrubs, parks and gardens.

BREEDING In large colonies, with a great number of nests clustered in the crown of a large tree. Individual nests are bulky, oval-shaped, suspended, sometimes several joined. Two to four bluish-white eggs, speckled brown and grey.

RANGE North-eastern Queensland; Cape York south to Townsville. Also in New Guinea and adjacent islands. Migratory.

STATUS Common.

▶ See also pages
85 94 94

607 COMMON STARLING

Sturnus vulgaris   Sturnidae

RECOGNITION Glossy black plumage, with a pale yellow bill. After breeding, moults to plumage that is flecked white beneath, and the bill becomes black. *Introduced species*. 21 cm.

VOICE Chatterings and twitterings, with some mimicry.

HABITAT Urban and country areas including cleared land, mallee, coastal, alpine, parks and gardens.

BREEDING Nest is a rough and untidy cup, in a tree hollow, stump, post hollow, hole in cliff, building. Four to five plain bluish-white eggs.

RANGE South-eastern Australia, Nullarbor to mid-eastern coast Queensland. Also in Europe, Africa, Asia. Nomadic or migratory.

STATUS Common. Introduced species.

608 COMMON MYNAH

Acridotheres tristis   Sturnidae

RECOGNITION Body almost entirely rich brown, shading to black on the head, and with white undertail-coverts. Large white wing patches are conspicuous in flight; show as small white patches on folded wing. Tail blackish with white tip. There is a bright patch of deep yellow skin behind the eye; bill and legs bright deep yellow. *Introduced species*. 23–25 cm.

VOICE Varied raucous and squeaky noises.

HABITAT Urban areas, and around towns and farm buildings of agricultural and pastoral areas; cane-fields.

BREEDING Nest is in a cavity or recess of a building, hollow of a tree; these lined with grass; sometimes as a cup nest in dense foliage. Four to five glossy, pale blue eggs.

RANGE Coastal eastern mainland Australia near State capitals, northern Queensland. Widespread in Asia, Africa.

STATUS Abundant. Introduced species.

ORIOLES, FIGBIRDS

Oriolidae Family of 27–34 species
3 in Australia, 3 breeding
Sibley-Ahlquist: Family Corvidae,
Subfamily Corvinae, Tribe Oriolini

A tropical family of medium-sized arboreal birds, plumaged in bright colours including bright yellow and black. The Australian species are comparatively softly coloured in yellow-greens and olive-greens. The Figbird has brightly coloured bare skin round the eye. In Australia, the members of this family are migratory or nomadic, moving in search of seasonal fruits.

609 YELLOW ORIOLE

Oriolus flavocinctus   Oriolidae

OTHER NAMES Yellow-bellied Oriole, Green Oriole, Green Mulberry

RECOGNITION Overall colour bright yellow-green (moss green or mustard yellow-green) both on upperparts and underparts, with head and breast finely streaked black. Primaries, secondaries and upperwing-coverts black, edged pale yellow to buffy-white. Tail feathers black, edged olive, tipped pale yellow to white. Eye bright red; bill moderately long and light brownish-pink; legs dark grey. Female: yellower; more streaked. Immatures: heavier dark streaks. 25–30 cm.

VOICE Loud, rich and fluid, with a bubbling quality, often repeated, of three to four uniform notes, as 'yok-yok-yoddle'; also a clear 'bee-queek'.

HABITAT Principally lowland rainforests and adjoining mangroves, lush watercourse vegetation, swamp-woodlands, and nearby plantations, gardens.

BREEDING July–March; usually September–January. The nest is a deep cup-shaped basket of interwoven bark strips, vine tendrils, with finer lining; usually slung in a slender horizontal fork at 2–15 m. Two creamy eggs, marked grey and brown.

RANGE Northern Australia; north-eastern Queensland to western Kimberley. Also in New Guinea and Aru Islands. Possibly locally nomadic.

STATUS Moderately common.

▶ See also pages
110 199 209 210
403

610 OLIVE-BACKED ORIOLE

Oriolus sagittatus   Oriolidae
OTHER NAMES Cedarbird, Cedar Pigeon, Greenback, Green Thrush, Oriole

RECOGNITION Upperparts olive-green, including face, and finely streaked black. Wings black, with feathers edged grey; tail dark grey, tipped white. Underparts white with conspicuous dark streaks, and washed olive-green on the throat and breast. Eye bright red; bill large, deep salmon pink; legs grey. Female: upperparts greyer; lacks olive wash to breast; tail tipped buff rather than white; wing feathers edged cinnamon. Immatures duller; bill darker. 25–28 cm.

VOICE A low-pitched, mellow rolling 'orry, orry-ole' or 'orry-orry-oo', frequently repeated. Also some scratchy warblings, mimicry, harsh scoldings.

HABITAT Eucalypt forests and woodlands, rainforest margins, swamp-woodlands, watercourse thickets, mallee, parks, gardens.

BREEDING Most months; most often recorded September–January. The nest is a deep, large, untidy looking cup of bark strips, leaves, grass, often wool; suspended by the rim in outer foliage. Two to four cream eggs, marked greys, browns.

RANGE Northern, eastern and south-eastern Australia; western Kimberley to south-eastern South Australia. Also in New Guinea and adjacent islands. Partially migratory.

STATUS Moderately common.

▶ See also pages
122 123 *126* 209

611 FIGBIRD

Sphecotheres viridis   Oriolidae
OTHER NAMES Southern Figbird, Green Figbird, Yellow Figbird, Banana-bird, Mulberry-bird

RECOGNITION Upperparts olive-green; head black; bare skin about eye red in breeding season otherwise yellow. Wings black edged grey; tail black tipped white. The northern subspecies (Yellow Figbird) has yellowish underparts; the southern subspecies (Green Figbird) has throat and breast grey, belly yellow-green fading to white under tail. Eye red-brown; bill black; legs buff. Female (both subspecies): grey round eye; back olive-brown; underparts whitish streaked brown. 28–30 cm.

VOICE Call is a squeaky yelp with downward inflection, 'jokyer', and clear 'see-kew, see-kew'; song is strong, mellow, 'tu-tu-heer, tu-heer-'.

HABITAT Rainforest, and its margins and clearings; also in eucalypt forests, swamp-woodlands, mangroves, denser vegetation of farms, gardens.

BREEDING August–April; usually October–January. The shallow cup-shaped nest of vine tendrils, fine twigs and rootlets is loosely woven; placed in a horizontal fork among foliage, usually quite high. Two to three dull olive eggs, spotted brown.

RANGE Northern and eastern Australia; western Kimberley to south-eastern New South Wales. Also in New Guinea, Timor and other islands to the north. Locally nomadic.

STATUS Moderately common.

▶ See also pages
77 79 175 209

**Dicruridae Family of 20 species
1 in Australia, 1 breeding
Sibley-Ahlquist: Family Corvidae,
Subfamily Monarchinae, Tribe
Dicrurini**

Medium-sized, black with iridescent gloss. Tails are typically flared out towards the forked tip, in fishtail shape, and usually quite long. They are restlessly active, with swooping, twisting flight in pursuit of flying insects. The stout, arched bill has numerous bristles about the base. Voices are usually harsh and metallic. Recent studies of DNA suggest the drongos to be part of the Corvidae, a large family of Australian origin.

612 SPANGLED DRONGO

Dicrurus hottentottus   Dicruridae
OTHER NAMES Hair-crested Drongo, King Crow, Drongo, Drongo-shrike, Fishtail

RECOGNITION Plumage overall black with greenish sheen to the wings and tail; and indistinct greenish spangles or streaks over the head, neck and breast; sometimes white spots on shoulders. Tail long, widening towards the tip in a fishtail shape. Eye bright red; bill and legs black. Immatures: head and nape duller, smoky black; eye brown; scattered white patches and spots on central abdomen, undertail, underwing. Active, noisy, pugnacious. 30–32 cm.

VOICE Harsh, tearing, cackling and metallic sounds, 'twanging' noises, both perched and while in flight; song a creaking whistle.

HABITAT Rainforests, eucalypt forests and woodlands, mangroves; favouring situations where there are high lookout perches from which to pursue insects.

BREEDING August–May; usually September–March. Nest is a shallow cup of vine tendrils and other plant fibres; built into a horizontal fork; usually well concealed in foliage at 10–20 m. Three to five pinkish-grey eggs, marked red and purple.

RANGE Northern and eastern Australia, mainly coastal. Also in New Guinea, Indonesia and southern Asia. Partially migratory.

STATUS Common in north; uncommon south of Sydney.

▶ See also pages
80 122 *403*

BOWERBIRDS

Ptilonorhynchidae Family of 17 species 9 in Australia, 9 breeding, 7 endemic Sibley-Ahlquist: Family Ptilonorhynchidae

A fascinating family confined to New Guinea and Australia. They are distinguished by the bowers which most species construct for displays and mating; forming the central focus of each male's territory. The building and elaborate decoration of such complex structures, with the displays, may establish the family as among the most advanced. Recent DNA studies indicate bowerbirds to be more closely related to scrub-birds, lyrebirds and treecreepers than, as previously thought, to the birds of paradise.

613 GOLDEN BOWERBIRD

Prionodura newtoniana Ptilonorhynchidae

OTHER NAMES Golden Gardener, Queensland Gardener, Newton's Bowerbird

RECOGNITION Upperparts golden-olive, including face and wings; with a short crest of golden yellow at rear of crown, and a larger patch at nape. Entire underparts bright yellow. Plumage has a remarkable glossy opalescent sheen, giving brilliant highlights where touched by sunlight. Central tail feathers are brownish; outer feathers entirely yellow. Eye pale yellow; bill olive-brown; legs black. Female: dull olive-brown upperparts; ash grey underparts. 23–25 cm.

VOICE Calls at or near bower: wheezing and frog-like croaks, strange mechanical ratchet-like rattlings, churrings, and occasional mimicry.

HABITAT Tropical rainforests, at altitudes 900–1500 m.

BREEDING September–March; usually October–January. The nest is a rough, solid cup of bark strips, leaves, twigs, rootlets, and vine tendrils. The site may be in a hole or large fork of a tree well away from bower, at 1–3 m. One to two creamy white eggs.

RANGE North-eastern Queensland, coastal ranges; approximately Cooktown to Townsville. Sedentary.

STATUS Moderately common within restricted range. Endemic.

▶ See also pages
85 94 95 97

614 SATIN BOWERBIRD

Ptilonorhynchus violaceus Ptilonorhynchidae

OTHER NAME Satinbird

RECOGNITION Entirely glossy blue-black, the blue as a surface sheen; eye lilac; bill deep, bluish-white blending to pale yellowish towards the tip. Legs and feet pale greenish-yellow. Female: lighter blue-grey to olive-grey upperparts; blending to tawny-brown on wings. Underparts creamy or fawny-white with dark grey crescent markings, giving scaly appearance. Immatures: as female to fourth year, when males begin to show greens and blues, full colour by seventh year. 28–33 cm.

VOICE Noisy in breeding season, territorial and alarm call a loud harsh wheezing. At bower, a great variety of buzzings, churrings, also mimicry.

HABITAT Rainforests, wet eucalypt forests; extending in autumn and winter to more open woodlands, parks and gardens.

BREEDING September–March; usually October–February. Nest is a shallow bowl of sticks, lined with leaves; built into a fork towards the crown of a forest tree or mistletoe clump; some distance from bower of male. One to three buff eggs, marked grey, brown.

RANGE Two subspecies: north-eastern Queensland, and south-eastern Queensland to Otway Range (Vic). Locally nomadic.

STATUS Common. Endemic.

▶ See also pages
115 122 127

615 REGENT BOWERBIRD

Sericulus chrysocephalus Ptilonorhynchidae

OTHER NAMES Australian Regent Bird, Regentbird

RECOGNITION Boldly plumaged black and deep yellow. Forehead to mantle rich yellow becoming orange on the forehead; wings with broad band of bright golden yellow. Rest of plumage entirely black, including face, with the bright yellow eye conspicuous. Female and immatures: upperparts olive-brown; mottled fawn on the upper back. Crown, nape and mantle blackish. Underparts fawny, heavily scalloped brown; throat blackish; eye dull yellow. Male plumage acquired after two years. 24–28 cm.

VOICE A harsh, scolding 'te-aarr', and scratchy or wheezy sounds, often with ventriloquial effects, soft whisper-songs, chatterings, hisses.

HABITAT Rainforests, and dense adjacent vegetation; coastal scrubs and thickets. Out of breeding season ventures into eucalypt forests, gardens.

BREEDING September–February; usually October–January. Nest attended by female only; built on a vine tangle at 3–15 m; usually well away from male's bower; a loose, frail saucer of twigs. Two pale grey eggs, with lines of umber and black.

RANGE South-eastern Queensland to central eastern New South Wales, coast and Great Dividing Range. Locally nomadic.

STATUS Moderately common. Endemic.

▶ See also pages
52 80 119–20 *120* 121 122 127

616 SPOTTED BOWERBIRD

Chlamydera maculata Ptilonorhynchidae

OTHER NAMES Western Spotted Bowerbird, Western Bowerbird, Mimicbird

RECOGNITION Upperparts dark brown to blackish-brown, heavily spotted cinnamon. Head almost entirely cinnamon, but on western subspecies *guttata*, blackish with finer cinnamon spots. On nape, a small fan-like pink crest, visible mainly in display. Underparts grey-buff or ochrebuff, lightly barred darker on the flanks; on throat darker cinnamon mottled darker brown, or on western subspecies black with cinnamon spots. Immatures paler. 25–31 cm.

VOICE Varied, with churring and grinding sounds, noisy near bower. Accomplished mimic, imitates other birds, feral cats, and other noises.

HABITAT Dense thickets in woodlands, along watercourses and in gorges of drier parts of its range; usually where there is water and native figs.

BREEDING August–January; usually October–December. The female builds a shallow saucer of twigs set on horizontal branches of tree or shrub, 2–15 m high; usually not very far from bower. Two light grey to grey-green eggs, with fine dark brown lines.

RANGE Eastern Australian interior; western subspecies from centre to north-west coast. Partially nomadic.

STATUS Moderately common. Endemic.

▶ See also pages
137 175 *176* 182 183 184 197 221 230 232 233

617 GREAT BOWERBIRD

Chlamydera nuchalis Ptilonorhynchidae

OTHER NAMES Great Grey Bowerbird, Queensland Bowerbird

RECOGNITION The largest bowerbird. Dominantly fawny-grey, mottled grey-brown on the back and crown. There is a lilac crest at the back of the nape, most noticeable during display, often lacking on females and immatures. Bill deep, strongly arched on the upper profile; eye brown; legs grey. Female: slightly smaller, often paler and faintly barred on belly. Immatures: lack lilac crest; mottled and barred underparts. 34–37 cm.

VOICE A mixture of contrasting sounds, including rasping, wheezing, crackling and churring noises, often loud, as well as extensive mimicry.

HABITAT Eucalypt woodlands and forests, favouring vicinity of thickets, often along watercourses, margins of rainforests, mangroves, tropical gardens.

BREEDING August–February; usually October–January. The female usually builds well away from the male's bower; the nest in a shrub or tree is a shallow bowl of sticks. One to two grey-green eggs, with lines of brown and purplish-grey.

RANGE Northern Australia; from western Kimberley to north-eastern Queensland. Sedentary.

STATUS Common. Endemic.

▶ See also pages
107 197 204 211

618 FAWN-BREASTED BOWERBIRD

Chlamydera cerviniventris
Ptilonorhynchidae

RECOGNITION Upperparts pale grey-brown, finely streaked off-white on forehead, face and throat, and with feathers of mantle and wings finely margined and tipped buffy-white. Breast fawn or pale fawn-ochre; remainder of underparts pale buff; often faintly barred on the flanks and scalloped on the breast in a slightly richer tone. Eye dark brown; bill black; legs grey-brown. Immatures: barrings and scallopings on plumage more obvious. 25–30 cm.

VOICE Alarm and contact calls harsh, rasping; song weak but penetrating. Male in display has metallic churrings, hisses; mimics other birds.

HABITAT Eucalypt and paperbark woodlands, vine scrubs, watercourse thickets, mangrove edges.

BREEDING Recorded all months; usually September–December. The nest is a shallow and flimsy bowl of twigs, vine tendrils, rootlets; placed in dense foliage of tree or pandanus. One to two pale olive to cream eggs, scribbled with umber, grey.

RANGE North-eastern Cape York. Also in New Guinea. Sedentary.

STATUS Locally moderately common.

▶ See also pages
106 107–8 110

619 TOOTH-BILLED CATBIRD

Ailuroedus dentirostris Ptilonorhynchidae
OTHER NAMES Stagemaker, Tooth-billed Bowerbird, Queensland Gardener

RECOGNITION Upperparts are dark olive-brown; underparts fawny, heavily streaked brown. Bill heavy, dark brown, deep and serrated near tips of both mandibles. Eye dark brown; legs grey-brown. Immatures: throat and breast paler, mottled. Usually solitary, but gathering in small parties in the non-breeding season; when quiet and unobtrusive in dense forests. 26–27 cm.

VOICE Noisy in breeding season, with song that is a strange mixture of low chucklings, attractive whistling notes, harsh tearing sounds, mimicry.

HABITAT Tropical rainforests and vine scrubs; extending to adjacent thickets, plantations, gardens.

BREEDING September–March; usually October–January. The nest, built by the female, is frail saucer of sticks; placed in a vine tangle or rainforest canopy at heights 3–25 m. Two plain eggs, creamy white to buff.

RANGE North-eastern Queensland, coast and ranges; from Cooktown south to Townsville. Sedentary.

STATUS Moderately common; locally common. Endemic species and genus.

▶ See also pages
85 94 95 97

620 SPOTTED CATBIRD

Ailuroedus melanotis Ptilonorhynchidae
OTHER NAME Black-eared Catbird

RECOGNITION Dominantly bright green, with brownish-black head. The dark head is lightened by buff spottings, and the face is buffy-white, particularly on the eyebrow and cheek; there is a prominent large black ear-patch. Nape and back dusky green; remainder of upperparts emerald green, with white on some shoulder and inner flight feathers. Chin black; upperparts light olive-green, streaked creamy white. Eye red; bill cream. Immatures duller. 26–29 cm.

VOICE A drawn-out, nasal cat-like meow, by both sexes. During the breeding season, also has a series of clicking sounds.

HABITAT Rainforests, most often observed

at rainforest edges, clearings, regrowth, where canopy is lower.

BREEDING August–April; usually September–January. The nest is a bulky cup of twigs and vine tendrils, with many leaves interwoven; usually sited in a vertical fork, or a tangle in dense vegetation, 2–20 m. Two to four creamy or buffy-white eggs.

RANGE Two subspecies: north-eastern Cape York and Atherton Region. Also occurs in New Guinea. Sedentary.

STATUS Moderately common.

▶ See also pages
95 95 97 111

621 GREEN CATBIRD

Ailuroedus crassirostris Ptilonorhynchidae
OTHER NAME Catbird

RECOGNITION Upperparts emerald green, blending to duller, olive-green on the head; prominent white tips to secondaries and tail-tips. Head lightly flecked buff and dark brown. Chin and throat dark olive, finely mottled black and streaked white; remainder of underparts light olive-green to yellow-green with extensive buffy-white streaks. Eye red; bill deep, creamy or fawny-white; legs grey. Immatures duller; less streaked; eye brown. 29–32 cm.

VOICE Loud, far-carrying and weird cat-like wailings, nasal, as in drawled-out 'here-I-are'. Also sharp clicking and low guttural sounds.

HABITAT Rainforests, occasionally densely foliaged adjoining eucalypt forest, dense watercourse vegetation.

BREEDING September–March; usually October–January. The nest is large, bulky, deeply cup-shaped; built of twigs, leaves, vine tendrils; placed in an upright fork, vine tangle, or crown of a tree-fern. Two to four plain creamy white to creamy-buff eggs.

RANGE South-eastern Queensland to south-eastern New South Wales, coast and Great Dividing Range. Mainly sedentary.

STATUS Common; becoming uncommon to the south-east of range. Endemic.

▶ See also pages
125 127

**Paradisaeidae Family of 43 species
4 in Australia, 4 breeding, 2 endemic
Sibley-Ahlquist: Family Corvidae,
Subfamily Corvinae, Tribe
Paradisaeini**

The birds of paradise reach their ulti-mate spectacular peak in New Guinea; just four species reach the rainforests of eastern Australia. The family dis-plays an extravaganza of lavish plumes and iridescent colours, used in elaborate courtship displays. The males of the Australian riflebirds are typical of, but far from the peak of, spectacular plumages evolved in New Guinea, while the Trumpet Manucode has less impressive plumage. DNA studies show these birds to be closely related to crows, magpies and orioles, and to be part of the old endemic parvorder Corvi, which originated within Australia.

622 ## PARADISE RIFLEBIRD

Ptiloris paradiseus   Paradisaeidae
OTHER NAME Riflebird

RECOGNITION Plumage velvety black with an iridescent metallic green sheen to crown, nape and central tail feathers. The centre of throat and upper breast has a triangular gorget of iridescent purplish-green. Remainder of underparts velvety black, with feathers tipped iridescent dark green. Bill long, strongly downcurved; tail very short. Female: grey-brown upper-parts, rufous on the wings; whitish eye-brow, throat. Underparts buff with black chevrons. 25–29 cm.

VOICE A loud rasping 'yaaa-a-a-ss', poss-ibly by both sexes, but given at much more frequent intervals by the male through the breeding season.

HABITAT Rainforests, including *Nothofagus* and also adjoining eucalypt forest; form-erly lowland forests, now largely restricted to highlands.

BREEDING September–February; usually October–January. The nest, attended by female alone, is a bulky, rough bowl of twigs, leaves, decorated with moss, or-chids, sometimes snakeskins; placed high in dense foliage. Two pinkish eggs, marked chestnut and grey.

RANGE South-eastern Queensland, north-eastern New South Wales, coast and coastal highlands. Sedentary.

STATUS Moderately common in north of range; uncommon in south. Endemic.

▶ **See also pages**
52 *119* 120 121 127

623 ## VICTORIA'S RIFLEBIRD

Ptiloris victoriae   Paradisaeidae
OTHER NAMES Lesser Riflebird, Queen Victoria Riflebird

RECOGNITION Plumage black, with iri-descent purplish-green on the crown, and triangular green throat-patch that is smaller than that of the Paradise Riflebird. There is a larger area of velvety black be-tween this throat-patch and the greenish-black of the lower breast, belly and flanks. Bill long, but shorter than other riflebirds. Female: dark olive-brown upperparts; buffy-white eyebrow line; underparts rich rufous-buff, with sparse brown markings. 23–25 cm.

VOICE A loud rasping 'ya-a-ar' or 'ya-a-as', especially by males.

HABITAT Rainforests and rainforest mar-gins; also similar vegetation of some offshore islands within its range.

BREEDING September–February; usually October–January. The nest is a large, rough, bulky bowl of sticks, leaves, some-times with a sloughed snakeskin round the rim; built in dense foliage, at 2–15 m. Two reddish-buff eggs, marked red, umber, grey.

RANGE North-eastern Queensland, in Atherton Region. Sedentary or partially locally nomadic.

STATUS Moderately common. Endemic.

▶ **See also pages**
85 95 97 *99*

624 ## MAGNIFICENT RIFLEBIRD

Ptiloris magnificus   Paradisaeidae
OTHER NAMES Albert Lyrebird, Prince Albert Lyrebird

RECOGNITION Dominantly velvety black, with iridescent blue-green crown, nape and central tail feathers. Centre of throat has iridescent green, scale-like feathers forming a wide triangular fan, which is separated from the black of the remainder of the underparts by narrow bands of black and green. There are long, black filamentous plumes on the flanks. Bill long, down-curved. Female: upperparts cinnamon brown; underparts whitish, finely barred brown. 26–33 cm.

VOICE Usually two powerful whistles, ex-tended in breeding season to four with the last more abrupt, deeper. Also rasping sounds.

HABITAT Tropical rainforests, monsoon forests, watercourse scrubs.

BREEDING September–March; usually Oct-ober–January. The nest is a deep, loosely constructed cup of twigs, vines, leaves; built into a tree fork, among leaves of a pandanus, at heights of 1–10 m. Two creamy eggs, streaked brown, grey.

RANGE Northern Cape York, south to Princess Charlotte Bay on east coast. Also in New Guinea. Sedentary.

STATUS Moderately common.

▶ **See also pages**
101 106 108–9 *108 109* 111

625 ## TRUMPET MANUCODE

Manucodia keraudrenii   Paradisaeidae
OTHER NAMES Trumpetbird, Manucode

RECOGNITION Glossy black with a sheen of iridescent green and purplish tones. Feathers of nape, neck and throat narrow, elongated and pointed; some of those of the nape forming quite long plumes. Tail moderately long. Eye bright vermilion; bill heavy and relatively short. Female: plu-mage slightly less highly glossed; nape plumes shorter. Immatures: plumage with less gloss; head plumes short. Species usually keeps to the upper canopy of veg-etation. 27–32 cm.

VOICE Male gives a drawn-out trumpet-call, likened to the squeaking of the hinges of a heavy door. Contact call a short met-allic 'gwaark'.

HABITAT Tropical lowland rainforests and monsoon forests; especially the rainforest edges and clearings.

BREEDING September–February; usually October–January. Nest a shallow, flimsy cup of twigs and vine tendrils, placed high in rainforest canopy. One to two dull pink to lilac-pink eggs, spotted and blotched red-brown, umber and grey-violet.

RANGE Cape York south to McIlwraith Range. Also in New Guinea and adjacent islands. Probably sedentary.

STATUS Moderately common.

▶ **See also pages**
109 *109* 111

**Corcoracidae Family of 2 species
2 in Australia, 2 breeding, endemic
family
Sibley-Ahlquist: Family Corvidae,
Subfamily Corcoracinae**

Highly gregarious birds; quite large to rather small; black or greyish; which build comparatively large bowl-shaped nests mainly of mud. The basis of the group is a dominant male, and several mature females whose nest construction and attendance is assisted by immature birds, the progeny of previous seasons. Much time is spent foraging on the ground, and the group wanders over a somewhat greater territory after the completion of nesting.

WHITE-WINGED CHOUGH

Corcorax melanorhamphos Corcoracidae

OTHER NAMES Apostlebird, Black Magpie, Black Jay

RECOGNITION Plumage entirely sooty grey-black except for a large white patch on each wing, conspicuous in flight, and sometimes just visible on the folded wing as a thin white streak. Tail long, without any white tips. Eye reddish; bill moderately long, strongly downcurved; legs black. Immatures: eye browner; tail shorter. The species is often seen in parties, usually five to 10 birds, and often feeding on the ground. 42–47 cm.

VOICE A double piping whistle, mellow, descending; also various grating and soft clicking sounds.

HABITAT Drier forest and woodland, mallee and mulga scrublands, watercourse and farmland timber.

BREEDING July–February; usually August–December. The nest is a large bowl of mud, reinforced by grass and other fibres, lined with grass, shredded bark, fur; placed on a horizontal limb, usually quite high. Three to five creamy white eggs, splotched brown.

RANGE Eastern and south-eastern Australia; Burdekin River, south-west to Eyre Peninsula. Sedentary or nomadic.

STATUS Common, but patchy. Endemic.

▶ **See also page** 136

APOSTLEBIRD

Struthidea cinerea Corcoracidae

OTHER NAMES CWA-bird, Grey Jumper, Happy Family, Lousy Jack, Twelve Apostles

RECOGNITION A dumpy bird of predominantly grey plumage and with short robust bill. Flight feathers grey-brown; tail long, black. The plumage of crown, back and breast is mottled with light grey. Bill and legs black. Immatures: smaller, tail slightly shorter. Apostlebirds are very sociable, usually in groups of about eight to 20 birds. Their restless aggressive behaviour and garrulous chatterings have earned them a number of descriptive names. 28–33 cm.

VOICE A variety of harsh, scratchy chatterings, likened to tearing sandpaper, as 'ch-

kew-ch-kew, creee-chew, creee-chew, cher-eer, cher-eer'.

HABITAT Eucalypt and native-pine woodlands, mallee country, watercourse timber such as red-gum and black-box; never far from water.

BREEDING August–February; usually September–January. The nest is a large bowl of grass, heavily plastered with mud; built on a horizontal branch at 3–20 m. Mem-

609 **Yellow Oriole** *Oriolus flavocinctus*
612 **Spangled Drongo** *Dicrurus hottentottus*
626 **White-winged Chough** *Corcorax melanorhamphos*
628 **Australian Magpie-lark** *Grallina cyanoleuca*
629 **White-breasted Woodswallow** *Artamus leucorhynchus*
639 **Australian Magpie** *Gymnorhina tibicen*
642 **Grey Currawong** *Strepera versicolor*
643 **Australian Raven** *Corvus coronoides*

bers of the group assist at nest. Two to five white eggs, streaked and blotched brown, grey.

RANGE Northern and eastern Australia, sub-interior, Northern Territory to Victoria, South Australia. Mainly sedentary.

STATUS Moderately common; localized and patchy. Endemic.

▶ See also pages
41 43 136

MAGPIE-LARKS

Grallinidae Family of 2 species
1 in Australia, 1 breeding
Sibley-Ahlquist: Family Corvidae,
Subfamily Monarchinae, Tribe
Monarchini

Black and white, long-legged, plover-like, mud-nest builders. They are neither magpies nor larks, taking their name from the plumage colour and pattern, and their loud musical calls. Often associated with other black-and-white birds, feeding on the ground, and walking with back-and-forward head movements. In flight, have long wingbeats, relatively slow yet acrobatic in the air. Usually the Australian Magpie-lark is placed with the Torrent Lark of New Guinea in the family Grallinidae. Recent DNA studies indicate the magpie-lark to be closely related to the monarch flycatchers, in the tribe Monarchini, and part of a proposed large family Corvidae.

628 AUSTRALIAN MAGPIE-LARK

Grallina cyanoleuca Grallinidae

OTHER NAMES Mudlark, Peewee, Peewit, Little Magpie, Murray Magpie

RECOGNITION Black-and-white plumage in bold clear-cut pattern. Upperparts black, with a broad white patch in the wing; rump, tip and base of tail white. Large white eyebrow line; black neck and breast separated from black of upperparts by a wide white panel down each side of the neck. Remainder of underparts white. Eye pale yellow; bill whitish. Female: forehead, face and front of neck white, black line vertically through eye. 26–30 cm.

VOICE Clear ringing calls, often as a duet between a pair, one beginning 'pee-wee' followed without break by the other with 'pee-o-wit, pee-o-wee'.

HABITAT Open country generally, from coastal to semi-desert; usually not far from

628 AUSTRALIAN MAGPIE-LARK
Grallina cyanoleuca

water, preferring vicinity of rivers, swamps and watercourses.

BREEDING Throughout year; mainly August–December. The nest is a deep bowl of mud, reinforced with grass, well lined with grass, fur, feathers; placed on a horizontal limb, often over water, 5–15 m. Three to five whitish eggs, marked brown, grey-violet.

RANGE Almost throughout Australia; absent from Tasmania and parts of most arid western deserts. Also in southern New Guinea, Timor. Sedentary.

STATUS Common.

▶ See also pages
325 403

WOODSWALLOWS

Artamidae Family of 10 species
6 in Australia, 6 breeding, 4 endemic
Sibley-Ahlquist: Family Corvidae,
Subfamily Corvinae, Tribe Cracticini

Small, superficially swallow-like songbirds which hawk gracefully for insects on pointed, backswept wings. They are solid-bodied, and typically fly with bursts of quick shallow wingbeats, alternating with gliding and soaring circling, on outstretched wings and tail. Their colours are in soft pastel tones, for they alone of passerines have powder-downs in the plumage. They are highly gregarious, and form swarms or clusters.

629 WHITE-BREASTED WOODSWALLOW

Artamus leucorhynchus Artamidae

OTHER NAMES White-rumped Woodswallow, Swallow-shrike

RECOGNITION Clear-cut two-toned plumage: upperparts including entire head, throat, back, wings and tail are dark blue-grey to brownish-grey. Large white rump patch; white breast meeting dark throat in a clear-cut line; remainder of underparts white except underwings pale grey. The folded wings extend beyond the tail-tip when bird is perched. Eye brown; bill blue-grey with black tip; legs blue-grey. Immatures: dark areas mottled. 17–18 cm.

VOICE Brisk 'pirt-pirt' or 'chyek-'; soft chatterings and a pleasant soft song.

HABITAT Forests, woodlands, watercourse timber-belts, mangroves on coast, Great Barrier Reef islands; always near water, often in trees over water.

BREEDING Throughout year; mostly August–December. Often nests in loose colonies, sometimes over water. The nest is a substantial bowl of twigs, grass; sited in a fork, shallow hollow, or old mud nest. Three to four white eggs, spotted red-brown.

RANGE Northern and eastern Australia; absent south-west, western interior, west of South Australia and Tasmania. Also in New Guinea, South-East Asia, western Pacific, Philippines. Partially migratory.

STATUS Moderately common.

▶ See also pages
175 223 403

630 MASKED WOODSWALLOW

Artamus personatus Artamidae

OTHER NAMES Bluebird, Blue Martin, Bush Martin, Skimmer

RECOGNITION Upperparts are blue-grey; darker on flight feathers; tail blue-grey tipped white; underparts pale grey. Forehead, lores, face and throat black, bordered white at the rear and below, forming a conspicuous and distinctive mask. Underwings pale grey. Eye dark brown; bill bluish, tipped black; legs black. Female: face, throat, underparts dusky brownish-grey; mask not sharply defined or white-edged. Immatures: upperparts mottled with white. 18–19 cm.

VOICE Chattered contact call, a musical 'chap-chap'; also notes like those of miners.

HABITAT Woodlands, open forests, coastal heaths, heath-woodlands, mulga and spinifex country, farmlands.

BREEDING Most months after rain; usually August–December. The nest is a sparse and flimsy bowl of fine twigs, grass, rootlets, placed in a tree fork, shallow hollow of tree stump, 1–5 m high. Two to three white to grey-green eggs, speckled and blotched brown, grey.

630 **MASKED WOODSWALLOW** *Artamus personatus*

HABITAT Eucalypt woodlands, mulga scrublands, spinifex, grasslands, farmlands.

BREEDING All months; usually August–December. The compact bowl of fine twigs, rootlets, and grass is well hidden in a shrub or small tree, occasionally on a stump or post. Three to four white eggs, spotted and blotched red-brown, purplish-grey.

RANGE Throughout Australia except Tasmania, south-east coastal, and extreme south-west. Also in New Guinea, Timor. Sedentary.

STATUS Common.

RANGE Throughout Australia except northern Cape York, south-western Australia and Tasmania. Nomadic, migratory.

STATUS Moderately common. Endemic.

▶ **See also page** 43

WHITE-BROWED WOODSWALLOW

631

Artamus superciliosus   Artamidae

OTHER NAMES Blue Martin, Summerbird or Sky Summerbird, Skimmer

RECOGNITION Upperparts deep blue-grey; blackish about the face, extending down onto the upper breast. Prominent long white eyebrow line; tail tipped white. Breast and belly rufous-chestnut; undertail and underwings pale grey. Eye dark brown; bill blue-white with black tip; legs black. Female: slightly paler upperparts; darker about the lores; shorter eyebrow line. Immatures: similar to female; upperparts mottled with white. 19–21 cm.

VOICE Flight call a soft musical 'chap-chap', becoming harsh and scolding in alarm or aggressive mobbing.

HABITAT Woodlands, open forests, semi-arid and arid scrublands. Wandering flocks may be encountered in a great diversity of habitats.

BREEDING Any month after rain; usually August–January. The nest is a rough and flimsy bowl of fine twigs, rootlets, grass;

built into a bushy shrub, low tree, hollow spout, stump. Two to three white to greenish eggs, blotched grey, brown.

RANGE Mainland Australia; sparse in Western Australia, absent in south-west of Western Australia and Cape York. Migratory.

STATUS Moderately common; locally abundant. Endemic.

▶ **See also pages** *41* 43

BLACK-FACED WOODSWALLOW

632

Artamus cinereus   Artamidae

OTHER NAMES Grey Woodswallow, Grey-breasted Woodswallow, White-bellied Woodswallow, White-vented Woodswallow

RECOGNITION Overall a brownish grey; darker on crown, nape, back and wings; rump and tail black. There is a small area of black round the base of the bill and extending back only as far as the eye. Underparts pale brownish-grey, undertail-coverts blackish tipped white, or wholly white (subspecies *hypoleucos*) in eastern Queensland. Eye dark brown; bill blue-grey with black tip; legs blue-grey. Immatures: speckled or mottled upperparts. 18–20 cm.

VOICE A scratchy and not very loud, 'chiff-chiff' or 'chep-chep', and soft chatterings.

632 **BLACK-FACED WOODSWALLOW** *Artamus cinereus*

DUSKY WOODSWALLOW

633

Artamus cyanopterus   Artamidae

OTHER NAMES Beebird, Bluey, Skimmer, Jacky Martin, Summerbird, Wood Martin

RECOGNITION Overall dusky grey-brown except wings and tail which are blue-black with a white streak along the leading edge of the wing, clearly visible when perched. In flight, the whitish underwings are in contrast against darker underbody; tail tipped white. Eye dark brown; bill blue-grey with black tip; legs slate-grey. Immatures: paler grey-brown, streaked and mottled grey-buff; bill brownish. Sometimes in company with other woodswallow species. 17–18 cm.

VOICE Frequent chatterings and contact calls, including a low soft 'vut-vut' and brisk 'peek-peek'; also an animated but quiet song.

HABITAT Woodlands, forest clearings, paddocks with standing dead trees, open coastal and inland scrublands.

BREEDING Recorded most months; usually August–December. The nest is a flimsy, untidy bowl of fine twigs, rootlets, grass; built into a fork, or shallow hollow of treetrunk or stump, 1–20 m high. Three to four buffy-white eggs, spotted browns and greys.

RANGE Eastern, south-eastern, south-western Australia and Tasmania. Sedentary in north; migratory in south-east.

STATUS Common. Endemic.

▶ **See also page** *157*

634 LITTLE WOODSWALLOW

Artamus minor **Artamidae**

RECOGNITION Body plumage dusky dark brown; wings grey; tail and rump blue-black; the tail tipped white. Eye dark brown; bill blue-grey with black tip; legs black. Immatures: speckled and streaked brown and cream. Lacks the white leading edge wing streak of the other overall dark species, the Dusky Woodswallow. In flight, whitish underwings in strong contrast to dark body. Often in small parties or colonies, hawking for insects in manner of swallows or martins. 12–14 cm.

VOICE A brisk, chattered 'peet-peet-', usually while in flight, softer than other woodswallows; also a soft twittering song.

HABITAT Acacia scrublands and spinifex country in rocky ranges where there are gorges with permanent water; also grassy woodlands, watercourse timbers.

BREEDING Most months; usually August–December. The shallow bowl of fine twigs and rootlets is built into a rock crevice, or hollow of treetrunk or broken limb. Three white or buffy-white eggs, spotted and blotched brown and dark grey.

RANGE Northern and inland Australia; absent in south and Tasmania. Nomadic; partially migratory.

STATUS Uncommon; locally common, patchy. Endemic.

▶ **See also pages** *136 169*

Cracticidae Family of 10 species 8 in Australia, 8 breeding, 5 endemic Sibley-Ahlquist: Family Corvidae, Subfamily Corvinae, Tribe Cracticini

Medium to moderately large, solidly built birds, with strong flight; and black, black-and-white or black-grey-and-white plumage. Song of some species is superb. The butcherbirds are aggressive predators, taking small birds, mammals, reptiles as well as insects. The Australian Magpie and the currawongs are more omnivorous, often on the ground digging for larvae, and also feeding on fruits and berries; currawongs also raid birds' nests.

635 BLACK BUTCHERBIRD

Cracticus quoyi **Cracticidae**

OTHER NAMES Black Crow-shrike, Rufous Crow-shrike

RECOGNITION Entirely blue-black, with metallic sheen. Bill robust, straight, tapering evenly to a strongly hooked tip, pale blue-grey at the base, remainder black. Eye dark brown; legs black. Immatures: wholly black, or in north-eastern Queensland subspecies *rufescens*, immatures are blackish, heavily streaked brown on upperparts; cinnamon-rufous barred black on underparts; apparently breeds while still in this plumage. In pairs or small parties. 42–44 cm.

VOICE A loud, rich, musical, flute-like yodelled 'ah-oo-ah, ah-oo-ah', and 'caw-caw-cooka-cook'; melodious song of interspersed loud and soft notes.

HABITAT Rainforests, monsoon forests, mangroves, riverine forests and scrubs; venturing to nearby open woodlands, farmlands, gardens.

BREEDING September–February. The nest is a substantial bowl of sticks, in an upright fork, 2–10 m high, in eucalypt, melaleuca, or mangrove. Two to four pale olive to grey-green or warm grey eggs, lightly spotted lavender, red-brown, and dark brown.

RANGE North-eastern Queensland south to Rockhampton, Top End (NT), north-eastern Kimberley. Also in New Guinea. Sedentary.

STATUS Moderately common.

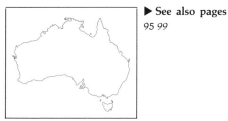

▶ **See also pages** *95 99*

---

636 GREY BUTCHERBIRD

Cracticus torquatus **Cracticidae**

OTHER NAMES Derwent Jackass, Tasmania Jackass, Silver-backed Butcherbird, Grey Shrike

RECOGNITION Upperparts grey, darkening to black on the head and tail; wings blackish-brown with white streak from shoulder to innerwing. The black of the head extends to the face and sides of neck, separated from the dark grey of upper back by a white collar; there is a small dull white patch in front of the eye. Underparts and rump white. Eye dark brown; bill blue-grey, black near hooked tip. Female: browner on crown. Immatures: upperparts mottled brown. 28–32 cm.

VOICE As a territorial song, a deep mellow piping, with mimicry included in quieter sub-song; duets by male and female. In aggression, harsh shrieks.

HABITAT Eucalypt woodlands, forest margins, clearings, including margins of rainforests, inland mallee and watercourse timber, roadside and farm trees.

BREEDING July–January; usually August–December. The nest is an untidy but substantial bowl of twigs, rootlets, dry grasses. It is usually placed in an upright fork, in dense foliage, 2–10 m high. Three to five dull pale green-brown eggs, spotted chestnut.

RANGE Almost throughout Australia, except northern interior to Cape York. Sedentary.

STATUS Moderately common. Endemic.

▶ **See also page** *159*

637 BLACK-BACKED BUTCHERBIRD

Cracticus mentalis **Cracticidae**

RECOGNITION Resembles the widespread Grey Butcherbird, but with back black instead of dark grey; white shoulder stripe continuing down centre of back onto wing; wider white collar. Rump pale grey; uppertail-coverts and tail-tip white; throat and underparts white. Eye brown; bill light grey with black hooked tip; legs dark grey. Immatures duller, with dark brown in place of black; shoulder stripe dull off-white. Often becomes tame around settlements. 25–28 cm.

VOICE Carolling calls like those of Grey Butcherbird, mellow, but weaker; an accomplished mimic.

HABITAT Eucalypt woodlands and open forests, watercourse vegetation; in vicinity of farms and other settlements.

BREEDING June–December. The nest is a shallow cup of sticks, rootlets, stems of creepers; built into a fork to 25 m high. Two to three green-grey eggs, spotted brown, grey.

RANGE Cape York south to Palmer River on east side and Coleman River on west side. Also in New Guinea. Sedentary.

STATUS Common.

▶ See also page
109

638 PIED BUTCHERBIRD

Cracticus nigrogularis   Cracticidae

OTHER NAMES Black-throated Butcherbird, Break-o'-Day Boy, Organbird

RECOGNITION Boldly plumaged. Head, neck, throat and breast entirely black; collar, rump and remainder of underparts white. Wings black with white bar; tail black tipped white. Eye dark brown; bill blue-grey, with hooked tip black. Immatures: brown replaces the black areas of the adult plumage, and very young birds have fawny-white replacing the black bib. Usually aggressive near the nest. 32–36 cm.

VOICE A superb songster, with flute-like notes, ranging from clear high whistles to deep mellow notes, far-carrying; often calls on moonlit nights.

HABITAT Eucalypt woodlands, mulga and mallee scrublands, watercourse and farmland timber.

BREEDING May–December; usually August–December. The nest is a deep cup of sticks, lined with rootlets, fine grass; built into a tree fork. Three to five brownish to dull green eggs, spotted and blotched brown and black.

RANGE Throughout Australia except extreme south-east coastal, Tasmania, southwest. Sedentary.

STATUS Common. Endemic.

▶ See also page
183

639 AUSTRALIAN MAGPIE

Gymnorhina tibicen   Cracticidae

OTHER NAMES Western Magpie, Black-backed Magpie, White-backed Magpie

RECOGNITION A familiar black-and-white bird with heavy, straight bill. Underparts black except white undertail-coverts and underwing. Head black, with broad white patch on nape. White shoulder-patch. Tail white, tipped black. Back pattern geographically variable: nominate subspecies has black back; subspecies *hypoleuca* (White-backed Magpie) and *dorsalis* (Western Magpie) white, female of latter more heavily mottled back. Females: nape and rump pale grey. 37–44 cm.

639 AUSTRALIAN MAGPIE *Gymnorhina tibicen hypoleuca*

VOICE Rich clear carolling notes, by single bird, or often taken up in chorus by others of group; often at night. Harsh loud alarm 'squark'.

HABITAT Eucalypt woodlands, mallee, mulga and other semi-arid scrub, watercourse timbers, forest clearings, farmlands, suburban parks and gardens.

BREEDING July–December; usually August–November. The nest is a large solid bowl of sticks, well lined with grass, hair, wool; usually quite well hidden in canopy of a tree, at 5–15 m. One to six blue, blue-green, or olive eggs, spotted and blotched brown.

RANGE Throughout Australia except Top End (NT), tip of Cape York Peninsula. Also in New Guinea; introduced to New Zealand. Sedentary.

STATUS Common to abundant.

▶ See also pages
213 325 *403* 406

640 PIED CURRAWONG

Strepera graculina   Cracticidae

OTHER NAMES Bell-magpie, Black Magpie, Mountain Magpie, Chillawong, Currawang

RECOGNITION Large, with heavy black bill. Plumage black except for a large white patch in wings; white undertail-coverts, base and tips of tail feathers. The eye deep yellow. Less white at south-east of range, more like Grey Currawong. Legs Black. Immatures greyer, with browner tone round throat; breast mottled, less white; eye dark. Singly or in pairs, or in flocks in autumn and winter. Often seen around campsites and picnic areas, where it becomes quite bold. 43–50 cm.

VOICE A loud ringing double-noted 'currawong', but variable, including 'jaba-wok', 'crik-crik-beware', 'currar-awok-awok-'; also drawn-out whistles.

HABITAT Forests and woodlands; including ranges, alpine woodlands, coastal and inland scrubs; extending mainly in winter to farmlands, suburbs.

BREEDING August–December; mainly September–November. The nest is a large, shallow bowl loosely constructed of sticks; lined with bark fibres, rootlets, grass; placed among foliage of a tree, 3–15 m high. Two to three buffy eggs, speckled and blotched brown.

RANGE Eastern Australia; Cape York to western Victoria. Sedentary in north; locally dispersive in south.

STATUS Common. Endemic.

▶ See also pages
119 149 325

641 BLACK CURRAWONG

Strepera fuliginosa   Cracticidae
OTHER NAMES Black Bell-magpie, Black Crow-shrike, Mountain Magpie, Sooty Crow-shrike

RECOGNITION Overall black plumage, with small, white wing patch; white tail-tip. Bill heavy, black; eye bright deep yellow; legs black. Immatures: gape yellow. In pairs or family parties, larger flocks in winter. 47–49 cm.

VOICE Loud, musical 'karweek, weekar', and various metallic calls.

HABITAT Rainforests, eucalypt forests, heaths, and in winter extending to the open eucalypt forests which are occupied by the Grey Currawong in eastern Tasmania.

BREEDING August–December; mainly September–November. The nest is a bulky, deep bowl of sticks, lined with rootlets and grass; built into an upright fork, usually high in a forest tree. Two to four pale brownish-grey to buff eggs, blotched red-brown, purple.

RANGE Confined to Tasmania and Bass Strait islands. Seasonal altitudinal migrant.

STATUS Common. Endemic.

▶ See also pages
142 149 *149* 151 152

642 GREY CURRAWONG

Strepera versicolor   Cracticidae
OTHER NAMES Black-winged Bell-magpie, Brown Currawong, Clinking Currawong, Black-winged Currawong

RECOGNITION Large, with dark but geographically variable plumage colour, brownish grey to near black. Nominate subspecies dark grey; darker on crown and round eye; large white wing patch; flight and tail feathers tipped white; undertail-coverts white. Tasmanian subspecies *arguta* largest, almost black. Progressively darker west of Melbourne: subspecies *intermedia* of Eyre and Yorke peninsulas (SA), darker brown; *melanoptera* of south-eastern mallee, is blackish; lacks white wing patches. 45–50 cm.

VOICE Loud, ringing metallic clinking 'chling-chling', and 'chlang-chlang'. Also varied quieter sounds. In Tasmania, local subspecies 'keer-keer-kink'.

HABITAT Eucalypt forest, woodlands, mallee, heath, roadside timber, treed farmlands; occasionally suburban areas.

BREEDING August–December; usually September–November. The large, shallow nest is of loose, bulky construction; made of sticks lined with fine rootlets, grass; placed at 3–15 m in tree or shrub. Two to four pale buff eggs, spotted dark grey, brown.

RANGE Southern Australia; south-eastern New South Wales to eastern Tasmania, South Australia, south of Western Australia. Locally nomadic.

STATUS Moderately common; locally common to sparse. Endemic.

▶ See also pages
149 213 *403*

RAVENS, CROWS

Corvidae Family of 102 species
6 in Australia, 5 breeding, 4 endemic,
1 vagrant
Sibley-Ahlquist: Family Corvidae,
Subfamily Corvinae, Tribe Corvini

Large and solidly built, with sleek contours and glossy black plumage; calls are harsh, mainly deep cawings. They are opportunistic predators of relatively weak and helpless prey, but rely very much upon carrion. Because they are highly adaptable and intelligent they are considered to be the most highly evolved of birds. Identification of the Australian species is difficult, relying largely upon calls, behaviour and distribution.

643 AUSTRALIAN RAVEN

Corvus coronoides   Corvidae
OTHER NAMES Crow, Kelly, Raven

RECOGNITION Large; plumage overall black, with purplish and greenish gloss. Long, loose floppy throat feathers that become conspicuous when the throat enlarges as the bird calls, especially in the horizontal posture adopted in giving territorial call. Eye white; bill massive, black. In hand, bases of feathers grey; loose bare skin under chin. Female slightly smaller. Immatures duller; breast and belly sooty black; eye brown. 46–52 cm.

VOICE Usual call a deep powerful 'aah-aah-aaaagh', the last part becoming very low, with strangled, fading gurgling.

HABITAT Varied, including drier forests, woodlands; absent from dense wet forests.

BREEDING July–October; usually August–September. The nest is a substantial shallow bowl of sticks; well lined with bark, hair and wool; usually placed towards crown of a tall tree. Three to five pale blue-green eggs, blotched and freckled olive and brown.

RANGE Eastern Australia except coastal Queensland and Tasmania; also in south-western Australia. Sedentary.

STATUS Common. Endemic.

▶ See also pages
403 409

644 FOREST RAVEN

Corvus tasmanicus   Corvidae
OTHER NAMES Tasmania Raven, New England Raven

RECOGNITION Large; black with a green and purple gloss; throat hackles indistinct; tail comparatively short. Bill massive, that of the southern (nominate) subspecies being the largest of any Australian corvid. In the hand, the bases of the feathers are grey. Eye white; bill and legs black. The northern subspecies *boreus*, confined to north-eastern New South Wales highlands, has a longer tail. Immatures: breast and belly feathers sooty brown; eye brown. 50–55 cm.

VOICE Extremely deep, harsh, slow, rolling 'korr-korr-korr-korr-rr-'; last note very low and drawn-out until fading away.

HABITAT In Tasmania, where it is the only corvid, it occupies wide range of habitats; forests, woodlands, coastal scrub; on mainland, mainly wet eucalypt forests.

BREEDING July–November; usually August–October. The nest is a large basket of sticks, lined with bark fibres, wool; placed in a high fork of a tree. Four pale greenish eggs, blotched and spotted olive and dark brown.

RANGE Tasmania, and adjacent southern Victoria, south-east South Australia; also

646 LITTLE CROW *Corvus bennetti*

in north-eastern New South Wales. Sedentary.

STATUS Common. Endemic.

► See also pages
145 151 153

► See also pages
145 151 153

645 LITTLE RAVEN

Corvus mellori   Corvidae

OTHER NAME Crow

RECOGNITION Slightly smaller than the Australian Raven. Throat hackles not as greatly elongated, this being most noticeable when comparing calling birds. When calling, gives a quick upward shuffle of both wings over the back as each note is uttered. Calls from varied perching postures, rather than the horizontal posture adopted by the Australian Raven. Down at base of body feathers ashy brown. Eye white. Immatures: underbody sooty brown; eye brown. 50 cm.

VOICE Short, quick notes, but harsh and guttural, 'kar-kar-kar-kar', or 'ark-ark-', notes clipped, not gradually fading away.

HABITAT Mulga and other semi-arid scrubs, spinifex, open plains, eucalypt forests and woodlands, including alpine, farmlands.

BREEDING April–December; usually Aug-

ust–October. Nest is a shallow but substantial cup of sticks, lined with bark, wool, grass; usually situated at moderate height in the outer canopy. Four to five pale green eggs, blotched and freckled olive and brown.

RANGE South-eastern Australia; central New South Wales to Eyre Peninsula. Nomadic to partially migratory.

STATUS Common. Endemic.

► See also page
157

► See also page
157

646 LITTLE CROW

Corvus bennetti   Corvidae

OTHER NAMES Bennett's Crow, Small-billed Crow, Kelly

RECOGNITION Smallest corvid, with slenderer bill. Plumage overall black with purplish-green gloss; general silhouette neater than other species. In the hand, the down at the base of the feathers is white. Eye white; bill and legs black. Immatures duller; eye brown. The Little Crow tends to be comparatively tame, the corvids generally being rather wary. In flight, wingbeats more rapid, shallow. Often in large flocks, breeds in scattered groups. 41–48 cm.

VOICE A prolonged nasal 'aark-aark-aark-', quite deep, monotonous, and though each note is prolonged, they are uttered in rapid succession.

HABITAT All kinds of semi-arid and arid environs; including spinifex, mulga scrublands, watercourse trees, around outback towns, homesteads.

BREEDING Almost throughout year; usually August–October. The nest of small sticks is usually plastered internally with mud or clay, and lined with soft bark, fur, feathers. Four to six greenish-blue eggs, speckled and blotched olive-brown.

RANGE Throughout Australian interior, and to north-west coast and to west of South Australia. Nomadic.

STATUS Common; locally abundant. Endemic.

647 TORRESIAN CROW

Corvus orru   Corvidae

OTHER NAMES Australian Crow, Crow, Kelly

RECOGNITION Closely resembles the Australian Raven in size, and glossy black plumage, but with throat hackles shorter, comparatively inconspicuous. In the hand, the underdown is white. Larger than Little Crow, and has the habit of repeatedly shuffling the wings upon landing rather than when calling; tail broader, more square-cut. Eye white; bill and legs black. Immatures: plumage brownish-black; eye brown to three years. 50–55 cm.

VOICE Short nasal 'ok-ok-ok-ok-' or 'uk-uk-', and 'oo-ah', not 'aaark', squeaky door sounds, notes drawled. Also long, harsh snarling calls.

HABITAT Open forests, woodlands. In arid regions, timbered watercourses, and gorges of ranges, taller areas of mulga. Also coastal scrubs, mudflats.

BREEDING August–April; usually August–October in south to February in north. The nest of twigs is sparsely lined, or unlined; usually placed high in the canopy. Three to five pale blue to pale greenish-blue eggs, spotted and blotched olive and dark brown.

RANGE Northern and arid Australia; absent south-west to south-east, Tasmania. Also in New Guinea, Moluccas, Bismark Archipelago. Mainly sedentary.

STATUS Common.

► See also page
179

► See also page
179

REGIONAL BIRDLIST

The fourteen regions shown on the list correspond to the regions discussed in this book. The birds listed cover the 647 species in the Bird Reference section, plus subspecies which are referred to in the text and are included in the entry for the relevant full species.

● Found in region

★ Endemic to region; substantially confined to region

○ Vagrant; few records of sightings; marginal

* Indicates subspecies

(I) Indicates introduced species

COMMON NAME	Eastern Qld	Atherton	Cape York	South East	Murray-Darling	Tasmania	Central South	Eastern Deserts	Central Deserts	Top End	Kimberley	Western Deserts	Pilbara	South West
Albatross, Black-browed				●		●	●							●
Royal				●		●	●							
Shy				●		●	●							●
Wandering				●		●	●							●
Yellow-nosed				●		●	●							●
Apostlebird	●	●		●			●		●					
Avocet, Red-necked	○			●	●		●	●	●	●	●	●	●	●
Babbler, Chestnut-crowned				●			●	●						
Grey-crowned	●	●	●	●				●	●	●	●	●	●	
Hall's				●			●							
White-browed				●			●	●	●			●	●	●
Baza, Pacific	●	●	●	●	●					●	●			
Bee-eater, Rainbow	●	●	●	●	●		●	●	●	●	●	●	●	●
Bellbird, Crested	●			●	●		●	●	●			●	●	
Bittern, Australasian				●	●	●	●							●
Black	●	●	●	●			●		●	●				●
Little	●	●		●	●				○					●
Black-Cockatoo, Glossy	●			●	●		●							
Long-billed														★
Red-tailed	●	●	●		●			●	●	●	●	○	●	●
*White-tailed													○	●
Yellow-tailed	●			●	●	●	●						○	●
Blue Bonnet			○	●		●		●	●				●	
Boatbill, Yellow-breasted		●	●											
Boobook, Southern	●	●	●	●	●	●	●	●	●	●	●	●	●	●
Booby, Brown	●	●	●							●	●	●		●
Masked	●	●	●							●	●			
Red-footed	○	○	●											
Bowerbird, Fawn-breasted			★											
Golden		★												
Great	●	●	●				●		●	●				
Regent	●			●										
Satin	●	●		●	●									
Spotted	●				●			●	●			●	●	
Bristlebird, Eastern				★										
Rufous				●		●								
Western														★
Brolga	●	●	●	●	●		●	●	●	●	●	●	●	
Bronze-Cuckoo, Gould's	●	●	●											
Horsfield's	●	●	●	●	●	●	●	●	●	●	●	●	●	●
Little	●	●	●	○					●	●				
Shining	●	●	●	●	●	●	●	●					○	●
Bronzewing, Brush	○			●	●	●	●							●
Common	●	●	●	●	●	●	●	●	●	●	●	●	●	●
Flock	○							●	●	○	●	●		
Brush-turkey, Australian	●	●	●											
Budgerigar	●			○	●		●	●	●	●	●	●	●	●
Bulbul, Red-whiskered (I)			●	○										
Bush-hen	●	●	●	○					●					
Bushlark, Singing	●	●	●	●	●		●	●	●	●	●	●	●	
Bustard, Australian	●	●	●		●		●	●	●	●	●	●	●	●

COMMON NAME	Eastern Qld	Atherton	Cape York	South East	Murray-Darling	Tasmania	Central South	Eastern Deserts	Central Deserts	Top End	Kimberley	Western Deserts	Pilbara	South West
Butcherbird, Black	●	●	●											
Black-backed		★												
Grey	●	●	○	●	●	●	●	●	●	●	●	●	●	●
Pied	●	●	●	●	●			●	●	●	●	●	●	●
Button-quail, Black-breasted	★													
Buff-breasted		★												
Chestnut-backed											★	○		
Little	●			●	●		●	●	●	○	○	●	●	●
Painted	●	●		●	●	●	●							●
Red-backed	●	●	●							●				
Red-chested	●	●	●	●	●		○	●	○	○	○			
Buzzard, Black-breasted	●	●	●	○			○	●	●	●	●	●	●	●
Cassowary, Southern		●	●											
Catbird, Green	●		●											
Spotted		●	●											
Tooth-billed		★												
Chat, Crimson	○			●			●	●	●			●	●	●
Orange	●			●			●	●	●			●	●	○
White-fronted				●	●	●	●	●	○			●	●	●
Yellow							●			●	●	●		
Chough, White-winged	●			●	●		●							
Chowchilla		★												
Cicadabird	●	●	●	●	●					●	●	○		
Cisticola, Golden-headed	●	●	●	●	●		●	●	○	●	●	○		
Zitting	●		●							●	●	○		
Cockatiel	●	●		○	●		●	●	●	●	●	●	●	●
Cockatoo, Gang-gang			●	○										
Palm		★												
Pink				●			●	●	●			●	●	●
Sulphur-crested	●	●	●	●	●	●	●	●	○	●	●			○
Coot, Eurasian	●	●	●	●	●	●	●	●	●	●	●	●	●	●
Corella, Little	●			○	●		●	●	●	●	●	●	●	●
Long-billed							●	●						
Western Long-billed														★
Cormorant, Great	●	●	●	●	●	●	●	●	●	●	●	●	●	●
Little Black	●	●	●	●	●	○	●	●	●	●	●	●	●	●
Little Pied	●	●	●	●	●	●	●	●	●	●	●	●	●	●
Pied	●	●	●	●	●	●	●	●	●	●	●	●	●	●
Coucal, Pheasant	●	●	●	●	●			○		●	●	○	●	
Crake, Australian	○			●	●	●	●	●	○			○	●	●
Baillon's	●	○	○	●	●	○	●	●	○	●	●	○	○	●
Red-necked		●	●											
Spotless	●	●	●	●	●	●	●	●		○			●	●
White-browed		●	●							●	●			
Crane, Sarus	●	●	●							●		●	○	
Crow, Little	●			●			●	●	●			●	●	●
Torresian	●	●	●	●	●			●	●	●	●	●	●	○
Cuckoo, Black-eared	●	●	●	●	●	○	●	●	●	●	●	●	●	●
Brush	●	●	●	●	●					●	●			
Channel-billed	●	●	●	●	●			●	○	●	●			
Chestnut-breasted		★												

COMMON NAME	Eastern Qld	Atherton	Cape York	South East	Murray-Darling	Tasmania	Central South	Eastern Deserts	Central Deserts	Top End	Kimberley	Western Deserts	Pilbara	South West
Fan-tailed	●	●	●	●	●	●	●	○				○		●
Oriental	●	●	●	○						●	●	○		
Pallid	●	●	●	●	●	●	●	●	●	●	●	●	●	●
Cuckoo-Dove, Brown	●	●	●	●										
Cuckoo-shrike, Black-faced	●	●	●	●	●	●	●	●	●	●	●	●	●	●
Ground	●	○		○	●		●	●	●	●	●	●	●	●
White-bellied	●	●	●	●	●			●	○	●	●			
Yellow-eyed	●	●	●	●										
Curlew, Eastern	●	●	●	●	○	●	●			●	●	●		
Little	●	●	●	●	○		●	○	○	●	●	●		○
Currawong, Black						★								
Grey				●	●	●	●						●	●
Pied	●	●	●	●	●									
Darter	●	●	●	●	●	○	●	●	●	●	●	●	●	●
Diving-Petrel, Common			●		●	○								○
Dollarbird	●	●	●	●	●			●	○	●	●	○		
Dotterel, Inland				●		●	●	●				●	●	●
Red-kneed	●	●	●	●	●	○	●	●	●	●	●	●	●	●
Dove, Bar-shouldered	●	●	●	●	●			●		●	●	●	○	
Diamond	●	●	●	●	●		●	●	●	●	●	●	●	○
Emerald	●	●	●	●						●	●			
Peaceful	●	●	●	●	●		●	●	●	●	●	●	●	
Drongo, Spangled	●	●	●	●						●	●			
Duck, Blue-billed	○			●	●	●	●	●	○					●
Freckled	○			●	●		●	●	○			○	○	●
Maned	●	●		●	●	●	●	●	●	●	○	○	○	●
Musk	○			●	●	●	●	●					●	●
Pacific Black	●	●	●	●	●	●	●	●	●	●	●	●	●	●
Pink-eared	●	●	●	●	●	●	●	●	●	●	●	●	●	●
Eagle, Little	●	●	●	●	●	●	●	●	●	●	●	●	●	●
Wedge-tailed	●	●	●	●	●	●	●	●	●	●	●	●	●	●
Egret, Cattle	●	●	●	●	●	●	●	○	○	●	●	○	●	○
Eastern Reef	●	●	●	●			●			●	●	●	●	●
Great	●	●	●	●	●	●	●	●	●	●	●	●	●	●
Intermediate	●	●	●	●	●	●	●	●	○	●	●	○		○
Little	●	●	●	●	●	●	●	●	○	●	●	●	●	●
Emu	●	●	●	●	●	●	●	●	●			●	●	●
Emu-wren, Rufous-crowned				●			●	●			●	●		
Southern				●		●	●							●
Fairy-wren, *Black-and-white													★	
Blue-breasted							●				●	●	●	
*Lavender-flanked										●	●			
Lovely		●	●											
Purple-crowned								●	○	●	●			
Red-backed	●	●	●	●				●	●	●	●			
Red-winged														★
Splendid	○				●		●	●	●			●	●	●
Superb	●			●	●	●	●							
Variegated	●			●	●		●	●	●	●	●	●	●	●
White-winged	●			●	●		●	●			●	●	●	●
Falcon, Black	●	●	●	●	●	●	●	●	●	●	●	○	○	○
Brown	●	●	●	●	●	●	●	●	●	●	●	●	●	●
Grey	●			○	●	●	●	●	●	●	●	●		○
Peregrine	●	●	●	●	●	●	●	●	●	●	●	●	●	●
Fantail, Grey	●	●	●	●	●	●	●	●	●	●	●	●	●	●
Northern		●	●					○		●	●			
Rufous	●	●	●	●	●					●	●			
Fernwren, Australian		★												
Fieldwren, Striated				●	●	●	●	●	●	●			●	●	●

COMMON NAME	Eastern Qld	Atherton	Cape York	South East	Murray-Darling	Tasmania	Central South	Eastern Deserts	Central Deserts	Top End	Kimberley	Western Deserts	Pilbara	South West
Fig-Parrot, Double-eyed	●	●	●	●										
*Coxen's	●			●										
*Marshall's			★											
*Macleay's		★												
Figbird	●	●	●	●						●	●			
Finch, Black-throated	●	●	●					●						
Blue-faced		★												
Crimson	●	●	●					●		●	●			
Double-barred	●	●	●	●	●			●		●	●			
Gouldian	●	○						○		●	●			
Long-tailed								●		●	●			
Masked	○	○	●					○		●	●			
Plum-headed	●	○		●	●			●						
Star	○	○	●							●	●	●	●	
Zebra	●	●	○	●	●		●	●	●	●	●	●	●	●
Firetail, Beautiful				●		●	●	●						
Diamond	●			●	●		●							
Painted					○	●	●		●	●	●			
Red-browed	●	●	●	●	●		●							
Red-eared														★
Flycatcher, Broad-billed		○	●							●	●			
*Kimberley											★			
Leaden	●	●	●	●	●		●			●	●			
Lemon-bellied	●	●	●							●	●			
Restless	●	●	●	●	●		●	●	●	●	●			●
Satin	●	●	●	●	●	●								
Shining	●	●	●							●	●			
Yellow-legged		★												
Friarbird, Helmeted	●	●	●					●						
Little	●	●	●	●	●			●	○	●	●			
Noisy	●	●	●	●	●									
Silver-crowned		●	●					●		●	●			
Frigatebird, Great	●	●	●	○						●				
Least	●	●	●							●	●	●		
Frogmouth, Marbled	●		★	●										
Papuan		●	●											
*Plumed	●			●										
Tawny	●	●	●	●	●	●	●	●	●	●	●	●	●	●
Fruit-Dove, Banded										★				
Rose-crowned	●	●	●	●						●	●			
Superb	●	●	●	●										
Wompoo	●	●	●	●										
Galah	●	●	●	●	●	●	●	●	●	●	●	●	●	●
Gannet, Australasian	●			●		●	●							●
Giant-Petrel, Northern				●		●	●							●
Southern				●		●	●						○	●
Gibberbird						●		●	●					
Godwit, Bar-tailed	●	●	●	●	●	●	●		○	●	●	●	●	●
Black-tailed	●	●	○	●	●	○	●	●	○	●	●	●	●	●
Goldfinch, European (I)				●	●	●	●							
Goose, Cape Barren				●	○	●	●							●
Magpie	●	●	●	○		○		○	○	●	●			
Goshawk, Brown	●	●	●	●	●	●	●	●	●	●	●	●	●	●
Grey	●	●	●	●	●	●	●			●	●			
Red	●	●	●	○						●	○			
Grassbird, Little	●	●		●	●	●	●	●	●			★	●	●
Tawny	●	●	●	●						●	○			
Grasswren, Black											★			
Carpentarian									★					

COMMON NAME	Eastern Qld	Atherton	Cape York	South East	Murray-Darling	Tasmania	Central South	Eastern Deserts	Central Deserts	Top End	Kimberley	Western Deserts	Pilbara	South West
Dusky							●	●						
Eyrean							★							
Grey				●			●							
Striated				●			●	○	●			●	●	
Thick-billed							●						●	
White-throated										★				
Grebe, Australasian	●	●	●	●	●	●	●	●	●	●	●	●	●	●
Great Crested	●	●	●	●	●	●	●	●	○	○		○	○	●
Hoary-headed	●	○		●	●	●	●	●	●	●	●	●	●	●
Greenfinch, European (I)				●	●	●	●							
Greenshank	●	●	●	●	●	●	●	●	●	●	●	●	●	●
Ground-thrush, Australian	●	●		●		●								
Russet-tailed	●	●		●										
Gull, Kelp				●		●	●							●
Pacific				●		●	●					●	●	●
Silver	●	●	●	●	●	●	●	●	●	●	●	●	●	●
Hardhead	●	●	●	●	●	●	●	●	●	●	●	●	●	●
Harrier, Marsh	●	●	●	●	●	●	●	●	●	●	●	○	●	●
Spotted	●	●	●	●	●	○	●	●	●	●	●	●	●	●
Heathwren, Chestnut-rumped				●	●		●							
Shy				●			●						○	●
Heron, Great-billed	●	●	●	●						●	●			
Pacific	●	●	●	●	●	●	●	●	●	●	●	●	●	●
Pied	●	●	●							●	●			
Striated	●	●	●	●	●					●	●	●	●	
White-faced	●	●	●	●	●	●	●	●	●	●	●	●	●	●
Hobby, Australian	●	●	●	●	●	●	●	●	●	●	●	●	●	●
Honeyeater, Banded	●	●	●					●		●	●			
Bar-breasted	●		●				○			●	●			
Black	●				●	○	●	●			●	●		
Black-chinned	●	●	●	●	●			●	●	●	●	●	●	
Black-headed					★									
Blue-faced	●	●	●	●	●		○			●	●			
Bridled		★												
Brown	●	●	●	●	●			●	●	●	●	●	●	●
Brown-backed		●	●											
Brown-headed	●			●	●		●						●	●
Crescent				●	●	●	●							
Dusky	●	●	●							●				
Eungella	★													
Fuscous	●	●		●	●									
*Golden-backed							●	●	●	●	●	●		
Graceful		●	●											
Green-backed			★											
Grey							○	●			●	●		
Grey-fronted	●		○		●			●	●	●	●	●	●	
Grey-headed	○							●	●	●	●	●	●	
*Helmeted				★										
Lewin's	●	●		●	●									
Macleay's		★												
Mangrove	●	●		●										
New Holland				●	●	●	●							●
Painted	●			●	●			●	○	●				
Pied				●			●	●	●		●	●		
Purple-gaped				●			●							●
Red-headed	●										●	●		
Regent				●	●									
Rufous-banded		●								●				
Rufous-throated	●	●	●					●	●	●	●			
Scarlet	●	●	○	●	●									

COMMON NAME	Eastern Qld	Atherton	Cape York	South East	Murray-Darling	Tasmania	Central South	Eastern Deserts	Central Deserts	Top End	Kimberley	Western Deserts	Pilbara	South West
Singing	●			●	●		●	●	●	●	●	●	●	●
Spiny-cheeked	●			●	●		●	●	●			●	●	●
Striped	●			●	●		●							
Strong-billed						★								
Tawny-breasted			★											
Tawny-crowned				●	●	●	●						○	●
Varied		●	●											
White-cheeked	●	●		●										●
White-eared	●			●	●		●						●	●
White-fronted				●			●	●	●			●	●	●
White-gaped	●	●	●					●		●	●			
White-lined										●	●			
White-naped	●	●		●	●		●							●
White-plumed	●			●	●		●	●	●		●	●	●	○
White-streaked		●	●											
White-throated	●	●	●	●						●	●			
Yellow	●	●	●											
Yellow-faced	●	●		●	●		●							
Yellow-plumed				●			●					●	●	●
Yellow-spotted		●	●											
Yellow-throated						★								
Yellow-tinted	●	○	○					●	●	●	●			
Yellow-tufted	●			●	●									
Ibis, Glossy	●	●	●	●	●	○	●	●	●	●	●	●	●	●
Sacred	●	●	●	●	●	○	●	●	○	●	●	○	○	●
Straw-necked	●	●	●	●	●	○	●	●	●	●	●	●	●	●
Imperial-Pigeon, Torresian	●	●	●							●	●			
Jacana, Comb-crested	●	●	●	●				○		●	●			
Jacky Winter	●	●	●	●	●		●	●	●	●	●	●	●	●
Jaeger, Arctic	○	○	○	●		●	●			○	○			●
Pomarine	○		○	●		●				○	●		○	
Kestrel, Australian	●	●	●	●	●	●	●	●	●	●	●	●	●	●
King-Parrot, Australian	●	●		●	●									
Kingfisher, Azure	●	●	●	●	●	●		○	○	●	●			
Collared	●	●	●							●	●	●	●	
Forest	●	●	●	●	○					●				
Little	●	●	●							●				
Red-backed	●	●	●	●	●			●	●	●	●	●	●	●
Sacred	●	●	●	●	●	●	●	●	●	●	●	●	●	●
Yellow-billed			★											
Kite, Black	●	●	●	●	●	○	●	●	●	●	●	●	●	●
Black-shouldered	●	●	●	●	●	●	●	●	●	●	●	●	●	●
Brahminy	●	●	●	●						●	●	●	○	●
Letter-winged	●			●	●		●	●	●	●	●		○	●
Square-tailed	●	●	●	●	●		○	●	●	●	●	○	●	●
Whistling	●	●	●	●	●		○	●	●	●	●	●	●	●
Knot, Great	●	●	●	●	●	●	●		○	●	●	●	●	●
Red	●	●	●	●	○	●	●			●	●	●	●	●
Koel, Common	●	●	●	●	●			○		●	●			
Kookaburra, Blue-winged	●	●	●							●	●	●	●	
Laughing	●	●	●	●	●	●								●
Lapwing, Banded	●			●	●	●	●	●	●			●	●	●
Masked	●	●	●	●	●	●	●	●	●	●	●	○	○	○
Logrunner	●			●										
Lorikeet, Little	●	●		●	●									
Musk	●			●	●	●	●							
Purple-crowned				●	●		●						●	●
Rainbow	●	●	●	●	●		●							
Red-collared										●	●			

COMMON NAME	Eastern Qld	Atherton	Cape York	South East	Murray-Darling	Tasmania	Central South	Eastern Deserts	Central Deserts	Top End	Kimberley	Western Deserts	Pilbara	South West
Scaly-breasted	●	●	●	●	●									
Varied	●		●				●	○	●	●				
Lyrebird, Albert's	●			●										
Superb				●	○	○								
Magpie, Australian	●	●	●	●	●	●	●	●	●	●	●	●	●	●
Magpie-lark, Australian	●	●	●	●	●		●	●	●	●	●	●	●	●
Mallard (I)	○			●	●	●	●						○	
Malleefowl					●		●						●	●
Mannikin, Chestnut-breasted	●	●	●	●						●	●			
Nutmeg	●	●		●										
Pictorella	○		○					●	●	●	●			
Yellow-rumped										●	●			
Manucode, Trumpet			★											
Martin, Fairy	●	●	●	●	●		●	●	●	●	●	●	●	●
Tree	●	●	●	●	●	●	●	●	●	●	●	●	●	●
Miner, Bell	●			●										
Black-eared					★									
Noisy	●	●	○	●	●	●	●	○						
Yellow-throated	●	●			●		●	●	●	●	●	●	●	●
Mistletoebird	●	●	●	●	●		●	●	●	●	●	●	●	●
Monarch, Black-faced	●	●	●	●										
Black-winged			★											
Frilled			★											
Pied		★												
Spectacled	●	●	●	●										
White-eared	●	●	●	○										
Moorhen, Dusky	●	●		●	●	●	●							●
Mynah, Common	●	●		●	○									
*Naretha Parrot												★		
Native-hen, Black-tailed	●	○		●	●		●	●	●	●				●
Tasmanian						★								
Needletail, White-throated	●	●	●	●	●	●	●	●	●	●	●	●	●	●
Night Heron, Rufous	●	●	●	●	●	●	●	●	●	●	●	●	●	●
Nightjar, Large-tailed	●	●	●							●				
Spotted	●	●	●	○	●		●	●	●	●	●	●	●	●
White-throated	●	●	●	●	●									
Noddy, Black	●	●	●	○										
Common	●	●	●	●						●	●	○	●	●
Lesser														★
Oriole, Olive-backed	●	●	●	●	●			●		●	●			
Yellow		●	●							●	●			
Osprey	●	●	●	●	○	○	●	○		●	●	●	●	●
Owl, Barking	●	●	●	●	●			●		●	●	●	●	●
Barn	●	●	●	●	●	○		●		●	●	●	●	●
Eastern Grass	●	●	●		○			●		●	○			
Masked	○	○		●	○	●				●		●		●
Powerful	●			●	●									
Rufous	●	●	●							●				
Sooty	●	●		●										
Owlet-nightjar, Australian	●	●	●	●	●	●	●	●	●	●	●	●	●	●
Oystercatcher, Pied	●	●	●	●			●	●			●	●	●	●
Sooty	●	●	●	●		●	●				●	●	●	●
Paradise-Kingfisher, Buff-breasted	○	●	●											
Pardalote, Forty-spotted						★								
Red-browed	●	●	●		●			●	●	●	●	●	●	
Spotted	●	●		●	●	●	●							●
Striated	●	●	●	●	●	●	●	●	●	●	●	●	●	●
Yellow-rumped					●	●							●	
Parrot, Alexandra's								●			●			

COMMON NAME	Eastern Qld	Atherton	Cape York	South East	Murray-Darling	Tasmania	Central South	Eastern Deserts	Central Deserts	Top End	Kimberley	Western Deserts	Pilbara	South West
Blue-winged				●	●		●	●						
Bourke's					●		●	●	●			●	●	
Eclectus			★											
Elegant					●		●							●
Golden-shouldered			★											
Ground	●		●		●									●
Hooded										★				
Mulga					●		●	●	●			●	●	●
Night							○		○		○			
Orange-bellied				●		○	○							
Paradise	○		○	○										
Red-capped														★
Red-cheeked			★											
Red-rumped	●			●	●		●	●						
Red-winged	●	●	●	○	●			●	●	●	●	●		
Regent					●		○						●	●
Rock							●							●
Scarlet-chested							○	●	○	●	●		●	
Superb				★										
Swift				●	●	●								
Turquoise				●	●									
Pelican, Australian	●	●	●	●	●	●	●	●	●	●	●	●	●	●
Penguin, Little				●		●	●							●
Petrel, Cape						●	●						●	○
Gould's						●	●							
Great-winged						●	●							●
Kerguelen						●	●							
White-headed						●	●							○
Pigeon, Crested	●	●	○	●	●		●	●	●	●	●	●	●	●
Partridge										●	●			
Spinifex								●	●	●	●	●		
Squatter	●	●	●		●									
Topknot	●	●	○	●										
White-headed	●	●	●											
Wonga	●		●											
Pilotbird				★										
Pipit, Richard's	●	●	●	●	●	●	●	●	●	●	●	●	●	●
Pitta, Noisy	●	●	●											
Rainbow										●	●			
Red-bellied			★											
Plains-wanderer				○	●		○							
Plover, Black-fronted	●	●	●	●	●		●	●	●	●	●	●	●	●
Double-banded	●	○		●	●	●	●							●
Grey	●	●	●	●	○	●	●			●	●	●	●	●
Hooded					●	●							●	●
Large Sand	●	●	●	●	●	○				●	●	●	●	●
Lesser Golden	●	●	●	●	●		●		○	●	●	●	●	●
Mongolian	●	●	●							●	●		●	●
Oriental	○	○	○	○	○									
Red-capped	●	●	●	●	●	●	●	●	●	●	●	●	●	●
Pratincole, Australian	●	●	●	○			●	●	●	●	●	●	●	○
Oriental	○						●	●	●	●	●	●	●	○
Prion, Antarctic						●	●							●
Fairy						●	●							○
Lesser Broad-billed						●	●							●
Slender-billed						●	●							●
Pygmy-Goose, Cotton	●	●	●											
Green	●	●	●						○	●	●			
Quail, Brown (includes Swamp Quail)	●	●	●	●	●	●				●	●	○		●

COMMON NAME	Eastern Qld	Atherton	Cape York	South East	Murray-Darling	Tasmania	Central South	Eastern Deserts	Central Deserts	Top End	Kimberley	Western Deserts	Pilbara	South West
King	●	●	●	●						●	●			
Stubble	●	○		●	●		●	●	●	○		○	●	●
Quail-thrush, Chestnut				●		●		●				●	●	●
Cinnamon				●		●	●	●				●	●	
Nullarbor												★		
Spotted	●			●	●	●	○							
Rail, Buff-banded	●	●	●	●	●		●	○	○	●	○	○	●	●
Chestnut										●	●			
Lewin's	●	●		●	●	●	●							
Raven, Australian	●	●	○	●	●		●	●	●				●	●
Forest				●		●	●	○						
Little				●	●		●							
Redthroat				●		●	●	●				●	●	●
Reed-Warbler, Clamorous	●	●	●	●	●	●	●	●	●	●	●	○	●	●
Riflebird, Magnificent			★											
Paradise	●			●										
Victoria's		★												
Ringneck, Mallee	●				●		●	●						
Port Lincoln					●	●	●				●	●	●	
Robin, Dusky						★								
Eastern Yellow	●	●		●	●									
Flame				●	●	●	●							
Grey-headed		★												
Hooded	●			●	●		●	●	●	●	●	●	●	●
Mangrove	●	●	●						●	●	●	●		
Pale-yellow	●	●		●										
Pink				●	●	●								
Red-capped	●			●	●		●	●	●			●	●	●
Rose	●			●	●		○							
Scarlet	○			●	●	●	●					○	●	
Western Yellow							●					○	●	
White-breasted														★
White-browed	●	●	●				●		●	●				
White-faced			★											
Rock-Pigeon, Chestnut-quilled									★					
White-quilled									●	●				
Rosella, *Adelaide						★								
Crimson	●	●		●	●	●								
Eastern	●			●	●	●	●							
Green						★								
Northern										●	●			
Pale-headed	●	●	●	●	●									
Western														★
*Yellow						★								
Ruff	○		○	●	●		●		●			○	○	
Sanderling	●	●	○	●		●	●		●	●	●	●	●	
Sandpiper, Broad-billed	●	●	○	●			○		○	○	○		○	
Common	●	●	●	●	●	●	●	●	●	●	●	●	●	●
Curlew	●	●	●	●	●	●	●	●	●	○	●	●	●	
Marsh	●	●	●	●	●		●	●	●	●	●	●	●	
Pectoral		●		●	●	●	●		○	○		○	●	
Sharp-tailed	●	●	●	●	●	●	●	●	●	●	●	●	●	
Terek	●	●	●	●			●		●	●	●	●	●	
Wood	●	○		●	●	○	●	●	●	●	●	●	●	
Scrub-bird, Noisy														★
Rufous				★										
Scrub-robin, Northern			●						○					
Southern					●		●				○	●	●	
Scrubfowl, Orange-footed	●	●	●							●	●			

COMMON NAME	Eastern Qld	Atherton	Cape York	South East	Murray-Darling	Tasmania	Central South	Eastern Deserts	Central Deserts	Top End	Kimberley	Western Deserts	Pilbara	South West
Scrubtit						★								
Scrubwren, Atherton		★												
Large-billed	●	●		●										
Tropical			★											
White-browed	●	●		●	●	●	●					●	●	●
Yellow-throated	●	●		●										
Sea-Eagle, White-bellied	●	●	●	●	●		●	●		●	●	●	●	●
Shag, Black-faced				●		●	●							●
Shearwater, Fleshy-footed				●		●	●					●	●	
Fluttering	○			●		●	●							○
Little				●										●
Short-tailed	○			●		●	●							●
Sooty				●		●	○						○	
Streaked			●							●	●			
Wedge-tailed	●	●	●	●						●	●	●	●	
Shelduck, Australian				●	●	●	●	●				○	●	●
Radjah	●	●	●							●	●			
Shoveler, Australasian	●	○	○	●	●	●	●					○	●	●
Shrike-thrush, Bower's		★												
Grey	●	●	●	●	●	●	●	●	●	●	●	●	●	●
Little	●	●	●	●							●	●		
Sandstone										●	●			
Shrike-tit, Crested	●	●		●	●		●							●
Silvereye	●	●	●	●		●	●	○			●	●	●	
Sittella, Varied	●	●	●	●		●	●	●	●	●	●	●	●	
Skua, Great				●		●	●						○	●
Skylark				●	●	●	●							
Snipe, Latham's (includes Pin-tailed and Swinhoe's)	●	●	●	●	●	●	●		○		●	○	○	○
Painted	●	○		●	●		●	●	○	○	○			
Songlark, Brown	●			●	●		●	●	●	●	●	●	●	●
Rufous	●	●	●	●	●		●	●	●	●	●	●	●	●
Sparrow, House (I)	●	●	●	●	●	●	●	●	○		○			
Tree (I)				●	●									
Sparrowhawk, Collared	●	●	●	●	●	●	●	●	●	●	●	●	●	●
Spinebill, Eastern	●	●		●	●	●	●							
Western														★
Spinifexbird								●	●		●	●		
Spoonbill, Royal	●	●	●	●	●		●	●	●	●	●		○	○
Yellow-billed	●	●	●	●	●	○	●	●	●	●	●	○	●	●
Starling, Common (I)	●	○		●	●	●	●	●			●			○
Metallic	●	●	●											
Stilt, Banded				●	●	●	●	●	●		●	●	●	
Black-winged	●	●	●	●	●		●	●	●	●	●	●	●	
Stint, Long-toed				●	●	○	●	○	○	○	●	●		
Red-necked	●	●	●	●	●	●	●	●	●	●	●	●	●	
Stork, Black-necked	●	●	●	●			●	●	●	●	●		○	
Storm-Petrel, White-faced				●		●	●						○	●
Wilson's				●		●	●							●
Sunbird, Yellow-bellied	●	●	●											
Swallow, Barn	●	●	○			○		○	○	●				
Welcome	●	●		●	●	●	●	●	●	○	○	●	●	●
White-backed	●			●	●		●	●	●		●	●	●	
Swamp-hen, Purple	●	●	●	●	●	●	●		●	●	●	○	○	●
Swan, Black	●	●	○	●	●	●	●		●		●	●	●	
Swift, Fork-tailed	●	●	●	●	●	●	●	●	●	●	●	●	●	
Swiftlet, White-rumped	●	●	●											
Tattler, Grey-tailed	●	●	●	●		●	●			●	●	●	●	●
Wandering	●	●	○	●					○					

COMMON NAME	Eastern Qld	Atherton	Cape York	South East	Murray-Darling	Tasmania	Central South	Eastern Deserts	Central Deserts	Top End	Kimberley	Western Deserts	Pilbara	South West
Teal, Chestnut	●			●	●	●	●	○	○			○	○	●
Grey	●	●	●	●	●	●	●	●	●	●	●	●	●	●
Tern, Black-naped	●	●	●							●				
Bridled	●	●	●							●	●	●	●	
Caspian	●	●	●	●	●	●	●	●	○	●	●	●	●	●
Common	●	●	●	●		●				●	○			
Crested	●	●	●	●		●	●			●	●	●	●	●
Fairy			●			●	●				●	●	●	●
Gull-billed	●	●	●	●	●	○	●	●	●	●	●	●	○	●
Lesser Crested	●	●	●							●	●	●	●	
Little	●	●	●	●		●	●			●	●	●	●	
Roseate	●	●	●							●	○	●	●	●
Sooty	●	●	●	●			○			●	●	●	●	●
Whiskered	●	●	●	●	●		●	●	●	●	●	●	●	●
White-fronted	○			●		●	●							
White-winged	●	○	●	●	●	●	●	○	○	●	●	●	●	○
Thick-knee, Beach	●	●	●	●						●	●	●		
Bush	●	●	●	●	●		●	●	●	●	●	●	●	●
Thornbill, Brown	●			●	●	●	●							
Buff-rumped	●	●		●	●									
Chestnut-rumped	●				●		●	●	●			●	●	●
Inland	●				●		●	●	●			●	●	●
Mountain			★											
Slaty-backed							●				●	●		
Slender-billed				●		●					●	●	●	
Striated	●			●	●		●							
Tasmanian						★								
Western														★
Yellow	●	●		●	●		●	○						
Yellow-rumped	●			●	●	●	●	●	●			●	●	●
Treecreeper, Black-tailed							●	●	●	●	●	●		
Brown	●	●		●	●		●							
*Little		★												
Red-browed	●			●	●									
Rufous						●			●			●	●	●
White-browed	○				●		●	○	●			●	●	
White-throated	●	●		●	●		●							
Triller, Varied	●	●	●	●							●	●		
White-winged	●	●	●	●	●	●	○	●	●	●	●	●	●	●
Tropicbird, Red-tailed		●								○	○		○	●
Turnstone, Ruddy	●	●	●	●	●	●	●			●	●	●	●	
Turtle-Dove, Laughing (I)													●	●

COMMON NAME	Eastern Qld	Atherton	Cape York	South East	Murray-Darling	Tasmania	Central South	Eastern Deserts	Central Deserts	Top End	Kimberley	Western Deserts	Pilbara	South West
Spotted (I)	●	●		●	●	●	●							●
Wagtail, Willie	●	●	●	●	●	○	●	●	●	●	●	●	●	●
Yellow			○		●					●	●			○
Warbler, Brown	●	●		●										
Dusky										●	●	●		
Fairy	●	●	●											
Green-backed										●	●			
Large-billed	●	●	●							●	●			
Mangrove	●	●	●	●						●	●			
Rock			★											
Speckled	●			●	●									
Western	●			○	●			●	●			●	●	●
White-throated	●	●	●	●	●		●			●	●			
Wattlebird, Little	●			●		●	●							●
Red	○			●	●		●					●	●	●
Yellow						★								
Wedgebill, Chiming							●	○	●			●	●	
Chirruping				●			●	●	●					
Weebill	●	●	●	●	●		●	●	●	●	●	●	●	●
Whimbrel	●	●	●	●	○	●	●	○		●	●	●	●	●
Whipbird, Eastern	●	●		●										
Western				○		●								●
Whistler, Gilbert's				●			●		●			●	●	●
Golden	●	●		●	●	●	●						●	●
Grey		●	●						●					
Mangrove Golden	●	●	●							●	●	●	●	
Olive				●	○	●	○							
Red-lored				★										
Rufous	●	●	●	●	●	○	●	●	●	●	●	●	●	●
White-breasted		○								●	●	●	●	
Whistling-Duck, Plumed	●	●	●	●	●			●	●	●	●	○	○	
Wandering	●	●	●	○	●			○		●	●			
White-eye, Pale			★											
Yellow	○	○	●							●	●	●	●	
Whiteface, Banded							●	●				●	●	
Chestnut-breasted							●	●	●					
Southern				●	●		●	●	●			●	●	
Woodswallow, Black-faced	●	●	●		●		●	●	●	●	●	●	●	●
Dusky	●	●		●	●	●	●	○				●	●	
Little	●	●	●		●		●	●	●	●	●	●	●	
Masked	●	●		●	●		●	●	●	●	●	●	●	
White-breasted	●	●	●	●	●		○	●	●	●	●	●		
White-browed	●	●		●	●		●	●	●	●		●	●	

Uncommon Vagrants and Introduced Species

Birds listed here are additional to the birds in the Bird Reference section.

◆ Uncommon vagrant

X Introduced

	Eastern Qld	Atherton	Cape York	South East	Murray-Darling	Tasmania	Central South	Eastern Deserts	Central Deserts	Top End	Kimberley	Western Deserts	Pilbara	South West
Albatross, Buller's			◆		◆	◆								
Grey-headed	◆		◆		◆	◆							X	X
Light-mantled Sooty			◆		◆	◆							◆	◆
Sooty			◆		◆	◆							◆	◆
Bishop, Red				◆		◆								
Blackbird				X	X	X	X							
Corncrake	◆													◆
Crake, Red-legged										◆				
Curlew, Eurasian									◆					
Diving-Petrel, South Georgian			◆											

	Eastern Qld	Atherton	Cape York	South East	Murray-Darling	Tasmania	Central South	Eastern Deserts	Central Deserts	Top End	Kimberley	Western Deserts	Pilbara	South West
Dowitcher, Asian	◆	◆		◆						◆		◆		
Dunlin		◆												
Fulmar, Southern				◆	◆									
Garganey	X		X							X				X
Greenshank, Spotted										◆				
Gull, Franklin's										◆				
Jaeger, Long-tailed	◆			◆		◆	◆			◆				
Ostrich					X									
Peafowl					X	X								X
Penguin, Adelie			◆											

COMMON NAME	Eastern Qld	Atherton	Cape York	South East	Murray-Darling	Tasmania	Central South	Eastern Deserts	Central Deserts	Top End	Kimberley	Western Deserts	Pilbara	South West
Erect-crested				◆		◆	◆							◆
Fiordland				◆		◆	◆							◆
King				◆		◆								
Rockhopper				◆		◆	◆							◆
Royal				◆		◆	◆							
Snares				◆		◆								
Petrel, Providence	◆			◆		◆								
Antarctic				◆		◆								
Black	◆			◆										
Blue				◆		◆	◆							◆
Cook's	◆			◆										
Grey				◆		◆	◆							◆
Herald	◆	◆	◆	◆										
Kermadec	◆													
Mottled				◆		◆	◆							
Snow				◆			◆							
Soft-plumaged				◆		◆	◆							◆
Tahiti	◆	◆	◆											
Westland				◆		◆								
White-chinned				◆		◆	◆							◆
Black-winged	◆			◆										
Phalarope, Red-necked				◆	◆		◆		◆		◆			
Wilson's				◆			◆							
Pheasant, Common						◆	◆							◆
Pigeon, Feral	X	X		X	X	X	X	X	◆	◆	◆	◆	X	X
Pitta, Blue-winged										◆				
Plover, Little Ringed					◆	◆				◆				◆
Ringed	◆			◆										
Prion, Lesser Broad-billed	◆			◆		◆	◆							◆
Broad-billed	◆			◆		◆	◆							◆
Redshank		◆				◆				◆	◆			

COMMON NAME	Eastern Qld	Atherton	Cape York	South East	Murray-Darling	Tasmania	Central South	Eastern Deserts	Central Deserts	Top End	Kimberley	Western Deserts	Pilbara	South West
Reed-Warbler, Great										◆				
Sandpiper, Baird's				◆	◆					◆				◆
Buff-breasted				◆	◆	◆								◆
Cox's				◆				◆						
White-rumped				◆										◆
Shearwater, Buller's				◆										
Hutton's	◆	◆	◆	◆			◆	◆		◆	◆	◆	◆	◆
Shoveler, Northern				◆					◆					◆
Skua, South Polar				◆										
Skylark				X	X	X	X							
Snipe, Pin-tailed										◆	◆			
Swinhoe's			◆							◆	◆			
Starling, Common	X	◆		X	X	X	X	X	◆			◆		◆
Stint, Little				◆	◆	◆	◆							◆
Storm-Petrel, Black-bellied	◆			◆		◆	◆							◆
Grey-backed				◆		◆	◆							
Sooty	◆			◆		◆	◆							◆
White-bellied	◆	◆		◆										
Swan, Mute							◆							◆
Swiftlet, Uniform			◆											
Glossy	◆		◆											
Tern, Arctic	◆			◆		◆	◆							◆
Ternlet, Grey				◆										
Thrush, Song				X										
Tropicbird, White-tailed	◆	◆	◆	◆						◆	◆	◆		
Turtle-Dove, Laughing													X	X
Spotted	X	X		X	X	X	X							X
Wagtail, Grey		◆								◆				
White											◆			◆
Yellow-headed				◆						◆				
Wydah, White-winged				◆										

ACKNOWLEDGEMENTS

During the many years of bird photography and several years of compiling the text for this book, I have received invaluable assistance from a great many people, to whom I wish to express my most sincere thanks. I would especially like to thank my wife, Irene, for her assistance and understanding through this lengthy and time-consuming project, and Mr Ron Johnstone, who read and commented upon a substantial part of the text. Considerable assistance was also received from the Royal Australasian Ornithologists Union through its publications, which include *The Emu*, newsletters, and reports on bird study projects including endangered species. Of valuable assistance was the *Atlas of Australian Birds*, a major study of the distribution of Australian birds. For membership and publications contact R.A.O.U., 21 Gladstone St., Moonee Ponds, Vic. 3039.

A variety of cameras have been used over the years, currently a Bronica for 6 × 4.5 cm transparencies, a Nikon for most of the 35 mm photos, and, more recently, Olympus equipment. Outback travel was with Range Rover and Landrover 110.

BIBLIOGRAPHY

Aston H.I., Balmford, R.A. *A Bird Atlas of the Melbourne Region, Victorian Ornithological Research Group.* Brown Prior Anderson Pty Ltd, Melbourne, 1978.

Australian Heritage Commission. *The Heritage of Australia.* Macmillan, Melbourne, 1981.

Beruldsen, G. *A Field Guide to Nests and Eggs of Australian Birds.* Rigby, Adelaide. 1980.

Blakers, M., Davies, S.J.J.F. & Reilly, P.N. *The Atlas of Australian Birds.* Melbourne University Press, Melbourne, 1984.

Breeden, S. & Breeden, K. *Tropical Queensland: A Natural History of Australia: 1.* Collins, Sydney, 1970.

Breeden, S. & Breeden, K. *Australia's South East: A Natural History of Australia: 2.* Collins, Sydney, 1972.

Breeden, S. & Breeden, K. *Australia's North: A Natural History of Australia: 3.* Collins, Sydney, 1975.

Breeden, S. & Slater, P. *Birds of Australia.* Angus & Robertson, Sydney, 1968.

Burton, J.A. & Risdon, D.H.S. *The Love of Birds.* Octopus, Sydney, 1975.

Busby, J.R. & Davies, S.J.J.F. *Distribution of Birds on the Australian Mainland.* Commonwealth Scientific and Industrial Research Organization, Canberra, 1977.

Cooper, W.T. & Forshaw, J.M. *The Birds of Paradise and Bowerbirds.* Collins, Sydney, 1977.

Cupper, J. & Cupper, L. *Hawks in Focus: A Study of Australia's Birds of Prey.* Jodin Enterprises, Mildura, 1981.

Curry, P. *A Survey of the Birds of Herdsman Lake.* Department of Conservation and Environment, Perth, 1981.

Fleay, D. *Nightwatchmen of Bush and Plain.* Jacaranda Press, Milton, Brisbane, 1968.

Forshaw, J.M. *Australian Parrots.* Lansdowne Press, Sydney, 1980.

Frith, H.J. *Pigeons and Doves of Australia.* Rigby, Adelaide, 1982.

Frith, H.J. *The Waterfowl in Australia.* Angus & Robertson, Sydney, 1982.

Garnett, S. *Birds of the Townsville Common.* S.T. Garnett & J.A. Cox, Townsville, 1983.

Garstone, R. *Birds of the Great Southern.* A.C. Blair, Perth.

Hindwood, K. *Australian Birds in Colour.* A.H. & A.W. Reed, Sydney, 1966.

Hollands, D. *Eagles, Hawks and Falcons of Australia.* Nelson, Melbourne, 1984.

Hutton, G. ed. *Australia's Natural Heritage.* Australian Conservation Foundation, Melbourne, 1981.

Keast, A., Recher, H.F., Ford, H. et. al. eds. *Birds of Eucalypt Forests and Woodlands: Ecology, Conservation, Management.* Surrey Beatty & Sons Pty Ltd, Sydney, 1985.

Lane, B.A., Schulz, M. & Wood, K.L. *Birds of Port Phillip Bay.* Ministry for Planning and Environment, Melbourne, 1984.

Learmonth, N. & Learmonth, A. *Regional Landscapes of Australia: Form, Function and Change.* Angus & Robertson, Sydney, 1971.

MacDonald, J.D. *Birds of Australia.* A.H. & A.W. Reed, Sydney, 1973.

MacDonald, J.D. *Understanding Australian Birds.* A.H. & A.W. Reed, Sydney, 1982.

Morcombe, I.M. & Morcombe, M.K. *Australian Bush Birds in Colour.* A.H. & A.W. Reed, Sydney, 1974.

Morcombe, I.M. & Morcombe, M.K. *Discover Australia's National Parks and Naturelands.* Lansdowne Press, Sydney, 1983.

Morcombe, M.K. *Birds of Australia.* Australian Universities Press Pty Ltd, Sydney, 1974.

National Photographic Index Australian Wildlife. *The Wrens and Warblers of Australia.* Angus & Robertson, Sydney, 1982.

National Photographic Index Australian Wildlife. *The Waterbirds of Australia.* Angus & Robertson, Sydney, 1985.

Officer, H.R. *Australian Flycatchers.* The Bird Observers Club, Melbourne, 1969.

Pescott, T. *Birds of Geelong.* Neptune Press, Newtown, 1983.

Prince, J.H. *A Superb Collection of Australian Parrots and Cockatoos.* A.H. & A.W. Reed, Sydney, 1982.

Reader's Digest. *Readers' Digest Atlas of Australia.* Reader's Digest Services, Sydney, 1977.

Rowley, I. *Birdlife.* Collins, Sydney, 1982.

Royal Australasian Ornithologists Union. *Eyre Bird Observatory, Report 1979–1981.* Royal Australasian Ornithologists Union, Perth, 1982.

Schodde, R. *The Fairy-Wrens: A Monograph of the Maluidae.* Lansdowne Press, Sydney, 1982.

Serventy, D.L. & Whittell, H.M. *Birds of Western Australia.* Paterson Brokensha, Perth, 1962.

Sharland, M. *A Guide to the Birds of Tasmania.* Drinkwater Publishing, Hobart, 1981.

Simpson, K. & Day, N. *The Birds of Australia: A Book of Identification.* Curry O'Neil, Melbourne, 1984.

Slater, P. *Rare and Vanishing Australian Birds.* Rigby, Adelaide, 1978.

Slater, P. *Masterpieces of Australian Bird Photography.* Rigby, Adelaide, 1980.

Smith, L.H. *The Lyrebird.* Lansdowne Press, Sydney, 1968.

Storr, G.M. *Birds of the Northern Territory: Western Australian Museum Special Publication No. 7.* Western Australian Museum, Perth, 1977.

Storr, G.M. *Birds of the Kimberley Division, Western Australia: Western Australian Museum Special Publication No. 11.* Western Australian Museum, Perth, 1980.

Storr, G.M. *Birds of the Pilbara Region, Western Australia.* Western Australian Museum, Perth, 1984.

Storr, G.M. & Johnstone, R.E. *A Field Guide to the Birds of Western Australia.* Western Australian Museum, Perth, 1985.

Storr, G.M. *Revised List of Queensland Birds: Records of the Western Australian Museum, supp. No. 19.* Western Australian Museum, Perth, 1984.

Thomas, R. & Wheeler, J. *Birds of the Ballarat Region: A Handbook.* Roger Thomas, Linton, 1983.

Vernon, D.P. *Birds of Brisbane and Environs: Museum Booklet No. 5.* Government Printer, Queensland, 1968.

Western Australian Museum. *Biological Survey of Mitchell Plateau and Admiralty Gulf, Kimberley.* Western Australian Museum, Perth, 1981.

Wheeler, R.W. *The Birds of Victoria and Where to Find Them.* Nelson, Melbourne, 1979.

Journals

Canberra Bird Notes 5–10. Canberra Ornithologists Group, Canberra, 1980–1985.

Corella 1–10. Australian Bird Study Association, Sydney, 1977–1986.

Emu 53–86. Royal Australasian Ornithologists Union, Melbourne, 1953–1986.

Northern Territory Naturalist 1–8. Northern Territory Field Naturalists Club, Darwin, 1978–1985.

Tasmanian Bird Report 5–14. Bird Observers Association of Tasmania, Hobart, 1975–1985.

The Australian Bird Bander 3–14. Bird Banders Association of Australia, Sydney, 1965–1976.

The Australian Bird Watcher 1–11. The Bird Observers Club, Melbourne, 1959.

The South Australian Ornithologist 1–13. South Australian Ornithologists Association, Adelaide, 1914–1936.

The South Australian Ornithologist 26–30. South Australian Ornithologists Association, Adelaide, 1974–1986.

The Sunbird 9–16. Queensland Ornithological Society, Brisbane, 1978–1986.

The Western Australian Naturalist 1–16. Western Australian Naturalists Club, Perth, 1947–1985.

GLOSSARY

Adult Birds which have reached breeding age. Adult plumage does not continue to change in appearance in subsequent moults, except for alternating eclipse plumages in some species.

Barred Transverse lines, usually quite fine.

Casque A helmet-like ridge or plate on the bill or skull.

Cere A bare fleshy structure around the base of the upper mandible, containing the nostrils.

Chevrons V-shaped transverse markings, usually on the underparts.

Cline A gradual change in the appearance or other characteristics of a bird across a geographic area.

Colour phase Varying colour within a single interbreeding population, unrelated to age, sex or season.

Eclipse Plumage, usually dull, acquired by many bird species during late summer, autumn or winter.

Endemic Native and confined to a particular geographical area, e.g. endemic to Australia; endemic to one of the defined regions of this book.

Extinct No individuals of the species remain in the wild or in captivity.

Facial disc The relatively flat, rounded or heart-shaped outline of the face of some birds, usually used in descriptions of owls.

Family The division of classification into which an Order is divided, and containing one or more genera.

Feral Having returned to the wild after domestication; usually a species introduced into the continent or region by man.

Fingers The finger-like outspread wingtip primaries; a description usually applied to soaring birds of prey.

Genus A division of classification into which a Family is divided and which contains one or more species.

Gular Part of the throat. A gular pouch is a distendible pocket of skin in the central area of the throat.

Hackles Relatively long neck feathers, often standing out from the general plumage surface.

Immature Birds not yet capable of breeding; immature plumages are those after juvenile plumage and preceding that usually worn by mature adults of breeding age.

Juvenile Young birds at and soon after fledging, with the feathers which first replaced the natal down; may still be under parental care.

Lamella A narrow layer of stiff hairs (membranes) along the inner edge of the bill, used to sieve food particles from water.

Mandible The upper or lower half of the bill.

Mantle Feathers of the upper back and onto the shoulders.

Mask A dark or black patch which encloses the eyes and part of the face.

Migratory Has regular geographical movements, between continents, or within a continent or other geographical area.

Mirrors White patches on the primary feathers of gulls.

Nail The hooked tip of the upper mandibles of albatrosses, petrels, waterfowl.

Nestling In or closely attached to the nest.

Nomadic Undertakes irregular and often erratic geographical movements.

Nominate Where a species has more than one subspecies, the nominate subspecies takes a subspecific name identical to the specific name of that species; it is known as the nominate subspecies and is listed first among the subspecies of that species.

Nuptial Of or pertaining to breeding, e.g. nuptial plumage.

Orbital ring A ring, fleshy or feathered, surrounding the eye.

Order A division of classification into which a Class is divided and having one or more Families.

Pellet The indigestible remains of prey, usually of feathers, hair, bone, scales, etc., regurgitated as a compact rounded pellet.

Piratic Steals food from other species, usually by attack or harassment.

Plumes Long, showy feathers, usually used in nuptial display.

Soft parts Unfeathered parts of the body, including feet, eye, cere and any bare skin.

Species A division of classification into which a genus is divided, the members of which can interbreed among themselves, but not usually with members of other species.

Speculum Iridescent colour patch on the wing, most commonly seen on ducks.

Striated Marked with fine longitudinal lines.

Subspecies Geographically restricted subdivisions of a species that are taxonomically different from other subdivisions of that species.

Tarsus The lower leg of birds; may be fully or partly feathered, or bare.

Underparts Undersurfaces from chin to undertail.

Upperparts The upper parts of the bird's body — the mantle, back, rump and base of tail.

Vagrant Found at a locality which is not within usual range, due to disorientation, adverse winds or other influence.

Ventral The undersurface of the body.

Wattle A fleshy lobe or appendage, often brightly coloured, hanging from throat or neck of some birds.

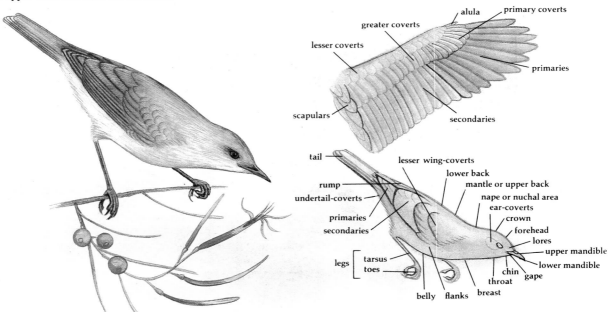

559 GREY HONEYEATER *Conopophila whitei*

INDEX

275 **WESTERN ROSELLA** *Platycercus icterotis*

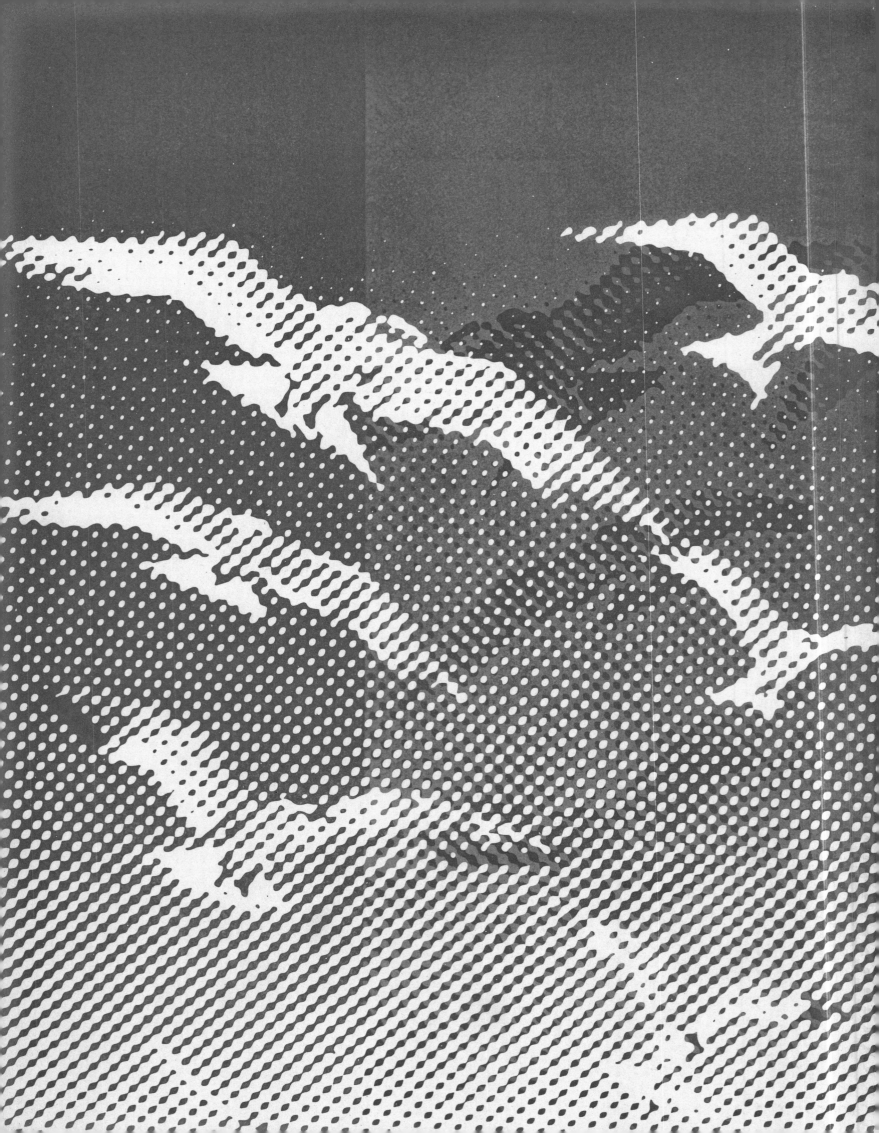